"This fourth edition is an exceptionally well written introduction to political theory, with the focus on principal concepts and excellent case studies. This book is a marvelous contribution to the field of Political Science. Yet above all, the book offers an outstanding basis of knowledge and motivation for university students learning about political theory."

**Katarzyna Stokłosa**, *University of Southern Denmark, Denmark*

"Hoffman and Graham's textbook is a success at many levels. It is admirably comprehensive, is not afraid of courting controversy (particularly in its refreshing scepticism about the state) and demonstrates how central normative theory is to a study of politics. Above all, perhaps, it manages, with the help of very useful case studies, to pull off the difficult task of making complex ideas eminently accessible. I highly recommend the book as an ideal introduction to the study of political theory."

**Robert Garner**, *University of Leicester, UK*

# Introduction to Political Theory

This vibrant and significantly revised new edition is a comprehensive and accessible text for studying political theory in a changing world.

Bringing together classic and contemporary political concepts and ideologies into one book, it introduces the major approaches to political issues that have shaped our world, and the ideas that form the currency of political debate. Consistently, it relates political ideas to political realities through effective use of examples and case studies making theory lively, contentious, and relevant.

With significant revisions which reflect the latest questions facing political theory in an increasingly international context key features and updates include:

- Two brand new chapters on Migration and Freedom of Speech and a significant new section on the radical right;
- Thought-provoking case studies to bring the theory to life including social media and internet regulation, Brexit and the EU, anti-vaxxer campaigns, surrogacy tourism, and autonomous anarchist zones;
- A revamped website, including podcasts, to aid study of, and reading around, the subject.

*Introduction to Political Theory*, Fourth Edition is the perfect accompaniment to undergraduate study in political theory, political philosophy, concepts and ideologies, and more broadly to the social sciences and philosophy.

**Paul Graham** teaches political theory at the University of Buckingham, UK.

**John Hoffman** is Emeritus Professor of Political Theory at the University of Leicester, UK.

# Introduction to Political Theory

Fourth Edition

Paul Graham and
John Hoffman

Routledge
Taylor & Francis Group

LONDON AND NEW YORK

Cover image: © Getty Images

Fourth edition published 2022
by Routledge
4 Park Square, Milton Park, Abingdon, Oxon OX14 4RN

and by Routledge
605 Third Avenue, New York, NY 10158

*Routledge is an imprint of the Taylor & Francis Group, an informa business*

© 2022 Paul Graham and John Hoffman

First edition published by Pearson Education Ltd. 2006
Third edition published by Routledge 2015

*British Library Cataloguing-in-Publication Data*
A catalogue record for this book is available from the British Library

*Library of Congress Cataloging-in-Publication Data*
Names: Graham, Paul, author. | Hoffman, John, author.
Title: Introduction to political theory / Paul Graham and John Hoffman.
Description: Fourth edition. | Abingdon, Oxon; New York, NY: Routledge,
2022. | "First edition published by Pearson Education Ltd. 2006. Third
edition published by Routledge 2015" — T.p. verso. | Includes
bibliographical references and index.
Identifiers: LCCN 2021050192 (print) | LCCN 2021050193 (ebook) |
ISBN 9781138389205 (hardback) | ISBN 9781138389212 (paperback) |
ISBN 9780429424106 (ebook)
Subjects: LCSH: Political science.
Classification: LCC JA71.H6133 2022 (print) | LCC JA71 (ebook) |
DDC 320.01—dc23
LC record available at https://lccn.loc.gov/2021050192
LC ebook record available at https://lccn.loc.gov/2021050193

ISBN: 978-1-138-38920-5 (hbk)
ISBN: 978-1-138-38921-2 (pbk)
ISBN: 978-0-429-42410-6 (ebk)

DOI: 10.4324/9780429424106

Typeset in Bembo Std
by codeMantra

Access the companion website: www.routledge.com/cw/graham

# Brief contents

# Contents

## Part 3    Classical ideologies

# Preface to the Fourth Edition

The First Edition of *Introduction to Political Theory* appeared in 2006. That year saw Twitter launched and Donald Trump began his fifth season hosting *The Apprentice*. The First Edition was written over the period 2004–6, during which the United States was embroiled in wars in Afghanistan and Iraq, and where the effects of 9/11 on politics were still keenly felt.

Political theory moves more slowly than empirical political science, and it is sometimes argued that it deals with perennial problems, so that revising a theory textbook might be less urgent than updating one in political science. Nonetheless, much has happened in 15 years, and it is important for political theorists to reflect on events. In our textbook, we have always stressed the real-world applications of what might appear abstract philosophical reflections.

The Fourth Edition was written during the lockdowns of 2020 and 2021, and Covid-19 raises issues of central importance to political theorists: about free speech (Covid scepticism and anti-vaxxer claims), restrictions on movement, the importance (or alternatively impotence) of borders, the fair distribution of vaccines, and the interdependence of nations. For the generation attending university and college, Covid-19 has been especially disruptive, and we hope that this book will allow you to reflect on some of its political aspects, perhaps with a view to preventing a future health crisis.

By the time we get to work on the Fifth Edition in the mid-2020s no doubt the media caravan will have moved on, and there will be other crises and challenges. Some might come out of a clear blue sky, such as a civil nuclear meltdown, or a terrorist attack that surpasses 9/11 in its level of destructiveness. Hopefully, the arguments in this book will allow you to think about how we might avoid such crises or at least mitigate their effects.

This edition is the most significant re-writing to date. Many of the chapters have been thoroughly re-written, in large part as a response to the useful feedback we have received on the Third Edition. The previous chapter on freedom is now split into two. The chapter on fascism and the radical right takes into account recent intellectual developments, and there is a completely new chapter on migration. Where chapters have been dropped, the very important issues raised in them have been integrated into the other chapters.

I have taken the lead on the Fourth Edition, but this textbook would not have been the success it is without my co-author Prof John Hoffman. I am extremely grateful to him.

I dedicate this new edition to the memory of my father, Revd Douglas Graham (1933–2020).

Paul Graham
Bicester, Oxfordshire
July 2021

# Introduction

## Politics and political theory

Three aspects of human life are central to politics and political activity:

1. Conflict between humans over the distribution of resources.
2. Despite such conflict, we can gain through cooperation – cooperation is often mutually beneficial.
3. We engage in conscious strategies to further our interests. These strategies are informed by political concepts, ideas, and theories.

Points 1 (conflict over resources) and 2 (gains through cooperation) apply to many – perhaps all – life-forms, from simple single-cell organisms to complex mammals, but point 3 is more specifically human. Ideas are means by which humans can advance their interests. Think of how often we seek to justify our behaviour through the use of moral language – arguing your case by appeal to your own self-interest is not normally a smart strategy. This raises the question of whether ideas (point 3) are reducible to material interests (point 1). For example, are egalitarians – believers in equality – driven by self-interest? Perhaps if they are poor, the answer is obvious, but what if they are wealthy? Maybe rich egalitarians gain non-monetary rewards from signalling their political beliefs. They are still motivated by a desire to maximise their resources; it is just that those 'resources' include such things as prestige or reputation.

Students of politics often believe that politics can be studied without theory. They take the view that we can focus upon the facts without worrying about ideas. But we should never underestimate how important theories and theorists are to professional politicians and other political actors. Just as in our everyday lives we are guided by notions of right and wrong, justice and injustice, so politicians are similarly guided. It is not a question of *whether* political actors follow theory, but a question of *which* theory or concept is supported when they present policies and undertake actions. We can argue as to whether the British prime minister or the United States president acts according to the right political concepts, but it is undeniable that their actions are linked to theory. Humans in general cannot act without ideas: indeed, it is a defining property of human activity that we can only act when we have ideas in our head as to what we should do.

In discussing the state or democracy or freedom in this book, we are talking about ideas or concepts or theories – we use the terms interchangeably – that guide and inform political action. Some universities and colleges offer courses in political *philosophy* and philosophical questions such as the nature of truth, free will, and determinism do play a crucial role in our argumentation, but we prefer the term 'theory' because it seems less daunting to many students, and it is less

DOI: 10.4324/9780429424106-1

abstract. However, we do not see any substantive difference between theory, on the one hand, and philosophy, on the other.

As for theory and ideology, here the difference is more tangible. Ideologies seek to persuade, theories to expound and explain, and in a way that encourages the reader to think for him- or herself. Of course, there is an overlap: ideologies are arguably more persuasive if the theory they draw upon is rigorous and accurate, but the two have different roles to play. It is vital that readers should feel encouraged and stimulated to form their own views, using logic, evidence, and rigour to present their case. A student may feel, for example, that there should be compulsory vaccination in the face of a virus, such as that which causes Covid-19. It is important that views are not put forward simply because it is felt that they will please peers or tutors.

## The structure of this book

The book has five parts and twenty chapters:

### Part 1: Coercion, Legitimacy, and Collective Choice

- The State
- Democracy
- Punishment
- Civil Disobedience and Conscientious Objection

### Part 2: Freedom, Equality, and Justice

- Equality
- Freedom of Action
- Freedom of Speech
- Distributive Justice

### Part 3: Classical Ideologies

- Liberalism
- Conservatism
- Socialism and Marxism
- Anarchism
- Nationalism
- Fascism and the Radical Right

### Part 4: Contemporary Ideologies

- Feminism
- Multiculturalism
- Ecologism

### Part 5: Global Political Theory

- Human Rights
- Global Justice
- Migration

Parts 1, 4, and 5 focus on concepts, while Parts 2 and 3 discuss ideologies.

# Theories and concepts

The four concepts discussed in Part 1 focus on the role of coercion in ensuring political outcomes. The state is by definition coercive, and it is at its most coercive when it punishes – or threatens to punish – law-breakers. Democracy might appear not to be coercive, but it is a method for agreeing laws and policies, and except for the unusual situation in which unanimity is required, the 'losers' in a vote have to accept the result. An important issue – central to the discussion of civil disobedience – is whether it makes a difference that a decision was made democratically: do we have a stronger obligation to obey democratically agreed laws than those handed down by a dictator or a set of oligarchs?

A key conclusion of Part 1 is that people can benefit from cooperation. In the language of game theory, politics is – or, at least, can be – a positive sum game. But some may gain more than others and that raises an important second-order issue: how do we distribute the benefits of cooperation? We might tend to think that the only benefits are material, such as money and similarly tangible goods, but there are other resources such as esteem and freedom. In Chapter 5 (equality), we discuss arguments for and against a range of principles of equality (equal distribution of resources). We then discuss freedom – freedom of action and freedom of speech – before bringing everything together in a discussion of distributive justice (not to be confused with retributive justice, which we discuss in Chapter 3, on punishment).

# Ideologies

In Parts 3 and 4, we switch from concepts to ideologies. Broadly speaking, the classical ideologies (Part 3) predate 1945, while the contemporary ones have emerged since the Second World War. However, most of the classical ideologies are still alive, and indeed liberalism (Chapter 9) has emerged as the world's dominant ideology. What is more, some of the contemporary ideologies have older roots – this is especially evident with feminism.

An ideology is a system of ideas, organised around an attempt to win power. Power is here defined in a broad sense. It is not restricted to acquiring political office. Ideology can be used in a neutral sense, but historically it acquired pejorative overtones. To understand why, we need to briefly outline its history.

The term was coined in the aftermath of the 1789 French Revolution by Antoine Destutt de Tracey to denote a science of ideas. It had positive connotations: the ideas were rational and progressive, based on empirical evidence, free from metaphysical and religious content. De Tracey was put in charge of the Institut de France, and he regarded the spreading of ideology as effectively the same thing as disseminating the ideas of the French and European Enlightenments.

However, the term soon became negative. Napoléon Bonaparte denounced ideology as dangerous radicalism – sinister and doctrinaire: a 'cloudy metaphysics' that ignores history and reality (McLellan, 1995: 5). And this seems to have been the view of Karl Marx and Friedrich Engels in their work *The German Ideology* (1845). They injected into the term two new connotations. First, ideologies are infused with idealism – they are a substitute for reality. Second, ideologies mask material interests. Marx and Engels contrasted their 'scientific socialism' to these reality-distorting and interest-concealing ideologies, on the ground that scientific socialism reflected the class interests of the proletariat. Because the proletariat was the class whose historical mission is to lead the struggle to convert capitalism into communism, its outlook (as interpreted by Marxists) is deemed scientific *and* ideological.

German sociologist Karl Mannheim wrote a classic book in 1929 entitled *Ideology and Utopia* (Mannheim, 1936). In this work, he raised an intriguing problem. Can we talk about ideology without being ideological ourselves? After all, if ideologies arise because of a person's social context, then is not the critique of ideology also situationally influenced, so that the critic of ideology is himself ideological? His argument raises the question as to whether we should define ideologies negatively or positively. If, as is common, we identify ideologies as negative bodies of thought, then we identify them as dogmas, authoritarian thought constructs that distort the real world, and are threats to an open-minded and tolerant approach to politics and political ideas. Yet, the negative definition seems naive because it implies that while our opponents are ideological, we are not.

The approach we adopt in this book is to accept that to some degree *ideologies* both distort reality and reflect interests, but with the use of *theory* we can achieve some degree of distance from our subjectivity and interests. It is for that reason that we try, as best we can, to discuss full range of political-ideological perspectives. Above all, we attempt to avoid 'name-calling' and encourage our readers to do likewise. There may be political positions discussed in this book with which you strongly disagree or that even make you uncomfortable. Our aim is not to convert you to any position but allow you to defend or criticise a theory with a degree of sophistication. Open discussion is critical to the study of political theory.

## Global political theory

We round off the book with three chapters that deal with global issues: human rights, global (or international) justice, and migration.

Political theory has traditionally been preoccupied with the relationship between the individual and the state, and that concern will be evident in Parts 1 and 2. Global (or international) political theory, on the other hand, is concerned with the relationship between states and between individuals across state boundaries. Issues discussed in Part 5 include whether there are universal human rights, what obligations wealthy states have to poor ones to transfer resources, and whether there should be a right to immigrate – that is, whether should there be open borders.

## How to read the book

Each chapter starts with a case study. The aim is for you to take a real-world example and think about it prior to reading the rest of the chapter. Political theory is a reflection on the real world and in that sense we are all political theorists, even if we have not studied the subject academically. In all but one of the chapters, we come back to the case study at the end (the exception is Chapter 19 – global justice – where we start the main discussion of the chapter with the case study, which is on famine). The aim of coming back to the case study is for you to think again about your initial response to it after having worked through the arguments of the chapter.

At the end of each chapter are suggestions for further reading. In addition, you will find a range of additional resources on the website: www.routledge.com/cw/graham.

Although each chapter has a broadly similar structure, we have avoided a cookie cutter approach, whereby every chapter has exactly the same structure. We let the topic dictate the approach of the chapter. For example, there are many strands of feminism, and debates within feminism are central to understanding it is an ideology. So we have structured that chapter around the various feminisms and allowed them to critique one another. On the other hand, there are many theories of multiculturalism, without there being much internal debate, and so in that chapter we outline six theories and offer some criticisms of each. In the chapter on fascism and the radical right there is a split between classical fascism (Italian fascism and German national socialism) and the contemporary radical right, and this is reflected in both the title and the chapter structure.

Throughout the book we use two types of references – references to other works, the full details of which can be found in the bibliography at the end of each chapter, and cross references to other parts of the book; these are indicated by an arrow (→) in the text.

## References

Mannheim, K. (1936) *Ideology and Utopia*, English translation. London: Routledge & Kegan Paul.

McLellan, D. (1995) *Ideology*, 2nd edn. Buckingham: Open University.

**Part 1**

# Coercion, legitimacy, and collective choice

# Chapter 1

# The State

## Introduction

The state is a central concept in politics. Sociologist Max Weber defined it as an entity that commands a monopoly on the legitimate use of violence in a particular territory. Much modern (post sixteenth century) political theory is concerned with the meaning of 'legitimacy' and in this chapter we set out a number of arguments for the legitimacy of the state, as articulated by major political thinkers: (1) Its legitimacy derives from self-interest (Hobbes). (2) It reconciles morality and self-interest (Rousseau, Kant, Hegel). (3) It is an expression of sovereignty and it cannot be reduced to morality, self-interest, or even law (Schmitt). While the primary focus is on the individual's relationship to a state, the chapter is rounded off with a discussion of the state in international relations – that is, the relationship between states.

## Key questions

- What is the state?
- What is the rationale for the state?
- Could the state be reduced in size? Does it (for example) need to provide policing?

## What is the state?

One of the most influential and useful definitions of the state was articulated by Max Weber (1864–1920): 'The state is the only human community, which within a determinate area success-fully *claims a monopoly on legitimate physical violence*' (Weber, 1994: 311).[1] The italicisation is Weber's and is the key part of the definition: what is a monopoly? What does it mean for this thing we call the state to be legitimate? And what is physical violence (*physische Gewaltsamkeit*)? Is there a difference between the state and a criminal gang? We start with the last of those questions.

A criminal gang can effectively impose its will within a particular locality. And it can extract payment, in the form of protection money. So how does it differ from the state?

1. State violence is based on laws, meaning that those who are subject to violence can predict how the state will behave. Of course, the success of organised criminal gangs also requires that their victims can plan: a business must know when and how much protection money it must pay, so this is not an entirely convincing distinction.

DOI: 10.4324/9780429424106-3

## Case study 1.1

## Do we need the police?

**PHOTO 1.1** © Marcin Rogozinski/Alamy Stock Photo.

In economically developed societies, the state provides many services including health, education, and roadbuilding. These are funded from taxation, which is a compulsory charge imposed on citizens. There are vigorous debates about the degree to which these services should be state-funded, as we can see in the controversy over the Affordable Care Act ('Obamacare') in the United States. Rare however is it advocated that policing should be privately provided and funded. Security – internal (policing) and external (the armed forces) – is taken to be the core function of the state. But why not privatise the police?

Before reading this chapter try to imagine a society without state-funded police. Note that security could be provided by non-state actors, so you are not being asked to imagine a society without security. The question is whether as a matter of fact in the absence of the state, such security would be produced.

2. The state uses violence, but it is constrained by a higher law, which may be positive (posited, created) or natural (not created). God's commands would be an example of the former, while natural rights (human rights) illustrate the latter. However, the idea of being constrained conflicts with the idea of a *monopoly* on the *legitimate* use of violence.

3. States emerge from criminal gangs but over time acquire legitimacy in the eyes of those subject to violence. Kurrild-Klitgaard and Svendsen argue that the Vikings, who raided England over

several centuries, changed in the period 850–925 from roving to stationary bandits as they real-ised more was gained by monopolising violence – 'taxing' people in return for protecting them against other bandits (Kurrild-Klitgaard and Svendsen, 2003: 256–7).

4. Perhaps we need to distinguish legitimate violence, exercised by the state, from illegitimate violence, practised by criminals. But then, Weber could have used a different phrase, such as a 'monopoly on authority'. Furthermore, the term 'authority' is ambiguous. We accept to a large degree the authority of experts – for example, deferring to medical practitioners. Yet, authority can also be coercive. There is a continuum from the relatively freely accepted authority of experts to the coercive authority of bodies that threaten violence.

5. We could distinguish between *de jure* and *de facto* states. The former is legally recognised but does not effectively practise coercion, while the latter lacks legitimacy but is effective in getting peo-ple to do what they want them to do. But Weber argues that the state must be both legitimate and effective. An ineffective state is a failed state.

It is difficult to get away from the idea of violence and the tension between legitimacy and violence. There are various strategies for addressing this. The first is to reject legitimacy: the state is no different to a criminal gang and can never be legitimate, even if psychologically 'citizens' have internalised their acceptance of the state and perceive it as legitimate. This is the anarchist position (see pp. 207–8) The second approach is to reconcile violence and legit-imacy through appeal to self-interest: we are all better off if we submit to the state. Its most famous advocate is Thomas Hobbes (1588–1679) and this position is discussed in the next section. The third is to identify the state with a community that is more than the sum of its members and so while violence – or the threat of violence – may be used against individuals, it is never ultimately used against the community. In different ways, we see this argument in the works of Jean-Jacques Rousseau (1712–78), Immanuel Kant (1720–1804), and G W F Hegel (1770–1831). The fourth can be found in the work of Carl Schmitt (1888–1985) and combines Hobbes, and his emphasis on power as a fact, with the German tradition of the community as above the individual.

## The state as the product of individual self-interest

One of the most important arguments for the state was advanced by Hobbes in *Leviathan* (published 1651), which is arguably the first significant work of modern political thought. The method he uses to justify the state is contractarian (see pp. 165–6): we imagine a situation in which there is no state – the state of nature – and ask ourselves whether it is better to remain in the state of nature or agree to submit to a sovereign (or state). In the twentieth century, Hobbes has been reinterpreted as a rational choice theorist (McLean, 1981). People are maximisers: they have preferences, and they seek to satisfy as many as possible. Other humans can frustrate them, but life is not pure conflict: through cooperation competitors can all gain. This competitive relationship can be thought of as a game – hence 'game theory'; the most famous game is the prisoner's dilemma.

*Leviathan* can be interpreted as an attempt to solve the prisoner's dilemma. We imagine two people arrested for a crime. If they remain silent, each will be convicted of a relatively minor offence and spend a year in prison. If both confess, each receives five years for a more serious offence. If one confesses but the other remains silent, the confessor goes free, while the other receives a ten-year sentence. Clearly, the actions of one affect the outcome for the other, as can be seen from the pay-off table:

| | Second prisoner Remains silent | Confesses |
|---|---|---|
| First prisoner | | |
| Remains silent | 1, 1 | 10, 0 |
| Confesses | 0, 10 | 5, 5 |

If we assume that the prisoners are self-interested, each will attempt to achieve his first prefer-ence. The preference-ordering of each can be tabulated:

| | 1st preference | 2nd preference | 3rd preference | 4th preference |
|---|---|---|---|---|
| First prisoner | 0, 10 | 1, 1 | 5, 5 | 10, 0 |
| Second prisoner | 10, 0 | 1, 1 | 5, 5 | 0, 10 |

It is not rational to remain silent while the other prisoner confesses and so the likely outcome is that each confesses, with the consequence that each satisfies only his third preference. This is termed the Nash equilibrium (or the unbeatable strategy): if you are the first prisoner, then no matter what the second prisoner does, you cannot do better than confess. If the second prisoner confesses you get five years. If he does not confess you go free.

What, however, makes the game interesting is that while from an individual perspective you cannot do better than confess, if you both cooperate and agree to remain silent, you could do better than five years in prison. The prisoner's dilemma is a non-zero sum game: a gain for one prisoner does not result in an equivalent loss for the other. The explanation of how, through cooperation, each prisoner might move from his third to his second preference is a contemporary rendition of the reasoning behind Hobbes's contract theory. The third preference represents the non-cooperation characteristic of the state of nature, the agreement to remain silent is equivalent to the contract itself, and the satisfaction of the second preference equates to life under a state. There are costs as well as benefits resulting from submission to a state – we are required to conform to laws which restrict our freedom. But we also gain the benefits of security, and with security comes increased prosperity, and a guarantee that we will enjoy a significant amount of (protected) personal freedom.

It might appear that the rational strategy is for each prisoner to give up his first preference to achieve his second preference. This is incorrect: for each prisoner, achieving his first preference should remain his goal. What he wants is an agreement with the other prisoner that each will remain silent, but then break the agreement in the hope the other prisoner will honour it. He wants to free-ride on the other's compliance, gaining the benefit of cooperation, which is the avoidance of four years (five less one) in prison, without paying the cost of cooperation, one year in prison. Of course, each prisoner understands the motivations of the other, so a voluntary agreement is ineffective. What they need is a third-party enforcer of the agreement. The enforcer imposes sanctions on free-riders, so there is an incentive to comply. If each can be assured of the enforcer's effectiveness a move from each prisoner's third preference to his second preference can be achieved. In political terms, the enforcer is the state.

Hobbes reduces the legitimacy of the state to self-interest. His starting point is a materialist con-ception of human nature: human beings are 'bodies in motion', continually desiring things, and never fully satisfied (Hobbes, 1991: 118–20). Because there is scarcity of desired objects, humans are brought into conflict with one another. Their greatest fear is death, and that fear is the key to understanding why the state of nature is a 'war of all against all' (1991: 185–6). Because even the weakest can kill the strongest, there is an equality of vulnerability that makes pre-emptive action rational: kill or be killed.

While there are 'laws of nature' in the state of nature, these are best interpreted as rational guidance rather than moral obligations. For example, we are required to seek peace, unless war is necessary for self-defence (1991: 190).

A twentieth century theorist, John Plamenatz, criticised Hobbes on grounds that if his description of the state of nature were accurate, people would be too nasty to stick to any agreement, and if they stick to the agreement the state of nature cannot be as Hobbes describes it (Plamenatz, 1992: 193–7). One of the several insights of game theory is to provide a solution to this apparent paradox: what we seek is an agreement, equivalent to the prisoners' agreement to remain silent, but what we fear is that other people will defect from the agreement. It follows that prisoner's dilemma-type situations are assurance games. In short, people are not nasty, but fearful. You do not pre-emptively kill another out of enjoyment but because you cannot be certain she will not kill you. The key point is that you know other people face the same dilemma – kill or be killed – and so you have no option but to kill. What is required is something more fearful than the other person, and that is the state.

## Goods – public, common, private, and club

Hobbes's most famous quotation is his description of life in the state of nature as 'solitary, poor, nasty, brutish, and short' (Hobbes, 1991: 186), but of more significance are the comments immediately proceeding that statement, where he lists all the things – largely economic goods – absent in the state of nature. These include security, industry, culture, established trade routes, significant buildings, large-scale mechanisation, scientific knowledge, and written history. This is a varied list and in principle some of these could be provided without the state, although arguably all depend on security.

Economic goods can be distinguished by two characteristics: excludability and rivalry. If you buy a can of *Coca Cola*, you can exclude others from consuming it and your consumption precludes others consuming it. Coca Cola is a *private good* because it is excludable and rivalrous. National defence on the other hand is a *public good* (non-excludable and non-rivalrous): you benefit from it even if you do not pay for it and although a larger population may require more defence it is at the non-rivalrous end of the scale – the same amount of national defence is sufficient to protect 10, 20, or 30 million people. *Club goods* are excludable and non-rivalrous: satellite TV is an example. Toll roads are another example. *Common goods* (common pool goods; congestible goods) are non-excludable and rivalrous, examples being fish stocks and any other potentially non-replenishable things access to which is hard to control. In summary:

|  | Excludable | Non-excludable |
| --- | --- | --- |
| Rivalrous | **Private** | **Common** |
| Non-rivalrous | **Club** | **Public** |

A couple of other points need to be made. The table represents pure types. There are, in fact, degrees of rivalry and excludability. A good can change its character over the course of a day: a toll road is a club good, but during the rush hour it becomes more congested and looks more like a private good. A second point is that we – collectively – can choose to create certain kinds of goods. Emergency numbers – 999 in the United Kingdom, 911 in the United States – are common goods, but they need not be. If charges were made for phoning the police, then it would be a private good. But some goods do seem more naturally to be one or other. Access to fish stocks in the open seas is hard to control, so there is a challenge in converting those stocks into a private good.

Core to the argument for the state is that security – internal (police) and external (army) – is a naturally occurring public good or common good. Non-payers cannot be excluded from bene-fitting from the good and so must be forced to pay through taxation. Taxation is state-extracted payment. Recall Hobbes's list of the things we will not have in a state of nature: many of them could be private or club goods, but the protection of those things depends on security. Your car may be private, but you need the police to ensure that it remains in your possession. Security is therefore an overriding good that can only be secured by the state. This suggests that there are two types of free-riders: (a) those who break the laws the state is created to deter, for example, house-breakers; (b) those who avoid paying for state services, with the obvious example being tax evaders.

Anarchists challenge this claim, maintaining that security can be generated without coer-cion. But even those who are not anarchists question the extent of state activities. In a famous example, Ronald Coase argues that what looks like a natural public good, a lighthouse, could in fact be a club good. Ships benefit from the light provided by the house and so lighthouses seem non-excludable. However, many – although not all – of those ships will be coming into port, and entry to a port is excludable. Coase's solution to the possible under-provision of lighthouses is to bundle up the cost of their construction and operation with the benefit of us-ing the port by charging port entry fees (Coase, 1974: 361–2). The port builds the lighthouses and charges docking ships. That not all passing ships will dock does not matter. Lighthouses generate positive externalities – benefits accruing to those who are not party to the transac-tion. The parties are the port/lighthouse and the docking ships; passing ships are third-party beneficiaries. If positive externalities are very large, then the good – the lighthouse – may not be built, but so long as it still pays for the contracting parties to produce the good, there is no problem. This will be an important argument when we discuss the case study – policing – at the end of the chapter.

## The state as ethical

In this section, we consider the work of a number of political philosophers who collectively argue that the state cannot in a straightforward way be reduced to self-interest: Rousseau, Kant, and Hegel.

## Rousseau

Although Rousseau was, like Hobbes, a contract theorist, he rejected the latter's idea of a sov-ereign (Leviathan) not bound by law and not identical with the people. In its place, Rousseau defends *popular* sovereignty. But the 'people' is singular; it is not – or they are not – a mere aggre-gate of individuals (Rousseau, 1986: 13). While he accepts that different kinds of societies exist, a political community under a sovereign state must be ethical.

To constitute themselves as a people, there must be a procedure for making decisions, but we face a problem of infinite regress: if a sovereign people does not already exist, there can be no pre-existing procedure for creating one because that procedure – set of rules – presupposes that a people exists. In this case, unanimity is the only acceptable rule: all individuals must consent to create the sovereign (the state). But people cannot consent to a blank cheque, so Rousseau sets out a number of rules that make up the contract (this list has been reconstructed by Noone, 1970: 699–701):

1. All members of the political association have a voice in the General Assembly.
2. Sovereignty is inalienable – it cannot be transferred to another entity.
3. Sovereignty is indivisible.
4. The Assembly cannot bind itself or future generations.
5. Except for the original contract, the majority binds the minority.
6. The Assembly is a permanent body and no form of government is privileged.
7. There must be periodic Assemblies.
8. All magistrates must be elected by universal franchise.
9. The criminal code can include any penalties, including death.
10. The government, not the Assembly, is the arbiter of fact and the application of law.
11. Legislation is limited to areas of common concern, although the Assembly determines what these are.
12. Laws must be universal and impersonal.
13. Citizens are to vote based on common interests, not their individual interests.
14. All laws must be fully enforced.

These rules are procedural (or formal) rather than substantive: they tell citizens *how* to make decisions, not *what* decisions to make. An aggregate of people becomes a sovereign people through an act of unanimous consent to the above contract. Once consent is given to the contract, laws passed by the Assembly are morally binding, even for the losing minority, and the government is obliged to enforce the law. All of this assumes that there is strict adherence to the terms of the contract.

Rousseau does not make sharp distinctions between law, politics, and morality. He is a conventionalist in morality – there is no natural law, independently of what exists in society: the contract creates morality (Melzer, 1983: 638–9). A common criticism of contractarianism is that the contract requires at least one natural moral duty: the obligation to keep your promise. But for Rousseau the meaning of the term 'moral obligation' is internal to the contract. A person who breaks the law can legitimately be punished, even though he himself does not recognise the legitimacy of the law. What the lawbreaker cannot say is that the law is immoral or illegitimate. From the perspective of the sovereign, the lawbreaker is in the state of nature, which is an amoral condition (Noone, 1970: 706).

# Kant

Rousseau was an important influence on Kant. Both were contractarians, and both stressed the idea of self-legislation: laws (including moral laws) are only binding on you if they can be conceived as the product of your will. That is not a reduction of morality to self-interest because moral autonomy – the idea of giving yourself law – assumes that rationality is universalisation. For example, you cannot universalise theft because that would legitimate the seizure of your own property; you cannot create a *law* that permits theft. Where Kant and Rousseau differ is that for the former, morality is universal, for the latter, conventional. Paradoxically, this makes Rousseau's political theory very rigid: if we do not keep to the contract, we are back in the state of nature (amorality). Kant can be more flexible because, at any point, an individual can adopt the moral standpoint. It also leads to a fusion of morality and politics in Rousseau, but their separation in Kant.

While Kant's moral theory and political theory are separate, he nonetheless wants to connect them. In part, this is because it should be possible for a good person to live under the state: the state should not demand immoral acts. How he connects politics and morality – and justifies the state – is through history. To understand his argument, we first need to explore what he means by morality.

In *Groundwork of the Metaphysics of Morals* (1785), Kant outlines a method for determining how we should behave – the categorical imperative (Kant, 1996: 37–108). He offers several formulations, the differences intended to capture various aspects of moral relationships. Simplifying a great deal, what is morally right is what would be chosen if we were to view a situation from an autonomous standpoint, unaffected by emotional, and other, attachments. If we abstract from those attachments, we will necessarily see the world from a universal perspective. Moral reasoning entails universalising a 'maxim', which is a claim that we intend to form the basis of a moral law. If we cannot universalise that maxim it cannot become a moral law.

Kant provides a simple example: a shopkeeper knows that he can get away with overcharging a customer but feels moved to inform the customer that he has been overcharged. The maxim is: 'I should always be honest' (Kant, 1996: 53). This maxim can form the basis of a moral law only if it can be universalised, meaning that anybody in the shopkeeper's situation can make the same judgement, and the shopkeeper in a different situation can apply that maxim. Universalisation involves abstraction from people and situations. Perhaps the customer is a friend, and friendship moves the shopkeeper to be honest, or alternatively, the customer is a child, and the shopkeeper feels bad about cheating a child, or maybe the shopkeeper 'just knows' that it is wrong to overcharge. These cannot justify the maxim because they depend on the identities of the agents or on particular emotions.

The categorical imperative is not a tool for making everyday judgements. This becomes clear when Kant, in one of the formulations, maintains that you should will that your maxim becomes a 'universal law of *nature*' (Kant, 1996: 73). The task is not to make case-by-case judgements but to think holistically: we imagine a *society* governed by universal laws. Such a society Kant describes as a Kingdom of Ends, for if we universalise we must necessarily treat other human beings as ends and not means (Kant, 1996: 80). These laws are not given to us by God, or through our senses, but are constructed by human beings exercising powers of reason (although they are nonetheless universal, not conventional). Through construction of moral laws we lift ourselves above our animal natures and prove our autonomy. There is an important political point here: we can be coerced into *conforming* with what morality requires, but not coerced into acting *for the right reasons*. The shopkeeper can be motivated to be honest by threat of punishment, but he would not be acting morally because he is not moved by reason.

Some contemporary political theorists draw an anarchist conclusion from Kant's argument. Robert Paul Wolff argues that we can never reconcile moral autonomy and the state (Wolff, 2020: 18–19). But Kant does defend the state. He even maintains that a civilised state is possible among a 'nation of devils . . . just so long as they get the constitution right' (Kant, 1996: 335). To understand the relationship between morality and politics we need to distinguish internal freedom and external freedom. The former – which can also be called autonomy – entails the ability to be motivated to act morally by the force of reason alone. The latter is the idea that the freedom of one person must coexist with the freedom of all others. This is expressed as a system of rights, coercively enforced by the state.

The state serves the end of morality by helping realise the Kingdom of Ends. The difficulty with this argument is that human agents will the creation of that Kingdom, whereas in a political community – under the state – we are coerced into behaving in accordance with other people's rights. One way of resolving the conflict between autonomy and coercion would be to think of two standpoints a citizen can adopt: as morally autonomous and as a subject of law. As an auton-omous agent, you will the creation of a political community in which each person's rights are respected, but you also know enough about human nature to recognise that rights will have to be protected through coercion, such that you are at the same time willing the creation of a *coercive* political community. This would, of course, create a divide within human psychology between moral autonomy and political subjectivity.

To overcome the divide between moral autonomy and political subjectivity, Kant appeals to the concept of unsocial sociability (Kant, 1991: 44). Competition is not necessarily the enemy of cooperation as it drives economic development. In the struggle between states, competition can lead to war, but it can also promote trade and trade is a positive-sum game: both trading partners can win. And states also come to realise that war undermines trade; the more trade develops the greater the costs of war. And this brings us back to the universal law of nature. Kant argues that we have a moral duty to create peace and order. At base, war is immoral. Our duty is to bring it about that the law of nature becomes a reality, and the pursuit of self-interest might be the best route to this. The task is to create political institutions that channel those unsocial drives in the direction of sociability, which is why even a 'nation of devils' can create a civilised state, just so long as they have the right constitution.

## Hegel

Hegel's argument for the legitimacy of the state draws on Kant's but is critical of it. As with Kant, he builds on the idea of unsocial sociability: the market (civil society) can unconsciously produce a common good through the pursuit of economic self-interest (Hegel, 1975: 89). But he differs from Kant in maintaining that the harmonisation of self-interest and the common good cannot be an accidental (or contingent) product of history but is in some way necessary (Kain, 1988: 348). How Hegel gets there is complicated – he is a harder philosopher to understand than Rousseau or Kant – but essentially it entails recognising the universal within the particular.

Morality (the universal) is not a constraint on self-interest (the particular) but is necessarily (not contingently) the product of self-interest. Hegel distinguishes *Sittlichkeit* and *Moralität*, with the former being standardly translated as 'ethical life' and the latter as the more straightforward word for morality, but which in Hegel's specific usage means abstract morality and equates to Kant's idea of morality as acting on the basis of a categorical imperative. *Sittlichkeit* denotes so-cially embodied morality; for example, the morality of market relations or of citizenship. It is not 'abstracted' from everyday life. Whereas to act morally (as per *Moralität*) we must be conscious, *Sittlichkeit*, on the other hand, may be unconscious: an ethical life can come about without people consciously attempting to bring it about. It is motivated by custom, habit, and tradition (Kain, 1988: 350). Indeed, humans may be unwitting tools of the process by which *Sittlichkeit* is realised. And while we ought to bring about *Moralität*, *Sittlichkeit* is already there: it makes no sense to say we should bring into existence what already exists.

Individual identity is made possible through social interaction, and society is the product of individual action, so self-interest (individuality) and morality (*Moralität*) affect one another, and the result is concrete ethical life (*Sittlichkeit*), of which living under a state – and a specific state located in space and time – is one important aspect. Underlying this process is *Geist* (Spirit), of which we (humanity) may not be conscious. The historical process is, despite appearances, ra-tional and as Hegel argues 'when we look at the world rationally, the world looks rationally back' (Hegel, 1956: 11). Perhaps confusingly, Hegel argues that *Geist* involves the synthesis of *Moralität* and *Sittlichkeit*, so the latter is no longer unconscious habit but is reflective: we are conscious of our concrete ethical life (Kain, 1988: 350–1). Synthesis (*Aufhebung*) is not merely combination, but the creation of something new. What historically pushes humans to this new, higher level is a recognition of the inadequacy of what exists, which in this case are *Moralität* and *Sittlichkeit*. The former makes no sense without the latter, and the latter is blind without the former. For example, you cannot – Hegel argues – understand the concept of moral duty without context: duties owed by parents to children are different to those owed by citizens to the state and those in their turn are different to duties owed by employers to employees. So *Moralität* presupposes *Sittlichkeit*, but as autonomous agents we should be capable of analysing our duties and being conscious of them.

Hegel reconciles individual freedom with state coercion in the following way:

1.  Individuals must be authors of the laws under which they live. That means they must be morally autonomous (in this he agrees with Kant).
2.  Autonomy can only be realised in a political community, under law (we need *Sittlichkeit* as well as *Moralität*).
3.  Customs must be adapted and moulded so they recognise individual interests but also lead the way to the universal (*Geist*). An example would be the guarantee of private property rights. Private property rights cannot be understood in negative terms as the limits of state power but rather by working on the world – for example, by creating a product – you not only claim ownership of that product but also make concrete your own individuality: you externalise yourself, and the product looks back at you as an expression of your identity (Knowles, 1983: 50–2).

Political institutions must be legitimated but they also legitimate. Once again, there is a sublation (*Aufhebung*) of two correct – but in themselves inadequate – ideas: individuals need to make the laws under which they live and in this sense contract theorists are right, but legitimation does not stop once the contract is (metaphorically) signed, but continues as a historical process. This also explains the relationship between the 'nation' and the 'state'. Nations are often the focus of positive sentiment and loyalty, whereas the state – in the Weberian sense – is hardly loveable. But while there could be stateless nations, the drive is to fuse the nation with the state. That said, nation-states can often appear historically arbitrary, with boundaries drawn in odd places. Why then should we feel loyalty to such historically contingent constructions? Hegel's answer is, first, states and nations go together – a stateless nation will not engender *Sittlichkeit* – and second, state institutions change the character of the nation (Kain, 1988: 358–9), so those peculiarly drawn nation-states can over time attract allegiance.

Individual obligation to the state results from a process of alienation, a process that precedes state-creation. When we (physically) labour, we confront something that is alien to us: the physical object. But as suggested above in the context of property rights we come to see ourselves in the object on which we have laboured. We have overcome our alienation, and our individuality moves from an abstract possibility to something concrete. This is one stage in the historical process of individual self-realisation. Living under a state is another. The state is alien: it threatens us with punishment. But by living under the state – a specific state – we become something else: citizens with a real history and sense of belonging. As the state gains loyalty and recognition from its citizens so it becomes more legitimate.

## The state and the politics of the exception

The third and final perspective on the state is influenced by Hobbes but rejects the rational-choice interpretation presented earlier in this chapter. Carl Schmitt (1888–1985) was a German academic lawyer who had a significant impact well beyond his native country. There was a resurgence of interest in his work in the 1980s, and he continues to exert influence. Among his many works, his most famous is *The Concept of the Political* (1927), which argued that politics exists where there is a distinction between friend and enemy.

Schmitt was clear that the state had to be legitimate. In his study of Hobbes, he argues that 'no political system can survive even a generation with only the naked techniques of holding power. . .there is no politics without authority and no authority without an ethos of belief [in that authority]' (Schmitt, 1996: 17). But politics cannot be reduced to law or to morality. What is legal is determined by legal norms, whereas politics is about friends and enemies. The application of legal norms presupposes a situation of social normality, but that may be absent. The sovereign is not defined legally but is the person who decides on the 'state of exception': the person capable of suspending law and using extra-legal force to normalise a situation (Schmitt, 2005: 5, 13). The sovereign does not need legal recognition because there is no background of social normality against which the law could legitimate his sovereignty.

In a divided society, the sovereign will inevitably side with one faction over another, and so creating a situation of normality entails suppressing some groups. The task for the sovereign is to create identity. A sovereign dictator does not defend an existing constitution but creates a new one and does so in the name of the people. This assumes that there is a people and here the friend-enemy distinction is central. Two groups find themselves in a situation of mutual enmity if there is a possibility of war between them. Membership of a group is denoted by the willing-ness to die for one's group and kill members of the other group.

Any distinction – linguistic, racial, cultural, or religious – can become a marker of group identity. There can be no external moral judgement of the validity of a group or its identity. It is for that group to decide who is friend and who is enemy. Modern liberal states tend not to distinguish between friend and enemy and so they extend membership (citizenship) rights to people who do not truly belong to the political community. For that reason, the boundaries of citizenship and the political community should coincide. In *The Concept of the Political*, Schmitt maintains that the state presupposes the concept of the political, meaning the friend-enemy distinction (Schmitt, 2007: 26). And one of the aims of the sovereign dictator in the process of creating social normality is to engender social homogeneity – if necessary, by force.

There is a tendency, Schmitt argues, to see all conflicts as soluble if institutions are created that work to everyone's advantage. The rational choice interpretation of Hobbes assumes this – Schmitt's interpretation of Hobbes is very different – and we saw the same thinking behind Kant's unsocial sociability. Underlying this criticism of modern thought – especially characteris-tic of liberal theory – is the idea that the political community is, for Schmitt, something worthy of personal sacrifice.

Schmitt emphasises the exceptional and the state of emergency, but after the normalisation brought about by the sovereign there will be a legal order. It follows that politics cannot be a permanent state of emergency. Schmitt argues that the new constitutional order can be demo-cratic and egalitarian, just so long as there is political identity (Schmitt, 2008: 257–64). However, he rejects the idea of universal equality. Citizens can be equal as members of the political com-munity, but that community rests on the friend-enemy distinction, and so equal rights cannot extend to outsiders.

There is an intense debate over Schmitt's relationship to German National Socialism (Caldwell, 2005). He was an important commentator on the Weimar Republic in the late 1920s and early 1930s and advocated for the use of Article 48 of the Weimar Constitution giving the President emergency powers (Hollerich, 2004: 108). However, he reconciled himself to the new nazi regime, and certainly some of the concepts outlined above have a superficial similarity to nazi doctrine. But there is a case to be made that his conception of the state is theological. Indeed, one of his major works is entitled *Political Theology* (1922), and in it he outlines elements of his theory of sovereignty. It could be argued that what he was fighting is the perceived despiritualisation (or disenchantment) of modernity, characterised by economic values – making money rather pursuing virtue – and by the fragmentation of politics through the power-play of interest groups (this was one of his major criticisms of the latter period of the Weimar Republic). And despite admiring his work, Schmitt argues that Hobbes was also guilty of pushing religion out of politics (Hollerich, 2004: 119). While Hobbes insisted that there should be one state religion – he did not support religious toleration – this was motivated entirely by considerations of public order (Hobbes, 1991: 405–6). Since religion was a cause of conflict, religious differences had to be suppressed, but what you believe privately – in your head – was a matter between you and God, and if it turns out that the state religion promotes false beliefs God will forgive you for openly professing that false faith (so long as you inwardly reject it).

Putting aside the controversial aspects of Schmitt's biography, the main problem with his theory of the state is that it does not seem to engage with everyday politics – despite his own very real engagement with everyday politics over a long life. Politics cannot be separated from economics, as Hobbes well saw. And while there may be spiritual aspects to politics – absent in modern, 'post-heroic' societies – the spiritual has always been in tension with the material. In other words, Schmitt's conception of politics – and, by extension, state authority – is one-sided.

## The state in international politics

The focus so far has been on the relationship of the individual to the state, but it is also important to understand the relationship between states in international politics. In the academic sub-discipline of international relations, there is no shortage of theories of the international system, but two are of particular relevance: realism and liberalism. Of the political thinkers discussed in this chapter Hobbes and Schmitt are clearly realists, whereas Kant certainly – and possibly also Rousseau and Hegel – are liberals.

## Realism

Realism comes in two versions – classical and structural, with a further sub-division of the latter – but both emphasise the interests of states. And power is a central concept in international politics. Influential international relations theory Hans Morgenthau (1904–80) argued in his book *Politics among Nations* (first published 1948) that the struggle for power between states takes three basic forms: keep power (status quo), increase power ('imperialism'; overthrow of the status quo), or demonstrate power (prestige) (Thompson and Morgenthau, 1985: 52–3). International law is not completely absent, but its effectiveness is dependent either on a balance of power or on how the interests of two or more states are aligned.

Structural realism emphasises that the structure of the international system determines state behaviour. There are five key tenets:

1. The international system is anarchical.
2. All states possess some offensive capacity.
3. States can never be certain of the intentions of other states.

4. The main goal of states is survival.
5. States are rational actors; they seek to maximise the satisfaction of their preferences (Waltz, 1979: 88–93).

The international equivalent of the prisoner's dilemma is the security dilemma. States can spend money on defence or on other goods. The best outcome would be to spend little on defence in the hope other states will do likewise, or if they do spend on defence, they will not use their military against you. The worst outcome would be to spend little on defence and be invaded and occupied. Since states cannot trust one another, they spend money on defence. Furthermore, even though one state believes that it is spending only on defensive – not offensive – forces, because of uncertainty other states should rationally interpret 'defence' spending as 'offence' spending. The result is an arms race.

Within structural realism, there is a division between defensive realism and offensive realism, with the leading representative of the former being Kenneth Waltz and of the latter John Mearsheimer. Both emphasise the importance of power but whereas Waltz argues that states can be satisfied with a certain level of power and their key objective is the maintenance of the status quo, Mearsheimer argues that there is no limit to the search for power (Mearsheimer, 2001: 21). Put rather simplistically, offensive realism says that states must keep running to stand still. What they seek is hegemonic power. Global hegemony is unlikely, as it would require a monopoly of nuclear weapons, but regional domination is possible (2001: 145). However, regional hegemons may face each other at the boundaries of regions, an example being China and the United States in the Pacific region.

Given the affinities between Hobbesianism and structural realism, it might be asked why there is not a war of all states against all states, parallel to what Hobbes thinks holds between individuals in the state of nature. Hobbes argued that there would be distrust but not necessarily war:

> . . .in all times kings and persons of sovereign authority, because of their independence, are in continual jealousies, and in the state and posture of gladiators, having their weapons pointing and their eyes fixed on one another – that is, their forts, garrisons and guns upon the frontiers of their kingdoms, and continual spies on their neighbours, which is a posture of war.
>
> (Hobbes, 1991: 187–8)

The world is anarchical and so is Hobbes's state of nature (life without a state), but there are differences between the 'domestic' state of nature and the 'global' one. The causes of conflict in the former are competition, diffidence, and glory-seeker (the last of these entails the pursuit of reputation despite the risks of death). Competition and glory-seeking will apply in the global state of nature, but diffidence may not. Human beings are roughly equal in the (domestic) state of nature, but states in the international system are not. The United States does not feel threatened by Tonga and so will not attack – or at least it will not attack as a pre-emptive act. Of course, where states are equal enough to feel threatened – again, think of China and the United States – there is a degree of diffidence.

## Liberalism

Liberal international relation theorists claim either that the structure of the international system is not anarchical or if it is, there are ways of solving the security dilemma and building trust between states. Michael Doyle argues that liberal-democratic states are different to non-liberal states. (Realists argue that regime type – liberal or authoritarian – makes no difference to the behaviour of states as all face the same challenges arising from anarchy.) He claims that no two 'constitutionally secure liberal states' have gone to war against one another (Doyle, 1983: 213). There are two interpretations of this claim. The first is that liberal democracies externalise their norms: because they treat their own citizens well, they also show a degree of respect for citizens in other liberal democracies. The second is that because of internal constraints – such as a relatively free press and parliamentary scrutiny – liberal states will not engage in offensive action which conflicts with the interests of their people. Since other liberal states know this, distrust is significantly reduced. The so-called democratic peace argument is not without its critics (Rosato, 2003), but it provides a counterweight to realism, which is arguably the dominant theory of state behaviour in international politics.

Doyle draws heavily on Kant's essay 'Perpetual Peace: A Philosophical Sketch' (1795). Kant argues that there are three 'Definitive Articles' forming the foundation of world peace:

1. The constitution of every state should be republican, that is, democratic or constitutional.
2. The law of nations should be founded on a federation of free states.
3. The law of world citizenship shall be limited to 'universal hospitality' (Kant, 2008: 74–85).

The last of these articles makes clear two things: (a) there is no world government and (b) individuals should be accorded protection when they travel. So, for example, businessmen travelling abroad should have the same basic rights before the law, short of citizenship, as citizens themselves. The development of embassies and diplomacy – a product of the Italian Renaissance – is also part of this process. The argument is tied closely to the gains from trade argument; not only is trade mutually beneficial, but war interferes with it.

## Schmitt on international relations

Given the importance of the friend-enemy distinction, it follows that international politics is a central aspect of Schmitt's understanding of the state. Schmitt does not defend war, nor does he reject the idea that one state can recognise the legitimacy of another state and both states can peacefully coexist (Schmitt, 2003: 42–9). But part of mutual recognition is the right of states to go to war (*jus ad bellum*); there are no international legal norms determining *jus ad bellum*. Any political community can go to war for whatever reason it thinks appropriate. In defending this, he appeals to the period of European history between the Treaty of Westphalia (1648) – the point at which the modern state system emerged – to 1914. This was governed by *jus publicum Europaeum*. In this legal order, there was no distinction between just and unjust wars. All sides in a war were recognised as legitimate belligerents. This meant that states could make peace without the need to allocate moral blame and it also gave states the freedom to choose sides (or keep out of conflicts). It also meant that the conduct of war was constrained by rules (*jus in bello*) (2003: 140–71).

The emergence of a 'discriminating concept of war', whereby sides were judged moral or immoral, undermined the *jus publicum Europaeum*. The condemnation of Germany in the First World War led to the use of tactics, such as a starvation blockade, that would have been deemed immoral (under *jus in bello*) in previous conflicts. Moralised wars become total wars. When one side is deemed evil there is no restriction on the means considered necessary for its elimination (Schmitt, 2007: 36).

Schmitt acknowledged that the days of *jus publicum Europaeum* were over, and in its place advocated a new global order analogous to it (Schmitt, 2014: 101–9). In his book *The Nomos of the Earth* (Schmitt, 2003), he outlined a framework of international politics in which enemy states could coexist without their enmity becoming 'absolute'. Essentially, conflicts should be reduced to territoriality and not ideas (or ideologies). Drawing on his earlier work he argues that territorialisation (or spatialisation) will work only if people who share the same territory share the same political identity (Schmitt, 2014: 86–8). He recognises the fact of great powers (superpowers) and argues that spatialisation entails regional hegemony. That is, superpowers control specific territory; in the 1950s that meant the Soviet Union in Eastern Europe and the United States in Western Europe.

## Should policing be privatised?

We return to the question asked at the start of the chapter. To be clear, the discussion is not simply about whether aspects of policing should be privatised, but whether *all* police activity should be privately supplied. We assume that there is a legal system, although this might take the form of natural rights in a state of nature. Any police service will be bound by law. We evaluate private security by its effectiveness in deterring crime, or, should crime happen, in apprehending criminals.

If we follow the arguments of Rousseau and Hegel – and perhaps also Kant – we would reject private policing as incompatible with the will of the people. Policing is not just of instrumental value but expresses the common good. Private interests must either be suppressed (Rousseau) or transcended (*aufgehoben* – Hegel). For Hobbes, policing is close to the raw exercise of coercion and is therefore the preserve of the sovereign, although that does not preclude him employing private agencies.

Perhaps the most interesting perspective on this question draws on the four goods discussed earlier. Recall that these goods are distinguished by two characteristics: excludability and rivalry. In practice, goods differ in the degree to which they have these characteristics; there are few pure types. That said, policing looks like something that is largely non-excludable. If your neighbour pays for police patrols but you do not, then you are free-riding on her contribution. Of course, house-breakers might know that you are a non-payer and that the police will not turn up to investigate a break-in, but the patrols might still deter them. What we have here is the standard Hobbesian argument for the state: we need security, which we can term a first-order issue. But then, we need to pay for it. This is a second-order issue.

Is the Hobbesian argument correct? Quite a lot of security is provided privately: burglar alarms; personal protection (guns; pepper spray); self-defence classes; gated communities; CCTV; security guards for shops and other businesses; private detective agencies. However, the question we posed was whether policing could be *fully* privatised.

A second line of argument is concerned with externalities. That your neighbour's payment for police patrols benefits you – that is, generates positive externalities – does not mean that the good (patrols) will be undersupplied. She might calculate that the direct benefits (internalities) are sufficient to justify paying. This argument could be extended to a wider territory. One concern about privatising policing is that there will be large areas where there is inadequate provision because people cannot afford to pay for it. But given that wealthy people value security – and often need to travel through poorer areas – they would likely pay for it, perhaps through not-for-profit social enterprises.

A third possibility is to draw on Coase's lighthouse argument and bundle policing up with some other good. Streets could be privatised and managed by residents' associations. If you buy a house, you might also have to buy security (landlords could include this in the rent charged).

Where it is not economically efficient to have competing agencies within a given territory, there might emerge monopoly providers, but if these fail, new security companies could emerge.

How realistic this is will depend on how high the barriers to entry are. A variant is 'voting with your feet': if you are not happy with the service provided in one municipality you move to another. Indeed, the threat of losing customers may be sufficient to maintain a good standard of service on the part of the monopoly provider.

## Conclusion

The state is a monopoliser of violence, but it needs to distinguish itself from other entities that use violence such as criminal organisations. It must be explained why it is rational for individuals to obey the state – arguments that are qualitatively different from the simple fact that people fear it. Hobbes argued from self-interest. Rousseau, Kant, and Hegel derived the legitimacy of the state from ethical conceptions, which while not reducible to self-interest could be comprehended by individuals. Schmitt abandons ideas of morality and legality and maintains that the state is identifiable with a sovereign who creates legitimacy where none exists.

## Note

1   In the original German: "Staat ist diejenige menschliche Gemeinschaft, welche innerhalb eines bestimmten Gebietes. . .das *Monopol legitimer physischer Gewaltsamkeit* für sich (mit Erfolg) beansprucht". Max Weber, *Politik als Beruf*, Duncker and Humblot, Second Edition, 1926, p.8.

## References

Caldwell, P. C. (2005). Controversies over Carl Schmitt: A Review of Recent Literature. *The Journal of Modern History*, 77(2), 357–87.

Coase, R. H. (1974). The Lighthouse in Economics. *The Journal of Law and Economics*, 17(2), 357–76.

Doyle, M. W. (1983). Kant, Liberal Legacies, and Foreign Affairs. *Philosophy & Public Affairs*, 12, 205–35.

Hegel, G. W. F. (1975). *Lectures on the Philosophy of World History: Introduction*. Ed. J Hoffmeister. Cambridge: Cambridge University Press.

Hegel G. W. F. (1956). *The Philosophy of History*. Translated by J. Sibree. New York: Dover

Hobbes, T. (1991). *Leviathan*. Ed. C.B. Macpherson. London: Penguin.

Hollerich, M. (2004). 'Carl Schmitt', in Peter Scott and William T. Cavanaugh (eds.). *The Blackwell Companion to Political Theology*. Oxford: Blackwell

Kain, P. (1988). Hegel's Political Theory and Philosophy of History. *Clio*, 17(4), 345–68.

Kant, I (1991). *Political Writings*. Ed. H Reiss. New York: Cambridge University Press. Second Edition.

Kant, I. (1996). *Practical Philosophy*. Ed. M. Gregor. Cambridge: Cambridge University Press.

Kant, I. (2008). *Toward Perpetual Peace and Other Writings on Politics, Peace, and History*. New Haven, CT: Yale University Press.

Knowles, D. (1983). Hegel on Property and Personality. *The Philosophical Quarterly (1950–)*, 33(130), 45–62.

Kurrild-Klitgaard, P., and Svendsen, G. T. (2003). Rational Bandits: Plunder, Public Goods, and the Vikings. *Public Choice*, *117*(3), 255–72.

McLean, I. (1981). The Social Contract in Leviathan and the Prisoner's Dilemma Supergame. *Political Studies*, *29*(3), 339–51.

Mearsheimer, J. J. (2001). *The Tragedy of Great Power Politics*. New York: WW Norton & Company.

Melzer, A. M. (1983). Rousseau's Moral Realism: Replacing Natural Law with the General Will. *The American Political Science Review*, *77*(3), 633–51.

Noone Jr, J. B. (1970). The Social Contract and the Idea of Sovereignty in Rousseau. *The Journal of Politics*, *32*(3), 696–708.

Plamenatz, J. (1992) *Man and Society: Political and Social Theories from Machiavelli to Marx. Vol. 1, From the Middle Ages to Locke*. London: Longman.

Rosato, S. (2003). The Flawed Logic of Democratic Peace Theory. *American Political Science Review*, *97*(4), 585–602.

Rousseau, J. J. (1986). 'The Social Contract', in *Rousseau: Political Writings*, trans. by Frederick Watkins. New York: Nelson.

Schmitt, C. (1996). *Roman Catholicism and Political Form* (No. 380). Westport, CT: Greenwood Publishing Group.

Schmitt, C. (2003). *The Nomos of the Earth in the International Law of the Jus Publicum Europaeum*. New York: Telos.

Schmitt, C. (2005). *Political Theology: Four Chapters on the Concept of Sovereignty*. Chicago, IL: University of Chicago Press.

Schmitt, C. (2007). *The Concept of the Political*. Chicago: University of Chicago Press.

Schmitt, C. (2008). *Constitutional Theory*. Durham, NC: Duke University Press.

Schmitt, C. (2014). *Writings on War*. London: John Wiley & Sons.

Thompson, K. and Morgenthau, H. (1985). *Politics among Nations: The Struggle for Power and Peace*. New York: Alfred A. Knopf.

Waltz, K. N. (1979). *Theory of International Politics*. New York: McGraw-Hill.

Weber, M. (1994). *Weber: Political Writings*. Cambridge: Cambridge University Press.

Wolff, R. P. (2020). *In Defense of Anarchism*. Berkeley and Los Angeles: University of California Press.

Waltz, K. N. (1979). *Theory of International Politics*. New York: McGraw-Hill.

## Further reading

Although they take a different approach to outlining theories of the state, the following are useful (if slightly dated): Colin Hay, Michael Lister, and David Marsh (eds.), *The State: Theories and Issues* (Palgrave Macmillan, 2005); David Held, *Political Theory and the Modern State: Essays on State, Power and Democracy* (Polity, 1989). Authority, power, and sovereignty are important concepts in discussion of the state, and these books are helpful: Fabian Wendt, *Authority* (Polity, 2018); Peter Morriss, *Power: A Philosophical Analysis* (Manchester University Press, 2002); Dieter Grimm, *Sovereignty: The Origin and Future of a Political Concept* (Columbia University Press, 2015). On international relations theory: Tim Dunne, Mijka Kurki, and Steve Smith (eds.), *International Relations Theories: Discipline and Diversity* (Oxford University Press, 2020), see especially Chapters 2, 3 and 4.

# Chapter 2

# Democracy

## Introduction

Democracy is a term so frequently used in everyday political debate and whose meaning has been extended to encompass so much of what is valued that it can be daunting defining it and assessing its merits. In this chapter, we argue for a narrow definition: it is a method for making collective decisions where each person's voice has (in principle) equal weight.

How effective is it as a decision-making method? Would a reduction in democracy produce better results? Indeed, what is a good result? There are two ways to approach this last question. Democracy is simply concerned with individuals' preferences: it is an instrument for preference-aggregation. Against this instrumental view of democracy, there is an alternative one: democracy is a means of arriving at the truth (the epistemic view). In this chapter, we will see how well democracy performs in both its instrumental and epistemic variants.

## Key questions

- What is democracy?
- How effective is democracy in achieving important political objectives?
- Should the scope of democracy be extended or reduced?

## What is democracy?

Democracy is a word widely used in everyday debate. It has been inflated to encompass liberalism, with its emphasis on freedom, although there are tensions between democracy and individual rights. In recognition of these tensions, the qualified term 'liberal-democracy' is often used. Another very strong association in the popular mind is democracy and majority rule: many people think democracy simply *is* majority rule. This is a mistake, although as we will see there are good reasons for granting majority decision-making special status within democratic theory. It is also tempting in defining the concept to reach for the dictionary and appeal to etymology: democracy as the rule of the people (*demos*). This is not wrong – and it is useful when studying ancient Greek thought (Liddel, 2009) – but it is of limited help in understanding contemporary applications of the concept.

DOI: 10.4324/9780429424106-4

Case study 2.1

## Was Brexit a mistake?

**PHOTO 2.1** © Jim Dyson/Getty Images.

In June 2016, the United Kingdom voted by 51.9% to 48.1%, on a 72.2% voter turnout, to leave the European Union. Of the four constituent parts of the United Kingdom, England and Wales voted to leave and Scotland and Northern Ireland to remain.

National referendums are rare in the United Kingdom. There have been only three UK-wide ones – a vote on whether to leave the EU (then the European Economic Community) in 1975, one on changing the electoral system in 2011, and the 2016 referendum. The 2011 referendum was legally binding; had it been successful, parliament would have been required to enact it. The 1975 and 2016 EU referendums were advisory, but almost all campaigners and participants treated them as if they were binding.

In March 2017, the British Prime Minister triggered Article 50 of the Lisbon Treaty and started a two-year transition period to leaving the EU. There were various further extensions, in part a result of parliamentary votes lost by the government, but on 31 January 2020, the United Kingdom finally ended its 47-year membership of the organisation.

Before reading the rest of this chapter, ask yourself: should there have been a referendum on leaving the EU? If so, should more than a simple majority have been required to leave? For example, it could have been stipulated that there must be 60% in favour of leaving or (alternatively) 50% of the electorate (not just those who voted). Was it right to have a binary leave/remain question, or should there have been more options on the ballot paper, and how would the votes then have been counted? If there was evidence that after the 2016 referendum opinion had shifted in favour of remaining in the EU should there have been a second referendum? Should there have been a second referendum in any case, on the grounds (it is claimed) that people did not know what they were voting for in 2016?

Rather than adopting the expansive sense of the term, the focus in this chapter will be on democracy narrowly defined as a method for making collective decisions where each person's vote (in principle) counts equally and no one person's opinion is intrinsically superior to that of another. This is the core definition of democracy. Other ideas may become attached to democracy, but it is helpful to keep in mind this core idea.

The core definition of democracy is compatible with both direct and indirect (representative) democracy. In a direct democracy, all those subject to laws are creators of those laws, whereas with indirect democracy, we vote for representatives. This is however a simplification. Take as an example a referendum – for example, the EU one. While all those on the electoral register vote directly on the proposition, the framing of the question is determined by elected representatives. Representative democracy itself is subject to degrees of directness. A famous debate in the British parliamentary tradition is between those who argue members of parliament are not delegates, mandated to follow the will of their electors, but representatives charged with using their judgement: we vote for people, not policies (see pp. 178–9).

Another distinction is between the constitutional level (second-order decision-making) and the legislative level (first-order). This may be less evident in the United Kingdom which, unusual among jurisdictions, lacks a codified constitution and much more obvious in the United States, which has possibly the most famous constitution in world history. But despite these differences, in both countries – and indeed all democracies – there is first-order decision-making (voting for parties and candidates; lawmakers voting on legislation) and there are 'decisions about decisions', which is second-order. Voting in a presidential election is a first-order act, whereas deciding the rules for how a president is elected is a second-order one. In the United States, the Electoral College system is laid down in the Constitution and to change it would require amending the Constitution, which is a complicated process (in essence, you need two-thirds of each house of Congress and three-quarters of the states).

## Majorities

As suggested above, democracy is a system in which there is 'one person, one vote'. That might be compatible with something other than majority rule. Perhaps unanimity could be required: everybody must agree (Gill and Gainous, 2002: 386). Imagine a community of 100 people deciding how many guns and how much butter to produce. Guns are on the x-axis and butter (in kg) is on the y-axis. Each person has a different preference along the Pareto Frontier, which marks the boundary of Pareto efficiency: nobody can be made better off without making someone else worse off. They keep negotiating until they settle upon a point (Figure 2.1).

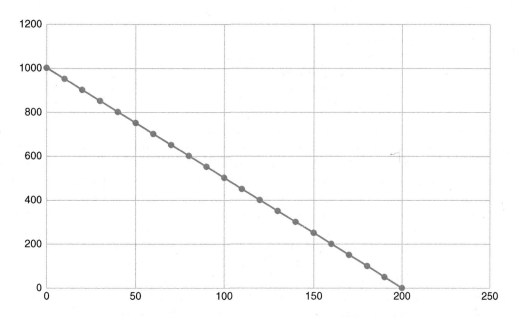

**FIGURE 2.1** The trade-off between guns (horizontal axis) and butter (in kg) (vertical axis).

Decisions might also be made by qualified majorities. There could be a rule requiring 60% of voters to agree to a law or policy rather than a bare majority. On the face of it, this appears unfair: if 58% vote in favour, then 42% are asserting their will over the 58%, and this does not seem compatible with votes counting equally. But we must think back to the first-order/second-order distinction: if the 60% rule was agreed in advance of voting, the 58% should accept the result. However, this pushes the issue back a stage, because quite often changing a constitution requires a qualified majority. Who decided that is how you change the constitution? There is infinite regress: each stage requires a previous one to legitimate subsequent ones. Indeed, we may be back to the problem of the state (Chapter 1): at some point the political (and legal) system was imposed by force.

One strategy common among political theorists is to set up a thought-experiment. We have already encountered one in Hobbes's theory of the state: we imagine there is no state and ask ourselves whether it would be rational to create one. In later chapters other such experiments will be presented, the most famous recent one being John Rawls's veil of ignorance: what would we choose if we did not know our identities? The details of the veil will be left to a later chapter (see p. 136), but the basic idea can be applied to the question of whether we would endorse a simple majority rule or go for a qualified majority rule. In deciding which rule to support, you must consider two things: (a) What are the gains from winning and what are the losses if you lose? (To make it easier, think in terms of monetary losses and gains); (b) What is the probability you will end up on the winning (or losing) side?

At the start of this chapter, we suggested that there is a tension between democracy and rights. The majority may vote to take away the rights of the minority. Using the veil of ignorance, we could in principle remove this tension. Consider the following options:

1. One person – a dictator – can remove your rights.
2. A minority can remove your rights. (The minority can range from two people to any number just below half of voters).

3. A simple majority (50 + 1) can remove your rights.
4. A qualified majority can remove your rights. (This majority can range from a bare majority plus one, to everybody minus one).
5. Your rights can only be removed by a unanimous vote.
6. One person – you – can remove your rights.
7. Nobody – including you – can remove your rights. This is what is meant by inalienable rights: you cannot give away – 'make alien' – your rights.

It might be tempting to endorse option 5. But that would make social change difficult: we might all be worse off if it is impossible to make any collective decisions. A better strategy is to weigh gains and losses by the probability of being on the winning side. Since you do not know your identity, you cannot calculate individual probabilities – you only know the probabilities for a person selected at random. Given this fact about probabilities, it would be rational to endorse a simple majority rule if the gains and losses are symmetrical: the gains from being on the winning side are exactly matched by any losses should you end up losing. If the loss is greater than the gain, it makes sense to set the bar higher. But how high? The higher you lift the bar the higher the probability you will be on the winning side: if there is a 60% majority rule, there is 60% chance of being on the winning side. But if the gains from winning are (only) marginally lower than the losses from losing, 60% may be too high. In effect, the balance between losses and gains for a random person will determine the threshold at which a decision is endorsed.

To put this in stark terms: if the seizure of all your property and its redistribution to the winning side is the price of losing, then you would want to set the bar very high (especially if the winners gain only a small amount from redistribution). This explains why constitutions often embody (or are linked to) a bill of rights and amending that bill of rights is made difficult.

The problem is that real people know their identities and can reasonably enough refuse to accept that the veil of ignorance argument has any moral significance. The closest we can get to the veil is the sense that there are vicissitudes in life: we can never be certain what the future holds and endorsing a qualified majority rule is a hedge against changing fortunes. We might also have vicarious preferences: you want things for other people, such as your children, and you would not want their vital interests placed at the mercy of a simple majority.

## The median voter

While preferences may count equally in the sense of 'one person, one vote', the outcome may not be equal. Imagine people are voting on one issue and there is a continuum of positions. The most straightforward example is tax-and-spend policy: we move from extreme left (high tax, high spend) to extreme right (low tax, low spend). Between these extremes, there are intermediate positions: as you move from left to right, the preferences gradually (monotonically) shift to lower taxes and lower spending. There are two political parties A and B, each having a precise position on the spectrum.

Voters are arranged along the spectrum. The median voter (M) is exactly halfway along the distribution: she has half of voters to the left of her and half to the right. The party that wins over the median voter wins the election because a party simply needs 50 + 1. Since party A's policy is closer to M than party B's policy, A wins. For B to win, the party needs to get closer than A to M. Two points follow: parties' policies will converge, and the median voter gets more of her preferences satisfied than a voter further away on the spectrum.

Various assumptions underlie the median voter theory, which was developed by, among others, Duncan Black (Black, 1948), and Anthony Downs (Rowley, 1984: 105–6):

1. There is only dimension – in this example, left to right on tax-and-spend.
2. Voters' preferences are single-peaked, meaning that for any voter distance from his preference is progressively worse (if a voter wanted to be highly taxed or lightly taxed but not moderately taxed his preferences would have more than one peak).
3. There are only two options – in this case parties A and B.
4. Parties (or candidates) only care about maximising votes (and thereby winning power) and not ideology.
5. All eligible voters vote.
6. Lobbying and campaign financing has no effect.
7. Parties (or candidates) have perfect information.

Many of these assumptions do not hold. Nonetheless, the median voter theory illuminates some real-world aspects of competitive elections, if only dimly. Politics in the United Kingdom since 1945 illustrate the election-winning power of the median voter. By the time of the next election (due in 2024), the Labour Party will have been in power for only 30 of the preceding 79 years. On losing office, it tends to move to the left and away from the median voter with bad consequences for its electability. As it keeps losing elections it gradually moves back to the centre. The Conservatives have been defter at tacking closer to the median voter. But note that the median voter – the famous 'centre ground' of politics – can shift. In the 1960s, the median British voter was closer to a policy package that included significant state intervention in the economy, whereas by the 1980s, the centre had shifted to free market solutions; today, it is possible that there has been a shift back to greater intervention in the economy.

## Interest groups

One of the assumptions of the median voter model is the absence of interest groups and campaign finance. In practice, they have significant influence. Interest groups use advocacy to pursue their objectives; those objectives may be value-based – for example, in favour of animal welfare – or economic, such as getting regulatory concessions in the automobile industry. They use money to finance their communication strategy, but they may also fund politicians directly through campaign donations.

The concept of collective action is central to understanding the role of interest groups. They face a free-rider problem. Imagine you own a restaurant and there is an interest group for restaurateurs to which you could belong were you to pay a subscription. If you benefit from the interest group's advocacy but do not pay your subscription you are a free-rider: you are getting benefits at no personal cost. In general, interest groups with fewer potential members are more effective at dealing with free-riders (Mueller, 2003: 473–4). Aerospace companies have far fewer members (potential beneficiaries) than the restaurant sector, and with fewer members, the gains from lobbying are more concentrated and the free-riders more exposed.

A problem for democracy arises where on one side you have a highly concentrated benefit which carries a cost for a highly dispersed and unorganised group on the other. This is evident in trade policy. Cyclists want cheap bikes. National bicycle manufacturers want to shut out international competition through hefty tariffs on imported bikes. The national manufacturers lobby politicians for tariffs and as a result gain a concentrated benefit. But that gain is at a cost to ordinary cyclists, who must pay higher prices. However, because the cost is dispersed, they might not notice, and even if they do, they face a free-rider problem: they could establish a cyclists' lobby to counter the power of the manufacturers but most cyclists will not pay for that lobbying effort. The best strategy for concerned cyclists is to bundle up lobbying with some club good (for a discussion of different kinds of goods, see p. 14). For example, in Britain there is an organisation for non-competitive cyclists – Cycling UK – which lobbies on behalf of ordinary cyclists, but packages that lobbying with some membership benefits, such as cheaper insurance.

Interest groups seem to have a distorting influence on democratic politics, but they do provide some benefits. Voters cannot influence the policy process, but they can use intermediaries – interest groups – to achieve this. These intermediaries are professionals who have the time and money to acquire detailed information on policies and on strategies to influence politicians – they are political professionals, whereas voters are amateurs. And voters often have more than one interest: cyclists are usually also workers, so that what is good for their employer is good for them.

## Log-rolling

There is a distinction between ordinal and cardinal voting. If you are asked to choose between apples, oranges, and bananas you can order your references: 1st – oranges; 2nd – bananas; 3rd – apples (or whatever order you prefer). But that ordering tells us nothing about the intensity of your preferences. You might only slightly prefer oranges to bananas and bananas to apples, or very strongly prefer one to the other. Cardinal measures attempt to express the intensity of your preference.

Most voting systems are not cardinal, and so there tends to be a do-it-yourself quality to expressing an intensity of preference. This is best illustrated in voting among elected representatives. Log-rolling is one such method (the origins of the terms seem to lie in the practice of neighbours assisting one another to move logs, rather than the balancing game).

| Voter | Project and value attached to each by three voters | | |
| | Project X | Project Y | Project Z |
|---|---|---|---|
| **A** | 15 | −3 | −8 |
| **B** | −8 | 18 | −13 |
| **C** | −5 | −4 | 30 |
| **Total net gain** | 2 | 11 | 9 |

There are three 'voters' (in fact, members of Congress, or of Parliament) and three projects. If the projects are voted on separately, all are defeated: B and C vote against X, A and C against Y, and A and B against Z. But if – for example – A votes for Y in return for B voting for X, they both gain a benefit. (For a technical discussion of log-rolling, see Mueller, 2003: 104–8.)

The negative side of this is pork barrel politics; that is, the channelling of public money for projects based on geographical electoral considerations rather than the overall public good. Imagine an election in a fictional country produces the following result: Red Party 90 seats, Blue Party 70 seats, Yellow Party 40 seats. The Blues hold mainly urban seats, and their priority is to increase hospital provision in those seats, while the Yellows have mainly rural and island seats, and they want more roads and bridges. The main competitor in all the Blue-held and Yellow-held seats is the Red Party, so the chance of the Blues and Yellows taking seats off one another is remote. A Blue-Yellow Coalition Government is formed. Under these circumstances, it is in the interests of Blues and Yellows to channel funds to each other's seats. The government will spend lots of money on hospitals in Blue seats, to the detriment of people in Red seats, and on roads and bridges in Yellow seats, even though few people will use them. These policies distort national priorities and reduce overall utility. (For the application of the concept to a specific example – India – see Sharma, 2017).

## Voting with your feet – Tiebout sorting

The problem of public goods was discussed in Chapter 1 (see pp. 13–14). A public good is one from which non-payers cannot be excluded and additional consumers do not reduce its consumption. The non-provision of public goods is thought to be a market failure: since the market will not produce the good, the state must do so through compulsory payment (taxation). One of the functions of elections is to work out how much of a public good we want: if we vote for a party that will increase spending on roads that signals we want more roads. But elections are often a poor signalling device because people vote for many different reasons, have poor information and, as we have seen, interest groups and pork barrel politics distort priorities. There is a *preference-revelation problem*: unlike the demand for (say) shoes (which is a private good), we cannot be sure what level of a public good is desired.

Economist Charles Tiebout proposed a solution, which has been called Tiebout sorting (or Tiebout migration). Different local municipalities offer different mixes of services, such as roads and policing. People then 'vote' for a particular mix by moving to that municipality. Municipalities compete through their taxation (and spending) policies and preferences are revealed through migration. This does not eliminate ballot-box style voting but it does offer an alternative way to express a preference. People vote with their feet.

As with many economic models, there are a number of unrealistic assumptions underpinning Tiebout sorting (Tiebout, 1956: 419–20):

1. People are mobile, and there are no costs to moving.
2. People have complete information on the services offered.
3. There are many municipalities from which to choose.
4. Employment is not a restriction (it is assumed people live off dividend income).
5. The benefits from one municipality do not spill over to another.
6. There is an optimal size for a municipality.

It may be possible to make Tiebout more realistic: there are costs to moving, but people balance those costs against the tax/public goods benefits of a particular locality. There is evidence of this in the United Kingdom, with school choice. While some people pay for private schooling, others also effectively pay for high-quality state schools through purchasing more expensive property in the catchment area of a good school. They might also be willing to commute longer distances to live in a better municipality. Evidence for Tiebout may also be found in the political resistance of certain wealthy suburbs to incorporation in larger, poorer municipalities. (For a discussion of whether there are Tiebout sorting effects, see Saltz and Capener, 2016).

## Is voting rational?

An assumption of the discussion so far is that voting is instrumental: we vote to satisfy our preferences. That voting might not be instrumental will be explored later but staying for now with the idea that it is, we come up against a problem: voting seems irrational. It carries costs, such as time spent queuing at the polling station and effort expended in getting information on how to vote and which parties or candidates to support. Yet, the chances of your vote making the difference are vanishingly small – 1 in 60 million in an American presidential election (Gelman, Silver and Edlin, 2010: 322–3), which is worse odds than those for the jackpot in a major national lottery. Yet, people vote.

One argument for voting is that it is a collective act: your vote for candidate X might not get her elected, but you are part of something bigger. To assess this argument, we need to focus on two types of voter: the altruistic voter and the self-interested voter. Preferences are often self-interested but need not be. A wealthy person might support redistributive economic policies, even if he thinks there is no personal gain, beyond a sense of satisfaction. A person already motivated to override his self-interest and act altruistically might also be motivated to vote, despite the costs. The self-interested voter would be more difficult to persuade: party X promotes his interests, and he wants it to win. The party will only win if enough people vote for it – so again, collective action is required – but it is still irrational to vote.

It is true that as fewer people vote the odds of your vote being decisive – making the difference between defeat and victory – increase. But turnout would have to drop very low for the odds to be attractive enough to counterbalance the costs, and obviously this is an argument against most people voting (unless the electorate is extremely small). If the rationality of voting depends on low turnout, then we have a negative frequency-dependent phenomenon, meaning that its value increases the fewer the number of voters.[1]

Another argument is that voting is less like a lottery and more like buying house insurance. There is a superficial similarity between the two, as both are concerned with remote possibilities – winning $1 million, your house burning down. However, people are loss averse. They are more concerned about losing than gaining and so the two are not equivalent. We should therefore apply the minimax regret rule (Blais et al., 1995). Applied to house insurance the rule compares two outcomes:

a)   You pay for insurance. Your house does not burn down. The insurance money is wasted. You feel regret.
b)   You did not pay for insurance. Your house burnt down. You feel regret.

And applied to voting:

a)   You vote. Your vote did not make a difference. You lost time voting. You feel regret.
b)   You did not vote. Your vote would have made the difference. You feel regret.

Which regret is greater (how do you minimise the maximum regret)? Although minimax regret is a sound principle for making decisions under conditions of uncertainty, it only goes so far in addressing the irrationality of voting argument. Regret must be balanced by probabilities. If the probability of something very bad happening is remote, it might still be irrational to insure against it. And people already psychologically predisposed to vote might well endorse the principle, but it would be a *post hoc* justification for their voting (Blais et al., 1995: 832–4).

Another possibility is that you gain from voting in ways unconnected to the success of your vote (Mueller, 2003: 306). You might enjoy voting (and politics in general). Voting may be socially approved in your peer group, such that stigma attaches to not voting. There is a parallel with buying a lottery ticket: the prospect of winning is an incentive.

## Voting paradoxes

Before turning to non-instrumental theories of democracy, consideration needs to be given to how preferences (votes) are combined. Democracy is a method for making collective decisions, but it is not always possible to convert individual sets of preferences into a collective preference-ordering. Imagine you and two friends want to eat out but have different preferences regarding cuisine. There are three restaurants in town: Greek, Thai, and Mexican. Where would you go? These are your preferences:

|  | You | Friend A | Friend B |
| --- | --- | --- | --- |
| 1st preference | Greek | Thai | Mexican |
| 2nd preference | Thai | Mexican | Greek |
| 3rd preference | Mexican | Greek | Thai |

If you vote on Greek, that will be defeated 2 to 1 because A and B prefer something else. If you then vote on Thai that will lose 2-1. And Mexican suffers the same fate. This is the phenomenon of cycling (or the Condorcet paradox).[2] As Kenneth Arrow established, no fair voting system can be guaranteed simultaneously to satisfy five 'reasonable' conditions (Maskin and Sen, 2014):

1. **Non-dictatorship.** The collective result should reflect the preferences of multiple voters and not the preferences of only one.
2. **Pareto efficiency** (unanimity). If all voters prefer X to Y, the collective preference should be for X over Y.
3. **Independence of irrelevant alternatives.** A voter's preference for X over Y should remain whether or not Z is available (Z may be preferred to both, but the preference for X over Y should be unchanged; Y should not be preferred over X in the presence of Z).
4. **Unrestricted domain.** All preferences must be ranked (and the result should be the same each time those preferences are expressed).
5. **Social ordering.** Voters should be able to rank their preferences in a complete and transitive way: if X is preferred to Y and Y to Z, then Z cannot be preferred to X.

In our example if we could eliminate one option (say, Mexican), it would be a straightforward choice between Thai and Greek. This violates unrestricted domain. One person could decide, but this breaks the non-dictatorship requirement. You might vote pairwise on the options, and the last option left standing is the victor, but again this is incompatible with unrestricted domain.

Arrow's Impossibility Theorem only applies to ordinal voting. If you could attach a value to each option, it might be possible to avoid the impossibility of a collective preference. Imagine each of you had 100 utils (units of utility) to distribute. Negative utils are possible but for summing purposes they must be treated as positive numbers, for otherwise one person's utility counts for more than another, which given our core definition of democracy as the equality of preferences would be a problem:

| You | Friend A | Friend B |
| --- | --- | --- |
| Greek +48 | Thai +60 | Mexican +35 |
| Thai +2 | Mexican +18 | Greek +33 |
| Mexican -50 | Greek +12 | Thai +32 |

The final scores are Thai 94, Greek 93, Mexican 3.

Most electoral systems are ordinal and in the real world of politics these force a choice, even if they violate one or more of Arrow's conditions. In French presidential elections, there are two rounds to voting – separated by two weeks – and the top two go into the run-off. In 2002, commentators were surprised – and many shocked – when in the first round, the Socialist Lionel Jospin came third with 16.2% of the vote to second-placed far-right candidate Jean-Marie Le Pen, who got 16.9%. There were 16 candidates in the first round, of which at least eight, in addition to Jospin, were on the left, with a combined total of around 45%. In the run-off, Le Pen faced centre-right incumbent President Jacques Chirac, who went on to defeat Le Pen by 82.2% to 17.8%. Putting ideological positions completely to one side and viewing this election simply as one of preference-aggregation it was clearly unsatisfactory.

## Brexit and voting paradoxes

The voting paradox issue can be illustrated by the debate over whether there should have been a second referendum on the UK's membership of the EU. At the end of the chapter, we discuss some broader issues, but here we focus on what voting system might have been used had there been a second referendum.

Whereas the June 2016 referendum was a binary leave/remain choice, many of those who advocated for a second referendum argued that it should contain three options: remain (R); leave with a deal (D); leave with no deal (N). Mathematician Bernhard von Stengel sets out a hypothetical distribution (we can think of each as equally sized blocs of voters) (von Stengel, 2019):

| 1. | R | R | R | R | N | N | N | D | D |
| --- | --- | --- | --- | --- | --- | --- | --- | --- | --- |
| 2. | D | D | D | D | D | D | D | R | N |
| 3. | N | N | N | N | R | R | R | N | R |

The numbers (rows) represent preferences, so the first four columns (blocs of voters) prefer Remain to Deal to No deal. We need to think about voting rules. If we use the plurality system (first-past-the-post), then R wins, even though a majority (N + D) want to leave the EU. Another system is the supplementary vote (instant run-off). Here, the least preferred option (D) is eliminated, and D's second preferences counted, so 1 goes to R and 1 to N and R wins 5-4. An important consideration is that rules can change preferences and lead to strategic voting. If it looks like the result will indeed be R5-N4, then N voters should put D as their first preference to force a run-off between R and D.

Another voting system is the Condorcet winner (pairwise comparison). We tried this with the cuisine example and ended up with the Condorcet paradox (cycling). Can we do better here? The voting would go: D5-R4, D6-N3, R5-N4. D wins two of the three contests, even though it was only the first preference of 2 of the 9 voters (or blocs). There could be cycling if the voter profile was as follows (note that we only need three blocs to make the point):

| 1. | R | D | N |
|----|---|---|---|
| 2. | D | N | R |
| 3. | N | R | D |

A third possible voting system is the Borda Count. Here, preferences get points: 2 for a first preference, 1 for a second, and 0 for a third (although you could have a 3, 2, 1 system). We get the following:

R = 2 + 2 + 2 + 2 + 0 + 0 + 0 + 1 + 0 = 9
N = 0 + 0 + 0 + 0 + 2 + 2 + 2 + 0 + 1 = 7
D = 1 + 1 + 1 + 1 + 1 + 1 + 1 + 2 + 2 = 11

D wins. But we have a problem if people do not express a full preference-ordering. Indeed, a person may have a preference between two of the options; for example, he favours N, but is indifferent between D and R.

It might be argued that most of these methods converge on leaving the EU with a deal and that does seem to be the majority view. Indeed, the UK government, led by Boris Johnson, did leave on 31 January 2020 with a deal. But there are two overall points. First, even when preferences are fixed, different voting systems can produce different outcomes. Second, voting systems can themselves change preferences, as we saw with strategic tactics in the use of the supplementary vote.

## Epistemic theories of democracy

We now shift the focus to a different way of understanding – and justifying – democracy: it is a method for pursuing the truth. Polymath Sir Francis Galton attended a country fair in 1906 and observed a competition in which country folk were asked to guess the weight of an ox. 787 people submitted guesses and even though nobody guessed correctly, the average of those guesses was 1,197lb. The correct weight was 1,198lb (Wallis, 2014). This story has now become rather clichéd, but nonetheless it illustrates an epistemic argument for democracy. The 787 were not expressing a preference but seeking to get at a correct answer.

Once again, Condorcet has given his name to a theorem: Condorcet's Jury Theorem. The larger the jury, the more likely it will arrive at the correct answer – for example, guilt or innocence. It assumes that the average competence is above 50%. If you have 250 voters with an average competence of 0.51, then you will have a group competence of 0.62 (meaning that 62% of the time they will get the correct answer). Ten thousand voters will have a group competence of 0.98 (Estlund, 1994: 131). It should be noted that the 0.51 competence need only be a mean average; within the group there could be considerable variation in competence.

One of the crucial assumptions of the theorem is that we do not influence one another, which makes the reference to a jury unfortunate, as the point of a jury is to deliberate. If we allow that in the real world there will be some influence, the Jury Theorem involves two considerations: the degree of competence and the degree of influence, with trade-offs between them. Indeed, the 'independence of judgement' is so important that you could improve the quality of the judgement by introducing less competent people into the group if they also happen to increase the level of independence (Vermeule, 2009: 6).

Clearly, the theorem assumes that there is an objectively correct answer. This is important, as the argument for the Jury Theorem is often subsumed under a larger discussion of 'many minds' (dispersed knowledge). It is a common argument in favour of markets (the price mechanism) that many minds are better than one. When people buy shoes, they are both expressing a preference and providing manufacturers with useful information as to what shoes to produce and at what price. No single mind contains that information, but it is distributed across many minds. If instead of a market you had central planning, you would need a single mind to determine what shoes to produce (Hayek, 1945). But in the Condorcet Theorem, voters are not expressing a preference but trying to establish a truth and it is questionable whether this is a many minds (distributed knowledge) phenomenon, rather than simply the Law of Large Numbers, where the average is accurate because it eliminates eccentricity and noise (Vermeule, 2009: 6).

## Economists and Brexit

Let us return to Brexit. There was an epistemic component to the vote, namely a judgement about how much better off the average person would be as a result. This, however, was not the only question. Other issues were immigration and political sovereignty. But for the sake of the current discussion, let us assume that economic growth was the sole issue, and this was something that had a correct answer. Most economists argued that the United Kingdom would be worse off by leaving the EU. Below are the predictions from various groups of economists on the change in Gross Domestic Product (GDP) of the United Kingdom on leaving the EU (adapted from Tetlow and Stojanovic, 2018: 64):

The Jury Theorem would suggest that the people will be right and the experts wrong. Partly, this is a case of numbers: even if the average voter is considerably less competent than a professional economist, in the mass – on average – the people will be superior in their judgement. It might also be a consequence of independence of judgement. Voters are less likely than professional economists to discuss economics with their neighbours. Indeed, there may be assumptions underpinning most economic models that if wrong will contaminate all the models. One such assumption is the gravity theory of trade, whereby the volume of trade two countries conduct is a function of their size multiplied by inverse distance. In other words, the closer you are, the more trade you do (allowing for the size of the economy) (Gudgin et al., 2017). The Economists for Free Trade (EFT) group explicitly rejected the model (Minford and Xu, 2018), but all the other models presupposed gravity effects, even if they disagreed about their magnitude. Given

Change in GDP relative to remaining in the European Union

| Economic modeller | Time-scale | Under four different scenarios | | | |
|---|---|---|---|---|---|
| | | European Economic Area (EEA) % change | Free trade agreement % change | World Trade Organization (WTO) rules % change | Unilateral free trade % change |
| Rabobank | To 2030 | −10 | −12.5 | −18 | |
| Treasury | To 2032 | −3.8 | −6.2 | −7.5 | |
| RAND | To 2030 | −1.7 | −1.9 | −4.9 | |
| NIESR | To 2030 | −1.8 | −2.1 | −3.2 | |
| PwC | To 2030 | | −1.2 | −3.5 | |
| Open Europe | To 2030 | | −0.8 | −2.2 | +1.6 |
| EFT | To 2032 | | | | +4.0 |

the UK's physical location, the gravity model predicts that increased trade with non-EU countries would not make up for the loss of trade with the EU resulting from increased UK-EU tariff and non-tariff barriers.

## Expertise and Heuristics

In assessing the Jury Theorem, we need to think about expertise. If two experts disagree would that not count against them being experts? And yet, across multiple fields – for example, economics, medicine, law, meteorology – experts often present quite different conclusions. The 'experts are useless' argument can be broken down into five steps (Shanteau and Hall, 2001: 230–1):

1. There is a ground-truth about something, but it is difficult to obtain. We cannot rely on everyday knowledge to get to that truth.
2. Because of their skills and experience, experts can get to that truth.
3. Since there can only be one ground-truth, experts should agree on it.
4. If experts disagree, then someone is wrong.
5. Since non-experts cannot know which experts are right or wrong, it is best to assume that they are all wrong.

Shanteau and Hall categorise experts from high to low competence (2001: 235–6). On the high end of the spectrum are experts who make aided decisions, meaning that they rely on computerised tools, an example being weather forecasters. Then come skilled, but unaided, experts, such as livestock judges. Then there are those with limited competence, such as clinical psychologists. Finally, there are experts whose conclusions are close to random, such as stockbrokers.

It is sometimes claimed that experts are less biased than ordinary people; they have a more objective view of the subject matter. Because the world is complicated and the costs, in time and effort, of trying to understand it are high, ordinary people use heuristics – short-cuts or 'rules of thumb' – to judge who to vote for and, by extension, which policies to endorse. Examples of heuristics include (Lau and Redlawsk, 2001: 953–4):

- Party identification: always vote for the same party.
- Ideology of the candidate based on easily accessible judgements. An example would that most Americans know Bernie Sanders is left-wing ('liberal' in American parlance), so there is no need to find out more about him.
- Endorsements of candidates by celebrities.
- Viability of a candidate or party as measured by opinion polls – a rule of thumb is not to waste time on losers.
- How a candidate sounds or appears.

Of the last of these, there is a considerable literature in psychology on the effects of voice pitch on electability, most of which suggests the deeper the voice, the better (Klofstad and Anderson, 2018). There have been fewer studies on the physical attractiveness of candidates, but research in Ireland (Buckley, Collins, and Reidy, 2007) and (separately) in Switzerland (Lutz, 2010) – both countries in which the pictures of candidates appear on the ballot paper – suggest that better looking candidates are at an advantage, although the Swiss study argues that it is not attractiveness *per se* that accounts for the advantage, but that voters linger longer over attractive images (2010: 476). Heuristics are used most often in low information elections, where candidates are little known or there are no very clear policy differences between them.

Are heuristics irrational? In this chapter, we have set out two alternative ways of determining the success of voting: preference-satisfaction (instrumental) or truth (epistemic). The success of heuristics must be judged against the achievement of one or other of these, but for the purposes of this discussion we will conflate them, and say a voter makes the right choice if she most effectively satisfies her preferences or if she comes to the correct answer about the truth of something. We can then say that heuristics are rational if by employing them she is correct above the level of chance, and if heuristic judgements are more efficient than cognitive ones.

Take voice pitch. A voter may subconsciously vote for the candidate with the lower pitch. This requires little effort on the part of the voter; it does not involve cognition and is fast. Let us assume, for the sake of argument, that voice pitch does indicate above the level of chance leadership qualities such as decisiveness, honesty, and competence. If we say that by using the voice pitch heuristic, the voter gets the right answer 55% of the time (and that is above chance), would she do any better if she spent time reading the candidates' platform statements and engaging in other time-consuming information-gathering? If she did so she might raise the probability of getting the right answer to 60%, but we must assess whether that 5% gain is worth the cost. Classical rational choice theory holds that it is rational to keep searching for information if the gain from getting a better 'product' (party, candidate) is greater than marginal cost of that increased search time. If it makes it easier to understand the argument, think about looking online for a product: is the effort of continuing your search justified by finding a better deal? It may be easier just to use a heuristic.

We can link the use of heuristics back to the question of whether experts make better judgements. The argument for experts is likely stronger on the epistemic theory of democracy, distinct from the instrumental theory, but even here there is a case to be made for letting ordinary people decide on a political issue, rather than an expert. The argument is summarised in the table. It is broken down into a series of considerations: cost of the information search; the probability of an individual arriving at the correct answer; the probability of a group arriving at the correct answer; and the extent to which judgements are independent of one another. Note that the percentages are arbitrary and put in simply to illustrate the argument.

| Consideration | Voters using heuristics | Experts using their specialist knowledge |
|---|---|---|
| Costs (measured by time and intellectual effort): | Very low. | High. |
| Probability of *each individual* arriving at a correct answer: | Lower than for an expert. Let us assume a 55% probability of any voter getting the correct answer. | Higher than for a voter. Let us assume a 65% probability of any expert getting the correct answer. |
| Probability of *a group* arriving at the correct answer, based on the Law of Large Numbers: | 55% for an individual rises to close to 100% for the group as the number of voters increases. | 65% will rise as more experts contribute to the collective outcome, but as there are fewer experts than voters, it may not rise as high as it could for voters. |
| Independence of judgement: | We assume relatively high, so reinforcing the effect of the Law of Large Numbers. | Since experts are trained, we assume *interdependence* of judgement is high, thus working against the Law of Large Numbers. |

We can conclude that the case is strongest for experts making political decisions, where voters have only a random chance of being right and when they are open to influence – or manipulation – that undermines their independence of judgement.

## Deliberative democracy

Deliberative theories of democracy place emphasis on the idea of the informed voter, where being informed is a result of discussion with other voters. There are several arguments in its favour. First, voters increase their civic skills and become 'better' citizens. Second, by debating issues with other voters a sense of civil community is fostered. Third, the decisions made have greater legitimacy because voters have been more involved in them. Fourth, the gap between leaders and voters is reduced as the latter come to a better appreciation of the compromises and trade-offs that must be made in politics (Michels, 2011: 278).

Citizens' juries embody the idea of deliberative decision-making. Juries can be selected through a snowball effect, whereby a few individuals are chosen, and they use their social networks to recruit more jury members. An alternative is to use a representative sample matched to demography (age, sex, ethnicity, and so on) (Ryfe, 2005: 51). Once selected, jurors hear expert evidence, discuss that evidence with the other jurors, and produce recommendations.

There are a number of problems with juries and similar mechanisms of deliberative democracy:

1. Snowballing is likely to lead to juries that are demographically unrepresentative. But representative samples – as used by polling agencies – presuppose that certain characteristics are important such as age, sex, class, and ethnicity.
2. Juries may attract distinct psychological types and thus skew the outcome of the deliberations.
3. Those who are not selected are unlikely to regard the decisions made as legitimate. Jury selection is not like a tombola, where you buy a ticket and hope your number comes up.
4. Even if deliberation is educative, only those who are selected benefit.
5. The agenda for discussion must be framed, and this is likely done either by dominant members of the jury or by external experts.
6. Experts – or expert evidence – must be selected. Who does that? More fundamentally, if you are not an expert, how can you determine who is an expert? This draws deliberative democracy back into the 'voters versus experts' problem.
7. Assuming Condorcet is right, his (misnamed) Jury Theorem works less effectively when people influence one another.

In short, deliberative democracy is unlikely to yield benefits, and it solves none of the problems identified in this chapter.

## Brexit (again)

Let us return to the case study set out at the beginning of this chapter. In the course of the chapter, we have already discussed several aspects of the EU referendum: the voting system that could have been used for a second, multi-option referendum and the role of experts. Related to the latter point is the claim – often implied, but sometimes explicitly stated – that Leave voters were less well-informed than Remain voters. A 2018 study found that this was not the case, although it did find that on a simple intelligence test Remainers scored higher than Leavers (Carl, Richards and Heath, 2019). The main part of their study asked for true/false answers to a list of statements. Some were neutral ('Switzerland is a member of the EU'), others were likely to engender an evaluative response ('the UK is a net contributor to the EU'; 'the EU is the world's second largest economy'). The statements which appealed to Leavers garnered a higher correct response from them, and conversely Remainers gave a higher correct response to statements placing EU membership in a positive light. This was a case of motivated reasoning, whereby we respond to statements by whether they fit our existing beliefs – not so much 'do I think this is true?', as 'how do I feel about this?' (Kahan, 2015: 2–3). All humans engage in motivated reasoning, but whether the average voter does so to a greater extent than an expert is an open question. A replication study found that Remain voters were indeed better informed, but the questions in this study were 'neutral' rather than ones that elicit a motivated response (Carl, 2019).

Connecting back to the discussion in the first part of the chapter: should the decision to leave or remain the EU have been by a simple majority vote or by a qualified majority? One consideration is whether certain groups would be disproportionately affected either by leaving or remaining. EU citizens resident in the United Kingdom – who were not in fact entitled to vote – could have lost a great deal, as would UK residents in other EU countries (many of whom did have a vote). If their rights were removed, then a higher approval threshold might have been justified. As it was, there was an understanding that EU citizens' rights would be guaranteed, thus removing this as a consideration.

A common theme in the period after the referendum was that voters were misled by the Leave campaign. Attention focused on the claim by the Leave side that after departing the EU, the United Kingdom would 'take back control' of roughly £350 million per week. The United Kingdom was a net contributor to the EU's budget, but received a rebate, which would reduce the figure to around £275 million. Around £115 million would return to the United Kingdom in EU grants, leaving a final contribution of £160 million. Since the United Kingdom did not control what that £115 million was spent on it would be accurate to say the United Kingdom was *taking back control* of £275 million. Whether the claim made the difference between victory and defeat for Leave is a matter of debate. But the broader question for political theorists is whether inaccuracies invalidate the right of people to choose in a referendum or indeed should invalidate an election or referendum result.

## Conclusion

Democracy as a procedure for making collective decisions has its strengths and weaknesses. The more people who participate in a decision, the greater the likelihood that eccentric views will not skew the outcome. And there is no compelling case for experts as better decision-makers than non-experts. On the other hand, how questions are put to voters will structure their responses, so that while preferences can remain unchanged, the voting rules will generate different outcomes. What is more, there is no guarantee of a collective preference, as evidenced by cycling. And there is no truly convincing answer to the charge that voting is irrational.

# Notes

1  Negative-frequency-dependent selection is a concept from evolutionary biology: the fewer people who have the trait, the more advantageous for its bearer, an example being left-handed in hand-to-hand combat and racket sports.
2  For a non-technical, but real-world discussion, see Kurrild-Klitgaard (2001).

# References

Black, D. (1948). On the Rationale of Group Decision-Making. *Journal of Political Economy, 56*(1), 23–34.

Blais, A., Young, R., Fleury, C., and Lapp, M. (1995). Do People Vote on the Basis of Minimax Regret? *Political Research Quarterly, 48*(4), 827–36.

Buckley, F., Collins, N., and Reidy, T. (2007). Ballot Paper Photographs and Low-Information Elections in Ireland. *Politics, 27*(3), 174–81.

Carl, N. (2019). Comparing EU knowledge among leave and remain voters: A replication study. *SocArXiv*: 15 Sept. 2019.

Carl, N., Richards, L., and Heath, A. (2019). Leave and Remain Voters' Knowledge of the EU after the Referendum of 2016. *Electoral Studies, 57*, 90–8.

Estlund, D. M. (1994). Opinion Leaders, Independence, and Condorcet's Jury Theorem. *Theory and Decision, 36*(2), 131–62.

Gelman, A., Silver, N., and Edlin, A. (2010). What is the Probability Your Vote will Make a Difference? *Economic Inquiry, 50*(2), 321–26.

Gill, J. and Gainous, J. (2002). Why Does Voting get so Complicated? A Review of Theories for Analyzing Democratic Participation. *Statistical Science, 17*(4), 383–404.

Gudgin, G., Coutts, K. J., Gibson, N., and Buchanan, J. (2017). *The Role of Gravity Models in Estimating the Economic Impact of Brexit*. Centre for Business Research, Cambridge: University of Cambridge.

Hayek, F. A. (1945). The Use of Knowledge in Society. *The American Economic Review, 35*(4), 519–30.

Kahan, D. M. (2015). The Politically Motivated Reasoning Paradigm, Part 1: What Politically Motivated Reasoning Is and How to Measure It, in R. Scott and S. Kosslyn (eds), *Emerging Trends in the Social and Behavioral Sciences: An Interdisciplinary, Searchable, and Linkable Resource*, London: John Wiley and Sons, 1–16.

Klofstad, C. A. and Anderson, R. C. (2018). Voice Pitch Predicts Electability, But Does Not Signal Leadership Ability. *Evolution and Human Behavior, 39*(3), 349–54.

Kurrild-Klitgaard, P. (2001). An Empirical Example of the Condorcet Paradox of Voting in a Large Electorate. *Public Choice, 107*(1–2), 135–145.

Lau, R. R. and Redlawsk, D. P. (2001). Advantages and Disadvantages of Cognitive Heuristics in Political Decision Making. *American Journal of Political Science, 45*(4), 951–71.

Liddel, P. (2009). 'Democracy Ancient and Modern' in R. K. Balot (ed.), *A Companion to Greek and Roman Political Thought*. Malden, MA: Wiley-Blackwell.

Lutz, G. (2010). The Electoral Success of Beauties and Beasts. *Swiss Political Science Review, 16*(3), 457–80.

Maskin, E. and Sen, A. (2014). 'The Arrow Impossibility Theorem: Where do We Go from Here?', in E Maskin and A Sen (eds), *The Arrow Impossibility Theorem*. New York: Columbia University Press, pp. 43–56.

Michels, A. (2011). Innovations in Democratic Governance: How does Citizen Participation Contribute to a Better Democracy? *International Review of Administrative Sciences, 77*(2), 275–93.

Minford, P. and Xu, Y. (2018). Classical or Gravity? Which Trade Model Best Matches the UK Facts? *Open Economies Review, 29*(3), 579–611.

Mueller, D. C. (2003). *Public Choice III.* Cambridge: Cambridge University Press.

Rowley, C. K. (1984). The Relevance of the Median Voter Theorem. *Zeitschrift für die gesamte Staatswissenschaft/Journal of Institutional and Theoretical Economics,* (H. 1), 104–26.

Ryfe, D. M. (2005). Does Deliberative Democracy Work? *Annual Review of Political Science, 8,* 49–71.

Saltz, I. S. and Capener, D. (2016). 60 years Later and Still Going Strong: The Continued Relevance of the Tiebout Hypothesis. *Journal of Regional Analysis and Policy, 46*(1100–2016–90019), 72–94.

Shanteau, J. and Hall, B. (2001). 'What Does It Mean When Experts Disagree?', in E. Salas and G. Klein (eds), *Linking Expertise and Naturalistic Decision Making,* Hove, England: Psychology Press, 229–44.

Sharma, C. K. (2017). A Situational Theory of Pork-Barrel Politics: The Shifting Logic of Discretionary Allocations in India. *India Review, 16*(1), 14–41.

Tetlow, G. and Stojanovic, A. (2018). *Understanding the Economic Impact of Brexit.* London: Institute for Government.

Tiebout, C. M. (1956). A Pure Theory of Local Expenditures. *Journal of Political Economy, 64*(5), 416–24.

Vermeule, A. (2009). Many-Minds Arguments in Legal Theory. *Journal of Legal Analysis, 1,* 1.

Von Stengel, B. (2019). A Mathematical View of the Will of the People. *Democratic Audit,* viewed 20 July 2021, https://www.democraticaudit.com/2019/02/21/a-mathematical-view-of-the-will-of-the-people/

Wallis, K. F. (2014). Revisiting Francis Galton's Forecasting Competition. *Statistical Science, 29*(3), 420–24.

## Further reading

There are number of useful introductions to, and discussions of, democracy: Albert Weale, *Democracy* (Palgrave, 2007); Frank Cunningham, *Theories of Democracy: A Critical Introduction* (Routledge, 2001); Ian O'Flynn, *Deliberative Democracy* (Polity, 2021); Frederick Whelan, *Democracy in Theory and Practice* (Routledge, 2018); Garett Jones, *10% Less Democracy: Why we Should Trust Elites a Little More and the Masses a Little Less* (Stanford University Press, 2021). On Condorcet's Jury Theorem and related themes, read the bestseller James Surowiecki, *The Wisdom of Crowds: Why the Many are Smarter than the Few.*

# Chapter 3

# Punishment

## Introduction

Punishment is the infliction of hard treatment by an authority on an individual in connection to a crime. But what justifies punishment? And how does it advance political objectives? Two theories dominate the debate: retributivism and consequentialism. But there is a third: restitutionism. Retributivists emphasise responsibility for the crime: the guilty – and only the guilty – should be punished. Consequentialism, as the label suggests, focuses on the positive consequences of punishment, primarily, but not exclusively, its effect in deterring people from committing crime. Restitutionists argue that the emphasis should be on the harm done to the victims of crime and punishment is compensation.

## Key questions

- What is punishment?
- What justifies punishment?
- Is the debate over punishment primarily a moral one, or does it have a political dimension?

## Defining punishment

In Chapter 1, we argued that the state is a coercive entity. In Max Weber's words, it successfully claims a monopoly on the legitimate use of violence in a given territory (see p. 9). And the state is most obviously coercive when it punishes – or threatens to punish – those residing on its territory. But as per Weber's conceptualisation, those threats are not a naked exercise of violence; the state claims the *right* to punish, implying that it can provide reasons for doing so. It is these reasons that concern us in this chapter.

Unlike some other concepts employed by political theorists, punishment is one widely used in everyday discussion. The person in the street would probably not offer an abstract definition but rather equate punishment with imprisonment or being fined. And although most people would no doubt accept that sometimes the innocent are punished it is considered outrageous *deliberately* to punish an innocent person. For most people, punishment is the infliction of something negative, such as prison time, on a person who deserves it, and the state should only punish those it is confident deserve it.

DOI: 10.4324/9780429424106-5

Case study 3.1

## Precrimes

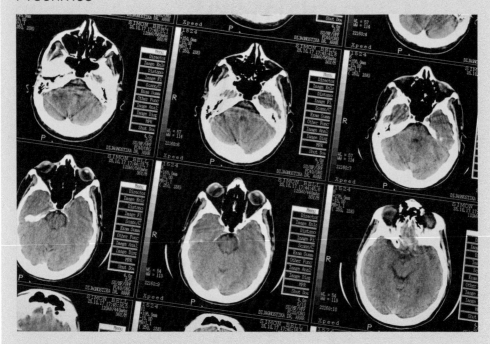

**PHOTO 3.1** © PhotoEdit/Alamy Stock Photo.

Should the population be screened to detect the propensity to commit crime and prevent those crimes being committed, even before the (potential) perpetrator is aware he or she is going to commit a crime?

While much crime may be attributed to social-environmental factors, and the appropriate response could be to address those causes of crime, people are still punished despite their poor upbringing. If we punish people even though they are not causally responsible for their upbringing, why not go a step back and prevent crime being committed in the first place? Prevention could take the form of restricting the movements of high risk individuals or putting them under permanent surveillance (through, for example, electronic tagging).

It may be argued that we cannot identify at-risk people. But there is neurological evidence that some people have deficits in those parts of the brain that affect empathy and impulse control. Furthermore, research suggests a (partial) genetic basis to some forms of behaviour. Genome sequencing and brain scans could assist in the identification of the relevant individuals.

However, another common argument for punishment is that it deters crime. Yet, as we will see later, if we punish to deter, then there are circumstances in which punishing an innocent person might be justified (of course, we – or most of us – must *believe* the person is guilty). Therefore, we cannot start by defining punishment as the infliction of a sanction by the state on a *guilty* (or deserving) person.

More broadly, how we define punishment is bound up with why we punish – we cannot operate with a morally neutral definition of punishment and then simply move on to its justification. That said, we will provide a rough, working definition (which will then have to be refined depending on how we justify it): **punishment is the infliction of 'hard treatment' where the suffering is *in some way* connected to the actual or potential violation of a law.** The phrase 'in some way' leaves open the possibility that an innocent person could justifiably be punished. And the phrase 'hard treatment' is standardly used in philosophical debate to denote what is done to the punished person – it leaves open the specifics of the treatment.

With that definition in mind, we can now consider what justifies the infliction of hard treatment, and, in the process, clarify the phrase 'in some way'. Traditionally, two theories dominate the debate over the justification of punishment – retributivism and consequentialism – but there is a third theory that we argue should take its place alongside these others: restitutivism.

Given the central role of the state in punishment, it seems an eminently relevant topic for political theory. However, the connection with politics needs some explanation. Much philosophical debate focuses on the morality of punishment, where morality is concerned with what we owe individuals, disconnected from the wider issue of political order. In this chapter, we emphasise the connection of punishment to the arguments about state power discussed in Chapter 1. And while the three theories of punishment do not map directly onto the three perspectives outlined in that chapter, there are connections.

## Retributivism

Most people equate retributivism with the slogan 'an eye for an eye, and a tooth for a tooth'. Punishment is payback, or, in more philosophical language, restitution, a word with roots in the idea of repaying a debt (Cottingham, 1979: 238). However, while equivalence between crime and punishment is an important aspect of retributivism, payback is a stronger element of *restitutionism*, a justification for punishment that focuses on the harm done to the victim, rather than the guilt of the criminal. We discuss restitution later.

There is a broad consensus that retributivism entails three claims:

1. Those who commit certain acts morally deserve to suffer in some defined way.
2. That such suffering is good in itself, independently of other goods that might arise through the act, such as deterring people from committing crime. This is an explicit rejection of consequentialism.
3. It is morally wrong to punish those who have not committed acts deserving of punishment or to punish to excess guilty acts or to impose inequitable punishments.

Why does a wrongdoer *deserve* to be punished? The most obvious answer appeals to human intuition: the average person just has a very strong sense that many criminals deserve punishment (and the innocent should definitely not be punished). Viewed from the perspective of human evolutionary history, such a sense may have been adaptive, meaning that it would have promoted human survival and reproduction: the equivalent for our ancestors of modern punishment would have been the killing of, or expulsion from the tribal band of, wrongdoers. Not only would this have directly benefited the band it would also have suppressed the reproduction of those genes implicated in anti-social behaviour. Furthermore, punishment facilitated increases in human group size (Boyd and Richerson, 1992: 173–5); the bigger a group gets, the harder it is to deal with free-riders, and so institutionalising punishment – rather than leaving it to individuals to carry out – enabled the kind of social organisation that has characterised the past 10,000 years of human history. However, even if this is a plausible explanation of our retributivist intuitions, it does not justify punishment because you cannot derive ought ('punish wrongdoers!') from is ('it was adaptive in human history').

To justify punishment – the 'ought' – retributivists use a rational procedure: universalisation. This was discussed in Chapter 1 in the context of state legitimacy (see pp. 15–16), and again, Kant and Hegel are important theorists. Although there are differences between them, we will present a composite of their retributivist arguments for punishment.[1] We present it as a series of steps:

> Step 1: Crime is egoistic (purely self-interest). It is an act of coercion of other citizens.
>
> Step 2: Punishment is the annulment (or negation) of the egoistic act. It is the *second act of coercion*. Unlike the crime itself, this second act of coercion is not an egoistic act, but the result of universalisation. We – all rational agents – think what it would be like to live in a society in which acts such as murder, were permitted. Given we would not accept murder, we have to annul the act.
>
> Step 3. The criminal is also a rational agent, so she must will the annulment of her act. Thus, she wills her own punishment. A person who has not committed a criminal act cannot (logically) will her own punishment. Therefore, you cannot punish an innocent person.

Retributivists hold that a person must have acted intentionally or recklessly. Standardly referred to as *mens rea* ('guilty mind') (Chan and Simester, 2011), the intention must then be combined with a harmful act – *actus reus* – for punishment to be applied (Sullivan, 1993). In addition, whereas retributivism is often thought of as an 'eye for an eye', the Kant-Hegel position does not require a qualitative equivalence between the criminal act and the punishment, but rather proportionality – the more serious the crime, the more severe the punishment. This is *lex talionis* (the law of proportionality) (Waldron, 1992).

Underlying the Kant-Hegel theory are complicated metaphysical claims about the nature of humans and human rationality (see pp. 15–18). Contemporary theorists of retributivism generally avoid these claims and offer more down-to-earth versions of universalisation, which draw on empirical psychology or rational choice theory. A psychological argument is presented by Michael Moore (1997: 145). He imagines that he has committed a horrible crime and hopes that he would feel 'guilty unto death' and so welcome punishment. His feeling that he ought to be punished provides a standpoint from which it is reasonable for him to infer that someone who does in fact commit such a horrible crime should be punished. As with the Kant-Hegel argument this involves universalisation: you put yourself in the shoes of another person and think what you would want for that person.

Moore's version of universalisation has much intuitive appeal. Ordinary people can think the same thought as Moore. It is not a highly abstract thought-experiment. But it is problematic. Perhaps the psychology of a criminal is just too different to that of someone not motivated to commit the crime Moore is imagining. The criminal may be morally unlucky. Thomas Nagel distinguishes four types of moral luck (Nagel, 2012: 24–38), the most relevant of which is constitutive luck: a person was unlucky enough to have the genetic endowment or upbringing that predisposed him to murder. For example, some people with the low activity version of the monoamine oxidase A (MAOA) gene exhibit, if they suffered abuse in childhood, a higher propensity to engage in violent acts than those with the high activity version of the gene or those with that allele but who have not suffered abuse (see Caspi et al., 2002). This is not an argument against holding people criminally responsible for their actions, but it is an objection to expecting others to think the way you do and from there to justify punishment.

Another variant of the universalisation argument is the appeal to fairness. Individuals gain benefits through cooperation, but cooperation depends on accepting certain restraints. Criminals free-ride on others' restraint (Morris, 1968: 33). They gain an unfair advantage. Punishment erases that advantage. The argument assumes that there is a payoff from crime. This may be clearer in the case of criminal enrichment, such as theft or tax evasion, and perhaps less so with violence and sexual coercion, although even these can have non-monetary rewards, as arguably in the case of rape (McKibbin et al., 2008; Vandermassen, 2011). The harm done by free-riding is direct – the person gains something through his actions – and indirect, in that compliance is weakened.

Criticism of this argument comes from retributivists who say that the sense of unfairness does not adequately capture how most people feel about criminals. If we think about a particularly vicious murderer, such as Ivan Milat (the 'Backpacker Murderer'), the sense that he was taking advantage of others implies that sadistic murder is the norm, and it is wrong because we have entered into an agreement with one another to refrain from it. Hobbes certainly argued that without the state, it would be a 'war of all against all', but that was because we feared others and we attacked (and killed) to pre-empt being attacked. We do not kill because we enjoy it. For the retributivist, there is pre-institutional desert, meaning that some actions are wrong independently of the fact that we live under a set of institutions, the existence of which benefits everyone. Milat's actions would have been deserving of punishment even in the state of nature.

The fairness argument also opens the door to consequentialism. If the popular view is indeed that criminals are taking advantage of law-abiding citizens, then we are judging the crime against a goal, which is the maintenance of the cooperative scheme. For example, tax evasion might not just trigger resentment among those who pay their taxes, it might also lead to increased tax evasion because it is irrational to comply with a rule ('pay your taxes!') while many others are not. But perhaps a certain amount of evasion does not undermine the production of public goods; people may still feel resentment, but nonetheless pay their taxes. The question then is whether you can detach that resentment ('I resent tax evaders') from the effects of evasion ('I am still going to pay my taxes'). If you cannot detach them, then in effect this is a consequentialist argument.

## Consequentialism

For a consequentialist, we punish to bring about good consequences or avoid bad ones. Consequentialism can be pluralistic or maximising: we could have a range of different consequences we seek to bring about, without adding them all up to determine what is the best outcome overall, or we could try to attach a single value to all the consequences. (The argument from fairness, discussed in the previous section, looks like a non-maximising consequentialist one). Utilitarianism, which is a major stream of moral and political theory, is a maximising form of consequentialism, with utility as the common value.

The positive consequences of punishment can include satisfaction on the part of victims and their families, and incapacitation and thus inability to commit further crimes. Most discussion focuses however on deterrence. Two key variables in reducing crime are the perceived chances of a crime being detected and the severity of the punishment (Friesen, 2012). Let us assume that criminals are rational: in deciding whether to commit a crime, they calculate the chances of getting caught and what will happen to them if they are caught. They might trade detection off against jail time: high detection but short sentences versus low detection but lengthy sentences.

Reflecting on what ordinary people – as against philosophers – think about punishment, alongside the sense that only the guilty should be punished, deterrence is a major reason given for punishment. However, there is a tension between the commitment to *mens rea* and the importance of deterrence. Consider this scenario:

A child has been murdered and somebody who has a criminal record of sexual offences against children has been arrested (call him A). Some very high-ranking police officers have evidence that proves he could not have murdered the child but believe the chances of apprehending the real killer (call him B) are remote. Although they know that A is innocent, they are confident they can construct a case against him such that lower-ranking police officers, the courts, and the general population will be convinced he is guilty.

In the absence of a conviction, there will be negative consequences: public disorder; attacks on anybody who looks like a paedophile; fear on the part of parents and their children; loss of respect for authority; the passing of poorly thought-out legislation; and – crucially – the loss of deterrence as the murder is seen by other potential offenders to have gone unpunished.

Although there is a risk that B will strike again, the police calculate that it is better A is arrested, tried, and convicted than for no arrest to be made. Obviously, if the truth were to emerge, there would be significant negative consequences, but the police can calculate probabilities – the less likely the truth will emerge, the more they discount the negative consequences of revelation.

For the punishment of A to work, the vast majority of people must believe that A is guilty and that requires a high level of deception and conspiracy. And, therefore, a crucial element of the scenario is secrecy. Not only should the utilitarian conspire to have an innocent person punished, he is obliged, metaphorically speaking, to keep two sets of moral accounts: one he presents to the populace, the other he keeps to himself (or to a small group). Henry Sidgwick – one of the most important utilitarian philosophers of the nineteenth century – argued for an esoteric morality, meaning a secret, as against a public (or exoteric) one. De Lazari-Radek and Singer summarise Sidgwick's argument (2010: 35):

1. Some acts are right if nobody – or virtually nobody – finds out about them.
2. Some people know better than others what to do in certain circumstances.
3. There are at least two different sets of instructions (moral codes), suitable for different categories of people.
4. While consequentialism is the correct moral theory, consequentialists may need to discourage others from embracing it.
5. Philosophers who support esoteric morality should not do so openly.

The consequentialist effectiveness of punishment therefore relies on the general population not fully embracing consequentialism – or at least not recognising the tension between *mens rea* and deterrence. In the next section, we discuss a strategy to avoid esoteric morality, but we conclude this section with some other implications of consequentialism:

- If deterrence is justified, then perhaps so is prevention. This leads to the *Minority Report* scenario, whereby the state seeks to identify crimes (precrimes) before they have been committed. That film was rather far-fetched in that it imagined the existence of pre-cognitions, but a less fanciful version of precrime would be the identification of social or behavioural characteristics that suggest an increased likelihood of committing crime. As suggested at the beginning of this chapter, brain scans could reveal deficits in the amygdala, which then trigger a tracking and prevention programme. We would not be punishing to deter, but rather to prevent crime. (We return to this topic at the end of the chapter.)
- There is a problem with equity. For example, one person might receive a six-year prison sentence and another a one-year sentence for what is essentially the same crime, on grounds that the six-year sentence is intended to 'send out a message' – and thus deter others.
- There is a weak sense of *lex talionis*. Some crimes may be more sensitive to deterrence than others: speeding offences may be more susceptible to reduction because of harsher punishment, whereas murder may not be. In this case, we should have draconian anti-speeding measures but relatively light sentences for murder.

Given that the two strong intuitions held by ordinary people – *mens rea* and deterrence – appear to conflict much effort has gone into reconciling them.

## Indirect consequentialism

Some theorists argue that it is, by definition, impossible to punish an innocent person – if you look up 'punishment' in the *Chambers Dictionary*, you will find this definition: 'to cause (someone) to suffer for an offence', with the implication that the preposition 'for' states a causal relationship. This argument is weak. First, dictionaries – indeed, everyday usage of words – do not settle philosophical arguments, and second, we could just invent another word to denote something like punishment.

A better starting point for dealing with the problems thrown up by consequentialism is to distinguish acts and rules, and thus act-utilitarianism and rule-utilitarianism. Act-utilitarianism requires (a) that utility be maximised and (b) that each person should on each occasion act to maximise utility. If we apply this to punishment, state officials (police, judiciary) should always have in mind the maximisation of utility. Rule-utilitarianism endorses (a) – we have a duty to maximise utility – but says that we should not always act as if we are utilitarians. So long as a person's (police officer's and judge's) actions contribute to the maximisation of utility, it is not necessary to *think* (be *motivated*) like a utilitarian. State officials could think like retributivists. At the core of rule-utilitarianism is the idea that by respecting rules – for example, *mens rea* – we maximise utility. To be clear, this is an empirical argument: we must show that it is in fact the case that respecting rules maximises utility. Some critics of utilitarianism are not convinced. In response, a further refinement of the theory has been made – we do not just follow rules, but we separate out roles. This theory has been termed institutional utilitarianism and has been advanced by H.L.A. Hart and by John Rawls (although as argued below, Rawls is not a utilitarian).

In his essay 'Prolegomena to the Principles of Punishment', Hart argued that three questions are central to the philosophical debate over punishment:

1. What is the 'general justifying aim' of punishment?
2. Who may properly be punished?
3. How should the appropriate amount of punishment be determined? (Hart, 1959: 3)

What is at issue is whether all of 1 through 3 can be adequately answered by reference to a single principle such as the moral requirement to maximise utility, or whether they require separate treatment. Indirect consequentialist theories maintain that different principles must be applied to address each of these questions. However, as the title of his essay suggests, Hart is not offering a fully-fledged theory of punishment (a 'prolegomena' is a preface or programmatic statement). Other theorists have offered more substantial contributions to the development of a compromise theory.

In his essay 'Two Concepts of Rules' (first published 1955), Rawls seeks to reconcile two moral intuitions: (a) only the guilty should be punished (a retributivist intuition) and (b) punishment should serve a purpose (a consequentialist one) (Rawls, 1999: 22). Rawls also makes the distinction between rules and actions mentioned above and from that distinction emerge two correspondingly roles: the legislator (who determines the rules) and the judge (who applies the rules to particular cases without considering the wider purpose of punishment). The rules require that only a person who has committed the crime be punished. The argument is a form of institutional utilitarianism rather than rule-utilitarianism because the latter would collapse into act-utilitarianism if we had perfect knowledge: if we could make precise judgements on each occasion of whether knowingly punishing an innocent person would maximise utility, then we could carve out exceptions to the rule that we should never punish an innocent person. Central to Rawls's argument is the idea that given imperfect knowledge it is better to have a moral division of labour between legislator and judge.

Rawls then tackles the problem of how a consequentialist can avoid punishing an innocent person. In response to the linguistic (or dictionary) objection, Rawls coins the word 'telishment': telishment allows for the imposition of hard treatment on an innocent person whenever the officials empowered by that institution judge that it will maximise utility. He argues that such an institution would require a very high level of deception, and so the legislator would never empower the judge to telish somebody (Rawls, 1999: 27).

Rawls occupied a somewhat unusual position between retributivism and utilitarianism. He is regarded as one of the most important political philosophers of the twentieth century, and his major work *A Theory of Justice* (first published 1971) is discussed at length in Chapter 8. In summary, the purpose of a theory of justice is to ascertain the fair distribution of the benefits and burdens of social cooperation. Benefits include freedom and material resources, and burdens are the advantages we forego by agreeing to cooperate. To establish a fair distribution, we must imagine a situation in which we do not know our identities (this is the veil of ignorance). And while, for reasons explained in Chapter 8 (see p. 68), Rawls does not discuss punishment in *A Theory of Justice*, the background assumptions of the veil of ignorance rule out esoteric morality: although people are free to propose any principles of justice, they are constrained by the fact that the principles must be public: there can be no secret principles.

*A Theory of Justice* was hailed as a revival of Kantianism and a rejection of utilitarianism, and the publicity requirement fits with universalism: we could never will that a moral elite operates with a utilitarian moral code, while simultaneously inculcating a belief in retributivism in the populace. Rule-utilitarianism really is utilitarianism; we are only trained to think like retributivists because it is claimed that as a matter of fact this is the best way to maximise utility. But so-called institutional utilitarianism is not really utilitarian because the imposition of publicity cannot itself be explained in utilitarian terms.

Another way to strengthen the utilitarian response to the charge that it justifies deliberately punishing an innocent person is to observe that retributivism itself does not entirely avoid something closely related: the danger of a miscarriage of justice. If you know there is a probability that a person did not commit a crime what justifies punishing him? In law, a jury is asked to make a guilty judgement if they are convinced 'beyond reasonable doubt' of his guilt. If the test were changed to 'no doubt at all', many criminals would go unpunished and for a retributivist that would be bad. But this does suggest that, for a retributivist, there is a consequentialist consideration: the effectiveness of the criminal justice system in identifying and punishing the guilty.

In response to this charge, a 'sophisticated' retributivist might draw a parallel with just war theory. One aspect of *jus in bello* (rules for the conduct of war) is that you should never deliberately target non-combatants. Without any subsidiary requirements this rule is weak; a belligerent state that killed non-combatants in a bombing raid could say that they did not deliberately target the non-combatants but they were unfortunate collateral damage. Likewise, a 'crude' retributivist might argue that victims of miscarriages are collateral victims. What is required in both cases – war and punishment – are secondary rules that require you to make stringent efforts to avoid harming innocent victims. In combat, this would require that your military forces avoid killing non-combatants, even if that increases the risks to those forces. And with criminal justice there must be strict laws of evidence.

## The argument so far

In this section, we take stock of the arguments set out above and set the scene for the discussion of the third theory of punishment: restitutionism.

In assessing theories of punishment, we should ask two questions:

1. Who is (or are) the focal actor(s) in the process of punishment? There are three possibilities: (a) victim; (b) perpetrator; (c) society.
2. What is the purpose of punishment?

We can tabulate the responses to these questions in this way:

|  | *Focal actor(s)* | *Purpose of punishment* |
| --- | --- | --- |
| **Retributivism** | **Criminal**. The concern is with his or her mental state – *mens rea*. | Addressing the will (or intention) of the criminal. |
| **Consequentialism** | **Society**. Punishment maximises the overall good. | Good consequences, through, for example, deterrence. |
| **Restitutivism** | **Victim**. Crime is harm to that individual's interests as the result of the violation of his or her rights. | Making good the harm done to individuals by the crime. |

While restitutivism looks a lot like retributivism, there are important differences. The latter is based on the idea of a public power that is not reducible to the interests of individuals, whereas the former is fully individualistic. By individualistic is meant that *in principle* all harms are traceable to individuals, and punishment should map onto the harm done – it should seek to restore the *status quo ante*. For example, if A steals from B, then C may be harmed because one crime makes another more likely. But we can still identify the harm done to C. There is no abstract entity called 'society' that is harmed by the criminal's act. Another difference is that there is no need to engage in a universalisation process to determine who should be punished. What distinguishes restitutivism above all from the other two theories is the focus on the victim, who is often forgotten in retributivism and consequentialism. Certainly, there might be a psychic compensation resulting from punishment – satisfaction that the perpetrator has suffered – but there is little in the way of material compensation.

## Restitutivism

Randy Barnett defends the idea of restitution and challenges the existing paradigm of punishment, which he argues is based on an outdated sovereignty model of the state. Crime, he maintains, entails harming an individual, not the state or community (Barnett, 1977: 287–8). He notes that restitution plays a minor role in existing law, taking the form of relatively small cash payments to victims. This is inadequate because it comes mostly out of tax; is discretionary rather than a right; is needs-assessed; is limited to certain crimes; and, finally, is assumed to be compatible with traditional theories of punishment. Barnett wants a complete 'paradigm-shift' to restitution: 'the idea of restitution is actually quite simple. . . it views crime as an offense by one individual against the rights of another' (Barnett, 1977: 287). The robber did not rob society, he robbed the victim.

Some critics regard restitutivism as atavistic. It is a throwback to an eye for an eye. And certainly we need to consider both historical examples and modern reworkings of the theory. English legal history illustrates the transition from restitutivism to retributivism. Simplifying somewhat, during much of the Anglo-Saxon period (410–1066), what is modern-day England had a loose structure of kingdoms and more decentralised organisations. In the absence of a strong central state, order was maintained by a system of group protection and compensation (*wergild*) (Sides, 2017):

1.  *Wergild* was blood-money.
2.  For murder, the money goes to the victim's family (although it could go to the king or abbot). In effect, the money goes to whoever protected the murdered man.
3.  You are under the protection of your sib (family) or others, but they are also responsible for your actions (in modern language, this is a community responsibility system).
4.  You can abandon a family member. That person literally became an outlaw – outside the protection of law.
5.  Blood-feud – mutual violence – was a social control mechanism. But it was less costly to threaten violence and accept money than to carry out the threat.
6.  How much should be paid was determined by law, which both sides accepted.

There were strong incentives not to commit crime, as the entire group suffered. The upshot was that the group controlled its own members. Blood-feuds were rational, as they incentivised the group to control its members. The development of centralised authority led to the King becoming the repository of compensation and the only person who could punish, and it marked the end of the blood-feud and the emergence of retributivism.

In the contemporary world, group-based punishment tends to be associated with fragile (failed) states and ungoverned spaces (Leeson, 2009). Their experience does not seem like a recommendation of restitutionism. However, a contemporary version could be developed which is not born out of necessity – the lack of effective state order – but is a conscious design feature of the legal system. Although some anarchists may be attracted to restitutionism, we will assume that there is a state. We are not dependent on small communities to generate order, and there is no reliance on blood-feuds as a threat. However, other features of the old system are relevant, especially an agreed scheme of compensation and the right of an individual to choose to press for compensation. This is how such a scheme could work (in a series of steps):

1.  Each person is insured. Insurance could be provided by the state or private companies and the amount may be fixed or vary dependent on how much coverage is desired.
2.  After a crime is committed the insurer pays out to the victim (or his estate).

3. The insurer seeks to recover damages from the perpetrator. Recovery can take various forms such as seizure of assets or being required to work to pay off the debt.
4. It might be possible to insure yourself against committing a crime, especially if you think you have a genetic predisposition to do so.

One of the obvious problems is how you compensate for certain crimes. As with *wergild*, monetary value would have to attach to the harm caused by, for example, murder. And the situation is more complex than in Anglo-Saxon England, where certain crimes, such as rape, were defined as the violation of the rights of the husband.

In the next section, we compare the three theories of punishment by focusing on whether capital punishment – state execution – is justified. Aside from the central issue of its justification, this debate is a useful way of bringing out the differences between the theories. By default, the discussion tends to focus on capital punishment for murder, but of course it could be applied as a punishment for other crimes.

## Capital punishment

## Retributivism and capital punishment

Kant argued that:

> ...even if civil society [i.e., the state] were to be dissolved by consent of all its members, the last murderer remaining in prison would first have to be executed, so that each has done to him what his deeds deserve and blood guilt does not cling to the people for not having insisted upon this punishment; for otherwise the people can be regarded as collaborators in this public violation of justice.
>
> (Kant, 1996: 474)

This is a very pure statement of retribution: (a) since society (or the state) is going to be dissolved it carries no practical consequences (primarily, deterrence) if the murderer is not executed; (b) the people have no choice but to execute the murderer: if they do not execute him, they are complicit in his act.

The act of murder is a universalisation by the murderer of the killing of an innocent person, such that the murderer wills his own death. The murderer's will cannot be allowed to stand, so the state must reassert its will by forcing the murderer to accept the consequences of his willing 'that innocent people be killed'. On the face of it, this argument seems odd: if we execute him we are legitimating the principle 'that innocent people be killed'. We surely do not think that the murderer is innocent, so in executing him, we are not acting out the principle of killing innocent people. Moreover, why should the murderer dictate to us what we should do? If the state is superior to the murderer it could choose not to execute him. This second point is important and allows for a retributivist rejection of capital punishment, but some clarification of Kant's position is required. What the murderer wants to do is to kill and get away with it. In executing him, we are forcing him to accept the logic of his action – it is not an eye for an eye, but an attempt to recognise the murderer as a responsible agent and force him to accept that responsibility.

However, even allowing for this clarification, Kant's position still seems crude, and Hegel's theory of punishment is an attempt to offer something more sophisticated. While Hegel supported the death penalty, he offered a way out of *requiring* the death penalty on retributivist grounds. Alan Brudner contrasts Kant's and Hegel's positions (Brudner, 1980: 345–8). For Kant, we are required by justice to execute murderers because to fail to do so is unjust to the victims. Hegel allows for clemency: 'pardon is the remission of punishment, but it does not annul the law. On the contrary, the law stands and the pardoned man remains a criminal as before' (Hegel cited in Brudner, 1980: 352). To pardon is an expression of the power of the state: to be able to apprehend, justly convict, and execute a person is enough. The state need not choose to execute the person. Justice does not require it. The authority of the state rests for Kant on a contractual relationship between the individual and the state, such that the state cannot disregard the rights of the victim. For Hegel, the legitimacy of the state is more complex: the individual realises himself in the state, such that his interests are bound up with the state (see pp. 17–18). To decide not to execute murderers is not a violation of the victim's rights.

## Consequentialism and capital punishment

Consequentialist arguments for and against the death penalty come down – unsurprisingly – to an assessment of the consequences of the practice. Popular debate is dominated by one issue: whether capital punishment deters murder. However, there are other possible consequences, including the feeling of satisfaction of the victim's family when the murderer is executed; the popular sense of satisfaction at the death of a murderer; and the reinforcement of a sense of legitimacy of the legal system (especially if there is majority support for the death penalty). But there are negative consequences to be weighed in the balance: the sense of injustice if it is found that an innocent person has been executed; the loss to the executed person, both the immediate pain and the loss of his future; the loss to the murderer's family; and the brutalising effects of capital punishment on state officials and the population in general. This not an exhaustive list of the consequences, but hopefully sufficient to get across the point that in assessing consequentialist arguments for and against the death penalty it is important not to concentrate entirely on the issue of deterrence.

## Restitutionism and capital punishment

Restitutionists would seem to have a particular problem with capital punishment. How do you compensate a person for the loss of his life? It is noteworthy that, in earlier Anglo-Saxon England – before the assertion of kingly authority in the ninth century – capital punishment was not widely practised. You could be threatened with death, but that was to motivate the payment of *wergild*, which was monetary compensation. There was a sliding scale for payments depending on the status of the person murdered, and that payment scheme itself was based not on the intrinsic worth of the murdered person, but his importance in maintain social order or *friþ* (Sides, 2017: 106). This was a very political consideration. A modern version of restitution would have to look to the value a person's life has for that person. One possibility is that the monetary value is attached to unrealised projects. A person's legal identity survives her death, and compensation would enable other people to pursue the projects she valued. But it is very difficult to compensate for the loss of consciousness. Perhaps, as with *wergild*, a society simply decides on a scheme of compensation without pretending it has any metaphysical status; such a scheme might calculate expected years lost, so a younger life lost results in higher compensation.

# The status of the executed person

Two questions:

1. Is capital punishment ever justified?
2. Even if your answer to question 1 is 'no', consider two scenarios: (a) a person is 'straightforwardly' executed with a bullet through the heart: death is instantaneous; (b) that person is executed with a bullet through the head (death is instantaneous), but then his or her organs are harvested for transplant operations. Are (a) and (b) equally bad, or is (b) worse/better than (a)? (Assume that, in both scenarios, the condemned person has not given consent for the use of his or her body parts.)

If we are concerned with good consequences, then why not? If a person is going to die, why not use her body parts? A consequentialist argument against this practice is that people might feel distaste towards it: it just seems unpleasant and for that reason is disutilitarian. Another consequentialist argument against the practice is that it might encourage the state to kill people for their body parts.

A retributivist would have a very clear answer: in executing a person we respect her. We do not use her as a means to an end, but simply give her what she deserves: she brought her execution on herself. Strange as it may sound, killing a person is not, morally speaking, a violation of that person's integrity – after all, it is her physical destruction. However, using her body parts *is* a violation. There is an interesting moment in the British film *Pierrepoint* (2005) when the state executioner Albert Pierrepoint is washing down and preparing for burial the woman he has just hanged, when his assistant asks why they should be doing this – why cannot it be left to the people at the morgue? Pierrepoint responds that they would not show sufficient respect: *she is innocent now because she has paid the price.* Whether the real Albert Pierrepoint actually said this, or the scriptwriter put the words in his mouth, is irrelevant: it encapsulates the retributivist view of the executed person.

## Prepunishment

We return to the question posed at the start of the chapter: should we prepunish?

Whether a person is responsible for any action is a popular topic of discussion in introductory philosophy courses (this is the free will and determinism problem). For the sake of this discussion, let us assume that we can be held responsible for at least some of our actions. And, furthermore, assume some actions are intentional and others unintentional. As we have seen, the *mens rea* test should establish whether an action is intentional – whether it was done with a 'guilty mind'. For a retributivist, *mens rea* is essential to holding someone responsible for his actions. On the other side, a consequentialist need not insist on the test being satisfied in order to punish a person. Indeed, the logic of consequentialism may require the test be set aside.

If a person can be subject to hard treatment without intending to commit a crime, this open the way to prepunishment: predicting the likelihood a person will commit a crime and acting to prevent it. We might not call this punishment, but it would look like a great deal like it, especially if it resulted in incarceration. There are historical precedents for it, even in liberal democracies. Internment of enemy aliens – or of citizens with dual nationality – in wartime is one example. Another is the prediction of gang membership. The London Metropolitan Police Gangs Matrix is a database with 3,000–4,000 people on it (Densley and Pyrooz, 2020: 11). Although an intelligence tool, as Densley and Pyrooz argue: 'a gang designation can immediately escalate a routine stop by police and the stigma and scrutiny of being named in a database can far outlast actual affiliation with a gang' (2020: 16).

We can assess prepunishment from a moral and a political perspective. From a moral perspective, prepunishment may jar with strongly held intuitions about who deserves punishment. But political theory is not identical with moral theory and has its own concerns, including a focus on social order and the trust that makes order possible. Would prepunishment facilitate or undermine trust? An argument for prepunishment is that it might make people feel safer if higher risk individuals were out of circulation; this has the effect of increasing trust even between low risk individuals since we cannot, in the normal course of life be sure of another person's propensity to commit crime. If there were experts who could assess risk and prepunish – *and if we trusted their judgement* – the overall level of trust in society would increase. Note that the experts could be wrong. What matters is the widespread belief they are right.

There are, however, reasons why prepunishment would reduce trust. There is a close relationship between reciprocity and trust (Evans and Krueger, 2009: 1013–14). Indeed, one way out of the prisoner's dilemma is to repeat it: recall that in a one-shot game the rational strategy is non-cooperation (see pp. 11–12). But if you have to interact with the same person on future occasions, you have an incentive to cooperate – you want to build a reputation for trustworthiness. This is why very small communities – in which there is repeated interaction – can sustain cooperation without a state. And indeed, there is evidence that cooperation is the default position for most people because the brain has been shaped by our ancestral past in which we lived in small hunter-gatherer bands (Hoffman, McCabe, and Smith, 1998: 350). Intentionality and reciprocity are closely related. A person who did not intend to harm another is treated more leniently than someone who did intend harm, and this makes sense. Intentional harm, once multiplied across society, would lead to a collapse in social order, whereas a few people, who for reasons of diminished responsibility, cannot be held responsible for their actions, do not pose such a great threat.

Prepunishment breaks the link between intentionality, reciprocity, and trust. What is wrong with prepunishment also allows us to see why both *mens rea* and deterrence are central to punishment and central to a political – and not just a moral – analysis of punishment. Punishment must serve some ends, hence the focus on its deterrent effect, but humans are also intentional agents, who respond to the perceived intentions of others.

## Conclusion

We have presented the two dominant justifications for punishment – retributivism and consequentialism – and a third one: restitutionism. No theory seems able to reconcile what to ordinary people are two important aspects of punishment: that only the guilty should be punished (and the guilty should not escape punishment) and punishment should deter crime. There is a third consideration which tends to be ignored in the practice of punishment and that is the harm done to the victims of crime, and for which there should be compensation.

It is important in assessing punishment to identify its distinctly political aspect: its role in securing social order. This links punishment back to arguments for the state (discussed in Chapter 1). Reciprocity – sensitivity to the potential for free-riding by others – is central to engendering the trust that makes political order possible. And even though we have struggled to reconcile *mens rea* and deterrence, reciprocity draws together these two ideas: in everyday life, we are conscious of whether someone acted intentionally and from intentionality comes reciprocity, which, in turn, is the basis of trust and order.

# Note

1   For an overview of Hegel, see Steinberger (1983). For Kant, see Hill (1999).

# References

Barnett, R. (1977). Restitution: A New Paradigm of Criminal Justice. *Ethics*, *87*(4), 279–301.

Boyd, R. and Richerson, P. J. (1992). Punishment Allows the Evolution of Cooperation (or Anything Else) in Sizable Groups. *Ethology and Sociobiology*, *13*(3), 171–95.

Brudner, A. (1980). Retributivism and the Death Penalty. *University of Toronto Law Journal*, *30*(4), 337–55.

Caspi, A., McClay, J., Moffitt, T. E., Mill, J., Martin, J., Craig, I. W.,. . . Poulton, R. (2002). Role of Genotype in the Cycle of Violence in Maltreated Children. *Science*, *297*(5582), 851–4.

Chan, W., and Simester, A. P. (2011). Four Functions of Mens Rea. *The Cambridge Law Journal*, *70*(2), 381–96.

Cottingham, J. (1979). Varieties of Retribution. *The Philosophical Quarterly (1950–)*, *29*(116), 238–246.

Densley, J. A. and Pyrooz, D. C. (2020). The Matrix in Context: Taking Stock of Police Gang Databases in London and Beyond. *Youth Justice*, *20*(1–2), 11–30.

De Lazari-Radek, K., and Singer, P. (2010). Secrecy in Consequentialism: A Defence of Esoteric Morality. *Ratio*, *23*(1), 34–58.

Evans, A. M. and Krueger, J. I. (2009). The Psychology (and Economics) of Trust. *Social and Personality Psychology Compass*, *3*(6), 1003–17.

Friesen, L. (2012). Certainty of Punishment versus Severity of Punishment: An Experimental Investigation. *Southern Economic Journal*, *79*(2), 399–421.

Hart, H.L.A. (1959). The Presidential Address: Prolegomenon to the Principles of Punishment, *Proceedings of the Aristotelian Society*, New Series, *60*, 1–26.

Hill, T. E. (1999). Kant on Wrongdoing, Desert, and Punishment. *Law and Philosophy*, *18*(4), 407–41.

Hoffman, E., McCabe, K. A., and Smith, V. L. (1998). Behavioral Foundations of Reciprocity: Experimental Economics and Evolutionary Psychology. *Economic Inquiry*, *36*(3), 335–52.

Kant, I. (1996). 'The Metaphysics of Morals', in M. Gregor (ed.), *Practical Philosophy* Cambridge: Cambridge University Press.

Leeson, P. T. (2009). The Laws of Lawlessness. *The Journal of Legal Studies*, *38*(2), 471–503.

Moore, M. (1997). *Placing Blame: A Theory of Criminal Law.* Oxford: Oxford University Press.

Morris, H. (1968). Persons and Punishment. *The Monist*, *52*(4), 475–501.

McKibbin, W. F., Shackelford, T. K., Goetz, A. T., and Starratt, V. G. (2008). Why Do Men Rape? An Evolutionary Psychological Perspective. *Review of General Psychology*, *12*(1), 86–97.

Nagel, T. (2012). *Mortal Questions.* Cambridge: Cambridge University Press.

Rawls, J. (1999). 'Two Concepts of Rules', in S. Freeman (ed.), *Collected Papers.* Cambridge MA and London: Harvard University Press, 20–46.

Sides, B. (2017). A Life's Worth: Reexamining Wergild in the Anglo-Saxon Royal Law Codes (c. 600–1035). *The Expositor: A Journal of Undergraduate Research in the Humanities*, *13*, 85–107.

Steinberger, P. J. (1983). Hegel on Crime and Punishment. *The American Political Science Review*, *77*(4),858–70.

Sullivan, G. R. (1993). Cause and the Contemporaneity of Actus Reus and Mens Rea. *The Cambridge Law Journal*, 52(3), 487–500.

Vandermassen, G. (2011). Evolution and Rape: A Feminist Darwinian Perspective. *Sex Roles*, *64*(9–10), 732–47.

Waldron, J. (1992). Lex talionis. *Arizona Law Journal*, *34*, 25.

## Further reading

A high-quality collection of contributions can be found in Farah Focquaert, Elizabeth Shaw, and Bruce Waller (eds.), *The Routledge Handbook of the Philosophy and Science of Punishment* (Routledge, 2020). Also useful are the following works: A John Simmons (ed.), *Punishment: A Philosophy and Public Affairs Reader* (Princeton University Press, 1994); Nicola Lacey, *State Punishment* (Routledge, 1994); David Boonin, *The Problem of Punishment* (Cambridge University Press, 2008); Bruce Waller, *The Injustice of Punishment* (Routledge, 2020); Erin Kelly, *The Limits of Blame: Rethinking Punishment and Responsibility* (Harvard University Press, 2018).

# Chapter 4

# Civil disobedience and conscientious objection

## Introduction

Civil disobedience is the non-violent breaking of a law on moral grounds. While there were theorists of civil disobedience in the nineteenth and early twentieth centuries, and the theory may be applicable to non-democratic societies, this chapter focuses on the post-war discussion of civil disobedience in a liberal-democratic society. Although few people engage in civil disobedience, it is not a peripheral concept, for the justification of civil disobedience touches on the moral basis of majoritarian democracy. Whereas in the pre-modern and early modern periods, political theory was concerned with the right to rebel, the fundamental question raised by civil disobedience to a modern audience is this: how is it possible to have a general respect for the rule of law and yet break specific laws?

## Key questions

- Are you ever morally justified in breaking the law?
- If you think you are justified, can you answer the question: what if everyone broke the law?
- Does law-breaking weaken or strengthen the state?

## Civil disobedience and law-breaking

This chapter is concerned with justifications for civil disobedience, and naturally, it makes sense to start with a definition. However, as we shall see, the definition and justification of civil disobedience are closely related, so that a particular definition implies a certain understanding of the role civil disobedience plays in the political system. What we offer here is an initial definition, which will require further clarification: civil disobedience is morally justified law-breaking, *normally* intended to change a law or policy. It has these components: (a) it involves breaking the law – it is not simply legal protest; (b) there are moral reasons justifying the action; (c) the aim is to change a law or policy rather than bring down the political system.

DOI: 10.4324/9780429424106-6

## Case study 4.1

## Refusing military service

**PHOTO 4.1** © Ulrich Baumgarrten/Getty Images.

Is a person justified in refusing to fight to defend his (or her) country when it is under attack (or is threatened with attack)? Is it right that the state should permit exemptions for individuals who refuse to fight?

Most liberal-democratic states permit exemptions, but it is not obvious why they should. If we benefit from living under a state, we should also bear the burdens, one of which is defending the state when it is under attack. And the burdens ought to be fairly distributed. If one person refuses to fight, it may make others reluctant to do so, as they perceive the refusenik to be a free-rider, who is taking advantage of those willing to fight.

If exemptions are granted, what criteria should be applied? Should exemptions be given only to those who refuse to fight in any wars or should selective objection – refusal to fight in a *particular* war, but not all wars – be accepted?

Of all the concepts discussed in this book, civil disobedience is among a relatively small group, where theory and practice are closely related, and indeed where some of the most important theorists of the concept have been its practitioners. American Henry David Thoreau (1817–62) is credited with offering the earliest theory of civil disobedience. Thoreau was imprisoned for refusing to pay a tax that was intended to fund what he regarded as an unjust war by the United States against Mexico. In his essay 'Civil Disobedience' (1849), he argued that an individual had a moral duty to break an unjust law – you should, he suggests, 'let your life be a counter-friction to stop the machine' (Thoreau, 1991: 36). In other words, civil disobedience was intended to obstruct the implementation of immoral policies. Thoreau's argument was highly influential. Mahatma Gandhi (1869–1948) read 'Civil Disobedience' while in prison and developed both its theory and practice in his struggle against British rule in India. But the theories of Thoreau and Gandhi are problematic because although they were directed at a political situation – war and occupation – they were motivated by a sense of personal integrity rather than an appeal to the sense of justice of their respective publics. A more *political* justification for civil disobedience was advanced by Martin Luther King.

As with Gandhi it was also from a prison cell that in 1963 King wrote what became known as the 'Letter from Birmingham City Jail' (King, 1991), a plea to fellow church leaders to accept the legitimacy of non-violent law-breaking in pursuit of equal rights for US citizens. Although inspired by Thoreau and Gandhi, King offers a two-level justification of civil disobedience: one level articulated in theological terms and directed at church leaders, the other level expressed in secular language and aimed at his fellow citizens.

In this chapter, we will explore King's argument, as well as Gandhi's *satyagraha*, a term Gandhi coined, which while not accurately translated as civil disobedience, is of relevance to the debate. Among philosophers, the most influential defence of civil disobedience was advanced by John Rawls, who argued that it was an appeal to the sense of justice of the majority. Before discussing the work of these theorists and practitioners, we need to explore the concept of morally motivated law-breaking.

## Law-breaking

Criminals break laws, and so do people who engage in civil disobedience. How do we distinguish the civilly disobedient from the merely criminal? In part, the distinction will rest on *how* the law is broken, in part on *why* it is broken. Reasons for breaking the law fall into four categories, although the fourth is a subcategory of the third:

1. Individual self-interest: a law is not in the individual's interests.
2. Group interest: a law is not in the interests of a particular group.
3. Morality: a law is morally wrong.
4. Justice: a law is unjust.

All defenders of civil disobedience reject the first category as justifying law-breaking – to break the law simply because it does not suit your interests is to engage in a criminal act. The second category is more complex. Marx and Engels argued that it was in the interests of the working class to overthrow the capitalist system and create a classless society (see p. 192). It follows that it is in the long-term interests of *all* human beings that the working class should succeed. But Marx and Engels advocated the complete transformation of society – revolution – and not simply the removal of certain laws. For them, there could be no appeal to morality, for morality is the product of existing, capitalist, society.

Civil disobedience, as distinct from revolution, must appeal to moral ideas held by those who support the existing laws. The willingness of the civilly disobedient to accept the penalties for their law-breaking assumes the majority, who may with varying degrees of awareness support the existing unjust laws, can be moved by their actions. Consequently, most theories of civil disobedience rest on the third and fourth categories. However, there is an important distinction, which we discuss later, between breaking a law because you judge it immoral and breaking it because you believe it is unjust.

Although self-interest is not a justification for civil disobedience, it may well be a motivating factor. For example, the segregation laws operative in the Southern states of the United States before the 1960s damaged the interests of *individual* blacks and blacks as a *group*. This does not invalidate the claims of people such as Martin Luther King that he and other blacks were morally justified in breaking the law.

## Civil disobedience versus rebellion

It is important to recognise how recent is the development of the concept of civil disobedience. Certainly, political philosophers prior to the twentieth century had much to say about rebellion, but the possibility that rebellion could be anything other than the overthrow of the political system was not seriously considered. It is important not to dismiss earlier thinkers, because their concerns about social order provide a backdrop to the more recent discussion of civil disobedience.

Hobbes (see pp. 11–13) rejected rebellion on several grounds. First, once you contract into the state, you give up your rights to private judgement regarding the justice or injustice of the state. Second, while you do not give up your intellectual capacity, any rational person will see that life under the state – under any regime, however authoritarian – is better than life in the state of nature. Third, law-breaking is a form of free-riding and will rapidly lead to a collapse in obedience to the state because the worst possible position for any individual is to obey the law while most others are breaking it.

Later, thinker John Locke (1632–1704), whose work is often compared with Hobbes, granted citizens more latitude. Like Hobbes, he presents a contract theory, and his argument starts with the state of nature (no state) and moves to the state. Locke's argument is discussed in more detail in Chapter 9 (see pp. 166–7), but in brief Locke split the creation of the state into two stages: we pool our individual rights to punish and create a sovereign power, and we then entrust that sovereign power to a group of individuals (a government), who exercise it on our behalf (Locke, 1997: 48–9, 54–5). It is important to understand that individuals have natural rights, and they enter a state so as better to protect these rights. Rebellion is justified if, first, the government either violates our natural rights or fails to defend us against their violation by others. Second, if the government does not promote the common good, meaning the provision of public goods (see pp. 13–14). Third, if the government hands over some, or all, of the sovereign power we invested in it to a foreign power. Finally, rebellion is justified if the government does not respect its own law – that is, positive law (law created – posited – rather than natural) (Thomas, 1995: 60–5).

Rebellion is a collective act of the people, as distinct from the later concept of civil disobedience, which is an individual act, or at least carried out by a section, rather than the whole, of the community. But it also distinguishes Locke from Hobbes. For Hobbes, there was nothing between the state (Leviathan) and individuals (there might be families, but these are not politically significant). It follows that for Hobbes rebellion can only be an act of an individual and presupposes that individuals retain the right of private judgement. Locke's theory of rebellion depends on interposing between the government and individuals what he calls the community (what we today would term the people). Both theorists pose an important question: who has the authority to challenge the legitimacy of the state (and its laws, policies, and actions)? Hobbes's answer was that nobody has the authority. Locke's response was to say the people as a collective had the authority, but then, the people require leadership and that raises the question of who has the right to lead a rebellion on behalf of the people.

# Democracy and obedience

In Chapter 2, we suggested that there was a possible conflict between majoritarian democracy and individual rights – the majority could vote to remove the rights of minorities. If we did not know our identities – we are placed behind a veil of ignorance (see p. 136) – the problem might be lessened, as we would ensure that safeguards, such as qualified majority requirements or bills of rights, were put in place. But in practice we are not behind a veil, and so we must deal with the real world, one in which the majority knows it is the majority and can oppress minorities.

Civil disobedience indicates the moral limits of majority rule but it also forces us to reflect on the justifications *for* majority rule. For these reasons, it is important to consider the relationship of civil disobedience to democracy. Are there stronger arguments for obeying laws produced by a democratic procedure than those created by a non-democratic one? Peter Singer thinks so. In his book *Democracy and Disobedience* (1973), he uses a very artificial example to illustrate his position; however, its artificiality helps to bring out the main lines of the argument.

Oxford University is a collegiate university, with most living and teaching centred around the individual colleges. Singer asks us to imagine that each college is equivalent to a state, and the colleges taken together represent the world system of states. The undergraduates in a college form what Singer calls the Association. Students cannot opt out of membership of the Association. A student could transfer to another college at the university, but she would be obliged to join *its* Association. Of course, she could leave the university, but we are to imagine the whole world is Oxford University, so that short of death there is no possibility of leaving. The Association of each college has been in existence for as long as anybody can remember – if there was ever a point at which it was set up, the records have been lost. The Association charges a subscription from each student, equivalent to a tax. There are two ways of making decisions on how much to charge and what the money is spent on:

- *The Leader.* Some time ago, one student who is now the Leader decided that decision-making was inefficient, and the decisions arrived at were stupid. He would now make the decisions, albeit guided by the interests of the other students (Singer, 1973: 14–15). Objectors would have to fight it out with the Leader's friends, who were the best fighters in the Association.
- *Democracy.* Decisions are taken by a majority vote of all members of the Association. At meetings, all are free to speak, subject to some essential procedural requirements, such as an agreed time limit on speeches. Meetings are conducted fairly, and the votes calculated correctly (1973: 16). (There is a third model – the Senior Member – but its introduction would unnecessarily complicate this discussion.)

An issue arises that causes serious dissension. The Association uses some of the subscription money to buy newspapers for general use in the student common room, and these must not be taken away. One day, it is decided that the common room should take *The News*. One member of the Association – the Dissenter – objects to this newspaper, arguing it is racist, and other members of the Association, less attuned to the paper's bigotry, will be influenced by it to the detriment of the few black students in the college. Consider now the two models:

- *The Leader.* The Dissenter asks the Leader to reconsider his decision, but the Leader is unmoved. The Dissenter takes things into his own hands by getting up early each morning and removing the paper before others have had a chance to read it.
- *Democracy.* It had been agreed after lengthy debate and by majority vote that the common room would take *The News*. The Dissenter finds himself in a minority. At the next and later

meetings, he attempts to get the decision reversed, but it becomes clear that a majority wants the paper. On realising this, the Dissenter behaves in the same way as under the other model: he removes the paper.

Thinking about the Dissenter, the initial question Singer poses is not whether he has moral reasons for removing *The News*, but whether under the Democracy model, there are special reasons for not removing it, reasons which do not exist under the Leader model. Participation, Singer suggests, is the key difference between democratic and non-democratic systems:

> ...the Dissenter, by voluntarily participating in the vote on the question of whether *The News* should be ordered, understanding that the purpose of the election is to enable the group to reach a decision on this issue, has behaved in such a way as to lead people reasonably to believe that he was accepting the democratic process as a suitable means of settling the issue.
>
> (Singer, 1973: 50)

Democratic decision-making is a *fair compromise* between people who have conflicting moral views. And while we cannot consent – either explicitly or tacitly – to the voting procedure itself, we can consent by our actions to the decisions made under it. Singer borrows a concept from law to express the moral bindingness of participation: estoppel. He quotes an English judge Lord Birkenhead:

> Where A has by his words or conduct justified B in believing that a certain state of affairs exists, and B has acted upon such belief to his prejudice, A is not permitted to affirm against B that a different state of facts existed at the same time.
>
> (Singer, 1973: 51)

An everyday, non-legal example would be the British convention of buying a round of drinks in a pub (bar): if four people go to the pub and the first person buys four pints of beer, and then the second person does so, and then the third person likewise, the fourth, who has accepted three pints, can reasonably be expected to buy a round. He has not consented to the rule or convention of buying a round, but his acceptance of the three pints has affected the behaviour of his three friends (1973: 49).

Singer anticipates the objection that the Dissenter can avoid being bound through estoppel simply by not participating in the democratic process. He argues that the notion of a fair compromise generates not only an obligation to accept the decision of the majority but also to participate in the process: it is not reasonable to sit it out. If you sit it out and then find the decision made is unacceptable, you cannot have grounds for refusing to accept the decision because you were unreasonable in prejudging the decision. People who do not vote can have no complaint against the decisions made by those who do.

## Problems with democracy

Singer's defence of obedience to a democratically agreed law is an 'all things being equal' defence. He does not argue that we should *always* obey such law. There are situations in which civil disobedience is justified even in a democracy. Some of the more obvious ones are these:

1. Most voting systems do not consider the intensity of a person's preferences. A minority may feel *very strongly* about an issue, but they are outvoted by an *apathetic* majority. Civil disobedience can be a means by which not only are views communicated but also the *intensity* of those views made apparent.

2. Some people find themselves in a permanent minority. This is exacerbated if electoral politics is based on one dominant social characteristic. For example, in Northern Ireland, voting is largely along religious lines. In the period 1922–73, there existed a devolved parliament in Northern Ireland with the Protestant Unionists always in the majority and Catholics entirely excluded from power.
3. Some people are denied the vote. The largest group is children. Their interests are affected by legislation over which they have no control. Civilly disobedient actions undertaken by children are rare but, arguably, groups of adults representing the interests of children could be justified in engaging in civil disobedience on their behalf.
4. It could be argued that animals have interests and that these are clearly affected by the democratic process. Some notable examples of civil disobedience have been based on concern for animal welfare; in the United Kingdom there has been a long-running campaign against the use of animals in what are seen by many as unnecessary experiments.
5. The decisions made today will affect future generations. The justification given for some acts of civil disobedience against the building of roads and airports is that fossil fuel emissions exacerbate global warming, which will have catastrophic consequences for future generations.

The implication of these objections is that democracy can on occasion break down, but that it can also be fixed. The more radical challenge lies in the rejection of majority decision-making: a person may believe that a law is simply wrong, and no amount of institutional reform can create a situation in which the majority makes it right. For example, defenders of animal experimentation for medical purposes will maintain that they have given due weight to non-human animals as beings worthy of moral respect, but that human beings have greater moral claims. Opponents of such experiments will disagree and maintain that actions such as breaking into laboratories and releasing animals are justified on moral grounds. It is very difficult to find common ground between these two positions.

We live in a pluralistic society in which there is not only conflict between various individual and group interests but also between different moral conceptions. The stability and legitimacy of the political system requires some agreement on moral principles. There need not be agreement on all moral issues, but there must be some agreement. In the next section, we reconsider the arguments of Rawls, who does provide an account of that shared morality, but also justifies civil disobedience.

## Rawls: civil disobedience and conscientious refusal

For Rawls, civil disobedience is an appeal to the sense of justice of the majority of citizenry. It is consistent with respect for – 'fidelity to' – the law. His argument is part of a wider political theory, which we discuss in Chapter 8 (see pp. 135–9). Our aim here is to set out the argument with minimal reference to that political theory. This is important because it might be possible to endorse Rawls's position on civil disobedience without necessarily accepting his other claims about what political principles we should live by, and how those principles are derived.

There are various stages in Rawls's argument (Rawls, 1972: 195–201), the first of which is dependent on his broader political theory:

1. **Original Position**: people agree on basic principles of justice from a position in which they do not know their identities (they are placed behind a veil of ignorance) – such ignorance extends to not knowing your society. Rawls argues that two principles would be agreed, which,

simplifying somewhat, are: (a) an equal set of rights; (b) equality of opportunity and a distribution of income that makes the worst-off as well off as possible. To be clear, the Original Position is a hypothetical position, not a real, historical process. It is a thought-experiment.

2. **Constitutional Convention**: now knowing their societies but not their individual identities, people are tasked with writing a constitution for their society. The constitution should embody the two principles of justice agreed at stage one.

3. **Legislative Stage**: specific laws are created but constrained by the constitution (Rawls argues that legislators do not know their identities – a more realistic model would be one in which they do, but feel the force of the principles of justice as embodied in the constitution).

4. **Judicial Stage**: rules (laws) are applied to specific cases by judges and administrators.

Although stage one is an idealisation – as is denying people knowledge of their individual identities at stage two – Rawls argues that his aim is to articulate by way of philosophical concepts a *sense of justice* which really exists in some societies. He distinguishes three kinds of society: just, nearly just, and unjust (Rawls, 1972: 363). Just societies are ideal-types and have never existed and likely never will. Nearly just societies are those in which there is a sense of justice; this is absent in unjust societies. It follows that civil disobedience only has a place in nearly just societies. There would be no cause for disobedience in a just society and no sense of justice to which you could appeal in an unjust society.

Importantly, people in the Original Position know that principles of justice will need to be put into practice in the real world, and laws can only be passed by majority rule. It is impossible to have unanimity. Therefore, the potential for injustice arises. There is a conflict between the effective endorsement of majority rule at stage one (the most just stage) and the fact that majoritarianism can cause injustice.

If an individual felt entitled, and even obliged, to break every law deemed unjust, majoritarian democracy would collapse, and in the process so would the possibility of a just society. The question, or challenge – 'what if everyone did that?' – can always reasonably be asked of someone engaged in civil disobedience. As Rawls puts it:

> At what point does the duty to comply with laws enacted by a legislative majority (or with executive acts supported by such a majority) cease to be binding in view of the right to defend one's liberties and the duty to oppose injustice? This involves the nature and limits of majority rule. For this reason the problem of civil disobedience is a crucial test for any theory of the moral basis of democracy.
>
> (Rawls, 1972: 363)

As suggested above, for Rawls the civilly disobedient are addressing, or appealing to, the sense of justice of the majority. All the other points that Rawls makes, including the important distinction between civil disobedience and conscientious refusal, lead back to this idea. He sets out a number of conditions on civil disobedience (1972: 363–8):

1. *Injustice must be clear.* What is unjust is determined by the principles of justice. Of the two, breaches of the first principle – equal liberty – are likely to be much clearer than denial of the second – which is about the distribution of material resources. For example, to deny a class of adults the right to vote on grounds of their ethnic or religious identity, or their gender, would be a clear infraction of the first principle. It is not only a clear injustice but also its remedy – granting the equal right to vote – is easy to grasp. On the other hand, significant economic inequality is much less *obviously* unjust, and the solution to the claimed injustice is not apparent.

2. *It involves breaking the law, rather than simply testing it.* Some laws are broken to force a judicial judgement, but this is not civil disobedience. As we will see, this might rule out classifying significant aspects of the struggle against segregation in the Southern states as civil disobedience.

3. *It need not involve breaking the law, which is the object of civil disobedience.* Laws are broken in the process of engaging in civil disobedience, but they need not be the direct object of the civilly disobedient action. For example, in order to protest against an unjust war, you might sit down in the middle of the road, thus violating traffic laws, but it is not the traffic laws that are the target of the action.

4. *It must be a public act.* Civil disobedience is a communicative act – the majority is being given 'fair notice' a law is unjust. The communicative act consists not simply in the transmission of information – that could be achieved through covert action – but in getting the majority to understand that the civilly disobedient are making an appeal. Indeed, there is a distinction between communicating something to the majority and *appealing* to it.

5. *It must be non-violent and not constitute a threat.* The reasoning behind this is similar to that behind (4) – the civilly disobedient want the majority to change the law for the right reason, namely because it is unjust and not because they fear the consequences of maintaining the law. But maybe this is naive: one group may be genuinely non-violent and non-threatening, but their actions could be unintentionally threatening insofar as they make the majority aware of the existence of other, less peaceful, groups.

6. *The civilly disobedient accept the penalties for law-breaking.* Once again, the reasoning behind this point is that the civilly disobedient are appealing to, rather than threatening, the majority. Willingness to accept the penalties for law-breaking – that is, not resisting arrest – demonstrates sincerity. Such behaviour may embarrass the majority, who must ask themselves whether they really want to punish, often in a draconian fashion, clearly peace-loving people.

7. *Even if laws are seriously unjust, civil disobedience must not threaten the stability of the political system.* The thinking behind this requirement is that a situation might arise where there are a number of groups justifiably engaged in civil disobedience, but the conjoint effects of their actions threaten the stability of the political system. In such a situation groups must show restraint. Although it is rather unrealistic, Rawls suggests that civilly disobedient groups might come to an agreement whereby groups take it in turns engaging in civil disobedience. One might wonder whether a political system that provokes so much civil disobedience is even partially just.

8. *Civil disobedience takes place within fidelity to law.* The civilly disobedient do not seek to bring down the existing system, but want to strengthen it by removing injustice, such that the system will win the loyalty of all citizens. In this sense, the civilly disobedient demonstrate fidelity – or faithfulness – to the law.

## Conscientious refusal

There is a distinction between disobedience on general moral grounds and disobedience on the narrower – but still moral – ground of injustice. Rawls's aim in *A Theory of Justice* was to articulate a morality appropriate to the political sphere. That political morality leaves open many other areas of morality. Conscientious refusal may be motivated by political morality, but it need not be; it may derive from 'religious or other principles at variance with the constitutional order' (Rawls, 1972: 369). The clearest modern example of conscientious refusal is objection to military service either for general pacifist reasons or because of opposition to a particular war. Rawls argues that such objections cannot be *automatically* accepted, for justice requires on occasion that people be prepared to defend – by force of arms – the political system. However, he concedes that the spirit of pacifism accords with the values underlying a just society – it is rare for nearly just societies to go to war against one another: this is the so-called democratic peace argument, discussed in Chapter 1 (see pp. 21–2). He also argues that an unjust war – a war that violates the laws of peoples – can quite properly be the object of civil disobedience. (We return to conscientious objection – which is a form of conscientious refusal – at the end of the chapter.)

The danger with conscientious refusal is that it undermines the political order by substituting individual moral judgement for the collective judgement of society. An example would be the refusal to pay taxes that go towards the development and maintenance of nuclear weapons. It is possible that most people are nuclear pacifists – while they might believe that a just war with conventional weapons is possible, the use of nuclear warheads represents a hugely disproportionate response to the aggression of another country. But among nuclear pacifists, a majority might judge that the *threat* to use – rather than actual use of – nuclear weapons is better than submission to a foreign power. Of course, this is a bluff and bluffing carries risks. Nonetheless, there can be reasonable moral disagreement, such that the majority view in favour of nuclear threats is justified.

## Criticisms of Rawls

Several criticisms of Rawls's theory can be made. First, civil disobedience may be intended simply to make a law unworkable. The tactic of the Civil Rights Movement whereby one wave of people sat down at a segregated lunch counter were arrested and were then replaced by a second wave had the result of filling the jails until the process of justice ground to a halt. The majority may calculate that it is not in their interests to continue to support unjust laws. Certainly, this tactic entails no appeal to the moral sense of the majority and Rawls may be concerned that motivating the majority through appeal to self-interest – in effect, telling the majority that their lives are going to be made uncomfortable – is a weak basis for long-term political stability.

Second, as Andrew Sabl argues, instead of 'nearly just' societies, it may be more accurate to talk of 'piecewise just societies': 'people can have a sense of justice and still, through prejudice or moral blindness, have a radically deficient conception of justice or of what justice entails in the particular circumstances' (Sabl, 2001: 316).

Third, if, as Thoreau argued, and contrary to Rawls's understanding, civil disobedience is intended to disable the state from carrying out its policies, then some of Rawls's conditions for what constitute civilly disobedient acts become redundant. It is no longer essential – although it may be desirable – that an action be public. Certainly, publicity may be important in achieving one's objective and covert action could blur the distinction between civil disobedience and mere criminality. Likewise, the willingness to bear the punishment is desirable – for the same reasons – but, again, would not be essential.

## Gandhi and *satyagraha*

Gandhi coined the term *satyagraha*, which translates as the insistence on truth (or firmness in the truth). While he was not a Jain, Gandhi was influenced by Jain ideas, especially *ahimsa* (non-violence). Non-violence extends far beyond its everyday meaning in the West. It is bound up with a particular view of the universe. It is significant that Jains take five main vows: *ahimsa*;

*satya* (truth; commitment to truth); *asteya* (not stealing); *brahmacharya* (sexual restraint); *aparigraha* (non-possessiveness).

As Alexander Livingston argues, the basis of political order in the West is violence. As we saw, Weber defines the state as a monopoliser of violence and Hobbes argues that it is rational to create something we fear more than other people: Leviathan. Even Rawls takes the existence of the Weberian state as a given. It is difficult to slot *satyagraha* into this world, although that is exactly what tends to be done in discussions of civil disobedience. As Livingstone maintains: 'fidelity to truth, by contrast [to Rawlsian fidelity to law], represents a break with the rationality of modern civilization through a practice of *ahimsa* that subordinates politics to ethics' (Livingston, 2018: 515).

Despite the misuse of *satyagraha* by Western legal and political theorists, its conceptualisation and practice could be supportive of Western liberal democracy. It would be an example of conscientious refusal, and as Rawls argues, conscientious refusal may be compatible with civil disobedience: a person might oppose unjust laws for reasons that extend far beyond political beliefs shared with other citizens, but just so long as the civilly disobedient act appeals to a sense of justice shared by the majority, then it is civil disobedience. Indeed, this duality – a deep moral view of the world and a narrower political conception of justice – is at the heart of Martin Luther King's campaign of civil disobedience, a campaign the justification of which drew on *satyagraha*.

## Martin Luther King and the Civil Rights Movement

The aim of this section is to apply the theoretical discussion of the previous sections to a case study of civil disobedience: Martin Luther King and the Civil Rights Movement in the United States in the 1950s and 1960s. It is the most famous example of civil disobedience and the one that influenced Rawls (*A Theory of Justice*, published in 1971, was written during the period of the Civil Rights Movement), and it is now over 50 years since the main objectives of the movement were achieved, so its impact can be assessed – if civil disobedience is an appeal to the majority to remove injustice *and so strengthen the political system*, it needs to be seen whether this was a result of the movement.

# Historical background to the Civil Rights Movement

The Civil Rights Movement has its roots in the struggle for emancipation from slavery in the nineteenth century. There were sporadic slave revolts before 1860, but it was during the Civil War of 1861–65 that the struggle for emancipation became a central focus of American life. During the Civil War, the Northern and Western states of America had remained within the Union, while the 11 Southern states formed the Confederacy. After President Abraham Lincoln issued the Emancipation Proclamation (1862), slavery became the main issue dividing the Union and the Confederacy.

The Union defeated the Confederacy and in 1866 Congress passed the Civil Rights Act (following the 13th Amendment to the Constitution, abolishing slavery), which declared that all persons born in the United States were citizens and so entitled to the 'full and equal benefit of the laws'. However, the Reconstruction period (1865–77) was a failure. By the beginning of the twentieth century, most blacks in the South had lost the right to vote, and there was widespread segregation of education, transport, and other services. The primary purpose of the Civil Rights Movement was to end segregation.

Not all the actions of the civil rights activists fall under the category of civil disobedience. Three strands can be discerned: (a) legal protests and actions, such as the Montgomery bus boycott (although, in fact, such actions soon became illegal); (b) actions through the courts, using or testing federal law against state law; (c) acts of peaceful law-breaking – that is, civil disobedience – such as refusing to obey police orders to disperse, and sitting at segregated lunch counters, where the proprietors could appeal to state law to enforce segregation. It is important to understand how the Civil Rights Movement took place within a context of constitutional conflict, which mirrored the federal versus states conflict of the nineteenth century. Repeatedly, the federal level attempted to force desegregation on the South, examples being *Brown v Board of Education of Topeka* (1954), 24th Amendment (which affected voting rights), Civil Rights Act (1964), Voting Rights Act (1965), and *Loving v Virginia* (1967).

Actions taken by the Civil Rights Movement included bus boycotts, 'freedom rides' (which were intended to desegregate interstate transportation), sit-ins at segregated lunch counters, and electoral registration campaigns. Some of these actions are difficult to categorise as civil disobedience. For example, the freedom rides are a grey area: the *political* aim of the action was to pressure President John F Kennedy, who was perceived at the 1960 Election to be sympathetic to civil rights, but who on taking office in January 1961 was much cooler about tackling the Southern states. The *legal* aim was to test the Supreme Court's 1946 ruling that segregation on interstate transportation was illegal. It is a matter for debate whether *testing* a law constitutes civil disobedience.

Sit-ins might go beyond civil disobedience. A common tactic of the activists was for one group to be ready to take the place of the arrested group at a lunch counter, with the consequence that the jails would soon fill up and the machinery of justice grind to a halt. But Rawls says that civil disobedience must not only be non-violent – and the sit-ins certainly were non-violent – but also non-coercive. Incapacitating the justice system might be coercive. Also, the reason why many actions, including the bus boycotts, worked was not because the majority became aware of injustice but because their interests were damaged – pressure came from bus companies and department stores to desegregate.

# Martin Luther King, 'Letter from Birmingham City Jail' (1963)

King's Letter was addressed to fellow – mainly Southern white – clergymen, some of whom had criticised King's campaign of civil disobedience. In setting out King's argument, we follow his narrative of events. His account should not be treated uncritically, but since the prime concern is with how he justified his actions from his perspective, the veracity of the historical details can be left to historians. King sets out 'four basic steps' in a campaign of civil disobedience (King, 1991: 69): the collection of facts to determine whether injustice is 'alive'; negotiation; self-purification; direct action.

The actions that resulted in King's imprisonment – and the occasion for the Letter – were illegal demonstrations in Birmingham, Alabama. These were directed against the 'whites only' and 'no coloreds' signs in shops, the segregated restaurants, and the negligence of the police in investigating 18 bombings of black homes and churches over the previous six years. With regard to the first step, there was little doubt that Birmingham had a poor record on civil rights.

The next step was to negotiate before engaging in civil disobedience. There were attempts to get the shopkeepers to remove their signs. Promises were made but not honoured.

A mayoral election in March 1963 between the reactionary Bull Connor and moderate – but still segregationist – Albert Boutwell resulted in the latter's victory, but because the three-man commission that had run Birmingham, and included Connor, refused to stand down, there was no movement on removal of discrimination. Negotiation had failed. The next step was 'self-purification'. This must be distinguished from what we identified as the introversion that sometimes characterises conscientious refusal (and also *satyagraha*). The aim of self-purification is to ascertain whether the protestors will be able to endure violence without reacting violently. To this end, workshops on non-violent protest were held.

Finally, we come to the act of civil disobedience. King argues that one of the aims of civil disobedience is to 'create such a crisis and establish such creative tension that a community which has constantly refused to negotiate is forced to confront the issue' (King, 1991: 71). The new Mayor Boutwell might be persuaded that resistance to desegregation was futile. It could be argued – and King was aware of this – that the effectiveness of civil disobedience rests on the existence of a violent alternative to it. Those engaged in civil disobedience need not intend to communicate this message for this message to be communicated through their actions. In 1963, the widely perceived alternative to King and the Southern Christian Leadership Conference (SCLC) was Malcolm X's Nation of Islam. Indeed, King indirectly cites this movement in his Letter, arguing that if civil rights activists are dismissed as 'rabble rousers' and 'outside agitators', then millions of blacks 'out of frustration and despair, will seek solace and security in black nationalist ideologies, a development that will lead inevitably to a frightening racial nightmare' (King, 1991: 77).

Responding to the question of how it is possible to obey some laws but disobey others, King argues that there are just laws and unjust laws:

> ...an unjust law is a human law that is not rooted in eternal and natural law. Any law that uplifts human personality is just. Any law that degrades human personality is unjust. All segregation statutes are unjust because segregation distorts the soul and damages the personality. It gives the segregator a false sense of superiority, and the segregated a false sense of inferiority.
>
> (King, 1991: 73)

In expanding on this distinction, King cites Augustine (354–430), Aquinas (1225–74), Jewish philosopher Martin Buber (1878–1965), and Protestant theologian Paul Tillich (1886–1965). It may appear that King is appealing to a particular moral conception, drawn from Judaism and Christianity, rather than a *political* morality. Three points should be made. First, so long as the underlying appeal extends beyond your own particular conception of what is ultimately valuable, which for King is rooted in Christian teaching, then enlisting Christian (and Jewish) thinkers is legitimate. In effect, King is saying 'I am a Christian, but you do not have to be a Christian to recognise the injustice I describe'. Insofar as we interpret King's argument for civil disobedience to be based on his Christian beliefs, it might be thought that he is engaged in what Rawls terms conscientious refusal, but conscientious refusal is not incompatible with civil disobedience – a person, such as King, can be motivated by a secular political morality *and* a Christian morality. What would be problematic is to appeal only to a non-political morality.

Second, the Letter was written to Christian clergy, so the Christian references are unsurprising. Third, King goes on to restate the argument in secular language:

> An unjust law is a code that a majority inflicts on a minority that is not binding on itself. This is difference made legal. On the other hand a just law is a code that a majority compels a minority to follow that it is willing to follow itself. This is sameness made legal.
>
> (King, 1991: 74)

He gives a couple of examples, the first of which is problematic. Because the state of Alabama had denied blacks the right to vote they could not be bound by its laws. The danger with this argument is that even if blacks had voted, being in a minority, they might have been subject to discriminatory laws. A better example is the denial of police permits to demonstrate: King accepts that there should be controls on demonstrations, but objects to the misuse of permits to deny civil rights activists the possibility of peaceful protest, while opponents of civil rights can protest unhindered.

King argues that a sign of the good faith of the civil rights activists is that they break the law openly and are willing to accept the penalties for law-breaking. These are, of course, on Rawls's list of conditions for civil disobedience. Finally, as if to underline the stabilising power of civil disobedience, King concludes his Letter with the following statement:

> One day the South will know that when the disinherited children of God sat down at lunch counters they were in reality standing up for the best in the American dream and the most sacred values in our Judeo-Christian heritage, and thusly, carrying our whole nation back to those great wells of democracy which were dug deep by the founding fathers in the formulation of the Constitution and the Declaration of Independence.
>
> (King, 1991: 84)

What makes the Civil Rights Movement an important example of civil disobedience is that in philosophical terms it took place in the space between the constitution and lower-level law. This may also, however, raise some definitional difficulties. The most visible aspect of the civil rights struggle was the clash between supporters and opponents of equal rights in the streets, on the buses and at the lunch counters. But behind that struggle was another: a struggle between federal law and constitutional judgements on the one side and the Southern states on the other. It is notable that when defenders of segregation organised themselves politically – at elections – they adopted the banner of States' Rights: the rights of the states against the President, Congress, and Supreme Court. Civil disobedience was made possible by (a) the existence of a (basically) just constitution and (b) the refusal at a lower level of law-making to respect the constitution. It could be argued that what the civil rights activists were doing was appealing, not to the majority of fellow Americans, but to the judiciary; in effect, they were forcing test cases for the legitimacy of state law. On the other hand, it might be maintained that it was through elected representatives in Congress – representatives of 'the majority' – that the great strides forward in civil rights were made.

The failure of the Civil Rights Movement to change Southerners' attitudes is revealed in the Congressional voting figures for the Civil Rights Act (1964). In the Senate, the Democrats divided 46–21 in favour (69% in favour), and the Republicans were 27–6 in favour (82%). All Southern Democratic Senators voted against. In the House of Representatives, the Democrats divided 152–96 in favour (61%) and the Republicans 138–34 in favour (80%). Of the Southern Democratic Congressman, 92 out of 103 (89%) voted against.

## Selective versus absolute pacifism

One of the questions posed at the start of the chapter was whether exemptions to do military service should be granted to absolute objectors (only) or (also) to selective objectors. This is a useful way into understanding the core political issue in conscientious objection, which is the effect the refusal to fight has on cooperation under the state.

At the height of the Vietnam War in 1971, a case came before the US Supreme Court: *Gillette v United States*. Guy Gillette was denied classification as an objector because his objection was 'political' and directed specifically at the Vietnam War rather than war in general (Malament, 1972). To understand why he lost his case requires a short outline of American law regarding conscientious objection. In the First World War, members of certain historic peace churches, such as the Quakers, were granted exemption from service. By 1940, reference was no longer made to specific churches, but the law provided exemption for those 'who by reason of religious training and belief, [are] conscientiously opposed to participation in war in any form' (1972: 373). A 1948 law inserted the qualification that the beliefs underpinning the objection to fighting must relate to a Supreme Being. An 'equivalency test' was added in 1965: you could be motivated by beliefs that occupied a place parallel to that of a Supreme Being. Thereafter, references to religion were deleted: in 1967, mention of a Supreme Being was removed, and in 1970, the insistence on 'religious training and belief' as proof of conviction was dropped. What remained however was a clear distinction between political and non-political objections to war. The question is: why the distinction?

Conscience is often accorded a high degree of respect. We hear phrases like 'my conscience does not allow me to do it' or 'in all conscience I cannot do it'. These phrases suggest an inner voice or a psychic pain caused by being forced to do the forbidden thing. But why should weight be attached to this inner voice or psychic pain, such that appeals to conscience release a person from military service? Consider two people. John has a reasoned and well-developed argument for not fighting but feels no pain when forced to do so. Adam has no reasoned argument, but nonetheless feels moral anguish when forced to fight. Should we not show greater respect for John than for Adam?

There are reasons for saying no. Conscience might be shorthand for sincerity. Those who are willing to fight do not want to be taken advantage of and so look for outward physical signs – emotions – indicating the objector is sincere and not motivated by self-interest. But the elimination of self-interest does not entirely solve the free-rider problem, as part of the 'burden' of living under the state is also accepting the state's right to make judgements on (some) matters of morality, such as whether to go to war. If everyone asserted the right to act on the basis of his own moral convictions, social order would be threatened. We are left in the position that a certain amount of latitude in allowing individuals the right to act on moral judgements at variance with those of the state will not lead to social collapse, as the majority is more open to sincere moral convictions than self-interest in assessing whether someone is taking advantage of the contributions made by others, but there are nonetheless limits even to appeals to morality.

## Conclusion

Civil disobedience may seem a marginal political issue, given that most citizens do not engage in it. However, the arguments for and against it go to the heart of the moral basis of democracy and, in particular, the only viable form of democracy in a modern society: representative majoritarian democracy. While Rawls's theory of civil disobedience does not really hold up when tested against historical reality it provides a useful framework within which to assess both the grounds, and the limits, of majoritarian democracy. More generally, the development of the concept of civil disobedience grew out of, but also represents a critique of, early liberal theories of political obligation; civil disobedience implies that human beings should retain a degree of moral autonomy *vis-à-vis* the state.

## References

King, M. L. (1991). 'Letter from Birmingham City Jail', in H.A. Bedau (ed.), *Civil Disobedience in Focus*. London: Routledge, 68–84.

Livingston, A. (2018). Fidelity to Truth: Gandhi and the Genealogy of Civil Disobedience. *Political Theory*, *46*(4), 511–36.

Locke, J. (1997). *Second Treatise of Government*. Ed. T. P. Peardon. Upper Saddle River, NJ: Prentice Hall.

Malament, D. (1972). Selective Conscientious Objection and Gillette Decision. *Philosophy & Public Affairs*, *1*(4), 363–86.

Thomas, D. L. (1995). *Routledge Philosophy Guidebook to Locke on Government*. London and New York: Routledge.

Thoreau, D. (1991). 'Civil Disobedience', in H.A. Bedau (ed.), *Civil Disobedience in Focus* London: Routledge, 28–48.

Rawls, J. (1972). *A Theory of Justice*. Oxford: Oxford University Press.

Sabl, A (2001). Looking Forward to Justice: Rawlsian Civil Disobedience and its Non-Rawlsian Lessons. *The Journal of Political Philosophy, 9*(3), 307–30.

Singer, P. (1973). *Democracy and Disobedience* Oxford: Clarendon Press.

## Further reading

An excellent collection of essays is William Scheuerman (ed.), *The Cambridge Companion to Civil Disobedience* (Cambridge University Press, 2021); Another, older collection, is Hugo Bedau (ed.), *Civil Disobedience in Focus* (Routledge, 1991) (it contains essays and extracts from Rawls, King, and others). Overviews and discussions of the concept include William Scheuerman, *Civil Disobedience* (Polity, 2018); Kimberley Brownlee, *Conscience and Conviction: The Case for Civil Disobedience* (Oxford University Press, 2012); Tony Milligan, *Civil Disobedience: Protest, Justification and the Law* (Bloomsbury Academic, 2013).

# Part 2

# Freedom, equality, and justice

# Chapter 5

# Equality

## Introduction

The core idea of equality is that people should be treated in the same way. However, there are many different principles of equality. The formal principle of 'treating like cases alike' does not advance the discussion very far, as we can always claim that people are not alike in key respects. Other principles have more substance, but they can range from treating people as morally equal, but not materially equal, to a very strong idea that outcomes should be equalised. Equality must then be reconciled with other political values such as freedom and efficiency. The aim of this chapter is to set out the conceptual challenges entailed by the claim that people should be treated equally and offer some arguments for and against equality. Further arguments will be set out in Chapter 8 (on distributive justice).

## Key questions

- What is equality?
- Should people be treated equally?
- What would treating people equally entail?
- Does equality conflict with other values such as freedom?

## Principles of equality

Equality is a widely used, but frequently misunderstood, concept in political debate. On the political left, it is a central value, with socialists and social democrats aiming to bring about if not an equal society, then a more equal one. On the political right, the attempt to create a more equal society is criticised as a drive to uniformity or a squeezing out of individual initiative. However, closer reflection on the nature of equality reveals several things. First, there is not one concept of equality, but a range of different types. Second, all the main ideological positions discussed in this book endorse at least one type of equality – formal equality – and most also endorse one or more substantive conceptions of equality. Third, principles of equality are often elliptical, meaning that there is an implicit claim that must be made explicit if we are to assess whether the claim is valid. To explain, since human beings possess more than one attribute or good, it is possible that equality in the possession of one will lead to, or imply, inequality in another. Anne

DOI: 10.4324/9780429424106-8

Case study 5.1

# Should the family be abolished?

**PHOTO 5.1** © Greg Balfour Evans/Alamy Stock Photo.

The family raises a host of equality-related issues. There is inequality within the family. Even in the most gender-equal societies women still undertake a disproportionate amount of domestic labour. The relationship between siblings is also marked by inequality, especially in certain traditional laws of inheritance, such as primogeniture, which favours the first-born male. And the family is a source of societal inequality, as it channels advantages to some and away from others.

Although in Western societies the term 'nepotism' – favouring your relatives – has negative connotations, as when for example jobs in government are handed out to a politician's children, in its generic sense it is at the heart of the traditional family: we expect parents to be partial towards their children. The question is whether there should be *any* nepotism, given that it leads to inequality.

Perhaps the family could be replaced by the collective upbringing of children – what Véronique Munoz-Dardé terms a 'generalised well-run orphanage' (Munoz-Dardé, 1999: 37). She defines the traditional family as 'a small intimate group where elders are responsible for raising and caring for children, and have authority over them' (1999: 39). The model is the two-parent, heterosexual nuclear biological family, but other family types – blended, one parent, same-sex – are modelled on that family. So the question is not about the success of these variants, but whether the model itself should be abandoned: ought the bringing up of children be collectivised along the lines Munoz-Dardé suggests? Material resources would be equally distributed among children and each child would have a range of teachers and mentors and not be reliant on his or her parents.

may be able-bodied, and John disabled. Each could be given equal amounts of resources, such as healthcare, and so with regard to healthcare they are treated equally, but John's needs are greater, so the equality of healthcare has unequal *effects*. If Anne and John were given resources commensurate with their needs, they would be being treated equally in one sphere (needs) but unequally in another (resources). The recognition of this plurality of goods, and therefore spheres within which people can be treated equally or unequally, is essential to grasping the complexity of the debate over equality and inequality.

We start by outlining principles of equality. Each principle is discussed in more detail in the chapter, but an initial outline of each will help elucidate the connections between them:

- *Formal equality.* To say that we should treat like cases alike states nothing more than a tautological truth. If two people are alike in all respects, we would have no reason to discriminate between them. However, no two people are alike, and the principle is indeed formal – it does not tell us how to treat dissimilar people. Racialists do not violate the principle of formal equality because they argue that racial groups are not similar and so need not, or should not, be treated in the same way.

- *Moral equality.* The concept of moral equality is sometimes presented in negative form as a rejection of natural hierarchy or natural inequality. In many societies, it is taken for granted that people are, in important respects, deserving of equal consideration. Much discussion in political theory – especially in the dominant liberal stream of the discipline (see Chapter 9) – is about the characterisation of moral equality, which, paradoxically, can take the form of *justifying inequality*: that is, if people are morally equal, how do we explain their unequal treatment in terms of the distribution of social goods, such as income? The very idea that such inequality must be justified assumes that people are morally equal – in a society where there is an overwhelming belief in natural inequality, such as a caste society, it would simply not occur to those in a higher stratum that they must justify their advantaged position or that those in a lower stratum should question their subordinate position.

- *Equality before the law.* That laws apply equally to those who are subject to them is widely accepted as a foundational belief of many, if not most, societies. Legal equality cuts both ways: there is equal protection before the law but also equal liability for your actions.

- *Equal liberty.* A common assumption, especially on the right, is that equality and liberty (freedom) conflict. Certainly, if we were in Hobbes's state of nature (see p. 12) and enjoyed pure liberty – that is, we were under no duties to refrain from behaving as we choose – then the exercise of liberty would reflect natural inequalities including any bad luck that might befall us. But under a state, while our liberty is restricted, the possibility exists for a degree of protection (through rights), such that a space is provided in which we are free to act without the danger of other people interfering in our actions. Once we move from pure liberty to protected liberty, an issue of distribution – and, therefore, a trade-off between equality and liberty – arises. Although the state cannot distribute the *exercise of choice*, it can distribute *rights* to do certain things.

- *Material equality.* The most significant disputes in many societies are connected with the distribution of income and other tangible material goods such as education and healthcare. The capacity to acquire material goods is to some extent, and perhaps a great extent, conditioned by structures that individuals do not control. From birth – and even before birth – a person is set on a course, at each stage of which he or she has some power to gain or lose material goods, but, arguably, the choices are restricted. Put simply, a person born into a wealthy family has more opportunities than someone with a poor background.
- *Equal access.* If a society places barriers in the way of certain groups acquiring material goods, such as jobs and services, as happened to blacks in the Southern states of the United States until the 1960s, then equal access is denied. On the face of it, guaranteeing equal access may appear closely connected with material equality, but in fact has more to do with equal civic and political rights or *liberty*: the liberty to compete for jobs and buy goods.
- *Equality of opportunity.* Unlike equal access this *is* a principle of material equality, and although it commands rhetorical support across the political spectrum, in any reasonably strong version, it has significant implications for the role of the state in individual and family life. If a society attempts to guarantee the equal opportunity to acquire, for example, a particular job, then it is going much further than simply removing legal obstacles to getting the job. Realising equal opportunity would require, among other things, substantial spending on education. Indeed, given the huge influence the family has on a child's prospects, to achieve equal opportunity may entail considerable intervention in family life, a point to which we return at the end of the chapter.
- *Equality of outcome.* Critics of equality frequently argue that egalitarians – that is, those who regard equality as a central political principle – want to create a society in which everybody is treated equally irrespective of personal differences or individual choice. This is a caricature, for it is possible to argue for equality of outcome as a *prima facie* principle, meaning that we should seek as far as possible to ensure an equal outcome consistent with other political principles. Equality of outcome may also function as a proxy for equality of opportunity: if there are significantly unequal outcomes, this indicates that there is not an adequate equality of opportunity. This last point leads us into a consideration of affirmative action.
- *Affirmative action.* Originating in the United States this is an umbrella term covering a range of policies intended to address the material deprivations suffered by (especially) black Americans. Although it embraces a wider range of policies, it is often used as a synonym for 'reverse discrimination' or 'positive discrimination'. Examples of reverse discrimination include the operation of quotas for jobs or a reduction in entry requirements for college places. Reverse discrimination is best understood as operating somewhere between equality of opportunity and equality of outcome: the principle acts directly on outcomes, but is intended to guarantee equality of opportunity.

## Moral equality

## Moral autonomy and moral equality

That people are morally equal is a central belief – often implicit rather than explicit – of societies influenced by the Enlightenment. Sometimes people talk of 'natural equality', but this has connotations of natural law – the belief that moral principles have a real existence, transcending time, and place. Moral equality can, minimally, be understood as a negative: people should be treated equally because there is no reason to believe in natural inequality. But the negative argument does not adequately capture the importance of moral equality: to be morally equal, that is, worthy of equal consideration, implies that you are a certain kind of being – a being to whom reasons, or justifications, can be given. This reflects the roots of the concept of moral equality in the Enlightenment, which challenges authority, and assumes that the human mind can understand the world. Among the political implications of this philosophical position are, first, that the social world is not natural – inequality must be justified and not dismissed as if it were simply the way the things are. Second, the Enlightenment stresses that human beings are *rational* – they can advance and understand arguments such that justifications for equality, or inequality, are always given to *individual* human beings.

It is a standard, but not necessary, starting point of liberalism – but also of other ideologies such as socialism, anarchism, feminism, and multiculturalism – that coercively enforced institutions must be justified to those who are subject to them (although anarchists conclude that coercion cannot be justified). That is, subjects should in some sense consent to those institutions. Since it is unrealistic to think that we can reach unanimity on how society should be organised, we must assume a moral standpoint distinct from the standpoints of 'real people'. The most famous recent elaboration of this idea can be found in the work of John Rawls, whose work we discuss in Chapter 8 (see pp. 135–9). Rawls asks us to imagine choosing a set of political principles without knowing our identities – that is, we do not know our natural abilities, class, gender, religious and other beliefs, and so on. This is the veil of ignorance. Because individuals do not know their identities they must, as a matter of reason, put themselves in the shoes of each other person and such role-reversal implies an equality of perspective. The idea of equality in Rawls's theory is highly abstract, and the use of the veil itself tells us little about how people should be treated. To generate more concrete principles of equality, Rawls makes certain claims not implied by the veil of ignorance, and in that sense he goes beyond moral equality; nonetheless, the starting point for Rawls is a situation of moral equality.

While Rawls draws strongly egalitarian conclusions from the idea of moral equality, other political theorists, while endorsing the idea of moral equality, derive different conclusions. Robert Nozick, in his book *Anarchy, State, and Utopia* (Nozick 1974), argues that individuals have strong rights to self-ownership, and they enjoy these rights equally, and for that reason, there are certain things we cannot do to people, including taxing their legitimate earnings, where legitimacy is established by certain principles of justice. Nozick's theory is discussed in more detail in Chapter 8 (see pp. 141–4), but the point is that a commitment to moral equality can lead in different directions in terms of whether we accept further principles of equality. Although Nozick's theory can only very loosely be described as Kantian, both Rawls and Nozick make explicit appeal to Kant's notion of respect for persons: treating people as ends in themselves and never merely as ends for others. In Rawls's case, this idea is expressed in the equality of the Original Position, whereas for Nozick it is implicit in the notion of (equal) property rights as constraints (or 'side constraints') on what others can do to us.

## Nietzsche contra moral equality

Although it has been open to significantly divergent interpretations, Friedrich Nietzsche's work has been the source of one of the most important critiques of moral equality in modern Western political thought. Rawls identifies him as a radical perfectionist, where 'perfectionism' is understood to be a theory whereby society is organised with the aim of advancing certain values or ways of life. In Nietzsche's case, this means that 'mankind must continually strive to produce great individuals . . . we give value to our lives by working for the good of the highest specimens' (Rawls 1972: 325). Other theorists have argued for a more liberal-democratic interpretation: what Nietzsche terms the 'will to power' ('Wille zur Macht') denotes an internal struggle: each individual should strive to overcome his weaknesses and pursue a higher good (Cavell, 1990: 50–1). The will to power does not necessarily entail domination over others. It follows that, on *this* interpretation, Nietzsche (implicitly) endorsed moral equality.

Nonetheless, there are many passages in Nietzsche's work which support an elitist and fundamentally anti-egalitarian position (Detwiler, 1990: 8). Even if we cannot decide finally on the interpretation of his work, it is clear that Nietzsche has inspired anti-egalitarian streams of thought and drawing on various concepts – in addition to the will to power – we will reconstruct the Nietzschean case against moral equality. Nietzsche's style is aphoristic rather than systematic, but among the more systematic works is *On the Genealogy of Morality* (published 1887). Divided into three Treatises, in the first, Nietzsche distinguishes the valuations good/bad and good/evil (Nietzsche, 1998: 14–17). Since 'good' can only be understood relative to its opposite, it follows that the 'good' in each pair does not mean the same thing. The good of the first pair denotes something powerful and life-affirming, whereas the good in the second pair corresponds to the Judaic (and Christian) notion of self-denial or meekness. Nietzsche traces the historical origins of goodness as self-denial to the slave revolt of the Jews against the Romans and through Judaism to Christianity. The slave does not take revenge against the master through physical action but through an imaginary – metaphysical – act (Nietzsche, 1998: 18–21). The slaves convince themselves that the meek will inherit the earth and they define the strong as 'evil'.

The struggle between slave and master is internalised with the construction of the 'soul'. The basic drive of human beings – the will to power – is turned inwards as human beings move from being nomadic 'birds of prey' to socially constricted citizens. Since the will to power cannot be extinguished, it is turned inwards and takes the form of guilt, as distinct from shame. Protestant Christianity is the clearest expression of a culture of guilt. Kant's moral philosophy is often described as securalised Protestantism: that the highest good for Kant is a pure will means that all those things that make us human – that, for Nietzsche, constitute 'life' – are devalued in favour of a characterless self. We are all morally equal but at the price of lacking any character. Kantian morality requires that we will a law that all rational agents could will – we put ourselves in the shoes of each other person – and we should feel guilt when we fail to do so. For Nietzsche, the internalisation of guilt entails forgetting the historical origins of this slave morality: the resentment (*ressentiment*) of the weak against the strong (Nietzsche 1998: 45–6).

In a culture of shame – distinct from guilt – we judge ourselves to have failed insofar as we fall short of a basically non-moral ideal. The soldier who shows cowardice in the face of the enemy feels ashamed without necessarily feeling guilt. Shame is outward-looking, whereas guilt is introspective. There is, for Nietzsche, no 'inwardness' in the Christian sense and therefore the idea of moral equality makes no sense.

Rawls may be right to argue that Nietzsche is committed to a strong perfectionist ideal of creating and serving great men, but such a perfectionism might also take a softer but still elitist form: what is of greatest value is the sustenance or transmission from one generation to the next, of cultural goods. This might well require a class-based society in which elites transmit values to the masses.

# Moral equality and the moralistic fallacy

Aside from Nietzsche's very specific critique, there are broader concerns about the concept of moral equality. The vagueness of the term may result in its overextension and a falling into the trap of the moralistic fallacy: deriving from what ought to be – 'people should be treated equally' – to a claim about what is: 'people are equal'. If Molly is richer than Willie but the two are morally equal, then the reasoning might be that their material inequality has resulted from a violation of the principle of moral equality.

But here it is important to stress how limited is the concept of moral equality: it is more than formal equality ('treat like cases alike') because it requires that inequality be justified, but it is significantly less than equal rights, or equality of access, or opportunity, or outcome. Mollie may be richer than Willie because she has a better genetic endowment, a superior upbringing, or has inherited wealth. Allowing these things to determine the distribution of resources may be unfair but that unfairness cannot be established by the principle of moral equality.

This is at the heart of popular discomfort with the concept of equality. It does not take much experience of life to see that people are factually unequal in their natural endowments such as intelligence, personality traits, physical strength, and stamina, and so on. Whether these differences should be allowed to determine the distribution of resources is something we discuss later in the chapter, but even if allowing wealth to track natural endowments is unfair – and thus Willie's inferior status to Molly is unjustified – we cannot make Molly and Willie factually equal. To commit the moralistic fallacy is to say because they *ought* to be treated equally, they *are* factually equal. Of course, there may be social benefits to promoting this fiction, justified by an esoteric morality (see p. 50) or an inversion of Plato's noble lie. Plato – through his mouthpiece Socrates – wants to convince people to accept their natural inequality. Rather than see themselves as born of parents, they are born from the earth, and their position in society reflects the earth's elements of gold, silver, bronze, or iron. Unlike other societies, where your position in society is determined by an accident of birth, the citizens of Plato's republic are allotted their place in society by the gods (Pappas, 2004: 71–2). It is a noble lie because it resembles the truth or put another way: by believing it is so, it becomes so. The egalitarian fiction reverses this: the noble lie is that, despite the inequalities arising from accidents of birth, people really are (factually) equal, and it is a good – noble – thing to believe this.

## Legal equality

We now move from moral equality to more specific principles of equality, although the concept of moral equality must always be in the background. A starting point for building up a more substantial political theory would be to distinguish the core legal–political institutions from broader socio-economic institutions. In most societies, but especially liberal-democratic ones, the core institutions of the state are divided into legislature, executive, and judiciary. Put simply, the legislature creates laws, the executive administers powers created through law, and the judiciary interprets and enforces the law. But a social institution is any large-scale, rule-governed activity and can include the economic organisation of society, such as the basic rules of property ownership, and various services provided by the state that extend beyond simply the creation and implementation of law. The wider concept of a social institution will be discussed later, but in this section, the focus is on the narrower concept.

We need to distinguish 'equality before the law' and 'equal civil liberties'. To be equal before the law is to be equally subject to the law, whereas to possess civil liberties is to be in a position to do certain things, such as vote or express an opinion, and obviously we are equal when we possess the same liberties. There is, however, a close relationship between equality before the law and equality of civil liberties, and a historical example will help to illustrate this. On 15 September 1935, the German Parliament (Reichstag) adopted the so-called Nuremberg Laws governing German citizenship, one of which defined German citizenship (citizenship law, or Reichsbürgergesetz). The law made a distinction between a subject of the state (Staatsange-höriger) and a citizen (Reichsbürger). Article 1 stated that 'a subject of the state is one who be-longs to the protective union of the German Reich', while Article 2 stated that 'a citizen of the Reich may be only one who is of German or kindred blood, and who, through his behaviour, shows that he is both desirous and personally fit to serve loyally the German people and the Re-ich'. Only citizens were to enjoy full, and equal, political rights. The First Supplementary Decree (14 November 1935) classified subjects by blood and denied citizenship to Jews, where Jewishness was defined by the state (Krošlák, 2015: 188–9).

It could be argued that these citizenship laws are compatible with equality before the law, since all are equally subject to the law, despite the fact the laws are themselves discriminatory. While on the face of it, this argument appears valid and seems to show how weak both the idea of moral equality and equality before the law are, there are grounds for arguing that nazi Germany could not maintain that all subjects were equal before the law. American legal theorist Lon Fuller, writing in the early post-war period, observed that nazi law was not really law at all because it violated certain requirements for any legal system. For Fuller, the essential function of law is to 'achieve order through subjecting people's conduct to the guidance of general rules by which they may themselves orient their behaviour' (Fuller, 1965: 657). To fulfil this function, law (or rules) must satisfy eight conditions (Fuller, 1969: 33–8):

1. The rules must be expressed in general terms.
2. The rules must be publicly promulgated.
3. The rules must be prospective in effect.
4. The rules must be expressed in understandable terms.
5. The rules must be consistent with one another.
6. The rules must not require conduct beyond the powers of the affected parties.
7. The rules must not be changed so frequently that the subject cannot rely on them.
8. The rules must be administered in a manner consistent with their wording.

Fuller's argument is not uncontroversial, and many legal theorists will reject these rules, but it is plausible to maintain that a condition of a law (so-called) being a law is that it is not arbitrary. Since the first article of the penal code of Nazi Germany asserted that the will of the Führer was the source of all law, it was impossible for subjects to determine what was required of them. Once it is accepted that law cannot be arbitrary then certain conditions follow, including at least a min-imal idea of equal basic civil liberties. Chief among the civil, or political, liberties are the right to vote and to hold office; significantly, both these rights were explicitly denied to non-citizens in the Nuremberg Laws.

There are other theories of law that do not rest on what Fuller terms an internal morality, and which presuppose neither moral equality nor equal liberties. Legal theorist John Austin charac-terised a 'law' as a general command issued by a 'sovereign' (or its agents), and that theory can be traced back to Hobbes (Dewey, 1894: 35). The sovereign is that person, or group of people, who receives 'habitual obedience' from the great majority of the population of a particular territory. Whereas Fuller would argue that (most) nazi laws were not really laws at all, Austin would have identified Hitler as the sovereign, who, insofar as he commands obedience, issues valid law. This does not mean that his laws were moral: Austin made a sharp distinction between legality and morality (1894: 35). The relationship between morality and legality will be discussed in later chapters and especially when we turn to the topic of human rights in Chapter 18.

## Equal liberties

As suggested above, the state cannot directly distribute choice, but it can distribute the conditions for choice by granting individuals rights or civil liberties. In liberal-democratic societies, the most important rights, or liberties, are freedom of expression, association, movement, and rights to a private life, career choice, a fair trial, vote, and to hold office if qualified. A couple of points are worth noting. First, it is difficult to distribute liberty *per se*; rather, what is distributed are specific rights-protected liberties. Second, you can have freedom without that freedom being recognised by the state, for no state can exercise complete control. However, when we talk about the distribution of liberty, it is not so much the freedom itself which is being distributed, but rather the *protection* of that liberty – if Sam is guaranteed that he will not be thrown in jail for expressing views critical of the state, but Amy is not given that guarantee, then clearly Sam and Amy are not being treated equally. It is the guarantee – the right to free expression – rather than the expression itself which is being distributed. The separation between the guarantee (protection of the capacity to choose; right to choose) and the action that is guaranteed does not hold for all liberties. For example, voting – a participatory, rather than a private or personal right – is something which is clearly susceptible to *direct* distribution in a way that the freedom to marry whoever you wish (a private right), or not get married, is not. Some people can be awarded more votes than others, or whole groups, such as workers or women, can be denied the vote (you can, of course, still choose not to vote).

## Do freedom and equality conflict?

Freedom (or liberty) necessarily entails choice, and individuals must make choices for themselves. It would follow that the state cannot – and indeed should not – attempt to control individual choice. At best, it can affect opportunities to make choices through the distribution of rights. Does this mean that freedom and equality necessarily conflict? In addressing this question, we need to make a further distinction to the one already made between choice and the capacity, or opportunity, to make choices, so that we have a threefold distinction:

1. Choice, which must be under the control of the individual, and for which the individual can be held responsible.
2. The capacity, or opportunity for choice, which is not under the control of the individual, and for which the individual should not be held responsible.
3. The outcome of the choices of individuals, where outcomes are determined to a large degree by the interactive nature of choice.

Consider this example from Nozick. Imagine 26 men and 26 women, one for each letter of the alphabet. Each person wants to marry, and each of the 26 men has the same preference-ordering of the women as the other men, and likewise each of the 26 women has the same prefer-ence-ordering of the men as the other women. So, if we name each person by a letter of the alphabet A, B, C, etc. for the men, and $A^1$, $B^1$, $C^1$, etc., for the women, each man prefers $A^1$ to $B^1$ and $B^1$ to $C^1$ and so on, down to the last preference $Z^1$. Likewise, each of the women prefers A to B and B to C, etc., down to Z. That means that all the women want to marry A, and so A has plenty of choice. Likewise, with regard to the men, $A^1$ has a full range of options. B and $B^1$ have one less option, but still a lot of choice, and so on, down to Z and $Z^1$ who have no choice but to marry one another (Nozick, 1974: 263–4). Are Z and $Z^1$ denied (a) freedom and (b) equality?

If we measure equality by the number of marriage partners available, there is an unequal dis-tribution: A and $A^1$ have the greatest number of options and Z and $Z^1$ the fewest. And if freedom is understood as choice, then arguably Z and $Z^1$ have no freedom because they have no choice but to marry each other. But, perhaps, the relevant liberty is determined by the relationship of each person to the *state*: in relation to the state, Z and $Z^1$ have as many options as A and $A^1$. It is the conjoint choices of individuals that create an inequality of outcome. Nozick can legitimately maintain that Z and $Z^1$ are as free as A and $A^1$ because his starting point is the concept of a nat-ural right to self-ownership. That right will always be held equally regardless of how individuals exercise the right.

Now consider a different example, this one advanced by Gerald Cohen. Ten of us are locked in a room. There is one exit at which there is a huge and heavily locked door. At roughly equal distances from each of us, there is a single heavy key (each of us is equally distant from the door). Whoever picks up the key (each is physically able to do so) and with very considerable effort opens the door can leave. But there is a sensor that will register when one person has left, and as soon as that person leaves, the door will slam shut and locked, and nobody else will be able to leave – *forever* (Cohen, 1979: 22). Are we free to leave?

If, prior to anyone leaving, a voice heard from outside asked each in turn 'are you free to leave?', we would be forced to say 'yes'. If we – plural – were asked whether we are free, the question is more difficult. Collectively, we are not free to leave: *each* is free to leave but *we* are not free to leave. Once again, conditionality is at work, but Cohen draws a different con-clusion to that of Nozick from this conditionality. Working with certain Marxist assump-tions, Cohen argues that a collectivist political order – one in which there is a much more equal distribution of income – would, in effect, enable more people to leave the room. In real-world terms, that means workers losing their subordinate class position. Unlike Nozick, Cohen is concerned with the choices people actually make rather than their legal position *vis-à-vis* the state.

## Material equality

In liberal societies, respect for equality before the law and equality of liberties is well embedded in the political culture – even though there is controversy over *particular* liberties, the majority of the population expresses support at least for the *principles*. The same cannot be said for principles of material equality. As was suggested earlier, while lip-service is paid to equality of opportunity, that term encompasses a great many possible principles of resource allocation, some of which en-tail radical state intervention in individuals' lives. More often than not, what is being advocated is equal access to jobs and services rather than equality of opportunity.

# Equal access

Equal access is sometimes referred to as formal equality of opportunity, but equal access is the better term, as it encompasses access not just to jobs but also services. In American jurisprudence, the term public accommodation is used; this is not to be confused with state (public) provision of housing, but is the idea that the general public must be accommodated. Shops, restaurants, and hotels cannot deny service to a person based on his or her sex, race, or other important ('protected') characteristics. Ensuring public accommodation was a central aspect of the Civil Rights Movement (see pp. 71–4).

The concept of equal access has subsequently been extended to address indirect discrimination. Examples of indirect discrimination in employment are the imposition of a height requirement, the prohibition on certain hairstyles, such as dreadlocks, the requirement to work on Saturdays, or the passing of certain tests of physical fitness. In relation to the provision of services, examples would be the failure to accommodate people with disabilities on public transport, the denial of certain methods of payment in shops, or the requirement to provide proof of identity for voting.

Discrimination may be justified if it is intrinsic to a job or the delivery of a service, or if accommodation would be so costly as to be unreasonable. On the latter point, a new train station should be designed for disabled access, but the cost of converting a small, Victorian-era station may be prohibitive. Certain discriminatory requirements such as a minimum height or a level of physical fitness could be essential to a job. Employment in a women's refuge would normally be restricted to women. And if there is evidence of widespread voter fraud, then proof of ID – such as a passport or driver's licence – at the polling place could be justified (although the state would then have to provide, free of charge, alternative ID to those without a passport or driver's licence).

# Equal access and freedom of association

Equal access may conflict with freedom of association. The right to associate with people of your choosing inevitably means by implication that others are excluded from that association. Most people accept that intimate associations – marriage, friendship, and so on – ought to be exclusive. We should not be forced to have personal relationships with people with whom we do not choose to associate. But what about larger, less intimate, associations? These include churches, synagogues, and mosques; sports clubs; youth clubs; political parties and pressure groups; professional associations; and shops.

The two most important cases regarding association to have come before the United States Supreme Court are *Roberts v United States Jaycees* (1984) and the *Boy Scouts of America (BSA) v Dale* (2000), and the reasoning in both cases has implications beyond the American legal context. The United States Junior Chamber (or Jaycees) is a leadership training and business networking association for those under the age of 40. At the time of the 1984 case, it did not admit women as full members. However, the Minnesota chapter of the Jaycees – in response to Minnesotan state law prohibiting discrimination – chose to admit women and were threatened with disaffiliation by the national organisation. The case wended its way through the court system, finally ending up in the US Supreme Court, which upheld the Minnesota law (Linder, 1983: 1878–80). Two issues were at the centre of discussion: whether the Jaycees were an intimate association and whether they were expressing a view, such that the admission of women under compulsion would entail the suppression of that viewpoint. The argument from intimacy was unconvincing as the organisation had at that time hundreds of thousands of members. The argument from free speech was more interesting: because the organisation was not overtly hostile to women it could not claim that it was promoting a message. Paradoxically, had it been explicitly hostile to women in business, it would have been on stronger ground (Marshall, 1986: 74).

The Boy Scouts case arose after scoutmaster James Dale was expelled after coming out as gay. New Jersey Supreme Court ruled the expulsion violated the state's public accommodation law, and that reinstating Dale would not violate the BSA's First Amendment – free speech – rights because it did not prevent the organisation carrying out its objectives. Readmitting Dale did not compel the BSA to communicate any specific message about homosexuality. On a 5-4 vote the US Supreme Court overruled the New Jersey decision. The majority decision maintained that opposition to homosexuality was part of the expressive message of the BSA. The evidence for this were the BSA's statements, including the Scout Promise and Scout Law, which talk about being 'morally straight' and 'clean'. While the four dissenting Justices argued that these documents did not refer to homosexuality, they did agree that the debate should focus on their interpretation (Johnson, 2000: 1641–47).

There are other arguments for (and against) freedom of association, and we discuss these in the final chapter, on migration (see Chapter 20). There we argue that association is central to the legitimacy or illegitimacy of restrictions on movement because the state itself is an association, and when it restricts access to its territory, it is determining who does, and who does not, belong to that association.

## Equality of opportunity

Equal opportunity is a much stronger principle of equality than equal access. As the name suggests, it requires that opportunities for acquiring favourable positions are equalised. This principle is attractive across the political spectrum because it seems to assume a meritocracy. For example, in Britain, there is much debate about the social composition of the student bodies in the highest-rated universities. Students educated at fee-paying secondary schools, or at state schools within relatively wealthy catchment areas, make up a disproportionately large part of the student intake of these universities. Even on the political right, this situation is condemned: the brightest students, rather than the wealthiest, should get, it is felt, the most desirable university places.

Although politicians disagree about the causes and the solutions to this situation, there is agreement that equal access alone does not ensure a meritocratic outcome. The difficulty is that an 18-year-old student has 18 years of education and socialisation behind her – every day she has been presented with opportunities that a peer may have been denied. Those opportunities include the emotional support necessary to achieve self-confidence and a sense of self-worth, stimulating conversation that enables her to develop a range of linguistic skills, interesting foreign holidays and activities, the presence of books in the family home, the imposition of a degree of parental discipline sufficient to encourage self-discipline, family networks and contacts, a good diet, and the provision of an adequate workspace. This list could go on, and none of these items relates to formal educational provision. Even parents who do not send their children to fee-paying schools may pay for such things as ballet classes or piano lessons. In short, every day of her life for the previous 18 years she has been given opportunities. To equalise such opportunities would require a very high degree of intervention in family life. (This is putting to one side the question of genetically determined advantages, which we discuss below.)

This description of a privileged child may overstate the requirement for an equalisation of opportunity. Perhaps it is not necessary that children have strictly equal opportunities, but rather that each child has a sufficient degree of opportunity to acquire advantageous positions. The idea is that there is a threshold level of opportunity below which a child should not fall.

Another point about equality of opportunity is that the principle presupposes that inequality can be justified, so long as any inequalities are the result of desert. We can distinguish social advantage, native ability (intelligence), and effort. It is a commonly held view that 'intelligence + effort' is an appropriate ground for discrimination, and that equal opportunity policies should endeavour to eliminate social advantage, but not the effects of heritable intelligence or effort as a cause of inequality. Against this view Rawls argues that people no more deserve their native abilities, including their propensity to work hard, than they do those advantages gained from their family and social background (Rawls, 1972: 104). Other theorists, such as Ronald Dworkin and David Miller, argue that Rawls's rejection of desert is inconsistent with other important aspects of his theory, which stress the importance of choice and responsibility (Miller, 1999: 131–55; Dworkin, 2000: 287–91). Nonetheless, Dworkin (especially) seeks to eliminate *natural ability* as a justification for inequality, while retaining responsibility for choices made. In this respect, both Rawls's and Dworkin's arguments are significantly at variance with popular attitudes.[1]

Not all liberal theorists defend equality of opportunity. Friedrich Hayek argues that the free market is an example of a 'spontaneous social order' that cannot be recreated by human minds, and that has no central direction. Some redistribution of wealth is justified, but the attempt to overcome inequality of opportunity is doomed to failure. Regardless of whether they deserve their wealth, the rich are the vanguard of socially useful change (Hayek, 1973: 88). Consider the high prices in today's values of cars in the 1920s, air travel in the 1930s, colour televisions in the 1960s, videotape machines in the 1970s, personal computers in the 1980s, or commercial DNA testing in the 1990s. Innovative companies had to make a profit in order to spur development, and a class had to exist capable of buying these things. What we call today the 'web' was not simply the product of one man's leap of imagination – Tim Berners-Lee's hypertext idea – but of a series of discrete technological developments, each requiring privileged consumers to make them commercially viable. Too much equality – including the attempt to achieve an elusive equality of opportunity – undermines the social conditions for innovation and progress.

## Equality of outcome

Equalisation of outcome seems, on the face of it, neither desirable nor coherent. It is not desirable because it would deny individual choice and responsibility: if one person chooses a life of leisure and another person chooses a life of hard work why should the state seek to equalise the outcome of those choices? The outcome may not, in fact, be susceptible to equalisation. If income level is the metric subject to distribution, then the outcome can be equalised *for that metric*; but welfare (or well-being) is also a relevant metric, and the person living a life of leisure has presumably enjoyed greater well-being than the hard worker, such that the only way the two can enjoy an equal level of well-being is if they had not lived their respective lives of leisure and hard work. The point is that equality is always equality *of something*, and the attempt to equalise along one metric, say income, may result in inequality along another metric.

Another difficulty with attempting to achieve equality of outcome is that some goods are 'positional': a positional good is one the enjoyment of which depends on the exclusion of others. For example, the slogan 'elite education for all' is a contradiction in terms. Likewise, eating at the best restaurant or driving the fastest car depends on that restaurant indeed being better than all the others and the car faster than all other cars. It follows that it is impossible to equalise positional goods.

Despite these objections, equality of outcome can play a role in political debate even if it cannot be made to work as a principle. Rawls justifies inequality by use of the difference principle (see pp. 138–9), but that principle rests on recognising that any inequalities must be to the benefit of the worst-off. This argument takes equality of outcome as the baseline against which alternative distributions are to be measured; in effect, moral equality will generate inequality of outcome if the worst-off consent to that inequality.

Rawls does not, therefore, defend equality of outcome as a substantive principle. Anne Phillips, on the other hand, does. Much of Phillips's work has been concerned with political representation and especially the underrepresentation of women and ethnic minorities in political institutions, and she takes the case of women in parliament as an example of the need for a principle of equal outcome. The underrepresentation of women in the British Parliament cannot, she argues, be attributed to lack of ability, or the conscious choice not to enter politics, but must be a consequence of the failure of equal opportunity (Phillips, 2004: 8). Women are not denied equal access to parliamentary representation, and many political parties now have dedicated support for female candidates, which include women's officers, training days, support networks, and the requirement to have at least one woman on every shortlist for candidate selection in a particular constituency (electoral district). Despite this, the only political party that, at the time Phillips was writing, that had been successful in increasing female representation in the House of Commons (the elected chamber) was the British Labour Party, and that success can be attributed to 'all-women' shortlists imposed on local constituencies by the central party.[2] The point being that all-women shortlists guarantee an increase in the number of candidates in Labour-held or winnable constituencies. The policy acts on outcomes and not on opportunities. The inequality of outcome in the other political parties is an indication that, despite various efforts, equality of opportunity has failed.

## Affirmative action

Affirmative action policies involve an explicit departure from the normal equal access and equal opportunity criteria for awarding a person a favoured position. The normal criteria include that (a) the position is open to all and (b) selection is by competence, which is measured by qualifications. There are various types of affirmative action policies:

- *Encouragement.* The job is advertised in newspapers read by particular communities such as ethnic minorities.
- *Tie-breaking.* If two people are 'equally qualified', then you choose the person from the 'disadvantaged group'.
- *Handicapping.* An example of this would be requiring higher entry points, or grades, for applicants to university from wealthy backgrounds.
- *Quota system.* A certain percentage of jobs must be filled by a particular group – this is usually subject to a requirement of minimum competence.

All-women shortlists are a version of the quota system and involve a setting aside of (a), and some critics would argue that it also entails setting aside (b). Affirmative action could, however, be defended on grounds that the evidence of qualification for a position cannot be taken as an accurate indication of a person's competence. To illustrate this point, let us imagine that entry to a good university normally requires 20 points in a school-leaving exam. Person A, from a poor background, scores 17 points, and person B, from a wealthy background, scores 21 points. However, evidence from the performance of previous cohorts of students suggests that (economically) poor students with lower entry points achieve a better final result on graduation than wealthy students with higher entry points, and so person A is predicted to do better than B, and therefore objectively is better qualified. Interestingly, this argument is meritocratic, and indeed is a technical, rather than a philosophical, objection to other principles of equality: existing evidence of competence is not reliable, so we have to broaden selection criteria to include prospective performance based not on the individual applicant's past behaviour but on the statistical behaviour of students from their background. However, distribution is still tied to the actions of individuals.

There are other ways of understanding affirmative action: it may be intended to provide role models; compensate a *group* for past injustices; or increase the level of welfare of a disadvantaged group. Some defences are backward-looking, in that they seek to redress something that happened in the past. Other defences, such as the one discussed above – prospective student performance – are forward-looking. An example of a backward-looking policy would be preferential access to loans for historically disadvantaged groups. It is argued that there is far less housing wealth (equity) in the hands of blacks relative to whites in the United States due (in part) to the historic policy of redlining. Redlining developed in the 1930s to minimise the risk of house foreclosure. Neighbourhoods were graded by credit risk, and this disproportionately affected blacks, who found it more difficult to borrow money, with long-term intergenerational effects (Krimmel, 2018: 30–1).

A common, everyday objection to affirmative action is that it undermines respect and creates resentment: if a person achieves a position through positive discrimination, then others may not respect that person, while the apparently better-qualified person passed over for the position will resent what seems an unfair selection procedure. This objection, whether valid or not, does identify an important aspect of equality (and inequality): there is an intersubjective dimension to human relationships, such that inequality can result in a lack of respect. Where that inequality seems unconnected to a person's actions – that is, when you end up in an unfavourable position regardless of what you have done – there is a feeling of resentment, rather than simply disappointment. This suggests that equality should not be understood merely as a mathematical question of who gets what, but is intimately connected to other concepts such as autonomy, responsibility, and well-being.

## Collectivising childcare

We began the chapter by posing the question: should the family be abolished? Recall that we defined the family as a unit in which there are elders who have special responsibility for children. The model is the two-parent, heterosexual biological family, but that model can be extended to single parents, and to blended, adoptive, and same-sex parent families. The question is not about these variants, but is more radical: should the bringing up of children be collectivised?

There are a number of arguments for abolition of the nuclear family. First, the bonds of family life would be transferred to a larger group, thus increasing social cohesion. The larger community – which could be a locality or even the nation – becomes (in effect) the family. Second, gender inequalities that exist within the family – the fact that women do most of the unpaid domestic labour – would be reduced, thus creating greater sexual equality in society. Third, sibling rivalries would be lessened. Fourth, the family would no longer be the conduit for the unequal transmission of wealth and other opportunities. Good parents with very modest incomes struggle to help their children, but even worse are bad parents who are often unemployed (and unemployable). Why should a child be disadvantaged by this natural lottery?

On the other hand, there are arguments against abolition. First, it is not clear how the family would be abolished. Would children be taken from their parents soon after birth? Or would reproduction be industrialised by, for example, mass sperm donation and gestational surrogacy? Would children (through DNA testing) ever discover the identities of their biological parents, or would such testing be prohibited? Perhaps incentivisation rather than coercion would be the strategy: parents would be paid to give up their children.

A second argument against abolition is that the family (it is claimed) is a brute fact of nature. It is the only institution not based on convention (Munoz-Dardé, 1999: 41). While this ignores the effects of law and state policy on the structure of the family, and the real cultural differences – even within Europe – between family structures (Todd, 2019: 1–33), nonetheless it does suggest that collectivisation would meet huge resistance.

A different line of criticism of the abolition proposal is that it would not achieve its objective. Parents may be partial to their children, but other carers – teachers in a boarding school – can also be partial. You would have to show that non-parental carers have enough incentive to provide the goods necessary for a child to grow up to be an intellectually and emotionally well-developed adult, and at the same time, not show partiality. Either carers do not care enough – and only the nuclear family can generate such care – or they care too much and are partial (Gheaus, 2018: 295).

## Conclusion

We have surveyed a number of principles of equality and sought to put them into some kind of order. A coherent defence of equality requires a number of things: (a) clear distinctions between different kinds of equality; (b) recognition that any principle of equality must explain what is being equalised because equality in one sphere (along one metric) can result in inequality in another; (c) a scheme for connecting different principles of equality together; (d) an explanation of how equality fits with other political principles, such as freedom and efficiency. One of the tasks of a theory of justice is to connect and order different political values and principles, and in Chapter 8, we set out several theories of justice. But before doing so, we need to discuss another major value: freedom.

## Notes

1   Recent work has suggested that there is a theological basis to Rawls's rejection of desert. Rawls lost his Christian faith in his early 20s, but retained an anti-Pelagian outlook, one that maintains that humans cannot save themselves, only Christ can. Pelagians – after theologian Pelagius (AD 354–418) – hold that we can save ourselves, and Eric Nelson argues that the thinkers who formed the liberal tradition, such as Locke and Kant, were Pelagians, believing that humans could perfect themselves. Rawls is unusual in his anti-Pelagian liberalism (Nelson, 2019: 49–72).

2 At the time Phillips was writing, 18% of Members of Parliament (MPs) were female: 23% of Labour MPs and 8% of Conservative MPs were women. Almost two decades (and five elections) later, the picture is: 34% of MPs are women – 24% of the Parliamentary Conservative Party and 51% of the Parliamentary Labour Party.

# References

Cavell, S. (1990). *Conditions Handsome and Unhandsome: The Constitution of Emersonian Perfectionism*. Chicago, IL: University of Chicago Press.

Cohen, G. (1979). 'Capitalism, Freedom, and the Proletariat', in A. Ryan (ed.), *The Idea of Freedom*. Oxford: Oxford University Press, 9–25.

Detwiler, B. (1990). *Nietzsche and the Politics of Aristocratic Radicalism*. Chicago, IL: University of Chicago Press.

Dewey, J. (1894). Austin's Theory of Sovereignty. *Political Science Quarterly*, 9(1), 31–52.

Dworkin, R. (2000). *Sovereign Virtue: The Theory and Practice of Equality*. London and Cambridge, MA: Harvard University Press.

Fuller, L. (1965). A Reply to Professors Cohen and Dworkin. *Villanova Law Review*, 10, 655–66.

Fuller, L. (1969). *The Morality of Law*. New Haven, CT: Yale University Press.

Gheaus, A. (2018). What Abolishing the Family would Not Do. *Critical Review of International Social and Political Philosophy*, 21(3), 284–300.

Hayek, F.A. (1973). *Law, Legislation and Liberty*. London: Routledge.

Johnson, S. N. (2000). Expressive Association and Organizational Autonomy. *Minnesota Law Review*, 85, 1639.

Krimmel, J. (2018). Persistence of Prejudice: Estimating the Long Term Effects of Redlining. Unpublished manuscript.

Krošlák, D. (2015). Nuremberg Laws. *The Lawyer Quarterly*, 5(3), 184–94.

Linder, D. O. (1983). Freedom of Association after Roberts v. United States Jaycees. *Michigan Law Review*, 82, 1878.

Marshall, W. P. (1986). Discrimination and the Right of Association. *Northwestern University Law Review*, 81, 68.

Miller, D. (1999). *Principles of Social Justice*. Cambridge, MA: Harvard University Press.

Munoz-Dardé, V. (1999, June). III—Is the Family to Be Abolished Then? *Proceedings of the Aristotelian Society*, 99, (1), 37–56.

Nelson, E. (2019). *The Theology of Liberalism: Political Philosophy and the Justice of God*. Cambridge, MA and London: The Belknap Press of Harvard University Press.

Nietzsche, F. (1998). *On the Genealogy of Morality*, translated by Maudemarie Clark and Alan J. Swenson. Indianapolis, IN: Hackett.

Nozick, R. (1974). *Anarchy, State, and Utopia*. Oxford: Blackwell.

Pappas, N. (2004). *Routledge Philosophy Guidebook to Plato and the Republic*. London and New York: Routledge.

Phillips, A. (2004). Defending Equality of Outcome. *Journal of Political Philosophy*, 12(1), 1–19.

Rawls, J. (1972). *A Theory of Justice*. Oxford: Clarendon Press.

Todd, E. (2019). *Lineages of Modernity: A History of Humanity from the Stone Age to Homo Americanus*. Cambridge: Polity.

## Further reading

The following are useful, and the subject matter of each is evident from the titles: Stuart White, *Equality* (Polity, 2006); Matt Cavanagh, *Against Equality of Opportunity* (Clarendon Press, 2003); John Roemer, *Equality of Opportunity* (Harvard University Press, 2000); Shlomi Segall, *Equality and Opportunity* (Oxford University Press, 2016); Carl Cohen and James Sterba, *Affirmative Action and Racial Preference: A Debate* (Oxford University Press, 2003); Kasper Lippert-Rasmussen, *Making Sense of Affirmative Action* (Oxford University Press, 2020); Sophia Moreau, *Faces of Inequality: A Theory of Wrongful Discrimination* (Oxford University Press, 2020); Kasper Lippert-Rasmussen, *Born Free and Equal? A Philosophical Inquiry into the Nature of Discrimination* (Oxford University Press, 2013).

# Chapter 6

# Freedom of action

## Introduction

Freedom is a central value in many societies. It is one of those concepts that, at least in the abstract, carries positive connotations. Because of this there is a danger of moralisation: we say that someone should be free to do only those things of which we approve. But if we the adopt the simplest definition of freedom as not being stopped from doing what you want to do, then we cannot prejudge people's desires. Murder is bad, but the prohibition on murder is still a restriction of the murderer's freedom. Of course, most people think that it is a justifiable restriction, and therefore much of the debate about freedom will be about its limits. How do we justify those limits? Why should a person not be free to do what he or she wants? In this chapter, we focus on the freedom to act and in Chapter 7 consider freedom of speech.

## Key questions

- What is freedom?
- Is freedom valuable?
- How do we decide when a person's freedom should be restricted?

## What is freedom?

A starting point is the distinction made by Isaiah Berlin between positive and negative freedom (or *liberty*; the terms freedom and liberty will be used interchangeably). Acknowledging that in the history of political thought there have been more than two concepts of freedom Berlin maintains 'negative liberty' and 'positive liberty' have had the greatest influence:

- *Negative liberty* is involved in the answer to the question: 'what is the area within which the subject – a person or group of persons – is or should be left to do or be what he is able to do or be, without interference by other persons?' (Berlin, 1991: 121–2)
- *Positive liberty* is involved in the answer to the question: 'what, or who, is the source of control or interference that can determine someone to do, or be, this rather than that?' (Berlin, 1991: 122).

Negative liberty is about being left alone, whereas positive liberty entails control over one's life. A person may be unfree to leave her home because she is under house arrest or unfree to leave

DOI: 10.4324/9780429424106-9

Case study 6.1

## Should there be a tax on sugar?

**PHOTO 6.1** © PS-I/Alamy Stock Photo.

Taxation reduces freedom, as it limits our capacity to choose what do with our money. That does not mean that taxes are not justified. They might be. Consider taxes ('duties') on cigarettes. Such taxes are well established and defended on two (separate) grounds: (a) they compensate non-smokers for the costs (negative externalities) imposed on them by smokers and tobacco producers and (b) they reduce the consumption of nicotine products, which is good for potential smokers.

In recent years, these arguments have been extended to high sugar content products. Are they valid arguments? Is one valid, but not the other? Are nicotine products and high sugar products comparable?

A sugar tax could take different forms: a tax on the raw product (prior to manufacture); an extra sales tax (reflecting the price rather than the sugar content of the product); a tax on each gram of sugar in the product; or a tax on specific products such as sugar-sweetened beverages. The level of tax could cover simply the costs imposed on other people or it could be set higher to deter consumption.

The arguments for and against will be discussed at the end of the chapter, but in the meantime, view this video presentation from Robert Lustig and colleagues on sugar – 'The Complete Skinny on Obesity' (University of California Television, 2014).

because she has a phobia that makes her fearful of leaving. In the first case, she is negatively un-free to leave, whereas in the second positively unfree. Of course, elements of both types of un-freedom could be evident: she may be fearful about leaving because she suspects that she is under surveillance and is at greater harm away from home. Perhaps she is paranoid, but if that paranoia has been caused by an actual experience the source of the unfreedom is not straightforwardly internal or external.

Berlin was hostile to positive liberty. He thought that it implied a belief in psychological sources of unfreedom concealed from the person who is deemed unfree and this belief forms the basis of a political theory in which people are 'forced to be free'. Although he identifies the concept in the writings of a long line of thinkers, the work of Immanuel Kant is representative of positive liberty. Kant defines freedom as self-government or self-direction: to be free is to act from laws (or reasons) that you give yourself. The self is split into two: you have a lower self, which is driven by desires, and a higher self, which is moved by reasons that transcend desire. You can have a reason to do something without having a desire to do it. For example, if you plan to spend six months in Italy a year from now and at present speak no Italian, you have a *reason* to enrol now in an Italian class even if you have no *desire* to do so (Nagel, 1970: 58–9). The reason is not explained by the desire, but rather the desire follows from the reason. For Kant, the rational is not something political, but Berlin sees in Kant's conception of freedom the danger that the ra-tional will become identified with the state, for if your desires are not a guide to what you should do then perhaps another agency – the state – can help you achieve 'true freedom'.

Some political theorists have dispensed with Berlin's two concepts and argue for just one. Gerald MacCallum suggests, 'freedom is . . . always *of* something (an agent or agents), *from* some-thing, *to* do, not do, become, or not become something' (MacCallum, 1991: 102). It is a triadic relationship: (a) the agent, or person, who is free (or unfree); (b) the constraints, restrictions, interferences, and barriers that make the agent free or unfree; and (c) what it is the person is free to do or not do. It is important that (c) means a person is free to do *or* not do something – he has a *choice*: an inmate of a jail is not prevented from residing there, but we would not say that he is free to be in jail.

MacCallum's definition is useful but does not tell us much about the source of (b). Must it be another person (or persons) who constrains or restricts your action? Could the source of un-freedom be yourself – your own weaknesses and irrationality? The difficulty with MacCallum's concept is not so much that it is wrong, but rather uninformative. Even if the triadic framework can be applied to all instances of freedom, the most interesting political questions are about the nature of the agent who is free or unfree, the source of that agent's (un)freedom, and what it is the agent is free or not free to do. Berlin's two concepts of liberty remain important.

## The value of freedom

In most societies, the term 'freedom' has positive connotations: freedom is thought to be a good thing. Is it? And if so, why? Consider the freedom to commit murder. Laws prohibiting murder are a restriction of freedom (defined as negative freedom). But most people would consider mur-der a bad thing.

There is a tendency for the evaluation of freedom to bleed into its definition. If we do not like something, we say that it is not freedom but something else – sometimes you hear peo-ple say: 'that isn't freedom, that's licence'. But it is important to avoid moralised definitions of freedom – saying something is not an instance of freedom just because we disapprove of the action enabled by that freedom (Oppenheim, 2004: 182–3).

While avoiding a moralised definition of freedom, it is possible that freedom could itself be valuable. There are three ways in which freedom could have value:

a) Intrinsically – it is a good thing to be free, independently of what we use our freedom to do.
b) Instrumentally – freedom is not itself valuable; it is what we do with our freedom that matters.
c) Constitutively – while freedom is valuable relative to what we want to do (it is instrumentally valuable), it does change the nature of the valued thing (there is an element of intrinsic value).

Imagine three possible (that is, alternative) worlds:

• In world 1 Amy and Jake are forced to marry.
• In world 2 Amy and Jake are free to marry but choose not to.
• In world 3 Amy and Jake are free to marry and do indeed marry.

How do these three worlds differ in terms of the value of freedom? In the table below, the worlds are ranked on each of the three measures of value:

| World | *Measures of the value of freedom* | | |
| | *Intrinsically valuable* | *Instrumentally valuable* | *Constitutively valuable* |
| --- | --- | --- | --- |
| 1 – forced to marry. | Worst situation. | As good as world 3 | Could be worse than world 2 (see comment below). |
| 2 – free to marry and choose not to marry. | As good as world 3 | Worst situation if the freedom not to marry has reduced the possibility Jake and Amy will marry. | Might be better than world, depending on how much value is attached to being free relative to being married. |
| 3 – free to marry and do so. | As good as world 2 | As good as world 1 | Better than world 1 |

While (c) – freedom as constitutively valuable – is more complicated than (a) and (b), it does help resolve a problem. To illustrate, consider religious freedom in Communist Albania and in the United States. Under Communism Albania went a considerable way to banning religion. On the other hand, because of a lack of traffic there were few traffic lights in the capital Tirana. We could say that religious believers had much less freedom in Albania than in the United States, but drivers had more freedom, as they were unimpeded in their journeys. Which freedom is more important? The answer may seem obvious – religious freedom trumps drivers' freedom – but if you have no predisposition to religious belief but love driving, you might prefer Communist Albania to the United States.

Another dimension to the debate is whether freedom is valuable to humans irrespective of the political system under which they live. Thomas Scanlon distinguishes artificial and natural arguments for freedom: artificial arguments depend on the existence of specific political institutions (Scanlon, 1972: 205–6). For example, if you have competitive elections, you need the freedom to communicate and to associate. In contrast, a natural argument might say freedom is essential to human development (or human dignity).

# Unfreedom versus inability

Human physiology combined with the laws of gravity make it impossible for human beings to fly unaided. Does this mean humans are not free – as distinct from unable – to fly? This is an important political question because some social conditions are attributed to inability rather than unfreedom. Gender identity is an example. There is now a vigorous debate about whether the binary distinction between male and female is constructed rather than a 'fact of nature', and whether somebody assigned male (or female) at birth is unfree – or simply unable – to change his/her/their gender identity.

David Miller provides a useful, although problematic, scheme for distinguishing unfreedom and inability. He asks us to imagine a room the door to which can only be opened from the outside and to consider six ways in which you might be trapped in the room (Miller, 1983: 70–1):

1. Person Y, knowing you are in the room, pushes the door shut. For Miller, this is a straightforward case of unfreedom, as you are prevented from leaving by the deliberate act of another agent.
2. Person Y, not knowing you are inside, pushes the door shut. This case is more complex than 1, but still a case of unfreedom – Y does not intend to imprison you, but is negligent, and so you are unfree.
3. The wind blows the door shut. Y is supposed to check the room at 7 p.m. each evening, but fails to do so on this evening. You are unfree to leave *from 7 p.m.*
4. The wind blows the door shut. At 6.30 p.m., you call to a passer-by X to unlock the door, but X, who knows Y's duties, is busy and pays no attention. In this case, X is causally, but not morally, responsible for your confinement from 6.30 p.m. to 7 p.m.
5. Y, whose job it is to check rooms, comes to your room, and looks around it. You have concealed yourself in a cupboard, and Y closes the door without having seen you. In contrast to the second scenario, Y here took all reasonable precautions, and so this cannot be described as a situation in which you are unfree, even though you are unable to leave.
6. The wind blows the door shut. There is no one assigned to check rooms and no passer-by within earshot. This situation is straightforward – the cause of your imprisonment is entirely the result of natural causes, thus you are unable to leave but not unfree to leave.

While helpful, this delineation of unfreedom and inability could be criticised as too restrictive. For Miller, unfreedom is caused by the actions of other agents, but it must also be the result of intent (or at least negligence). A more expansive way of understanding unfreedom is that it is caused by the actions of other human beings, where different social arrangements could have resulted in greater freedom. To return to the example of gender identity: except in a few cases – such as XY females – development will tend to produce humans with recognisable primary and secondary sexual characteristics (although there are significant intrasexual differences in, for example, the level of androgens, such as testosterone). Added to biology are cultural markers of sexual differentiation, such as dress and social expectations. We might tend to believe that culture is the sphere of freedom and biology the sphere of inability, but we need to distinguish omission and commission.

Consider the case of a child unhappy with the gender to which he or she has been assigned at birth. Parents who dress the children in ways that conform to gender expectations are committing an act: they are positively doing something, and this fits with Miller's understanding of unfreedom. On the other hand, refusing to intervene in the child's biological development by agreeing to hormone treatment ('puberty blockers') is more like an act of omission. It might be argued that the child is – following Miller's scheme – unable to change gender rather than un-free. However, the possibility of gender reassignment means that if denied such intervention one is unfree. (Whether children should be given this freedom is a separate issue; the point here is a conceptual one about the distinction between freedom and ability.)

## J.S. Mill and the harm principle

Mill's essay *On Liberty* has been hugely influential in discussions of political freedom. Mill was a utilitarian:

> Utility, or the Greatest Happiness Principle, holds that actions are right in proportion as they tend to promote happiness, wrong as they tend to produce the reverse of happiness.
>
> By happiness is intended pleasure, and the absence of pain; by unhappiness, pain, and the privation of pleasure.
>
> (Mill, 1991: 137)

Mill's definition of utility is ambiguous, for pleasure and happiness are not identical. Elsewhere he contrasts satisfaction and happiness: 'better to be a human dissatisfied than a pig satisfied; better to be Socrates dissatisfied than a fool satisfied' (Mill, 1991: 140). Mill argues that freedom advances the Greatest Happiness Principle, but what if freedom made people unhappy? Would that not justify restricting it? Furthermore, if it is a certain kind of pleasure that matters – higher pleasure – then why not force people to cultivate that? These problems become more acute if we interpret Mill as primarily a theorist of negative liberty. His statement of negative liberty is encapsulated in his famous harm principle:

> . . .the sole end for which mankind are warranted, individually or collectively, in interfering with the liberty of action of any of their number, is self-protection. [...] The only purpose for which power can be rightfully exercised over any member of a civilized community, against his will, is to prevent harm to others. His own good, either physical or moral, is not a sufficient warrant.
>
> (Mill, 1991: 14)

Mill's aim is to establish what rights people should have by determining when it is legitimate to interfere with their actions: only *non-consensual* harm-to-others is a ground for limiting a person's freedom. The phrase 'against his will' allows that a person may consent to be harmed. And the final sentence of the quotation is a rejection of paternalism: only (non-consensual) harm-to-others should be prohibited and not the harm you might do to yourself. It should also be noted that non-consensual harm-to-others is the only reason for restricting a person's freedom but that does not mean all such acts are prohibited.

You do not need to identify a harmer for the harm principle to hold. A person who contracts lung cancer as the result of environmental pollution (for example, cigarette smoke) is still harmed even if no specific causal agent (an individual smoker) can be identified. The harm results from the conjoint effects of the actions of many individuals.

But what is harm? Joel Feinberg – who defends Mill, with some modifications – defines it is a setback to one's ultimate interests, which are:

. . .the continuance for a foreseeable interval of one's life, and the interests in one's own physical health and vigor, the integrity and normal functioning of one's body, the absence of absorbing pain and suffering or grotesque disfigurement, minimal intellectual acuity, emotional stability, the absence of groundless anxieties and resentments, the capacity to engage normally in social intercourse and to enjoy and maintain friendships, at least minimal income and financial security, a tolerable social and physical environment, and a certain amount of freedom from interference and coercion.

(Feinberg, 1984: 37)

You could reject Feinberg's list approach and say simply that harm is a setback to the satisfaction of your preferences: harm is not getting what you want. But it would be odd to argue that stopping a serial killer killing harms the killer. Unlike freedom, harm is a normative concept: it is a ground for restricting freedom. However, even if we accept the idea of a list, we might disagree about the specific items on the list. The point, nonetheless, is that we need a list if the harm principle is to be useful. What we put on the list could depend on a societal consensus.

## Consent

As suggested above, the harm principle does not preclude a person consenting to be harmed. Consent could take different forms, the first two of which are relatively uncontroversial:

*Explicit consent.* There must be some explicit act such as signing a contract or swearing an oath.
*Tacit consent.* There need not be an explicit act, but the parties must be conscious consent is being given (and can be withheld).
*Presumed consent.* We assume a person would have given consent had she been able to do so. Giving a blood transfusion to an unconscious person is the classic example.
*Hypothetical consent.* A person would have given consent had she been rational.

Many political theorists reject hypothetical consent. An immature person, such as a child, might be forced to go to school against her express will, on the grounds that the mature person she will become would consent to go to school and her later gratitude at being forced to go to school is retroactive proof of consent. But this is stretching the notion of consent.

Even presumed consent – a standard concept in medical ethics – is problematic. In the absence of expressly forbidding a blood transfusion – some people carry anti-transfusion documents on their person – medics presume unconscious patients want to live and giving a blood transfusion increases the probability of survival. But then what has *consent* got to do with it? The medics are just saying 'it's good to have a blood transfusion'. The doctors might argue that the absence of proof of an objection is proof of consent. But since most people do not think about these scenarios – except in end-of-life situations – it is difficult to interpret the absence of an objection as assent.

Mill – and other political theorists – restricts the consent argument to those capable of giving consent (Mill, 1991: 14). As indicated, consent is a key concept in surgery and in the biomedical sciences. There are protocols for getting consent from potential research subjects in the development of drugs and vaccines and from patients in respect of medical procedures. Broadly, consent depends on the subject understanding the facts and appreciating the significance of the decision to be made. The latter point requires an ability to imagine future scenarios and understand in at least basic terms, probabilities – that is, risks.

Another area in which consent is so important that it is extensively discussed is sex, with rape as the paradigm of non-consensual sex. In England, the Sexual Offences Act (2003) defines rape in this way (Legislation.gov.uk):

1. A person (A) commits an offence if—

    a) he intentionally penetrates the vagina, anus, or mouth of another person (B) with his penis,
    b) B does not consent to the penetration, and
    c) A does not reasonably believe that B consents.

2. Whether a belief is reasonable is to be determined having regard to all the circumstances, including any steps A has taken to ascertain whether B consents.

Rape is not the only sexual offence and there is also statutory rape, which is sex with a minor, where only the ages of those having sex need be established and not whether consent has been given – it is presumed that one of the parties is not capable of giving consent, which is why there is an 'age of consent' (often set at 16 years).

Although there is a debate about the low prosecution rate for rape (BBC, 2019a), the underlying requirements of consent are relatively demanding and provide a useful practical guide to consent, which can be used to compare other areas of life.

Consent to sex requires both a state of mind (attitudinal) and an act (performative). In other words, all parties must want sex and indicate that they want it. 'No' cannot mean 'yes' – you cannot claim another person really wants sex (attitudinal) in the absence of an explicit sign of consent (performative). Both these elements must be 'common knowledge' between the relevant parties. Consent cannot be inferred from previous sexual relations, dress or behaviour, flirting, the discussion of the possibility of having sex (falling short of saying yes to sex), or being in a sexually charged atmosphere. Apparent consent is negated by fraud: *fraud in factum* (person A consents to activity X, which turns out to be activity Y) or fraud in the inducement (X is indeed X, but false inducements were given) (Dougherty, 2013). While there can be a conflict between freedom and equality, there is a link between them: an inequality of power invalidates any apparent consent. Person A coerces B if A makes a credible threat to leave B worse off if she does not have sex with him. The threat need not be one of violence. Nor is it necessary for the threat to be explicit – there could be (to use the legal phrase) an 'atmosphere of menace and fear'.

We can draw some general lessons from sexual consent, relevant to areas of human interaction where the bar is set lower:

1. A person must be of an age at which he or she has the capacity to consent. Where the line is drawn will depend on the area of life (we discuss children later).
2. There must be a consent situation (although this is problematic in some medical contexts).
3. Closely related to the last point, there must be a shared understanding that consent has been given: A recognises that B has consented, and B recognises that A knows that B has consented.
4. Deception negates apparent consent.
5. Coercion negates apparent consent.

One of the central questions in debates over freedom is the extent to which we can consent to harmful activities. Mill certainly thought that we should be free to do so, but we do not have to accept this claim. The problem cases are where a person satisfies the conditions of consent outlined above, but the activity itself is dangerous.

# Paternalism

Should the state protect people against themselves – that is, should the state act paternalistically? Richard Arneson defines paternalism in this way:

> Paternalistic policies are restrictions on a person's liberty which are justified exclusively by consideration of that person's own good or welfare, and which are carried out either against his present will (when his present will is not explicitly overridden by his own prior commitment) or against his prior commitment (when his present will is explicitly overridden by his own prior commitment).
>
> (Arneson, 1980: 471)

Present will is straightforward: it means what you want to do now. Prior commitment is a decision made at time $t$ to be prevented from doing x at $t + 1$ (or, alternatively, made to do y at $t + 1$). Arneson thinks that forcing someone to do something for which he granted prior authorisation does not amount to paternalism. An example of prior commitment is the stickK website (stickk. com), through which you lodge money and sign a contract committing you to a certain goal such as weight loss or smoking cessation. If you fail to achieve your goal – there is usually independent verification – your money goes to your chosen charity; indeed, you can opt – in advance – for the money to go to a charity you dislike (an anti-charity).

There are several positions on paternalism:

*Anti-paternalism.* Paternalism is not justified.
*Soft paternalism.* Paternalism is justified if the person's action is non-voluntary or if we need to establish whether it is voluntary.
*Hard paternalism.* Paternalism is justified if it increases a person's capacity to lead a rationally ordered life.

Mill endorses the first position. He illustrates his argument with the example of a dangerous bridge (Mill, 1991: 106–7). If we see a person about to cross a dangerous bridge – imagine it is a rope bridge – we can stop him if we think he is unaware of the danger. This might look like soft paternalism, as it opens the way to stopping people doing things because of their deficiencies in knowledge. If we can stop him crossing the bridge why not prevent him eating unhealthy foods, if we can convince ourselves he does not understand the dangers? But Mill's argument is about time, not knowledge. There simply is not enough time to explain the dangers and so we can (physically) intervene.

However, while the bridge example may be consistent with anti-paternalism, Mill's discussion of voluntary slavery is more problematic (Mill, 1991: 113–14). Mill argues that you cannot sign a slavery contract because you would be removing your capacity to withdraw consent later. This raises an interesting question about time and rationality. If you are the same person over time[1] – for example, at the age of 20 and 60 – then an action taken at 20 could harm the person you will be at 60. While economic models of rationality avoid explaining the origins of preferences, it seems that to have a preference means wanting or *desiring* something, and desire is always immediate – it is about *now* and not the future. You now want to be a slave, but at a future point you might not want to be a slave (of course, you can have desires for the future but those are still present desires about some future state). Paternalism could be justified on grounds of protecting your future self. But the personal identity argument opens the way to other paternalistic interventions: any action that harms your future self could be subject to restriction. To counter this extension of the anti-slavery contract argument, Mill would have to show that there is something qualitatively different between stopping people selling themselves into slavery and preventing them from (say) consuming unhealthy foods. He might be able to do this if eating unhealthy foods does not destroy your capacity for choice, whereas slavery and other, even more extreme acts, such as apparently voluntary cannibalism, as in the case of Bernd Brandes (Bergelson, 2007: 724–5), do extinguish that capacity.

Soft paternalism adds the element of voluntariness. Take rooftopping (or roofing): young people (usually male) climb to the top of tall structures without any ropes or other protective equipment. If we assume that they are adults, should the state intervene to prevent them? In fact, they are (often) breaking the law, but at issue is whether their actions *should* be illegal. Watching videos of these activities, one senses a degree of peer encouragement, but is it peer *pressure* and does that render their actions involuntary?

A hard paternalist might argue that even if roofers are acting voluntarily, they are not acting in their interests. The loss of utility due to death is huge and the risks of falling to your death are high. There are nonetheless plenty of reasons for roofing. First, it is enjoyable, as is the risk associated with it (obviously, the gain in utility from the risk must be balanced against any future loss of utility). Second, roofers are building an 'experiential CV (resume)' – laying down memories which will give them future utility. Third, they achieve fame, often through viral videos. Fourth, successful roofers can intentionally (or unintentionally) signal high intelligence. Roofing requires complex thought and good spatiovisual cognitive ability. And linked to the last point, there may be sexual signalling. Young men (especially) are signalling their sexual desirability. Indeed, this is a major explanation for why young men are high risk-takers. From an evolutionary perspective risk-taking may have increased reproduction and thus the propagation of genes – risk-taking is 'selected' in a Darwinian sense. That said, evidence suggests that women value heroic, rather than non-heroic, risk-taking (Farthing, 2005).

It is irrational to minimise risk: risk-minimisers will not fulfil many of their preferences. But can actions be too risky? It depends on whether you can calculate the risks. Roofers may underestimate the risks and think that they are invincible. On the other hand, they might also be living in an uncertain environment. Risk and uncertainty are distinct; with risk you can calculate probabilities (think of the odds of winning a lottery), but with uncertainty you cannot. There are strategies for making decisions under conditions of uncertainty. You could minimise the worst possible outcome; that is, maximin: the maximisation of the minimum (worst) position. Alternatively, you could minimise regret – minimax regret: minimisation of the maximum regret.

Let us say the options for the roofers are:

a)   Climb and get kudos – respect from peers, fame, sexual opportunities, and so on.
b)   Do not climb and forgo the kudos.

The worst outcome of each is, respectively, death and loss of kudos. Even if we assume death is worse than a loss of kudos, we need to decide *how much worse* it is. We must then calculate the probabilities of each outcome happening. Put crudely, if the probability of death is very low but the probability of lost kudos high, then – depending on the exact numbers – roofing might be rational. If we cannot work out the probabilities – and are thus faced with uncertainty – then you have either to maximin or work out the maximum regret, with a view to minimising it.

Time is also a consideration. As suggested above, philosophers have debated whether persons (or selves) endure through time – whether you are the same person at 20 and 60. These are debates in the philosophy of mind and ontology, and perhaps political theorists could avoid taking a position on which position is correct; we could leave it to individuals to decide what weight they attach to their 'future selves' (or even if they believe in identity-through-time). Economists talk of time preference and discount rates. A person with a high time preference emphasises the now or near future. Someone with a low time preference delays gratification. High time preference will lead to a high discount rate: there is a steep decay in concern for the future. For example, if you accord the current time 100 units of value and have an annual discount rate of 20%, then you keep multiplying the annual units by 0.8. If your discount rate is 3%, then multiply by 0.97. On the higher rate you value your life in five years from now at roughly 33% of its current value. With the lower rate you have it at around 86%.

Advocates of paternalism could argue that humans are bad at calculating probabilities and thus risk, and intervention – stopping people doing certain things, such as roofing – reduces risks. Hard paternalists may go further: even if roofers have a reasonably good sense of the risks, they should still be stopped because interests have an objective component.

## Paternalism and public policy

The above examples – roofing, voluntary slavery contracts, bridge crossing – all focus on rather specific, individual actions. They are useful in testing our reactions, but in the real world of politics paternalism is an intervention intended to change behaviour on a large scale. Here is a list of paternalistic policies (it is illustrative, rather than exhaustive):

1. Laws requiring motorcyclists to wear helmets.
2. Laws requiring the wearing of car seatbelts.
3. Laws prohibiting self-medication.
4. Laws requiring the testing of drugs before sale.
5. Laws prohibiting the sale of pornography to minors.
6. Laws prohibiting certain kinds of child labour.
7. Curfews on children.
8. Prohibition on duelling.
9. Compulsory education of the young.
10. Prohibition on assistance in cases of requested suicide.
11. Compulsory vaccination.
12. Compulsory participation in social security schemes.
13. Prohibition on voluntary self-enslavement.
14. Sectioning (civil commitment of the mentally ill).
15. Distribution of welfare in kind rather than cash.
16. Fluoridation of water.
17. Compulsory folic acid fortification of bread.
18. Prohibition on purchase of fireworks (usually to minors).
19. Waiting periods for divorce.
20. Smoking bans in public places.
21. Taxes on high sugar content products.

A few points should be made. First, most of these cases are taken from Van de Veer (1986: 13–15). He lists 40 examples; however, some do not refer to legal paternalism (state coercion), but to medical paternalism (for example, not informing a patient of the seriousness of his condition for fear the anxiety will worsen it). Second, many of the policies could be justified on non-paternalistic – harm-to-others – grounds. We need to separate the paternalistic and non-paternalistic reasons for these policies. Third, some of them focus on the protection of children (5–7, 9, 18). Discussions of paternalism often ignore children and assume that it is acceptable to prevent children harming themselves. Indeed, there is often an implicit appeal to the etymology of the word – the authority of the father: treating children as children is appropriate but treating adults as children is not. We discuss children in the next section.

In approaching the use of paternalism in public policy, we need a framework – a series of questions we ask in respect of each policy. Take as an example number 20, smoking bans in public places (such as bars):

| Question: | | Responses by Anti-Paternalists, Soft Paternalists, and Hard Paternalists. | | |
|---|---|---|---|---|
| 1. Do non-smokers consent to be harmed by smokers? | YES: | Anti-paternalists reject bans. | NO: | All three go to Q2 |
| 2. Can the non-consensual harm done to non-smokers be eliminated by alternative policies? | YES: | **Anti-paternalists reject bans and stop here.** | NO: | **All three: support bans (and stop here).** |
| 3. Is the smoker's decision to smoke genuinely voluntary? | YES: | **Soft paternalists reject bans and stop here.** | NO: | **Soft and hard paternalists support bans (and stop here).** |
| 4. Have smokers weighed up the risks of smoking? | YES: | Necessary but insufficient condition for a hard paternalist to oppose bans. | NO: | *Hard paternalists have already supported bans (see Q3 above), but this would be an additional reason in support of a ban.* |
| 5. Do smokers operate with a reasonable time preference (and discount rate)? | YES: | **Hard paternalists reject bans and stop here.** | NO: | *Hard paternalists have already supported bans (see Q3 above), but this would be yet another reason to support a ban.* |

As we can see, while anti-paternalists never go beyond question 2, and soft paternalists beyond question 3, hard paternalists may go to question 5. A key consideration for all three positions – Anti, Soft, and Hard – is whether any non-consensual harm-to-others is caused by smokers rather than just harm to the smokers themselves. As argued above, the 21 policies listed above are not pure examples of paternalism: almost all have some elements of harm-to-others.

## Paternalism towards children

Children have preferences, which will likely change over time. But should they be allowed to act on those preferences? Do they have the capacity to determine what is in their interests and consent to certain things?

The human brain is distinct from other primate brains in that the parts most strongly associated with human interaction – such as the prefrontal lobe – are significantly larger than would be expected, given human body mass and in relation to other species (Schoenemann, 2006: 383). The brain takes a long time to mature and this requires a long period of altriciality and so dependence on parents (or guardians).

While children have preferences, these need to be contextualised. Certainly, there are domains in which a child's judgements are superior to his or her guardian. There is, for example, evidence of a significant gender difference in toy preferences, with boys preferring stereotypically male toys and girls preferring stereotypically female toys (Davis and Hines, 2020). These effects are independent of parental influence. Forcing a boy to play with dolls, or a girl with trucks is arguably a violation of the child's autonomy. We might say that here the child's preferences should override that of the parents. The same could be said of friendships. Children are better judges of the personalities of their peers than are their guardians. Again, to force a friendship seems like an unjustifiable imposition.

Children are sometimes portrayed as lacking the ability to delay gratification, but depending on the age and given a goal children can exercise considerable self-discipline. This is seen in how hard a child trains for a sport or similar activity. Furthermore, there are individual differences between children, as evidenced by the Stamford Marshmallow Experiment. In the experiment, children were given the choice between an immediate reward, such as a marshmallow or pretzel stick, or if they waited, two of the selected rewards. The study was longitudinal and delayed gratification predicted better life outcomes (Mischel, Shoda and Peake, 1988).

Paternalism towards children needs to be sensitive to context – toy preference, friendships – and make some allowance for individual differences in motivation and self-control, although taking account of individual differences may be difficult as ages of consent need to be uniform, even if they appear arbitrary.

The standard model applied to children is trusteeship: others – adults, usually but not always parents – make choices on behalf of children. But the interests of parents may conflict with their children's. Some have advocated that each child should have a 'named person' – such as a health worker or teacher – as a point of reference, additional to the parent. Such an idea was debated in Scotland, but eventually dropped (BBC, 2019b).

## Is consent enough? Is harm the only consideration?

The discussion so far has assumed that consent is the central issue. Restrictions on freedom are justified if a person has not consented or could not consent. But some theorists argue that consent – and the avoidance of non-consensual harm-to-others – is not enough to justify an activity. The intrinsic qualities of the practice are important. A case from the United Kingdom illustrates the argument.

In 1990, a number of men were charged with assault occasioning actual bodily harm (R. v. Brown and Others (1993); the arrest was codenamed Operation Spanner (Moran, 1995). The men had engaged in a protracted session of sadomasochistic sexual activity, which they had filmed. Their defence – that they all consented – was dismissed by the court. The parallel of boxing was used as part of the defence: if two men can beat each other up, then why can they not get sexual pleasure from inflicting pain on each other? The judge argued that consent was a ground for permitting harm, but it had to be backed up by a justification of the activity itself, and the following were legitimate: surgery; a 'properly conducted game or sport'; tattooing and ear-piercing. On sport, Foster's Crown Law (Foster, 1792) was cited: boxing and wrestling are 'manly diversions, they intend to give strength, skill and activity, and may fit people for defence, public as well as personal, in time of need'. The court deemed consent was a necessary but insufficient ground for the action. The correct analogy was between sadomasochism and bare-knuckle fighting, which is illegal, and not with boxing.

While not part of the prosecution case there are further arguments against the sufficiency of consent to justify sadomasochism. Thinking back to Weber's definition of the state as a monopoliser of the legitimate use of violence (see p. 9), it could be argued that the use of violence is always by permission of the state, and it permits some violent activities and not others. But this argument only takes you so far. Unless you endorse the idea that the state's use of violence is arbitrary – and thus the permission it grants to individuals to use violence is arbitrary – then it has to give a *reason* why boxing is legal and other activities are illegal. What is more, the monopolisation of violence implies that the state's permission is required for *all* activities, and not simply ones that are violent in the ordinary, everyday sense of that word.

The Operation Spanner case leads us to the idea of harmless wrongdoing, which is a difficult concept to grasp. In part, the difficulty lies in its formulation: if wrongness is defined as 'that which is harmful', then harmless wrongdoing is a contradiction in terms. But perhaps there are wrongs that cannot be traced to harms done to individuals. This could be a free-floating good (Duff, 2001). It is however hard to make sense of this concept, without any reference to harm.

In Mill's lifetime, a view was articulated – by James Fitzjames Stephen (Stephen, 1993; originally published 1873) – that to permit an 'immoral' act is equivalent to allowing an act of treason to go unpunished: the good of society was at risk. This view was rearticulated in the 1960s by Patrick (Lord) Devlin (Devlin, 1965) in response to the recommendation of a commission (Wolfenden, 1957) that laws on homosexuality should be liberalised. Devlin argued that there was a shared morality and that permitting 'immoral acts' in private threatened that morality (Devlin, 1965: 13–14). There was a danger of social disintegration. Actions may not have discernibly harmful effects, but cumulatively they erode social norms, and that erosion is *seriously* harmful. This philosophical position is termed legal moralism. However, it still seems to be concerned with harm.

A more recent strand of thought is new natural law theory (Crowe, 2011). A central claim is that if certain things are objectively valuable, then any rational mind, contrary to Mill's fallibility argument, will recognise them to be so. John Finnis argues that there are seven basic goods: life, knowledge, play, aesthetic experience, friendship, practical reasonableness, and religion (meaning speculation on the order of things). One of the principles of practical reason is non-violation – respect every basic good in every act. In practice, this means that you cannot mix the goods. *Life* means reproduction, so sex must be reproductive. If the primary aim of sex is enjoyment – *play* – then you are mixing up the goods and this is violative (Finnis, 1980: 86–9).

Stephen, Devlin, and Finnis would not reject the idea that people should have a sphere of freedom ('private sphere'), but maintain that it is a function of the state to change human behaviour, and law should reflect morality. For example, Finnis is a vocal critic of laws which treat homosexuals and heterosexuals equally, arguing that equal treatment implies that they are equally valid: a position he rejects, maintaining homosexuality is contrary to natural law (Perry, 1995). There is a parallel between legal moralism and the judgement made in the Operation Spanner case. The men involved in sadomasochism had, according to the trial judge, to justify the practice of sadomasochism. Legal moralists would argue that such an activity cannot be justified.[2]

The difficulty with legal moralism (and new natural law theory) is that it assumes more than just a shared morality – it assumes a shared conception of what is *ultimately valuable*. Many defenders of freedom would agree that we need a shared morality: respecting other people, and not harming them without their consent, *is* a moral position. But such a morality leaves open many questions of what is truly valuable in life. Individuals must find their own way to what is valuable. This does not mean that there are no objectively valuable ends, but simply that coercion, by definition, will not help us to get there: the state can stop people harming one another, but it cannot make people good.

## A tax on sugar

After considering arguments for freedom and its limitation, let us return to the case study: should there be a tax on high sugar content products?

There was a 'war' in the 1970s over whether obesity was caused by saturated fat – the view of influential physiologist Ancel Keys (Keys et al., 1986) – or by sugar, as argued by John Yudkin in his book *Pure, White and Deadly* (Yudkin, 2013; first published 1974). Yudkin 'lost', but now sugar is back in the frame as the prime culprit in the obesity epidemic and there have been calls to tax sugar. Two lines of argument are identifiable. One is about harm-to-others: the costs imposed on society by the consumption of sugar and the other is concerned with the harm done to the consumer. More accurately, the social costs are negative externalities; costs imposed on non-consenting third parties, that is people who neither produce nor consume the harmful product. Of course, we all consume sugar, so the harm results from *excessive* consumption.

Endocrinologist Robert Lustig – one of the leading figures in the fight against sugar – argues for the parallel between sugar and alcohol, both of which are 'no ordinary commodities', and which should be subject to regulation. Alcohol and sugar share four features in common: they are pervasive throughout society (unavoidable); toxic (sugar is a chronic, dose-dependent hepato toxin); have the potential for abuse (sugar interferes with signalling hormones, such as ghrelin and leptin); and they have negative effects on society (Lustig et al., 2012: 28).

If you endorse Mill's harm principle, then you seek to separate out harm-to-others (negative externalities) and harm-to-self. One way to do this is through a Pigouvian tax (Fleischer, 2015: 1683–4). A Pigouvian tax should raise the price, which could do either of two things (or a combination of both): reduce demand or raise money. Both are intended to address the negative externality. If you reduce demand, there is less of the harmful product consumed. And if you increase tax revenue, you can use the money to pay for the health resources required to address the consequences of obesity.

The concept of a Pigouvian tax leaves open exactly how you tax sugar. You could tax the raw product, prior to food manufacture. A sales tax is a possibility, but then you are taxing the price of the product, not the sugar content. Another option is to tax per gram of sugar. In parallel with alcohol minimum unit pricing, you might ensure that the price of the product never drops below a particular level and is tied to the grams of sugar in that product. Finally – and, in practice, the most widely adopted – is a tax on sugar-sweetened beverages. There is now a significant body of research on many of these policies, with the consensus being that they are modestly to significantly effective at reducing demand for the harmful products (Escobar et al., 2013; Allcott, Lockwood, and Taubinsky, 2019; Teng et al., 2019). However, we will focus here on the broad principles.

While the taxes may cut demand, and thus reduce harm, do they target the person or entity causing the harm? Take guns and domestic wood-burning. In the United Kingdom, around 8% of people have a wood fire, and it is now the biggest cause of small particle air pollution (Carrington, 2021). The harm caused is greater in an urban environment, so some home-owners cause more harm than others, but a standard rate Pigouvian tax would roughly equate to the harm done by individuals. Compare that with guns, which can also cause harm, through deliberate or accidental homicide. Some gun-owners are highly responsible, while others are not, and so the sources of the harm vary significantly. If we follow the harm principle, then you should only be prohibited from causing (non-consensual) harm-to-others. The responsible gun-owner is not harming others (and might even generate a positive externality by deterring crime) (Fleischer,

2015: 1677). Is sugar consumption more like wood-burning or gun ownership? If more like the former, then the freedom-consistent case for a Pigouvian tax on sugar is stronger.

Taxes on sugar are often attacked as 'nanny state' policies, but this phrase trivialises the issue. As Lustig argues, obesity causes harm-to-others, even in countries with private insurance-based healthcare, such as the United States (Lustig, Schmidt, and Brindis, 2012: 28). It may be possible to construct a tax that targets only the negative externalities – in other words, the harm caused to others – and as such is not paternalistic. The key point – and the reason why we have used sugar as the case study for this chapter – is that the focus should be on separating out harm-to-self from harm-to-others. If you believe, contra Mill, that paternalism is justified, then you can use taxation to stop people harming themselves, but it is still important to distinguish restrictions on freedom that are motivated by the aim of preventing harm-to-others from those intended to prevent harm-to-self.

## Conclusion

The core of freedom is the choice to do what you want to do unimpeded by others. But your freedom can harm others, and so much of the debate is focused on justifications for limiting freedom. And we need to separate out the harm done to other people from the harm done to the actor. Some political theorists reject the idea that the state should stop people harming themselves, although it requires some resolve to be consistently anti-paternalistic. Even Mill – who is often presented as an Anti-paternalist – thought that people should not be allowed to sign slavery contracts.

## Notes

1  Not all philosophers accept individuals survive through time. See, for example, Parfit (1971).
2  One response is to accept the judge's challenge and provide a justification of consensual sadomasochism. Based on empirical observations, Klement et al. (2017) argue that participants in sadomasochism experience deepened interpersonal connections, reduced stress, and altered states of consciousness.

## References

Allcott, H., Lockwood, B. B., and Taubinsky, D. (2019). Should We Tax Sugar-Sweetened Beverages? An Overview of Theory and Evidence. *Journal of Economic Perspectives, 33*(3), 202–27.

Arneson, R. (1980). Mill versus Paternalism. *Ethics 90*(4), 470–89.

BBC (2019a). Why Are Rape Prosecutions Falling? *British Broadcasting Corporation (BBC) News,* viewed 2 June 2021, https://www.bbc.co.uk/news/uk-48095118

BBC (2019b). Named Person Scheme Scrapped by Scottish Government. *British Broadcasting Corporation (BBC) News,* viewed 2 June 2021, https://www.bbc.co.uk/news/uk-scotland-scotland-politics-49753980

Berlin, I. (1991). 'Two Concepts of Liberty', in D. Miller (ed.), *Liberty.* Oxford: Oxford University Press, 33–57.

Bergelson, V. (2007). Autonomy, Dignity, and Consent to Harm. *Rutgers Law Review, 60,* 723.

Carrington, D (2021). Wood Burning at Home Now Biggest Cause of UK Particle Pollution. *The Guardian*, viewed 2 June 2021, https://www.theguardian.com/environment/2021/feb/16/home-wood-burning-biggest-cause-particle-pollution-fires

Crowe, J. (2011). Natural Law beyond Finnis. *Jurisprudence, 2*(2), 293–308.

Davis, J. T., and Hines, M. (2020). How Large Are Gender Differences in Toy Preferences? A Systematic Review and Meta-analysis of Toy Preference Research. *Archives of Sexual Behavior, 49*(2), 373–94.

Devlin, P. (1965). *The Enforcement of Morals.* London: Oxford University Press.

Dougherty, T. (2013). Sex, Lies, and Consent. *Ethics, 123*(4), 717–44.

Duff, R. A. (2001). Harms and Wrongs. *Buffalo Criminal Law Review, 5*(1), 13–45.

Escobar, M. A. C., Veerman, J. L., Tollman, S. M., Bertram, M. Y., and Hofman, K. J. (2013). Evidence that a Tax on Sugar Sweetened Beverages Reduces the Obesity Rate: A Meta-analysis. *BMC Public Health, 13*(1), 1–10.

Farthing, G. W. (2005). Attitudes toward Heroic and Nonheroic Physical Risk Takers as Mates and as Friends. *Evolution and Human Behavior, 26*(2), 171–85.

Feinberg, J. (1984). *The Moral Limits of the Criminal Law, Vol. 1: Harm to Others.* New York: Oxford University Press.

Finnis, J. (1980). *Natural Law and Natural Rights.* Oxford: Clarendon Press.

Fleischer, V. (2015). Curb your Enthusiasm for Pigovian Taxes. *Vanderbilt Law Review, 68*, 1673.

Foster, M. (1792). *A Report on Crown Cases and Discourses on the Crown Law,* 3rd edn. London: M. Dodson.

Keys, A., Mienotti, A., Karvonen, M. J., Aravanis, C., Blackburn, H., Buzina, R., . . . and Toshima, H. (1986). The Diet and 15-year Death Rate in the Seven Countries Study. *American Journal of Epidemiology, 124*(6), 903–15.

Klement, K. R., Lee, E. M., Ambler, J. K., Hanson, S. A., Comber, E., Wietting, D., . . . and Sagarin, B. J. (2017). Extreme Rituals in a BDSM Context: The Physiological and Psychological Effects of the 'Dance of Souls'. *Culture, Health & Sexuality, 19*(4), 453–69.

Legislation.gov.uk. Sexual Offences Act 2003. Legislation.gov.uk, viewed 2 June 2021, https://www.legislation.gov.uk/ukpga/2003/42/contents

Lustig, R. H., Schmidt, L. A., and Brindis, C. D. (2012). The Toxic Truth about Sugar. *Nature, 482*(7383), 27–9.

MacCallum, G. (1991). 'Negative and Positive Freedom', in D. Miller (ed.), *Liberty* Oxford: Oxford University Press, 100–22.

Mill, J. S. (1991). *On Liberty and Other Essays.* Ed. John Gray. Oxford: Oxford University Press.

Miller, D. (1983). Constraints on Freedom. *Ethics, 94*, 66–86.

Mischel, W., Shoda, Y., and Peake, P. K. (1988). The Nature of Adolescent Competencies Predicted by Preschool Delay of Gratification. *Journal of Personality and Social Psychology, 54*(4), 687.

Moran, L. J. (1995). Violence and the Law: The Case of Sadomasochism. *Social & Legal Studies, 4*(2), 225–51.

Nagel, T. (1970). *The Possibility of Altruism.* Princeton, NJ: Princeton University Press.

Oppenheim, F. E. (2004). Social Freedom: Definition, Measurability, Valuation. *Social Choice and Welfare, 22*(1), 175–85.

Parfit, D. (1971). Personal Identity. *The Philosophical Review, 80*(1), 3–27.

Perry, M. J. (1995). The Morality of Homosexual Conduct: A Response to John Finnis. *Notre Dame Journal of Law, Ethics and Public Policy, 9*, 41.

Scanlon, T. (1972). A Theory of Freedom of Expression. *Philosophy and Public Affairs, 1*(2), 204–26.

Schoenemann, P. T. (2006). Evolution of the Size and Functional Areas of the Human Brain. *Annual Review of Anthropology, 35*, 379–406.

Stephen, J.F. (1873, 1993). *Liberty, Equality, Fraternity.* Indianapolis: Liberty Fund.

Teng, A. M., Jones, A. C., Mizdrak, A., Signal, L., Genç, M., and Wilson, N. (2019). Impact of Sugar-sweetened Beverage Taxes on Purchases and Dietary Intake: Systematic Review and Meta-analysis. *Obesity Reviews, 20*(9), 1187–204.

University of California Television (2014). *The Complete Skinny on Obesity.* Available at: https://www.youtube.com/results?search_query=skinny+on+obesity, accessed 2 June 2021.

Van de Veer D. (1986). *Paternalistic Intervention: The Moral Bounds of Benevolence.* Princeton, NJ: Princeton University Press.

Wolfenden, J. (1957). *Report of the Committee on Homosexual Offences and Prostitution.* London: HMSO.

Yudkin, J. (2013). *Pure, White, and Deadly: How Sugar Is Killing Us and What We Can Do to Stop It.* London: Penguin.

# Further reading

On Isaiah Berlin and the two concepts of liberty: Bruce Baum (ed.), *Isaiah Berlin and the Politics of Freedom: 'Two Concepts of Liberty' 50 Years Later* (Routledge, 2015); Maria Dimova-Cookson, *Rethinking Positive and Negative Liberty* (Routledge, 2021). Broader discussions of freedom: Philip Pettit, *A Theory of Freedom: From the Psychology to the Politics of Freedom* (Polity, 2001); Katrin Flikschuh, *Freedom: Contemporary Liberal Perspectives* (Polity, 2007). On consent: Franklin Miller and Alan Wertheimer (eds.), *The Ethics of Consent: Theory and Practice* (Oxford University Press, 2009); Alan Wertheimer, *Consent to Sexual Relations* (Cambridge University Press, 2003). On paternalism: Christian Coons (ed.), *Paternalism: Theory and Practice* (Cambridge University Press, 2013); Kalle Grill and Jason Hanna (eds.), *The Routledge Handbook of the Philosophy of Paternalism* (Routledge, 2020).

# Chapter 7

# Freedom of speech

## Introduction

Free speech is much valued, at least in the abstract. However, just as action can be harmful, so can speech. Indeed, speech may simply be another kind of action, and the restrictions on freedom discussed in Chapter 6 could straightforwardly be applied to speech. That said, speech does seem special. In this chapter, we offer a definition of speech, suggest reasons why speech might be important, and discuss principled arguments for its limitation.

## Key questions

- What is speech?
- Is there something special about speech, such that it requires extra protection?
- Are there principled ways of limiting speech – in other words, arguments that do not simply rely on whether you like what is being expressed?

## Is there such a thing as free speech?

Access any news website on any day, and you can be sure to find at least one story that touches on the topic of this chapter. And in many countries and cultures, free speech is highly valued – at least in the abstract. People, it is said, should be free to say whatever they want; if you do not like what they are saying, then challenge it through speech and do not suppress it through law. However, once we shift attention to more specific examples, this absolutist position tends to weaken. Inciting violence or hatred, trashing somebody's reputation, passing on information useful to criminals, and downloading certain kinds of pornography are all considered activities which should be restricted. When presented with these kind of cases, people begin to say things like 'liberty isn't licence', or 'speech must be used responsibly', or 'there is no such thing as absolute free speech', or 'nobody should be allowed to shout "Fire!" in a crowded theatre'. These statements are often made in a rhetorical way – they are intended to end discussion rather than invite further exploration of the scope and limits of speech. They are then met in turn with other clichéd phrases, such as the quote falsely attributed to Voltaire 'I disapprove

DOI: 10.4324/9780429424106-10

## Case study 7.1

# Anti-vaxxers and free speech

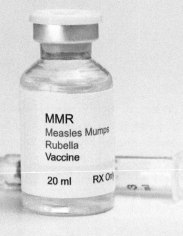

**PHOTO 7.1** © MedStockPhotos/Alamy Stock Photo.

In 1998, British doctor Andrew Wakefield (and twelve others) published a study in the highly regarded medical journal *The Lancet* claiming that there was a link between the Measles, Mumps, and Rubella (MMR) vaccination and autism (and some other health conditions). At a press conference, Wakefield advocated the use of single vaccines rather than the combined shot. In 2001, the *Daily Mail* came out in support of Wakefield after he repeated his claims about the MMR vaccine. By 2004, ten of the authors of the original paper had retracted the interpretation section of the paper and in 2007 the UK's General Medical Council (GMC) began disciplinary action against Wakefield and two co-authors. In 2010, *The Lancet* took the rare step of retracting the paper, and later that year Wakefield was found guilty by the GMC of serious professional misconduct and was struck off the medical register.

In 2019 cases of mumps among college-age students in the United Kingdom quadrupled from the previous year. Whether there is a link between the fall in children getting the full, combined vaccination in the period between 1998 and 2004 and the surge in mumps in 2019 is unclear, but the general view is that Wakefield's claims led to a reduction in the uptake of the MMR jab with detrimental consequences.

The Wakefield case raises questions about free speech:

1. Should he have been subject to criminal prosecution and not simply disciplinary action from the GMC? Or:

2. Should he in fact have been protected from action by the GMC? After all, he may have been wrong but there could be benefits to encouraging a culture of debate over scientific and medical issues.

For a useful discussion, see Offit and Coffin (2003). At the end of the chapter, we will discuss the expression of anti-vaxxer arguments, primarily in the context of Covid-19 vaccines.

of what *you say*, but I will defend to the death your right to *say* it'. However, it is discovering the limits of speech that is at the heart of debates in legal and political theory. What we need are *principled* reasons for limiting speech, not rhetoric.

A starting point might be *a presumption in favour of free speech*: people ought to be free to say what they want unless there are reasons for restricting their expression. And it is those reasons that concern us in this chapter. This approach is not, however, uncontroversial, for it presupposes that we can identify something called 'speech', which is then limited by the state. American literary theorist Stanley Fish argues that there is no such thing as free speech (in the abstract). 'Free speech' is the name we give to verbal behaviour that serves our agenda (Fish, 1994: 102). The First Amendment to the American Constitution – which dominates debates over free speech in the United States – states that 'Congress shall make no law respecting an establishment of religion, or prohibiting the free exercise thereof; or *abridging the freedom of speech*, or of the press; or the right of the people peaceably to assemble, and to petition the Government for a redress of grievances' (emphasis added). Fish argues that the apparent absolutism of this defence of free speech conceals the fact that the Supreme Court can quite easily find ways of limiting speech by redefining it as a form of action ('fighting words'). At a more basic level, the Supreme Court Justices do not limit free speech but *create* it through classifying some actions as speech and some as action (Fish, 1994: 106). All speech, Fish argues, is the product of context. For example, the idea of academic freedom – the right of students and professors to express unpopular or controversial views – only makes sense if you understand the purpose of a university. In short, Fish rejects the presumption in favour of free speech.

## Speech-acts

While Fish is right to reject an absolute distinction between speech and action, it is possible to identify a specific kind of act which has certain features. Thomas Scanlon expresses this well when he defines speech (or expression) as 'any act that is intended by its agent to communicate to one or more person some proposition or attitude':

…this is an extremely broad class. In addition to many acts of speech and publication it includes displays of symbols, failures to display them, demonstrations, many musical performances, and some bombings, assassinations, and self-immolations. In order for any act to be classified as an act of expression it is sufficient that it be linked with some proposition or attitude which it is intended to convey.

(Scanlon 1972: 206)

What linguists[1] call a 'speech-act' often has three features:

1. It has a meaning. It is not just a load of sounds or incomprehensible scribbles.
2. It entails doing something by saying something.
3. It has an effect on the audience (Austin, 1975: 101).

We can do lots of different things with speech: communicate a proposition ('it is raining') or an attitude ('I hate you') or an emotion ('I am hurt by that comment') or an order ('do it!'). And while we can intend a particular effect on the audience, some speech-acts have unintentional effects. Consider two scenarios:

1. You are taking a university course in Middle East Politics and in one class you say that while you condemn all political violence, you understand why a particular organisation commits acts of violence. And you set out the historical detail justifying your position. You make clear that you do not want anybody to emulate the actions of that organisation. However, your contribution sets off a process of discovery on the part of another student that eventually leads him to engage in a terrorist act. On its own, your speech-act did not cause him to commit violence, but it contributed to a process of radicalisation.
2. You are a chemistry student and knowing the terrorist sympathies of that same student you tell him how to make a bomb, knowing there is a high likelihood he will follow your instructions and carry out a terrorist act.

In the first scenario, there is a long causal chain between your speech-act and violence, whereas, in the second, it is short. These are extremes, but where you draw the line and say speech is likely to cause harm is a central issue in discussions of speech regulation.

A final definitional point: the term 'speech' is used widely to include visual phenomena. This chapter could have been entitled 'freedom of expression', and indeed, many writers use that term, but 'speech' is more commonly used. In large part, this reflects the influence of American First Amendment jurisprudence. In practical terms, free speech issues include incitement to violence, incitement to hatred, pornography, blasphemy, the glorification of terrorism, marches, offensiveness in the public sphere, privacy (as a restriction on speech), the expression of heterodox views of historical events, reputation (defamation), film violence, and scientific debate.

## Restrictions on speech

Restrictions on speech can include censorship (an *ex-ante* – 'before the event' – restriction), criminal sanctions (an *ex-post* – 'after the event' – restriction), civil law sanctions, informal sanctions (the 'weight of public opinion'), the absence of employment protections, and private restrictions such as exercised by social media companies. In addition, being forced to express a view is also a restriction on speech (conscious non-expression – deliberately remaining silent – is an act of expression).

Censorship and criminal sanctions involve the state acting directly as an agent. With civil law sanctions, the state facilitates the legal action of private individuals and imposes damages. It may be thought that the other restrictions have nothing to do with politics. If you are ostracised because of your views, that seems an entirely private matter well beyond the scope of state action. If you are fired from your job because of your views then again this looks like a case of private individuals exercising their contractual rights – in this case, your employer's right to terminate your employment. And social media companies, such as Twitter or Facebook, are private companies, who can decide with whom they want to transact business.

But by deciding not to intervene the state is making a decision. It could encourage diversity of opinion as a way of counteracting the ostracisation of unpopular views. It could pass employment laws that protect the expression of views. And it could require social media companies to act in the same way as telecommunications companies, where the company is not responsible for the views expressed on its platforms, but at the same time prohibit those companies from censoring speech.

## Mill's defence of free speech

John Stuart Mill's defence of freedom was discussed in the previous chapter. Mill distinguishes speech and action, although ultimately, the arguments for both rest on what he claims are the long-term benefits to humankind of protecting and encouraging freedom in action and in speech.

Even if a person finds himself alone in expressing an opinion he should, according to Mill, be free to express it. If the opinion is true, suppressing it deprives humanity of the truth. If the opinion is false, humanity again loses because while false, its expression forces the majority to restate the reasons for their (true) beliefs. A competition of ideas is healthy (Mill 1991: 21). The third possibility is that the truth in a particular case is eclectic, meaning complex (Mill 1991: 52) – it is composed of different claims, some of which might be true, others false, and we need to sift what is true from what is false.

Those who suppress opinion assume that their beliefs are infallible; they confuse *their* certainty with *absolute* certainty. Mill accepts that people must make decisions and act on them, and those decisions are based on beliefs. It would be irrational to jump off a cliff if that action were based on the belief you could fly unaided; a rational person is guided by a belief in the laws of gravity. However, Mill distinguishes holding a belief to be certain from not permitting others to refute it – people should be free to question the laws of gravity, and this is consistent with the rest of us acting as if the law were true. (Isaac Newton's laws of gravity were later challenged and found not to hold at the sub-atomic level; the challenge to Newton is a good example of Mill's point.)

As argued in the last chapter, Mill is a utilitarian – the aim is to maximise utility. Free speech, he claims, is a means to that end: through a competition of ideas, we get to the truth, and truth is one way to maximise utility. It is also a natural, rather than an artificial, defence of free speech; free speech is good for everyone rather than its value being tied to specific institutions (Scanlon, 1972: 205–6).

There are objections to Mill's argument. First, knowledge of the truth could be bad for society – it might reduce utility. Second, his argument seems to violate the harm principle, set out in the last chapter: a person's freedom can be restricted if he causes non-consensual harm-to-others. That said, Mill's free speech argument could be compatible with the harm principle if we recall that the only actions that are prohibited are non-consensually harmful ones, *not that all such actions are prohibited*. Harm caused by speech could be one type of exception. Nonetheless, Mill must justify harm done to others through speech. Indeed, he says speech should not incite violence (Mill, 1991: 55). The third – and much more radical challenge – is that there is no truth. This is the postmodern position. For the purposes of the current discussion, it will be assumed that there are truths, and the focus will be on the first two points and especially the problem of harmful speech.

## Harm

The implication of Mill's argument is that some people may be harmed through speech, but humanity in the long-run benefits from relatively unrestrained expression. The 'victims' of speech must bear the cost of this benefit to humanity. And as per the first criticism discussed above, this assumes that Mill is actually right about the historic benefits of speech; if he is wrong, then these costs are not even beneficial to others.

Richard Posner suggests a formula for determining whether speech should be permitted or restricted (Posner, 1986: 8). Speech should be prohibited if:

$$B < PL.$$

B is the cost of the regulation, including the loss of valuable information. P is the probability the speech is harmful. L is the magnitude of the harm. Expressed in words the formula states that we should regulate speech if the cost of the regulation is less than the probability the speech is harmful multiplied by the magnitude of the harm. A more complicated version is:

$$V + E < P \times L/(1 + i)n.$$

B (in the simpler formula) is composed of V (valuable information) plus E (error: the legal costs involved in trying to distinguish the information society wishes to suppress from valuable information). $L/(1 + i)n$ allows for the fact that the harmful costs may not be immediate: the larger n and i are, the less the harm; i is a discount rate – the further in the future the effects of speech the less weight we attach to them.

There are *positive externalities* to speech – that is, people benefit who have not 'paid' for its production:

1.  It informs political choices such as the decision how to vote.
2.  It allows for the communication of valuable beliefs – for example, over the causes of, and avoidance of, transmittable diseases.
3.  It provides government with useful feedback on their performance.
4.  It may benefit a specific group in society. For example, advocating for gay rights in 1950s Britain carried personal costs but helped other gay people.
5.  It may generate economic benefits. For example, pornography is big business, and historically, it sped up the propagation of technology.[2]
6.  It informs consumer choice.

But there can also be negative externalities, meaning that third parties carry costs resulting from the production of the speech:

1.  It can lead to dangerous behaviour, such as the transmission of disease.
2.  It can lead to mass panic – the classic 'shouting "Fire!" in a crowded theatre'.
3.  It can inconvenience people. Streets must be closed for demonstrations. Loud hailers cause noise. Leafletting creates litter.
4.  It can harm specific individuals through defamation.
5.  It can harm identifiable groups through stereotyping. Even if there is truth in the claims, harm is still caused. We cannot assume – as Mill does – that communicating the truth is beneficial (although to be clear, Mill argues that it is beneficial over the long term, not that each instance of speech is beneficial).

6. It can aid criminal activity. This may be directly through providing information, such as where to get guns or how to make a bomb, or indirectly by incentivising crime. An example of the latter is making money from the publication of crime memoirs.
7. It can be offensive.
8. It can undermine security, as in the case of passing state military secrets to an enemy state.

If only the speaker – and a consenting audience – bore the costs and benefits of the speech-act, then the debate over free speech would reduce to the discussion of freedom of action. For example, if all the costs and benefits of pornography were internalised, you could argue that a consumer is harming himself but then restrictions on his consumption could only be justified on paternalistic grounds (see p. 105). Of course, the production and consumption of products can generate negative externalities, as we saw with sugar. And in many ways, pornography is more like sugar than it is like political speech.

Mill argued that we cannot judge the value of a speech-act ahead of its expression. Free speech is *how* we work out what is valuable. This may be overstated. We can recognise patterns. Low value and/or high-cost speech-acts include expletive-laden speech, passing on commercially sensitive information to a rival (the recipient might benefit but there will be an overall loss of trust), incitement to *violence*, monetising crime through selling accounts of your criminal acts, and causing panic. Other examples are more complicated. Hatred sounds bad, and so its incitement looks like a good candidate for restriction, but there is considerable disagreement over what constitutes 'hate'. Trashing a person's reputation also seems like something that should be prohibited, but there may be unintended consequences in providing protection to the wealthy and powerful. And while the MMR scare was hugely damaging, there may be benefits to a culture in which people can raise alerts about the possible effects of vaccines.

While it may be difficult to do a full cost-benefit analysis of speech, there are several arguments in favour of analysing speech in this way. First, it provides a way of tackling the charge that some people (and groups) disproportionately bear the costs of speech. If this is so we can add a distribution requirement: not only must speech generate an overall benefit, but its costs also have to be distributed across society. Second, all the costs and benefits are put on the same scale. To explain, a distinction is drawn – especially in American legal debate – between viewpoint-neutral (or content-neutral) and non-neutral restrictions on speech (Altman, 1993: 303–6). Typical neutral ones are 'time, place and manner' (TPM) restrictions: protestors cannot permanently block the road or use loud hailers through the night; in debates you have to take turns in speaking and the time allotted to each speaker may be limited. Non-neutral restrictions would be based on objections to what is being said: a far-left protest is permitted, but a far-right one banned. It should be noted however that TPM restrictions may be neutral in intent but non-neutral in their effect: groups more reliant on public demonstrations to get their views across will be affected more by TPM restrictions than those, such as lobbyists, who are not.

The third advantage of a cost-benefit approach is that it allows for even small and dispersed costs (or harms) to be counted. Joel Feinberg distinguishes harm and offence, arguing that an expressive act could be offensive but not harmful, and so we need an offence principle to supplement the harm principle.

Finally – and this motivates Posner's discussion – a cost-benefit model allows us to think about speech in economic terms. In Chapter 1, we outlined four kinds of (economic) good – public, club, common, and private (see pp. 13–14). What kind of good is free speech? Answering this question helps us to think about the effects of restrictions on speech.

## Is speech a public good?

A public good is non-excludable and non-rivalrous, meaning that people can benefit from it without contributing to its production. Because of this, it is *likely* to be underproduced (it is not *necessarily* underproduced if it still pays to produce it even in the presence of free-riders, as we saw in the discussion of policing; see p. 23).

Think about someone expressing an unpopular opinion. What benefits does he get from doing this? There could be psychic benefits – he is the only person to have the guts to express this opinion, and that makes him feel good. In addition, assuming a few other people hold his views, he might feel the solidarity of a small group bound together by their shared beliefs in opposition to wider society (the internet may help in developing this sense of community). He might also aim for a future reputation (even if posthumous): future generations will, he believes, recognise both the truth of his views and his courage in expressing them in a hostile environment. Again, the prospect of a future benefit is a psychic benefit. But there are also costs. He might be prosecuted. He could lose his family and friends. He could be dismissed from his job and unable to pay his bills. He could end up homeless.

If Mill is right that society benefits from the expression of unpopular views, then others are free-riding on his contribution. Unless the personal gains outweigh the costs, a rational person will either join the majority – whether sincerely or not – or else remain silent. Given that being forced to conform to majority beliefs you think are untrue is painful, a rational person might seek to bring it about that he believes the majority opinion. That isolated person may come to believe that because he is alone in his opinion, he must be wrong; this process of self-doubt was tested in the 1950s in psychologist Solomon Asch's conformity experiments (Asch, 1955). If a minority view is in decline, then there might also be a 'spiral of silence' effect, whereby the very act of remaining silent reduces the number of people who hold that view (Noelle-Neumann, 1977: 143–4).

It should be noted however that each additional person expressing a view reduces the 'unit cost' of the speech. This was found in Asch's experiment (Morris and Miller, 1975). More recent computer modelling has suggested that if 10% hold an unshakable belief, it will spread to become the majority view (Xie et al., 2011). The potential for a belief to reach a tipping point at a relatively low level might explain the zeal with which certain beliefs are suppressed.

Not all speech-acts are public goods. Below is a scheme setting out the four goods, defined by the two parameters of rivalry and excludability, with examples of speech falling under each category:

|  | Excludable | Non-excludable |
|---|---|---|
| **Rivalrous** | *Private*<br>Individual lobbying of politicians.<br>Hard copy newspapers. | *Common* (or Common Pool; Congestible)<br>Street protests. |
| **Non-rivalrous** | *Club*<br>Pay-to-view products, such as films, music, and pornography.<br>Interest group lobbying of politicians.<br>Media behind a paywall. | *Public*<br>Political debate (insofar as it aids voters).<br>Scientific debate (assuming no subscription to publications).<br>Media, not behind a paywall. |

All forms of communication count as speech. When a businesswoman lobbies a politician for a favour that is speech. If all such communication must be logged and made public the effectiveness of lobbying is reduced, and although it would be odd to say speech (lobbying) is *suppressed* it is nonetheless being *regulated*. Small groups are more effective at lobbying than large ones (see pp. 31–2); this is because the benefits are relatively concentrated and free-riders (non-paying, non-excludable beneficiaries) controlled. Lobbying is either a private good or (more likely) a club good. More dispersed interests must take their chances in an arena where there are many more free-riders and where – even worse – they must compete for attention. Where there is a cacophony of voices, there is congestion. You can create a blog but how many people will read it?

## The offence principle

As has been argued, Mill maintains that only non-consensual harm-to-others justifies restricting freedom. However, he also maintains that:

> There are many acts which, being directly injurious only to the agents themselves, ought not to be legally interdicted, but which, if done publicly, are a violation of good manners, and coming thus within the category of offences against others, may rightfully be prohibited. Of this kind are offences against decency; on which it is unnecessary to dwell.
>
> (Mill, 1991: 109)

Feinberg argues that Mill should have articulated an offence principle, separate from his harm principle. He seeks to fill that gap. Whereas harm can be defined as a setback to one's interests, offence is shorthand for a 'miscellany of disliked states' including disgust, shame, hurt, anxiety, disappointment, embarrassment, resentment, humiliation, and anger (Feinberg, 1985: 1). While you can be harmed without your knowledge – as when someone hacks into your bank account and steals money, even though you are unaware of this happening – offence must be experienced. Feinberg relies on the concept of nuisance to develop an offence principle. In tort law, public nuisance relates to actions that materially affect the 'reasonable comfort and convenience of life' of others (Reynolds, 1992: 78n). Some offence is immediate, in that the offending action affects the senses. But offence can also be mediated, as when something is offensive against a background set of beliefs, and historical experiences.

Feinberg sets out his offence principle, arguing that we need to weigh the *seriousness* of the offence caused against the *reasonableness* of the offender's conduct (Feinberg, 1985: 26, 35). Seriousness is measured by: (1) magnitude (intensity, duration, and extent); (2) avoidability; (3) impact on a person of average sensibility. The reasonableness of the offender's conduct is determined by (1) its importance to the offender; (2) its social value; (3) the extent to which free expression is involved; (4) the availability of alternative outlets; (5) the role of malice or spite as a motive; (6) how common the conduct is in the locality in which it occurs. Feinberg is keen to avoid appeal to underlying moral values: the principle must be self-standing. We assess the value of the action to the person causing offence and the harm done to the offended in terms of *their* values rather than judging the offending action or offended response in terms of values we – who are not participants – hold.

We can consider a couple of examples to test the application of the offence principle. The first is whether an interracial couple holding hands in public would be deemed offensive. Clearly, for many people, even asking the question might be offensive, but Feinberg must show that the application of the principle alone – and not underlying values, such as racial equality or freedom of association – can determine what should, or should not be, prohibited. The other example is walking around naked in public. There has been a celebrated case in the United Kingdom with

Steve Gough (the so-called Naked Rambler). Gough has insisted on walking naked from one end of Britain to the other with nothing but boots, a hat, and a backpack:

|  | *Interracial couple* | *The Naked Rambler* |
|---|---|---|
| **Seriousness:** | | |
| Magnitude | Intermittent | Intermittent |
| Avoidability | No. | No. |
| Impact on a person of average sensibility | This will depend on the norms in the area. | Probably negative – for some shock, for others embarrassment (which could be vicarious). |
| **Reasonableness:** | | |
| Importance to the offender | High. | High – Gough argues walking around naked is a human right. |
| Social value | This would depend on your beliefs. For a racialist, interracial relationships are a threat to racial survival. For a liberal, freedom of association is important. For others, interracial relationships are the route to overcoming racism. | Possibly low, although a case can be made that walking around naked is liberating and educational. |
| Extent of free expression | High – the relationship is unlikely to be coerced. | In the case of Gough very high. |
| Availability of alternative outlets | No – the point is to hold hands in public. | Nudist beaches (etc.) are not for Gough an alternative. |
| The role of spite or malice as a motive | Unlikely, unless the aim is to spite people perceived as racist. | It is largely accepted that Gough is not motivated by spite or malice. |
| How common the conduct is in the locality in which it takes place | This will vary. | In the United Kingdom, not at all common. |

It can be left to the reader to decide the merits of these cases, but the point is that this exercise must be carried out if the offence principle is to be put into practice. The problem of value remains, and it may be that what is at issue are not moral values (right/wrong, good/bad), but charientic values – a word coined from the Charites (three graces) (Ellis, 1984: 15). Something is uncharientic if it is uncouth, or lacking in good taste, rather than immoral (Glassen, 1958). But charientic values can be as controversial as moral values.

## Quality uncertainty

There has been much discussion of fake news, especially after Donald Trump emerged as a presidential candidate in 2015, with Trump accusing the mainstream media of being 'fake news' and his opponents countering with the same charge against him. In a study of the 2016 Presidential Election, Allcott and Gentzkow found that 62% of American adults got their political news from social media (2017: 122). The most popular fake news stories were more widely shared on Facebook than the most popular mainstream news stories, and many people who saw fake news stories believed them. Fake news stories tended to favour Trump over his opponent Hillary Clinton.

Allcott and Gentzkow define as fake any news stories that are verifiably false and could mislead readers (Allcott and Gentzkow, 2017: 213–14). They include intentionally fabricated stories and stories that might be misunderstood as factual. They exclude from the definition unintentional reporting mistakes; rumours that do not originate from a specific news source; conspiracy theories, which, they claim, are by their nature difficult to prove as true or false; false statements by politicians; and reports that are slanted but not outright false.

Whether fake news is harmful is not straightforward. While it might seem obvious that it is better to know the truth, lies can be satisfying and the truth painful. It is a common observation from psychological research that we seek out information that supports our existing beliefs (confirmation bias) (Nickerson, 1998: 175–6) and approach new information by (implicitly) asking not whether it is true or false, but whether we like it or not (motivated reasoning) (Kahan, 2012: 408). That said, acting on false information could ultimately be harmful. Voting for a candidate A over B in the belief A will make you better off may turn out to be both false and harmful.

If in the long run truth matters, then media outlets concerned with their long-term reputation will want to avoid fake news. But not all media outlets are concerned with their long-run reputation. Fake news outlets operate on a shorter cycle. They want clicks. They also have a low cost base. They do not stay around long enough to be worried about their reputation. But fake news carries costs:

1. Consumers cannot distinguish between high-quality and low-quality media providers.
2. Whereas true stories generate positive externalities, false stories reduce those externalities.
3. Consumers become more sceptical of news stories in general.
4. A reduced demand for high-precision reporting reduces the incentives to invest in it (Allcott and Gentzkow, 2017: 219).

These points taken together raise the issue of quality uncertainty. In a famous article economist George Akerlof discusses the market for lemons (used cars) (Akerlof, 1978). That market is intended as an example of any market in which there is an information asymmetry: sellers of a product know whether the product is good or bad. Buyers do not. Therefore, it is rational to sell a bad product at the same price as a good one. Over time, bad products will drive out good ones (Akerlof, 1978: 488). This is a market failure. Applied to the market for news, we can say that quality journalism is expensive. It requires paying good money to people with credentials (good university and journalism school qualifications) and funding investigative journalism. Investigative journalism carries business risks: it takes time, requires the corroboration of evidence, and there is a danger of being scooped. If consumers cannot work out true from false reporting, then good quality journalism will decline as it will not pay to produce it.

Akerlof's solutions to the market for lemons problem included providing time-limited guarantees (or warrantees); developing a brand name; creating chains (e.g., of restaurants or hotels); and licensing (e.g., of doctors or lawyers) (Akerlof, 1978: 499–500). Could any of these be employed to counteract fake news? Each is a kind of self-regulation, although in many countries there are statutory guarantees. There are brand names such as the major broadcasters and newspapers. It could be argued that media outlets should be held financially responsible for what they publish, but the likely effect of this would be to deter publication by high-quality outlets. As much news reporting has moved online the Big Tech companies, such as Facebook, have become the arbiters of truth and quality, and that raises a set of additional problems, which we discuss in the final part of the chapter.

## Incitement to hatred

Incitement to hatred laws were developed from the 1960s onwards, and most Western – and many non-Western countries – have such laws, with the United States being a notable outlier. While the use of the term 'hatred' in a legal context is novel, there were precursors. For example, in England, there was a common law crime of seditious libel, which made it an offence 'to promote feelings of ill-will and hostility between different classes of His Majesty's subjects'. A famous case was *R v Osborne* (1732), which concerned claims made against the Sephardic Jewish community (Lasson, 1987: 162). And – allowing for translation – there are across different jurisdictions synonyms for hatred (and its incitement): ridicule; insults; abuse; offence and offensiveness; 'attack on the dignity of a person'; (more archaically) 'attack on the honour of a person'; 'spreading false news'; group libel; incitement of the people (*Volksverhetzung*).[3]

Incitement to hatred was enshrined in UK law with the 1965 Race Relations Act. Section 6 of the Act made it an offence for a person intentionally to stir up hatred against a section of public based on colour, race, or ethnic origins (Lasson, 1987: 266–7). In the law as originally stated, there had to be *both* a subjective intent to stir up hatred *and* an objective likelihood of stirring up hatred. Intentionality was removed in a later law (1976 Race Relations Act). Crucially, truth was no defence, although in this respect the new law was no different from the older one of seditious libel. The genesis of the 1965 law can be traced 30 years earlier to the battle between the British Union of Fascists (BUF), led by Oswald Mosley, and the Communist Party of Great Britain (CPGB). The 1936 Public Order Act was passed in an attempt to control clashes between the BUF and CPGB, where the Fascists' mass gatherings were disrupted by the Communists (Cullen, 1993: 254). Section 5 of the Public Order Act prohibited 'threatening, abusive or insulting words or behaviour, with intent to provoke a breach of the peace, or whereby a breach of the peace is likely to be occasioned' (Lasson, 1987: 165). The impetus for the 1965 Act came from the desire to control anti-Semitism, which had increased in the 1940s (Kushner, 1989: 166). The law was strengthened by later Acts of Parliament and, in the 2000s, extended to religious hatred and hatred on grounds of sexual orientation.

While the 1965 law referenced 'stirring up hatred', the term 'hate speech', understood as something potentially requiring regulation, only really gained widespread currency in the 1980s (Brown, 2017a: 424). 'Hate' is, of course, a common, everyday word, and most people would think hate speech communicates an emotion, or an emotion accompanies the speech-act. However, as Brown argues, hatred need not be present for a communicative act to be deemed hate speech. Hate speech laws identify and control forms of speech that:

1. Harm already disadvantaged or victimised members of society.
2. Are very socially divisive in a diverse society.
3. Undermine the victim's sense of self-respect.
4. Are incompatible with the norms of acceptable speech and work against civilised political debate.
5. Run contrary to – or even threaten – fundamental democratic values (Brown, 2017b: 569).

The problem is that an emotionally laden word is being employed to justify the attempt to eliminate very different types of harm. This lack of precision has several consequences. First, it leads to an emphasis on the subjective over the objective: instead of independent verification that a person has been harmed the victim determines whether he or she has been harmed, to the detriment of the person accused of hate speech. Second, the vagueness of the concept has the potential to inflate its application. Vague laws are bad laws, as Lon Fuller argued (see p. 86). Third, while, as Brown argues, hatred need not be present to identify something as hate speech (Brown, 2017a: 440), the emotional force of the word creates an unfair advantage to advocates of further restrictions on speech, which – paradoxically – is incompatible with point 4 above: the importance of civilised political debate. Fourth, because hatred is hard to measure, the cost-benefit analysis discussed earlier cannot be easily applied to instances of speech. Fifth, non-criminal regulation of hate speech by social media companies draws its inspiration from the law, and so the problems just identified – subjectivity over objectivity, inflation, the disadvantaging of opponents of regulation, the lack of measurability – carry over to online censorship.

# Social media

Earlier in the chapter we argued that speech can be restricted in a number of ways, one of which is by the state choosing *not* to intervene. This is arguably the case in relation to Big Tech companies such as Google, Amazon, Facebook, Twitter, and YouTube. Given how much speech is mediated by these companies, the question of the role of the state in intervening in their activities, or not, is an important one. Key issues are whether these companies are monopolies, whether they are publishers or simply neutral bulletin boards and if the former, whether they exercise their power to the detriment of certain voices in the political sphere.

In law, a monopoly can be identified in two ways: control of market shares and barriers to entry. On the first criterion, it is open to debate whether Big Tech companies are monopolies. In the United States, a 70% market share will trigger an investigation by the antitrust authorities and in the European Union the minimum figure is around 40% (Davie, 2014). Amazon controls around 51% of US digital sales (PYMNTS, 2021). Google facilitates 92% of online searches (Oberlo, 2021). Google, Amazon, and Facebook together generate 64% of US digital advertising revenue (Statista, 2021).

It is on the second criterion – barriers to entry – that these companies may be deemed monopolistic. Network effects mean that once a company has achieved a certain market share it is extremely difficult for competitors to break through. There are alternative video uploading sites to YouTube, but videos on those sites will never reach a large audience because nodes (individual users) are simply not tied (connected) to other nodes. After the first commercial web browser became available in 1993 there was much optimism that networks would be decentralised or even fully distributed, and so, for example, there would be multiple online booksellers and video sites. It turns out that centralised networks are more efficient and so we have the current media landscape.

We can summarise the problem of trying to establish whether Big Tech companies have a monopolistic position as follows:

1. We need to work out the market shares of the companies, but share of what? It could be digital news. It may be all news. It might be advertising. For the sake of argument, let us assume that it is news – the communication of political information.
2. We then need to investigate who is excluded: is it producers of political information or its consumers?
3. Even if the market share of political information can be established and is high enough to trigger concern, it might be insufficient to conclude that Big Tech companies are monopolies. Facebook, as an example, may not be creating a structure that excludes rivals: they are not stopping rivals entering the market.
4. The structure that disadvantages rivals may be network effects – consumers want to connect with others, so they go with the biggest network. But this seems like a free choice rather than Facebook forcing out competitors.
5. One argument against monopolies is that they can inflate prices. But what if the product is ostensibly free? (Of course, the price we pay for joining a network is the use of our personal data).
6. It might be that because of network effects – and the lack of competitors – the quality of the product is reduced.

The last steps – 5 and 6 – would not convince a court of law that intervention is required, but they might be relevant to the morality of speech regulation. If due to their dominant position Big Tech companies reduce the quality of the product – in this case, political information – then intervention may be justified.

There is evidence that Google, as one example, ranks right-wing bloggers below left-wing ones (UnGoogleUs, 2020). The counterargument is that Google's algorithm is not biased but that left-wing sites do better with backlinks to universities, whose top-level domain '.edu' ranks high, and also with mainstream media outlets (Gotch, 2020). Since academic institutions skew left (Honeycutt and Freberg, 2017), Google simply amplifies a bias inherent in modern opinion-forming institutions.

What could be done? Section 230 of the Communications Decency Act 1996 is a key piece of American legislation, and given that most Big Tech companies are headquartered in the United States, it is also relevant for the rest of the world. Section 230 gives immunity to platforms for what third parties publish on them. In effect, the social media companies are not publishers: 'no provider or user of an interactive computer service shall be treated as the publisher or speaker of any information provided by another information content provider' (Legal Information Institute). But there is a Good Samaritan clause enabling companies to delete content in the interests of the common good – even if that speech is constitutionally protected (under the First Amendment) – just so long as they act 'in good faith'. If companies can make these decisions, it would imply that they are publishers, but the point of Section 230 is to close off that argument: censoring does not make them publishers.

When the web began to grow in the mid-1990s lawmakers faced a dilemma: they could treat platforms as passive conduits of the views expressed on them, much in the same way that a telephone company is not responsible for conversations transmitted over its service or the platforms were publishers (curators) of the content uploaded to them (Skorup and Huddleston, 2019: 650). The background to the 1996 Act – and the explanation of the name – was concern that the web would lead to an explosion in pornography (which it did). While Section 230 was something of an afterthought to that main concern, it has turned out to be its most significant element. The Good Samaritan clause was the tool by which platforms navigated between allowing all content, however problematic, being uploaded, or curating content, but then taking on liability as a publisher. Legal phrases such as 'in good faith' are always problematic because of their vagueness, but if the state tried to define more narrowly the term, then it would end up as a regulator.

Because of network effects, there are no simple solutions to the problem of political bias by, and on, social media platforms. Some possibilities are to allow relatively unrestricted speech to those willing to identify themselves, rather than hide behind a moniker, on the grounds that with identity comes responsibility for what you say. But the (relative) anonymity of online activity may be necessary for unpopular views to be expressed. Another policy would be to require social media companies to be more open about those who flag up speech that purportedly violates 'community standards'; there are often organised lobby groups that swarm on content, particularly on certain sensitive political or historical topics. Although their identities should not be revealed, more (suitably anonymised) data on patterns of complaints could be produced in order to reveal organised campaigns.

## Anti-vaxxers

The debate over free expression for those sceptical about vaccination illustrates the effects of speech on behaviour. At the time of writing – mid-2021 – most of the world has not been vaccinated against Severe Acute Respiratory Syndrome Coronavirus 2 (SARSCoV2), the virus that causes Covid-19. Indeed, only a few countries have given more than half their population one shot. The main vaccines – for example, Pfizer, AstraZeneca, and Moderna – have high efficacy, as measured by the avoidance of contracting Covid-19, or if contracted, avoiding hospitalisation, serious illness, and death. That is obviously good for those who are vaccinated, but it is also good for others, who do not then have to bear the financial costs of treating sufferers or are forced into costly lockdowns (where lockdowns are imposed to avoid health providers being overwhelmed with patients). In addition, the vaccines may reduce the spread of the virus through reducing viral loads and so reducing the emission of the virus. Eventually, herd immunity can be achieved (Fine, Eames and Heymann, 2011: 911–12).

There is an altruistic component to vaccination – that is, a benefit to others at a cost to oneself. Awareness of people around you who cannot, for health reasons, risk vaccination, but who also need to be protected through herd immunity, increases the willingness to be vaccinated (Cucciniello et al., 2020; see also Rieger, 2020). Anti-vaxxer arguments give people plausible reasons for not getting vaccinated, even if the real motivation to avoid vaccination is self-interested. But obviously there are genuine concerns about vaccines, and following the logic of Mill's argument, minority views should be heard. Although concerns were raised by medical professionals rather than anti-vaxxers, the problem of rare blood clots with vector vaccines such as AstraZeneca and Johnson & Johnson was not picked up in the clinical trials (Gross, 2021).

To assess the extent to which vaccine scepticism – be it over the MMR shot or the Covid-19 ones – should be tolerated we can apply Posner's algorithm: $V + E < P \times L/(1 + i)n$. Let us break it down into its components. Remember that if $V + E$ are less than $P \times L/(1 + i)n$, then the speech should be suppressed.

| | |
|---|---|
| **V**<br>Valuable information | Anti-vaxxers may have important things to say about the dangers of a particular vaccine. More generally, they could encourage a culture in which the producers of vaccines are challenged, which forces them to maintain high standards. Suppression of speech spills over into other areas of biomedical research such as the dangers of vaccine escape from laboratories resulting from gain of function research (Wade, 2021). |
| **+ E**<br>Error involved in trying to suppress information | There are legal and administrative costs involved in suppressing the anti-vaxxers. In addition, there are chilling effects – meaning that if people are uncertain about whether what they are saying is prohibited, they will remain silent. Concerned medics might keep quiet. These count against suppression of anti-vaxxer expression. |
| **< P**<br>Probability of harm | How likely is it that anti-vaxxer arguments will cause harm? Value (V), probability (P), and magnitude (L) may seem inextricably linked. To distinguish P, L, and V, let us contrast Mr Jones, who has no medical credentials, and Dr Smith, who does. Both advance an identical argument against vaccines, but people listen to Dr Smith, but not Mr Jones. Dr Smith's speech-act has a higher probability of harm than Mr Jones's. While it would be unfair to criminalise Dr Smith on grounds that he has caused more harm, professional regulations may penalise Dr Smith, and the state will not intervene to protect him. This is indeed what happened in the case of Andrew Wakefield. |
| **L**<br>Magnitude of harm | Anti-vaxxer arguments may reduce vaccine uptake and increase the risk of disease and death. In addition, an uncontrollable virus triggers lockdowns, which cause economic damage. |

| | |
|---|---|
| **(1+i)**<br>Discount rate | If the harm (L) is in the distant future, then we can reduce it by a certain amount. For example, if we apply a discount rate of 10%, then 1 is multiplied by 0.9 each year. It might seem odd to use discount rates. Compare Covid-19 vaccine scepticism with Wakefield's anti-MMR arguments. With Covid-19, the effects come within weeks and months, whereas with the MMR shot, it was experienced around 15 years later (assuming that the surge in mumps in 2019 was caused by the drop-off in vaccination in 1999–2004). The logic of a discount rate would be to prohibit Covid-19 anti-vaxxer expression, but be more tolerant of discussion of the MMR vaccine. The case for a discount rate is that 'pro-vaxxers' have more time to regroup and offer counter-arguments before the full effects of anti-vaxxer movements are felt. In the case of MMR, it may be possible to remedy missed vaccinations. With Covid-19, it is a race against time. |
| **N**<br>Multiply discount rate by years | This connects closely to the discount rate – it is the temporal extent of the harm. Harm may be equally spread out over a number of years, decline in a predictable way, or it may be lumpy: for example, little harm in year 1, a lot in year 2, less in year 3, and a surge in year 4. |

## Conclusion

We hope that you have come away from this discussion better able to assess the value of free speech and determine when it is appropriate to limit speech, by how much, and in what way. Speech would have no value if it did not have effects on behaviour, but obviously those effects can be harmful, and so we need principled arguments for regulating speech. We have suggested that a useful way to think about regulation is to conceptualise speech as an economic good (even if it is not a good in the narrow sense of something traded in a market). And developing that idea we can categorise different kinds of speech in terms of whether they are public, private, club, or common goods. Speech-acts that are public goods, and generate positive externalities, are in greatest need of protection.

## Notes

1  This scheme is a simplification of linguist John Austin's famous distinctions between locutionary, illocutionary, and perlocutionary acts. See Austin.
2  For example: Super 8 cameras in the 1960s; VHS (over Betamax) in the 1970s and 1980s; scaling up of the web in the 1990s; streaming video; online payment systems; Blu-Ray over HD DVD; webcams.
3  Section 130 of the German criminal code. The official English translation is 'incitement to hatred'.

## References

Akerlof, G. A. (1978). 'The Market for "lemons": Quality Uncertainty and the Market Mechanism', in P. Diamond and M. Rothschild (eds), *Uncertainty in Economics*. New York: Academic Press, 235–51.

Allcott, H., and Gentzkow, M. (2017). Social Media and Fake News in the 2016 Election. *Journal of Economic Perspectives, 31*(2), 211–36.

Altman, A. (1993). Liberalism and Campus Hate Speech: A Philosophical Examination. *Ethics, 103*(2), 302–17.

Asch, S. E. (1955). Opinions and Social Pressure. *Scientific American, 193*(5), 31–5.

Austin, J. L. (1975). *How to Do Things with Words* (Vol. 88). Oxford university press.

Brown, A. (2017a). What Is Hate Speech? Part 1: The Myth of Hate. *Law and Philosophy, 36*(4), 419–68.

Brown, A. (2017b). What Is Hate Speech? Part 2: Family Resemblances. *Law and Philosophy, 36*(5), 561–613.

Cucciniello, M., Pin, P., Imre, B., Porumbescu, G., and Melegaro, A. (2020). Altruism and Vaccination Intentions: Evidence from Behavioral Experiments. *medRxiv.*

Cullen, S. M. (1993). Political Violence: The Case of the British Union of Fascists. *Journal of Contemporary History, 28*(2), 245–67.

Davie, I. (2014). EU and US Antitrust: Converging Approaches to Monopolies? Le Petite Jurist, viewed 31 May 2021. https://www.lepetitjuriste.fr/eu-and-us-antitrust-converging-approaches-to-monopolies/

Ellis, A. (1984). Offense and the Liberal Conception of Law. *Philosophy and Public Affairs, 13*(1), 3–23.

Feinberg, J. (1985). *The Moral Limits of the Criminal Law, Vol. 2: Offense to Others.* New York: Oxford University Press.

Fine, P., Eames, K., and Heymann, D. L. (2011). "Herd immunity": A Rough Guide. *Clinical Infectious Diseases, 52*(7), 911–16.

Fish, S. (1994). *There Is No Such Thing as Free Speech and that is a Good Thing, Too.* New York and Oxford: Oxford University Press

Glassen, P. (1958). "Charientic" Judgments. *Philosophy, 33*(125), 138–46.

Gotch, N. (2020). Is Google Biased? We Analyzed 50 Key Politically-Driven Topics to Find Out. Gotch SEO, viewed 31 May 2021. https://www.gotchseo.com/google-biased/

Gross, A. (2021). Scientists Claim to Have Solved Covid Vaccine Blood-clot Puzzle. *Financial Times,* viewed 2 June 2021. https://www.ft.com/content/f76eb802-ec05-4461-9956-b250115d0577

Honeycutt, N., and Freberg, L. (2017). The Liberal and Conservative Experience across Academic Disciplines: An Extension of Inbar and Lammers. *Social Psychological and Personality Science, 8*(2), 115–23.

Kahan, D. M. (2012). Ideology, Motivated Reasoning, and Cognitive Reflection: An Experimental Study. *Judgment and Decision Making, 8,* 407–24.

Kushner, T. (1989). *The Persistence of Prejudice: Antisemitism in British Society during the Second World War.* Manchester: Manchester University Press.

Lasson, K. (1987). Racism in Great Britain: Drawing the Line on Free Speech. *Boston College Third World Law Journal, 7,* 161.

Legal Information Institute. 47 U.S. Code § 230- Protection for Private Blocking and Screening of Offensive Material. Legal Information Institute (Cornell Law School), viewed 31 May 2021. https://www.law.cornell.edu/uscode/text/47/230

Mill, J.S. (1991). *On Liberty and Other Essays.* Ed. John Gray. Oxford: Oxford University Press.

Morris, W. N., and Miller, R. S. (1975). The Effects of Consensus-Breaking and Consensus-Preempting Partners on Reduction of Conformity. *Journal of Experimental Social Psychology, 11*(3), 215–23.

Nickerson, R. S. (1998). Confirmation Bias: A Ubiquitous Phenomenon in Many Guises. *Review of General Psychology, 2*(2), 175–220.

Noelle-Neumann, E. (1977). Turbulences in the Climate of Opinion: Methodological Applications of the Spiral of Silence Theory. *Public Opinion Quarterly, 41*(2), 143–58.

Oberlo (2021). Search Engine Market Share in 2021. *Oberlo,* viewed 2 June 2021, https://www.oberlo.co.uk/statistics/search-engine-market-share

Offit, P. A., and Coffin, S. E. (2003). Communicating Science to the Public: MMR Vaccine and Autism. *Vaccine*, 22(1), 1–6.

Posner, R. A. (1986). Free Speech in an Economic Perspective. *Suffolk University Law Review, 20*, 1.

PYMNTS (2021). Amazon and Walmart Are Nearly Tied in Full-Year Share of Retail Sales. *Payments News and Mobile Payments Trends*, viewed 31 May 2021. https://www.pymnts.com/news/retail/2021/amazon-walmart-nearly-tied-in-full-year-share-of-retail-sales/

Reynolds Jr, O. M. (1992). Of Time and Feedlots: The Effect of Spur Industries on Nuisance Law. *Washington University Journal of Urban and Contemporary Law, 41*, 75.

Rieger, M. O. (2020). Triggering Altruism Increases the Willingness to Get Vaccinated against COVID-19. *Social Health and Behavior, 3*(3), 78.

Scanlon, T. (1972). A Theory of Freedom of Expression. *Philosophy and Public Affairs, 1*(2), 204–26.

Skorup, B., and Huddleston, J. (2019). The Erosion of Publisher Liability in American Law, Section 230, and the Future of Online Curation. *Oklahoma Law Review, 72*, 635.

Statista (2021). Distribution of Net Digital ad Revenue in the United States in 2019 and 2020, by Company. *Statista*, viewed 31 May 2021. https://www.statista.com/statistics/242549/digital-ad-market-share-of-major-ad-selling-companies-in-the-us-by-revenue/

UnGoogleUs (2020). Yes, Google Puts its Thumb on the Scale. UnGoogleUs, viewed 31 May 2021. https://ungoogle.us/index.php

Wade, N. (2021). The Origin of COVID: Did People or Nature Open Pandora's Box at Wuhan? *Bulletin of the Atomic Scientists*, viewed 4 June 2021. https://thebulletin.org/2021/05/the-origin-of-covid-did-people-or-nature-open-pandoras-box-at-wuhan/

Xie, J., Sreenivasan, S., Korniss, G., Zhang, W., Lim, C., and Szymanski, B. K. (2011). Social Consensus through the Influence of Committed Minorities. *Physical Review E, 84*(1), 011130.

## Further reading

General overviews and collections include: Eric Barendt, *Freedom of Speech* (Oxford University Press, 2007); Adrienne Stone and Frederick Schauer (eds.), *The Oxford Handbook of Freedom of Speech* (Oxford University Press, 2021); Ellen F Paul, Fred Miller, and Jeffrey Paul (eds.), *Freedom of Speech* (Cambridge University Press, 2004). On hate speech laws: David Renton, *No Free Speech for Fascists: Exploring 'No Platform' in History, Law and Politics* (Routledge, 2021); Ivan Hare (ed.), *Extreme Speech and Democracy* (Oxford University Press, 2011); Nadine Strossen, *Hate: Why we Should Resist it with Free Speech, not Censorship* (Oxford University Press, 2018); Jeremy Waldron, *The Harm in Hate Speech* (Harvard University Press, 2014); Eric Heinze, *Hate Speech and Democratic Citizenship* (Oxford University Press, 2017); Alexander Brown, *Hate Speech Law: A Philosophical Examination* (Routledge, 2017). On offence: Andrew Sneddon, *Offense and Offensiveness: A Philosophical Account* (Routledge, 2020).

# Chapter 8

# Distributive justice

## Introduction

Distributive justice is concerned with the fair – or 'just' – distribution of resources. In the early modern period, the focus was on property rights as the moral basis for the distribution of resources. In this chapter, we concentrate on contemporary theories of justice, in which private property rights are often regarded as problematic – although one of the three theories discussed is a contemporary restatement and defence of strong private property rights. The primary focus is on the work of John Rawls, Robert Nozick, and Gerald Cohen.

## Key questions

- What is distributive justice (as a concept)?
- What is a fair distribution of resources?
- How do we decide what is a fair distribution of resources?

## Theories of just distribution

Distributive justice is, as the name suggests, concerned with the just distribution of resources. It must be distinguished from *retributive* justice, which is concerned with how a punishment fits a crime (see pp. 47–8). What might be the basis for the distribution of resources? Here are some possibilities:

- *Threat advantage.* The amount a person earns is the result of that person's relative bargaining power.
- *Need.* Everyone should have their needs satisfied – there should be a guaranteed minimum set of resources equivalent to that required to satisfy those needs.
- *Desert.* If you work hard and as a consequence increase your earnings relative to others, you deserve to keep those additional earnings.
- *Freedom.* The pattern of distribution is the result of the choices people make – if you have a product that others *choose* to buy, in buying the product other people have *consented* to the income you gain from selling it and therefore also to any resulting inequality.
- *Labour.* The profit made from the sale of commodities should reflect the contribution that the producer (labourer) makes to the commodity.

DOI: 10.4324/9780429424106-11

Case study 8.1

# Fair taxes

**PHOTO 8.1** © Philip Lewis/Alamy Stock Photo.

Should the state tax people? That is, should it be allowed to appropriate resources through coercion? If so, are some types of tax fairer than others?

First, read this overview – Tax Basics 2021: https://files.taxfoundation.org/20210115115229/Tax-Basics-The-Three-Basic-Tax-Types.pdf

The focus in the Tax Basics document is the United States, but the types of tax discussed are operative in many countries. They place taxes in three categories: on what you earn; on what you buy; and on what you own.

Using the Tax Basics guide rank the following types of tax from what you consider to be the fairest to the least fair:

1. Progressive income tax.

2. Corporate income tax (known in the United Kingdom as Corporation tax).

3. Capital gains tax.

4. Sales tax. Value added tax (VAT) is slightly different, but for the purposes of this discussion can be lumped together with a sales tax. Europeans are more familiar with VAT.

5. Property tax intended to fund local services.

6. Estate tax – paid on an estate prior to its disbursement.

7. Inheritance tax – paid by those who inherit.

8. Wealth tax.

Provide reasons for your rankings.

- *Maximise utility.* We should aim to maximise the overall level of utility in society; 'utility' may be defined as happiness or pleasure or welfare or preference satisfaction.
- *Equality.* Resources should be distributed equally.
- *Priority to the worst-off.* The worst-off should be as well off as possible.

Rather than run through all these options we will focus on the work of three thinkers – John Rawls, Robert Nozick, and Gerald Cohen. In the course of the discussion, comments will be made on all the above options. Although the focus on social justice,[1] distinct from justice as an individual virtue, is a very recent development, there is a history to these contemporary debates, as will be particularly evident in the discussion of Nozick. Furthermore, the debate over social justice set out in this chapter connects to an even more recent development: the concern with global justice, which we discuss in Chapter 19.

## Rawls and priority to the worst-off

Rawls's book *A Theory of Justice* (Rawls, 1972) had a big impact on political theory. In it, he advances a method for making decisions about the distribution of resources – not just material resources, but also freedom and political power – and argues that the operation of that method would result in giving priority to the worst-off.

Rawls's work falls within the social contract tradition of Locke, Rousseau, and Kant, and indeed, he is credited with reviving this tradition, which had gone into decline after about 1800. The contract was a device by which power was legitimated: it is rational from the standpoint of the individual to hand over some (most, all) of the rights he enjoys in the state of nature to a coercive authority. Rawls differs from the classical theorists by taking it for granted that social cooperation under a state is normally a good thing. The focus is not the justification of the state, but the distribution of the benefits and burdens of cooperation under a state. The *benefits* are material goods, freedom, and political power. The *burdens* include not only any inequality which may arise but also the fact that principles will be coercively enforced.

A theory of justice applies to the basic structure of society. This consists of those institutions fundamentally affecting a person's life. Included are the structure of the economy – the rules of ownership and exchange – and the provision of services such as health and education, as well as constitutional rights.

## The original position

Rawls's theory has two parts: an explanation of how we decide what is just and a discussion of what he believes we would decide is just. Starting with the first part, he employs what he terms the original position. This is a thought experiment – you are asking a 'what if?' question: what if such-and-such were the case? It is not a 'place' – you only 'go into' the original position in a figurative sense. The most important feature of the original position is the veil of ignorance: you do not know your class and social position, natural assets and abilities, strength and intelligence, particular psychological characteristics, gender, to which generation you belong, who your family and friends are, and your conception of the good – that is, your ideas about what makes life valuable or worth living, such as your religious and philosophical beliefs (Rawls, 1972: 12). You do however know you live in a society characterised by moderate scarcity: there are enough resources to satisfy basic needs and leave a significant surplus to be distributed, but that surplus is not sufficient to overcome conflict between people over its distribution. Rawls assumes that people want more rather than fewer of the benefits generated by cooperation. As well as knowing your society is marked by moderate scarcity, you also have a general knowledge of psychology and economics.

## Motivation in the original position

Rawls attributes to people in the original position a set of motivations. He makes these assumptions for the purposes of his theory; he does not claim that real people – that is, people who know their identities – have these motivations. In the original position, the following holds:

- We value the (social) primary goods. These are rights, liberties, powers and opportunities, income and wealth, and the bases of self-respect. The primary goods are valuable to many different ends, so if you choose a career trading in stocks and shares, or, alternatively, living in a self-sufficient community on a remote island, you will value these things (Rawls, 1972: 93).
- We seek to maximise our share of the primary social goods (Rawls, 1972: 142).
- We are not gamblers. Rawls tries to avoid assuming a particular attitude to risk; nonetheless, the way the original position is set up would suggest that we would be risk-averse (Rawls, 2001: 106–7).
- We are not envious of other people (Rawls, 1972: 143).
- We are mutually disinterested: we are not interested in one another's welfare. You do know, however, that once the veil has been lifted you will have family and friends who you do care about (Rawls, 1972: 144–5).
- We live in a closed society – entered at birth and exited at death. Again, this point can easily be misunderstood. We do not know what principles of justice will be chosen – we have not got to that point yet – but it is highly likely that among the principles will be a right to emigrate. The reason Rawls assumes we live our whole lives in one society is that it makes the choice of principles very serious; John Locke is often interpreted – perhaps wrongly – as arguing that remaining in a society and using the state's resources constituted tacit consent to the state (Thomas, 1995: 38–9). Rawls rejects that argument: for an individual to leave a society and seek asylum elsewhere is such a major step that deciding not to seek asylum cannot be taken to constitute consent to the existing regime. This generates two motivational points: because the choice of principles is a serious one, we would (a) not gamble our interests (a point

already made) and (b) we accept that the chosen principles will be binding on us once the veil has been lifted – Rawls terms the acceptance of the principles the strains of commitment (Rawls, 1972: 145).

It has probably struck you that there is something odd about the motivation of people in the original position. On the one hand, they are purely self-interested – they seek to maximise their individual shares of the primary goods. On the other hand, because they do not know their identities they are forced to be impartial, that is, each individual can only advance his or her interests by viewing the choice of principles from the standpoint of each other individual.

## What would be chosen in the original position?

Now, we come to the second part of Rawls's theory: the choice of principles. Agents in the original position are free to choose whatever they wish, but Rawls discusses some candidates (Rawls, 1972: 124). These are expressed in philosophical language. He does not talk about choosing state socialism or a free market economy, although in later work he has things to say about these economic systems. The competing principles are:

1. Everyone serves my interests – I get what I want (first-person dictatorship).
2. Everyone acts fairly except me (free-rider).
3. Everyone can advance his or her interests as he or she wishes (general egoism).
4. We maximise the aggregate level of goods (classical utilitarianism).
5. Option 4 but with a minimum level of goods for each individual.
6. We maximise the average (per capita) level of goods (average utilitarianism).
7. Option 6 but with a minimum level of goods for each individual.
8. Certain ways of life are to be privileged because they have greater intrinsic value (perfectionism).
9. We balance a list of prima facie valid principles; that is, we make an intuitive judgement about the correct trade-off between freedom and equality should they conflict (intuitionism).
10. The two principles of justice (democratic conception).

Rawls argues that we would choose option 10: the democratic conception. Option 1 is incoherent. Because you can only have one dictator, we would never agree to dictatorship. Option 2 contradicts the strains of commitment and option 3 is unstable. Options 4–7 represent utilitarianism. Utilitarians hold that what we ought to do is maximise the overall level of well-being (utility). They are not concerned with the distribution of utility (although options 5 and 7 do give some weight to individuals – they create a floor below which nobody should fall). Classical utilitarianism measures the level of welfare without reference to the number of utility-generating beings (we say 'beings' because non-human animals might generate utility), whereas average utilitarianism divides the level of welfare by the number of utility-generating beings. Compare the following two situations:

a)   2,000 units of welfare divided by 500 beings.
b)   1,000 units of welfare divided by 20 beings.

For a classical utilitarian, (a) is superior to (b), whereas for an average utilitarian, (b) is superior to (a): 50 units versus 4 units.

Perfectionists (option 8) maintain that there are certain ways of life worthy of pursuit, and the state should aim to bring these ways of life about (to 'perfect' means to complete or bring to fruition). This argument does not have great significance for the distribution of income, but it certainly affects what amount of freedom we should have. Rawls argues that because we are denied knowledge of our particular conceptions of the good we would not opt for perfectionism; we would not, for example, choose to give a particular religion special status. Intuitionism (option 9) entails resolving conflicts of values and interests on an *ad hoc*, case-by-case basis – we have no method for resolving them. The aim of Rawls's theory is to provide just such a method.

## The two principles of justice

Rawls argues that agents in the original position would choose the democratic conception. He distinguishes a special and a general conception, which are versions of the democratic conception. The general conception is: 'all social primary goods . . . are to be distributed equally unless an unequal distribution of any or all of these goods is to the advantage of the least favoured' (Rawls, 1972: 303). He hopes he can persuade the reader that the general conception would be endorsed even if the special conception, as one version of it, is rejected. The special conception consists of the two principles of justice. As Rawls's original presentation of the two principles was slightly confusing, we will use, in abbreviated form, his revised version from *Justice as Fairness: A Restatement* (Rawls, 2001: 42–3):

1.  Equal liberty: each person is guaranteed a set of basic liberties.
2a. Equal opportunity: there must be equal access to jobs and services under fair equality of opportunity.
2b. Difference principle: inequalities are only justified if they benefit the least advantaged members of society. (In addition to the two principles – 1 and 2a/2b – there is also the just savings principle, which is intended to determine how much should be saved for future generations.)

The first principle is a familiar one – each person has an equal right to free speech, association, conscience, thought, property, a fair trial, vote, hold political office if qualified, and so on. Principle 2a is also familiar – jobs and services should be open to all (equal access), but furthermore society should be so arranged that as far as possible people have an equal *opportunity* to get jobs and gain access to services. 2b – the difference principle – is novel and is the one we shall focus on in the next section.

Rawls maintains that there is a lexical priority of 1 over 2a and 2a over 2b: you cannot sacrifice liberty for economic justice – you must satisfy fully the equal liberty principle before applying equality of opportunity, and equal opportunity takes priority over the difference principle (Rawls, 1972: 42–3). For example, the greatest source of unequal opportunity is the family – parents favouring their children – but Rawls argues that even though people in the original position are mutually disinterested, they do value personal freedom, which includes the freedom to form personal relationships, marry, have a family, and enjoy a private sphere of life. They would, therefore, opt to protect this private sphere even if it resulted in unequal opportunity.

## The difference principle

Consider this table. There are three distributions (A, B, C) of income (the numbers are units of income) and under each distribution you have an equal (1 in 4) chance of ending up with one of the incomes. If you did not know your identity, which distribution in this table would you choose (A, B, or C)?

| A | B | C |
|---|---|---|
| 80 | 50 | 10 |
| 45 | 32 | 8 |
| 20 | 22 | 7 |
| 15 | 20 | 6 |

Rational agents in the original position, recognising the seriousness of the choice, will, Rawls maintains, ensure that should they end up in the bottom quarter of society they will be as well off as possible. The reasoning behind this is termed 'maximin': *maximum minimorum* or the *maxi*misation of the *min*imum position (Rawls, 1972: 154). Although Rawls avoids committing himself to any particular view on agents' attitude to risk, only high risk takers would select A over B. Note that expected utility theory treats A and B as identical: in B, there is a guaranteed 20, while in A, there is 1 in 4 chance of 80 (80/4 = 20). However, the risk is greater in A than B.

In C, everybody is worse off relative to how they could have done had they ended up in the equivalent position in a different distribution. However, this is a more equal society – the lower distributions range from 60% to 80% of the top income. If inequality mattered in itself or if people were envious, then the case for choosing C would be stronger. Rawls argues that the poor will accept greater income differentials if they gain in absolute (distinct from relative) terms.

The biggest challenge for Rawls is to show that people would choose B over A. The average income in A is 40, whereas the average for B is 31. It is only the very strong veil of ignorance that skews the choice to B. As Bernard Williams argues, there is a similarity between Rawls's argument and Pascal's Wager (Williams, 1981: 96–7). Blaise Pascal (1623–62) was an important contributor to decision-making under conditions of uncertainty. He argued that it was rational to believe in God – more accurately, to try to bring it about that you believe in God – because if there is no God, there might be at most a small loss of utility (we have to lead more austere lives), but if God exists, there is infinite utility. Even on the slightest probability that God exists, it pays to believe (or try to believe) in his existence (Hájek, 2003). The parallel with Rawls is not exact because he does not offer the prospect of infinite utility, but there is some similarity: we face uncertainty, and the negative utility of ending up in a very bad place is enough to motivate us to choose the difference principle.

## Rawls, Meade, and a property-owning democracy

In his later work, Rawls worried that the difference principle could undermine self-respect by making the poor dependent on wealth transfers and correspondingly engender resentment in the rich who pay high taxes to fund those transfers. To address this problem he picked up on idea from British economist James Meade (1907–95): property-owning democracy (Rawls, 2001: 135–6). Meade was active on the centre-left in the United Kingdom and rather cheekily took the phrase 'a property-owning democracy' from the Conservative Party. However, for Meade, in contrast to the Conservatives, the idea of a property-owning democracy entailed a much more radical transfer of capital.

Capital is a crucial concept. Marx defined capital narrowly as ownership of the means of production (either directly in the form of private companies or through share-ownership). He also distinguished it from labour. For Meade, capital is a wider concept and can include human capital acquired through education, in addition to material assets. It does not, however, include cash receipts, unless those receipts become a source of expanding value as against simply funding current consumption.

While Meade was a man of the left, he was somewhat unusual in combining a strong commitment to the price mechanism – free markets – with a concern for what he perceived to be the growing inequality in the ownership of capital, which he maintained was exacerbated by the technological revolution. The price mechanism maximises efficiency, but not equality. For reasons of efficiency, he was opposed to rent controls, capping of utility prices, or a minimum wage. Achieving equality requires measures that do not distort prices. He sets out his arguments in *Efficiency, Equality and the Ownership of Property* (Meade, 2013; first published 1964).

On taxation, Meade was in favour of a wealth tax and a lifetime consumption tax rather than income tax. In respect of inheritance, he argued for a reform of death duties (estate tax). Rather than taxing estates, the *recipients* of bequests should be taxed relative to the total income they have received; a record would have to be kept of such gifts (the infrastructure required for a wealth tax could serve also for this record-keeping). In this way, it would be possible for a wealthy person to avoid any inheritance tax just so long as he spread his wealth around.

A more controversial aspect of his work was his advocacy of eugenics. Meade became treasurer of the Eugenics Society in the 1960s. He was well aware of how controversial eugenics had become, but continued to use the term into the 1960s, although by the time he published *The Intelligent Radical's Guide to Economic Policy* in 1974 (Meade, 2012), while still advocating the same policies, he avoided the term. His specific recommendations were sex education and the widespread use of contraception, combined with tax policies that encouraged wealthier – and by extension more intelligent – individuals to have more children. Tax policies would be targeted at the wealthy childless. Such policies were to have a neutral effect on the tax burden on the poor *vis-à-vis* the rich, but alter the balance within the higher income groups (Meade, 2012: 80–1). It is not clear whether such taxation is intended to incentivise those without children to reproduce or is a way of subsidising the reproduction of their fellow class members.

Meade links this eugenic policy to his inheritance tax proposal: if the wealthy have more children, their high wealth will be transmitted in more small bundles. He is adamant that his 'moderate eugenic policy' (Meade 2013: 65) does not involve compulsion. Any parent should be free to determine the size of his or her family. But it is also clear that 'social-demographic changes which reduce the fertility of the unfortunate relative to the fertility of the fortunate families will…help the equalisation of economic wealth' (Meade, 2012: 81).

Drawing on Meade, Rawls distinguishes welfare state capitalism and a property-owning democracy; the key difference is that the former redistributes wealth after it has been generated, while the latter aims for a more equal distribution of earning power (capital) and thus less reliance on post-production transfers of income. His adoption of the property-owning democracy concept is motivated by a concern that his theory of justice is not adequately realised under welfare state capitalism.

Rawls himself was vague on the details of a property-owning democracy, and it has been left to others to elaborate. Martin O'Neill and Thad Williamson argue that such a system would have three elements: (a) a wide dispersal of capital through workers' ownership of the means of production; (b) the blocking of intergenerational transmission of advantage through various types of inheritance tax; (c) safeguards against the corruption of politics through campaign finance reform and the public provision of forums for debate (O'Neill and Williamson, 2009: 5).

O'Neill and Williamson make no reference – even negatively – to eugenics, but, in fact, Rawls was aware that one way to increase human capital and create a more equal society without redistribution was to increase native ability. In the only place in *A Theory of Justice* where Rawls discusses eugenics, he says that, for the purposes of his argument, he has taken the distribution of natural assets as a 'fact of nature', but also acknowledges that it can be affected by the social system. A caste system, for example, divides society into separate biological populations, while 'an open society encourages the widest genetic diversity' (Rawls, 1972: 107). In addition, it is not to the advantage of the less fortunate to propose policies that reduce the talents of others; under the difference principle, the position of the worst-off is maximised by taking advantage of those talents. In addition, Rawls argues that we owe it to future generations to maintain or increase the stock of natural assets. This is not an overwhelming rejection of eugenics.

## Nozick: a libertarian theory of justice

Robert Nozick advanced an alternative to Rawls's egalitarian theory of justice; one that lays stress on the importance of private property rights. In his book *Anarchy, State, and Utopia* Nozick defends the minimal state against philosophical anarchists, who reject the state. A minimal state is a monopoly provider of security services. A more extensive state – one that intervenes in the economy and supplies welfare benefits – cannot be justified. Utopia would be a world in which diverse lifestyles and communities would flourish under the protection of the minimal state.

## Nozick's starting point: private property rights

The very first line of *Anarchy, State, and Utopia* reads: 'individuals have rights, and there are things no person or group may do to them (without violating their rights)' (Nozick 1974: ix). Jonathan Wolff argues that Nozick is a one-value political philosopher (Wolff, 1991: 3–4). Other philosophers claim that there is more than one value; for example, they might say that freedom is important, but so is equality, and since freedom and equality often conflict, we need a method for resolving that conflict. Rawls's *two* principles of justice express this idea. Wolff maintains that Nozick's one value is private property or more precisely the right to private property. Property here means the legally sanctioned (or morally legitimate) appropriation of things. A right is an advantage held against another person – if you have a right, then another person has a duty to do something (or not do something: that is, not interfere), so a right is a relationship between people (see pp. 325–6). Bringing together the two concepts – private property and rights – a right to private property entails the exclusion of other people from the use of something. Nozick's entitlement theory of justice is based on the inviolability of private property rights. There are three parts to it:

Part 1: Just acquisition
Part 2: Just transfer
Part 3: Rectification.

## Just acquisition – Locke and Nozick

The first question to ask is: how did anybody acquire the right to exclude other people from something? Nozick draws on the work of John Locke, specifically, his defence of private property, and especially his argument for first acquisition. We must imagine a historical situation in which nobody owns anything and then explain (justify) the parcelling up of that which has hitherto been held in common. The standard interpretation of Locke is that he was attempting to reconcile Christianity and capitalism at a time – the seventeenth century – when capitalism was beginning to replace feudalism as the dominant form of economic organisation. Locke began with three Christian premises:

1. God had entrusted the material world to human beings, who were its stewards and thus had a duty to respect it.
2. The implication of 1 is that the world is owned in common by humanity.
3. God as creator had rights to what he created. As God's creatures, human beings have a duty to God to preserve themselves.

Capitalism poses a challenge because it was wasteful of natural resources, which violates stewardship. And capitalism entails private, not common, ownership, and it threatened to push large numbers of people into poverty and starvation, thus undermining their capacity to fulfil their duty to God to preserve themselves. For example, in seventeenth century England, we begin to see the movement from smallholdings to large estates, with smallholders (serfs) forced to hire out their labour for a daily wage, thus becoming wage labourers. The creation of a class of rural wage labourers presaged the development of an urban working class with the industrialisation of the eighteenth and (especially) the nineteenth centuries. The risks of starvation were significantly greater for the wage labourers than for their earlier counterparts, the serfs.

Christian theology, Locke argued, did not strictly require common ownership, but rather promotion of the common good, and capitalism, through its capacity to generate wealth, did indeed promote it (Locke, 1988: 291). Locke's starting point for a defence of capitalism is his account of how we go from common ownership to private ownership: if a person mixes his labour with something external to himself, he acquires rights in that thing. Mixing one's labour is sufficient to establish ownership so long as two provisos are satisfied:

- *Sufficiency proviso.* There must be 'enough and as good left for others' (Locke, 1988: 288).
- *Spoilage proviso.* There must be no wasting away of the product (Locke, 1988: 290).

In practice, these two provisos are easily met because of the development of wage labour and money (Locke, 1988: 293). Wage labour is premised on the notion of having property rights in your own body – rights which you cannot alienate, that is, you cannot sell your body – but the product of the use of your body (that is, labour) can be sold, such that your labour becomes a commodity which is hired out.

Wage labour is important for Locke because it enables the buyer of labour to say to the potential seller of labour (wage labourer) that you can acquire sufficient goods to preserve yourself if you sell your labour to me. If you do not, *you* (not me) are violating your duty to God to preserve yourself. Crucially, that labour does not create rights for the labourer in the product since what the labourer sells to the buyer is an extension of the buyer's body; Locke argued that 'the turfs my servant has cut are *my* turfs' (Locke, 1988: 289). Wage labour, therefore, satisfies the sufficiency proviso. Money deals with the spoilage proviso – a person's property can be held in this abstract form and will not spoil, unlike, say, crops, which rot, or animals, who die.

Nozick draws heavily on Locke's acquisition argument, but without its theological basis. He begins with the assumption of self-ownership, that is, you own your body, and everything associated with it – brain states, genetic make-up, and so on – but this is no longer based on God's rights as creator. He then adopts Locke's mixed labour device, but he alters the provisos:

- *Sufficiency proviso.* Locke was worried that there would come a point in the development of capitalism where some people really did not have enough to survive on, even with the possibility of wage labour. Nozick is not so concerned: so long as everyone is *better off* after appropriation, then that appropriation is just (Nozick, 1974: 175–6).

- *Spoilage proviso.* Nozick is not worried about spoilage, but does insist that a person cannot acquire a monopoly control over certain goods such as a water supply (Nozick, 1974: 180–1).

## Just transfer

Just transfer is dependent upon just acquisition because you cannot justly transfer what you have not justly acquired. Furthermore, acquisition is a very strong idea – it entails full control over the thing acquired, including the power to transfer it to another person. Nozick takes the example of basketball player Wilt Chamberlain (1936–99). Imagine a basketball match watched by 3,000 people, each of whom pays $20 to see Chamberlain play and $8 of that $20 goes directly to Chamberlain (the $8 is Chamberlain's marginal value: if he were not playing the organisers would have to sell the tickets at $12). Assume each of the 3,000 spectators and Chamberlain earns $40,000. This is, of course, unrealistic, but it is intended to make a point. We can compare earnings – what Nozick calls holdings – before and after the tickets were bought:

|  | *Spectators' holdings* | *Chamberlain's holdings* |
|---|---|---|
| Before the purchase | $40,000 × 3,000 | $40,000 |
| After the purchase | $39,980 × 3,000 | $64,000 |

Nozick argues that so long as Chamberlain did not use threats or fraud to acquire each $8, his additional earning is legitimately his by simple transfer (Nozick, 1974: 161–3). The fact that such transfers will over time create significant inequalities is irrelevant, for what matters is that individuals have consented to the transfer. Those who object to such transfers want, in Nozick's words, 'to forbid capitalist acts between consenting adults' (Nozick, 1974: 163). To evaluate the force of Nozick's argument we need to compare his theory of justice with the alternatives.

## Types of theory

Nozick divides theories of justice into two groups – end-state and historical (Nozick, 1974: 153–5) – with a sub-division of the second into patterned and unpatterned theories (Nozick, 1974: 155–60).

End-state theories are not concerned with what people *do*, but only with the *end result*. Utilitarian theories fall into this category – the aim is to maximise total, or alternatively, average utility. Who gets what under this arrangement is irrelevant: person A may get 25 units and person B 10, and the total is 35 (and average 17.5), but if A got 10 and B 25, the end result would be the same.

Historical theories focus on what people have done. For example, distribution according to desert, that is, hard work, is a historical principle (actually, 'historical' is a bad label – it would have been better, though less elegant, to talk of *person-regarding* theories because it is not necessarily what a person has *done* that is relevant – need would be person-regarding). Historical theories are further divided into patterned and unpatterned:

- Any principle that involves the phrase 'to each according to _____' (fill in the blank: desert, need, labour, and so on) will create a pattern (Nozick, 1974: 159–60). Nozick includes Rawls's theory as patterned: priority to the worst-off (maximin) generates a pattern.
- Nozick calls his own theory unpatterned because whatever distribution exists should be the result of choice. You could argue that this is patterned with the blank filled in as 'choice', but 'choice' is not really the same as desert or need – the latter two provide objective criteria that can be used by a redistributive agency (the state), whereas you choose to do whatever you like.

Individuals may, under Nozick's utopian framework, aim to bring about an end-state or patterned distribution, but what may not happen is that the state *coerces* people into creating that end-state or pattern. To appropriate some of Chamberlain's $24,000 is tantamount to forcing him to labour (Nozick, 1974: 172).

# Rectification

Nozick's comments on the third part of his theory are brief and underdeveloped. If something was acquired or transferred as the result of fraud or theft or force, then some mechanism is required to rectify the situation (Nozick, 1974: 152–3). All that Nozick offers in the way of a theory is the suggestion that counterfactual reasoning be applied: what would be the pattern of holdings if the unjust acquisition/transfer had not taken place? This raises the problem of increased value: if you steal a dollar and make a million dollars as a result, what should you pay back – the dollar or the million dollars? This is a live issue, for unlike Locke, who argued that the United States was unowned prior to European colonisation (Locke, 1988: 299–301), Nozick maintains that Native Americans had rights to their land, and these were violated and so rectification is required. But Manhattan – whose only trace of native ownership is its name – has increased vastly in value since it was acquired by Europeans: how do we rectify that injustice? Nozick provides no answer.

## Left libertarianism

A distinction is made between right libertarianism and left libertarianism. Self-ownership is the starting point for all libertarians, but right and left libertarians divide over its implications for the ownership of external things. One of the most influential left libertarians – Hillel Steiner – argues, against Nozick, that the natural right to self-ownership does not 'ground' a right to ownership of the external world:

a)  A set of rights must be compossible, meaning that it is logically impossible for one individual's exercise of rights to constitute an interference in another person's exercise of their rights (within the same set);
b)  For a right to be natural, it cannot be the result of a contract;
c)  All actions consist in some kind of motion (material and special components of an action are its *physical components*);
d)  One individual's actions cannot interfere with another's if none of their physical components is identical (Steiner, 1974: 42–4).

Two points follow from these claims. First, self-ownership is a natural right, but Nozickian ownership of the external world is not. Second, if you impose any constraint on acquisition, such as Locke's 'enough and as good left for others' or Nozick's 'no monopolies' requirements, then the first owner must be capable of predicting the effect of his action on all future people – first ownership is only retroactively legitimate – but this is impossible to do. Self-ownership does not suffer from these problems. Although Steiner does not endorse his argument, many left libertarians follow Henry George's idea of a site (or land) value tax as a means by which a person's acquisition of external things can be made compatible with the idea that nobody has a natural right to the world.

Henry George (1839–97) was an American self-taught economist remembered primarily for his proposal that there should be just one tax – on land. George noted that the poor of New York were considerably poorer than those of California and concluded that exploitation had its roots in monopolistic control of land rents, which were determined by supply and demand. Land is in limited supply, whereas the value humans can add to land is indeterminate, and so we distinguish (a) the site value – which is determined by externalities and (b) the value added to the land by the owner. We should tax only (a) (Carter, 1982: 24–5). Many things affect the site value including location, natural beauty, and mineral deposits, and we calculate site value by using a similar but 'empty' or undeveloped plot – the site value of such a plot should (ideally) account for its full value and so we can use market prices. Site value tax revenues should be used to compensate those who are not able to acquire land because of the history of acquisition and transfer. The idea is that the value we add is 'ours' because it is an extension of ourselves, whereas the land itself can never be ours.

## Cohen: a Marxist perspective on distributive justice

Marx's critique of private property must be located in his theory of history: human beings have a drive to increase productivity, and this generates two struggles. The first is a struggle against nature, and the second a struggle between human beings. The two are related, for how we organise production will determine how effective we are at using nature to our advantage. Over time, the particular organisation – mode of production – changes, but what characterises all modes is a class relationship in which one class exploits another. Exploitation is made possible by the unequal ownership of the two things that enable an increase in production: the means of production and labour power. The former includes factories and tools, while the latter consists of the skills of labour, both physical and mental. At the time Marx was writing – the mid- to late-nineteenth century – capitalism had emerged as the dominant mode of production. For Marx, the key features of capitalism are as follows.

- *Ownership.* Under capitalism, in contrast to previous modes of production, every person owns his own labour power. However, a minority class – the capitalists or bourgeoisie – own a monopoly of the means of production, with the consequence that the majority class – the working class, or proletariat – can survive only by selling their labour power to the capitalists.
- *Capital.* This is something that is an 'expanding source of value' and is unequally owned: one class (capitalists or the bourgeoisie) are in a position to benefit from this expansion of value by virtue of their ownership of the means of production.
- *Exploitation.* The true value of labour is not the price it commands in the market (the wage) but the amount of time that goes into the production of the commodity (labour value). The

worker does not receive the full value of his product – the difference between the wage and labour value is the amount creamed off by the capitalist. This is what Marx means by exploitation.

- *Use value and exchange value.* A distinction is drawn between the value we get from a commodity (use value) and its price (exchange value). Every commodity has a use value, but not everything that has a use value is a commodity. For example, air has a use value but is not a commodity and hence does not have an exchange value. If pollution became very bad, and everybody had to carry a supply of clean air, and somebody started bottling and selling it, then it would acquire an exchange value, in addition to its use value.
- *Markets.* Interaction between individuals takes place through the laws of supply and demand. These laws fulfil two functions: (a) to provide information on how much of a product should be produced and at what price and (b) to provide incentives to produce, and these incentives derive from self-interested motivations. Marx argues that the market is not in long-term equilibrium and is subject to increasingly severe depressions. He further argues that capitalism assumes that people are *by nature* selfish; this he rejects as an ontologisation of historical experience – that is, turning something transitory into an ahistorical fact.

Marxists have tended not to engage in debate with liberals (or libertarians), rejecting as they do certain fundamental claims about the nature of human motivation and political epistemology. On human motivation, for example, Rawls maintains the principles of justice apply to a society characterised by moderate scarcity in which people are in conflict over the distribution of those (moderately) scarce resources. A Marxist maintains that when production levels reach a certain point – and capitalism is historically useful because it massively increases productivity – we will be in a position to say that there is no longer scarcity, and the causes of social conflict will be removed. Regarding political *epistemology* – that is, how we *know* what is just – Marxists maintain that it is only in a post-scarcity situation that we will be able to determine the correct distribution of resources. Gerald Cohen is unusual amongst Marxists in his engagement with liberal (libertarian) thinkers such as Rawls and Nozick. What makes his argument interesting is that he attacks liberals on what they believe to be their strongest ground: freedom.

## Cohen against Nozick

Cohen does not deny that capitalism gives people freedom to buy and sell labour, but argues that defenders of capitalism make the illegitimate claim that their society is comprehensively free: they falsely equate capitalism with the free society. Cohen maintains liberals – both left-wing (egalitarian) and right-wing (libertarian) – are wrong. Capitalism does not guarantee the maximum amount of freedom possible. A moralised definition of freedom is used – the validity of private property rights is taken for granted, such that freedom comes to be defined in terms of private property and any infringement of it a reduction of freedom. Cohen provides an example to illustrate his point: Mr Morgan owns a yacht. You want to sail it for one day, returning it without any damage done to it. If you take it, you will be violating Mr Morgan's rights, but which situation creates more *freedom*, Mr Morgan's exclusive use of the boat, or your one-day use combined with his 364-days-a-year use (Cohen, 1979: 11–12)?

For *one day*, Mr Morgan is prevented from using his yacht and is forced not to use it – his freedom has indeed been restricted. But Mr Morgan's private property rights prevent you from using the yacht for *365 days* in the year and force you not to use it (Cohen, 1979: 12). Capitalism – the exercise of private property rights – is a complex system of freedom and unfreedom. One could, of course, maintain that the difference between Mr Morgan's use of the yacht and your use of the yacht is precisely that it is *his* yacht; but then, we need to justify Mr Morgan's acquisition of the yacht – to say Mr Morgan ought to own the yacht because he does own that the yacht is a circular argument.

A more restricted defence of capitalism is then considered by Cohen: capitalists do not maintain that their preferred economic system promotes freedom in general, but merely economic freedom. Mr Morgan's property rights do not restrict your economic freedom, and a capitalist society is better able than any alternative to maximise *economic* freedom (Cohen, 1979: 14). To grasp Cohen's response, we need to refer back to the distinction between use value and exchange value:

a) If economic freedom is defined as the freedom to *use* goods and services, then it restricts freedom whenever it grants it – Mr Morgan's freedom to use his yacht corresponds to your unfreedom to use it.

b) If economic freedom is the freedom to buy and sell – that is, exchange products – then this looks better for capitalists, but is a restricted definition of economic freedom.

Is there then an alternative to capitalism and – crucially – one that increases freedom? Cohen gives a 'homespun' example. Persons A and B are neighbours, and each owns a set of household implements such as a lawnmower, saws, paintbrushes and so on. Each owns what the other lacks. We now imagine a rule is imposed, whereby when A is not using something he owns, B has the right to use it, just so long as he returns it when A needs it, and vice-versa. This communising rule will, Cohen maintains, increase implement-using freedom (Cohen, 1979: 16–17).

A capitalist response to this example would be that A and B could increase their implement-using freedom by entering a contract, either a kind of barter, or a money-based relationship. Cohen's counter-response is to argue that in the example A and B are roughly equal and therefore capable of entering a freedom-enhancing contract, but if you generalise across society, such equality does not exist. In fact, there is another response to Cohen, which appeals to efficiency and *indirectly* to freedom: while Cohen's argument is in many ways sound – capitalism entails unfreedom as well as freedom – one has to look at the empirical consequences of different economic systems. Cohen's 'homespun' example does not help because it is a very simple situation in which there are no communication problems. One argument for capitalism is that it avoids an excessively powerful state. The history of socialism has been characterised by an attempt to acquire the advantages of coordination associated with the market, while avoiding the inequalities generated by it.

## Cohen against Rawls

As we have seen, Rawls does not defend unregulated capitalism and advances a theory of justice that would entail a significant redistribution of income to the worst-off. What then is wrong with Rawls? There are three main Marxist objections:

1. Rawls has an incoherent model of human psychology (motivation).
2. Rawls restricts the principles of justice to the basic structure of society and that conceals exploitation.
3. Rawls rejects self-ownership as morally irrelevant to the distribution of resources. Curiously enough, on this point, Cohen sides with the 'right-wing' libertarian Nozick against Rawls.

The first two objections are closely related. People in the original position are motivated to maximise their share of the primary goods, but from behind a veil of ignorance, meaning that although they are self-interested, they are forced by the way the original position is set up to be impartial. Rational people will, Rawls argues, select the two principles of justice, including the difference principle, which entails maximising the position of the worst-off (maximin). The original position is intended to model how real people *could* behave. The difficulty is that the theory pulls in two different directions: on the one hand, Rawls assumes that we – that is, 'we' in the real world, and not in the original position – can develop a commitment to giving priority to the worst-off in society, and the difference principle is the structural device by which this is achieved. But how much the worst-off actually receive will depend on everyday human behaviour. Consider the distribution table on p. 139: under maximin, the richest quarter get 50 units and the poorest quarter get 20 units. Imagine you are in the top quarter. What motivations will you have in the real world, assuming you endorse Rawls's theory?

a)   You will be committed to giving priority to the worst-off and so will regard redistributive income tax as legitimate.
b)   You will be motivated to maximise your income.

These two motivations do not necessarily conflict if we assume – as Rawls does – that inequality generates incentives to produce and thus help the worst-off, but if you are really committed to helping the worst-off do you not have a moral duty to:

a)   Give *directly* – not just through tax – to the poor; and:
b)   Work to bring about a society in which the poorest earn more than 20 units?

Cohen borrows a slogan from the feminist movement: the 'personal is political' (Cohen, 2000: 122–3). How you behave in your personal life is a political issue. Rawls, along with most liberals, rejects this claim, arguing that the distinction between public and private is essential to a pluralistic society, and not all aspects of morality should be enforced by the state: while it is right to require people to pay taxes to help the worst-off, it is for individuals to decide what they do with their post-tax income. This may not resolve the tension that Cohen identifies between, crudely expressed, public generosity and private avarice, but the onus is on Cohen to explain the role of the state in 'encouraging' private generosity.

   This brings us to the second criticism, which relates to the basic structure argument. The rich fulfil their duties to the poor by accepting the legitimacy of taxation, and taxation is used to fund certain institutions, such as the pre-university education system, money transfers (social security, pensions, and so on), and healthcare. Outside the scope of the original position is a private sphere that includes the family. Rawls accepts that the family is a major source of inequality – the transmission from parent to child of privilege undermines equality of opportunity (Rawls 1972: 511; see p. 90) – but because liberty (the first principle of justice) takes priority over equality (the second principle), there has to be a legally protected private sphere. Not only is the private sphere a source of inequality, it also produces within itself inequality. Here, Cohen joins forces with feminist critics of Rawls: families are based on a division of labour, and one loaded against women, but because the recipient of redistribution is the household, and not the individual, there is a class of people – mostly women – who are worse off than that class which Rawls identifies as the 'worst-off'.

   Cohen argues that what Rawls includes in the basic structure is arbitrary – Rawls cannot give clear criteria for what should or should not be included. He cannot say that the basic structure consists of those institutions which are coercively enforced, that is, we are forced to fund through taxation because the basic structure is defined *before* we choose the principles of justice, whereas what is coercively enforced is a decision to be made in the original position (Cohen, 2000: 136–7). The basic Marxist point is this: Rawls assumes that human motivations are relatively constant – certainly, people can develop a moral consciousness, but they will remain self-interested. Motivations will always be a mix of self-interest and morality. Marxists reject this, maintaining that social structures determine how people behave.

We come, finally, to the third criticism. Marx argued that the workers do not get the full value of their labour. This argument assumes that there is something a person owns which generates a moral right to other things: in effect, as a Marxist, Cohen, along with Nozick (who is not a Marxist!), endorses Locke's mixed labour formula. What Cohen rejects is the idea that mixing your labour establishes merely first acquisition. For Locke and Nozick, once the world is divided into private property, the mixed labour formula ceases to be of any use. Cohen argues that a worker *constantly* mixes his labour, such that there is a *continuous* claim on the product. Locke's argument that 'the turfs my servant has cut are *my* turfs' is rejected by Cohen; insofar as the servant (worker) does not get the full value of his labour he is exploited, and the resulting distribution is unjust. Rawls implicitly rejects the notion of self-ownership; that does not mean we do not have rights over our bodies, but rather, we have no pre-social rights. The rights we have are the result of a choice made in the original position. This becomes clearer if we look at the concept of desert.

Desert is tied to effort: we get something if we do something. Rawls argues that because we are not responsible for our natural endowments – strength, looks, intelligence, personality traits – we cannot claim the product generated by those natural endowments. Under the difference principle, one person may earn 50 units and another 20 units, but not a single unit of that 30 unit difference is justified by reference to desert. Of course, in causal terms, the difference may be attributed, at least in part, to native ability, but that does not justify the difference. Rawls goes as far as to say that natural endowments are a social resource to be used for the benefit of the worst-off (Rawls, 1972: 179). It is strange that on desert Rawls is the radical, whereas Cohen sides with Nozick. It is true that Nozick does not believe that the rich are rich because they deserve to be rich – Wilt Chamberlain was rich because *other people chose to give him money* to play basketball – but the idea of self-ownership (private property rights) does imply a right to keep the fruit of your labour.

Whether you accept Cohen's argument against Rawls depends to some extent on whether you endorse Marx's labour theory of value. Many people would, however, follow Thomas Nagel in arguing that the value of a product is not the result of the amount of labour that went into it, but rather the other way round: the value of labour is the result of the contribution that labour makes to the product (Nagel, 1991: 99). Ask yourself this: if you have a firm making smartphones, which group of workers do you *least* want to lose: the canteen staff? Cleaners? Assembly line workers? Phone designers? Venture capitalists? It could be argued that the last two groups are the most important. The conclusion to be drawn is that if we want to justify an egalitarian distribution of wealth we need what Rawls attempts to offer, which is a moral justification that assumes that many of the poorest will get *more* than that to which their labour entitles them.

## Fair taxes

At the beginning of the chapter we listed eight types of taxation. We asked you to rank them from what you judged to be the fairest to the least fair and to provide reasons for your ranking.

You may agree with Nozick that all taxation is illegitimate. If Chamberlain's earnings were taxed then, according to Nozick, this is tantamount to forced labour (Nozick, 1974: 169). This is an exaggeration. If tax rates are published in advance, then Chamberlain can adapt his behaviour. This is a long way from slave labour, where you cannot predict how you will be treated. Furthermore, as we discuss in a later chapter (see pp. 209–10), Nozick defends a minimal state – one focused on providing security – and security has to be funded through what in effect is taxation.

Let us – for the sake of argument – accept that some taxation is justified and focus on the choice between different types. One complication of this exercise is that a particular tax might in itself be fair, but combined with another is quite unfair. For example, progressive income tax and estate tax, when combined would entail double-taxation of the same income. This might also apply to the combination of income tax and sales tax, although you could avoid the latter by not purchasing goods and services. Complexity is another consideration. Income tax may in itself be fair, but if the tax code is complicated, then the potential for avoidance is increased, and those who have the wherewithal to employ lawyers are at an advantage.

Beyond the double-taxation and complexity problems, we can focus on the effects of tax. For Rawls, progressive income taxes are fairer than sales taxes, as the latter are regressive – poorer people pay a greater proportion of their income in sales tax than do rich people. The *level* of tax is determined by its efficiency in raising the position of the worst-off. A famous argument of those opposed to significant redistribution is that high taxes simply reduce the tax yield and so benefit nobody. This is the famous Laffer Curve (Laffer, 2004). Rawls's difference principle entails raising tax to the point where the worst-off are as well off as possible and so provides a neat response to the Laffer Curve argument.

As suggested earlier, Rawls was increasingly concerned about the effects of redistribution on the taxed, who resent transferring their wealth to the poor, and on the recipients of transfers, whose self-respect is undermined by their dependence on state largesse. This had implications for which taxes should be employed. Under the influence of Meade, he argued that the aim should be to put people in a position where they have the human capital to get good jobs. In the long run, estate and wealth taxes are preferable to income tax. And inheritance tax is better than estate tax because it encourages the spread of wealth.

## Conclusion

We have discussed a range of theories of distributive justice, from egalitarian (Rawls and Meade) to anti-egalitarian 'right libertarianism' (Nozick), with 'left libertarianism' (Steiner) sharing some premises, such as self-ownership, with their rightist counterparts, but largely coming to egalitarian conclusions, due to the split between self-ownership and the ownership of things in the world. We also discussed a Marxist critique (Cohen) of Rawls and Nozick. The debate in political theory operates at a certain level of abstraction. It is not concerned with the nitty-gritty of socio-economic systems, but obviously, it cannot be entirely detached from the question of who owns what in the real world. Another limitation is that, traditionally, the debate has focused on the distribution of resources between individuals living under a state and not the global distribution of resources or economic relations between states. The concern with global justice is more recent and is discussed in Chapter 19.

## Note

1  The term social justice has within the last ten years acquired a specific, pejorative meaning – as in Social Justice Warrior (SJW) (Intellectual Takeout, 2018). Before then, although it had a left-wing hue, the term was mostly used by social democrats to indicate a relatively more distributive set of economic arrangements, and that is how we employ the term. Even the older term was, however, subject to criticism. Friedrich Hayek argued that justice was an individual virtue and made no sense when applied to social organisations (Lister, 2013).

## References

Carter, W. S. (1982). 'An Introduction to Henry George', in R. W. Lindholm and A. D. Jr. Lynn (eds.), *Land Value Taxation: The Progress and Poverty Centenary*, Madison, WI: University of Wisconsin Press, 19–31.

Cohen, G. A. (1979). 'Capitalism, Freedom, and the Proletariat', in A. Ryan (ed.), *The Idea of Freedom*. Oxford: Oxford University Press.

Cohen, G. A. (2000). *If You're An Egalitarian, How Come You're So Rich?* Cambridge, MA: Harvard University Press.

Hájek, A. (2003). Waging War on Pascal's Wager. *The Philosophical Review, 112*(1), 27–56.

Intellectual Takeout (2018). How the Term 'Social Justice Warrior' Became an Insult. *Intellectual Takeout*, viewed 2 June 2021. https://www.intellectualtakeout.org/article/how-term-social-justice-warrior-became-insult/

Laffer, A. B. (2004). The Laffer Curve: Past, Present, and Future. *Backgrounder, 1765*(1), 1–16.

Lister, A. (2013). The "mirage" of Social Justice: Hayek against (and for) Rawls. *Critical Review, 25*(3–4), 409–44.

Locke, J. (1988). *Two Treatises of Government*. Ed. P. Laslett, student edn. Cambridge: Cambridge University Press.

Meade, J. E. (2012). *The Intelligent Radical's Guide to Economic Policy: The Mixed Economy*. Abingdon and New York: Routledge.

Meade, J. E. (2013). *Efficiency, Equality and the Ownership of Property (Routledge Revivals)*. Abingdon and New York: Routledge.

Nagel, T. (1991). *Equality and Partiality*. New York: Oxford University Press.

Nozick, R. (1974). *Anarchy, State, and Utopia*. New York: Basic Books.

O'Neill, M. and Williamson, T. (2009). Property-owning Democracy and the Demands of Justice. Working Paper.

Rawls, J. (1972). *A Theory of Justice*. Oxford: Oxford University Press.

Rawls, J. (2001). *Justice as Fairness: A Restatement*. Cambridge, MA: Harvard University Press.

Steiner, H. (1974). The Natural Right to Equal Freedom. *Mind, 83*(330), 41–9.

Tax Foundation (2019). The Three Basic Tax Types. *Tax Foundation*, viewed 2 June 2021, https://files.taxfoundation.org/20210115115229/Tax-Basics-The-Three-Basic-Tax-Types.pdf

Thomas, D. L. (1995). *Routledge Philosophy Guidebook to Locke on Government*. London and New York: Routledge.

Williams, B. (1981). *Moral Luck: Philosophical Papers 1973–1980*. Cambridge: Cambridge University Press.

Wolff, J. (1991). *Robert Nozick: Property, Justice and the Minimal State*. Oxford: Polity Press.

## Further reading

The following are useful overviews: Jeppe Platz, *Theories of Distributive Justice: Who Gets What and Why* (Routledge, 2020); Michael Allingham, *Distributive Justice* (Routledge, 2014). A good collection is Serena Olsaretti (ed.), *The Oxford Handbook of Distributive Justice* (Oxford University Press, 2018). There are many commentaries on Rawls – this is a selection for students coming to Rawls for the first time: Thomas Pogge, *John Rawls: His Life and Theory of Justice* (Oxford University Press, 2007); Jon Mandle, *Rawls's 'A Theory of Justice': An Introduction* (Cambridge University Press, 2009); Paul Graham, *Rawls* (OneWorld:, 2015); Ruth Abbey (ed.), *Feminist Interpretations of John Rawls* (Pennsylvania State University Press, 2013); Samuel Freeman (ed.), *The Cambridge Companion to Rawls* (Cambridge University Press, 2002); Jon Mandle (ed.), *John Rawls: Debating the Major Questions* (Oxford University Press, 2020). On Nozick: Ralf Bader and John Meadowcroft (eds.), *The Cambridge Companion to Nozick's Anarchy, State, and Utopia* (Cambridge University Press, 2011); Alan Lacey, *Robert Nozick* (Routledge, 2014); Jonathan Wolff, *Robert Nozick: Property, Justice and the Minimal State* (Polity, 2013).

# Part 3

# Classical ideologies

# Chapter 9

# Liberalism

## Introduction

Liberalism has emerged as the world's dominant ideology, and much political debate takes place within liberal parameters. For liberals, freedom (liberty) is a fundamental value, and although a person's freedom can be limited – because it clashes with the freedom of others or with other values – what defines liberalism is the *presumption* that freedom is a good thing, meaning that limitations on freedom must be justified. A less obvious aspect of liberalism is its emphasis on equality, and again, the presumption is that people are equal. Although this appears to generate a major contradiction at the heart of liberalism – after all, the exercise of freedom will often lead to inequality – the two can (it is argued) be reconciled if we assume people are *morally* equal. Moral equality may be compatible with material, or social, inequality.

## Key questions

- What is liberalism?
- Is there one liberalism or many liberalisms?
- Can liberals believe in both freedom *and* equality?

## The meaning of liberalism

Liberalism has emerged as the world's dominant ideology. Europe provides a good example of the spread of liberal-democratic values and institutions: the 1970s saw the transition from right-wing, military regimes in Greece, Spain, and Portugal, and in 1989–91, the process of democratisation spread to Eastern Europe in the dramatic overthrow of state socialism from the Baltic states to Romania. While the depth of commitment at elite and popular levels to liberal-democratic values in the emergent democracies of Eastern Europe is a matter of much debate among political scientists, all these states and their leaders have at least until now subscribed to a liberal ideology, a recent exception being Hungarian leader Viktor Orbán, who in a 2014 speech advocated for what he termed 'illiberal democracy' (Tóth, 2014).

The very dominance of liberalism can make it a difficult ideology to grasp. In the history of political thought quite different bodies of thought are identified as 'liberal'. And, in popular, political discourse confusion can be caused when the term is applied to political parties,

DOI: 10.4324/9780429424106-13

Case study 9.1

# Should it be illegal to buy sex?

**PHOTO 9.1** Until its closure in 2020, the Pascha in Cologne, Germany, was the largest brothel in the world. © Hackenberg-Photo-Cologne/Alamy Stock Photo.

In 1998, the Swedish Parliament passed the Prohibition of the Purchase of Sexual Services Act. The law does what its title suggests: it prohibits the sale of sexual services. Most countries have legal controls on prostitution, which often include banning brothels, pimping, kerb-crawling, and advertising. The Swedish law tightened up on these aspects, but it achieved international attention because it went further than other European countries: it made it illegal to purchase or attempt to purchase 'casual sexual services'. The prohibition applied not only to street prostitution, brothels, and massage parlours but also to escort services or 'any other circumstances' in which sexual services are sold. Obviously, existing laws captured many of these aspects of prostitution, but the new law was a catch-all, and so quite radical. A crucial point was that the buyer, rather than the seller, was criminalised.

In contrast, the Netherlands has adopted a quite different approach: there, prostitution is defined as a profession, at least for those from European Union (EU) countries. Sex workers have access to welfare services and pay tax on their earnings. Whereas in Sweden prostitution is viewed primarily as violence against women, in the Netherlands, so long as coercion is not used, it is a voluntary exchange. Both Sweden and the Netherlands have long histories as liberal democracies, and in defending their respective policies, they draw on liberal arguments; yet, they come to quite different conclusions on the regulation of prostitution.

Which country has the right approach and why?

movements, or strands of thought *within* a liberal democracy. For example, many parties have the word 'liberal' in their name; in Canada, the Liberal Party is towards the left of the political spectrum, while in Australia, the Liberal Party is on the right. In many European countries, liberalism is associated with a strong commitment to the free market, whereas in the United States, the term denotes a belief in central – that is, federal – state intervention in society and the economy, and so 'liberals' are on the left. Clarification is sometimes provided by a qualifying adjective: *economic* liberalism or *social* liberalism. Occasionally, the term *classical* liberalism is employed to denote support for free trade and the free market.

Some distinctions will help to cut through the confusions of popular usage:

- *Justification* Political institutions can be described as 'liberal', but so can the method by which they are justified. Hobbes's defence of the state (see pp. 11–13) is a good example of this distinction. The institutions he defends appear highly illiberal but his method of justifying those institutions – contractarianism – is liberal. State authority is justified because we, as rational individuals, would calculate that it is in our interests to submit to it. Most of our attention in this chapter will be on the justification of institutions, with a particular focus on the problem of the state. As argued in Chapter 1, the state is by its nature coercive. If liberals are committed to freedom, then how is coercion justified? We offered some arguments in that first chapter, but liberals, historically, have been very conscious of the need to limit the state's role.

- *Constitution and policy* Turning to institutions, we can distinguish between the constitution and policy (or law-making). The constitution determines the procedure by which laws are passed, while to a large extent leaving open the content of those laws. Although there may be debate about the constitution, most people are implicitly liberal on the essentials of the constitution: the division of powers and the basic rights of individuals. They may not, however, support parties that describe themselves as liberal. The struggle between political parties normally operates *within* the constitution rather than being a battle over the constitution. In short, at the constitutional level, most of us are liberals, but at the policy level, this may not be the case.

- *Attitudes* There is a distinction between how political theorists have defended – justified – liberal principles and institutions, and popular attitudes to those institutions. Understanding such attitudes is primarily the focus of empirical political science, using quantitative methods such as surveys. Although we do not discuss it here, the work of political scientists provides a useful perspective on liberalism – if people find it difficult to endorse liberal values, then it should force liberals to reconsider how they defend liberal institutions.

Keeping these distinctions in mind, we offer a rough definition of liberalism. As the etymology of the word implies, liberals emphasise liberty (freedom). A less obvious aspect of liberal thought is its emphasis on equality – not necessarily material equality, but moral equality. A more precise definition of liberalism carries the risk of excluding from the liberal tradition important strands of thought. The best approach then is to look at a number of liberalisms. We discuss four: liberalism as neutrality (or *modus vivendi* liberalism), perfectionist liberalism, contractarianism (and contractualism), and utilitarianism. These are not mutually exclusive positions. There can be cross-fertilisation between them. For example, contractarianism can be combined with utilitarianism as well as with liberal neutrality, and there are perfectionist utilitarians. The two that are least combinable are perfectionism and neutrality. As a means of orientation, the perspectives can be summarised:

- *Neutrality* The state should as far as possible avoid taking a position on comprehensive views of the world, which can include both religious and secular systems of belief.

- **Perfectionism** The state should promote a set of values or ideals, centred on human autonomy. (There are non-liberal forms of perfectionism.)
- **Utilitarianism** The state should seek to maximise utility. (There are different definitions of utility.)
- **Contractarianism** The state (or political principles) can be modelled as the product of an agreement (contract) between individuals in a fair bargaining situation.

## Liberalism as neutrality

## The historical background

Liberalism is a body of ideas, but those ideas have a history. Many historians of political thought locate the origins of liberal discourse in the struggle for religious toleration generated by the Reformation and subsequent Wars of Religion. Although the term 'Wars of Religion' is sometimes reserved for a series of civil wars fought in France between 1562 and 1598, it can be used more widely to include the struggle of the Protestant Netherlands (United Provinces) to free themselves from Catholic Spain and the Thirty Years War (1618–48) in Germany.

Theological dispute centred on the nature of salvation, and the role of the church in offering, or perhaps even guaranteeing, salvation.[1] Simplifying somewhat, the Reformers ('Protestants') argued for a reduced role for the church (with the radical wing of the Reformation Movement almost eliminating the church). This, in turn, affected church-state relations, and more broadly, politics. The immediate impact was on the relationship of the secular and spiritual powers. In the longer term, the theological ideas generated by Reformed Christianity gave rise to secular equivalents. For example, the theological individualism of Protestantism was translated into a secular, philosophical individualism, which stressed individual responsibility.

Political power in mediaeval Europe was characterised by two overarching power structures. On the one side, there was the spiritual authority of the pontiff (Pope), and on the other, his secular equivalent, the Holy Roman Emperor. The latter was relatively weak, and most secular power resided in the nations and city-states. Nonetheless, the loyalties of individual citizens were split between the pontiff and the national (or local) secular powers.

Throughout the fourteenth century, there were continual pressures on the Church to reform itself, and this was expressed as a demand for a general council (a council of lay people) to discuss reform, a demand which was rejected. The religious intolerance that eventually hardened into war cannot be attributed to the Church of Rome's attempt to suppress dissent. Rather, the institutional break created a legitimation crisis for the secular authorities. In states where the prince (or elector) had embraced Lutheranism or Calvinism (two variants of mainstream Protestantism), the continuing allegiance of some of their citizens to Rome was a threat to the prince's authority. Conversely, where the prince had remained loyal to Rome but some of his subjects had embraced Reformed religion there was a loss of spiritual authority – an authority that had underwritten secular authority in the pre-Reformation period. In addition, the mediaeval division of spiritual and secular power had resulted in two sources of law, with much domestic law – for example, marriage law – the responsibility of church courts rather than secular courts. In Reformed states, the legitimacy of that domestic law was now in question.

The first Europe-wide attempt to address, rather than suppress, this conflict of loyalties was the Treaty of Augsburg (1555), which produced the formula: *cujus regio, eius religio* – loosely translated as 'the ruler determines the religion'. Two points should be made. First, it tolerated rulers and not individual citizens. Second, it was a mere *modus vivendi* – that is, a way of living together, but without any underlying respect for the other person's beliefs or way of life. It was a recognition of the reality of power: neither side could destroy the other, and it was in neither's interest for there to be continual war, so they agreed to disagree. However, once the balance of power shifted, the newly dominant side had no reason not to suppress the other. Not surprisingly, the Augsburg settlement proved unstable, and it took a century more of conflict before the so-called Peace of Westphalia (1648) created a new and relatively stable, European order. The Peace of Westphalia is the name given to a series of treaties that ended the last of the great wars of religion – the Thirty Years War (1618–48). It reaffirmed the formula of *cujus regio, eius religio*, but made some concession to toleration of individuals by respecting the beliefs of those resident in a particular territory prior to 1618.

## Toleration

The settlement of the Wars of Religion is credited with making toleration a central concept of political life and in the process, generating a body of political reflection and writing that can be described as liberal. The term toleration has, to twenty first century ears, a negative connotation. It suggests grudging acceptance rather than respect. However, toleration remains an important concept.

Toleration appears to require approving and disapproving of something at the same time. For example, person A:

1. believes that salvation can only be achieved by being a member of the Church (of Rome), so that outside the Church there can be no salvation, but:
2. accepts person B has the right to express her religious (or other) beliefs – person B is justified in not seeking salvation through the Church (of Rome).

The apparent tension between 1 and 2 is resolved if we recognise that they refer to different actions: 2 is not direct approval of person B's choices because that would contradict 1. The approval in 2 might be of B's capacity to make a choice ('might' because other reasons are possible). Nonetheless, there is still a tension between 1 and 2; what is required is a bridge between them.

One bridge could be the acceptance of the sheer fact of religious difference. This is the Augsburg *modus vivendi* argument applied to toleration of individuals: torture will not force (some) people to abandon their religious beliefs and practices, so it is both useless and politically destabilising to oppress them. Toleration grows out of recognition of this reality. But this is not really a justification for toleration – it does not provide reasons for toleration. To go beyond a *modus vivendi* person, A would have to find something in his own religious beliefs that enables him to accept B's dissent from those beliefs. In the history of the development of religious toleration in the sixteenth and seventeenth centuries, a range of such arguments were advanced. They included the following:

- *Latitudinarianism*: the belief in a minimal set of Christian doctrines and the acceptance of dissent beyond that minimum.
- *Catholicism* (in the generic sense): the importance of Christian unity over uniformity.
- *Christian choice*: God gives us a choice, and so we are not entitled to deny people choice.

The list is far from exhaustive. What is striking, however, is that there is assumed an underlying commitment to Christianity. Insofar as there was toleration in the sixteenth and seventeenth centuries it tended to be limited to Catholicism and the two major branches of the mainstream Reformation – Lutheranism and Calvinism. It was rarely extended to radical Reformers, Jews, and atheists.

In the eighteenth and nineteenth centuries, the circle of toleration is extended to include previously untolerated groups, and the justification of toleration shifts from religious to secular grounds. Here are a few secular arguments:

- *Scepticism*: it is impossible to prove the existence of God.
- *Progress*: humanity progresses if there is a competition of ideas.
- *Autonomy*: how we should behave can be determined rationally through the exercise of human reason.

Some contemporary theorists argue that these secular arguments are themselves intolerant and incompatible with a pluralistic society: scepticism is a rejection of religious belief, and autonomy, while not a rejection, cannot be endorsed by someone who believes revelation or natural law is the source for guidance on moral conduct. Because of this there has been a 'rediscovery' of *modus vivendi* toleration.

## Toleration as neutrality

Debates in political theory tend to come in waves, and in the 1980s there was much discussion of the idea of neutrality. The state should avoid as far as possible endorsing a particular conception of the good. The good can be contrasted with the right. These terms are attributed to Kant, but the precise definition was given by moral philosopher David Ross. He defined the right as 'that which is obligatory' and the good as 'that which is worth pursuing' (Ross, 1930: 3). There are many different forms of goodness: aesthetic evaluation, friendship, and the pursuit of truth are but a few.

For neutralists, because people disagree about the good, the state should not endorse or promote one conception over another. This does not mean liberalism lacks value, and of course we have the old problem of how you tolerate the intolerant, which is sometimes advanced as if it were a knock-down argument against liberalism. It is not. Neutrality means that *as far as possible* we remove a dispute from the scope of state power, not that the state can or should avoid all conflicts.

Think of a contentious issue, such as abortion, or same-sex marriage, or transgender rights, or gun ownership. How contentious a specific issue is will vary across countries, even between those categorised as liberal democracies. For example, gun ownership is an issue in the United States, but not so much in Europe. So pick an issue that is 'live' in your society and ask how – procedurally – it could be resolved. One strategy is to privatise it. While we disagree about the right thing to do, we agree that it is for individuals to decide – it should be treated as a private rather than a public matter. For example, while a person might believe that abortion is wrong, he accepts that a woman should have the right to choose whether or not to have an abortion. The right will be coupled with free speech, such that an opponent of abortion has the ability to communicate his opposition and seek to persuade women not to have an abortion.

However, abortion is problematic because the primary arguments against it are focused on the status of the foetus, and so we have a conflict of rights, which gets simplified into the slogans the 'right to life' versus the 'right to choose', or simplified even further to 'pro-life' and 'pro-choice'. It looks like we have an irreconcilable conflict. But all is not lost. We can try to identify areas of common agreement and also acknowledge the complexity within the 'pro-life' and 'pro-choice' camps. Some areas of agreement could be:

1. The foetus has (some) moral status.
2. The mother has moral status.
3. Women bear the greater burden of bringing children into existence.
4. The reasons for an abortion can vary in weight. For example, rape or the threat to the mother's life carries greater weight than other reasons for having an abortion.
5. Empirical evidence can play a part in assessing the status of the foetus as well as the effects of abortion on the mother.

The suggestion is not that all supporters and opponents of abortion will agree on the above, even in the deliberately loose, vague, and tentative way the reasons have been expressed. But rather that there can be some crossover between the 'two sides' (although that phrase misleadingly implies there are two monolithic positions). In the end, abortion may just be a hard issue, and different countries will tackle it in different ways, either through primary legislation, such as the UK's 1967 Abortion Act, or through judicial ruling, as in the 1973 *Roe v Wade* decision. But political debate is not just about the end result – whether abortion is legal or not – but how you reason your way to that result. If you are a protagonist in a political conflict, to what extent do you treat your opponents as reasonable people, whose arguments carry some weight (even if ultimately you reject those arguments or at least think there are stronger counter-arguments)?

John Rawls argues that reasonable people can disagree (Rawls, 1996: 56), and we face the 'fact of pluralism': 'no general and comprehensive view can provide a publicly acceptable basis for a political conception of justice' (1996: 4). Since there is a conflict of values, only oppression would ensure conformity to a single conception of the good. In a liberal society, stability is only possible on the basis of a broad consensus. But while there may exist disagreement about moral or theological truths, there can still be points of agreement. These include broad – not necessarily unanimous – agreement that most people are capable of developing plans for their lives, are able to reason about what they should do, and that they possess a sense of fairness, which allows for a significant degree of interpersonal trust.

What is important is that these ideas are not themselves derived from 'controversial' philosophical ideas. Indeed, this point explains the trigger for the 1980s debate over state neutrality. Rawls's 1971 book *A Theory of Justice*, which we discussed in Chapter 8, had a big impact. Some interpreted it as offering a comprehensive liberalism, one derived from just the kind of controversial ideas Rawls was later to reject. In subsequent publications, he stresses that liberalism should be 'political, not metaphysical' (Rawls, 1985). Take the idea of human autonomy, to which, as suggested above, many people in a liberal democracy attach value. When pressed why they subscribe to this idea, many different positions might be advanced. The most common could be that people behave as if they were responsible for their actions. More intellectually refined people might appeal to a Kantian conception of moral autonomy, or a utilitarian rational-choice model, or a theological idea derived from humans' relationship to God, or a belief in *moksha* and the breaking of the chains of *karma*. These are metaphysical beliefs. Political agreement should be built on what Rawls terms an 'overlapping consensus' (Rawls, 1987) between these beliefs: each person – the Kantian, the utilitarian, the Christian, and the Jain – need not give up her metaphysical beliefs but finds common ground with each of the others.

Joseph Raz objects to the overlapping consensus, arguing that it entails the promotion by the state of 'epistemic abstinence': the liberal state must act for good reasons but should not be concerned with the truth of the doctrine(s) which guides it (Raz, 1990: 4, 9). The overlap just looks like an accident, much like the fortuitous balance of power in seventeenth century Europe. So, Rawls must do two seemingly incompatible things: demonstrate that liberalism is valuable in its own terms – for example, that freedom is a good – and yet ensure citizens can accept liberal values without giving up their own religious or metaphysical beliefs.

He does suggest that liberalism is valuable in itself, but there is a stage at which citizens – perhaps through socialisation into the political culture – take up liberal values and fit them into their own comprehensive conception of the good (Rawls, 1996: 12–13). While he never gives specific examples, we can illustrate this with the case of Muslims in a liberal democracy. What we need to show is how liberalism can be compatible with Islam by focusing on different aspects of Islam and working out whether or not they are compatible with liberalism (Graham, 2015: 151–3):

| Concept | Incompatible with liberalism | Compatible with liberalism |
| --- | --- | --- |
| Dar-al-Islam versus dar-al-harb | Intolerance of non-Muslims. | Third concept: dar-al-Sulh. Liberal society? |
| Shariah | Totalitarian – no respect for the private sphere. | Secular law only has to be compatible with Shariah. |
| Islam as submission | Conflicts with autonomy. | Self-imposed discipline. |
| Jihad | Violence towards non-believers. | Spiritual struggle. |
| Behaviour as: (a) required; (b) prohibited; (c) recommended; (d) discouraged; (e) morally indifferent. | (b) Raises difficulties. Alcohol consumption; illicit sex. | Prohibited actions could receive 'spiritual punishment'. |
| Attitude towards women | Gender inequality. | Largely symbolic and modesty is also expected of men. |

On a neutralist theory, Muslims cannot be told how to interpret their religious beliefs, but liberal theory can work with people from diverse backgrounds to map the overlap between them, and by doing so, people become conscious of what they share. That new awareness is itself valuable.

## Liberal perfectionism

To perfect means to complete or to achieve to a maximal extent. In reality, humans often have to trade off different goods, such that it is conceptually impossible to achieve perfection. For example, you might seek to be the best lawyer you possibly can be, but in so doing you sacrifice a family life, which is also a good. If you make trade-offs between career and family, then you cannot perfect either, even if a life based on trade-offs is better than monomaniacal commitment.

Neutralists do not reject perfectionism as a non-political ideal. Indeed, the aim is to create a state structure in which people are free to engage in valuable pursuits and ways of life. However, perfectionists attack neutrality in one of two ways: either by arguing that there are goods the state ought to promote, or that, in fact, the 'neutral' state is not neutral because it places value on consensus and reasonable disagreement, which themselves are values. Furthermore, the logic of Rawlsian neutrality, with its emphasis on reasonable disagreement, is that the state could endorse a conception of the good if there were agreement. Imagine everybody subscribed, without coercion, to the same set of religious beliefs. While reasonable people *could* reject that religion, *as a matter of fact*, they do not. That said, agreement to a single position is not the same thing as perfectionism, for the latter holds there are things that are valuable even if nobody recognises such value, so this second objection fails. The charge that neutralists place (excessive) value on consensus nonetheless stands and illustrates for perfectionists the absurdity of the (supposedly) neutral state.

There are, it should be noted, non-liberal forms of perfectionism. In Chapter 5, we discussed Nietzsche's critique of moral equality (see pp. 83–4), and although contemporary interpreters have put a liberal gloss on his argument, it is essentially a rejection of liberalism. A *liberal* perfectionism would emphasise not only that each person is capable of achieving value but that he or she should also be encouraged to do so. We do not exist to serve great men and there is no natural hierarchy. Furthermore, liberal perfectionism need not be competitive or conflictual. For example, if knowledge is a public good, meaning that it is non-rivalrous – there is no limit to the number of people who can consume knowledge (see pp. 13–14) – then the pursuit of learning is not competitive. With the development of the internet this may well be true, although there is still competition in the production of knowledge, and the desire to impress others with your intellectual prowess also generates conflicts.

Both liberal and non-liberal perfectionists maintain that some ways of life are more valuable than others. This contrast with a preference-based conception of the good – goodness here defined as the maximisation of the satisfaction of preferences. Perfectionists argue that some preferences are bad, so that we cannot equate goodness with preference-satisfaction. But there is a distinction between monists and pluralists, and preferences may still play some role in determining value. Monists maintain that there is a single set of goods, whereas pluralists hold that what is good for one person may not be good for another, in part because we are born with different aptitudes. A person with athletic ability – cardiovascular strength and spatiovisual ability – should pursue sport, while a person with good interpersonal skills, such as empathetic identification, would be better advised to enter a caring profession. Of course, there may be generic values common to both, such as conscientiousness, and so part of defining what is valuable is deciding what level of generality is being applied when judging whether a way of life is valuable.

A particular focus of liberal perfectionism is human autonomy. This is closely related to, but not identical with, freedom. Autonomy is independence, but also self-unity: you see your life as a whole and are capable of putting together a plan for it. You do not focus on one set of preferences or treat preferences in an additive fashion, but you think about how everything fits together and how preferences interact. A perfectionist concerned with autonomy would very likely rule out selling yourself into slavery, as Mill argued (see p. 105). Although Mill is a utilitarian, there are perfectionist elements in his defence of liberty – he argues that individuality is valuable (Mill, 1991: 62–82). The problem is that while Mill explicitly rejects paternalism, the logic of treating autonomy as a good is that you have duties to yourself – negative duties not to harm yourself, such as signing a slavery contract, and positive duties to develop your autonomous capacities.

Neutralists think that perfectionism is both self-defeating and an illegitimate use of state power. It is self-defeating insofar as autonomy implies desire: if you are forced to do something against your will, then this does not seem like independence in judgement and action. Perhaps, the idea is that people through coercion can acquire autonomy. This is often an aim of education, but there the focus is on children and not adults, so using state power to encourage certain habits of thought in adults – so as to 'become autonomous' – is problematic. A less coercive form of perfectionism is the funding of things the existence of which are valuable. An example would be state subsidy of the arts. Simply giving money to theatres and orchestras seems non-coercive – after all, you are not forcing people to go to the theatre or the concert hall. However, you are taxing people to fund these things and that is coercive. What is more, by shaping the public environment – subsidising the arts – the state is manipulating people's choices.

# Utilitarianism

Utilitarians hold that political institutions function to increase the overall level of welfare – or utility – of a society. At first sight, this appears incompatible with a liberal emphasis on individual freedom and equality: utility-maximisation implies that there is a thing called 'society', which has aims over and above those of individuals, or that the aims and interests of individuals are subsumed in 'society'. While there are tensions between utilitarianism and individualism, there are shared historical roots, and most utilitarians argue that no one person's utility should take priority over that of another. So utilitarians, in common with other liberals, do endorse moral equality.

The claim that utilitarianism entails the maximisation of utility requires elaboration: what is utility? How do we maximise it? What does utilitarianism require of individuals? Different utilitarian thinkers have defined utility in different ways: Jeremy Bentham defined it as pleasure or the avoidance of pain (Kahneman, Wakker and Sarin, 1997: 375) as did J.S. Mill (Mill, 1991: 137), whereas in contrast G.E. Moore argued that the whole can be more than the sum of the parts (Skelton, 2019: 301), and this position has been dubbed ideal-utilitarianism. All these definitions conceptualise utility as something experiential – a feeling or state of mind. This raises an epistemological question: how do we know someone is happy, or feeling pleasure, or has the right state of mind? Contemporary utilitarians avoid the epistemological question by defining utility as preference-satisfaction. This has the advantage that there are available real-world systems for ordering preferences: voting and markets. When we cast a vote or buy a pair of shoes, other people can see we are expressing a preference – they do not need access to our state of mind.

To maximise utility, we must measure it, and two options are available: either we add up instances of utility (cardinal measurement) or we rank instances of it (ordinal measurement). The definition of utility affects how we go about measuring it: experiential definitions lend themselves to cardinal measurement, while preference-satisfaction fits best with ordinal measurement. In fact, it was the difficulty of measuring pleasure or happiness that led to a shift to defining utility as preference-satisfaction.

We now come to the third – and most obviously political – question: if we are utilitarians, how should we behave, and more specifically, what justifies the use of coercion by the state? There are some common criticisms of utilitarianism:

- What makes people happy, gives them pleasure, or what they prefer is completely open: if torturing another person gives you pleasure, then it must be counted into the maximand (that which is to be maximised).
- We cannot respect the law if breaking it will increase utility.
- Utilitarians cannot respect individual rights – Mill's attempt to establish a 'sphere of non-interference' (rights) on the basis of utility-maximisation is incoherent.
- One person could be made to suffer excruciating pain so as to give a million people each a minuscule amount of pleasure. A less extravagant criticism is that utilitarians cannot be concerned about the distribution of welfare, but merely its overall level.
- You are as much responsible for what you allow to happen as what you do in a more direct sense of doing. For example, given the choice between (a) killing one person and 'allowing' 19 to live or (b) 'standing by' while all 20 are killed, utilitarianism requires you to kill that one person (Williams and Smart, 1973: 98–9).

These criticisms are dismissed by utilitarians as unrealistic. The way to avoid them, it is claimed, is to distinguish between direct and indirect utilitarianism. Direct utilitarianism – or 'act utilitarianism' – requires that you seek to maximise utility on every occasion. Indirect utilitarianism, which includes 'rule utilitarianism' and 'institutional utilitarianism', separates action and justification: what we should do is follow rules, such as respecting individual rights, and the consequence of doing so is that utility will be maximised. Institutional utilitarianism is compatible with contractarianism: in the contract situation, we agree to a set of institutions, the operation of which will maximise utility. We applied this idea to punishment in chapter 3 (see pp. 51–2).

There is no doubt that since the early nineteenth century, utilitarianism has developed in sophistication. However, our concern is with the relationship of utilitarianism to the other types of liberalism. What makes utilitarianism liberal?

a)   Utilitarians reject 'natural authority'. Utilitarianism developed out of a secular, natural–scientific, world view. The calculability of pleasure or happiness fits neatly with the rise of science and the rejection of the idea that there are forces beyond human consciousness.
b)   Utilitarians still hold to the liberal presumption in favour of freedom and the presumption of natural equality. People are free to express their preferences, and coercion is only justified to bring about the greatest good. And people are equally generators of utility – Mill attributed this formula to the earlier utilitarian thinker Jeremy Bentham: 'each to count for one and nobody for more than one' (Mill, 1991: 198–9).
c)   In concrete political terms, utilitarians have invariably been progressive or radical in their attitudes to social problems.
d)   Most important of all, utilitarianism grew in parallel with the development of democracy. The high point of utilitarian thought was the nineteenth century, although it continued to be the dominant philosophical method for justifying political principles until the 1960s' when there was a revival in contractarianism, and remains a central philosophical position. The decline of contract thinking around 1800 went hand in hand with scepticism about using the contract – actual or hypothetical – to explain political obligation in a *mass* society. Utilitarianism seemed to provide a much more convincing method of justification in democratic societies: the calculation of utility dovetails with the counting of votes, although it was only in the twentieth century, with the development of preference-satisfaction as the definition of utility, that a more direct link between utilitarianism and democracy was established.

## Contractarianism

We have discussed contractarian theories in previous chapters. Hobbes's derivation of the state is contractarian (see pp. 11–13), as is Rousseau's (see pp. 14–15). Rawls's theory of justice is also contractarian, and he clearly situates his theory in that tradition, although he makes the interesting observation that 'for all its greatness, Hobbes's *Leviathan* raises special problems' (Rawls, 1972: 11). Hobbes is a problem because while his method is eminently compatible with liberalism – we contract into the state because it is in our individual interest to do so – the outcome is anything but liberal. But putting to one side the ambivalent status of Hobbes's contract theory – and perhaps also Rousseau's idea that we can be forced to be free – most contract theorists are squarely within the liberal tradition.

Liberal or not, all contract theories have three main stages:

1. An initial bargaining situation (the state of nature in Hobbes and Locke; the original position in Rawls).
2. An outline of the procedure for either submitting to a state or agreeing to a certain set of coercively enforced political principles – this is the 'contract';
3. A description of what is chosen – the state, political institutions, or political principles (such as principles of justice).

Contract theory holds that we can gain from cooperation, and it is rational to sign up to the contract. This assumes that we can measure gains and losses – there is a 'currency', utility for example, or defined resources such as primary goods (see p. 136). It also assumes a degree of interdependence. For Hobbes, you only have reason to enter an agreement with another person if he can affect your interests, for better or worse. For example, if he can kill you, then you have a reason to negotiate with him. Given the need for Leviathan to be effective, the group of bargainers will be quite large, such as the whole of England. But in the seventeenth century, a person in China or Africa would have no effect on your fate, and so he is not part of the bargaining group. Today, this claim would be controversial, and we will return to it in our discussion of global justice (see p. 343).

We argued at the start of the chapter that liberalism can be approached at different levels. We outlined three: justification, constitution (or institutions), and attitudes. Contract theories differ in what comes out of the contractual process; that is, what constitutional arrangements are chosen. There is Hobbes's all-powerful Leviathan (which we have suggested is not liberal), Rousseau's general assembly (which might be), and Rawls's two principles of justice (which are). But there is also the level of justification, and for contract theorists, the initial bargaining conditions are crucial. How you set up the bargaining situation will determine what comes out of it. Rawls calls his theory 'justice as fairness' because he claims that the principles of justice are indeed just precisely because they emerge from a starting point – the original position – that is fair. On the other hand, Hobbes's starting point is the desire for self-preservation and the fear of death, so that, in effect, threat advantage determines the outcome. This contrasts not only with Rawls's 'justice as fairness' but also with a thinker closer in time to Hobbes – Locke.

## Locke

Most courses in the history of political thought link together Hobbes and Locke and compare and contrast their contract theories. A simplistic comparison would describe Locke's state of nature as a rather less unpleasant place than the Hobbesian equivalent, and this affects their attitude to the contract, and to the rights individuals should enjoy under the state. Locke, for example, thinks that we have a right to rebel against the state, whereas Hobbes rejects such a right. But these superficial differences conceal more significant ones, such that it is possible to say that Locke was not simply the next in line in the contract tradition, but articulated a distinct stream of contractarian thought, one which emphasised moral rights. This idea had a huge impact not only on political thought in Locke's native England but also, and perhaps especially, in the United States.

Hobbes maintained that people were free and equal in the state of nature, and there existed natural laws. Locke offers a similar description of the state of nature, but his understanding of freedom, equality, and natural law is quite different to that of Hobbes:

- Hobbes's liberty is simply the absence of restraint, whereas Locke's liberty takes the form of actionable rights.
- Hobbes understood equality in naturalistic rather than moral terms: the weakest can kill the strongest, so we are equally vulnerable. For Locke, we are equal because no person has a natural right to subordinate another.
- Unlike Hobbes's laws of nature, Locke's laws have a theological basis – we have a natural duty to preserve ourselves, a duty owed to God, who created us.

For Locke, moral rights precede the contract to create a state, and the role of the state is to settle disputes over the interpretation of those rights and ensure that violations of the rights are punished. The most important among the rights are those to private property, which are an extension of rights in one's body. Self-ownership is, however, derivative of God's right, as creator, in his creatures.

Economic and social life is possible in the state of nature. People can enter contracts – that is, exercise their powers – and individuals have the right to enforce them. Furthermore, at an early stage in the economic development of society, individuals are materially satisfied – they do not compete for scarce resources. Only later, with a rise in population, does the problem of scarcity emerge (Locke, 1988: 297–8).

What makes the state of nature 'inconvenient' is the absence of a body that can *authoritatively* determine when rights have been violated and *effectively* enforce a remedy (Locke, 1988: 329–30). Hobbes was obsessed with effectiveness, but as there was no pre-contractual law in Hobbes's state of nature there was nothing to adjudicate. Because individuals in Locke's state of nature have the capacity to recognise the moral law, and the state is created as a judge and enforcer, it follows that should the state fail in these tasks individuals are justified in rebelling against it (see pp. 64).

There is much that is anachronistic in Locke. His claim that Native Americans do not possess property because they cannot recognise natural law, and thus America was 'unowned' (Locke, 1988: 293), is an embarrassment to contemporary defenders of Locke, as his defence of slavery (Uzgalis, 2017). Also, the Christian basis of his thought is problematic in modern, pluralistic societies, although his appeal to natural law does provide a route to a secularised notion of human rights. However, overall, Locke made key contributions to liberal thought:

a)  The idea that there are what Robert Nozick calls 'side constraints' which limit what the state, or society in general, can do to human beings (Nozick, 1974: ix).
b)  That natural (or moral) rights provide a standpoint from which we can judge the state. Unlike Hobbes, obligation to obey the state is not for Locke an all-or-nothing matter. Although we give up a certain degree of moral judgement when we contract into the state, we do not hand over all our autonomy.
c)  There is much more discussion of the institutions of liberal democracy in Locke than in Hobbes and that discussion has been hugely influential. Locke is identified as a key influence on the formation of the American Constitution.

Overall, contractarianism has been an influential strand in liberalism, but we need to distinguish two ideas: (a) that it is derived entirely from self-interest and (b) that it presupposes certain moral ideas – constraints on the pursuit of self-interest. As we have discussed elsewhere, we face a prisoner's dilemma (see pp. 11–12): it is rational to break agreements. Knowing that, nobody would make an agreement unless they were guaranteed that others will comply. We have to split the prisoner's dilemma into two problems: the bargaining problem – how an agreement is reached, and the compliance problem – how and why the agreement is maintained.

## Liberals and sex workers

We began this chapter with a discussion of anti-prostitution laws in Sweden, and especially the prohibition on the purchase of sexual services. This may have seemed an odd case study to head a chapter on liberalism, but it reveals tensions within liberal thought, especially when the Swedish policy is compared to the Dutch one. A number of arguments have been advanced by the Swedish government for the law (Gender Equality, 2016):

1. Human trafficking is a violation of human rights. Of those trafficked, 80% are women and children.
2. Demand is the key driver for prostitution, and the law is intended to reduce it.
3. In a transaction for sexual services, the seller is the weaker party in the bargaining process.
4. A report published in 2010 assessed the first ten years of the policy and found that prostitution had been halved in that time.
5. That report also highlighted a change in attitudes among people towards prostitution, with now much greater hostility than had previously been the case. Support for the law stood at 72%.
6. Those who have left prostitution say that 'criminalisation of [the] purchase of sexual services has made them stronger'. And they claim that there is no such thing as voluntary prostitution: 'the buyer always has the power and the people selling their bodies are always the ones being exploited'.

The first point to make is that critics of the law would argue for a distinction between public and private: it is possible to disapprove of prostitution but believe that consenting adults should have the right to make choices. This is a development of the argument for toleration, but extended far beyond religious toleration. It may appear that the Swedish state has simply rejected toleration, but, in fact, the language used to justify the law is an implicit acknowledgement that the limitation on the purchaser's freedom requires justification. Points 3 and 6 claim that prostitution does not entail consent. The power imbalance between prostitute and client is, they claim, so great that the former cannot be deemed to be a consenting adult. Obviously, one can disagree with this assessment, but the debate over the harm caused by prostitution, and whether prostitutes can really consent, is fought out in liberal terms.

Several of the arguments – points 2, 4, and 5 – reference the good *consequences* of banning the sale of sexual services. It is often commented that Sweden has a particularly strong idea of the 'common good', and this has resulted in laws which seem to impinge on individual freedom. There are a number of reasons for this, one being the dominance of the centre-left Social Democrats in post-war Sweden. The general point is that utilitarian – or consequentialist – reasoning is clearly evident in the justification for the anti-prostitution law.

The Swedish state is using its coercive power to motivate people and change attitudes and thus to bring about a 'good' state of affairs. For a rights-based, Lockean, liberal this is an illegitimate extension of state power. And it is important to distinguish the motivation argument from the harm argument. A defender of rights-based liberalism might accept that prostitutes cannot consent, and so buying their services is a form of harm and should be illegal, but motivating people – that is, changing their attitudes – even if it were successful, would be incompatible with moral autonomy.

In the Netherlands, by contrast, prostitution is accepted as a fact, and the task is to manage it in order to avoid its worst consequence. Although toleration of prostitution may seem a long way from religious toleration, the Dutch policy implicitly draws on a tradition that has deep roots in the Netherlands: *modus vivendi* liberalism. Although they have broken down, until relatively, recently, Dutch society was characterised by 'pillarisation' (*verzuiling*), whereby social institutions were vertically divided between Protestants, Catholics, and 'social-democrats' (embracing the 'secular'). That meant that Catholics had their own political parties, schools, universities, newspapers, TV stations, and trade unions, and this was, likewise, the case for the other two pillars. Whether this constituted a pure *modus vivendi* or whether there were moral and political values underlying all pillars and guaranteeing social stability is a matter of debate. Nonetheless, in contrast to Sweden – with its powerful social democratic and egalitarian ethos – the Netherlands has always been more willing to *tolerate* moral, religious, and political difference.

## Conclusion

At the heart of liberalism is the belief that people are naturally free and equal. That does not mean that there are no limitations on freedom, or that people must be equal, or treated equally, in all respects. Rather, we are presumed to be free and equal, and departures from freedom and equality require justification. Viewed historically, liberalism developed out of the settlement of the Wars of Religion, with the emphasis on toleration of religious difference. Such toleration was gradually extended beyond the sphere of religion to other aspects of belief and lifestyle. Several strands of liberalism emerged after the seventeenth century, and we have identified four: liberalism as neutrality, perfectionism, utilitarianism, and contractarianism. Although there are significant philosophical differences between them, they are all clearly part of the 'liberal family'. Much of the left–right debate in contemporary politics operates around different interpretations of liberalism.

## Note

1   For a discussion of the theological issues, see McGrath (1988).

## References

Gender Equality (2016). Gender Equality Policy in Sweden, *Government Offices of Sweden*, viewed 26 November 2021. https://www.government.se/4a7738/contentassets/efcc5a15ef154522a872d8e46ad69148/gender-equality-policy-in-sweden

Graham, P. (2015). *Rawls*. Oxford: Oneworld.

Kahneman, D., Wakker, P. P., and Sarin, R. (1997). Back to Bentham? Explorations of Experienced Utility. *The Quarterly Journal of Economics, 112*(2), 375–406.

Locke, J. (1988). *Two Treatises of Government*. Ed. Peter Laslett. Cambridge: Cambridge University Press.

McGrath, A. (1988). *Reformation Thought: An Introduction* Oxford: Blackwell.

Mill, J.S. (1991). *On Liberty and Other Essays*. Ed. J. Gray. Oxford: Oxford University Press.

Nozick, R. (1974). *Anarchy, State, and Utopia*, New York: Basic Books.

Rawls, J. (1972). *A Theory of Justice*. Oxford: Oxford University Press.

Rawls, J. (1985). Justice as Fairness: Political not Metaphysical. *Philosophy and Public Affairs*, *14*(3), 223–51.

Rawls, J. (1987). The Idea of an Overlapping Consensus. *Oxford Journal of Legal Studies*, 7, 1.

Rawls, J. (1996). *Political Liberalism*. New York: Columbia University Press.

Raz, J. (1990). Facing Diversity: The Case of Epistemic Abstinence. *Philosophy & Public Affairs*, *19*(1), 3–46.

Ross, W. (1930). *The Right and the Good*. Oxford: Oxford University Press.

Skelton, A. (2019). 'Late Utilitarian Moral Theory and Its Development: Sidgwick, Moore', in J. Shand (ed.), *A Companion to Nineteenth-Century Philosophy*. Oxford: Wiley-Blackwell, 281–310.

Tóth, C. (2014). Full Text of Viktor Orbán's Speech at Băile Tuşnad (Tusnádfürdő) of 26 July 2014. *The Budapest Beacon*, viewed 6 June 2021, https://budapestbeacon.com/full-text-of-viktor-orbans-speech-at-baile-tusnad-tusnadfurdo-of-26-july-2014/

Uzgalis, W. (2017). 'John Locke, Racism, Slavery, and Indian Lands', in *The Oxford Handbook of Philosophy and Race*. New York: Oxford University Press, 21.

Williams, B. and Smart, J.J.C. (1973). *Utilitarianism: For and Against*. Cambridge: Cambridge University Press.

## Further reading

Broad discussions: John Charvet, *Liberalism: The Basics* (Routledge, 2018); Edmund Fawcett, *Liberalism: The Life of an Idea* (Princeton University Press, 2018); Michael Freeden, *Liberalism: A Very short Introduction* (Oxford University Press, 2015); Alan Ryan, *The Making of Modern Liberalism* (Princeton University Press, 2014); Jonathan Quong, *Liberalism without Perfection* (Oxford University Press, 2020). On utilitarianism: Robert Goodin, *Utilitarianism as a Public Policy* (Cambridge University Press, 2010); Ben Eggleston and Dale Miller (eds.), *The Cambridge Companion to Utilitarianism* (Cambridge University Press, 2014); Tim Mulgan, *Understanding Utilitarianism* (Routledge, 2007). On contractarianism: Stephen Darwall (ed.), *Contractarianism/Contractualism* (John Wiley, 2002); Michael Moehler, *Contractarianism* (Cambridge University Press, 2020).

# Chapter 10

# Conservatism

## Introduction

Conservatism is an elusive ideology. Although there are conservative streams of thought in parties and movements calling themselves 'conservative', the main ideology of these movements is a combination of liberalism and nationalism, with the former particularly dominant. There are far fewer 'small c' than 'big c' conservatives. Yet, despite its marginalisation, conservatism is a distinct ideology, and conservative thinkers present arguments of continuing relevance. Above all, conservatives challenge the idea that society can be planned in a rational way without regard to tradition and historical experience. This core idea leads them to support national institutions, but not radical nationalism; individual liberty against state power, but not the natural rights that many liberals defend; spontaneous order, but not anarchism; community, but not socialist collectivism.

## Key questions

- What is conservatism?
- There are political parties with conservative in their name, but are there any genuine conservatives?
- Does conservatism provide a political blueprint or is it just a style of argument?

## Conservatism: an elusive ideology?

Anybody with a basic knowledge of party politics, but coming to political theory for the first time, may assume that 'conservatism' is simply the ideology of political parties calling themselves 'conservative' such as the Conservative Party in Britain or the Conservatives in Canada. However, an analysis of the aims and policies of these parties would suggest that their ideological make-up is hybrid and changeable. Take the British Conservative Party, which was during the twentieth century the most electorally successful 'conservative' party in the world; its ideology shifted to such an extent that under Margaret Thatcher (British Prime Minister, 1979–90), it would be best described as 'national liberal'. The Thatcher government was economically liberal: it extended the use of market mechanisms in the domestic arena and pursued a pro-free trade policy in the international sphere. It was 'national' in that emphasis was placed on the restoration

DOI: 10.4324/9780429424106-14

## Case study 10.1

## Reforming the House of Lords

**PHOTO 10.1** © Jack Hill - WPA Pool/Getty Images.

Only the United Kingdom, Tonga, and Lesotho have hereditary members in their parliaments. Only Iran and the United Kingdom have seats reserved for representatives of the state religion (Garland, 2018). The House of Lords is the only upper chamber of a bicameral parliament to be larger than the lower chamber. In size, it is second only to the Chinese National People's Congress.

Reform of the Lords has been a political issue for over 100 years. The Liberal Government at the turn of the twentieth century oversaw the passage of the 1911 Parliament Act, which removed the right of the Lords to veto finance bills, and only allowed delaying powers for other legislation. In the preamble to the Act, it is stated that it is intended 'to substitute for the House of Lords as it at present exists a Second Chamber constituted on a popular instead of hereditary basis, but such substitution cannot be immediately brought into operation' (Parliament Act 1911).

It was only in 1999 that the hereditary principle was removed, and most existing hereditary lords (peers) removed. However, there are still 83, along with 678 life peers and 25 bishops of the Church of England. Legislation requires the approval of the elected chamber (Commons), the Lords (which has only delaying powers, except over the extension of the term of life of the Commons, which it can veto), and the monarch, who must give Royal Assent (last denied in 1708).

To most people outside the United Kingdom, and a large proportion of the British population, the idea of having hereditary members of the legislature seems bizarre (notwithstanding popular support for a hereditary Head of State). But is there a case for the hereditary principle? And what is the correct approach to parliamentary reform? How fast or slow should you go with change? Should Lords reform be reversed – why not bring back the hereditary peers?

of national pride after what was perceived to be a policy of 'managed decline' in the period 1945–79. Although parties carrying the name 'liberal' tend to have a stronger social dimension, maintaining that welfare provision is necessary to enable people to live autonomous lives, social liberalism and economic liberalism are members of the same ideological family. They are not conservative.

If the Thatcher government was not really conservative, then what is conservatism? Etymology can mislead, but it is useful to start with the word 'conservative'. The idea of 'conservation' or 'preservation' suggests that conservatives stand opposed to progress. An earlier Conservative Prime Minister, Robert Gascoyne-Cecil, the 3rd Marquess of Salisbury (1830–1903), held to the credo that 'whatever happens will be for the worse, and therefore it is in our interest that as little should happen as possible' (Roberts, 2012: 328). Not coincidentally, the leading conservative journal, *The Salisbury Review*, is named in his honour.

But conservatives can be progressive. What is distinctive about conservatism is its attitude – progress must be careful, tentative, respectful of past practices, pragmatic, and go with the grain of human nature. If conservatism has an enemy, it is 'rationalism' – an approach to political problems derived from the application of abstract concepts. Quite often, conservative thinkers appear to reject abstract thought altogether, with the consequence that it is difficult to talk of a conservative political *theory*. However, it is still possible to identify features of conservative thought that allow us to describe conservatism as a distinct ideology.

## Basic elements of conservatism

As with all ideologies, there are significant differences between thinkers and streams of thought, but there are also some common themes in conservatism. We can start with the most philosophical of the elements and gradually move to the more concrete, political ones:

1. *Rejection of 'rationalism'* Conservatives often use the metaphor of a ship at sea to explain their objections to what they call 'rationalism': you are at sea and your ship develops a fault, which if not dealt with will result in the ship sinking. The 'ship' is the state, or the set of political institutions that make up the state, while the 'sea' is society or culture in the widest sense. The 'fault' is a metaphor intended to illustrate the stresses and strains that political institutions frequently face. Rationalism would entail analysing – or breaking down – the ship into its components in the hope of understanding the source of the fault and so rectifying it. The conservatives' point is not hard to discern: we cannot deconstruct the ship while at sea, but we must do something about the fault or we will sink.

2. ***Experience matters*** Continuing with the metaphor of the ship, our response to the fault must be based on experience and, if necessary, a cautious process of trial and error. The 'conservatism' of conservatives rests not on irrational veneration of the past but on recognition of the limits of human reason, and this is why conservatives can be progressive and embrace change. What they fear are radical experiments: human beings cannot adequately predict the full consequences of their actions and while some experiments may make the world a better place we cannot be sure they will.

3. ***Human nature*** While there are some marked differences within conservative thought concerning human behaviour, capabilities, and motivation, there is a broad agreement that human beings are limited in their capacity to comprehend the society in which they live. This does not mean that humans are stupid, but rather, that no individual mind can understand the complexity of social relations, and there is no 'supermind' capable of doing so. Here, the conservative critique of socialism is most apparent: socialist planning presupposes a mind capable of making complex economic decisions. Socialism is doomed to failure because it is inefficient, and – perhaps more worryingly – requires a concentration of power in the hands of the state. Conservatives tend to support the free market on grounds that the distribution of goods depends on the decisions made by millions of individuals without the necessity for central control. This brings them close to libertarianism (see p. 141) but, importantly, conservative support for markets is not based on the individualist premise of moral rights to private property but on a claim about the limits of human capabilities.

4. ***Rejection of 'visionary politics'*** Conservative thinker Edmund Burke famously observed that 'at the end of every vista, you see nothing but the gallows' (Burke, 1975: 344). He had in mind the visionary politics of the French Revolution. Visionaries do not recognise the pluralism of everyday life – the fact that individuals have conflicting needs, desires, and values. A vision implies a common project for society which overrides that pluralism. A later thinker, Michael Oakeshott, makes a distinction between society as a 'civic association' and an 'enterprise association': an enterprise implies a common purpose, whereas a civic association rests on certain rules of conduct that allow individuals to live together.

5. ***Respect for institutions*** An institution is a rule-governed activity. Conservatives maintain institutions evolve, rather than being created at a determinate point in time. This may seem to misdescribe the history of many national institutions. For example, the United States and modern France had 'founding moments' – 1776 and 1789 – and the process of decolonisation in the period after 1945 resulted in the creation of many new states. However, conservatives argue, first, that the instability of many newly created states is evidence of the importance of evolution, and, second, where institutions appear to be successful, it is because they have adapted over time. The American political system is a good example – contemporary US institutions are radically different to those created by the founding fathers. The fact that many Americans do not recognise this fact and hold that their institutions are continuous reinforces the conservatives' argument: a belief in continuity, alongside adaptation, is a 'necessary fiction'.

6. ***Suspicion of authority*** This feature of conservatism may seem to contradict the last one; however, to say conservatives are suspicious of authority does not entail its rejection. What conservatives are wary of is the accumulation of state power, which for reasons discussed above is incompatible with a recognition of the limits of individuals to grasp complex social relations. Although politicians calling themselves 'conservatives' are not shy about using state power to suppress movements they consider to be a threat to social order, more reflective conservatives will argue that institutions are not abstract entities, but have to be run by human beings, who are always in

danger either of abusing their position or, even if well-meaning, of putting into practice policies which have unintended, bad consequences. From this position, conservatives can make some interesting alliances – while rejecting statements of universal human rights detached from a social or legal system, they nonetheless stress 'our ancient liberties' and will join forces with civil liberties groups against, for example, measures aimed at combatting terrorism.

These points are intended to provide an overview of conservatism. To get a better idea of conservative thought and to understand its strengths and weaknesses, it is best to consider the work of specific thinkers. We focus on four: David Hume (1711–76), Edmund Burke (1729–97), Michael Oakeshott (1901–90), and Leo Strauss (1899–1973). Of the four Leo Strauss's work least manifests the above elements of thought. However, he is an important influence on neoconservatism – a largely American phenomenon – and the discussion of Strauss allows us to assess the degree to which neoconservatism is really conservative.

## The conservative revolution

There is a fifth position: revolutionary conservatism. This sounds oxymoronic: how can conservatives be revolutionaries? Because of its distinct intellectual origins, we discuss it in more detail in another chapter – on Fascism and the Radical Right (see p. 249). The Conservative Revolution is a name given to a group of thinkers in Germany writing from the end of the First World War to the rise of Adolf Hitler. For the purpose of this chapter, a British (or English) perspective will cast some light on it. British political history from the eighteenth to the twentieth centuries (and beyond) can be seen as a compromise between conservatism and liberalism, here using those terms both as indicating political philosophies and as party political labels, with the Tories becoming the Conservative Party (they are still colloquially called Tories) and Whigs evolving into the Liberal Party (supplanted in the twentieth century by the Labour Party).

Tories defended the 'estates' – that is, a social structure with a distinct hierarchy, with some limited social mobility. Central to this structure was the hereditary principle, and the gradations of inherited rank, as well as the privileges of the established Church of England, which entailed discriminating against Catholics (although there were Catholic aristocrats) and non-conformist Protestants (Baptists, Methodists, and others). The rise of capitalism and the propagation of the ideas of the rights of man was a challenge to this view of society. There were demands for Catholic and non-conformist emancipation and for an extension of the vote to the working class. Eventually, the (now) Conservative (no longer Tory) Party embraced change, and indeed, the 1867 Reform Act – which doubled the electorate – was initiated by a Conservative Government, and again in 1928, it was a Conservative Government that effectively brought in sexual equality in voting.

Essentially, but without conscious design, Britain affected a great compromise between liberalism and conservatism. While conservatives gave up their vision of an estate-based, organic society, liberals accepted that in practice people could not be materially equal. Both camps embraced the idea of moral equality and a vaguely progressive view of history, but stopped short of the kind of radical change demanded from the far left or a return to hierarchy demanded by a putative far right (that has never really existed in Britain). For various reasons, many other European countries – especially Germany – did not experience this level of mutual assimilation of liberalism and conservatism, with powerful far left and far right challenges to any such compromise.

# Hume

Eighteenth century Scottish philosopher David Hume is often described as the first conservative political theorist. Certainly, he is the first major thinker to offer a *philosophical* defence of conservatism. For that reason, it is necessary to explain how Hume derives his political theory from his epistemology (what we can know) and practical philosophy (how we should behave or what motivates us to act in certain ways).

Although their relevance to politics may not, at first sight, be obvious, it is necessary to set out a number of Hume's philosophical claims:

1. Human understanding must be drawn from experience. All the materials of thinking – perceptions – are derived either from sensations or from reflection. Although 'reflection' will generate complex ideas, which we do not directly experience, all such ideas are combinations of simple sensations. If philosophers use a term, such as 'cause' or 'freedom', then we can test whether it has any meaning by breaking the idea down to its simple sensations or 'impressions'.
2. Simple impressions must be connected or 'associated'. At any moment, there is a great deal going on in a person's mind, but you cannot reason if the contents of your mind are arbitrary: you need to connect, or associate, ideas. There are three principles of association: resemblance, contiguity, and causation. The last is problematic because it takes us beyond experience: Johnny throws a brick through the window and so 'causes' the window to break, but all we *see* are Johnny and his body movements, the trajectory of the brick, and the breaking window.
3. We attribute causes to events based on experience, and more specifically, habit. For example, we grasp the causal properties of gravity by observing falling objects. Beliefs are built on habits, but a belief is itself a sensation and not something external to experience. Although every occurrence is a simple or unique sensation, the observation of repetition creates an 'internal impression' or reflection.

In summary, Hume rejects the idea that 'reason' transcends or goes beyond, what can be observed. To grasp the political significance of this rejection, we need to consider Hume's moral philosophy. Morality is concerned with action, but not simply action, for a person's motives – reasons for action – are important in assessing whether an act is right or wrong, good or bad. In keeping with his emphasis on experience as the basis of knowledge and applying it to action, Hume argues that any assessment of a person's actions, and that person's own assessment of what he should do, cannot be based on something which transcends experience. Indeed, reasoning about what should be done is itself severely limited: one can at best assess the most effective means to a given end, but the end itself is beyond assessment. If Jane wants to murder John, then reason can be used to determine the most effective means – shooting, poisoning, strangulation, and so on – but it cannot be employed to assess the end itself, that is, whether Jane *ought* to kill John. Hume is not arguing that murder is acceptable, but rather that what stops Jane murdering John is *sentiment*: to twenty first century ears this word has slightly saccharine overtones, but in the eighteenth century it was an important philosophical concept. A sentiment is a pre-rational feeling towards somebody or something. Against Hobbes's theory, Hume does not believe that human beings are motivated purely by self-interest, but rather, their sentiments are limited: they are concerned with their own interests, or those very close to them, such as family, but they are capable of sympathy, and so are moved to act in ways beneficial to other people.

Human beings' motives are mixed: although they are self-interested, they are capable of limited sacrifices of their own self-interest for the benefit of others, and it is important that such beneficence is based on sympathy rather than (concealed) self-interest. In Hobbes's political theory, although each person is better off under a – any – state than under no state, the absence of genuine moral sentiments made people distrustful of one another and rendered society unstable. As does Hobbes, Hume argues that we are better off under a state, especially a state guaranteeing protection of private property. But, for Hume, the very success of such mutual advantage depends on a suspension of self-interest. This observation leads to Hume's famous rejection of the social contract and, by extension, his rejection of the liberal tradition.

The social contract is a fiction: no political society was ever created by a contract. More important than Hume's historical observation is his discussion of the implications for political legitimacy of holding the view that society was the result of a contract. Political authority, or legitimacy, arises from the habit of obedience to a power that initially is recognised as neither legitimate nor illegitimate, but as simply 'given' (Hume, 1963: 462). The implication of Hobbes's argument was that any monopolistic political power was preferable to none, such that this distinction is invalid: whatever gets us out of the state of nature is 'legitimate'. Hume, in part, endorses Hobbes's argument for the state over anarchy, but because Hume ties legitimacy to sentiment, and sentiment only develops gradually, the state acquires legitimacy after the fact of its existence (Hume, 1963: 538). Crucially, the degree to which it is legitimate depends on how effective it is in protecting individuals' interests and engendering moral sentiments conducive to social order. While Hume rejects revolution as a leap into the unknown, the implication of his argument is that repressive, authoritarian states will have limited success in building legitimacy.

Justice is a virtue operating in any society in which strangers come into contact with one another. The rules of justice are the product of artifice and contrivance and are intended to protect private property. Crucially, the rules evolve over time as people become habituated to them. We recognise that they serve our interests, but our allegiance to them cannot be reduced to self-interest, for we respect them even when it might be in our interest to break them. There develops an 'intercourse of sentiments' – a 'conversation' between citizens out of which emerges a limited benevolence detached from narrow self-interest (Hume, 1978: 602). Many critics suspect that moral sentiments, or sympathy, are still egoistic, for what human beings care about is that they will be held in esteem by others, and therefore, doing the right thing is pleasurable. Hume himself seems to suggest this: 'every quality of the mind, which is *useful* or *agreeable* to the *person himself* or to *others*, communicates a pleasure to the spectator, engages his esteem, and is admitted under the honourable denomination of virtue or merit' (Hume, 1978: 277). However, pleasure is compatible with sociability in a way that self-interest is not.

## Burke

If Hume was the first great conservative thinker, then Edmund Burke must be the most famous. As with Hume, the philosophical starting point for Burke's conservatism is his rejection of abstractions such as the natural rights proclaimed by the French Revolutionaries in 1789. Abstractions become embodied in theories, and theories become dogma, and a dogmatic approach will not permit criticism. The political consequence of abstract thought, Burke argues, is terror. Against abstraction, theory, and dogma, Burke defends habit, taste, and prejudice. The concept of prejudice is the single most important concept in Burke's conservative political theory. Today, 'prejudice' is a pejorative term, so it is important to understand how Burke uses it. A prejudice is a pre-judgement or a judgement made without recourse to theoretical abstractions. In contemporary philosophical language, we might use the term 'intuition' rather than prejudice. For Burke, the wisdom of other people, including previous generations, is a resource that must be respected if we are to avoid disastrous social consequences. The main thrust of Burke's *Reflections on the Revolution in France* is to contrast a society – France – which has abandoned prejudice in favour of 'theory', with a society – Britain – which has remained close to its traditions, to which it is prejudiced. Burke, claiming to speak on behalf of his fellow countrymen, observes:

> …that we have made no discoveries, and we think that no discoveries are to be made, in morality; not many in the great principles of government, nor in the ideas of liberty, which were understood long before we were born, altogether as well as they will be after the grave has heaped its mould upon our presumption, and the silent tomb shall have imposed its law on our pert loquacity.
>
> (Burke, 1969: 84)

To mid twentieth century conservatives, faced with what they termed 'totalitarian societies', Burke seemed ahead of his time, with the terror he predicted would follow the French Revolution being repeated in a more organised form in Stalin's Soviet Union and Hitler's Germany. However, it should be noted that Burke opposed the extension of democracy which would take place in the nineteenth century, and although there are, as John Stuart Mill observed, dangers in majoritarian democracy, the combination of civil liberties and participatory political structures – what later political scientists would term the 'civic culture' (Almond and Verba, 1963: 5–10) – has served as a bulwark against political authoritarianism. And, of course, while post-1789 French history has been complex, the Revolution did lay the groundwork for a strong liberal-democratic system.

Burke, like Hume, rejects the liberal idea that duties – or political obligations – are derived from a contract. Furthermore, unlike liberals, Burke does not make a sharp distinction between state and society: the 'state' is the political organisation of society, and for that reason it emerges from society. Although Burke himself does not pursue this line, a consequence of this argument is that the state has, for many conservatives, a role in shaping human behaviour, even in what liberals term the private sphere. The legal moralism of James Fitzjames Stephen and Patrick Devlin has its roots in a Burkean view of the relationship between state and society (see p. 110). Although he was highly ecumenical in his religious beliefs – he admired Hinduism and defended Irish Catholics – Burke does value religious belief and organisation, arguing that they are central to a prosperous, stable society.

Burke's conservatism is often misunderstood. He is sometimes assumed to be a straightforward reactionary. Yet, his interventions on policy towards the American colonies, India, and Ireland would suggest that he was, in the context of his time, a progressive. In addition, he argued strongly for parliamentary control over the Crown. Finally, he was not opposed to all revolutions, maintaining that the Glorious Revolution of 1688 in England was an historic achievement (although he denied that the Glorious Revolution was, in fact, a revolution at all, but rather a reassertion and restoration of 'ancient liberties'). He also defended the American Revolution. While Burke is sometimes wrongly painted as a reactionary, there is another danger, and that is using Burke's arguments out of their historical context. Burke's famous 'Speech to the Electors of Bristol' has been quoted in subsequent centuries by elected representatives who vote in ways contrary to the wishes of their electors (as measured by such things as opinion polls). On his election to the House of Commons as the representative for the English city of Bristol, Burke addressed his 5,000 electors:

> Parliament is not a congress of ambassadors from different and hostile interests; which interests each must maintain, as an agent and advocate, against other agents and advocates;

but parliament is a deliberative assembly of one nation, with one interest, that of the whole; where, not local purposes, not local prejudices, ought to guide, but the general good, resulting from the general reason of the whole. You choose a member indeed; but when you have chosen him, he is not member of Bristol, but he is a member of parliament. If the local constituents should have an interest, or should form a hasty opinion, evidently opposite to the real good of the rest of the community, the member for that place ought to be as far, as any other, from any endeavour to give it effect.

(Burke, 1975: 158)

Burke believes that parliament as an *institution* is what matters. Individuals do not have natural rights, the use of which transfers the individuals' authority on to the institution, but rather the institution has shaped individuals' rights, such as the right to vote. This also explains why Burke was prepared to submit himself to the electors of Bristol and yet at the same time ignore their wishes if they conflicted with the collective judgement of parliament (in fact, faced with defeat at the subsequent election, in 1780, Burke decided against submitting himself once again to the electors of Bristol). When Burke is quoted today, it is without adequate understanding of his conservatism. While a (philosophical, ideological) liberal may defend the idea that constituents' wishes on occasion be set aside, the reasons for doing so, and the mode in which it is done, will be quite different to that of a (philosophical, ideological) conservative. For a liberal, the strongest grounds for a representative to reject the majority preference of their constituents would be to defend minority rights; but, equally, a liberal would maintain that the representative should explain, or justify, his or her position to the constituents.

## Oakeshott

Hume and Burke were, in approximate terms, contemporaries, writing as they were in the eighteenth century. We now, however, jump a century to consider the work of Michael Oakeshott. Among Anglophone political theorists, Oakeshott is generally regarded as the key conservative thinker of the twentieth century. However, his philosophical position underwent a significant shift in the 40 years between his first major work, *Experience and its Modes* (published in 1933), and his last major work, *On Human Conduct* (1975). Our focus will be on one highly influential 1947 essay 'Rationalism in Politics' (Oakeshott, 1962), with a few comments on the latter book.

The 'rationalism' to which Oakeshott refers characterises Western culture as a whole and not simply one particular ideology or party. Oakeshott's critique is not, therefore, directed solely at socialism, but at modern 'conservatives' who are, in fact, liberal rationalists. A rationalist 'stands (he always stands) for independence of mind on all occasions, for thought free from obligation to any authority save the authority of reason' (Oakeshott, 1962: 1).

The rationalist rejects (Burkean) prejudice, custom, and habit and believes in the 'open mind, the mind free from prejudice and its relic, habit' (Oakeshott, 1962: 3). The rationalist holds that it is possible to reason about political institutions, and the fact that something exists, and has existed for a long time, is no ground for respecting or retaining it. This lack of respect for the familiar engenders a political attitude of radical change rather than gradual reform. Conservatives, who respect the familiar, will seek to patch up existing institutions. The rationalist disrespect for institutions extends to the world of ideas; instead of a careful engagement with the complex intellectual traditions that have shaped Western societies, a rationalist engages in a simplification – an 'abridgement' – of those traditions in the form of an 'ideology' (Oakeshott, 1962: 7). The rationalist in politics is essentially an engineer, obsessed with the correct technique for solving the problem he perceives to be immediately at hand. Politics is a series of crises to be solved. Because he rejects appeal to tradition, and tradition is specific to a particular culture, the rationalist assumes that there are universal solutions to problems, and political institutions cannot be peculiar to this or that culture. Under the umbrella term of rationalism, Oakeshott places together what appear to be diverse political positions, theories, projects, and ideologies: the early nineteenth century utopian socialism of Robert Owen; the League of Nations and the United Nations; all statements of universal human rights; the right to national or racial self-determination; the Christian ecumenical movement; a meritocratic civil service. He even goes on to list 'votes for women' as a rationalist project (Oakeshott, 1962: 6–7). We have not reproduced the entire list – it is long – but it is worth noting that it is so heterogeneous, and its items almost arbitrary, that one cannot help wondering whether Oakeshott himself is guilty of abridging traditions of thought by subsuming diverse phenomena under the pejorative label of rationalism. Aware of this charge, later in the essay, he maintains that rationalism, like an architectural style, 'emerges almost imperceptibly', and that it is a mistake to attempt to locate its origin (Oakeshott, 1962: 13).

In Part 2 of his essay Oakeshott's argument becomes more interesting as he advances a theory of knowledge. He distinguishes two kinds of knowledge: technical and practical (Oakeshott, 1962: 7–8). Technical knowledge is formulated as rules that are deliberately learnt, remembered, and put into practice. Whether or not such knowledge has *in fact* been formulated, its chief characteristic is that it *could* be. An example of technical knowledge is driving a car, the rules of which are, in many countries, set out in books such as, in Britain, *The Highway Code*. Another example is cooking, where the rules can be found in cookery books. Practical knowledge, on the other hand, is acquired only in use. It is not reflective and cannot be formulated as rules. Most activities involve the use of both types of knowledge, so a good cook will draw on both technical and practical knowledge. If you want to be a cook, technical knowledge will be insufficient, for what you need is practice. The acquisition of practical knowledge requires an apprenticeship, but the key feature of an apprenticeship is not subordination to a 'master', but continuous contact with the object of the practice: it is the food that is important, not the master chef. This argument gives Oakeshott's observations a libertarian, even an anarchist, cast.

Rationalists reject practical knowledge and recognise only technical knowledge. Because the latter can be contained between the covers of a book, it seems to guarantee certainty, whereas practical knowledge is diffuse. An ideology, which is a form of technical knowledge, can be expressed in a set of propositions, whereas a tradition of thought – which is a kind of practical knowledge – cannot be. The list of features of conservatism provided in the first section of this chapter might be an example of rationalism, as it appears to reduce conservatism to a set of propositions or elements – so we are guilty of rationalism!

At the time of writing – 1947 – Britain, as with most other Western European democracies, was in the process of creating a relatively comprehensive welfare state and developing more state interventionist economic policies such as the nationalisation of key industries. The essay 'Rationalism in Politics' is part of a broader intellectual intervention. It is notable that a number of works critical of the extension of state planning and state power were published at this time, including Friedrich von Hayek's *Road to Serfdom* (1944) and Karl Popper's *The Open Society and its Enemies* (1945). However, both works were clearly in the liberal (or libertarian) 'rationalist' tradition. Oakeshott observes that Hayek's book, although critical of state planning, exemplifies rationalism, for it develops one rationalist doctrine – free market libertarianism – to counter another, namely, state socialism (Oakeshott, 1962: 21–2). What this shows is that one can only participate in contemporary – that is, 1940s – politics by advancing a doctrine. This argument is leant retrospective force by the fact that Hayek became one of the major influences on the free market, or neo-liberal, reaction to the welfare state in both Britain, under Margaret Thatcher, and in the United States, under President Ronald Reagan. As we suggested at the beginning of this chapter, the Thatcher Government (1979–90) was not really conservative, and despite the Republicans' use of the term, the Reagan Administration (1981–9) was likewise not, in Oakeshott's terms, conservative, but rationalist.

Oakeshott is quite rude about politicians:

> . . . book in hand (because, though a technique can be learned by rote, they have not always learned their lesson well), the politicians of Europe pore over the simmering banquet they are preparing for the future; but, like jumped-up kitchen-porters deputizing for an absent cook, their knowledge does not extend beyond the written word which they read mechanically – it generates ideas in their heads but no tastes in their mouths.
>
> (Oakeshott, 1962: 22)

Rationalism is the politics of the 'inexperienced'. He uses the term 'experience' in a philosophical sense, meaning contact with tradition – certainly, politicians who have held office are experienced in the everyday sense of the word, but it is experience in problem-solving rather than the recognition of the importance of tradition. Oakeshott argues that the history of Europe from the fifteenth century onwards has suffered from the incursion of three types of political inexperience: the new ruler, the new ruling class, and the new political society. If a person does not belong to a family with a tradition of ruling, then he requires a 'book' – a 'crib' – to tell him what to do. Machiavelli provided an early example, with *The Prince*. Later 'books' include Locke's *Second Treatise of Civil Government*, but in the history of rationalism nothing compares with the work of Marx and Engels, who wrote for a class 'less politically educated . . . than any other that has ever come to have the illusion of exercising political power' (Oakeshott, 1962: 26). This is a crude caricature of Marx and Engels, and indeed of their readership, although it does contain an element of truth: the recitation of doctrine can relieve people of the effort of thought.

Interesting in the light of Burke's support for American independence is Oakeshott's critique of the American political tradition. The newly independent United States had the advantage of a tradition of European thought to draw upon, but unfortunately, the 'intellectual gifts' of Europe largely consisted of rationalist ideas. Combined with the mentality of a 'pioneer people' creating political society from scratch this has given rise to a rationalist political system with, unsurprisingly, a powerful emphasis on legal documents such as the Constitution. Somewhat ambivalently, Oakeshott suggests that this gave the United States an advantage; he does not develop this thought, but he might mean that the United States was eminently suited to the increasing rationalisation of domestic and world politics and so was on track to become a superpower.

Oakeshott's critique is radical. Indeed, it is difficult from a reading of 'Rationalism in Politics' to see what political order could reconcile technical and practical knowledge. The attack on the 'new class' of politicians is so comprehensive as to imply that even Burke was insufficiently conservative. Oakeshott's argument would suggest a rejection of democracy. Since any return to a non-rationalist political project would itself be rationalist – for that non-rationalist order would have to be set out in a programme – his argument appears purely negative, and its negativity creates a contradiction: is not rationalism itself a tradition? This is a standard problem with conservative thought: if what matters is what exists, and if what exists is an apparently rationalist political order, then on what grounds can a conservative criticise it? The restoration of the 'old order' is not, and cannot be, a conservative project. Oakeshott's distinction between technical and practical knowledge and the idea of an increasing predominance of the former over the latter are interesting ideas, but they are not necessarily conservative ones.

In his book *On Human Conduct* he presents a more 'positive' conception of politics. In it, he makes the distinction between a civil association and an enterprise association. An enterprise association exists for, and justifies its existence in terms of, a particular end or relatively coherent set of ends (Oakeshott, 1975: 108–18). These ends may be abstract, such as the maximisation of utility, or more concrete, such as the desire to maintain a particular cultural community. The enterprise association may not have a fully comprehensive set of aims – it might grant that individuals pursue different projects – but it will have some common aims. The commonly expressed desire to 'make the world a better place' would imply an enterprise attitude, even if people disagree over the best means of achieving it. A civil association, on the other hand, is a situation of mutual freedom under the rule of law. It is more than a Hobbesian state, for it implies mutual respect, and as such is a moral conception, but it is less than an enterprise. The best way to think about a civil association is as a set of rules that command respect not simply because they serve each person's self-interest, but because they allow human beings to choose how to live their lives. Although Oakeshott appears reactionary with regard to democratic politics, his argument in *On Human Conduct* comes close to being a liberal one.

## Strauss and American neoconservatism

An émigré from Nazi Germany to the United States, Leo Strauss is regarded as an important influence on what is called neoconservatism. Given the prominence of neoconservative ideas in US political debate, this makes Strauss a controversial figure and, as his ideas have become popularised, also a misunderstood one.

To understand Strauss's conservatism, it is necessary to start with his approach to the history of ideas and the interpretation of texts. As we will see, Strauss's conservatism is very different to that of Hume, Burke, and Oakeshott, and it reflects the culture of both his adopted home of the United States and the history of his country of origin, Germany. After a brief discussion of Strauss's work, we consider its influence on contemporary neoconservative thought in the United States.

Strauss sought to revive both the reading of texts in the history of political thought and the natural right tradition (note the singular 'right', and not 'rights'). The relationship between *reading* and *natural right* may not, at first sight, be obvious, and even less their relationship to *conservatism*, but the three are closely entwined. Natural right stands opposed to cultural relativism. Modern thought, according to Strauss, is characterised by a rejection of objective validity in favour of relativism (Strauss, 1953: 9). The starting point for a defence of natural right is the claim that radical historicism – that is, the view that morality is the product of immediate historical circumstances – must hold at least one thing as given by nature, and that is experience. There are many definitions of nature, but Strauss identifies two relevant ones: nature as the beginning of all things and nature as the character of something. For human beings, recognition of the first must depend on authority. For example, in Judaism and Christianity, the book of Genesis provides an account of humankind's origins. A refusal to accept the authority of the Bible undermines the force of that account and leads to disagreement about human origins. Recognition of the second – nature as the character of something – depends upon human experience. Hume exemplifies this approach: there must be a sensation in order to have confidence a thing exists. Since moral ideas – right and wrong – cannot be observed, modern political thinkers deny their existence.

Natural right teaching, which can be traced back to the ancient Greeks, holds that the good life is that which perfects human nature – we become what, by nature, we should be ('nature' is here used in the second sense of 'character', rather than the first sense of 'origin'). The logic of natural right is that those possessing the greatest wisdom should rule, and their power should be in proportion to their possession of the virtue of wisdom (Strauss, 1953: 102). This is incompatible with the modern – post-Hobbesian – emphasis on consent: the rulers rule by the consent of the ruled and not by appeal to the rulers' superior wisdom. Strauss argues that under modern conditions, the conflict can be reconciled by the rulers drawing up a code – or constitution – to which the people consent and to which they pledge allegiance. It is not difficult to see where this argument is heading: the recognition of the United States Constitution as the expression of natural right, and the Constitution should not be interpreted simply as a framework through which conflicts are settled, but understood as embodying religious virtue. Commitment to a 'politics of virtue' requires the resistance of tyranny, and this has practical implications for foreign policy, which we discuss briefly at the end of this section.

Strauss links his defence of natural right with a particular interpretation of the history of political thought. Drawing on Judaic ideas, Strauss argues that when we read pre-modern – and some modern – political texts, we must 'read between the lines' (Strauss, 1973: 490). Writing has two levels: a popular or edifying teaching directed to a contemporary audience (the exoteric) and a 'hidden' or secret teaching that is only revealed on careful reading (the esoteric). The great political thinkers had a storehouse of literary devices allowing them to obscure the meanings of their texts. The reason why they had to do this is made clear in the title of Strauss's *Persecution and the Art of Writing*. Thought is the enemy of tyranny, but it can only fight tyranny in its own way, and on its own terms, and that is in a literary way. Esoteric writing survives tyranny and transmits its message between political thinkers and to their intelligent readers, across the centuries. Quite clearly, a cultural relativist will reject this claim and argue that the only audience capable of being moved by a writer is the contemporary, or near-contemporary, one.

Strauss died in 1973, but if you do a keyword search of 'Leo Strauss', you will encounter a heated debate over his influence. Like much online debate, the subtleties of thought tend to be lost. However, it is interesting to explore the connections between Strauss and neoconservatism. Although the term 'neoconservative' – or 'neocon' – is more often used as a pejorative term by its opponents than by those identified as neoconservative, it still has validity. The prefix neo- is intended to identify the movement as a distinct stream within US conservatism. It indicates that adherents are new to conservatism, but also that traditional conservatism is the subject of critique and must be infused with novel policy positions.

Many, but not all, leading neoconservatives began their political life supporting what, in American terms, is the left: state intervention in the economy, policies to overcome poverty, and the civil rights movement. In demographic terms, neoconservatives are drawn disproportionately from the Jewish and the Catholic communities of mainland European origin. This is significant, because traditional conservatism was perceived to be dominated by the so-called WASPs (white Anglo-Saxon Protestants) who were hostile to the waves of immigrants who came to the United States in the late nineteenth and early twentieth centuries. Those waves of immigrants were subjected to 'assimilationist' policies (the 'great melting pot'), and neoconservatives place great value on the idea of a common US culture against what they see as the separatist multiculturalist policies in operation since the 1960s. While many neoconservatives strongly believe that the civil rights movement was justified in its aims, they oppose affirmative action policies. Furthermore, neoconservatives are much more prepared to support state spending if it will enable people to become responsible citizens, but this is combined with an emphasis on rewarding hard work through reductions in taxation. This twin-track approach was manifested in several key domestic policies of the administration of President George W Bush in the first decade of this century: the 'No Child Left Behind Act', which involved increased intervention by the centre (federal government) in the education system in order to improve educational standards among deprived groups; large tax cuts for the well-off; and partial privatisation of the state pension system. There is a Straussian influence here: objective natural right presupposes common standards and a common culture on which is based a political community that promotes virtue. The discrimination against black (and other) Americans is morally wrong, but so is what neoconservatives believe to be the separatism inherent in multiculturalism. Individual initiative should be rewarded because it reflects a perfectionist ideal: that is, we realise, or perfect, our nature through virtuous acts.

It is, however, in foreign policy that the influence of neoconservatives is most keenly felt. As suggested above, Strauss argued that tyranny should be resisted, and resistance must sometimes be in the face of widespread opposition. International institutions such as the United Nations simply reflect cultural relativism, such that a vote in the UN General Assembly or by the Security Council signifies nothing more than the balancing of interests or cultural differences. A just nation must find the justification for its actions out of a reflection on natural right and not through the support of international organisations, although it should attempt to persuade other nations to join it in a 'coalition of the willing'. What drove many thinkers and political activists from the Democratic Party to the Republicans was the perceived weakness of the left in confronting the Soviet Union in the 1970s – whereas the left sought containment of the USSR, the neoconservatives argued for a roll-back of Soviet power. In policy terms, the left supported Strategic Arms Limitation Treaties (SALT), whereas the neoconservatives argued for an aggressive arms war so as to force the Soviet Union to spend beyond its means. Significantly, this critique of perceived weakness extended to traditional conservatives such as President Richard Nixon (US President, 1969–74), who initiated the SALT talks and famously engaged with (Communist) China. At the beginning of the twenty first century, neoconservatives see fundamentalist Islam as the main source of tyranny and liken the refusal of many European countries to engage with this perceived threat as a political manifestation of a deeper cultural relativism and decadence.

## Lords reform

Constitutional debates are not unusual, and the United Kingdom is not alone in arguing over its institutional arrangements. Some countries, such as Denmark, Israel, and New Zealand, have unicameral parliaments. Larger countries tend to be bicameral, and most have some form of election for the upper (less powerful) chamber, either directly by voters or indirectly through seats allocated to provinces, based on their most recent elections, as in the case of the German Bundesrat. The difficulty all bicameral systems face is how to endow the upper chamber with sufficient legitimacy without it challenging the lower chamber. To do this, it has to be very different to the lower chamber. The German split between the lower Bundestag and upper Bundesrat seems to carry this off with some success.

The House of Lords is largely appointed, with seats for life, which creates inflationary pressure as the governing party can only increase its representation through adding new members (although a recent, but minor, innovation is the possibility of resignation). The non-appointed members are Bishops and the remaining hereditary peers, whose membership was winnowed down to an agreed number using an election among the hereditaries (a kind of balloon election, where those in balloon – the hereditary peers – decide which of their fellow hereditaries to throw over the side). The sense of legitimacy of the Lords varies depending on the times. In the middle of the first decade of the twenty first century, it was often praised for resisting what was perceived to be illiberal legislation coming from the Labour Government led by Tony Blair, especially around issues of free speech. At other times, it was seen as out of step with (especially) younger people, over issues such as the repeal of Section 28 (prohibiting the 'promotion' of homosexuality) and equalisation of the age of consent (Russell and Sciara, 2007).

Many critics see the Lords as an embarrassment. But equally, it could be a sign of just how successful the British constitution has been in ensuring stability. That the 'estates' gradually ceded power to the people meant that *popular* revolution – distinct from the Glorious Revolution of 1688, which was a *constitutional* act – was avoided. Burke made much of this in his critique of the 1789 French Revolution. The piecemeal reform of the Lords started with the 1911 Parliament Act and was amended by the 1949 Parliament Act, which further reduced the time the Lords could delay legislation. This was combined with the Salisbury Convention, which was an accepted agreement not to wreck legislation that had been set out in the governing party's election manifesto (or platform). The 1999 House of Lords Act further changed the nature of the upper chamber.

We can view the Lords as an example of Oakeshott's 'problem at sea': the ship (Lords) has developed faults, which if not rectified will become serious. A rationalist would start with abstract principles, such as the idea that legitimacy only comes from the universal franchise, or that once a decision is made by the elected chamber it should be put into law and so there is no place for bicameralism. In his more reactionary phase, Oakeshott would have argued the case for 'political families', where (male) children are brought up to govern. Indeed, he might observe that even the highly politically egalitarian United States produces dynasties such as the Kennedy or Bush families. Americans might have rejected the hereditary principle, but they cannot help but rely on some kind of inherited governing acumen.

Conservatives, such as Hume, Burke, and Oakeshott, are very sensitive to the unintended consequences of radical (and rationalist) change. A radical shift from a largely appointed Chamber to an elected one could result in gridlock if the Lords now felt emboldened by its new democratic credentials to challenge the House of Commons. And removing the bishops (the Lords Spiritual) might call into the question the status of the Church of England as the 'established' church, with wide-ranging implications. And elections to the Lords could result in the loss of expertise that some see as a strength of the chamber and just make it another route to power for career politicians.

## Conclusion

The contemporary relevance of traditional conservatism is seen less as an active ideology – party political conservatives are not really conservatives – but as an important source of ideas critical of the dominant liberal ideology. The core of conservatism is its critique of rationalism. While American conservatism – specifically, neoconservatism – is difficult to reconcile with British conservatism, there is an underlying respect for institutions and doubts about radical forms of democracy and egalitarianism. That said, apart from a common emphasis on the interpenetration of state and society, and consequently the recognition that politics is concerned with the development of virtue and not simply the resolution of conflicting interests, there is little that holds the four thinkers together (and Oakeshott, in his later work, rejects the idea that politics should promote virtue).

# References

Almond, G. and Verba, S. (1963). *The Civic Culture: Political Attitudes and Democracy in Five Nations*. Princeton, NJ: Princeton University Press.

Burke, E. (1969). *Reflections on the Revolution in France*. Ed. Conor Cruise O'Brien. Harmondsworth: Penguin.

Burke, E. (1975). *On Government, Politics and Society*. Ed. B.W. Hill. London: Fontana/The Harvester Press.

Garland, J. (2018). The UK's Parliament Is in Danger of Backsliding – but Current Policy Proposals Are Not the Right Fix. *Democratic Audit*, viewed 19 June 2021, https://www.democraticaudit.com/2018/11/15/the-uks-democracy-is-in-danger-of-backsliding-but-current-policy-proposals-are-not-the-right-fix/

Hume, D. (1963). *Essays, Moral, Political and Literary*. Oxford: Oxford University Press.

Hume, D. (1978). *A Treatise of Human Nature*. Ed. L.A. Selby-Bigge. Oxford: Clarendon Press.

Oakeshott, M. (1933). *Experience and its Modes*. Cambridge: Cambridge University Press.

Oakeshott, M. (1962). *Rationalism in Politics and Other Essays*. London: Methuen.

Oakeshott, M. (1975). *On Human Conduct*. Oxford: Clarendon Press.

Parliament Act 1911. Legislation.gov.uk, viewed 19 June 2021, https://www.legislation.gov.uk/ukpga/Geo5/1-2/13/introduction

Roberts, A. (2012). *Salisbury: Victorian Titan*. London: Faber & Faber.

Russell, M. and Sciara, M. (2007). Why Does the Government get Defeated in the House of Lords? The Lords, the Party System and British Politics. *British Politics*, 2, 299–322.

Strauss, L. (1953). *Natural Right and History*. Chicago, IL: University of Chicago Press.

Strauss, L. (1973). *Persecution and the Art of Writing*. Westport, CT: Greenwood Press.

# Further reading

Overviews of conservative thought: Edmund Fawcett, *Conservatism: The Fight for a Tradition* (Princeton University Press, 2020); Edmund Neill, *Conservatism* (Polity, 2021); Robert Nisbet, *Conservatism: Dream and Reality* (Routledge, 2017). On specific thinkers: Scott Yenor, *David Hume's Humanity: The Philosophy of Common Life and its Limits* (Palgrave Macmillan, 2017); Jesse Norman, *Edmund Burke: The Visionary who Invented Modern Politics* (HarperCollins, 2014); Emily Jones, *Edmund Burke and the Invention of Modern Conservatism, 1830–1914* (Oxford University Press, 2019); Edmund Neill, *Michael Oakeshott* (Bloomsbury, 2013); Eric Kos (ed.), *Michael Oakeshott on Authority, Governance, and the State* (Palgrave Macmillan, 2020); Neil Robertson, *Leo Strauss: An Introduction* (Polity, 2021); Steven Smith (ed.), *The Cambridge Companion to Leo Strauss* (Cambridge University Press, 2009).

# Chapter 11

# Socialism and Marxism

## Introduction

Is socialism dead? The collapse of Communist Party (CP) states in Eastern Europe and Russia in 1989–91 has left only China, Cuba, Laos, and Vietnam as CP states, and even those have embraced capitalism to such an extent that characterising them as communist is problematic. The difficulty in deciding whether socialism is dead is that socialism comes in so many varieties. The category of 'socialism' contains much more than communism, and in the post-Cold War era social-democratic parties have had considerable electoral success across the Western world – although even they appear now to be in retreat (*The Week*, 2021). Is there a generic socialism that encompasses both the most hardline forms of democratic centralism (Leninism) and the softest, most liberal – and capitalist-friendly – social democracy? Is part of the problem with socialism its utopianism? Or, if it is realistic rather than utopian, its indistinguishability from liberalism? And why have some forms of socialism resulted, directly or indirectly, in so many deaths?

## Defining socialism

The term 'socialist' covers a wide range of contradictory movements. Some socialists are religious, while others are atheist. Some advocate revolution, others reform. Nor are the alignments simple. Authoritarian socialisms may be atheistic – as in the communist tradition – but they need not be (Saddam Hussein's Iraqi regime claimed adherence to Islamic tradition). Some socialists have admired the parliamentary tradition, while others see parliamentary democracy as an obstacle to socialist advance.

The distinction between Marxism and social democracy is the major fault-line among socialisms. It has been argued that the differences between Marxism and social democracy are so substantial that communism should be distinguished from socialism. Since Marxists referred to themselves as 'scientific socialists', we will reject this distinction, although we have acknowledged the distinction in this chapter's title, and the differences between revolutionary and evolutionary varieties of socialism will be highlighted.

While the terms social democracy and democratic socialism will be used interchangeably, there are difficulties with treating them as synonyms. The history of socialist thought is thick with accusations of betrayal. Lenin believed that social democrats were traitors to socialism because they supported the First World War and opposed the Russian Revolution. Socialists influenced by libertarian or anarchist ideas claim that Lenin and the Bolsheviks betrayed the Soviet experiment by crushing the rebellion of Bolshevik sailors that took place in Kronstadt in 1921.

DOI: 10.4324/9780429424106-15

Case study 11.1

## Why so many deaths?

**PHOTO 11.1** A stack of Mao Tse-Tung's Little Red Book. © MARK RALSTON/AFP via
Getty Images.

The authors of *The Black Book of Communism* (Albert et al., 1999) maintain that the
death toll from communism (and 'state socialism') in the twentieth century was 94
million (1999: 4):

USSR – 20 million deaths.
China – 65 million deaths.
Vietnam – 1 million deaths.
North Korea – 2 million deaths.
Cambodia – 2 million deaths.
Eastern Europe – 1 million deaths.
Latin America – 150,000 deaths.
Africa – 1.7 million deaths.
Afghanistan – 1.5 million deaths.

The book's analysis and argument have been criticised, with a particular focus on
how these figures were arrived at, and what counts as murder, distinct from death.
Furthermore, some argue that communism – or Marxism – as a body of ideas needs to
be distinguished from the 'practice' of communism and state socialism. We return to
these issues at the end of the chapter.

However, even if the death count is considerably lower, it would still be very high. And so it is reasonable to pose the question: why has socialism – or at least, certain of its variants – led to so many deaths? Is there something in the ideology itself that accounts for this?

Trotsky and his supporters felt that Stalin had reneged on the revolutionary traditions of Lenin by seeking to build socialism in one country. Mao and many Chinese communists believed that the Russians had surrendered to capitalism and the market after 1956.

These differences have deeply divided socialists. The British Labour Party repeatedly refused the request for affiliation from the Communist Party of Great Britain (CPGB) on the grounds that the latter supported dictatorship against democracy. The Soviet Union's interventions in Hungary in 1956 and Czechoslovakia in 1968 were intended to stifle reform communists, and Western communists influenced by social democratic and liberal ideas called themselves 'Euro-communists' to distance themselves from the Soviet system.

There are however things most socialists share:

a) *an optimistic view of human nature* – human nature is either changeable or does not constitute a barrier to social regulation or ownership;
b) *a stress on cooperation* – people can and should work together so that market capitalism at the very least needs some adjustment to facilitate cooperation;
c) *support for material equality* – socialists define equality in dramatically different ways, but all must subscribe to a relatively strong form of material equality.

## The problem of utopia

All socialists are vulnerable to the charge of utopianism – of trying to create a society that is contrary to human experience and historical development. Socialists disagree as to whether utopianism is a good or bad thing. In his famous book *Utopia*, Thomas More (1478–1535) articulated the concept of a good society (eutopia) that is nowhere (utopia = no place) (Geoghegan, 1987: 1). Karl Mannheim in *Ideology and Utopia* (1936) defined utopia as an idea that was 'situation transcending' or 'incongruent with reality'; it 'breaks the bonds of the existing order' (1960: 173).

While some socialists have seen utopia as a good thing, liberals and conservatives regard utopia as negative – an irresponsible idealism incompatible with the hard facts of reality that can at worst lead to nightmarish regimes of a highly oppressive and totalitarian kind (see Burke's critique of the French Revolution, X-ref). Andrew Heywood argues that all socialists are utopians since they develop 'better visions of a better society in which human beings can achieve genuine emancipation and fulfilment as members of a community' (1992: 96). He even extends this to Marxism where he describes communism as 'a utopian vision of a future society envisaged and described by Marx and Engels'. On the other hand, he acknowledges that the issue is controversial since he also notes that Marx and Engels supported 'scientific socialism' and rejected what they called 'utopian socialism' (Heywood, 1992: 115, 127).

If socialism is utopian, can it never be put into practice? Zygmunt Bauman argues that we should view utopias positively – as a necessary condition of historical change (1976: 13). He insists that a utopia 'sets the stage for a genuinely realistic politics'. It extends the meaning of realism to encompass the full range of possible options (1976: 13). Utopias make consensus the major divisions of interest within society: the future is portrayed as a set of competing projects (1976: 15). But it is still unclear whether we can have a socialist society. Bauman argues that socialism is the counterculture of capitalist society (1976: 36), and it cannot be empirical reality, a society in its own right.

## Science and the 'utopian socialists'

Three socialists were singled out by Engels as being utopian – in contrast to his and Marx's scientific socialism: Henri Saint Simon (1760–1825); Charles Fourier (1773–1837); and Robert Owen (1771–1858).

In fact, each considered his own work scientific and practical. Saint Simon argued that the French Revolution had neglected class structure in the name of human rights. He included industrialists and bankers in the producing class, believing workers and capitalists have similar interests. Saint Simon believed that the old order had unintentionally produced the basis for a new order and in arguing this he sounds like a Marxist. His argument that the state gives way to administration – a central claim of Marxist theory – was based on a belief that the modern credit and banking system had already demonstrated its attachment to scientific principles, and that these could exert a discipline that would make the state redundant. Saint Simon does not fit into Engels' view that modern socialism is based on class antagonism between capitalist and wage worker (Marx and Engels, 1968: 399). But it does seem incorrect to ascribe to Saint Simon – as Engels does to the utopians in general – the view that socialism is not an inevitable event but a happy accident, when Saint Simon had laid so much emphasis on science and historical development.

Fourier, on the other hand, did consider the worker and the capitalist to have conflicting interests. He was particularly concerned at the way the industrial revolution has stripped work of its pleasure. His solution was to establish 'phalanteres' – cooperative communities of some 1,600 people working in areas of around 5,000 acres in the countryside or small towns. Fourier was adamant that his was not a utopian socialism. He described utopias as 'dreams', schemes without an effective method that have 'led people to the very opposite of the state of well-being they promised them' (Geoghegan, 1987: 17). He believed that his socialism was based on a scientific project for reconstruction. Indeed, so precise a science was socialism that Fourier took the view that civilised society has 144 evils; humans have 12 basic passions; they do 12 different jobs; and need 9 meals to sustain them.

As for Robert Owen, he saw himself as a practical, hard-headed person of business, and he owned cotton mills in New Lanark in Scotland. He was struck as to how under rational socialist management, they could still be profitable, and he decided to advocate village cooperatives between 300 and 2,000 people working land between 600 and 1,800 acres. It is true that his schemes were dogged by failure. The community he established at New Harmony in the United States collapsed after three years in 1827, and his labour bazaars at which goods were to be exchanged according to the amount of labour embodied in them did not survive the economic crisis of 1834. His national trade union was called a 'grand national moral union for the productive classes', but his dictatorial leadership demonstrated the problem with his theory of character. As Geoghegan points out, Owen thought that only an exceptional person (like himself) could initiate reform for a relatively passive population (Geoghegan, 1987: 14).

He had however a lasting effect on the British labour movement as a practical reformer, and the consumer cooperatives he advocated – the Co-op stores – still exist in British cities today. Although Owen's notion of science stems from an uncritical reading of the Enlightenment, he regarded himself as a person of scientific, secular, and empirical values. Indeed, a youthful Engels was to describe Owen's views as 'the most practical and fully worked out' of all the socialists (Geoghegan, 1987: 23).

## Introducing Marxism

The belief that socialism should be scientific and not utopian is highly contentious. There is a terminological point that should be tackled right away. In the *Communist Manifesto* of 1848, Engels explains that the term 'communism' was preferred because it was seen as a working-class movement from below. Socialism, he argued, was a respectable movement initiated from above (Marx and Engels, 1967: 62). Later, Marxists called themselves socialists and social democrats. It was only after 1917 when Lenin and the Bolsheviks wanted to distance themselves from other socialists – who had supported the First World War and opposed the Russian Revolution – that the term 'communist' was resurrected.

R.N. Berki has argued that Marx transformed socialism from underdog to a 'fully grown part of the modern landscape' (1974: 56). Marx was a philosopher, who devoted most of his life to studying political economy and in 1863 published *Capital* (or *Das Kapital*), a work that Engels was to describe as the bible of the working class. Engels, for his part, read and wrote widely about natural science, anthropology, history, politics, and economics, and both regarded science not as the pursuit of facts, rather than values, but simply as coherent and systematic thought.

Why did Engels see Saint Simon, Fourier, and Owen as utopians? In the *Communist Manifesto*, Marx and Engels praised the 'utopians' for producing 'the most valuable materials for the enlightenment of the working class'. Measures like the abolition of the distinction between town and country, the disappearance of the family, the wages system, the private ownership of industry, the dying out of the state, and a positive relationship between the individual and society were suggested by the utopians and became part of Marx and Engels' own arguments. Nevertheless, the label is contentious, for Marx and Engels clearly regarded the utopians as painting 'fantastic pictures of a future society', a fantasy which reflected the historically undeveloped state of the working class itself (1967: 116).

Why then was Marxism seen as scientific? Marxism, Marx and Engels argued, is a scientific socialism because it is:

- *A theory of class conflict* It holds that in class-divided societies there are incompatible social interests that lead to exploitation. Class is both an economic and a political reality since, between the classes, there is war. In contrast, the utopians seek change through general principles of 'reason' and 'justice'.
- *A theory of revolution* Such is the incompatibility of class interests, change can only come through revolution. Although the *Communist Manifesto* describes revolution in violent terms, Marx's later position was that revolutions can be peaceful, even constitutional, but they will be violent if necessary. Because classes are political as well as economic entities, they seek to control the state in their own interest, so the state has a class character. Utopians, by contrast, seek peaceful and sometimes piecemeal change, appealing to all classes

in society for support, and invariably see the state as part of the solution rather than the problem.

- **A theory of history** All societies are moulded by the conflict between the forces of production (which embrace science and technology) and the relations of production (the system of ownership). These two elements form a basis (or base) upon which arises a 'superstructure' that incorporates political institutions, educational systems, culture, and ideas. In class-divided societies, the conflict between the forces and relations of production creates the need for revolution so that under capitalism the social character of the forces of production comes into sharp and increasing conflict with the private relations of production. That is why revolution is inevitable. After this revolution, class divisions disappear, and with the disappearance of these divisions, the need for a state itself withers.
- **A theory of society** People enter relations of production 'independent of their will', meaning that while human activity is conscious, the consequences of this activity are never the same as those intended. Capitalism unintentionally creates the working class, educates them through factory production, goads them into struggle, and ultimately drives them to revolution. By way of contrast, utopians do not see capitalism as a contradictory system, a system that is self-destructive. They see no special role for the workers, nor do they accept the need for a communist or socialist party to provide leadership for revolution. Socialism, as far as they see it, is merely desirable and not inevitable.

## The authoritarian consequences of 'scientific socialism'

There are a number of problems with the theory – and not merely the practice – of scientific socialism:

a)  the argument of inevitability – this is the major problem;
b)  the theory of class war;
c)  a rejection of morality (characterised as 'moralism');
d)  the question of leadership – a relatively minor problem.

It will be argued that together these problems explain why CP states following the theory of 'scientific socialism' have proved vulnerable to popular – even proletarian – protest. Attempts to make CP states more democratic were resisted by the Soviet leadership in 1968, and today, only North Korea, Cuba, China, and Vietnam remain as CP states. Former CPs changed their names – usually to include democracy in their title – and they invariably describe themselves as socialist rather than communist. What relationship exists between the hapless fate of these states and the theory of scientific socialism? It is worth giving this question some thought.

## The inevitability argument

In Part I of the *Communist Manifesto*, the victory of the proletariat is described as 'inevitable', as in the famous comment that 'what the bourgeoisie . . . produces, above all, is its own grave-diggers. Its fall and the victory of the proletariat are equally inevitable' (Marx and Engels, 1967: 94). This has become a central theme of Marxism in general, and Engels was to argue that revolutions are 'the necessary outcome of circumstances, quite independent of the will or guide of particular parties' (Hoffman, 1995: 135). Marxism is 'scientific' because it arises from the real movement of history that compels people to do things whether they like it or not. Revolution is – in some sense of the term – a 'natural' process, driven by the antagonistic conflict between the forces and relations of production at the heart of society. It is therefore unavoidable. There are several problems with the 'inevitability argument'.

## What happens when revolutions are 'bourgeois' in character?

In the *Communist Manifesto*, Marx and Engels declare that 'Communists everywhere support every revolutionary movement against the existing order of things' (1967: 120). Contrary to the utopians who support socialism rather than capitalism, Marxists will support a 'bourgeois revolution' in countries where liberal constitutionalism has yet to prevail: in Germany, as the *Communist Manifesto* points out, communists will fight with the bourgeoisie where the latter are acting in a revolutionary way. This notion is of the utmost importance, for it explains the attraction of Marxism in colonial countries or in autocratic regimes of a feudal or semi-feudal kind. But what has a liberal revolution to do with communism?

One of the most contentious aspects of the *Communist Manifesto* derives from the argument that, once the old absolutist regime has fallen, 'the fight against the bourgeoisie itself may immediately begin'. The argument here focuses on Germany in 1848. Given the much more advanced conditions of European civilisation and 'a much more developed proletariat', 'the bourgeois revolution in Germany will be but the prelude to an immediately following proletarian revolution' (Marx and Engels, 1967: 120). This sentence was seen by the Bolsheviks as giving the October revolution its classical Marxist credentials since Russia of 1917 was deemed analogous to Germany of 1848 because of the combination of material backwardness and heightened political consciousness. The destruction of Tsarism – the bourgeois revolution – could then be 'the prelude to an immediately following proletarian revolution'.

Richard Hunt has argued that this formulation – which nowhere else occurs in Marx's writing – was put in to appease the members of the Communist League who commissioned the *Manifesto*. They did not like the idea of a bourgeois revolution anyway, but a bourgeois revolution immediately followed by a proletarian one was enough to sugar the pill. Hunt's argument is that this notion of permanent revolution – that a bourgeois revolution becomes relatively quickly a proletarian one – does not square with classical Marxism and the emphasis placed elsewhere in the *Communist Manifesto* on the gradual, step by step, education of the proletariat preparing them for revolution and power (Hunt, 1975: 180, 246). Whatever tactical considerations played their part in this fateful formulation, the argument is never actually repudiated by Marx and Engels, although they did later speak of the *Communist Manifesto* as an 'historical document which we have no longer any right to alter' (Marx and Engels, 1967: 54). Whether one finds Hunt's argument convincing, the point is that the notion that one revolution can immediately follow another has had significant historical consequences and has come to be seen as part and parcel of Marxist theory.

The implication is that relatively undeveloped countries can become socialist or communist without the lengthy period of preparation which capitalism unwittingly and normally allows the proletariat. Since this period is precisely the one in which workers become familiar with liberal ideas and institutions, it is not difficult to see that the omission or dramatic compression of such a period can only increase the need for the authoritarian leadership of a 'vanguard' party, and authoritarian political institutions themselves. It is not surprising then that the USSR, and later, the People's Republic of China, followed a development in which the liberal tradition was suppressed rather than made the basis for further political advance.

## What happens when revolutions are 'pre-mature'?

Engels told the German socialist Joseph Weydemeyer that 'we shall find ourselves compelled to make communist experiments and leaps which no-one knows better than ourselves to be untimely' (Hoffman, 1995: 135). But if revolution is deemed inevitable, then Marxists will 'find themselves' compelled to support 'experiments' and 'leaps' which are not only untimely but can only be sustained by authoritarian institutions. A good example of this problem can be seen in relation to Marx and Engels' attitude towards the Paris Commune. Because of the perceived heroism of the Communards, Marx extolled the virtues of the Commune. This he did in a book called *The Civil War in France*, which outlined a radical polity that became the basis of Lenin's blueprint in *The State and Revolution* written in 1918.

Yet, the Commune was in reality influenced by Blanquism – a rather elitist and coercive egalitarianism named after the French socialist Louis Blanqui (1805–81) – and by anarchist trends and reflected what has been called 'an unsophisticated anti-bureaucratism' (Hoffman, 1995: 137) – an anti-bureaucratism that enshrined anti-liberal political practices. Despite his private reservations, Marx felt obliged publicly to support an 'experiment' that could only have succeeded if power had been concentrated in an unambiguously authoritarian manner.

## Rosa Luxemburg, the Bolshevik Revolution, and Stalinism

Marx's support for the Paris Commune is not an isolated example. The Polish Marxist, Rosa Luxemburg, was to defend the Bolshevik Revolution in the same way and for the same reasons that Marx and Engels had praised the Paris Commune. The Bolsheviks, she argued, have acted with immense heroism: the revolution was an act of proletarian courage, and she supported it. On the other hand, she was alarmed by the authoritarianism of Lenin and Trotsky and she was particularly critical when the two leaders dispersed the Constituent Assembly in 1918, after it was returned with a socialist, but not a Bolshevik majority. She thought that the revolution was bound to fail. In fact, the Russian Revolution succeeded by crushing its opponents, and Luxemburg, who was assassinated by German soldiers in 1919, never lived to see how a virtue was made of necessity first by Lenin and then by Stalin.

A whole generation of communists in liberal countries were prepared to support Stalin and Stalinism on the grounds that such rule was 'inevitable'. This position also created a grave dilemma for Stalin's critics like Trotsky who supported the Russian Revolution and had shown his own illiberal tendencies. Bernard Crick expresses quite a common view when he says that 'it would have made little difference had Trotsky, not Stalin succeeded Lenin' (1987: 62). Engels was to argue – in response to the anarchists – that 'revolution is the most authoritarian thing there is' (Tucker, 1978: 733).

### The dilemma of democratic socialism

Until 1914, the term social democrat was widely adopted. It was used both by the Bolsheviks and the British Labour Party. In 1914, a great schism occurred. Some socialists supported the First World War, and this divide was deepened when the Bolshevik Revolution took place in 1917. Although socialists generally welcomed the fall of Tsarism in February 1917, many – including those who considered themselves Marxists – saw the seizure of power by Lenin in October 1917 as the act of mad man, a *coup d'état* rather than a genuine revolution, a pre-mature act which ignored the unripe conditions in Russia.

From then on, the concept of a social democrat became a term of differentiation, with the emphasis now on democracy. Socialists who opposed the Russian Revolution and subsequent Leninist and Stalinist rule invariably called themselves democratic socialists. Socialism, it was argued, is concerned with reform, not revolution: it must develop through parliamentary democracy, not through workers' councils or soviets. It must express itself through electoral victory, not a seizure of power: nor should socialists tie themselves to the leadership of the working class. Socialism involves the whole nation – not simply a part of it – and socialism must be realistic, attained through piecemeal reforms and in a manner that works with, and respects, the liberal tradition. As the French socialist, Jean Jaures put it, 'the great majority of the nation can be won over to our side by propaganda and lawful action and led to socialism' (Berki, 1974: 91–2).

Social democracy sees itself as everything that Marxism is not: democratic, reformist, realistic, open-minded, and concerned with the moral case for socialism. What is its dilemma? It is so anti-utopian that it is vulnerable to the charge that it is no different in essence from liberalism. Is it a movement in its own right? Berki makes the point that, just as in Aristotle, aristocracy can turn into its degenerate form, oligarchy, so social democracy can turn into its degenerate form, which is electoralism (1974: 104), that is, a concern to win elections without worrying about principles at all.

In other words, social democracy suffers from a serious identity problem. It is so pragmatic and flexible, so concerned with avoiding divisiveness and outraging, as Durbin puts it, 'the conservative sections of all classes' (Berki, 1974: 103), that it becomes a form of conservatism itself – or liberalism – and cannot be called socialism at all. Socialism is vulnerable to the charge of utopianism: but a forthright rebuttal of utopianism of any kind may mean that the transformative element in socialism is lost, and socialism degenerates.

## Eduard Bernstein and the German socialists

Eduard Bernstein is a significant figure to examine, for his critique of classical Marxism formed the theory and practice of what came to be called social democracy. He influenced a tradition that was resistant to theory. In his work, social democracy is not only contrasted explicitly and in detail to Marxism, but its own premises are lucidly displayed. Indeed, the book that has the English title of *Evolutionary Socialism* was actually called (if one translates the German directly) *The Premises of Socialism and the Task of Social Democracy.*

Bernstein joined the German Socialists in 1872. When the warring groups united, the party went from electoral success to electoral success. In 1876, it won 9% of the votes cast (Gay, 1962: 38–9). Bismarck, the German Chancellor, used the attempt to assassinate the Emperor – not it should be said by socialists – to harass the party. Bernstein, who was in Switzerland at the time, became converted to Marxism.

Despite the problems caused by Bismarck's anti-socialist law (which only lapsed in 1890), the party polled 12% of the vote in the elections of 1881 (1962: 52). In 1884, the party sent 24 members to the German parliament (the Reichstag). Under renewed pressure from Bismarck, Bernstein was forced to leave Switzerland and went to London. In 1890, the party secured nearly 20% of the vote in the national elections and increased its number of MPs to 35. By 1903, the SPD had 81 seats in parliament (1962: 230).

# Bernstein, revisionism, and the British tradition

Engels, who died in 1895, had already expressed his concern over Bernstein's enthusiasm for the Fabians – British socialists who explicitly rejected Marxism and named themselves after the Roman emperor Fabius famed for his step-by-step approach to fighting war. Engels was to accuse the Fabians – whose society was established in London in 1874 – of 'hushing up the class struggle' (Gay, 1962: 106). Bernstein was impressed by the tolerance and liberalism he found in London, so much so that Karl Kautsky, then the great champion of Marxist orthodoxy, was to declare Bernstein 'a representative of English socialism' (1962: 80).

In 1899, Bernstein wrote his *Evolutionary Socialism* – described as the 'bible of revisionism'. Bernstein had been asked by Engels to be one of the executors of the Marxist papers, and Bernstein was reluctant to accept that he had – in the quasi-theological jargon which Marxists embrace – 'revised' Marxism. He argued that his critique was a way of further developing Marxism: he was not destroying Marxism, since, as he put it, 'it is Marx who carries the point against Marx' (1961: 27). But what he argued was certainly explosive, and a different kind of socialism emerged in his critique.

# Bernstein's argument

Bernstein took the view that:

- Small and medium-sized enterprises were proving themselves viable. Hence members of the possessing classes were increasing, not diminishing (1961: xxv). Society was not becoming more simplified – as the *Communist Manifesto* declared – but more graduated and differentiated (1961: 49). Moreover, the constantly rising national product was distributed, albeit unequally, over all segments of the population, so that the position of the worker was improving (1961: 207). In agriculture, the small and medium landholding was increasing, and the large and very large decreasing (1961: 71).
- He followed the Fabians by arguing that the theory of value or surplus value in Marxist theory was unnecessary. Depressions are becoming milder. Modern banking and the internationalisation of trade create adjustment and flexibility in capitalism, not breakdown.
- He saw Marx's emphasis on dialectics – the world consists of opposing forces – as a snare, uncritically taken over from Hegel. Why not assume cooperation is just as important as struggle? Socialism must be based on facts, and it is a fact that there is compromise and cooperation between the classes.
- Ethical factors, in his view, create much greater space for independent activity than was seen to be the case in classical Marxism (Bernstein, 1961: 15). The notion of inevitability – a fusion of what is and what ought to be – must be decisively rejected. 'No ism is a science' (Gay, 1962: 158). Socialism is about what is ethically desirable, whereas science is about what is.
- Democracy, for Bernstein, is 'an absence of class government' – it avoids both the tyranny of the majority and the tyranny of the minority. Democracy is the high school of compromise and moderation (1961: 142–4). The notion of the 'dictatorship of the proletariat' has become redundant. Socialism seeks to make the proletarian into a citizen 'and to thus make citizenship universal' (1961: 146).
- Socialism, declared Bernstein, is 'the legitimate heir' to liberalism 'as a great historical movement' (1961: 149). There is no liberal thought that does not also belong to socialism. Industrial courts and trade councils involve democratic self-government (1961: 152). Socialism is

'organising liberalism' and requires the constant increase of municipal freedom (1961: 159). He was devoted to liberal parliamentarism (1961: 299), and if this parliamentarism becomes excessive, the antidote is local self-government.

- Social Democratic parties must fight for all those reforms that increase the power of the workers and give the state a more democratic form (Gay, 1962: 225). Bernstein described the Sozialistische Partei Deutschands (SPD) as a 'democratic-Socialist reform party'. Hence the trade unions (labour unions), far from being schools for socialism (in Marx's revolutionary sense), were concerned with practical and non-revolutionary improvements. Trade unions are, declared Bernstein, 'indispensable organs of democracy' (1961: 139–40).
- He linked the practicality of trade unions with the empirical orientation of the cooperative movement (1961: 204). The class struggle continues, but it is taking ever-milder forms. Cooperatives, particularly consumer co-ops, encourage democratic and egalitarian forms of management.

Bernstein exemplifies the dilemma of democratic socialism. How can social democrats navigate between what Gay called the Scylla of impotence and the Charybdis of betrayal of their cause (Gay, 1962: 302)? How can they be 'realistic' and yet remain socialist?

## The British Labour Party and the Fabians

The British Labour Party has never been a party of theory. Although its members may not even have heard of Bernstein, it is Bernsteinism that provides the underpinning for its practice.

The Fabians have already been mentioned. They became a kind of think-tank for the Labour Party and were influenced by the same theories that so appealed to Bernstein – empiricism, a philosophy that argues our knowledge comes through the observation of facts – and a belief in piecemeal reform through parliamentary democracy. Socialism was not a philosophy for life, but a highly focused doctrine that concerns itself with the organisation of industry and the distribution of wealth. Examine Fabian pamphlets today and what you find are specific proposals for organising the civil service, the health service, tax reforms, welfare benefits, and the like. Beatrice Webb (1858–1943), who played a key role in the Fabian Society and in the formation of the Labour Party, took the view that the whole nation was sliding into social democracy.

## The Labour Party, constitutionalism, and the trade unions

The Labour Representative Committee in 1900 was formed by trade unions. These unions felt that they needed a political voice and would cooperate with any party engaged in promoting legislation 'in the direct interest of labour' (Miliband, 1973: 19). The Liberal Party did not oppose the two Labour candidates who won their seats in 1900. After the formation of the Labour Party in 1906, a Trade Disputes Act was passed which strengthened the right of unions to strike, while the Trade Union Act of 1913 allowed trade unions to affiliate to the Labour Party. Ramsay MacDonald, the Party leader, made it clear that political weapons are to be found in the ballot box and the Act of Parliament – not in collective bargaining (Miliband, 1973: 35).

The party itself received a constitution in 1918, and the famous Clause IV that spoke of common ownership of the means of production was (rather cynically) inserted by the Webbs to give the party some kind of ideological distance from the conservatives and the liberals. Sidney Webb would, Tony Blair commented in 1995, be astonished to find that the clause was still in existence some 70 years later (1995: 12). It was not intended, Blair argued, to be taken seriously.

The 1922 programme made it clear that Labour stood neither for Bolshevism, nor Communism, but 'common sense and justice' (Miliband, 1973: 94). It is true that it suited the liberals and conservatives to present, in Winston Churchill's words, Labour as 'the party of revolution' (Miliband, 1973: 99), but, in fact, Labour's politics were always of a liberal and constitutional nature. It is revealing that during the crisis of 1931 when Prime Minister Ramsey MacDonald was expelled from the Labour Party for entering into a national government with the Conservatives, the Liberal leader, Sir Herbert Samuel, argued that it would be in the general interest if unpalatable social measures to deal with the economic crisis were imposed by a Labour Government (Miliband, 1973: 176).

Although conservative novelist and publicist Evelyn Waugh saw the country under occupation after the Labour electoral victory of 1945, in fact, Deputy Labour Leader Herbert Morrison made it clear that the socialisation of industry would only work 'on the merits of their specific cases. That is how the British mind works. It does not work in a vacuum or in abstract theories' (Miliband, 1973: 279).

## Blair's socialism

The position of Tony Blair (British Prime Minister, 1997–2007) – and this stance was also that of his successor Gordon Brown (Prime Minister, 2007–10) – followed this tradition of pragmatism, moralism, and constitutionalism. Indeed, Blair made it clear that the elimination of the old Clause IV was to facilitate a return to Labour's ethical roots (Wright, 1996: x). We must retain, he argues, the values and principles underlying democratic socialism but apply them entirely afresh to the modern world (Blair, 1992: 3). The values of democratic socialism are 'social justice, the equal worth of each citizen, equality of opportunity, community'. Socialism is, if you will, social-ism (Blair, 1994: 4). In the 50th-anniversary lecture of the 1945 Labour election victory, Blair described socialism as 'the political heir of radical liberalism' (1995: 8), which was the left wing of the once dominant Liberal Party (which was displaced by the Labour Party). He saw the New Liberals as social democrats, and he defines socialism as a form of politics through which to fight poverty, prejudice, and unemployment and to create the conditions in which to build one nation – tolerant, fair, enterprising, and inclusive. Socialists must be both moralists and empiricists. They need, on the one hand, to be concerned with values, but at the same time, they must address themselves to a world as it is and not as we would like it to be (Blair, 1995: 12–13). While after losing power in 2010, the Labour Party moved back to the left – especially under Jeremy Corbyn (Leader, 2015–20) – there was no serious attempt to reinstate the old Clause IV, and if anything Labour attempted to entice voters with 'retail politics', such as free superfast broadband.

## International social democrats

The German SPD sternly repudiated communism, and in its Bad Godesberg Resolution of 1959 – described by Berki as 'one of the boldest, most impressive "liberal" party manifestoes ever written' – it argues for competition where possible, planning 'as far as it is necessary'. It follows what the Swedish social democrats have called a 'matter-of-fact conception of man' (Berki, 1974: 98–9).

These comments capture the dilemma. Berki suggests that in a way social democracy can be characterised as 'utopian socialism minus utopian expectations' since it does not believe that ideals like justice, goodwill, brotherliness, and compassion could be 'unreservedly realised' (1974: 101). Is social democracy so pragmatic and flexible that it cannot be called socialism at all?

## Socialism in America

Commentators have often wondered why socialism has never really taken root in the United States. Factors that deserve emphasis are the following:

- Although the United States certainly had a war of independence against the British, those who supported the British were generally driven out and so the American republics had little class structure, certainly among free-born men.
- A high degree of mobility meant free men acquired private property so that a cultural ethos of individualism rather than collectivism prevailed.
- Even after the Civil War (1861–65), when class divisions became stark realities, emancipatory movements championed the rights of the 'small man', rather than an oppressed class, and labour unions often supported free enterprise in a way that Europeans found surprising.
- President Franklin D. Roosevelt's New Deal, although seen by its enemies as 'socialist' in character, embraced a social or new liberalism that never really challenged the capitalist nature of the economy.

## Can Marxism be rescued?

The aim of this final part of the chapter is to set out how a Marxist, or someone sympathetic to (at least some of) the tenets of Marxism, might seek to save Marxism. Obviously, someone who does not accept Marxist ideas will disagree. But since this is a chapter on socialism and Marxism, it is a valid approach. Readers unsympathetic to Marxism and socialism should view this as a hypothetical exercise in setting out the conditions under which Marxism (and socialism) might be salvaged. At the end, you can assess how successful the exercise has been.

## The notion of revolution

The concept of revolution as a dramatic element focused around a seizure of power is problematic. Marx uses the term revolution in different ways. He and Engels speak in the *Communist Manifesto* of the constant 'revolutionising of production' under capitalism (1967: 83) and in that sense, revolutions are occurring all the time. But revolution is also used to denote a transformation of state and class power – an event in which the character of society as a whole changes.

It is true that Marx argued that such an event need not be violent, and he even puts the view in 1882 that if in Britain 'the unavoidable evolution' turns into a revolution, that would not only be the fault of the ruling classes but also of the working class. Every peaceful concession has been wrung out through pressure, and the workers must wield their power and use their liberties, 'both of which they possess legally'. That suggests that each step forward is a kind of revolution in its own right and that the notion of revolution as a dramatic event that inevitably changes the character of society is redundant (Hoffman, 1975: 211).

This is not typical of Marx's view. The notion of revolution as a dramatic event linked to a seizure of power was inherited uncritically from the French Revolution of 1789. It creates a polarisation that makes the assertion of common interests and consensus more, not less, difficult. Engels is right: revolutions are authoritarian events, and they create a new state that clearly distinguishes between revolution and counter-revolution and this leads to the kind of insecurity and division that generates despotism rather than democracy.

## The inevitability problem and the liberal tradition

Clearly, the notion of revolution as inevitable creates the problem of supporting revolutions that generate authoritarian states and the consequent abuse of human rights. A scathing attitude towards morality can only aggravate the problem, but it does not follow from this that all elements of Marxism are authoritarian in orientation. Here the attitude towards liberalism is crucial. Not only did Marx begin his political career as a liberal steeped in the ideals of the European Enlightenment, but when he becomes a communist, he seeks to go beyond, rather than reject, liberal values.

The distinction between 'transcending' and 'rejecting' liberalism is crucial. To transcend liberalism is to build upon its values and institutions: it is to develop a theory and practice that extends freedom and equality more consistently and comprehensively than liberalism can do. Socialism as a 'post-liberalism' seeks to turn liberal values into concrete realities so that those excluded by classical liberalism – the workers, the poor, women, dependants – become free and equal, as part of an historical process which has no grand culminating moment or climax. Socialism as a 'pre-liberalism', on the other hand, negates liberal values by introducing a system that imposes despotic controls upon the population at large (whatever its claim to speak in the name of the workers), and it is well described in the *Communist Manifesto* as a reactionary socialism because it hurls 'traditional anathemas' against liberalism and representative government (Marx and Engels, 1967: 111).

The problem with Marxism is that it is an amalgam of pre-liberalism and post-liberalism. It is post-liberal in so far as it stresses the need to build upon, rather than reject, capitalist achievements. But while (conventionally defined) revolutions make sense in situations in which legal rights to change society are blocked, in societies that have, or are attempting to build, liberal institutions, revolutions lead to elitism, despotism, and a contempt for democracy. The notion of class war does not place enough emphasis on the need to create and consolidate common interests to campaign in a way that isolates those who oppose progress.

Again, there is a tension here in Marx's writings between his view that a classless society will eliminate alienation for all, and his argument that the bourgeoisie are the 'enemy' who must be overthrown. This leads to the privileging of the proletariat as the agent of revolution and hostility to all who are not proletarians.

## The question of class and agency

Socialists see class as something that is negative; freedom for all, they argue, is only possible in a classless society. Class privileges come at the expense of others. In liberal societies, it encourages an abstract approach to be taken to equality and power so that moral equality coexists with the significant inequalities of power and material resources (see pp. 90–2). Class is thus divisive, and it generates the kind of antagonisms that require force (and therefore the state) to tackle them.

For this reason, Marx argues that if we want to dispense with the need for an institution claiming a monopoly of legitimate force, we must dispense with classes. In a well-known comment, Marx argues that, in class-divided societies, social relations are not 'relations between individual and individual, but between worker and capitalist, between farmer and landlord, etc. Wipe out these relations and you annihilate all society' (Marx and Engels, 1975a: 77).

It may, however, be argued that this comment is not concrete enough, for workers also have a gender and national identity, and this materially affects how they relate to others. It is not that the class identity is unimportant: it is rather that it fuses with other identities since these other iden-tities are also a crucial part of the process that creates class. Brown argues that class has become invisible and inarticulate, rarely theorised or developed in the multiculturalist mantra 'race, class, gender, sexuality' (Brown, 1995: 61). The point is that we do not need to present these other identities as though they are separate from class.

Socialists must, in other words, seek to mobilise all those who are excluded by contemporary institutions. This goes well beyond the concept of a 'proletariat', although those who are poor and must subject themselves to the 'despotic' rules of employers are an obvious constituency in the struggle to govern one's own life. It is impossible to be free and equal if one is subject to ag-gressive pressures from employers and managers. Democratising the workplace to allow greater security, transparency, and participation is critical, and all those who suffer from these problems are natural constituents in the struggle for socialism.

Marxists might argue that with divisiveness in the world increasing through a kind of globali-sation that increases inequality, the notion of a proletariat must be viewed internationally rather than simply nationally. However, the danger still remains that such a perspective will take a narrow view of class and underplay the problem of cementing common interests across the globe.

## Socialism and inevitability

Marx sometimes makes it seem that socialism will arrive come what may. He speaks of 'the nat-ural laws of capitalist production' 'working with iron necessity towards inevitable results', and in a famous passage, he likens the birth of socialism to pregnancy (1970: 10). The development of socialism is as inevitable as the birth of a child. This argument is, however, only defensible as a conditional inevitability – not an absolute certainty independent of circumstances. In the *Communist Manifesto*, Marx and Engels comment that class struggle might end 'in a revolutionary constitution of society at large' or 'the common ruin of the contending classes' (Marx and Engels, 1967: 79). Not only is it impossible to establish a timescale for socialism but also its inevitability is conditional upon, for example, humanity avoiding a nuclear conflagration which wipes out humans, or the destruction of the environment which makes production impossible. Nor can it be said that liberal societies might not turn to the right before they turn to the left.

What a conditional inevitability merely states is that if humanity survives, then sooner or later, it will have to regulate its affairs in a socially conscious manner, and that, broadly speaking, is socialism. Only in this qualified and conditional sense, can it be said that socialism is inevitable. Marxism can be rescued if it makes it clear that 'inevitability' is conditional, drops the notion of revolution as a concentrated political event, and with it, a polarised and narrow notion of class. Whether it would still be Marxism is a moot point.

## The problem of utopianism

It has been argued that a credible socialism must draw upon social democratic and Marxist ideas. The problem with 'pure' social democrats as well as 'pure' Marxists is that they can be said to either embrace a (liberal) empiricist framework or they simply turn such a framework inside out.

Bernstein is a case in point. On the one hand, he saw himself as a positivist who stuck rigor-ously to the facts. On the other hand, he was living in a society which was clearly not socialist. Socialism is, he tells us, a piece of the beyond – something which ought to be, but is not (Gay, 1962: 158, 163). Abstract 'realism' coexists with abstract utopianism. The role of ethics is not integrated into a concern with the facts, and such a theory can pay too much attention to 'short-run developments', ruling out in a dogmatic fashion, dramatic, and unanticipated actions, 'apparently contradicted by the happenings of the day' (1962: 162).

Bernstein's position on economic concentration bears this out. As Gay comments, after 1924, German industry centralised and cartelised as never before (1962: 172). The trends that he analysed in 1899 were not irreversible. In the same way, Bernstein assumed that a new middle class would be democratic and pro-socialist. Yet, anyone who knows anything about German history after the First World War comments Gay 'will recognize the fallacious assumptions of Bernstein's theory'. Inflation and the world depression traumatised large groups within the German middle classes: they saw descent into the proletariat as a horrendous possibility (Gay, 1962: 215). Bernstein's analysis put into the context of Germany between the wars, turned out to be wishful thinking. Whether government through a representative parliament can work depends upon the social structure and political institutions of a country – it allows of no dogmatic answer (Gay, 1962: 236). Once we see that reality is in movement, then we can fuse utopia and realism. Utopia derives from the transformation of existing realities: but this utopia is not to be located outside existing realities, it is part of them. In arguing that socialism must be a 'utopian realism', there is avoided the dualism between facts and values, utopia and reality, a dualism that bedevils so many exponents of socialism, whether of the right or the left.

As has been argued in the chapter on anarchism, we need a state as long as humanity cannot resolve its conflicts of interest in a peaceful manner (see pp. 217–8). For Bernstein, because the state exists, it is here to stay. The 'so-called coercive associations, the state and the communities, will retain their great tasks in any future I can see' (Gay, 1962: 246). But to identify the state with community and regard its mechanisms for settling difference as only apparently 'coercive' shows how far 'pure' social democracy is still steeped in the abstract aspects of the liberal tradition.

Gay is surely right when he comments that Bernstein's optimism was not well founded: it took short-run prosperity and converted it into a law of capitalist development (1962: 299). If, as A.J. Taylor has said, Marx was a dogmatic optimist (Marx and Engels, 1967: 47), so was Bernstein. Socialism requires a conditional concept of inevitability and a dialectical determinism – one that takes full account of human agency – so that it is neither optimistic, nor pessimistic, but is a utopian realism.

## Death and socialism

We return to the question posed at the start: why so many deaths under communism? In the final chapter of the *Black Book of Communism*, Stéphane Courtois offers a range of explanations. Courtois's analysis is not uncontroversial (Weiner, 2002; Reid, 2005). However, he and his co-authors offer some interesting arguments. First, the appeal of the nihilistic Russian Sergei Nechaev to some Communists is significant. It is worth quoting Nechaev:

> This whole sick society must be divided into several categories. In the first category are the people who will be killed immediately…the second should include individuals who are to be allowed to continue living for a while, so that by their monstrous acts they merely accelerate the inevitable uprising of the people.
>
> (quoted in Albert et al., 1999: 730)

Courtois argues that the French Revolution of 1789 provided the model, or template, for revolution. Through terror, new humans would be forged. But in France the terror stopped with the ousting of Robespierre, and the Revolution became the basis of a liberal-democratic polity.

While Marx distanced himself from violence and interpreted revolution as radical change that could be affected by forces already present in society – by, for example, parliamentary institutions, as in the case of Britain – the eliminationist logic of the French Revolution resurfaced at the start of the twentieth century and was made more virulent by its being grafted onto a Russian tradition of violence. Lenin, while influenced by the relatively non-violent tradition of Western Marxism, was also deeply embedded in the revolutionary Russian land movement. Added to this was the fact that Russia was not 'ripe' for revolution, in the sense that it had not developed capitalism, and so communism became a 'development ideology' – a way of jumping from feudalism to modernity. There developed a strategy of combining mass insurrection from below with elite terror from above (Albert et al., 1999: 731).

That Leninism had a purely theoretical conception of class meant the elite defined who was revolutionary and who was counter-revolutionary, with the latter marked out for elimination (1999: 737). By creating abstractions, rather than recognising real flesh-and-blood human beings, killing became easy (1999: 740). And since law was associated with the bourgeois state – which was necessarily repressive – it could be suspended in favour of 'proletarian democracy', which in effect meant the party elite.

Most people find killing difficult, and so a process of psychological hardening is required. The creation of enemies through abstraction aids that process. And when the abstractions do not accord with reality, there is potentially no end to violence. Unless some fortunate historical events result in the violence being ended – as happened in post-revolutionary France – then every social, economic, and military disappointment will result in the search for new enemies. If utopia is not achieved, then it must be because there are traitors among us, and they must be rooted out. Of course, total economic collapse can also end the violence, but this requires recognition from the governing elite, and the discovery of suitable scapegoats, as happened with China's Cultural Revolution, which lasted from 1966 to 1976, and only ended with Mao's death. Because it would have undermined the legitimacy of the communist regime to blame Mao directly, the so-called Gang of Four – Jiang Qing, Zhang Chunqiao, Yao Wenyuan, and Wang Hongwen – were held responsible. Thereafter, China started on its path to authoritarian capitalism.

## Conclusion

Socialism is certainly a broad church, but underlying its numerous forms is a concern with co-operation and equality, a belief that human nature can change and that freedom requires an adequate provision of resources. Socialism is peculiarly prone to the problem of utopianism because it seeks to establish a society that differs from the world of the present. The work of Saint Simon, Fourier, and Robert Owen demonstrates that socialists who were labelled 'utopian' by their Marxist critics did not regard themselves in this light. Marxism is a variant of socialism that leads to authoritarianism insofar as it emphasises an unconditional inevitability, has a particular notion of revolution, and appears disdainful of moral judgement. Social democracy or democratic socialism rejects utopianism but runs the risk being indistinguishable from liberalism.

Marxism can only be rescued from the problem of authoritarianism if it rejects the notion of revolution as a single political event and adopts a broader view of class and a conditional notion of inevitability. The problem of utopia in socialism needs to be meaningfully addressed by constructing socialism as a utopian realism so that neither half of this construct is stressed at the expense of the other.

# References

Albert, G. P., Courtois, S., Werth, N., Paczkowski, A., Panné, J. L., Bartosek, K., and Margolin, J. L. (1999). *The Black Book of Communism: Crimes, Terror, Repression*. Harvard University Press.

Bauman, Z. (1976). *Socialism as Utopia*. London: George Allen and Unwin.

Berki, R. (1974). *Socialism*. London: Dent.

Bernstein, E. (1961). *Evolutionary Socialism*. New York: Schocken.

Blair, T. (1992). Pride without Prejudice. *Fabian Review, 104*(3), 3.

Blair, T. (1994). *Socialism*. Fabian Pamphlet 565, London.

Blair, T. (1995). *Let Us Face the Future*. Fabian Pamphlet 571, London.

Brown, W. (1995). *States of Injury*. Princeton, NJ: Princeton University Press.

Crick, B. (1987). *Socialism*. Milton Keynes: Open University Press.

Gay, P. (1962). *The Dilemma of Democratic Socialism*. New York: Collier.

Geoghegan, V. (1987). *Utopianism and Marxism*. London and New York: Methuen.

Heywood, A. (1992). *Political Ideologies*. Basingstoke: Macmillan.

Hoffman, J. (1975). *Marxism and the Theory of Praxis*. New York: International Publishers.

Hoffman, J. (1995). *Beyond the State*. Cambridge: Polity.

Hunt, R. (1975). *The Political Ideas of Marx and Engels*, vol. 1, Basingstoke: Macmillan.

Mannheim, K. (1960). *Ideology and Utopia*. London: Routledge and Kegan Paul.

Marx, K. (1970). *Capital*, vol. 1. London: Lawrence and Wishart.

Marx, K. and Engels, F. (1967). *The Communist Manifesto*. Harmondsworth: Penguin.

Marx, K. and Engels, F. (1968). *Selected Works*. London: Lawrence and Wishart.

Marx, K. and Engels, F. (1975a). *Collected Works*, vol. 4. London: Lawrence and Wishart.

Miliband, R. (1973). *Parliamentary Socialism*, 2nd edn. London: Merlin.

Reid, D. (2005). In Search of the Communist Syndrome: Opening the Black Book of the New Anti-communism in France. *The International History Review, 27*(2), 295–318.

The Week (2021). The Decline and Fall of Europe's Centre-left. *The Week*, viewed 24 June 2021, https://www.theweek.co.uk/news/world-news/952956/decline-fall-of-europe-centre-left

Tucker, R. (ed.) (1978). *The Marx-Engels Reader*, 2nd edn. New York and London: W.W. Norton.

Weiner, A. (2002). The Black Book of Communism: Crimes, Terror, Repression. *Journal of Interdisciplinary History, 32*(3), 450–52.

Wright, T. (1996). *Socialisms*. London and New York: Routledge.

# Further reading

Recently published overviews of socialism: Jeremy Gilbert, *Twenty-First Century Socialism* (Polity, 2020); Michael Newman, *Socialism: A Very Short Introduction* (Oxford University Press, 2020); Peter Lamb, *Socialism* (Polity, 2019). On Marxism: Gregory Claeys, *Marx and Marxism* (Pelican, 2018); Alex Callinicos, Stathis Kouvelakis, and Lucia Pradella (eds.), *Routledge Handbook of Marxism and Post-Marxism* (Routledge, 2020); Leszek Kolakowski, *Main Currents of Marxism* (Norton, 2008) (this is a classic study of the origins and development of Marxism).

# Chapter 12

# Anarchism

## Introduction

The term anarchism is much used in popular debates, especially in relation to anti-capitalist and Antifa protests. 'Anarchist' is often a term of abuse and is sometimes misused – but what exactly does it mean? What does it stand for and why have some argued that anarchism has enjoyed a resurgence in recent years? On the face of it, it seems like a self-defeating political ideology, as it seeks to get rid of the state, which is the entity within which, or around which, political activity takes place. So why does anarchism remain influential? Who does it attract and why?

## Key questions

- What is anarchism?
- Is anarchism a coherent ideology?
- Why is anarchism popularly associated with violence and is there any conceptual or theoretical justification for that linkage?

## What is anarchism?

For once, the etymology of a political concept is useful. At its most basic level, anarchy means 'without state', from the Greek *anarkhos*, without (*an*) chief (*arkhos*). That is the core idea. And if you believe that the absence of the state means the absence of rules and arbitrary violence, then you will be led to the popular definition of anarchy as violent disorder.

It is a rare political theorist who would value disorder (except as a tactic), and so anarchist political theory makes the claim that you can have stateless order. While the theories discussed in this chapter differ greatly from one another, they all hold to this idea. The nagging doubt is that, without a state, there will be arbitrary violence. Of course, the state uses violence – violence is one of its defining characteristics (see p. 9) – and that is a central focus of the anarchist critique of the state, but we need to distinguish the reasoned and controlled use of violence, as practiced in, for example, the institution of punishment and arbitrary violence.

DOI: 10.4324/9780429424106-16

Case study 12.1

# CHAZ or CHOP?

**PHOTO 12.1** © Noah Riffe/Anadolu Agency via Getty Images.

On 8 June 2020, in the wake of the death of George Floyd, protestors in Seattle established the Capitol Hill Autonomous Zone (CHAZ), later renamed the Capitol Hill Occupied Protest (CHOP). CHAZ/CHOP was a self-organised space, without official leadership. Their demands included cutting the Seattle Police Department's budget by 50%, redirecting that money to community programmes in historically black parts of the city, providing naturalisation services for irregular migrants, guaranteeing free public housing and education, release of prisoners serving drug-possession-related offences, mandatory retrials for people of colour serving sentences for violent crimes, a focus on black and minority history, and ensuring that protestors will not be charged with offences.

A Black Lives Matter (BLM) mural was created, free film screenings put on, and live music performed. A 'No Cop Co-op' was formed, giving out free supplies, and a community vegetable garden created. Decisions were made through a general assembly, with daily meetings and discussion groups.

What exactly happened between CHAZ/CHOP's formation on 8 June and its clearance by the police on 1 July is a matter of dispute – there were shootings in or around the zone and accusations that businesses were intimidated. With a highly partisan and polarised media, it is difficult to get an accurate picture, but of interest for us is the ambiguity around the name: was it a genuinely autonomous zone – CHAZ – or simply a protest, with a few gestures towards autonomy – CHOP? And the deeper question is whether anarchism can ever be a viable form of political organisation or is simply a style of politics.

## Anarchism and its relationship to socialism

In her book *Using Political Ideas* (Goodwin, 1997), Barbara Goodwin has a separate chapter on anarchism and argues that the anarchist is 'not merely a socialist who happens to dislike the state'. She concedes, however, that there is much overlap and that many anarchists have analysed capitalism in a way that resembles that of socialists (1997: 122).

R.N. Berki, however, in his influential book *Socialism*, treats anarchism as a current within socialism and notes, for example, that it was Pierre-Joseph Proudhon, a key anarchist discussed later in this chapter, who first called his doctrine 'scientific socialism' (Berki, 1974: 12), and that Proudhon's significance for socialism is enormous (1974: 84). Berki makes many acute observations about anarchism in the context of his chapter on the evolution of socialism. In a section on socialist thought at the turn of the century, he describes Michel Bakunin as a precursor to both Russian socialism and anarcho-syndicalism (1974: 83–8), about which more will be said later.

Andrew Vincent, like Goodwin, has a separate chapter on anarchism and makes the point that the doctrine overlaps with both liberalism and socialism (Goodwin, 1997: 114). But whatever the overlap between some kinds of anarchism and socialism, there is also an anarchism that is explicitly non-socialist and in some of its forms anti-socialist. It will be useful to say something about these first since they are dramatically different from 'socialist' forms of anarchism.

## Philosophical anarchists

Although anarchism is a very old theory, it only emerged in systematic form in the eighteenth century as part of the Enlightenment. William Godwin's *Enquiry Concerning Political Justice* (1793) is widely agreed to be the first comprehensive account of anarchist principles.

Godwin was really a liberal, even though he abandoned the classical liberal view of natural rights and a state of nature. He argues that humans are social beings, moulded by their environment and imbued with a capacity to reason. True happiness, as far as Godwin was concerned, lies with the development of individuality. All individuals have a right to private judgement. Everything understood by social organisation is 'in some degree evil', and he argued that communal institutions, even theatre and musical performances, could be seen as an invasion of our individuality. Society should be regarded as a 'luxury' rather than a 'necessity' and can never be more than the sum of its parts (Vincent, 1995: 125). Compulsory restraint violates a privately determined pursuit of happiness, and it is said that Godwin ends where Hobbes begins: for Hobbes, a decent life is only possible under the state (see pp. 12–13). While Godwin sees the state as vicious, evil, and tyrannical, the premises of his theory are strongly individualistic. If this atomistic view of the individual leads to radical insecurity and arbitrariness in Hobbes's state of nature, in Godwin, it generates the 'unspeakably beautiful vision of a world' in which individuals freely exercise their private judgement (Hoffman, 1995: 114).

Godwin was opposed to property, the market and acquisitiveness, in general, but he was no socialist. His opposition to the state extends to social relationships, and all individuals retain a sphere of private judgement that shuts society out. He may have hoped that small face-to-face communities would replace the state – with temporary coordinating bodies being transitionally necessary to resolve disputes and repel invaders – but he has been rightly called a 'philosophical anarchist' since his main preoccupation is with principles rather than practice.

Max Stirner is often bracketed with Godwin as a philosophical anarchist, but unlike Godwin, Stirner does not see individuals as benevolent and rational. He enthusiastically embraces the argument that consciousness – which is always 'alienated' – is the source of our oppression. In Stirner's case, concepts like humanism, communism, and liberalism are inherently oppressive because they are necessarily imposed upon the sovereign individual. The state of nature adhered to by classical liberals was essentially social in character, but individuals constitute the highest reality. People have no rights of any kind. As a conscious egoist, the individual, in Stirner's view, is beyond good and evil, and the oppressiveness of the state is no different in essence from the oppressiveness of all social relationships, indeed of ideologies. All subject the ego to some 'generality or other' (Hoffman, 1995: 115).

Stirner sees the natural world as a war of all against all, but unlike Hobbes who posits a powerful state to tackle this problem, Stirner advocates the formation of an association of sovereign individuals – a union of conscious egoists – who would spontaneously and voluntarily come together out of mutual interest. All teleological categories – goals, purposes, and ends – are oppressive even if they are imposed by individuals upon themselves. This means that even a system of direct democracy is unacceptable. His union of egoists would enable individuals to accomplish more than they could on their own, and though Stirner's world is one without rights and morality, the union would create security and put an end to poverty. Marx and Engels in their lengthy critique of Stirner's *The Ego and His Own* point out that Stirner employs a concept of the unique individual which in practice morally obliges other individuals, so that he is in the hapless position of attacking authority from moral premises which are not supposed to exist (Hoffman, 1995: 115).

In a more recent exposition of philosophical anarchism, Robert Paul Wolff argues that all adults are responsible beings who have a capacity for choice and a potential for autonomy that they lose if they obey the dictates of another. A person's primary obligation is to be autonomous. However, unlike Stirner and Godwin, Wolff accepts the case for a direct democracy, and he argues that people are bound by the decisions they have taken. The advantage of such a system is that the authority to which each citizen submits 'is not of himself simply, but that of the entire community taken collectively'. Not only does this sound rather authoritarian, but Wolff argues that each person encounters 'his better self in the form of the state, for its dictates are simply the laws which he has, after due deliberation willed to be enacted' (cited by Dahl, 1989: 348).

All philosophical anarchists have the problem of moving from the individual to some kind of collective organisation which, on the one hand, is deemed necessary to realise anarchism, but which, on the other, contradicts anarchist principles. We will see if the free market anarchists are better able to tackle this problem.

## Free market anarchists

Nineteenth century Americans like Lysander Spooner and Benjamin Tucker argued for an anarchism that was an extension of liberalism: if individuals are free and equal, why should they accept the compulsion of the state? Locke's state of nature (see p. 64) was a world in which individuals are not subject to external discipline: why should things not stay that way? But whereas nineteenth century free market anarchists were concerned about the structural inequalities that the market might generate – and they took the view that everyone should be an entrepreneur – more recent free market anarchists have accepted capitalism, arguing that exploitation and coercion are simply the product of the state rather than the market.

Free market anarchists like Murray Rothbard take the view that state welfare is as pernicious as state warfare. Any attempt to regulate production prevents consumers from purchasing commodities that *they* wish to buy, while goods that everybody wants, like sanitation, roads, and street lighting, are best provided by private enterprise. Disadvantaged groups, like the elderly, the unemployed, and the disabled, should be catered for by charity since state provision is invariably wasteful and open to abuse (Hoffman, 1995: 117).

It is not only the provision of such things as roads, schools, and hospitals that should be privatised. As far as modern-day free market anarchists are concerned, the market should take over the state's security role as well. Rothbard contends that people could insure themselves against bodily assault in the same way that they currently insure their possessions against theft. Aggrieved parties could then seek compensation and redress for injury through private tribunals, with the free market ensuring that arbitrators or judges with the best record in settling disputes would be hired. These arguments were discussed in Chapters 1 (see pp. 23–4) and 3 (see pp.54–5).

But how would these judgements be enforced? Recalitrants who refused to abide by tribunal decisions would be subject to boycott and ostracism, and in more serious cases, guards and police could be hired to defend injured parties and enforce judgements. People who refused to comply with judgements could be placed in private prisons, and aggrieved individuals might decide (with the help of friends and relatives) to retaliate in person. Rothbard describes the state as 'the great legalized and socially legitimated channel of all manner of social crime', and getting rid of the state would strengthen the 'good' in human nature and discourage the bad (Hoffman, 1995: 118). Humans remain possessive individualists by nature, and it is this assumption that leads the libertarian thinker Robert Nozick to make the case for the minimal state (Nozick, 1974).

## Nozick's minarchism

Nozick is not an anarchist, but rather advocates for a minimal state, one restricted to providing security. He is a critic of anything more than a minimal state, and we discussed his critique of egalitarian theories of redistributive justice in Chapter 8 (see pp. 143–4). Despite his rejection of anarchism, he does attempt to derive the minimal state from anarchist premises. His starting point is the idea of natural rights, and following a secularised version of Locke's argument, he argues that we have primary rights in our bodies (self-ownership) and secondary rights to punish those who violate those primary rights. Crucially, you can empower a third party to exercise your right to punish.

In Locke's theory, it is through a contract we pool our rights to punish and entrust those pooled rights to the state (see p. 64). For Nozick, in contrast, that enforcer (protection agency) emerges through the operation of the market. He distinguishes an ultraminimal from a minimal state (1974: 26–8). With the former, one protection agency monopolises force in a given geographical area and does not allow individuals to enforce their own rights, while with the latter that dominant agency protects everybody, even if they have not paid for security. This he terms compensation — those who do not accept the dominant agency must, he argues, be compensated. So, the key characteristic of the ultraminimal state is monopoly and of the minimal state monopoly plus compensation (1974: 78–84). There are a series of steps in the development of the minimal state:

1. The state of nature, with no protection agencies.
2. The state of nature with many agencies.
3. One dominant (but not monopolistic) agency.
4. One monopolistic agency.
5. A monopolistic agency, with compensation.

Nozick believes that we can get to 5 without violating anybody's rights. For his argument to be successful, he has to respond convincingly to the charge that the rights of two groups are threatened: (a) those who refuse to join the dominant agency, either preferring to go with a competing agency or enforce their own rights (he calls these 'independents'); (b) those who have to pay to compensate the independents.

Ultimately, it is difficult to see how the minimal state does not violate the rights of some individuals. The compensation problem may be less pressing if people still pay for the service. We discussed this issue in the Chapter 1 case study (see pp. 23–4). But the monopoly problem seems intractable, as choice is being taken away from people.

## Anti-capitalist anarchists: Proudhon, Bakunin, and Kropotkin

Proudhon was certainly a socialist, although he objected to communism on the grounds that it subordinates the individual to the collective (Marshall, 1993: 238). It is the unequal distribution of property that creates disorder, but the answer, as he saw it, was mutualism – a system that avoided the vices of both private property and collective ownership and was based upon exchange and credit. Exchange would occur through associations that calculated the necessary labour time involved in a product. People could start businesses by borrowing from a mutual credit bank, and this economic reorganisation would make the state redundant. In Proudhon's view, parliamentary democracy is futile and counter-productive – 'universal suffrage is counter revolution' is one of his many celebrated dictums (1993: 244).

Proudhon aroused the wrath of Marx who wrote his *Poverty of Philosophy* against Proudhon's *Philosophy of Poverty*. Marx objected to Proudhon's opposition to political involvement and trade unionism and regarded his principles of justice and equality as unhistorical. Proudhon's rejection of liberal principles of government meant that he regarded all forms of the state as anathema. He was also strongly nationalistic, patriarchal, and for a period supported the autocratic Emperor Napoleon III who suspended parliamentary politics. Proudhon popularised the view that anarchy stood for order – despite the frequent use of the word as a synonym for chaos – and is widely regarded as the father of anarchism.

Influenced by Proudhon, but strongly collectivist in orientation, was the Russian anarchist, Mikhail Bakunin. Bakunin declares with an anti-Hobbesian fervour that 'man is born into society, just as ant is born into an ant-hill and bee into its hive' (Marshall, 1993: 291). The analogy with nature is important for Bakunin since he takes the view that sociability and the desire to revolt are *instinctive*. They are both universal and stronger among some rather than others. He argued that the instinct for revolt was particularly strong among the Latins and the Slavs and weak among Germanic peoples. He saw revolution as a violent process, and what Marshall calls his 'apocalyptic fantasies' (1993: 306) manifest themselves in his belief that to create is to destroy. This slogan reappears during the May events – the student rebellion – in 1968 in Paris, and Berki notes that Bakunin's ideas became very fashionable in the 1970s in Western libertarian socialist circles (1974: 84).

Bakunin clashed with Marx in the First International, and he was expelled in 1872. Nevertheless, although he and the 'authoritarian' Marx disagreed over strategy, he greatly admired Marx's critique of capital and was opposed not simply to the repressive hierarchy of the state, but to the inequalities and exploitation identified with capitalism. He was, however, passionately opposed to Marx's notion of the workers becoming a ruling class and having to control a transitional state. The workers' state, he insisted, would be nothing but a barracks; a regime where working men and women are regimented. We will have 'despotic rule over the toiling masses by a new, numerically small aristocracy of genuine or sham scientists. The people . . . will be wholly regimented into one common herd of governed people. Emancipation indeed!' (Maximoff, 1953: 287). Not only was Bakunin sceptical about the 'authority' of science, but he regarded religion and the notion of God as inherently statist and authoritarian.

Yet, Bakunin argued the case for a secret association in which a revolutionary general staff would serve as intermediaries 'between the revolutionary idea and the instincts of the people', and this presumably accounts for his temporary attraction to Sergei Nechaev, a nihilist, who believed the revolution should be pursued by any means necessary (see pp. 202). Against one's will, declared Bakunin, one is obliged to use 'force, cunning and deception' (Marshall, 1993: 282–4). Bakunin was hugely influential. Not only did he make an enormous impact upon French labour, Italian revolutionaries, and as we shall see, the socialist movement in Spain, but his anti-capitalism attracted support among those who espoused what was called anarcho-syndicalism.

Bertrand Russell has referred to syndicalism as 'the anarchism of the marketplace' (Berki, 1974: 87), and it focuses on the role of industrial workers who are to organise themselves into revolutionary syndicates, making 'war on the bosses' and not bothering with politics (Marshall, 1993: 441). The general strike is seen as the best weapon for ushering in the new order. Syndicates should take on social functions as the germ of the stateless, socialist society. But not all anarchists agreed with syndicalism. Emma Goldman feared that syndicalism trampled upon the rights of the individual by accepting a principle of majority rule, while the Italian Errico Malatesta saw syndicalism simply as one of the many means to achieve anarchist ends (1993: 444).

The contrast between Pyotr Kropotkin and Bakunin is striking. Although they were both Russian and both influenced by Marx's critique of capitalism, Kropotkin had great respect for science and was an accomplished geographer. Kropotkin espoused the ideal of a federal and de-centralised society with the land and factories owned by the producers. He was sympathetic to syndicalism and argued that the great gains in the past had been made by the force of popular revolution, not through 'an evolution created by an elite' (Marshall, 1993: 317).

Anarchism must proceed with the method of the natural scientists. Mutual aid was far more important to the evolution of the species than mutual struggle. The species that cooperates the most is most likely to survive. Humans are, by nature, social and moral, and the greatest individual development comes through practising the 'highest communist sociability'. The socialist notion of a 'people's state' – here he agreed with Bakunin – is 'as great a danger to liberty as any form of autocracy' (Marshall, 1993: 321–6). Whereas Bakunin saw distribution as linked to the performance of work, Kropotkin also stressed need: production and distribution are integrated in communal enterprises so as to meet the physical and cultural needs of all (Vincent, 1995: 133).

He was offered a cabinet position – which he turned down – in the Provisional Government of Alexander Kerensky after the overthrow of Tsarism in 1917 and was bitterly critical both of the Bolshevik Revolution and the tactics adopted after the revolution. Kropotkin called himself a communist anarchist, whereas Bakunin preferred to see himself as a collectivist, while Proudhon regarded himself as a mutualist. But all three were critical of capitalism. All saw anarchism as a solution to the kind of inequality generated by a capitalist society.

## Republican Spain and the anarchist experience

The Spanish Republic has become a valuable historical laboratory for trying to understand an-archism because it is the only example in the twentieth century in which anarchism succeeded in constructing a new society, at least in particular regions and for a few years. As Thomas comments, 'the Spanish Anarchists are the only Anarchists in European history to have made any mark upon events' (1965: 279).

The liberal tradition was weak in Spain. During the nineteenth century, the church and the army had intervened to prevent or paralyse a liberal constitution, and this had strengthened the widespread scepticism towards conventional political processes. Anarchist strength centred on Barcelona in the north where it was reinforced by separatist sentiments among the Catalans (and took the form of anarcho-syndicalism), and it was also strong among the impoverished peasantry in the south. When a Spanish Communist Party was formed in 1921, the anarchists were four times more numerous than the socialists. In Spain, the mass of workers and peasants had followed Bakunin when he broke with Marx. The Confederación Nacional del Trabajo (CNT) had over a million members at the time of the First World War, and in 1933, the anarchist weekly *Tierra y Libertad* declared grandly:

> Workers! Do not vote! The vote is a negation of your personality. . .All the politicians are enemies. . .we need neither state nor government. . .Do not be concerned whether the Right or the Left emerge triumphant from this farce. . .Parliament. . .is a filthy house of prostitution. . .Destroy the ballots! Destroy the ballot boxes. . .hack off the heads of the ballot supervisors as well of the candidates. . ..
>
> (Thomas, 1965: 95)

One could well argue that revolutions do not have to be violent, but this was not how Spanish anarchists saw the issue. The Communists had, following the Seventh Comintern Congress, thrown their weight behind the idea of a Popular Front (an alliance of liberal and left-wing forces), and in 1936, the left won a substantial electoral victory on a programme of radical reform. Francisco Franco, with the army mostly loyal to him, led a rebellion. The socialists (and communists) were strong in Madrid, but the anarchists retained control of Barcelona, where all large industries passed to the CNT, and expropriation was considered the rule. Large numbers of people belonging to the old order were killed, and churches were destroyed. In some places, money was replaced by coupons, while in Andalusia in the south, where the anarchists were also strong, each town acted on its own responsibility. By 1937, some three million people were living in rural collectives.

The anarchists adopted military methods of organisation, and Miller cites Franz Borkenau's comment that, in one of the villages of Aragon, the agrarian revolution was almost the automatic consequence of executions (1974: 106–7). In September 1936, the anarchists entered the Catalan government calling it the Revolutionary Defence Council so as to avoid giving the impression 'to their already alarmed extremist followers' that they had joined a real government (Thomas, 1965: 367). Marshall argues that in so doing, they had started down the slippery slide to parliamentary participation, and this meant sacrificing the social revolution to the war against Franco (Marshall, 1993: 461).

As the crisis continued, the anarchists entered the government in Madrid, with the anarchist Garcia Oliver becoming Minister of Justice and the CNT recognising the republican state as 'an instrument of struggle' (Thomas, 1965: 404). The defence of this action by the CNT's daily newspaper is regarded by Marshall as 'an unparalleled bout of dissimulation' (Marshall, 1993: 465). Oliver, 'for all his devotion to Bakunin', proceeded to establish a new code of state laws and defended the need for iron discipline in the popular army (Thomas, 1965: 470; Marshall, 1993: 465). In late April 1937, a civil war between the anarchists and the communist-backed government broke out in Barcelona, and some 500 were killed. Anarchist influence ebbed away, and although the CNT continued to collaborate with the government, they no longer took even nominal responsibility for its actions (Thomas, 1965: 558).

On 18 March 1938, the CNT signed an agreement with the socialist Unión General de Trabajadores (UGT) to subject industry to central economic planning – collectivisation everywhere was giving way to state control (Thomas, 1965: 671). In Madrid, the anarchists backed attacks on the communists, putting the blame for the perilous military position on the Popular Front government (Thomas, 1965: 750). By the end of March, Franco's victory was secured.

## The problem of violence

The question of violence is linked to the question of transition – how gradual is the movement towards a stateless society to be? Can a dramatic transformation of society take place bit by bit?

Godwin believed that it would take considerable time before society became sufficiently enlightened to adopt anarchist institutions, and Marshall has suggested that different types of anarchist organisation could be taken to secure progression towards the anarchist goal. Thus, Proudhon's mutualism – involving the regulation of different private producers – could give way to Bakunin's collectivism – where people are rewarded according to their work – which, in turn, might yield to the more egalitarian idea of Kropotkin's communism where each is rewarded according to their needs (Hoffman, 1995: 124).

It is true that many anarchists have seen that violence involves an intolerable conflict between ends and means. The Russian anarchist and novelist, Leo Tolstoy (1828–1910) rejected all forms of violence, whether revolutionary or statist: is there any difference, he asked between killing a revolutionary and killing a policeman? 'The difference is between cat-shit and dog-shit . . . I don't like the smell of either' (cited in Marshall, 1993: 377). Mahatma Gandhi, influenced by Tolstoy, also espoused a militant pacifism (see pp. 70–1). April Carter argues that there are elements within anarchism that are peculiarly receptive to violence. The belief that many anarchists held, that a golden age might be realised through one apocalyptic outburst, an all-embracing revolution, can only encourage what Bakunin called the 'poetry of destruction' (Carter, 1978: 337).

Part of this utopianism is the shunning of political organisation in its conventional form, for it might be argued – as was the case with the anarchists in Spain – that it is worse to cast a ballot than fire a bullet. If constitutional procedures are identified with 'statist' liberalism, then the alternative may have to be despotism and violence. It is revealing that Robert Michels turned from anarchism to authoritarianism, arguing that because the German Social Democratic Party was too hierarchical, all organisation is oligarchical in character. One sympathetic commentator has argued ruefully that 'a streak of pathological violence' runs through anarchism (Hoffman, 1995: 126). We see how after the crushing of the Paris Commune in 1871, many anarchists resorted to a 'propaganda by deed' – dramatic action designed to shake the masses out of their passivity – and these propagandist deeds often degenerated into acts of terror. A belief that everything is right which is not 'legal' can easily lead to violence, even if it is justified as a way of avenging wrongs against the people, inspiring fear in the enemy and highlighting the evil practices of the state (Miller, 1974: 98–9).

Marshall quotes a passage from the CNT constitution printed on the membership card which states that 'the adversary does not discuss: he acts' (1993: 457), and even Kropotkin, whose personal life is often described in saint-like terms, displays what Marshall calls 'an uncomfortable mixture of quietism and aggressive elements'. Indeed, at one point in his life, Kropotkin supports the argument of the anarcho-syndicalist Georges Sorel that violence is the revolutionary whirlwind that energises 'sluggish hearts' (Hoffman, 1995: 126).

The problem of abolishing the state and authority seems to lead inevitably to the resort to violence; the perpetuation of the state in a new form and a legacy of division and mistrust. But how are people to free themselves when they are oppressed? Oppression arises when a person is deprived of material and social resources and lacks esteem: how is this emancipation to be secured without organisation? Marshall argues that anarchists only reject authoritarian organisation, but it could be argued that all organisation requires some hierarchy and leadership – the very political qualities that anarchists reject (Hoffman, 1995: 124).

Miller cites the sad reflections of Emma Goldman as she compares the weaknesses of Russian anarchists when set against the organisational strengths of the Bolsheviks. The work of the anarchists, she remarks, 'would have been of infinitely greater value had they been better organized' (Miller, 1974: 97–8), but she fails to ask herself whether these weaknesses were a product of anarchist theory itself. What are anarchists to do if the masses fail to rise in revolt? Two responses are possible. Either anarchists simply wait – as Godwin seems to argue – until the spirit of rational enlightenment takes root in the minds of the masses, or as in Bakunin's case, the people need a helping hand.

Certainly, it is difficult to see how anarchists can combine revolutionary effectiveness without resort to force, given the fact that politics in terms of organisation, representation, leadership, and compromise are ruled out by the theory adopted. This is a problem not only for left-wing anarchists but it also afflicts anarcho-capitalists who see the market as a source of freedom, but have the problem of tackling those who have vested interests in perpetuating concentrations of state power. Rothbard notes that anarchists have to contemplate 'the extremely difficult course of a revolution against a power with all the guns in its hands' (Hoffman, 1995: 124).

Despite Marshall's argument that the civil war in Spain demonstrated the strengths and not the weaknesses of anarchist theory, it is difficult not to see that event pointing to the fact that anarchists in practice can only operate in contradiction to their own theory. Those who see anarchism as having a built-in propensity to violence whatever the pacifist claims of some of its adherents are right. The theory cannot be understood without seeing a contradiction between ends and means.

## Anarchism and the new social movements

Anarchism continues to be influential, with adherents like Herbert Read stressing the relevance of anarchism to various contemporary social movements. Alex Comfort argued the case for sexual freedom, while Paul Goodman before his death in 1972 influenced many who took part in the counter-culture movements of the 1960s and 1970s. The relevance of anarchism to green movements and a concern about the deterioration of the urban and rural environment has been stressed in the work of Murray Bookchin. Nature, he argues, is a 'complex of life', charged with ethical meaning. Nature is essentially creative, directive, mutualistic, and fecund (Marshall, 1993: 605–6). This confirms the sociability and decency of humans. Without anarchism, there will be ecological disaster.

Bookchin's work is particularly important because many of his positions have been adopted in the new social movements by people who may be unfamiliar with anarchism and would not regard themselves as anarchists. The new social movements concern themselves with a wide array of causes – animal rights and ecology, peace and women's rights, anti-road building and private transport, to name just some of them. New social movements are characterised – or at least characterise themselves – as anti-authoritarian, and opposed to conventional politics, which they regard as stifling and treacherous; by a concern with breaking down barriers between the personal and political; and adopting a style of campaigning that unites ends and means and links enjoyment to efficiency. All this suggests that anarchist ideas have made a huge impact, even if anarchism considered as a comprehensive philosophy and systematic movement has not.

Green parties, like that in Germany, have enjoyed some electoral success and have built into their procedures a libertarian distrust of authoritarianism, and what are regarded as the dangers inherent in conventional political organisation (see pp. 299–300). At the same time, they have not ignored parliament or the state, and they have treated anarchism less as a dogma, and more as a set of values, some of which are more relevant and valid than others.

The philosophy of direct action – that laws and private property are not sacrosanct – stems from an anarchist suspicion of the state. When people in Britain refused to pay the poll tax (community charge) in the 1980s or occupied military and nuclear bases, many were acting according to anarchist values – understood in the sense of particular attitudes that may be appropriate for particular situations.

Classical anarchism is seen as being in the same boat as classical Marxism: rigid, dogmatic; old-fashioned; weak on issues of gender, children's rights, and the environment; too concerned with ideological rectitude and theoretical rigour. Anarchists often link their dislike for large organisations to a belief that the market is corrupting and capitalism unfair. Turner argues that the natural supporters of anarchist values are those who are excluded from consumerist society and who see politicians as an elite and incapable of engineering real change. He speaks of anarchism having a more receptive and permanent home among an underclass that might include 'disaffected youth, the long term unemployed and inner-city dwellers in perpetual poverty' (1993: 32).

## Organisation and relationships

It has been said that anarchism 'owes more to conventional liberalism than some of its adherents are willing to admit' (Hoffman, 1995: 113). It is not only philosophical and free market anarchists who embody the problems of the liberal tradition, so too do the anti-capitalist anarchists. The problem is that even when liberalism is militantly opposed, liberal values are turned inside out – they are inverted, but never meaningfully transcended or moved beyond.

Marshall captures the problem in a graphic way when he criticises Bookchin and Kropotkin for committing the naturalistic fallacy of deriving an 'is' from an 'ought'. 'There is', he argues, 'no logical connection to make us move from fact to value' (1993: 620). But from an anarchist standpoint, this is a misuse of the notion of a naturalistic fallacy. For an anarchist, the naturalistic fallacy refers to an erroneous belief in the timelessness of nature and of human links with nature. It is however quite another thing to argue that we cannot move from facts to value. This is a positivist (or empiricist) dictum – rejected by anarchists – that arises because thinkers cannot see that facts themselves embody relationships. Indeed, it is the relational nature of facts that gives them their evaluative or normative content.

From an anarchist perspective, this suggests that Marshall, an apparently enthusiastic anarchist, is still committed to a liberal methodology, and to a liberal opposition to understanding individuals in terms of the relationships that identify them. This can be seen in his attitude to organisation. Marshall may insist that he does not reject organisation per se, but only authoritarian organisation. The fact remains, however, that he accepts a philosophical standpoint that makes it impossible to see organisation as deriving from the relational character of humans. Even anarchists like Kropotkin and Bookchin fail to go along with the full implications of seeing humans as relational beings. By arguing that anarchism is based upon 'a mechanistic explanation of all phenomena' (Marshall, 1993: 318), Kropotkin accepts a static view of humanity – to which (like Bakunin) he ascribes an 'instinct' for sociability. His notion of the natural sciences is positivist and appears to argue that because humans have evolved from nature, they are simply the same as other natural beings. The specificity of human relationships is not understood.

While Bookchin does stress that humans have a 'second nature' – different from but linked to their biology and their 'first nature' – it is revealing that he calls his blending of anarchism and ecology an 'ecotopia'. He proclaims that 'our Science is Utopia' without seeing that (traditionally defined) utopias 'on their own' are static and ahistorical and postulate some kind of final end of history (Marshall, 1993: 621). This emphasises the ideal at the expense of the facts and ignores the dynamic and fluid nature of the real world. This abstract approach makes it impossible to account for relationships and the need for organisation – not simply to achieve a utopia – but as an ongoing expression of human relationships.

## The problem of hierarchy

Anarchists, in general, use the term 'hierarchy' in a negative way, but hierarchy itself is part and parcel of human relationships. Turner notes the work of A.S. Neil, who believed that education was possible without any hierarchy. Neil was the founder of the 'free school' movement, whose designs for education modelled at his Summerhill School conformed to anarchist prescriptions. There were to be no compulsory lessons; no authority of teachers over pupils; an emphasis upon self-development rather than 'instruction'; no testing of knowledge against prescribed targets; and no need to attend anything (Turner, 1993: 31).

While Summerhill School may have avoided authoritarianism, did it really avoid hierarchy as such? While it might be true that the use of force in relationships is counter-productive and is incompatible with the nature of relationships themselves, it does not follow that hierarchy in itself is wrong or oppressive. On the contrary, it exists in all relationships. The term 'authority' can be taken to assume persuasion and consent, but an authoritative relationship is one based on hierarchy. Surely when one goes to a doctor, you accept her authority, not because you are unwilling to question her advice, but because *in this situation*, there is a hierarchy born of the fact that the doctor has a specialist knowledge of health which you lack. This is not a static hierarchy – you may become more knowledgeable yourself – nor is it a comprehensive hierarchy. If you are a motor mechanic, the doctor may well come to you for help, and the hierarchy is reversed.

## The question of self-determination and constraint

Anarchists argue for self-determination and this is a valid objective to aim at, but it is misleading to imagine that self-determination, like autonomy or emancipation (to take just two related concepts), is a condition that we 'finally' reach, for like the notion of perfection, emancipation would turn into a nightmare if it ever 'arrived'. For what would happen to those deemed unemancipated? They would inevitably be 'forced to be free'.

What makes emancipatory concepts absolute as well as relative is the fact that our relationships with other humans, like our relationships with the wider world of nature, are continually changing. We are absolute in the sense that all humans are the same – they must relate to nature and to one another in order to survive – but we are also relative to one another. The way we relate depends upon the world we find ourselves in, and the world we construct, and this makes us different.

Not only are humans both absolute and relative in their rights, but we are agents whose freedom derives from the recognition and transformation of necessity. The kind of pressures that arise from being in society are better conceived of as a constraint, and these constraints arise out of relationships and are part and parcel of the price we pay as social beings, who can only become conscious of our individuality through relationships with others.

It is crucial to make the distinction which anarchism fails to make, between force and constraint. Force disrupts relationships because one party loses his subjectivity and becomes a mere 'thing'. Constraint on the other hand, while sometimes unpleasant, is unavoidable and a condition for freedom. It is not possible to be free without recognising and transforming the constraints that act upon us, and even the most spontaneous act can only succeed if it acknowledges and works to change a world of constraint. When Bakunin took part in the uprising in the French city of Lyon and proclaimed 'that the administrative and governmental machinery of the state' have been abolished (Marshall, 1993: 286), he learnt that it takes more than words to overthrow a despotic state, and unsurprisingly, the rising was speedily crushed. The point is that alliances must be formed; existing institutions utilised; the people must be prepared and feel that such an action is justified; and the forces of the opponent must be marginalised and neutralised – all the things which require organisation and the acknowledgement of constraints are crucial if a political action is to meet with hope of success.

## Anarchism and the distinction between state and government

The distinction between force and constraint translates into the opposition between state and government, and by condemning both, anarchists again leave themselves open to the charge that they are being utopian without at the same time being realistic.

The distinction between state and government is a crucial one to make. Anarchists tend to regard the two as synonyms. Godwin finds that government is opposed to society. It is static and oppressive – 'the only perennial causes of the vices of mankind' – and looks towards its 'true euthanasia' (Marshall, 1993: 206–7). Kropotkin makes a distinction between state and government, but considers both equally oppressive and both should be abolished. Representative government is no more than rule by the capitalists (Marshall, 1993: 325). It is not difficult to see that this negative view of government as well as the state is linked to a failure to distinguish between force and constraint.

Godwin saw public opinion as oppressive and irresistible as whips and chains. George Orwell is cited sympathetically as an anarchist who found Tolstoy's pacifism potentially coercive, while Gandhi's doctrine of non-violence has coercive overtones which Marshall sees as bullying and constituting a 'totalitarian danger' (Marshall, 1993: 650). It is one thing to warn – as J.S. Mill did – that public opinion can be intolerant and needlessly intrusive, but it is quite another to suggest that moral pressures are a kind of 'coercion' and as unacceptable as brute force. If the constraints imposed by Mill's natural penalties and the use of moral pressures are deemed authoritarian, then constitutionalism and the rule of law have to be rejected, even when these institutions operate in a purely governmental, as opposed to an oppressively statist, way (Hoffman, 1995: 127).

Government, it could be argued, is inherent in organisation and relationships. It involves the use of constraint to resolve conflicts that arise from the fact that each of us is different from the other and has different interests. For this reason, conflict is inevitable and so is government, but just as a sharp distinction needs to be drawn between constraint and force, so a distinction needs to be made between state and government. To link the state and government as twin enemies of freedom is to ignore the fact that stateless societies have governments, and that even in state-centred societies, the role of government can be positive and empowering.

Anarchist attacks on the 'welfare state' as bureaucratic and oppressive can only be legitimately described as *anti-statist* if they are able to show that the provision of welfare and security undermines self-development and is thus part and parcel of the state's exercise of force. If this cannot be shown, then the provision of welfare and security – to the extent that it is genuinely developmental – is governmental rather than statist in character. The existence of 'interference' and constraint is not in itself evidence of oppression since such attributes are inherent in all organisations and in relationships.

Carter is right to argue that administration in itself does not require the use of violence (1978: 324), although, of course, administrators may act in a high-handed and undemocratic fashion and thus contribute to the alienation which causes the use of force both by the opponents of the state and by the state itself. Nevertheless, we need to keep government and the state conceptually separate since it is wrong and counter productive to identify government with oppression, simply because it involves pressures and sanctions of a constraining kind.

## CHAZ (or CHOP) revisited

There is evidence that CHAZ/CHOP was influenced by anarchist ideas. Aris Roussinous – a war correspondent – noted the influence of the Autonomous Administration of Northeast Syria (AAENES), formerly known as Rojava. It operates in the most ethnically diverse part of Syria and is the area with the greatest wheat production and the largest oil fields. AAENES is very much environmentally aware and is reforesting the area's arid plains (Roussinous, 2020). Although policing is technically neighbourhood-based, in reality it looks like a normal force:

> Over the seven years that I have been visiting northeastern Syria as a journalist, policing has become increasingly professionalised. There are separate and well-armed militias for the purposes of general crime prevention, traffic police, highly-trained and well-equipped special forces teams for counterterrorism operations and military police to find and detain draft-dodgers and return them to their units. It is not a slight on the region's genuine achievements to observe that, for all its ideological basis in anarchist thought, it is a highly bureaucratic security state, and far from the policing abolitionist demands of American protestors.

Roussinous observes that AAENES is very experimental and pragmatic: if an aspect of anarchist theory does not work, then it is abandoned. In terms of theory, Bookchin (discussed earlier) is a significant influence. His thought 'filtered through the idiosyncratic readings of the jailed PKK leader Abdullah Ocalan have become the region's governing philosophy'. A central aspect of Bookchin's theory was the importance of the decentralisation of power.

One of the CHOP/CHAZ demands was resistance to gentrification of Capitol Hill, and this fits with a broader anarchist resistance to global capitalism, which is seen as a force for homogenisation. But the logic of this would be the acceptance that other communities – for example white separatist ones – should also have the right to autonomy. There is a tension between a progressive universalism and the demand for autonomy.

More broadly, AAENES differs from CHAZ in that it is a genuinely autonomous entity, operating in a very hostile environment. Whatever objections the Seattle protestors might raise against the local police and Federal agencies, the United States is a stable country with a high level of popular confidence in its legal institutions.

## Conclusion

Anarchism is often analysed as part of socialism, but anarchism is so distinctive that it deserves treatment in its own right. Philosophical anarchists are concerned with the autonomy of the individual as a theoretical problem, while free market anarchists argue the case for replacing the state with an unrestricted market.

Anti–capitalist anarchists are critical of Marxism either because, like Proudhon, they dislike collectivist solutions to the problem of inequality or because, in the case of anarchists like Bakunin and Kropotkin, they are unconvinced by the need for a dictatorship of the proletariat in the transformation of capitalism into communism. The Spanish Civil War constitutes a veritable historical laboratory in understanding anarchism. Anarchists were extremely influential during this period and their clashes with other sections of the left, and the tactics they adopted, are extremely instructive.

Anarchism is unable to handle the problem of violence, but it has played a significant role in the formation of new social movements. Anarchism runs into particular difficulty in its treatment of the problem of hierarchy and organisation. It is weakened through its failure to distinguish between state and government, and force and constraint.

## References

Berki, R. (1974). *Socialism*. London: Dent.

Carter, A. (1978). 'Anarchism and Violence' in J. Pennock and J. Chapman (eds), *Anarchism*. New York: New York University Press, 320–40.

Dahl, R. (1989). *Democracy and its Critics*. New Haven, CT and London: Yale University Press.

Goodwin, B. (1997). *Using Political Ideas*, 4th edn Chichester, New York, Toronto: John Wiley and Sons.

Hoffman, J. (1995). *Beyond the State*. Cambridge: Polity.

Marshall, P. (1993). *Demanding the Impossible*. London: Fontana.

Maximoff, G. (ed.) (1953). *The Political Philosophy of Bakunin*. New York: The Free Press.

Miller, D. (1974). *Anarchism*. London: Dent.

Nozick, R. (1974). *Anarchy, State, and Utopia*. Oxford: Basil Blackwell.

Roussinous, A. (2020). The Case for Tory Anarchism. *UnHerd*, viewed 24 June 2021, https://unherd.com/2020/06/the-case-for-tory-anarchism/

Thomas, H. (1965). *The Spanish Civil War*. Harmondsworth: Penguin.

Turner, R. (1993). Anarchism: What Is It? *Politics Review* 3(1), 28–32.

Vincent, A. (1995). *Modern Political Ideologies*. Oxford: Blackwell.

## Further reading

Useful overviews: Carissa Honeywell, *Anarchism* (Polity, 2020); Ruth Kinna, *Anarchism* (OneWorld, 2009); Ruth Kinna, *The Government of No One: The Theory and Practice of* Anarchism (Pelican, 2020); Colin Ward, *Anarchism: A Very Short Introduction* (Oxford University Press, 2004). Excellent collection: Gary Chartier and Chad Van Schoelandt (eds.), *The Routledge Handbook of Anarchy and Anarchist Thought* (Routledge, 2020). Approaches from philosophy: Nathan Jun, Leonard Williams, and Benjamin Franks (eds.), *Anarchism: A Conceptual Approach* (Routledge, 2018); Benjamin Franks, *Anarchisms, Postanarchisms and Ethics* (Rowman and Littlefield, 2018).

# Chapter 13

# Nationalism

## Introduction

Nationalism has been a powerful force in modern history. It arouses strong feelings – for some, it is tantamount to racism, but for others, nationalist sentiment creates solidarity and stability, which are preconditions for political freedom. These two perspectives are informed by history: in its most extreme form, nationalism has been, it is claimed, at the root of genocidal policies, and yet, it has also been the basis of liberation movements in such regions as Eastern Europe, Africa, and Asia. The challenge for political theorists is to explain how the nation can be a source of value and an object of allegiance. This is indeed a challenge: most liberals – and liberalism is the dominant ideology of our time – hold that the *individual human being* is the ultimate source of value, and the individual has claims against collective entities such as the nation; many socialists are collectivists, but for them, it is *class*, or *humanity* as a whole, that is the proper object of concern.

## Key questions

- What is the nation?
- What is nationalism?
- What value should we attach to the nation? What value should you attach to your nation?

## Nations and nationalism

In the period from around 1850 to the start of the First World War in 1914, there was a marked rise in popular nationalist consciousness across Europe, with the unification of Italy in 1861 and Germany in 1871, and the so-called 'scramble for Africa' pitting the European nations against one another on that continent, while a precarious balance of power was maintained within Europe. After its defeat in the First World War, the Austro-Hungarian Empire fragmented into new nations such as Czechoslovakia and Hungary. And there was much discussion of the right to national self-determination.

In the period after the Second World War, there was less theoretical interest in nationalism, with ideological debate centred on the struggle between liberal capitalism and state socialism. This was despite the fact that it was a period of significant nation-building in Africa and Asia in

DOI: 10.4324/9780429424106-17

## Who is Scottish?

**PHOTO 13.1** © Colin McPherson/Corbis via Getty Images.

In September 2014 Scotland held a referendum on whether to become an independent state, separate from the United Kingdom, to which it had been in union since 1707. The result was No (to independence) 55.3% against Yes 44.7%, on a very high voter turnout of 84.6%.

The leading party of independence, the Scottish National Party (SNP), was formed in 1934 as a merger of the right-wing and imperialist Scottish Party, which wanted dominion status for Scotland akin to what had been given to Canada, Australia, and New Zealand and the left-wing National Party of Scotland.

The current party leader and First Minister of Scotland Nicola Sturgeon has said that she wishes she could turn back time and re-name her party. Scottish nationalism is, she argues, very different to other nationalisms: 'it doesn't matter where you come from, if Scotland is your home and you live here and you feel you have a stake in the country, you are Scottish and you have as much say over the future of the country as I do' (BBC, 2017).

The idea that if you live in Scotland then you are Scottish is reflected in beliefs about who can vote in a referendum. In the last three Scottish Parliament elections, a majority of seats have been won by pro-independence parties, and in 2016 Scotland voted 62% to remain in the European Union (that an independent Scotland could not automatically remain in the EU had been a central claim of the 2014 No campaign). Although another referendum requires permission from the UK parliament, given these facts, there is a reasonably high likelihood of a second (legal) independence referendum sometime in the 2020s.

If that referendum is run on the same line as the last one, then those eligible to vote in a Scottish Parliament election will determine the destiny of Scotland. That includes all those aged over 16 registered to vote in Scotland, all Irish citizens resident in Scotland, and European Union citizens who have settled status. In 2014 there had to be a special register for 16- and 17-year-olds as they did not yet have the right to vote in Scottish Parliament elections, and EU citizens had the automatic right to vote, but since the UK has left the EU, it is necessary to establish a right to reside.

Missing from the list of eligible voters are Scots living outside Scotland, which in 2014 included the late actor and strong SNP supporter Sean Connery, who lived in the Bahamas. There are practical problems in extending the franchise to Scots outside of Scotland, but Sturgeon's comments suggest a deeper philosophical objection: to be Scottish is to live in Scotland. Ancestry and ethnicity play no role.

Is Sturgeon right? What does it mean to be Scottish? And what should be the basis of citizenship law in an independent Scotland? Should ancestry count for anything in claiming citizenship?

We have focused on Scotland, but these questions are of wider significance: what does it mean to belong to a nation? What makes you a citizen?

the wake of decolonisation. Since the dramatic events in Eastern Europe in 1989, there has been an extraordinary resurgence of interest in nationalism; in large part, this has been due to the recognition that powerful nationalist sentiments survived 40 years of state socialism in Eastern Europe. So, while nationalism is a 'traditional ideology', it is very much one the study of which is in the ascendant.

In previous chapters we have cautioned against overreliance on dictionary definitions in trying to understand concepts in political theory. While it can be useful to trace the etymology of words, everyday usage is too diverse and conflicting to provide guidance on the correct employment of concepts, the meanings of which are bound up with particular theories. The word 'nation' is a good example of the dangers of dictionary definitions. Dictionaries trace the word 'nation' to the Latin *natio*, and the Latin term was certainly used in the mediaeval period. For example, there is a debate about whether Scotland was really a nation before the Act of Union with England in 1707. One of the documents used in favour of the claim Scotland was indeed a nation is the Declaration of Arbroath (1320), which was written in Latin and uses the term *natio*. The difficulty with this argument is that *natio* can be translated as 'place of birth' – note the English word 'natal' – and the 37 signatories when they make reference to themselves as a 'nation' may not necessarily have possessed the modern consciousness of nationhood (Davidson, 2000: 48–9). The point is that words do not, in themselves, settle arguments over the nature of nationalism. Meanings are embedded in theories. However, it is useful to set out a variety of alternative definitions of 'nation' and of 'nationalism' and try to identify commonalities and divergences. We start with 'nation':

The totality of people who are united by a common fate so that they possess a common (national) character. The common fate is . . . primarily a common history; the common national character involves almost necessarily a uniformity of language.

(Otto Bauer in Davis, 1967: 150)

A nation is a community of sentiment that could adequately manifest itself in a state of its own: hence a nation is a community which normally tends to produce a state of its own.

(Max Weber in Hutchinson and Smith, 1994: 25)

[A nation is] a named human population that shares myths and memories, a mass public culture, a designated homeland, economic unity and equal rights and duties for all members.

(Smith, 1991: 43)

[A nation] is an imagined political community – and imagined as both inherently limited and sovereign . . . all communities larger than primordial villages of face-to-face contact (and perhaps even these) are imagined. Communities are to be distinguished, not by their falsity/ genuineness, but by the style in which they are imagined.

(Anderson, 1991: 6)

A nation is a group of people who feel themselves to be a community bound together by ties of history, culture and common ancestry. Nations have 'objective' characteristics that may include a territory, a language, a religion or common descent (though not all of these are always present), and 'subjective' characteristics, essentially a people's awareness of their nationality and affection for it.

(Kellas, 1998: 3)

All five definitions begin with the idea of a 'collective': 'totality of people', 'community of sentiment', 'named human population', 'imagined political community', and 'group of people . . . community', but disagreement exists on how this collective is held together. Bauer maintains that the nation possesses a 'common character' or 'common fate', which necessarily entails a shared language. Weber argues that sentiment – or fellow-feeling – holds the collective together, but that it also has a political project, namely the drive to create a state. Smith is more pluralistic in his understanding of what makes the collective cohere: myths, memories, mass public culture, homeland, economic unity, rights, and duties. The last basis is, however, distinctly political: the nation has a legal dimension. Anderson argues that because we will never meet more than a tiny fraction of our fellow citizens, the national community is imaginary, constructed above all through the medium of literature. Finally, Kellas stresses the objective *and* subjective dimensions of nationhood – nations require 'objective materials' such as territory or language, but there must also be a corresponding consciousness of belonging to a nation.

Is consciousness an essential requirement of nationhood? Can a group of people constitute a nation without being conscious of it? The five definitions imply not: Bauer talks of 'national character', Weber of a 'community of sentiment', Smith of '[shared] myths and memories', Anderson of the nation as an 'imagined political community', and Kellas of 'subjective characteristics'. However, people can have latent interests – that is, interests of which they are unaware or only dimly aware. Certainly, political theorists are concerned with articulating reasons for action, and this requires a high level of consciousness: a 'nation' that existed outside the consciousness of its 'members' would be of little interest to political theorists: it is the act of valuing the nation, or more precisely, the sense that we *ought* to value the – or *our* – nation or that it is *permissible* (even if not required) to be partial to our compatriots, that is the focus of our concern in this chapter.

We have talked of nations but what then of 'nationalism'? Again, we have competing understandings of nationalism:

It is a theory of political legitimacy, which requires that ethnic boundaries should not cut across political ones, and in particular, that ethnic boundaries within a given state . . . should not separate the power holders from the rest.

(Gellner, 1983: 1)

Nationalism is a doctrine invented in Europe at the beginning of the nineteenth century. It pretends to supply criteria for the determination of the unit of population proper to enjoy a government exclusively of its own, for the legitimate exercise of power in the state and for the right organisation of a society of states. Briefly, the doctrine holds that humanity is naturally divided into nations, that nations are known by certain characteristics which can be ascertained, and that the only legitimate type of government is national self-government.

(Kedourie, 1993: 9)

By nationalism I mean the sentiment of belonging to a community whose members identify with a set of symbols, beliefs and ways of life and have the will to decide upon their common political destiny.

(Guibernau, 1996: 47)

Whereas 'nation' refers to an entity, nationalism is a body of doctrine, theory, or beliefs about the nation, its historical significance, and moral importance.

Political theorists, who tend to operate with *universalist* concepts such as freedom, equality, and justice, have found it difficult to explain nationalism, which is, essentially, *particularist* – that is, it assumes that national boundaries are morally significant. At best, nationalism has been incorporated into other ideologies, such as liberalism or socialism, as a derivative concern. For example, liberals or socialists may argue that all human beings are equally worthy of moral concern, but the world is a better place if it is organised into nations – world government would be inefficient, or dangerous, because it would concentrate rather than disperse power. It might be possible to reconcile nationalism and universalism if we distinguish the appropriate level at which universal treatment should hold. Rather than argue that all individuals should be equal citizens under some kind of world regime, we could advocate universal nationalism: the world is divided up into nation-states, each of which carries a significant level of responsibility for its citizens, but all nations have equal standing in the world. We might seek to limit the powers of individual states by maintaining that individuals have rights simply in virtue of being human (universal human rights), and furthermore that there are some duties to redistribute wealth between states (global justice).

As a starting point to the debate over nationalism, we can say that all nationalisms have three characteristics: they imply a relationship of an individual to the collective that is in significant ways non-voluntary; they entail partiality; and they involve exclusion. So, you may be free to leave your country but you never chose to be a citizen of your country, unless you are a naturalised citizen. And, as a citizen, you stand in a special relationship to your country: nationalism implies that you are *permitted* to be partial to your compatriots (some types of nationalism may entail a *requirement* to show partiality). Finally, although a 'civic nation' may succeed in providing non-racial or non-ethnic criteria for citizenship, all nations involve belonging, and belonging implies its opposite: not belonging or exclusion. From the perspective of political theory, a nationalist must defend these three features of nationalism: non-voluntariness, partiality, and exclusion. In the remainder of this chapter, we explore a number of attempts to do this. We start with two important nineteenth century liberal thinkers – Mill and Herder – move on to a nineteenth century socialist perspective (Marx and Engels) and then explore contemporary approaches to nationalism.

## Liberalism and nationalism: Mill and Herder

As we have suggested, liberalism and nationalism seem to be an odd couple: for nationalists, the most significant moral entity is the nation, whereas for liberals, the most significant is the individual human being. Where there is a conflict between the claims of the individual and those of the nation, liberals and nationalists will diverge over which should take precedence. Furthermore, the priority given to the individual by liberals normally rests on features all human beings share, such that the logic of liberal individualism is moral *universalism*. In contrast, nationalists are *particularists*: although some nationalists will argue there is a universal need to belong to a nation, nationalism entails regarding one's own nation as special.

The difficulty with this apparent rejection of nationalism is that historically, liberalism and nationalism have often been combined into a single political programme: the struggle for national self-determination has been expressed in the language of freedom, self-government, and accountability. The question is whether the apparent affinity of liberalism and nationalism is simply a historical accident or whether there is a deeper philosophical compatibility that is not captured by an oversimplistic derivation of universalism from individualism.

Jean-Jacques Rousseau may be interpreted as the first significant liberal thinker to make an explicit case for nationalism. His defence of nationalism was based on the importance of a 'people' possessing a general will, the recognition of which supposedly guarantees individual freedom. The general will is not reducible to the wills of individuals or to a simple aggregation of wills (Rousseau, 1968: 247–9; see pp. 14–15). Rousseau's theory is highly abstract and seems unconnected to the political realities of his time, but it has been influential in the development of a popular nationalism based on democratic self-government. What provides the link between liberalism and nationalism in Rousseau's theory is the idea of democracy.

However, there are still difficulties reconciling nationalism and liberalism. Democracy and liberalism can conflict: while democracy implies that each person's interests should be given equal consideration, to make decisions we have to rely on a voting system, such that some people's preferences will almost inevitably be overridden. To protect individual freedom, we need rights that cannot be removed by the majority (see pp. 29–30). The threat from majorities exists whether or not there is strong nationalist sentiment but is deepened by the existence of such sentiment. Second, even if we can guarantee the rights of individuals within a democracy, a world divided into nation-states raises issues of international justice: there are strong and wealthy nations, and there are weak and poor nations. If individuals matter, then they matter irrespective of their nationality.

While the nation *may* be a threat to liberty and to global justice, there are grounds for holding that a world of nation-states is more likely to guarantee liberty and justice than some other form of political organisation. Two quite different lines of argument suggest themselves; both are liberal, but, in fact, correspond, respectively, to civic and communitarian forms of nationalism. The civic position is that the world is more stable and efficient if organised around nation-states, where each nation respects the territorial integrity of the others. As we suggested earlier, this argument attaches *instrumental* value to the nation: that is, the nation serves the purposes of individuals. The communitarian position is that individuals need culture as a means of self-expression, and the nation-state is the embodiment of culture. Such an argument assumes that nations have *intrinsic* value – valuing individual lives means respecting an individual's culture, the political expression of which is the nation-state. In the history of political thought, John Stuart Mill was an important exponent of the first position, while Johann Gottfried von Herder defended the second.

# John Stuart Mill

In his book *Considerations on Representative Government* (published 1859), Mill argues that 'free institutions are next to impossible in a country made up of different nationalities' (Mill, 1991: 428). A 'nation' Mill defines as a portion of humankind united 'among themselves' by common sympathies, which make them cooperate with each other more willingly than with those of other nations. These common sympathies may be based on race and descent, language, religion, shared memory, or political antecedents. Mill states that the last of these is the most important, and yet his brief discussion of nationalism focuses more on the need for a shared language than the existence of historic political institutions. Without a shared language a 'united public opinion' cannot exist; if, say, two major languages coexist, then public life is vertically divided, with each group reading different newspapers, books, and pamphlets, and each looking to its own political class, which speaks to them in their own language.

The danger with a multinational – meaning, a multilingual – state is that the army, as the security wing of the state, is held together by obedience to its officers and not by a shared sympathy with the people. Although Mill does not argue for a popular militia, he does imply that the army, and other security forces, must have popular legitimacy. Faced with popular discontent, an army made up of one ethnic–linguistic group will just as soon 'mow down' the members of another group as they will foreigners (Mill, 1991: 429). In a multinational state, the objective of the government will be the maintenance of stability and that will entail balancing competing linguistic groups, such that instead of developing fellow-feeling, differences will become institutionalised. Mill concedes that there are successful multinational states, the best example being Switzerland, and he also accepts that geographical 'intermingling' can be such that some states must be multinational. But he considers it preferable that 'peripheral' minorities be absorbed by larger nations: a Breton is better to share 'the advantages of French protection, and the dignity and prestige of French power, than to sulk on his own rocks, the half-savage relic of past times' (Mill, 1991: 431). Similarly, Wales and the Scottish Highlands are better absorbed into Britain. Today, these remarks seem anachronistic: the emphasis now is on respecting differences within the nation-state and ensuring that threatened languages such as Breton, Welsh, and Scots Gaelic survive. However, the anti-ethnic basis of Mill's argument is significant: the admixture and blending of nationalities is to the benefit of humanity because it softens the extremes between people (Mill, 1991: 432). In essence, Mill's nationalism is assimilationist – nations are culturally hybrid, but the political project must be to create fellow-feeling because this guarantees the development and reinforcement of individual freedom.

# Johann Gottfried von Herder

Herder is a major point of reference within the tradition that takes the nation to be a pre-modern ethnic community. For this reason, it might be thought that he cannot also be a liberal. Yet, in fact, Herder has been influential among those liberals who see human beings as necessarily cultural beings. At the heart of culture is language, and Herder anticipates one of the dominant themes of twentieth century philosophy in arguing that human self-consciousness is dependent on language: the very capacity to think presupposes language. Furthermore, language is necessarily collective, and while it is possible to identify universal features, languages are particular; a language is not simply a means by which we name things, but in writing, reading, and speaking a particular language, such as English or German, we locate ourselves and others in a particular world of emotion and sentiment. (For a modern application of Herder's reflections, see Breuilly, 1993: 55–9.)

Herder is attempting to reconcile Enlightenment and Romanticist views of human nature. Under the influence of the former, he argues that to be autonomous agents we need language, but under the influence of the latter, maintains that language summons up an emotional world. He also attempts to reconcile progress and tradition: the transmission of culture from one generation to another involves both the preservation of culture, or tradition, and the confrontation of the old with the new. This has implications for his understanding of nationalism: since newness is part of tradition and can come from outside a culture as a 'foreign influence', nations should not be chauvinistic. However, while Herder distances himself from extreme nationalism, he also maintains that cultures cannot be manufactured out of nothing, and that each culture – or nation – has a distinct character which should be preserved.

While language is one of the most fundamental capacities of human beings, the roots of political organisation lie in the family, and this is what gives rise to his organic view of the nation: the nation is not an organism in the sense that there is an interaction of parts within a relatively closed system, as the metaphor of the human body would imply, but rather the nation develops from its most basic unit of organisation. Herder draws an egalitarian and non-authoritarian conclusion from this: elites cannot create nations, and they must not impose their wills on individuals, but rather individuals must be free to develop themselves. Like the growth of an oak tree from an acorn, national development must come from 'within'. The difficulty with Herder's argument is that the family inevitably has paternalistic, if not patriarchal, overtones, and derivation of the nation from the family is problematic, for citizenship involves relationships with people you have never met and will never meet. Ethnic nationalism embodies all the limitedness of the family without preserving its positive features as a small-scale, 'face-to-face' community, based, at its best, on ties of affection.

## Socialism and nationalism: Marx and Engels

Marx and Engels make various comments on nationalism in the *Communist Manifesto*: responding to the charge that communists want to abolish the nation-state they argue the workers have no nation of their own, and national divisions have become increasingly irrelevant as capitalism has developed – the capitalists have created a single world bound together by free trade. Marx and Engels were 'collectivists', but the historically significant 'collective' was the working class, as the most advanced, and first 'truly revolutionary', class (see pp. 191–2). Although they avoid using the language of morality, holding that moral beliefs are the product of existing (capitalist) society, and the task is to create a new society, it is possible to discern a moral message in their work: the task is to create a classless society in which human beings recognise their common humanity. In his early work, Marx called this 'species consciousness'. The historical task is to develop (proletarian) class consciousness, and the ultimate moral aim is to overcome human alienation. This appears to leave little room for nationalism.

Marx and Engels do, however, argue that during the revolutionary phase the workers must 'make themselves into a nation': 'since the proletariat must first of all acquire supremacy, must rise to be *the* national class, must constitute itself the nation, it is, so far, itself national, though not in the bourgeois sense of the word' (Marx and Engels, 1967: 23). During what they call the 'dictatorship of the proletariat', it is necessary to take hold of the state and use it both to defeat counter-revolutionaries and to transform the relations of production. But this is a temporary phase, and just as the aim is for the state 'to lose its political character', that is, its coercive character, so it is necessary that the nation loses what might be termed its 'particular' character – in the latter phases of the process the national revolutions will become international. Because Marx and Engels said very little about what a classless society would look like, it is unclear what place nationalist consciousness would have in such a society. Cultural differences would not necessarily disappear, but they could not determine the distribution of resources. Nonetheless, even if the future of nationalism is unclear, nationalist consciousness does play a role in the revolutionary period, and broadly speaking, Marx and Engels argued that if nationalist movements serve the class struggle, they should be supported. More specifically, they maintained:

1.  Nations must have a certain *minimum size*, and large and powerful ones were to be encouraged – what Engels called the 'miserable remnants of former nations' should dissolve. A distinction is drawn between historic and non-historic nations, where 'history' is understood as actions and movements possessing class significance. The 'miserable remnants', examples of which include the Basques, Bretons, and Gaels, have no historic significance. Marx and Engels argue that, after a workers' revolution, there will always be the danger of counter-revolution, led by 'conservative' elements in society, and that these 'rotting remnants' would be among them. Interestingly, Mill also maintained that these peoples are better absorbed into larger nations.
2.  National self-determination was to be encouraged if it helped revolution. In the main, Marx and Engels believed that national struggles should only be encouraged in the big nations of Central and West Europe: France, Britain, and Germany. Struggles on the 'edge of Europe' were not generally supported. Which means, for example, that they did not in 1848 support the Irish struggle against the British – they later changed their views, and the reasons for the shift in their position are briefly discussed below.
3.  They opposed Russia, which they saw as the primary source of reaction in Europe, and so tactically supported the Habsburg (Austro-Hungarian) Empire – which meant opposing nationalist movements among, for example, the Czechs, Slovaks, and Serbs (Mill supported these struggles).
4.  Ireland: from an orthodox Marxist perspective, Ireland in the nineteenth century appears backward – Engels describes it as the agricultural appendage of Britain, or more specifically, England. Except in a small north-eastern corner of the country, it had not developed capitalism – which was a precondition of a workers' revolution. What is more, the Catholic Church was a source of 'false consciousness'. But Marx and Engels gradually shifted to the view that the liberation of Ireland was a condition for revolution in Britain: Britain (or England) was the nation most likely to experience revolution, but the Irish constituted a source of competition to British workers, which worsened the conditions of the latter, but without fuelling revolution because British workers saw their struggle against Irish labour as nationalist (and religious) in character. Paradoxically, through granting Ireland independence, British and Irish workers would develop class solidarity and recognise that the bourgeoisie was their true enemy.

## The contemporary debate

## Civic nationalism

In the rest of this chapter, we consider more recent discussions of nationalism, with the focus on civic, communitarian, and ethnic nationalisms. Michael Ignatieff defines a civic nation as 'a community of equal, rights-bearing citizens, united in patriotic attachment to a shared set of political practices and values' (Ignatieff, 1993: 7). For a civic nationalist, 'belonging' to a nation entails a rational choice rather than an inheritance. In contrast, a communitarian nationalist or ethnic nationalist maintains 'that an individual's deepest attachments are inherited, not chosen' (Ignatieff, 1993: 7). The distinction between civic and other forms of nationalism has been attributed to Hans Kohn, who, in his discussion of nationalism in the nineteenth century defined 'Western' nations, such as France, Britain, and the United States as civic and 'Eastern' nations, such as Germany and Russia, as ethnic.

Civic nationalism appears an expression of, or at least compatible with, the liberal values of freedom (autonomy, choice) and equality (equality of individuals and equality of nations). The concept of ethnic nationalism – the counterpoint of civic nationalism – is however more complex than Ignatieff suggests. Ethnicity might be understood as a cultural or a biological concept (or both). Among cultural traits are religion, food, dress, language, and family structures. Biology, on the other hand, is essentially about genetic relatedness and continuity. Two people can be native speakers of a language but be genetically very distant from one another. Given the distinction between culture and biology, it is preferable to distinguish two forms of ethnic nationalism, communitarian and ethnic (proper), where the latter necessarily entails some notion of genetic relatedness. In the next section, we focus on communitarian nationalism and its relationship to liberalism, while in the final section we discuss ethnonationalism.

## Liberalism and communitarian nationalism

Contemporary liberal debates over the status of the nation focus on several questions:

1. What is the nature of the human person or 'self'? Is he or she in some sense independent of his or her community (where one such community is the nation), or constituted by that community?
2. Does the existence of the nation carry special moral duties to our fellow citizens? To what extent do such duties limit our freedom?
3. Does the existence of the nation give us a reason to favour our compatriots over others? What are the implications of such partiality for the distribution of resources between nations?

Yael Tamir makes the point that liberals cannot ignore the nation: it forms the sociological basis of our political life. The world is organised around nations. Liberals may have problems *thinking* like nationalists, but they certainly *act* like them. Nations, Tamir suggests, provide contexts in which people live their lives. Following Benedict Anderson's definition, she views the nation as an 'imaginary community' (Tamir, 1993: 8). This implies an active capacity to identify. So, in answer to the first question, a person is (partially) constituted by his or her attachments, but in response to the second, the duties entailed in belonging to a nation are largely self-assumed. This has two practical consequences: individual choice must be valued, and the right to national self-determination is a right held by individuals and not by a collective. It is individual Kurds who (should) claim the right to nationhood rather than an entity called Kurdistan. Kurdistan exists because it is imagined as a community by individuals identifying themselves as Kurds. There is, however, a problem of circularity: Kurds identify with Kurdistan because they believe Kurdistan exists, such that their believing Kurdistan exists does not bring Kurdistan into existence. In response, it could be argued that Kurds have to believe that Kurdistan exists independently of their beliefs even if, in fact, it only exists because lots of people style themselves 'Kurds' and identify with a particular land mass, language, customs, and so on. On this argument, all 'social entities' are necessary fictions.

Whether social entities exist independently of individual beliefs and actions is a problem for philosophers of social science (see, for example, Ruben, 1985), but our concern is primarily with the ethical question: what is the moral status of this social entity we call a nation? The question of the constructedness of the nation is relevant, in that it could reasonably be argued that it is individuals, who, through their beliefs, construct the nation. This may lessen the claims the nation has on the individual: if a Kurd can say that Kurdistan only exists because a group of individuals 'construct' that nation, then it would appear to give moral primacy, or authority, to the individual over the collective. However, this argument may be less compelling than it appears, in that the nation may be constructed but the process of socialisation might be so strong that an individual cannot imagine him- or herself as anything other than Kurdish, or English, or French, or whatever.

There is another problem with the claim that because the nation is constructed somehow the individual is free to belong, or not belong, to it. The 'necessary fiction' of the nation implies that nationalism depends upon the myth of a really existing social entity. The word 'myth' is not an entirely pejorative term, for, as Anderson argues, there is a need for 'sacred stories' which purport to explain the 'origins' of the nation (Anderson, 1991). Nationalism depends on forgetfulness: forgetting the factual, highly contingent formation of the nation. The problem for liberal political theorists is less one of the authoritarian implications of elevating the nation over the individual – although that is a concern – but much more the deception necessarily entailed in effectively constructing the nation.

At the heart of both these problems – the implicit authoritarianism and the mythology of nationalism – is the question of the nature of the self. If individual human beings are the source of authority, then the claims of any collective are limited or constrained by our individual rights, and the idea that political institutions must be justified to each individual requires 'transparency'. In the 1980s, there was a significant debate within Anglo-American political philosophy between 'individualists' and 'communitarians'. John Rawls was taken to be representative of liberal individualism: the derivation of political principles from the original position (see p. 136) was individualist in that each individual 'chose' the principles through his or her own powers of reason independently of any prior attachments such as family, culture, or religion. In his influential critique Michael Sandel argued that Rawls's model of the individual was flawed because a person denied knowledge of his or her identity is in no position to value anything at all (Sandel, 1998: 179). How can you know what you want if you do not know what social ties or religious beliefs you have?

One of the problems with communitarianism is that, taken to its logical conclusion, there is no individual standpoint from which we can criticise 'our community', and values are entirely relative to 'my' community.[1] Given that we may belong to more than one community, we need to be able to negotiate our conflicting loyalties: this is evident in the conflict that, historically, Catholics have felt between Church and nation, and which many Muslims feel between Islam as a universal community of believers (*ummah*) and the nations to which they belong. There is another implication of communitarianism that was not pursued to the same degree within that debate, but which has been a topic of discussion within the broader justice debate: communitarianism implies that it is legitimate to show partiality towards members of 'our community', which in this case means the nation.

Thomas Nagel makes a distinction between agent-relative and agent-neutral reasons for action, and correspondingly between two attitudes we can adopt to our lives: partiality and impartiality (Nagel, 1991: 10–20). You can view your life as special to you or you can view your life as 'just one among many'. Emerging from these two standpoints are the two kinds of reasons (or motivations). A parent is acting partially – to be more precise, is acting from agent-relative reasons – when he shows a concern for his children which he does not bestow on other people's children. His justification is that they are *his* children, meaning that the identity of the children is of central importance. Their identity as *his* children explains his partiality towards them. Let us assume that the parent is very wealthy, such that his partiality results in significant material benefits for his children. But let us also assume that he has egalitarian beliefs: he thinks that all children should get a 'fair deal', and as a rich person, he should pay high levels of tax in order to fund an extensive and effective education system. Insofar as he is motivated by concern for all children in accepting as legitimate high taxes he is acting from agent-neutral reasons: other parent's children are of equal value to his own. Nagel thinks that there is an ineliminable conflict between partiality and impartiality, but – and this is the interesting point – each presupposes the other (Nagel, 1991: 14). When a parent shows partiality to his children, he is necessarily committed to the view that '(all) parents should show special concern for their children'. In reverse, impartiality implies partiality. This mutual implication of partiality and impartiality clarifies but does not resolve the tension between the two standpoints.

We have taken the parent–child relationship as one example, but Nagel argues that the tension manifests itself across the social and political field. Nationalists – of all types – must assume that membership of a nation implies the legitimacy of agent-relative reasons: you can show special concern for *your* compatriots (Nagel, 1991: 170–71). This suggests a lesser concern for members of other nations, even if partiality entails impartiality, meaning that you have to accept 'multiple partialities': a French person's partiality towards other French people commits him to accepting a Japanese person is 'entitled' to show partiality towards fellow Japanese. As suggested above, this does not resolve the conflict: at most, it might commit members of rich countries to avoid exploiting poorer ones. It does not commit the rich nations to a significant redistribution of resources. One response is to reject partiality altogether and argue for global impartiality. In other words, there is nothing special – morally significant – about our compatriots. Within the justice debate this position is termed 'cosmopolitanism', and we explore it in more detail in Chapter 19 (see pp. 343–4). Since the concern in this chapter is with nationalism, we will focus on the opposing position: particularism; the 'particular' here being the nation.

David Miller, in his book *On Nationality*, offers what he terms a discriminating defence of nationalism. He suggests that it is possible to 'acknowledge the claims of national identity without succumbing to an unthinking nationalism which simply tells us to follow the feelings of our blood' (Miller, 1995: 183–4). He endorses the communitarian argument that we are in part constituted by our social attachments – in this case, our nation – and this gives us reason to act partially towards our fellow nationals. The nation should not be confused with the state. The national community has five characteristics: (a) there is a shared belief that the members belong together by virtue of what they believe they hold in common; (b) the nation has a history, and the members of the nation are conscious of that history; (c) it is 'active in character'; (d) it is associated with a particular geographical space or 'homeland'; (e) it has a public culture (Miller, 1995: 27). Miller argues that national myths may be essential to reinforcing a sense of community and to the successful transmission of moral values across generations.

German President Gustav Heinemann (1899–1976: President 1969–74) once responded to the question whether he loved his country: 'I don't love my country; I love my wife' (Rosenberg, 2009). He might have been joking, but the implication was that you might love somebody with whom you have freely entered a relationship or feel pride in one's own achievements, but you cannot love what you have not chosen or be proud of something you have not yourself done. Miller would accept that this is true but nonetheless you can, as a result of self-reflection, identify with your nation, such that membership of the nation becomes integral to your conception of a good life. Identification through self-reflection is analogous to free choice and personal achievement.

Miller makes a distinction between ethical universalism and ethical particularism. The first leads to cosmopolitanism, and that entails rejecting the nation as ethically significant, while the latter allows space for partiality towards one's compatriots. However, that partiality is not absolute: nation A may be morally required to intervene in the affairs of nation B to prevent human rights violations so long as A's interests are not significantly damaged. Put negatively, one nation should not intervene in the affairs of another without compelling reasons for doing so. Miller's argument may be viewed less as an outline of what nations require and permit of us, but more an attempt to establish a moral space in which we can pursue particularist aims.

## Missionary nationalism

Before rounding off our review of theories of nationalism with a discussion of ethnonationalism, it is worth reflecting on whether nationalism is the preserve of the political right. There is a kind of civic nationalism much practised – perhaps without awareness – by people who identify with the political left. Eric Kaufmann dubs this 'missionary nationalism': being recognised in the eyes of the world as leaders in progressive values (Kaufmann, 2018: 154–7). So, British progressives take pride in the diversity of London, Swedes (or at least Swedish political elites) like to think of their country as a 'humanitarian superpower' (Simons and Manoilo, 2019), and there was much pride among (many) Germans during the 2015 migrant crisis in their *Willkommenskultur* (Akrap, 2015). Heading up league tables on gender development, racial equality, or being a positive influence in the world evokes pride. On the other hand, voting to leave the European Union, electing the Alternative für Deutschland (AfD) to parliament, or putting Donald Trump in the White House are sources of embarrassment for progressives.

What distinguishes missionary from ethnic nationalism is that the latter has a greater sense of place, both spatially and temporally. Ethnic nationalists see the nation as extended in time, as the home of their ancestors, and in space: they move out from the local – their town – to the country. Geordies (inhabitants of the city of Newcastle-upon-Tyne) will identify first with their city, then their county or region (North-East England), and then England, which:

> . . .fills most of their imagined canvass of Britain. They gain self-esteem from their collective identity by taking pride in their local particularity as 'truly English', an authentic expression of the nation. The audience for this expression of pride is national, not international.
>
> (153)

In contrast, the real or imagined audience for missionary nationalists is international. This is especially true for university graduates, for whom – with the massive expansion of higher education since the late 1980s – graduate status has become a base for social identification, as reflected in the demographics of the EU referendum result, in which 68% of graduates voted Remain (Ipsos Mori, 2016).

## Ethnonationalism

The revival of interest in Darwinism among social scientists in the 1970s provides the intellectual backdrop to the contemporary restatement of ethnonationalism, although that certainly does not mean that all social scientists influenced by Darwinian thought are ethnonationalists, or all ethnonationalists are Darwinists. What is popularly termed evolution is based on the work of Charles Darwin (1809–82) – particularly evolution by natural selection and by sexual selection – combined with genetics, with the gene being the basic unit of inheritance (a gene is a discrete units of code which carries instructions for the production of various things, primarily proteins). Darwin knew nothing about genes, so this second element is owed to the work of Gregor Mendel (1822–84), whose work was rediscovered by biologists in the twentieth century (although the molecular structure of genes was only discovered in the 1940s). Modern evolutionary theory is a synthesis and extension of the work of Darwin and Mendel and is often referred as the 'modern evolutionary synthesis'. In the 1970s, Edward O Wilson extended the application of evolutionary theory from biology to the social sciences and coined the term 'sociobiology'.

At a most general level, evolution only requires that traits are the product of a selection process, whereby those traits better adapted to a particular environment survive at a greater rate than less adaptive ones. It is possible to be a Darwinist without assuming that it is genes that are selected. Alternatives to genes would be organisms (which are composed of genes, among other things) and groups. Most evolutionary theorists do assume that genes are the primary carriers of heritable information. Some, such as Richard Dawkins, believe that genes are the only things subject to selection. Other writers allow that groups (as well as organisms) can be subject to selection. Darwin himself seemed to subscribe to this view. In his book *The Descent of Man*, he wrote:

> It must not be forgotten that although a high standard of morality gives but a slight or no advantage to each individual man and his children over the other men of the same tribe, yet that an increase in the number of well-endowed men and advancement in the standard of morality will certainly give an immense advantage to one tribe over another. There can be no doubt that a tribe including many members who, from possessing in a high degree the spirit of patriotism, fidelity, obedience, courage, and sympathy, were always ready to aid one another, and to sacrifice themselves for the common good, would be victorious over most other tribes; and this would be natural selection. At all times throughout the world tribes have supplanted other tribes; and as morality is one important element in their success, the standard of morality and the number of well-endowed men will thus everywhere tend to rise and increase.
>
> (Darwin cited in Sober and Wilson, 1998: 4)

In other words, when individuals act altruistically towards one another within a group (tribe), the group benefits. The standard criticism is that any altruists within the group are liable to have fewer children because they are directing resources towards less closely related members of the tribe and so pass on their genes at a lower rate than the non-altruist, with the consequence that genes for altruism will be selected out of the gene pool (Wilson, 2015: 31–45).

Although not entirely satisfactory, attempts have been made to explain the survival of altruism not by direct appeal to group benefits – which is Darwin's position in the above quotation – but to the survival of genes in individuals closely, but not directly, related to you. Belonging to a group of people who are relatively closely related helps in the reproduction of one's genes. The nation can then be defined as a relatively closed population of interbreeding individuals. While the state – as in *nation-state* – has only existed for a very short part of the 240,000-year history of anatomically modern humans, it is the successor to the tribal bands of our ancestors, and crucially, we have inherited their psychology. The primary function of the state is coercively to police territorial boundaries, and for ethnonationalists, the absence of a territory makes the reproduction of a group's genes very difficult.

J. Philippe Rushton claimed that nationalism – or 'ethnic nepotism' – can be explained by the ability of individuals to detect genetic closeness or similarity. He provides a range of empirical evidence for the general theory of genetic similarity (Rushton, 1989; Rushton, 2005), although these claims have been subject to considerable criticism. As a general point, Rushton has to show, first, that the average degree of relatedness between sexually reproducing mates (and also non-sexual friends) is higher than it is in the population as a whole, and, second, choices are made on the basis of genetic similarity. Finding the right control group ('population') is difficult. Proximity could explain mating. Most mating is between people who live – and were born – close by each other. It follows that the correct control group should be from a circumscribed – localised – community (Graves and Byrne, 1989: 12). To test whether we recognise genetic similarity in others, it has to be restricted to times when only unrelated but genetically similar individuals will be encountered. It is hard to see the circumstances under which this would happen (Hepper, 1989: 530).

Whatever the weaknesses of genetic similarity theory, one interesting point is that we share genes by descent (genes identical-by-descent, IBD), or without descent (identical-by-state, IBS) (all genes IBD must be IBS, but not all genes IBS will be IBD). Direct-to-consumer genetic testing companies, such as Ancestry.com or 23andme, calculate distance between individuals using centimorgans (cM). Crudely speaking, cM is a measure of identical stretches of deoxyribonucleic acid (DNA). More shared stretches between two individuals would imply a closer relationship.

The problem is that because of genetic recombination, the further you move away from first-degree relatives (parents, children, etc.) the less confidence there is that cMs predict a specific relationship. For example, a range of 3,330–3,720 cM indicates a parent (or child), whereas a third cousin could be anything from 0 to 173 cM. The point of political significance is this: trying to identify your third cousin may be challenging – there will be false positives and false negatives – but within a larger genetic cluster, there is a clearer probability that a sample of people picked at random will share stretches of DNA (by IBS, not IBD). Indeed, this is what underlies the 'ethnicity scores' (and corresponding maps) produced by Ancestry.com and 23andme. You might not share any genes with your great-great-grandparents, but you will share genes with an average 'co-ethnic'. If genetic similarity matters, then your ethnic group may be more important than your family. You can with greater precision increase your inclusive fitness (the reproduction of copies of your genes) by bestowing help across a large number of co-ethnics rather than concentrating it on your family.

It is this last idea that underlies Frank Salter's idea of ethnies as sources of value. In elaborating his argument, Salter employs the work of population geneticist Luigi Cavalli-Sforza, who conducted a global survey (assay) of the distribution of genes within and between populations. Salter argues that relatedness is a relative concept, such that how closely two cousins are related depends on the genetic distances existing in a particular population. Two people randomly selected from a population will have a relatedness of zero. If two people share fewer genes than average for the relevant population, they are negatively related. And 'if the world consisted of only one ethny, the relatedness of random pairs would effectively be zero for the purposes of estimating genetic interests; only genealogical kin would have higher kinship' (Salter, 2002: 119). In such a situation, it would make sense simply to care for your own family (and genes IBD). However, in a world of ethnies, it may be rational to act in ways that are partial towards your ethnic compatriots. Using Cavalli-Sforza's data, he argues that in a world consisting of just two ethnies – English and Danes – two random English people would have a positive kinship of 0.0021, which is slightly closer than the kinship of eight linear generations. What this means is that the English and the Danes are quite closely related. However, Australian Aborigines and the Mbuti people of Africa are not closely related, such that in a world in which only these two ethnies existed two random Aborigines are almost as closely related (0.43) as identical twins (0.5) (2002: 120–1).

We will return to Salter's argument in the final chapter on migration (see pp. 364–5), and we have further discussion of the concept of race ('ethny' in Salter's language) in Chapter 16 (see pp. 282–3), but a couple of problems are worth noting. First, as Salter is aware (Salter, 2007: 11–13), there is the problem of how you derive ought from is: why should we care about genetic related-ness? At the start of the chapter, we discussed latent interests – the idea you can have interests of which you are unaware. Salter implies that people have latent genetic interests. But what if you do not care about these 'interests', or indeed are an anti-natalist, who believes that being brought into existence is harmful (Benatar, 1997)? What reasons do they have for caring about the repro-duction of copies of their genes? Even if Rushton's genetic similarity theory was empirically well supported, it would not turn 'is' into 'ought': that people favour those most genetically closely re-lated does not mean that they should. Second, it follows from his idea of relatedness that the balance between care for your family relative to care for your ethny is determined by the degree to which your ethny is in conflict with another ethny and the genetic distance between the two ethnies. Where that distance is significant, then a co-ethnic is almost family (Salter, 2002: 121–2). But there is arguably a sleight of hand here: parents and children may feel affection quite independently of genetic relatedness – as in the case of adopted children. Salter is testing his reader's intuitions: if you are prepared to make sacrifices for immediate family, and co-ethnics are genetically almost family, then you should show the same commitment to your ethny you show to your family.

## Scottish nationalism

In rejecting ethnic nationalism, Nicola Sturgeon was articulating the consensus view, but now we have discussed a number of theories (and justifications) of nationalism we can take a second look at her view that you are Scottish if you live in Scotland.

Let us start where we finished – with genetics. A 2015 study of genetic patterns in the British Isles produced interesting results (Leslie et al., 2015). Based on a sample of 2,000 people, each of whom had a full set of grandparents born within a certain proximity of one another, they first split the sample into the two most distinct groups, then repeated the procedure. The first split identified the Orkney Islands as distinct from the rest of the British Isles, with strong Nordic input. The second split Wales from the rest, with a Celtic base. At the third split, northern Eng-land and Scotland separate from the rest of England, with latter then splitting. There is no clear genetic separation between modern England and Scotland, so perhaps we should not look to genetic patterns for a basis for Scottishness. (Although independence for the Shetland Islands and Orkney Islands cannot be dismissed, and with that a lot of North Sea oil revenue.)

But if not genes, then why not culture as the basis of Scottishness? Paradoxically, the rise of Scottish nationalism has run in parallel with a narrowing of differences in attitudes, traditions, and institutions between England and Scotland. For example, universities north and south of the border are more alike in degree organisation, curriculum, and faculty employed than they were 30 or 40 years ago. However, even though they owe a great deal to Sir Walter Scott, there are certain powerful symbols of Scottishness, such as the kilt and tartan, bagpipes, and Burns night. And as with all nations, there is the landscape, most especially the Highlands and Islands. Despite living outside Scotland, it is hard to argue that people for whom these images are part of their identity are not really Scottish.

The danger with Sturgeon's civic nationalism is that it lacks emotional appeal. It is perhaps one reason why despite such a favourable environment, little progress has been made in moving towards a second referendum (Campbell, 2021). Even if tinged with some element of England as the 'other' – with attendant problems for English people resident in Scotland – the 'old' Scotland is much more likely to engender allegiance as the cultural basis of a newly independent state. Indeed, there are distinct elements of missionary nationalism in the modern SNP; for example, trans rights has become a contentious debating point, but it is also a way of marking Scotland as 'progressive' relative to England (Lewis, 2021).

## Conclusion

For political theorists, nationalist sentiment is problematic because it seems to resist universalist concepts. Even the 'softest', most civic, nationalist will be forced to concede that their nation is special, for how else can they explain the value of nationhood? Of course, if we say, as liberals do, that the individual is the ultimate source of value and focus of concern, a similar objection can be raised to personal identity: your individual life is especially valuable to *you*. However, because the nation-state entails a massive concentration of power, the ethical particularism within nationalism is of special concern. On the other hand, a world of nation-states may offer the best way to realise values such as freedom, justice, and equality, and a history of nationalism that focused on cases of virulent nationalisms may fail to do justice to nationalism as a liberationist ideology.

## Note

1   Sandel recognised this problem and in a 1998 re-issue of his book maintained that what was important were objective 'ends', such as friendship or the pursuit of certain forms of excellence (Sandel, 1998: xi). Rather than being a communitarian, Sandel appears to be a perfectionist.

## References

Akrap, D. (2015). Germany's Response to the Refugee Crisis Is Admirable. But I Fear it Cannot Last. *The Guardian*, viewed 22 June 2021, https://www.theguardian.com/commentisfree/2015/sep/06/germany-refugee-crisis-syrian

Anderson, B. (1991). *Imagined Communities: Reflections on the Origin and Spread of Nationalism.* London: Verso.

BBC (2017). Nicola Sturgeon would Change SNP Name. *BBC News*, viewed 21 June 2021, https://www.bbc.co.uk/news/uk-scotland-scotland-politics-40975105

Benatar, D. (1997). Why it is Better Never to Come into Existence. *American Philosophical Quarterly*, *34*(3), 345–55.

Breuilly, J. (1993). *Nationalism and the State.* Manchester: Manchester University Press.

Campbell, S. (2021). How it Started and How it's Going, Wings over Scotland, viewed 23 June 2021, https://wingsoverscotland.com/how-it-started-and-how-its-going/

Davidson, N. (2000). *The Origins of Scottish Nationhood.* London: Pluto Press.

Davis, H. (1967). *Nationalism and Socialism: Marxist and Labor Theories of Nationalism to 1917.* New York: Monthly Review Press.

Gellner, E. (1983). *Nations and Nationalism.* Oxford: Basil Blackwell.

Graves, J. and Byrne, R. W. (1989). Mate Selection: The Wrong Control Group. *Behavioral and Brain Sciences, 12*(3), 527–8.

Guibernau, M. (1996). *Nationalisms: The Nation-State and Nationalism in the Twentieth Century* Cambridge: Polity Press.

Hepper, P. G. (1989). Recognising kin = Recognising Genetic Similarity. *Behavioral and Brain Sciences, 12*(3), 530.

Hutchinson, J. and Smith, A. (eds) (1994). *Nationalism.* Oxford: Oxford University Press.

Ignatieff, M. (1993). *Blood and Belonging: Journeys into the New Nationalism.* London: BBC Books and Chatto & Windus.

Ipsos MORI. (2016). How Britain Voted in the 2016 Referendum. *Ipsos MORI*, viewed 22 June 2021, https://www.ipsos.com/ipsos-mori/en-uk/how-britain-voted-2016-eu-referendum

Kaufmann, E. (2018). *Whiteshift: Populism, Immigration and the Future of White Majorities.* London: Penguin UK.

Kedourie, E. (1993). *Nationalism.* Oxford and Cambridge, MA: Blackwell.

Kellas, J. (1998). *The Politics of Nationalism and Ethnicity.* Basingstoke: Macmillan.

Leslie, S., Winney, B., Hellenthal, G., Davison, D., Boumertit, A., Day, T., . . . and Bodmer, W. (2015). The Fine-scale Genetic Structure of the British Population. *Nature*, 519(7543), 309–14.

Lewis, H. (2021). The Party Whose Success Is a Problem. *The Atlantic*, viewed 23 June 2021, https://www.theatlantic.com/international/archive/2021/05/nicola-sturgeon-scotland-election/618790/

Marx, K. and Engels, F. (1967). *The Communist Manifesto.* Introduction and notes by A.J.P. Taylor. London: Penguin.

Mill, J.S. (1991). *On Liberty and Other Essays.* Ed. J. Gray. Oxford: Oxford University Press.

Miller, D. (1995). *On Nationality.* Oxford: Clarendon Press.

Nagel, T. (1991). *Equality and Partiality.* Oxford and New York: Oxford University Press.

Rosenberg, S. (2009). Renewed Pride at Germany's Birthday Party. *BBC News*, viewed 23 June 2021, http://news.bbc.co.uk/1/hi/world/europe/8065504.stm

Rousseau J.-J. (1968). *The Social Contract.* Translated and introduced by Maurice Cranston. Harmondsworth: Penguin Books.

Ruben, D.-H. (1985). *The Metaphysics of the Social World.* London: Routledge and Kegan Paul.

Rushton, J. P. (1989). Genetic Similarity, Human Altruism, and Group Selection. *Behavioral and Brain Sciences, 12*, 503–18.

Rushton, J. P. (2005). Ethnic Nationalism, Evolutionary Psychology and Genetic Similarity Theory. *Nations and Nationalism, 11*(4), 489–507.

Salter, F. (2002). Estimating Ethnic Genetic Interests: Is it Adaptive to Resist Replacement Migration? *Population and Environment, 24*(2), 111–140.

Salter, F. (2007). *On Genetic Interests: Family, Ethnicity and Humanity in an Age of Mass Migration.* New Brunswick: Transaction Publishers.

Sandel, M. (1998). *Liberalism and the Limits of Justice*, 2nd edn. Cambridge: Cambridge University Press.

Simons, G. and Manoilo, A. (2019). Sweden's Self-perceived Global Role: Promises and Contradictions. *Research in Globalization, 1*, 100008.

Smith, A. (1991). *National Identity*. London: Penguin.

Sober, E. and Wilson, D. (1998). *Unto Others: The Evolution and Psychology of Unselfish Behavior*. Cambridge MA: Harvard University Press.

Tamir, Y. (1993). *Liberal Nationalism*. Princeton, NJ: Princeton University Press.

Wilson, D. (2015). *Does Altruism Exist? Culture, Genes, and the Welfare of Others*. New Haven, CT: Yale University Press.

## Further reading

Introductory, critical, and historical overviews: Richard Bosworth, *Nationalism* (Routledge, 2007); Steven Grosby, *Nationalism: A Very Short Introduction* (Oxford University Press, 2005); Philip Spencer and Howard Wollman, *Nationalism: A Critical Introduction* (Sage, 2002); Umut Özkirimli, *Theories of Nationalism: A Critical Introduction* (Red Globe Press, 2017); Anthony D Smith, *Nationalism: Theory, Ideology, History* (Polity, 2010); Yael Tamir, *Why Nationalism* (Princeton University Press, 2020). Good collection: John Breuilly (ed.), *The Oxford Handbook of the History of Nationalism* (Oxford University Press, 2016). More focused: David McCrone and Frank Bechhofer, *Understanding National Identity* (Cambridge University Press, 2015); Richard Lebow, *National Identities and International Relations* (Cambridge University Press, 2019).

# Chapter 14

# Fascism and the radical right

## Introduction

The word 'fascist' is often used as a term of abuse. Fascists are seen as people who act in authoritarian ways and seek to impose their views and values on others – and are often 'white supremacists' – but fascism is more complicated than this. First, because fascism needs to be more precisely defined, and second, the question arises as to whether it is a movement of the past or can be said to still exist today. Everyone has heard of Adolf Hitler (1889–1945), but Hitler called his party the National Socialist German Workers' Party: can he still be called a fascist? Not many movements have come to power since 1945 that can unambiguously be called fascist – but can we describe movements in these terms when they do not declare themselves in favour of Hitler or the founder of Italian fascism, Benito Mussolini?

## Key questions

- What is fascism? What is national socialism (nazism)?
- Is race (and racialism) central, or peripheral, to fascism and/or to nazism?
- To what extent – if at all – is the contemporary radical right (in popular terminology, the 'far right') ideologically continuous with older fascist and nazi movements?

## Defining fascism

Defining fascism raises a problem. Fascism as a movement extols ideas and aesthetics over theory. It can combine socialist ideas, avant-garde positions, anti-capitalist rhetoric, and ecological arguments. Hugh Trevor Roper described fascist ideology as 'an ill-sorted hodge-podge of ideas', and Harold Laski argued that any attempt to find a 'philosophy of fascism' is a waste of time (Griffin, 1995: 1, 276). However, while fascism is unusually flexible as an ideology, there are certain features that characterise it, so that a general view – or 'generic theory' – of fascism is possible.

The term fascism derives from the *fasces* – the bundle of rods carried by the consuls of ancient Rome, and the word *fascio* was used in Italy in the 1890s to indicate a political group or band, usually of revolutionary socialists (Heywood, 1992: 171). National defence groups organised after the Italian defeat at Caparetto in 1917, also called themselves *fasci* (Vincent, 1995: 141).

DOI: 10.4324/9780429424106-18

Case study 14.1

## The 'threat' from the far right

**PHOTO 14.1** Members of the Identitarian Movement, Vienna, Austria, 2017.
© JOE KLAMAR/AFP via Getty Images.

In 2020, Ken McCallum, the head of MI5, the UK's domestic security agency, claimed that nearly 30% (that is, 8 out of 27) of the 'major terror plots' that had been disrupted since 2017 had come from 'far right extremists'. He went on to argue that the pan-European threat from the far right was increasing with 'bitty, but meaningful international connectivity', and that 'quite a few young people [are] attracted to this ideology' (Paton Walsh, 2020). He claimed that, as with Islamist extremism, its adoption was the result of a psychological crisis: 'If you look either at right-wing extremism or Islamist extremism, it's not a coherent ideology that really stands up to much scrutiny. People are nonetheless, sadly, attracted to the seeming certainty that they seek to provide'.

Several points can be made. The pathologisation of extreme political beliefs is common in the security field. The idea of radicalisation is premised on certain psychological theories (see King and Taylor, 2011). This may be based on an observation of people who come to the attention of the security services, but lack of coherence likely characterises most people's political beliefs, whether they are moderate or extremist. That beliefs might also be a response to a psychological need is also not unique to extremism.

There are three questions to think about:

1.  What is the far right? And what is far right extremism?

> 2. Is there any ideological connection between people defined as 'far right' by the media and security services and 'classical' (pre-1945) fascists and nazis?
>
> 3. Is classical fascism dead?
>
> A way to think about these questions is to list all the attributes that you would associate with the terms nazi, neo-nazi, and fascist. Try then to answer the questions. After working through the chapter, come back to these questions.

Italian fascism saw itself as resurrecting the glories of the Roman Empire and Alfredo Rocco, an Italian fascist, identified Machiavelli as a founding father of fascist theory. German national socialism (nazism) was an extreme form of fascism and was seen by its advocates as rooted in the history of the Nordic peoples; a people now locked in a struggle with Jews. But not all fascist movements were anti-Semitic; Mussolini's movement in its original form was not.

Marxists maintain that fascism has particular appeal to those with a modest amount of property, who fear that they might be plunged into the ranks of the working class. However, as Roger Griffin argues, there is nothing in principle that precludes an employed or unemployed member of the working class, an aristocrat, city dweller or peasant, or a graduate from becoming a fascist (1995: 7). Fascism is a movement resistant to universalist ideas – resistant to what historian Ernst Nolte termed 'transcendence' (Kitchen, 1974: 139). The idea that people are divided by class is rejected in favour of the unity of the nation or people, so that industry is organised in a way that expresses the common interest between business and labour.

Fascists vary in their attitude towards the Church. Some fascists see religious organisations as a threat to the state, but may regard religion in a loose sense as being a useful way to instil order. And certainly, they use a religious style of language in invoking the need for sacrifice, redemption, and spiritual virtue and in attacking materialism, consumerism, and hedonism as decadent.

The term decadence has multiple meanings; etymologically, it is related to 'decay', but more specifically, it is a loss of form and purpose. For example, the rejection of modern abstract art was in part premised on the perceived decline in technical skill and realistic representation as well as its Jewish associations. It cannot be stressed enough that aesthetics is central to fascism, as the Marxist Walter Benjamin observed. Benjamin is credited with coining the term the 'aestheticisation of politics' and argued that the 'spectacle' was central to fascism (Jay, 1992: 42). The image is more powerful than the word. That said, the aesthetic commitments of different fascist groups varied enormously. Italian fascists were strongly influenced by avant-garde movements, such as Futurism, and modernist architecture was popular in Italy, whereas German national socialism was notably more hostile to modernism.

Fascism stands opposed to liberalism, which it regards as an embodiment of universalism and of abstract thought. Whereas liberalism derives its legitimacy from the consent of individuals, fascism takes as its starting point the collective – the national group, where the nation is often defined in racial or ethnic terms. Liberalism is perceived as a way in which anti-national elements, such as bolshevism, could inveigle their way into the political culture. The emphasis on the individual weakens the power of the national group.

Fascists see themselves as revolutionary in that they are concerned to rejuvenate a tired and decadent society, and some fascists speak of creating a 'new man' in a new society. They are, therefore, anti-conservative as well as anti-liberal, although, as we shall see, they may form tactical alliances with other sections of the right where they can establish momentary common ground. Many regimes, loosely called fascist, are in fact conservative – Franco's Spain, Petain's 'Vichy' France, and Japan under Hideki Tojo. They may have fascist elements within them, but they are not really anti-conservative in character.

## Fascism in Italy

Commentators generally agree that there was no fascism before the First World War and that it began in 1922–3 with the emergence of the Italian fascist party. The fascist movement was in power in Italy for 18 years (1925–43). Benito Mussolini, the leader of the Italian fascists, had campaigned for Italy's entry into the First World War. The parliamentary Fascio of National Defence was formed in 1917 and drew heavily upon veterans from the war to make up its ex-tra-parliamentary forces. The movement took off when the left organised factory occupations in Milan during the 'red years' of 1919–20, and in November 1920, a fascist party was formed. In October 1922, Mussolini persuaded the king, Victor Emmanuel III, by means of a threatened putsch – dramatised by the March on Rome – to allow him to become Prime Minister in a coalition government.

The action squads, veteran soldiers from an elite battalion, were in theory absorbed into the Voluntary Militia of National Security, but dissatisfied elements in June 1924 killed the socialist deputy, Giacomo Matteotti, who was a major parliamentary critic of Mussolini. Mussolini then suppressed all the other parliamentary parties and created a regime made up purely of fascists. Until 1929, Mussolini was concerned to consolidate the new system, and in the next decade he embarked upon the conquest of Abyssinia and formed an alliance with Hitler's Germany. Although Italy joined the Second World War on Hitler's side, in July 1943 Mussolini was ousted by the king and disaffected fascist leaders and Italy sued for peace with the anti-German allies. Mussolini was rescued by German troops and in a small town near Lake Garda, the Italian Social Republic (Republic of Salò) was proclaimed.

## Nationalism and war

Mussolini had argued strongly for intervention in the First World War, and war was treated by the fascists in Italy as a force for rejuvenation and life. War enabled the nation to constitute itself as a vital, living force, hence Filippo Maronetti (1876–1944), leader of the Futurist movement, spoke of the need for a nationalism that was 'ultra-violent, anti-traditionist and anti-clericalist', a nationalism based on 'the inexhaustible vitality of Italian blood' (Griffin, 1995: 26). The First World War was crucial to win the battle for civilisation and freedom. Maronetti believed that the war would enrich Italy with 'men of action', while Mussolini in 1914 broke with the 'cowards' who opposed it and declared in 1917 that those who fought in the trenches were the 'aristocracy of tomorrow', 'the aristocracy in action' (Griffin, 1995: 26–8). The regime's slogans were 'believe, obey, fight'.

The war was regarded by Roberto Farinacci (1892–1945) as the creator of a new Italian nation, and in Mussolini's view, the First World War brought about a profound psychological transformation among the peasants in the countryside, with veterans becoming leaders in the rural areas.

Physical exercise was to develop skills, according to the Italian leader, 'which may be necessary in a future war'. War was linked to nationalism. The nation, Mussolini declared shortly before the March on Rome, is a myth to which all must be subordinated, and Carlo Costamagna (1881–1965) insisted that, from a cultural point of view, only the individual nation constitutes a *universum*, a concrete universal. The Italian nation, argued the National Association in 1920, embraces people of the future as well as the present, in a venture that is both domestic as well as international in character: the nation either perishes or dominates. War has, said Luigi Federzoni (1878–1967) of the same Association, 'regenerating properties', which 'have taken effect miraculously and mysteriously in the soul of the Italian people'. War is 'the sole hygiene of the world' (Griffin, 1995: 38; 41–2; 44–5; 71, 85).

## Corporativism, violence, and the state

There is a strong economic imperative for fascism. Gabriele D'Annunzio, a fervent nationalist and military leader who had occupied the Adriatic port of Fiume in September 1919, argued for a corporate structure that embraced employees and employers, public and private, within a state that expressed the common will of the people. Mussolini organised the whole country into 22 corporations. Adrian Lyttelton argues that these were held up as fascism's 'most imposing creation': in fact, they served no serious function except as a front for groups of leading industrialists to control raw material allocations and investment decisions (Griffin, 1995: 97).

The trade (labour) unions were seen as contributing loyal employees within this structure – strikes and lockouts were banned – and syndicalists like Sergio Panunzio (1886–1944) saw in revolutionary trade unionism or syndicalism, a force that would transcend its adolescent phase by building up the state. A new national class was to be created – the essence of a civilisation that is neither bourgeois nor proletarian. Mussolini spoke of 'conscious class collaboration', and the tiny Italian Social Republic declared that it aimed to abolish the whole international capitalist system (Griffin, 1995: 47, 49, 64, 87).

Maronetti spoke of 'violence, rehabilitated as a decisive argument', and when links were forged with Hitler's Germany, Mussolini declared that both fascists and nazis believe in violence 'as the dynamo of their history'. The work of the French anarcho-syndicalist Georges Sorel was hugely influential because he extolled both the importance of myth and the need for violence (Griffin, 1995: 36, 45, 79).

Not surprisingly, the state was given a pivotal role, a spiritual and moral entity that, Mussolini declared, is the conscience of the nation. The state is the foundation of fascism: the state organises the nation and is concerned with the growth of empire. Giovanni Gentile (1875–1944) was the key intellectual of the regime, and drawing upon a version of Hegelian idealism, he pronounced the Fascist state to be an 'ethical state': it is the state of 'man himself'. The leader is revered with a capital 'L'. Mussolini ridiculed the 'demo-liberal' civilisation, while praising Hitler for creating 'a unitary, authoritarian, totalitarian state, i.e., a fascist one', although he acknowledges that Hitler operated in a different historical context.

## Intellectual roots

Although fascist intellectuals drew upon Machiavelli, Nietzsche, and Hegel, there was an important tradition of elitism in Italian political thought that was more recent and more influential.

Gaetano Mosca (1858–1941) had taught constitutional law at a number of leading Italian universities. In 1884, he published *Theory of Governments and Parliamentary Government*, but is best known for his book *The Ruling Class*, that appeared in 1896. All societies, he argued, are governed by minorities whether these are military, hereditary, priestly, or based on merit or wealth. He accepted that ownership of property could be a factor in accounting for elite rule, but he rejected the Marxist account that sought to privilege this particular factor. The ruling class or elite owes its superiority to organisational factors, he argued, and its skills alter according to circumstance. What he called the 'political formula' or the ideological mechanisms of rule varied, but whatever the form, all states are necessarily elitist in character, whether their legitimating myth is the divine right of kings, popular sovereignty, or the dictatorship of the proletariat.

Democracy, in his view, is simply a more subtle form of manipulation, and the parties offered inducements for people to vote for them. The political class must be distinguished from other sections of the elite, like industrialists, but in 1923, Mosca introduced in his work the argument that elites could compete through rival political parties. People of lower socio-economic origin can be recruited to renew elites. Unlike other elitists, he was, however, fiercely critical of Mussolini, and his theory is best described as conservative rather than fascist.

Rather more hawkish was Vilfredo Pareto (1848–1923). Pareto had taken the chair in political economy at the University of Lausanne in 1894, publishing his *Cours d'économie politique* (1896, 1897). In 1900, he declared himself an anti-democrat, arguing that the political movements in Italy and France were simply seeking to replace one elite with another. While he approved of Marx's emphasis upon struggle, he rejected completely the notion that a classless society was possible. In 1906, Pareto published his *Manual of Political Economy*, where he presented pure economics in mathematical form.

As far as he was concerned, human action is mostly non-logical in character and stems from non-rational sentiments and impulses: what Pareto called underlying 'residues'. In his most important political and sociological work, the *Mind and Society*, which he wrote in 1916, he distinguishes Class I residues, inventive, imaginative capacities, and Class II residues, conservative, persistent tendencies.

All government is government by an elite who use a combination of coercion and consent. Class I residues predominate when 'foxes' are in control – manipulative politicians who create consent – and Class II residues when violence is necessary. Each of these residues has its strengths and weaknesses, and the 'circulation of elites' can be explained as 'lions' – those who rule through brute force – replacing 'foxes'. He saw in Mussolini a politician with a lion-like character who had displaced wily politicians.

Perhaps most important of all in analysing the intellectual roots of fascism was the work of Robert Michels (1876–1936), a disillusioned German socialist who gained an academic position in Turin and was greatly influenced by syndicalism. In 1911 he published *Political Parties*. Here, he argues that all societies and all organisations are subject to 'an iron law of oligarchy', that is, a small group controlling the masses. Struck by what he saw as the contrast between the official statements of the German Social Democratic Party and the timidity of its political practice, he argued that oligarchy is present even in parties apparently committed to the norms of democracy. The fact that leaders are in practice autonomous from their followers derives from the constraints of organisation. Although he wrote a good deal about psychology, Michels argued that oligarchic tendencies are based upon organisational rather than psychological factors. The complexity of organisations can only be grasped by professional leaders who have communication skills and who understand the rules of elections and other external pressures. This leadership is made all the more entrenched by what Michels regarded as the incompetence and emotional vulnerability of their mass membership.

In 1914 Michels wrote a study of Italian imperialism and published widely on politics and sociology. In 1930 he wrote the entry on 'Authority' for the *Encyclopaedia of the Social Sciences*. He admired fascism and argued that, as with bolshevism, it was a reflection of the general tendency to oligarchy. Michels also wrote a good deal on nationalism, with his later writings becoming increasingly anti-democratic in tone (Beetham, 1977).

## Fascism in Germany – national socialism

## A brief history

Since the clauses of the Versailles Treaty limited the Reichswehr (the German army) to 100,000, Hitler was demobilised in 1920. He became leader of the German Workers' Party (DAP), which was then renamed the National Socialist German Workers' Party (NSDAP). A putsch was attempted in 1923, and Hitler was given a short prison sentence. Nazis were widely regarded as isolated fanatics until 1930. In 1928, the NSDAP won only 2.6% of the popular vote; yet by 1933 the movement had seized power. The Versailles Treaty which ended the First World War had punitive effects on Germany: all colonies were lost while it is calculated that the reparations bill equalled 1.5 times the total gross national product of Germany in 1929. Although the economy had improved in the 1920s, the depression had catastrophic effects. Investment and industry collapsed, and unemployment was officially estimated at some 30%: the real figure was nearer half.

The Social Democratic Party of Germany (SPD) had headed a coalition government until 1930: when this fell apart, the President ruled by decree for three years, real wages were halved, and Hitler had meanwhile stressed the need for a party capable of winning elections and conducting effective mass propaganda. In the elections in 1930, the nazis came second to the SPD, and two years later, they received 37% of the vote. Large employers began to support the nazis, and although many thought Hitler 'tactless' and his economic policies 'utopian', his militant anti-bolshevism appealed to them, and they backed him for Chancellor. He was appointed to the position in 1933, and the nazis received three posts in an 11-strong cabinet. Joseph Goebbels vowed that 1933 would strike the French revolutionary year of 1789 out of history.

## The 'socialism' in national socialism

Although clearly anti-bolshevist, the nazi movement was in the 1920s strongly anti-capitalist as well. The first programme of the party spoke of the need to share profits, nationalise the trusts, increase pensions, and provide free education. Hitler referred to the need to make the working people national, while Gregor Strasser, killed in the purges of 1934, attacked capitalism and argued for the emancipation of the worker through 'participation in profits, property and management'. Günther Gründel saw the creation of a new type of human being as constituting the end of the property-owning bourgeoisie (Griffin, 1995: 117, 123, 128), while Goebbels had said in 1928 that 'no honest thinking person today would want to deny the justification of the workers' movements'. Indeed, he had complained in 1926 that Hitler wanted to 'compensate the aristocrats' and not 'disturb private property. Horrendous! . . . we are Socialists. We don't want to have been so in vain'!

The body particularly concerned with advancing nazi interests among trade unionists – the National Socialist Factory Cell Organisation (NSBO) – became an increasing embarrassment to the nazi leadership. The 'Night of the Long Knives' that saw the liquidation of the leadership of the Sturmabteilung (stormtroopers) (SA) was justified by Hitler on the grounds that a second revolution had to be avoided at all costs. Socialism continued in the party's title, but it was mere rhetoric. The nazi economic programme was presented as a form of 'soldierly socialism', but the real target was Marxism and liberal democracy. Marxism, it was said, always follows capitalism as its shadow. Christoph Steding nonetheless spoke contemptuously of 'the purely mercenary capitalism of the stock exchange' (Griffin, 1995: 141, 152), and nazi policies often involved taking away certain freedoms from employers. For example, the introduction of some labour-saving machinery was banned, and government permission had to be obtained before firms could reduce their labour force. The government also tended to give work contracts to those companies that relied on manual labour rather than machines. The German economy however remained capitalist, although with extensive state control.

## The broad outlines of national socialist thought

Although Germany is famously the country of poets and thinkers ('Dichter und Denker'), it is fair to say that national socialism did not attract the explicit support of any high calibre philosophers. But that is not say that themes cannot be discerned, and the writings of 'lesser' theoreticians can be mined to reconstruct these themes. In his book *The Law of Blood: Thinking and Acting Like a Nazi*, Johann Chapoutot draws on a huge range of primary work published before 1945 – around 1,200 books and articles and around 50 films – to create a *Gestalt* of national socialism.

Borrowing a phrase from Kant, Chapoutot argues that there were three categorical imperatives at the heart of nazism, all three intended to ensure eternal life for Germany and the German people (Chapoutot, 2018: 19–20):

1. **Procreation**: have as many children as possible, but they must be of good quality and free from racial admixture.
2. **Intergroup conflict**: history is a struggle between races or racial groups. The war must be won for the German people.
3. **Eschatology**: after the struggle has been won, Germany must escape history and enjoy the bountiful plenty of its new, vast territories.

While Darwinism is often misunderstood and misused by political theorists, underpinning these three imperatives is a kind of 'social Darwinism' – a biocentric view of politics. But nature is also endowed with spiritual qualities, and while 'eco-fascism' has become a term of abuse, there is a clear ecological vision in nazism. While possibly used strategically – and not entirely sincerely – the nazis argued that Judaism (and by extension, Christianity) had denatured the world by restricting the spiritual to an absolute God (Jews) or a triune God (Christians). The losers had been non-human animals, and one of the early acts of Hitler's government was the passing of the Reich Animal Protection Act (November 1933). Chapoutot questions whether in practice animals really fared better in Germany than elsewhere (2018: 31), but nonetheless, animal protection was part of a holistic world view and a rejection of individualism and materialism, and not simply the instrumentalisation of popular sentiments towards animals in order to attack Jews, with their practice of ritual slaughter, as illustrated in the propaganda film *Der Ewige Jude* (2018: 24). The nazis' ecological vision can be summed up: 'the same thing that bound the living to the dead bound the living to the living. To be sure, those now living would die, but biological substance was eternal, so long as its health and purity were preserved' (2018: 28). Fritz Lenz argued that nazism stood for what he termed gentilism (from the Latin *gens*, people), against individualism and humanism (or universalism). Individuals had no capacities independently of their race, and humanity was a meaningless abstraction (2018: 87–88).

This ecological world view drew national socialists closer to Eastern thought – Hinduism and Buddhism – and away from the Abrahamic religions (2018: 29–30). And the concept of the Aryan race provided a racial bridge between East and West. In a vague sense, it equates to the contemporary concept of the Indo-European peoples, but whereas the origins of those peoples were the Pontic-Caspian steppe region, the nazis shifted their putative origins to Europe.

Law should also be informed by the naturalistic world view. In place of a cold, rationalistic legal code (2018: 98), supported by a legal profession in which Jews were overrepresented,[1] the nazis emphasised immediacy and the intuitive sense of justice of the German people. An important inspiration was the mediaeval document, the *Sachsenspiegel*. Written between 1220 and 1235, it codified customary law: it was literally putting a mirror (*Spiegel*) up to the Saxon people (2018: 41). And it is interesting to consider the role of the state. Whereas Italian fascism placed emphasis on the state as central to the formation of a people, nazism implies a pre-political – or at least pre-state – conception of the people as a biological entity. The *Sachsenspiegel* was interpreted not as the imposition of law – the positing of law, as in the phrase 'legal positivism' – but as the expression of what already existed. On the other side, it stood opposed to the idea of natural law, in the sense of universal laws applicable to 'humanity'. It was a fusion of legality and morality, but morality consisted solely of duties to the German people, and:

> Each race possessed its 'value system' (*Wertordnung*): race produced culture; values were dictated by blood. There was no need for lengthy reflection: natural norms were instinctive – immediate, animal, spontaneous – they 'do not think, they do not split hairs, they don't hesitate'. A sound mind born of unmixed biology and still faithful to its racial identity would produce pure thoughts and know how to act.
>
> (Chapoutot, 2018: 51)

Mixed-race people lacked the instinct for this fusion of morality and law. Jews, it was argued, were not a pure race, and thus heteronomous – dependent on an external legal code, such as Talmudic handbooks (2018: 52).

We suggested earlier that despite using the language of socialism, nazism did not fundamentally challenge capitalism. Nonetheless, anti-capitalism was rhetorically of great importance and was boiled down to gold versus blood. The Western nations – Britain and America, especially – were in thrall to gold, and to the Jews, as mediators of gold. Gold was a universal equaliser, which eliminated the particular, whereas blood could never be universalised (Chapoutot, 2018: 78).

This biocentric view required that Germans overcome their traditional divisions. Hostility to Protestant–Catholic marriages should end. Catholic priestly celibacy was dysgenic and should also end. Homosexuality was perceived as the product of all-male environments, and so early heterosexual experimentation should be permitted. Children born out of wedlock should be – if they are of pure race – looked after by the state. And the Lebensborn programme, started in 1935, was a product of that concern (2018: 110–11). And, of course, infamously, the nazis enacted the Aktion T4 euthanasia programme, which involved the sterilisation or – often – the killing of people with mental and physical disabilities. Ultimately, all policy should aim to reproduce the German people and allow Germans to outcompete other groups. What comes across in the documents Chapoutot cites is that harsh things had to be done in the name of a higher good, with a stoic sense of duty.

## Radical right thought

Italian fascism and German national socialism are the two 'classic' variants of (generic) fascism. The year 1945 marked the end of their worlds, and despite the popular use of the terms 'fascist' and 'nazi', it could reasonably be argued that fascism is a dead ideology, and its only afterlife is as a source of images intended to frighten people or gain in a political struggle by labelling your opponents in ways likely to stigmatise them and their beliefs, even if in fact those beliefs bear little or no connection to classical fascism. However, there is a contemporary radical right, and in the rest of this chapter, we outline its features and consider the extent to which it is continuous, or not, with classical fascism.

Although our focus is on the contemporary radical right, our starting point is an interwar movement that became dubbed the Conservative Revolution. In his book *The Conservative Revolution in Germany, 1918–1932*, Armin Mohler – who was sympathetic to the movement – identifies a number of groups and thinkers forming a nationalist right, distinct from national socialism (Mohler, 2018). Just how distinct is a matter of some debate. Key thinkers in the Conservative Revolution, and who are much discussed on the contemporary radical right scene, are cultural theorist Oswald Spengler (1880–1936), novelist Ernst Jünger (1895–1998), and legal theorist Carl Schmitt (1888–1985). We discussed Schmitt in Chapter 1 (see pp. 18–20). We will focus here on Spengler and Jünger and, in addition, discuss another important thinker who straddles the period before and after 1945: Julius Evola (1898–1974).

We briefly outline key aspects of the work of these three thinkers – Spengler, Jünger, and Evola – and then offer an overall picture of the world view that informs the contemporary radical right. Of course, there will be tensions within the radical right, but we argue that there are some distinct themes, and these can be found in the writings of the three thinkers.

## Spengler and decline

Spengler is most famous for his two-volume work *Der Untergang des Abendlandes* (translated as *The Decline of the West*), which was first published in 1918 (volume 1) and 1922 (volume 2). Although academic historians were hostile, the book sold extremely well through the 1920s and into the 1930s, and Spengler's ideas entered the public consciousness. The most provocative idea is in the title – that the West is in decline. However, in this context, 'Untergang' is tricky to translate. The standard translation is downfall ('going under'), but even in German, this was misleading, as Spengler did not envisage a catastrophe, but rather a gradual decline. And even that is misleading, as it is more a fulfilment (*Vollendung*) of the West's destiny rather than decline.

Spengler distinguishes culture and civilisation (Wei, 2011: 4). The former turns into the latter as its creative impulses wane, and critique – rationality – takes over (Rowland, 2015: 7). The intellect supplants the soul, and culture becomes disenchanted – it loses its spiritual qualities. Spengler rejects epochs, such as those standardly used by historians. Instead of ancient, mediaeval, and modern periods, he sees whole cultures as the units of history (Morley, 2004: 574). He identifies a number of 'high cultures', but his primary focus is on two: the Apollonian (or Classical) and the Faustian (or Western). The Apollonian, centred on Ancient Greece, is characterised by an appreciation for the human body. It is ahistorical in that it has no interest in what happened before. The Faustian emerged around the tenth century in Western Europe and has expanded to cover almost the entire earth, with the exception of the Islamic world. In the legend – most famously re-told by Goethe – Faustus makes a pact with the devil in return for unlimited knowledge, and for Spengler Faustian man seeks out infinity.

Cultures are inwardly focused and growing, whereas civilisations look outwards and expand physically or in terms of resources, but not spiritually. Whereas Ancient Greece grew culturally, the Roman Empire simply expanded, often without any significant resistance. Greece was a culture. Rome became a civilisation. Civilisation is the destiny of all cultures and is marked by a lack of creativity and by insincerity. Spengler also distinguishes the world-city and the countryside, these bearing some analogy to civilisation and culture. The countryside has order and hierarchy. City-dwellers are coldly intelligent, contemptuous of the provinces, but decadent, exemplified by lavish entertainment and a naturalism with regard to sex, which is, in fact, a return to primitive instincts.

Spengler rejects biological race, but emphasises rootedness in the landscape, arguing that a race does not migrate, only individual men migrate (Spengler, 1962: 254). People must be *conscious* of belonging to a race, so physical (biological) origin is of interest only to scientists. Cultures make people, and in the early phase of a culture 'prototypes' are produced, which then evolve into Englishmen, Italians, Germans, and so on. Religion is also crucial to culture. All cultures, he argues, begin from a religious impulse, that starts in the countryside and eventually spreads to the city, which then ultimately turns materialistic. And the Enlightenment, which begins with unlimited optimism in human power, devolves into scepticism. Liberal democracy is simply plutocracy, with the masses subjected to manipulation by political parties and interest groups. It is a cover for class war between the bourgeoisie and the aristocracy. In the end, Spengler predicts that democracy will collapse into Caesarism (Rowland, 2015: 12).

## Jünger, technology, and the individual

Jünger's long life traversed multiple incarnations of the German nation: the German Empire – Kaiserreich (until 1918), Weimar (1918–33), the Third Reich (1933–45), the divided (1945–89), and then reunified (post-1990), Germany. And in his literary output – mainly novels, but also diaries and political writings – there are significant shifts and turns, such that it is not possible to offer a single outline of his world view. There are, however, themes: the relationship between the individual and technology being a key one.

Born in 1895, Jünger served with distinction in the First World War (Neaman, 2019: 23–4). He was wounded multiple times and was awarded the highest medal for gallantry, the Pour le mérite. His memoir *In Stahlgewittern* (*Storm of Steel*), published 1920, ranks alongside Erich Maria Remarque's *Im Western nichts Neues* (*All Quiet on the Western Front*), as one of the most famous accounts of the war. Unlike Remarque's book, it cannot be described as pacifist. But neither is it exactly a glorification of the conflict. It is best described as an aestheticisation of war, not in the sense of beautifying it, but rather describing the appearance (*Schein*) or surface, such as descriptions of dead bodies. To use a term popular among the contemporary radical right: it was metapolitical. It does not argue the rights or wrongs of the war, but sees in it the future of humanity, specifically, the smallness of the individual in the face of technology, with the likely loss of notions of heroism in any future conflict.

Technology is also central to Jünger's 1932 novel *Der Arbeiter* (*The Worker*). Modernisation means that romantic ideas of individual subjectivity and sovereignty are giving way to the 'worker-type' (Bullock, 2012: 457–8). Jünger holds that there can be no turning back to a pre-modern society, and while work is a threat to sovereignty, it might ultimately be the route by which humans regain their individuality. This is achieved by confronting the external world through labour, just as the soldier regained his sovereignty through facing death (Pan, 2008). While the bourgeois individual sees his individuality as an expression of his universal humanity, the worker is not free in that sense, but can achieve individuality through skill. Indeed, the soldier and worker merge. Writing at a time when air war was developing at a rapid pace, Jünger sees in the airman a new, post-Feudal, but non-liberal individuality. A pilot can rise through the ranks of the air force based on skill, which in large part is technical. In his essay 'Total Mobilisation', Jünger advocates for the concentration of power into a self-preserving unity (Costea and Amiridis, 2017: 13). This is not a military mobilisation, nor a modelling of industry on military organisation – both ideas associated with the nazi use of the term – but is a more abstract idea.

Based on his war memoirs, Jünger was a famous man by the 1920s – even though he was barely in his 30s – and Hitler tried to persuade him to stand for election under the NSDAP label. Jünger declined, and while other leading nazis decided that he was an aesthete rather a serious political activist, he nonetheless enjoyed a certain protection, something that became important in the Second World War. In 1939, he published a barely disguised attack on nazism in his allegorical work *Auf den Marmorklippen* (*On the Marble Cliffs*). During most of the war, he served as a Wehrmacht officer in Paris, and he was on the margins of the Stauffenberg 20 July (1944) Plot to assassinate Hitler.[2] After the war, Jünger was banned from publishing for four years because of his refusal to submit to the 'denazification' process. By the 1950s, his reputation was largely restored. (That said, even commentators who accept he was not a nazi – despite the seemingly totalitarian implications of *The Worker* – hold him, and other nationalists, responsible for weakening Weimar democracy.)

Two post-war works are of particular significance: *Der Waldgang* (*The Forest Passage*) and *Eumeswil*. Published in 1951 and 1977, respectively, they outline a third 'type', alongside the soldier and the worker: the anarch. While not to be confused with the anarchist – which describes an ideological position – Jünger was nonetheless influenced by Max Stirner and his idea of the *Einzige* (the unique) (see pp. 207–8). The anarch is someone who lives in the world but is not of the world. Such a person achieves sovereignty either through withdrawal – by going into the forest – or, in the central figure of Venator in *Eumeswil*, being a faithful servant of those in power, while also building a refuge in the mountains, and achieving a kind of ironic, psychological distance from power (Jünger, 2015).

## Evola and tradition

Julius Evola is the single most referenced thinker on the contemporary radical right (Hakl, 2019). He has also been popular in occult circles, and underlying his philosophical system is a notion of the spiritual which politically has been expressed as 'tradition' (or 'traditionalism'). The term tradition carries rather soft, moderate conservative overtones, but is much more radical for Evola: it entails a neo-Platonic reality that, in the modern world, only a few people are capable of grasping. Evola is anti-egalitarian, anti-democratic, and elitist. The task is to return to an organic and hierarchical society – to an imperium, in which certain people are by nature rulers.

Evola, as with Spengler, interprets history as cyclical, not linear (and progressive). In his most famous work *Rivolta contro il Mondo moderno* (*Revolt against the Modern World*), first published in 1934, he sets out a view of history as a process of regression, from a society governed by a priestly class that held spiritual power, to one in which the warrior caste is in the ascendent, to the modern world where power is effectively in the hands of merchants.

As with Jünger and nazism, so Evola was part tolerated and part distrusted by Mussolini and the fascists. Evola thought that nazism and fascism were too democratic – they gave too much weight to the people, distinct from an elite (Wolff, 2014: 261). He developed his own racial theory, which he termed traditional racialism: the spirit – one's attitude to life and to action – are more important than physical, biological criteria. The aim was to create a super-race through selection, capable of world domination (Hakl, 2019: 63–4). He also rejected the geographical or linguistic concept of the nation in favour of a spiritual community focused on tradition. The Church (of Rome) might have provided the basis for such a community, but it would have had to turn completely against modernity – it would have to be, literally, reactionary (Wolff, 2014: 267).

Evola makes no attempt in his writings to persuade those who do not accept his premises to embrace tradition. His work is much more aimed at the initiated, and this fits with his broader occultism. He identifies three groups of people, and correspondingly, three ways of 'living among the ruins'. The first is composed of people who keep tradition alive, even in ignorance that there are other like-minded individuals. They retreat into an apolitical state, somewhat akin to Jünger's anarch. A second group is less aware and assured, but can be helped along the way to the realisation of the value of tradition. The third group – perhaps, the most interesting politically – are accelerationists. They adopt the most destructive tactics of modernity in order to speed up its day of reckoning – they 'ride the tiger' of modernity.[3]

## Strands and tensions in radical right thought

The work of these, and other, thinkers have achieved great popularity on the intellectual radical right. Whereas Spengler and Jünger are sufficiently mainstream to have had their work translated into other languages and published by mainstream outlets – Jünger is especially popular in France – it is only recently that Evola has appeared in translation, largely thanks to Swedish businessman Daniel Friberg and his publishing house Arktos Media (Teitelbaum, 2019: 269–70). In addition, the website Counter-Currents, established in 2010 (Macklin, 2019: 206–9), has helped to propagate the work of Evola and others.

What emerges through these endeavours is a picture of the radical right somewhat at variance to the popular image of the far right. Because the *Zeitgeist* is hostile to their world view, such that they cannot advance their cause through academia or the mainstream media, they are seeking to build a parallel structure. And there are practical issues here. Websites are reliant on not being downgraded on search engines and payments are dependent on PayPal and similar invoicing systems. The risk of being taken off social media platforms or demonetised or denied access to payment systems is such that they are seeking to build an autonomous, fully integrated alternative technology (Macklin, 2019: 207). Their hope is that they can sustain themselves long enough to achieve critical mass and break through to a larger audience. And given threats of 'doxing', many contributors to radical right websites use pseudonyms.

That is the organisational context in which the radical right operates. As to themes, the first – and obvious one – is race. For some on the radical right, the struggle is straightforward: it is to halt and reverse the demographic changes happening across the Western world. French novelist Renaud Camus' 2011 book *Le Grand Remplacement* (self-translated into English under the title *You will not Replace Us!*), dismissed by opponents as a conspiracy theory, articulates this theme (McAuley, 2019). Camus argues 'replaceism' – that everything has become substitutable – is extended to entire peoples.

While the radical right is racialist – using that term in a neutral sense as a belief in the reality and normative significance of race – there are different interpretations of 'race'. The Identitarian

Movement has eschewed the biological concept of race in favour of culture (Guenther et al., 2020: 1–2). Given the stigma attached to racism (using that term pejoratively), this may be strategic rather than sincere. Or it could be an attempt to turn the tables on the left, by using the language of multiculturalism and identity politics to advance the interests of white people. By focusing on the perceived double-standards of multiculturalism, whereby all groups except whites can advance their interests (see pp. 291–2), Identitarians can reach a wider – and, importantly, younger – audience. Those who have read Spengler, Jünger, and Evola will see in their work a cultural, rather than biological, concept of race, in contrast to the biocentric world view of national socialism.

While demographic change may be the fuel in the tank of the radical right two other themes articulated by the three thinkers are also important: a rejection of a progressive view of history, and the importance of the metapolitical. Spengler and Evola have a cyclical view of history. Phrases popular on the left, such as 'being progressive' or 'being on the right side of history' imply a linear view of history whereby things are getting better. This can be seen in the American self-consciousness of 'a more perfect union', and of the United States as unique due to its post-ethnic nature. If history is cyclical, then America may well be in the vanguard – but the vanguard of regression to formlessness. America is decadent. To some extent, this view of history might also serve as a coping strategy, and this fits with a perhaps surprising sub-theme of the radical right: the retreat to inwardness, as exemplified by Jünger's anarch. For someone out of sympathy with the times, the question he must ask is: should I withdraw (as far as is possible) from the world and wait for it to collapse? Or should I resist 'progressive' forces? Or, should I, in fact, engage with, and accelerate, the decline? All these positions – withdrawal, resistance, and acceleration – make sense against the background belief that progressive views of history are false.

Withdrawal entails retaining one's personal integrity in the face of what are perceived as socially enforced lies. Resistance would be engaging with that hostile culture. This could take the form of trying to persuade 'normies' – those who, in the language of *The Matrix*, have not yet been 'red-pilled' – of the contradictions in the progressive world view, and the threats posed by it. Somewhere between resistance and acceleration is delegitimisation: the more people who believe social media, mainstream news outlets, academia, police and security services, the justice system, and political elites are biased, the better. Weakening social and political institutions is a prerequisite to their overthrow. Acceleration entails speeding up what the radical right opposes, such as immigration, racial quotas, and restrictions on speech, with the intention of creating an environment of such conflict and tension that there will be revolution.

The other theme is metapolitics. In part, this is a strategy to 'red-pill' individuals and, in part, a reverse 'long march through the institutions'. That term is attributed to Communist student Rudi Dutschke (1940–79) and is based on the ideas of Antonio Gramsci (1891–1937), who argued that the ruling class use cultural institutions – universities, media, and so on – to establish and reinforce their 'hegemony'. The 'long march' is a struggle by the left to capture those cultural institutions, a struggle the radical right believes has been successful. Metapolitics is concerned not with politics in the narrow sense of electioneering and winning votes, but with changing the underlying culture. Changing, for example, how we describe things. The words we use. The cultural left describes all resistance to immigration as racist and advocating for immigration restrictions as hate speech. Racism and hate speech are powerful terms, and the targets of such terms are constantly on the defensive – 'I am not racist'. Success for the radical right would be measured by the extent to which these terms lose their power.

## The intelligence services and the far right

We started by asking you to reflect on the popular usage of the terms 'fascist', 'nazi', and 'neo-nazi', in the light of the head of MI5's comments about the threat from the far right. It is highly unlikely that the individuals who come to the attention of the intelligence and security services spend a great deal of their time discussing Julius Evola. That said, it could be argued that all intellectual reflection has effects, some of which may be to weaken liberal democracy. This raises issues of free speech, which we discussed in an earlier chapter (see Chapter 7).

The key question is whether classical fascism is continuous with the contemporary radical right. A few teenagers with swastikas on their bedroom walls does not amount to a resurgence of the ideology. Of course, there have been large-scale attacks in the past decade. Anders Breivik murdered 69 people in Norway in July 2011. His long manifesto, published under the lightly pseudonymous name Andrew Berwick, draws on some radical right themes, but is largely focused on Muslims – Muslims in Europe – and much of the imagery is from the Crusades. This is not classical fascism.

In March 2019, Brenton Tarrant murdered 51 people at the Al Noor Mosque in Christchurch, New Zealand. He also wrote a manifesto. Borrowing the title 'The Great Replacement', it largely adopts a 'question and answer' form such as 'was the attack "racist" in origin?'. Obviously written before the attack, the questions cover many of the talking points of the radical right, with the primary focus on the demographic displacement of whites in traditionally white-majority countries. The manifesto demonstrates considerable awareness of issues at the centre of online discussion. None of his statements invoke *classical* nazi or fascist imagery or language, although they do express biologically based ideas of intergroup conflict, with particular emphasis on immigration and fertility rates. Whether or not Tarrant is a 'fascist', the fact is that he used violence to achieve his ends, and it might be better to focus attention on that fact – and how to prevent such violent acts – than on ideological categorisation.

## Conclusion

Fascism arose first in Italy. The development of fascism in Italy needs to be explained, since this was the particular movement that gave the general movement its name. Nazism – German national socialism – is a form of fascism and not simply a historically unique movement. It is an extreme kind of fascism, emphasising the racial character of nationalism. Its anti-capitalism was ultimately rhetorical as the liquidation of the leaders of the nazi 'left' in 1934 demonstrates. Although fascism acquired mass support through espousing a rhetorical anti-capitalism, once in power, fascist movements consolidated their links with big business. Fascism rejects liberalism and the Enlightenment. Ideas of reason, equality, and emancipation are dismissed. Fascists see the state itself as central to human identity and vital to the idea of community (although German national socialism posits a pre-state racial community).

The contemporary radical right cannot be entirely detached from fascism, but at least in its intellectually developed form it draws inspiration from revolutionary nationalism and from what it terms 'traditionalism'. Race – understood in biological terms – is a concern for many, but not all, on the radical right.

# Notes

1 According to Slezkine, at the turn of the twentieth century, 62 per cent of lawyers in Vienna were Jewish, and in Prussia, as of 1925, one-quarter were Jewish (2019: 50).
2 Claus von Stauffenberg and others were deeply sympathetic to the ideas of the Conservative Revolution.
3 Another two of Evola's books carry the titles *Gli uomini e le rovine* (published 1953) (English title: *Men among the Ruins: Post-War Reflections of a Radical Traditionalist*) and *Cavalcare la tigre* (1961) (*Ride the Tiger: A Survival Manual for the Aristocrats of the Soul*).

# References

Beetham, D. (1977). From Socialism to Fascism: the Relation between Theory and Practice in the Work of Robert Michels. *Political Studies, 25*(3–24), 161–81.

Bullock, M. P. (2012). Flight Forward: The World of Ernst Jünger's Worker. *Utopian Studies, 23*(2), 450–71.

Chapoutot, J. (2018). *The Law of Blood: Thinking and Acting as a Nazi*. Trans. M R Mouillot. Cambridge, MA: Harvard University Press.

Costea, B., and Amiridis, K. (2017). Ernst Jünger, Total Mobilisation and the Work of War. *Organization, 24*(4), 475–90.

Griffin, R. (1995). *Fascism*. Oxford, New York: Oxford University Press.

Guenther, L., Ruhrmann, G., Bischoff, J., Penzel, T., and Weber, A. (2020). Strategic Framing and Social Media Engagement: Analyzing Memes Posted by the German Identitarian Movement on Facebook. *Social Media+ Society, 6*(1), 1–13.

Hakl, H. T. (2019). 'Julius Evola and Tradition', in *Key Thinkers of the Radical Right*. New York: Oxford University Press, 54–70.

Heywood, A. (1992). *Political Ideologies*. Basingstoke: Palgrave.

Jay, M. (1992). 'The Aesthetic Ideology' as Ideology; Or, What Does It Mean to Aestheticize Politics? *Cultural Critique, 21*, 41–61.

Jünger, E. (2015). *Eumeswil*. Trans Joachim Neugroschel. Candor, NY: Telos Press.

King, M., and Taylor, D. M. (2011). The Radicalization of Homegrown Jihadists: A Review of Theoretical Models and Social Psychological Evidence. *Terrorism and Political Violence, 23*(4), 602–22.

Kitchen, M. (1974). Ernst Nolte and the Phenomenology of Fascism. *Science & Society*, 130–49.

McAuley, J. (2019). How Gay Icon Renaud Camus Became the Idealogue of White Supremacy. *The Nation*, viewed 26 July 2021, https://www.thenation.com/article/archive/renaud-camus-great- replacement-brenton-tarrant/

Macklin, G. (2019). 'Greg Johnson and Counter-Currents', in M. Sedgwick (ed.), *Key Thinkers of the Radical Right*. New York: Oxford University Press, 204–23.

Mohler, A. (2018). *The Conservative Revolution in Germany, 1918–1932*. Whitefish, MT: Washington Summit Publishers.

Morley, N. (2004). Decadence as a Theory of History. *New Literary History, 35*(4), 573–85.

Neaman, E (2019). 'Ernst Jünger and Storms of Steel', in M. Sedgwick (ed.), *Key Thinkers of the Radical Right*. New York: Oxford University Press, 22–35.

Pan, D. (2008). The Sovereignty of the Individual in Ernst Junger's The Worker. *Telos, 144*(144), 66–74.

Paton Walsh, N. (2020). 30% of UK Terror Plots Disrupted by MI5 were Far Right. *CNN*, viewed 10 July 2021, https://edition.cnn.com/2020/10/14/uk/mi5-far-right-terror-plots-gbr-intl/index.html

Rowland, B. M. (2015). Spengler's Decline of the West Revisited, in B. Rowland (ed.), *Is the West in Decline? Historical, Military, and Economic Perspectives*, 3–17.

Slezkine, Y. (2019). *The Jewish Century*, 2nd edn. Princeton: Princeton University Press.

Spengler, O. (1962). *The Decline of the West*. New York: Alfred Knopf

Teitelbaum, B. (2019). 'Daniel Friberg and Metapolitics in Action', in M. Sedgwick (ed.), *Key Thinkers of the Radical Right*. New York: Oxford University Press, 259–76.

Vincent, A. (1995). *Modern Political Ideologies*, 2nd edn. Oxford: Blackwell.

Wei, R. (2011). 'Civilization' and 'Culture'. *International Review of Social Sciences and Humanities, 1*(1), 1–14.

Wolff, E. C. (2014). Apolitìa and Tradition in Julius Evola as Reaction to Nihilism. *European Review, 22*(2), 258–73.

## Further Reading

Useful overviews: Kevin Passmore, *Fascism: A Very Short Introduction* (Oxford University Press, 2014); Roger Griffin, *Fascism* (Polity, 2018); Renzo de Felice, *Fascism: An Informal Introduction to its Theory and Practice* (Transaction Publishers, 1977); Daniel Woodley, *Fascism and Political Theory* (Routledge, 2009); Carlos Martins, *From Hitler to Codreanu: The Ideology of Fascist Leaders* (Routledge, 2020). On the contemporary radical right: Mark Sedgwick (ed.), *Key Thinkers of the Radical Right* (Oxford University, 2019). On Julius Evola: Paul Furlong, *Social and Political Thought of Julius Evola* (Routledge, 2011).

# Part 4

# Contemporary ideologies

# Chapter 15

# Feminism

## Introduction

Feminism is an ideology that has always been controversial. It asks such questions as: do women have too much or too little power? It is not only controversial as far as traditional defenders of the status quo are concerned. Some women feel that they are in favour of equality with men, but do not like the idea of feminism. It has been said that we live in a post-feminist age and some contend that the main goals of feminism have been realised, so that it is quite unnecessary for feminists to continue their argument against male domination.

Feminism is however also controversial in the sense that different feminists mean different things by the term. There are different varieties that seem to have little in common. Just as writers have spoken of socialisms, so feminism has also been presented in the plural to indicate the diversity involved. In this chapter, we follow the example of many writers in trying to explain these different feminisms and also try to suggest a way of extracting some kind of unity out of this formidable diversity.

## Key questions

- What is feminism? Is it a distinct ideology?
- Is there a generic feminism, or just a plurality of feminisms?
- If there are feminisms, are there tensions between them?

## Feminism or feminisms?

It is commonplace to say there is no single feminism, but rather feminisms. In this chapter, we discuss liberal, radical, socialist, black, philosophical, and empirical forms of feminism. The strategy we use is to outline each and then discuss criticisms that other forms of feminism make of the form under discussion. In the case study – gestational surrogacy – we apply some of these feminist perspectives to that issue.

DOI: 10.4324/9780429424106-20

## Case study 15.1

## Fertility outsourcing

**PHOTO 15.1** © Vijayanand Gupta/Hindustan Times via Getty Images.

Couples who struggle to have children often – if they can afford it – resort to reproductive technology, such as in vitro fertilisation (IVF). More controversial is surrogacy, especially where it takes the form of 'reproductive tourism'. India has become one of the centres for gestational surrogacy, where the carrying woman is not genetically related to the child. Other significant suppliers of such services are Thailand and Ukraine (Deonandan, 2015: 111). Markets for surrogacy tend to be in the West, especially in countries with strict regulation, such as Germany.

As of 2014, it cost an estimated $20,000–$60,000 for the services of a surrogate in India (which compares to $80,000–$150,000 in the United States). While only a fraction goes to the surrogate, nonetheless it is still a significant amount – around $6,500, equivalent to five years of household income (Harrison, 2014: 146). Arguably, the work is less physically stressful than working in the garment industry, which is from where many surrogates are recruited. As part of the guarantee to the parents of the child, surrogates are expected to spend the pregnancy closely monitored in the clinic's hostel (2014: 147).

Laws on surrogacy can be grouped into four categories: (a) the practice is outlawed on the grounds that women are being used as 'means to an end'; (b) only 'altruistic' surrogacy is permitted, as it is a 'gift from one woman to another'; (c) it is a financial transaction; and (d) there is no regulation (Fenton-Glynn, 2019).

What should the law be on gestational surrogacy?

Should there be greater international regulation?

Are women who use surrogacy services exploiting other women?

## Liberal feminism

Liberal feminism would appear to be the earliest form of feminism. Feminism has a particular relationship to liberalism, and it has been said that all feminism is 'liberal at root' (Eisenstein, 1981: 4). We are assuming here not only that earlier treatments of women were anti-feminist in character, but that the ancient Greek philosopher Plato does not count as a feminist even though his views on women were remarkably atypical at the time.

Plato argues in *The Republic* that women can be among the elite who rule philosophically in his ideal state. Whereas Aristotle had contended that 'the relation of male to female is naturally that of superior to inferior, of the ruling to the ruled' (Coole, 1988: 44–5), Plato adopted (at least in *The Republic*) a gender-free view of political capacities. On the other hand, what makes his feminist credentials suspect is his explicit elitism. Only a tiny number of women would have been eligible to become rulers, and those that did, would (it is said) have to act just like men.

The position of women in mediaeval theory is depicted in explicitly hierarchical terms with women seen as more sinful than men, inferior to them, and not equipped to take part in political processes. Aquinas follows Aristotle in arguing that a wife 'is something belonging to her husband', although she is more distinct from him than a son from his father or a slave from his master (1953: 103). Had not the Bible made the inferiority of women clear?

## Mary Wollstonecraft

The liberal tradition challenges the notion that hierarchies are natural. It thus opens the way for the feminist argument that if all are free and equal individuals, why can women not be equal to men? It is true that Mary Astell had contended, as early as 1694, that women should be educated instead of being nursed in the vices for which they are then upbraided (Brody, 1992: 28). However, Mary Wollstonecraft is rightly regarded as the first major feminist, and in her *Vindication of the Rights of Women* (first published in 1792), she argues for women's economic independence and legal equality. At the time she wrote, a married woman could not own property in her own right, enter into legal contracts or have any claim over the rights of her children. History, philosophy, and classical languages were considered too rigorous for women to learn; botany and biology were proscribed from their educational curriculum, and physical exercise was thought unsuitable.

Wollstonecraft directs her argument to middle-class women – women in what she calls the 'natural state'. The middle-class woman is the woman who is neither dissipated by inherited wealth, nor brutalised by poverty. Wollstonecraft had taken from Richard Price the Enlightenment principle that all people are rational. The problem lay with the environment. Physical frailty derives from a cloistered upbringing, and this was thought to impact negatively upon intellectual ability. She tackles Rousseau's traditionalist view that women are inferior, seeing this as a betrayal of the liberal assumptions of his political theory. What Rousseau thought charming, Wollstonecraft considered immoral and dangerous. It is inconsistent to value independence and autonomy in men but not in women, particularly as patriarchy, or male domination, degrades men as well – 'the blind lead the blind' (Brody, 1992: 104).

Women, Wollstonecraft argues, are placed on a pedestal but within a prison (Brody, 1992: 50–1). Women ought to be represented in government and have a 'civil existence in the State' (Wollstonecraft, 1992: 265, 267). They should not be excluded from civil and political employments (1992: 291). The enlightened woman must be an 'active citizen' 'intent to manage her family, educate her children and assist her neighbours' (1992: 259). Friendship rather than gentleness, docility, and a spaniel-like affection 'should prevail between the sexes'. The emancipation of women is, in Wollstonecraft's view, part and parcel of the case against autocracy and arbitrariness in general: why contest the divine right of kings if one continues to subscribe to the divine right of husbands (1992: 118, 119)?

Wollstonecraft's position has a number of shortcomings that we will deal with later, but it is generally acknowledged that she tended to juxtapose reason to feeling, identifying feelings with animal appetites that men exploited. Moreover, she saw perfection as a realisable ideal, a position undoubtedly influenced by the intensely religious character of her argument. Wollstonecraft's position was complex – and she has been seen by some writers as 'ambivalent, contradictory and paradoxical' – reformer and revolutionary, rationalist and woman of feeling (Brody, 1992: 67, 70).

## John Stuart Mill

John Stuart Mill, influenced by his partner Harriet Taylor, wrote *The Subjection of Women* in 1869. In it, he argues women should enjoy equal rights with men – including the right to vote. Women, he contended, were still slaves in many respects, and to argue that they are inferior by 'nature' is to presume knowledge of nature: until equality has been established, how do we know what woman's nature is? It cannot be said that women are housewives and mothers by nature, although Mill does say – and this position is controversial among feminists today – that they are 'most suitable for this role', and he feels that female suffrage can only assist women in supervising domestic expenditure (Coole, 1988: 144; Bryson, 1992: 55–63). Mill, it is suggested, contributed to liberal feminism by extending his liberal principles to the position of women (Shanley and Pateman, 1991: 6), and like Wollstonecraft, he argued that the family must become a school for learning the values of freedom and independence.

## Liberal feminism in Britain and the United States

Throughout the nineteenth century, liberal feminism had developed often as an extension of other emancipatory movements. In the United States, figures like Elizabeth Cady Stanton (1815–1902) and her lifelong friend, Susan Anthony (1820–1906), raised the issue of women's freedom and equality as a result of experience in anti-slavery movements. Both edited a feminist journal in the 1860s called *The Revolution*. A National Women's Suffrage Association was set up after the Civil War and women's suffrage was attained in the United States through the Nineteenth Amendment to the constitution in 1920. In Britain, Mill's classic work had been preceded by the campaign against the 1864 Contagious Diseases Act that gave the police draconian powers to arrest prostitutes and those considered prostitutes, and when limited suffrage for women was achieved after the First World War, the struggle for its further extension was consolidated in the National Union of Societies for Equal Citizenship.

Liberal feminism appeared to have its greatest triumph in Britain when all women became eligible to vote in 1928. In other countries, this was attained later – in France after the Second World War – while in Switzerland, women only received the vote in 1970. In Britain, the Sex Discrimination Act and the Equal Opportunities Commission were established in the mid-1970s.

Liberal feminism identifies itself, in the words of Winifred Holtby, 'with the motto Equality First' (Humm, 1992: 43), and it extended its concerns with the publication of Betty Friedan's *The Feminine Mystique* (1963), which argued that middle-class American women suffered from depression and alienation as a result of giving up a career outside the home. They were incarcerated in a 'comfortable concentration camp' – Friedan's dramatic name for the home. She was instrumental in setting up the National Organization of Women in 1966 that not only campaigned for equal rights (including 'reproductive rights' – a right to abortion and birth control), but also assisted American women in re-entering the labour market and supported the establishment of childcare facilities in workplaces.

Liberal feminism has been criticised on a number of perspectives and in the next three sections we consider a number of these.

## Radical feminist critiques

Radical feminists claim liberal feminism is too superficial in its approach. All feminisms agree with the extension of liberal principles to women in terms of the vote and civil liberties, but radicals argue that the notion of equality is too abstract to be serviceable. The point about women is that they are different from men, and to argue for equality implies they aspire to be like men. But why?

Men not only oppress women but are responsible for war, violence, hierarchy, and the exploitation of nature and their fellows. Is this the model to which women should aspire? Radicals argue it is not equality which women should want, but liberation – and freedom for women means being separate and apart from men. It means celebrating their difference from men and their own distinctive sexuality. Liberal feminists not only regard sexuality as irrational and emotional, but uncritically accept that feelings should be transcended and they adopt a notion of reason that reflects male experience.

Feminism is not an extension of another ideology. It is concerned with the interests of women, and a new set of words needs to be developed to reflect the separateness of women. Some radicals like Mary Daly adopt a different style of writing to make it clear feminism represents as total a break as possible with male-constructed society. Politics is not simply about the law and state, as liberals think but about human activity in general and the celebrated slogan – 'the personal is political' – captures the radical feminist argument that interpersonal relations are as political as voting in elections. Radicals encourage women to meet separately – to voice their problems without men – and to take personal experience much more seriously than the liberal tradition allows.

Radicals see themselves as sexual revolutionaries, and thus very different from liberal feminists who work within the system. We shall see later that radicals have very different views from liberals on questions like prostitution and pornography.

## Socialist feminist critiques

The socialist critique of liberal feminism argues that liberal feminists ignore or marginalise the position of working-class women and the problems they have with exploitation and poor conditions in the workplace. The question of gender needs to be linked to the question of class – and legal and political equality, though important, does not address the differential in real power that exists in capitalist society.

Marxist feminists challenge the view of the state as a benevolent reformer, and argue the state is an expression of class domination. The freedom of women must be linked to the emancipation of the working class in general, with a much greater concentration on the social and economic dimensions of gender discrimination. Why should the right to join the armed forces and the police be a positive development if the police are used to oppress people at home and the army to oppress peoples abroad? Liberal feminism neglects the question of production and reproduction that lies at the heart of human activity.

## Other critiques

The black feminist critique particularly takes issue with the tendency of liberal feminists to treat women in an abstract fashion, and to assume women are not only middle class, but white as well. Many of the objections that liberal feminists raise to the hypocritical politeness of men hardly apply to women who are subject to racist abuse and treated in a derogatory fashion because they are black.

The feminisms looked at so far can be called 'ideological' feminisms, and they overlap with what can be labelled 'philosophical feminisms': feminist empiricism, standpoint feminism, and postmodern feminism.

Feminist empiricists take the view that feminism should be treated as an objective science which concentrates on the *facts* relating to discrimination. Feminist empiricists feel it is unnecessary and counterproductive to hitch feminism to an ideological position, and that the norms of liberalism involve a value commitment that narrows the appeal of feminist analysis.

Standpoint feminists take the view that the position of women gives rise to a different outlook so that liberal feminists are wrong to argue simply for equality with men, and to concern themselves only with legal and political rights.

As for postmodern feminists, they consider the tradition of the Enlightenment and liberalism to be hopelessly abstract. Not only is liberalism oblivious to the importance of difference – both between women and men and among women themselves – but the notion of freedom and autonomy as universal values reflects a prejudice which is part of the modern as opposed to the postmodern tradition.

## Socialist feminism

Socialist feminism arose out of the belief that feminism is not simply a legal and political question – though socialists, by which we mean socialist feminists, do support the case for the legal and political emancipation of women. Socialists take the view that women's emancipation is also – and primarily – a *social* question, so that the movement for women's freedom needs to be linked with the struggle to transform capitalism itself.

Early socialists like the Frenchman, Charles Fourier, saw the liberation of women as integral to redefining the labour process so that it becomes pleasurable and fulfilling, and he saw, as Marx did, the position of women as symptomatic of the level of civilisation of a given society. Marx tended to see women as the victims of market forces, and he argues in an early text that the prostitution of women is only a specific expression of the general prostitution of the labourer (Marx and Engels, 1975: 295). In the *Communist Manifesto*, for example, Marx takes the view that women under capitalism are mere instruments of production, but Marx showed little interest in the position of women and regarded the relation of men and women as 'natural' rather than moulded by class relationships.

## Engels' contribution

Engels was much more interested in women, and in his celebrated work, *The Origin of the Family, Private Property and the State*, published in 1894, he argues that in early tribal societies men, women and children lived together as part of larger households in which production was for use rather than exchange. Decision-making involved both men and women and because paternity or the position of a particular man as father could not be established in group marriage, collective property descended through women (i.e., matrilineally). 'The world-historical defeat of female sex', as Engels graphically describes it, occurs when men begin to domesticate animals and breed herds. Women seek monogamous relations in marriage (one wife–one husband) and the family is privatised. In the later bourgeois family, the woman's formal right to consent to marriage is neutralised by her lack of economic independence, and in the working-class family, the husband represents the bourgeois and the wife the proletarian – what nineteenth century socialists liked to call the 'slave of a slave'.

In Engels' view, male domination would only disappear with the socialisation of production. With women involved in paid employment outside the home, housework itself would become a public and collectivised activity (Sacks, 1974: 207).

## Bebel and later socialists

August Bebel of the German Social Democratic Party wrote a much more influential book than that of Engels – *Woman Under Socialism* (1878) – which followed the argument that women could only be emancipated through a proletarian revolution which resulted in their economic independence and the collectivisation of housework and childcare. However, unlike Engels, he was also conscious of the problems that were peculiar to women. Capitalist employment resulted in women being paid less than men, and women suffered from the problem of having to do all or most of the housework. Bebel also noted that economic subordination was linked to non-economic forms of oppression like a double standard of sexual morality, and inconvenient forms of dress (Bryson, 1992: 121).

Clara Zetkin, a German socialist who was to be a founder member of the German Communist Party, argued that class must take primacy over gender interests. She refused to cooperate with other women in campaigns for improved education, employment prospects, and legal status, on the grounds that proletarian and 'bourgeois' women had nothing in common. Lenin was to declare at the time of the Russian Revolution, that 'the proletariat cannot have complete liberty until it has won complete liberty for women' (Rowbotham, 1972: 163) but this did not prevent him from extracting a pledge from Zetkin that personal matters would not be raised in political discussions (Bryson, 1992: 125). It is true that the new Soviet government was the first in history to write women's emancipation into the law (in 1918), but the right to abortion was removed in 1936 and the family which radical bolsheviks had sought to abolish was idealised under Stalin as a crucial part of the disciplinary mechanism of the state.

Alexandra Kollontai was commissar or minister of social welfare in the first bolshevik government and she sought to encourage women to set up, with state help, nurseries, laundries, and educational campaigns. She fell from power in 1921 and the women's department that she headed, was abolished in 1929. She is also interesting because she argued for a new kind of relationship between men and women – one that would be less exclusive and not monogamous (Bryson, 1992: 137–40).

## The domestic labour debate

Of course, many socialists disagreed vehemently with the Communist Party states, even while they maintained a loyalty to Marxism. The domestic labour debate which took place in the pages of the British journal, *New Left Review*, sought to examine the position of women in the home and their relationship to the capitalist economy. Some argued that domestic labour produces value in the same way that other labour does, and therefore, women who work at home should be paid. Despite controversy on this point, there was general agreement that the family is linked to capitalism, and that domestic labour and who does it is an important issue for feminists to tackle (Bryson, 1992: 241).

As with liberal feminism there are a range of critiques of socialist feminism.

## Liberal feminist critique

Liberal feminists like Betty Friedan and Naomi Wolf argue socialist feminists are divisive in not accepting that some women might go into, and make a success of, business. Their dynamism and entrepreneurial flair should be both rewarded and acknowledged, and to regard feminism as a class question is unhelpful and narrowing. All women will benefit from a free system of production, based on the market and capitalism.

Women are individuals who should be entitled to exercise choice, and the tendency by socialist feminists to see work outside the home as crucial for emancipation is not borne out by the many women who choose to stay at home and live fulfilled and happy lives. Liberal feminists are not opposed to reforms that facilitate working outside the home, but they are opposed to an ideological position that seems to privilege this.

Liberal feminists would – like many other feminists – point to the authoritarian character of Communist Party states as evidence, not only of the generally problematic character of socialism, but of the negative way in which it impacts women's lives.

## Radical feminist critique

Radicals are sceptical that the problems facing women are simply due to capitalism. It is true that some socialist feminists have argued there is a dual system that oppresses women – capitalism *and* patriarchy. Capitalism may reward men as 'breadwinners', thereby creating a division of labour that disadvantages women, and writers like Ann Ferguson see patriarchy as semi-autonomous – sexual oppression exists alongside class oppression and is not 'reducible' to it (Bryson, 1992: 243–5). Radicals feel this argument merely serves to deepen the theoretical crisis faced by socialist feminists since there is no reason to believe that pornography, prostitution, and male chauvinist attitudes are specifically linked to a particular mode of production.

Indeed, many radical feminists developed their position as a result of experience in socialist movements where they were expected to take menial and 'feminine' roles by socialist men. Attempts to introduce the concept of patriarchy alongside the analysis of capitalism fail to get to grips with the fact that the former is wholly independent of the latter, and that when Marx treats the relations between men and women as natural, this is symptomatic of an inadequate methodology that cannot be rectified by simply tacking a critique of sexism onto Marxism or socialism. Catherine MacKinnon, in a much-quoted comment, argues that 'sexuality is to feminism, what work is to Marxism' (Humm, 1992: 117). The logics of the two are quite different, and any attempt to 'synthesise' Marxism and feminism, or feminism with socialism more generally, is bound to fail.

## Black feminist and philosophical feminist critiques

Black feminists believe that socialist emphasis upon class is as abstract as liberal emphasis upon the individual. Socialist feminism does not take the question of ethnicity seriously: it suffers from the problem of abstract universalism that means that it unthinkingly privileges a particular group or culture.

Feminist empiricists see in socialism the problem of ideological bias, and although some standpoint feminists like Nancy Hartsock are sympathetic to Marxism, standpoint feminism in general is unhappy with any privileging of class. After all, women experience oppression as women, and Carol Gilligan argues in *In a Different Voice* (1992) that because women are socialised differently from men, they grow up with quite different notions of morality and relationships. This occurs in both working class and bourgeois homes.

As for postmodern feminists, socialism has what they call an emancipatory 'metanarrative' – particularly strident in Marxism – that stems from the Enlightenment and expresses an absolutist prejudice. The belief in progress, equality, and autonomy, though different from the views of liberal feminists, still reflects a belief in a 'philosophy of history' that is ultimately arbitrary and implausible.

## Radical feminism

Radical feminism, as indicated from its critiques of other positions, takes the view that feminism ought to deal with the position of women independently of other ideological commitments. As MacKinnon argues, 'feminism is the first theory to emerge from those whose interests it affirms' (Humm, 1992: 119).

Radical feminists argue women are oppressed because women are women, and men are men. Male domination permeates all aspects of society – from sport to literature, dress to philosophy, entertainment to sexual mores. As Mary Daly argues, 'we live in a profoundly anti-female society, a misogynistic "civilization" in which men collectively victimize women, attacking us as personifications of their own paranoid fears' (Humm, 1992: 168).

This ubiquity of 'maleness' extends to the state itself. Weber's view of the state as an institution which claims a monopoly of legitimate force is too limited, in MacKinnon's view, since this monopoly 'describes the power of men over women in the home, in the bedroom, on the job, in the street, through social life' (1989: 169). Patriarchy is a comprehensive system of male power and it arises from men. Oppression, as the *Manifesto of the New York Redstockings* in 1969 declared, is total, 'affecting every facet of our lives' (Bryson, 1992: 183–4).

Moreover, the radicals argue that women's oppression is the oldest and most basic form of oppression, and whether it arises from socialists who expect women to make tea while men develop political strategy, or is expressed through black men like Stokely Carmichael who see women as having only bodies and not minds, the same point holds: all men oppress women, and all receive psychological, sexual, and material benefits from so doing. Germaine Greer, writing in 2000, argued that her proposition in *The Female Eunuch* (1970) still held 30 years later – men hate women at least some of the time. Indeed, she reckoned that in the year 2000 'more men hate more women more bitterly than in 1970' (1999: 14). Greer gives as good as she believes that women get and argues that 'to be male is to be a kind of idiot savant, full of queer obsessions about fetishistic activities and fantasy goals – a freak of nature, fragile, fantastic, bizarre' (1999: 327).

Why does the antagonism between men and women arise? Brownmiller appears to suggest the root is biological, and she speaks of the 'anatomical fact that the male sex organ has been misused as a weapon of terror' (Humm, 1992: 73), but radical feminists are aware of the dangers of a naturalist argument that reduces male domination to biology. Although MacKinnon speaks highly of Robert Dahl and endorses his view of politics as a system of power, authority, and control, she almost certainly would not endorse his once-expressed view that women's subordination arises from the superior physical strength of males (Hoffman, 2001: 97). The relation of man and women is a social product, she argues, and a 'naturalist' view fails to see these relationships as historical and transitory (MacKinnon 1989: 56). Nevertheless, radical feminists reject Marxist accounts that male domination arose historically from class divisions, and they argue that patriarchy has always been around. Although radicals disagree as to how and when patriarchy came about, they all agree that it exists and it has done so in every known society (Bryson, 1992: 188).

What can be done about it? Radical feminists developed in the late 1960s the idea of an all-women's 'consciousness-raising' group. Indeed, MacKinnon describes consciousness-raising as the 'feminist method' (Humm, 1992: 119) – a coming together by women to describe problems collectively so that the existence of oppression can be confirmed. The solution can only be separatism, for the consequence of the fact that the personal is political – and by political is meant the exercise of repressive power – is that men and women should live their lives as separately as possible. As Greer puts it rather wittily, 'both could do without each other if it were not for the pesky business of sexual reproduction' (1999: 68).

Indeed, one radical famously argued that the basis of women's oppression lies with child-bearing, as well as child-rearing, and the conception of love (Bryson, 1992: 204, 201). Others are doubtful that this 'pesky business' can be so easily avoided. But sexuality is seen as an expression of power so that the distinction between rape and sexual activity is not a meaningful one, and the reason why radical feminists are so passionately opposed to pornography and prostitution is that they see these institutions as fundamentally linked to a demeaning view and treatment of women. Whether men intend to oppress women is beside the point: patriarchy is a structural system of male oppression which operates, whether men are conscious of oppressing women or not.

Radical feminists have sometimes advocated lesbianism as a solution to the problem of oppressive encounters with men. Feminists in general would accept that lesbianism is a legitimate lifestyle choice, but radicals often go further and argue that it is a necessary way of preventing male domination. Rich advocates a broader notion of lesbianism so that it does not have to embrace genital activity, but denotes a rejection of compulsory heterosexuality imposed to prevent women from being individuals in their own right (Humm, 1992: 176–7). Because patriarchy is seen as a comprehensive system of male domination, even the most intimate of relationships becomes a matter for political scrutiny.

MacKinnon sees the whole notion of the public/private divide as oppressive and nothing more than a dangerous myth. The public is the private, just as the personal is political. Women's interest lies in overthrowing the distinction itself (1989: 120–1). Radical feminism is revolutionary. It is averse to differentiating one kind of patriarchy from another, and it is opposed to the kind of reforms that do not tackle the problem at its root. Radical feminists tend to identify pornography with sexual violence, and they regard prostitution as an act of force (Hoffman, 2001: 193). Women, in the view of radical feminists, do not want equality with men. They want liberation, and liberation is only possible if patriarchy is overthrown.

Again, there are a range of critiques of radical feminism.

## Liberal feminist critique

Liberal feminists disagree with radical feminists on a range of grounds. The first is that they see the idea that there is a war between the sexes as unfruitful. Men can be sympathetic to feminism – as J S Mill famously was – and it is wrong to assume men cannot become adherents to the feminist cause. The notion of separatism is pessimistic and self-defeating.

Nor are liberal feminists persuaded by the arguments for patriarchy. The notion that male domination enters into the very fibre of relationships ignores the importance of privacy and choice. Women are, or can be, agents, and the notion that the personal is political is a totalitarian credo that does not allow individuals to decide matters for themselves.

Some liberal feminists argue that prostitutes are sex workers who choose a profession that others dislike, and the full legalisation of prostitution would enable women who wish to pursue careers in this area to do so without hindrance and condemnation (see pp. 168–9). Liberal feminists see the campaigns against pornography as oppressive and authoritarian. Not only do such campaigners find themselves working with extremely conservative pressure groups, but the attempt to ban pornography leads to censorship – the prevention of people acting in unconventional ways which, liberal feminists insist, do not harm others.

Their attitude, in the eyes of liberal feminists, towards the state and legal reform is generally negative, and radical feminists suffer from an absolutist outlook that prevents them from seeing that gradual change, based upon rational discussion, is far more effective than utopian fantasies.

## Socialist feminist critique

Socialist feminists have no difficulty in extending the notion of politics at least to workplaces and the family, but they see the idea of sisterhood as dangerously abstract. Socialist feminists want to stress that women belong to different classes and their interests vary according to their class position. Socialist feminists are not necessarily opposed to the notion of patriarchy, but they insist it is much more complex than the radicals imagine.

In the first place, it is a system that arises historically, and even if Engels' account is not wholly plausible, he is correct to assume that patriarchy has not always existed and that it is connected with private property and the state. Second, socialist feminists want to distinguish between different kinds of patriarchy. There is an important distinction to be made between the kind of explicit patriarchy that exists in mediaeval and slave-owning societies, and a liberal patriarchy in which male domination coexists with liberal notions of consent and freedom. In fact, it is the gulf between theory and practice that makes the socialist critique possible, for women in developed liberal societies enjoy formal rights that contrast with their lack of real power. This kind of analysis is only possible if patriarchy itself is placed in a very specific historical context.

Socialist feminists, like liberal feminists, see no problem in forming alliances with men since men can be in favour of emancipation just as privileged women can be opposed to it. It is true that men benefit from patriarchy, but the socialist emphasis upon *relationships* means that men have their own lives limited and warped as a result of patriarchal prejudices which regard women, for example, as the natural guardians of children.

Even though socialist feminists would not accept extreme left-wing strictures against feminism as being inherently bourgeois and a distraction from class struggle, they tend to see the concern of radical feminists with lifestyle and sexuality as the product of a middle-class outlook that ignores the problems faced by women workers.

## Black feminist and philosophical feminist critiques

Black feminists are sceptical about a supra-ethnic notion of sisterhood. All women are not the same and the notion they are fundamentally oppressed by men could only be advanced by those who have never suffered from racist stereotyping. Women themselves can be racists and oppress black women – as well as black men – and the experience of subject-women under slavery and colonialism demonstrate very different patterns of family and economic life to those assumed by radical feminists.

Audre Lorde puts the matter in a nutshell in her open letter to Mary Daly, when she comments: 'The oppression of women knows no ethnic nor racial boundaries, true, but that does not mean that it is identical within those differences' (Humm, 1992: 139). A feminism that ignores ethnic or racial differences is a feminism that unthinkingly privileges one group over others.

Feminist empiricists reject the notion that science and objectivity are male activities. It is true that patriarchal prejudices can claim scientific warranty, but this is poor science. Science is not to blame for male domination but is a powerful weapon for exposing and combating it. Facts which point to discrimination and inequality are crucial to the arsenal of feminist argument and make it much more difficult for unsympathetic men to dismiss feminism as a man-hating, irrational doctrine.

Standpoint feminists are, it seems to us, more likely to be influenced by radical feminists and they can only distance themselves from radical feminism where they defend an argument that a woman's standpoint depends upon the particular social experience she has.

Postmodern feminists hold to the fact that power is exercised at every level in society, and it would seem therefore that they should be sympathetic to the radical feminist argument that male domination extends to apparently private as well as public institutions. However, in reality, postmodern feminists are particularly hostile to radical feminism since, as we shall see, they regard the whole notion of a 'woman' as problematically universalist in character. Radical feminism, in their eyes, suffers from deep-rooted binary divides – between men and women, reason and emotion – which leads these feminists to invert patriarchal arguments by accepting there is a fundamental sexual divide. Instead of demonising women, they demonise men, but the same absolutist logic is at work.

## Black feminism

Black feminists are acutely aware of the question of difference. Indeed, the very existence of 'black feminism' is a protest against the idea that women are all the same. Beneath the supposedly universal notion is to be found women who are often white, university-educated, and of middle-class background.

Black feminists argue that there is sufficient in common in Britain between Afro-Caribbean women, African women, and Asian women to assert a common identity. Of course, each of these categories is itself extremely diverse, but black women are considered to have a common experience. In the case of Britain, they are all 'outsiders', regarded as 'invisible' by the dominant culture and judged to be 'ethnic' and abnormal, as though the majority community is itself without an ethnic identity and embodies normality.

It is true that many white women turned to feminism as a result of their experience in anti-slavery and civil rights movements, but they failed to see that oppression is never simply universal – it always takes differential and particular forms. The notion that there is an *analogy* between women and blacks – Gayle Rubin wrote an essay in 1970 entitled *Woman as Nigger* – assumes that somehow black women do not exist!

The specific existence of black feminism contributes significantly to feminist theory as a whole by stressing the importance of a concrete approach that takes account of people's real-life situations and differences. By noting that some women are black in societies where whiteness is seen as the norm, one is more likely to observe that women may also be poor, disabled, or illiterate.

The assumption that the family is problematic for women is invariably made without taking account of the particular features of the black family that, in the United States, for example, is often headed by women who also have to work outside the home. Barrett and McIntosh have conceded that their own study of the family ignored the very different structures that exist in the families of Afro-Caribbean and Asian people in Britain (Bryson, 1992: 254). As for rape and sexuality, quite different assumptions are made of black women, and in Whelehan's view, black women suffer from poorer mental health than their white counterparts (Whelehan, 1995: 117).

Black feminists have argued that it is not just a question of disadvantages accumulating alongside one another – as independent entities – so that a black women may suffer from gender, ethnic, and class attributes. It is a question of developing a theory of oppression in which these 'multiple oppressions' reinforce one another and lie at the root of stereotyping. This warns us against absolutising one kind of oppression and opens the way to multiple alliances – of some women with some men for specific purposes. As the African-American writer, bell hooks has argued, black feminism stresses the value of solidarity – which unites similarity and difference – over the oppressively homogenous notion of sisterhood (Bryson, 1999: 35).

Whelehan has noted that during the 1970s it was commonly felt by radical feminists that analysis of related issues needed to be shelved so that full attention could be given to the question of women. As she comments, this kind of argument ignores the fact that women can also suffer oppression because of their class, racial, gender, and sexual orientation (Whelehan, 1995: 111). Not only does black feminism provide a challenge to a theory of domination, but it also poses a challenge to political theory as a whole. It invites a reconceptualisation of the notion of power and freedom, since those who are the subjects of black feminism have no, in Bryson's words, 'institutionalised inferiors' (1999: 34). Given the fact that there are relatively few black feminist academics, black feminism also poses the challenge of mobilising the considerable knowledge which the community has but has not produced in what Whelehan calls 'high theoretical' form (1995: 120).

Black feminism has been subjected to a number of critiques.

## Liberal, socialist, and radical feminist critiques

Liberal feminists are concerned about what they see as the divisiveness of black feminism as a distinct variety of feminist arguments. Black feminists are rightly opposed to racism but the answer to exclusion and marginalisation is to expand the notion of the individual to incorporate groups like blacks whose experience of repression has been very different.

Lynne Segal speaks for many socialist feminists who express concern at the fragmentation that has taken place within the women's movement and notes in particular the problem of the growth of 'Black feminist perspectives' (Whelehan, 1995: 121). What about the real class differences that exist within black communities – will they not be ignored if a feminism is created which highlights blackness as the defining criterion?

Radical feminists are concerned that the opposition to male domination is diffused by a concern with difference. Although MacKinnon does not address herself to black feminism as such, she is suspicious of the argument about difference. Inequality comes first, she insists; difference comes after: difference, she says, is the velvet glove on the iron fist of domination (1989: 219). In other words, difference can distract us from the force and repression inherent in patriarchy, and distinguishing between black and white women, can – radical feminists argue – play into the hands of men who are anxious to downgrade the plight of all women.

## Philosophical feminist critiques

Feminist empiricists believe that anything that ideologises feminism is a mistake. The statistic that 80 per cent of the mortality rate of illegal abortions came from women of colour – slightly broader than 'black' women – in the years preceding its decriminalisation in the United States (Whelehan, 1995: 117) is a revealing fact, and the danger is that it will not be as widely known as it deserves to be, if it is presented by a feminism perceived to be separatist and extremist. Standpoint feminists would acknowledge that different experiences are important and need to be considered, but this should not be juxtaposed to the common experiences which all women have, and which mould their particular outlook.

Although postmodern feminists are sympathetic to the point about difference, they argue 'blackness' represents another form of 'essentialism', i.e., the belief in an abstract 'essence'. Some black women might not only reveal class differences, as the socialists warn: what about hierarchies in the communities that lead black Americans to be suspicious of Asian-Americans? Differences like these are simply swept under the proverbial carpet if blackness becomes the criterion for a particular kind of feminism. Whatever black feminists may say in theory, in practice the notion of a black feminism inevitably privileges blackness over other differences, while the idea that race must be explored in relation to gender and class ignores the other differences – of sexual orientation, region, religion, and so on – which problematise the very existence of the notion of woman.

## Philosophical feminisms

## Feminist empiricism

Feminist empiricists take the view that sexist and 'androcentric' (male) biases can be eliminated from scholarship and statements if there is a strict adherence to existing norms of scientific inquiry. If projects are rigorously designed, hypotheses properly tested, and data soundly interpreted, then sexist prejudices can be dealt with alongside all other prejudices – as thoroughly unscientific in character (Hoffman, 2001: 55).

The more female researchers there are in the profession, the better since women are likely to be more sensitive to sexist prejudices than men. However, the question is not one of female science, but of sound science. The fact is that women are dramatically under-represented in the decision-making structures of the United Nations or in legislative bodies or in the world of business – indeed in the 'public' world in general, except perhaps in certain new social movements like the peace movement and in certain professions. These facts can only be established through sound statistical techniques, and they establish the existence of discrimination in ways that cannot be ignored.

Feminist empiricism ensures that feminism has come of age, entering into mainstream argument and debate.

## Standpoint feminism

Standpoint feminism arose initially as a feminist version of the Marxist argument that the proletariat had a superior view of society because it was the victim rather than the beneficiary of the market. Standpoint theorists argue that because women have been excluded from power – whether within societies or in international organisations – they see the world differently from men.

Standpoint theorists differ in explaining *why* women have an alternative outlook. Do women have a more respectful attitude towards nature than men, because they menstruate and can give birth to children, or is it because they are socialised differently, so that nature seems more precious to them than it does to many men? Peace activists may likewise differ in accounting for the fact that women in general are more likely to oppose war than men.

Whatever the emphasis placed upon nature or nurture, standpoint feminists generally believe women are different to men. One of the reasons why standpoint feminists see women as more practically minded than men is because they often have to undertake activity of a rather menial kind. Bryson refers to Marilyn French's novel *The Women's Room* (1978) (quoted by Hartsock) in which a woman has the job of washing a toilet and the floor and walls around it: an activity, says French, which brings women 'in touch with necessity', and this is why they 'are saner than men' (Bryson, 1999: 23). Indeed, Hartsock seeks to redefine power as a capacity and not as domination, arguing that women's experience stresses connection and relationship rather than individuality and competition (Hartsock, 1983: 253).

## Postmodern feminism

Some make a distinction between postmodern feminism and feminist postmodernism. Those who say they are postmodern feminists but not feminist postmodernists sometimes define post-modern feminism as 'postmodernism with a standpoint bent' (Hoffman, 2001: 63), but the question of a 'standpoint bent' is best understood by looking at the section preceding this one.

Postmodernists seek to overcome the dualistic character of traditional theory. We should refuse to accept that we are either critical (and want to overturn everything) or conservative (and want to keep things as they are). We need to be both subjective and objective, valuing the individual *and* society. In this way, we avoid making the kind of choices that postmodernists call 'binary' and absolutist. This leads postmodernists to stress the importance of difference and plurality, and this is why postmodern feminists or feminist postmodernists argue that the notion of feminism as the emancipation of women is doubly problematic. First, because emancipation sounds as though at some privileged point in time women will finally be free and autonomous, and second, because the very term woman implies that what unites women is more important than what divides them.

This, postmodernists argue, violates the logic of both/and, since it privileges sameness over difference. Indeed, Kate Nash argues that because postmodernism commits us to argue that woman 'is not a fixed category with specific characteristics', we have to be committed to the concept of woman as a 'fiction' in order to be a feminist at all (Hoffman, 2001: 78).

One last time we have to consider a range of critiques.

## Liberal feminist critique

Liberal feminists are sympathetic to feminist empiricism. Indeed, one writer has described feminist empiricism as the 'philosophical underpinning of liberal feminism' (Hoffman, 2001: 56), and naturally liberal feminists are attracted to the stress on rationality, science, and evidence. On the other hand, liberal feminists argue that questions of freedom and autonomy, the rule of law, and individual rights involve values, and feminist empiricists seem to be committed to a notion of science that excludes values, basing their hypotheses and findings simply on facts.

Standpoint feminists suffer from the same one-sidedness that afflicts radical feminism. By probing women's experience in general, it does not respect the division between the public and the private, and by arguing for the superiority of the female standpoint, it makes alliances with well-meaning men more difficult. Both factors make standpoint feminists liable to embrace an authoritarian style of politics.

As for postmodern feminism, liberal feminists feel that its aversion to absolutes and modernism leads to scepticism and renders problematic the whole concern with women's rights.

## Socialist, radical, and black feminist critiques

Socialist feminism challenges the feminist empiricist notion of science as value-free and not itself ideological. An emphasis upon relationships leads to the view that facts do not speak for themselves but imply evaluation, and therefore it is naive to imagine that a purely scientific – rather than explicitly ideological – presentation of feminism will be more persuasive.

As for standpoint feminism, socialists argue that an emphasis upon women's experience needs to take more specific account of the impact of class and capitalism, while postmodern feminism leads to a kind of academic conservatism that makes emancipatory politics impossible.

Radical feminists feel the emphasis upon science is male-oriented and that feminist empiricists underestimate the extent to which male mores have penetrated the academy. Radicals are more sympathetic to standpoint feminism, particularly where the difference and even superiority of women are emphasised, while postmodernist feminism is seen as a betrayal of women's interests and a rejection of the need for feminism at all.

To black feminists, feminist empiricism seems elitist and very 'white' since most black women find it difficult to obtain academic positions. As for standpoint feminism, it speaks (like radical feminism) of women in abstract terms and therefore unthinkingly adopts the position of white women. Postmodern feminism is seen as indulgent and sceptical and, for all its emphasis upon difference, ignores the problems which black women face and which make the notion of emancipation a meaningful ideal. Deconstructing modernity seems a rather hollow enterprise when women who are black have yet to obtain modernist goals of equality and autonomy.

## Reproductive tourism

Now that we have discussed a full range of feminisms let us return to our case study. Putting gender at the centre of the discussion, how should we view gestational surrogacy? We will focus on empiricist, liberal, radical, socialist, and black perspectives.

An empiricist wants to understand the facts underlying commercial surrogacy. What drives it? Who benefits? What would be the effects of intervention, by, for example, making it illegal or requiring that the child, at an appropriate age, be informed of the surrogate's identity? Would intervention worsen the position of women in India?

A liberal feminist would be concerned with the freedom to choose. Is Germany restricting the freedom of its citizens in a way inconsistent with (for example) J S Mill's harm principle? Is India adequately protecting surrogates from 'consenting' to something over which they have weak bargaining power? When a woman who is either illiterate or cannot read English signs a contract (Harrison, 2014: 148), is she really consenting (see pp. 103–4)?

A significant strand of feminist thought – whether liberal or radical – focuses on a woman's right to control her own body and reproduction. So long as the surrogate knows what she is agreeing to, then most liberals would argue that surrogacy is compatible with self-ownership. Radical feminists argue, however, that gestational surrogacy carries with it a particular conception of the female body: 'the uterus is technically and legally isolated as a component that can be contractually ordered, detached from the selfhood of the surrogate and repositioned in a production chain at the behest of the clinic and commissioning couple' (Cooper and Waldby, cited in Harrison, 2014: 148). This decoupling of a body part from the whole self is despite the fact that, as Laura Harrison found from her research, surrogates felt the child was to some degree a part of them – there was an emotional bond. (Harrison does not say this – because she wants to de-emphasise genetics – but the surrogate can in fact affect the expression of genes, through the hormonal environment of the womb.)

Finally, the liberal emphasis on individuals freely contracting to provide and pay for a service ignores the global division of labour, which has both class and racial characteristics. Socialist feminists (and also black feminists) argue that liberals see only individuals, and not *social structures*.

Women do most of the 'intimate labour', but the young, poor Indian women who provide surrogacy are doubly oppressed:

> Surrogates in India are performing intimate labor. . .with little or no connection with the couples commissioning their labor. Surrogacy in India has all the hallmarks of intimate labor described by Boris and Parrenas – embodied intimacy, the 'messiness' of birth, the class and often racial 'Otherness' of the surrogate – resulting in conflicting demands between the expectations of nurturing and caring about the fetus during pregnancy and immediate affective disengagement after the birth.
>
> (Harrison, 2014: 147)

Surrogacy is the commodification of attributes that are stereotypically associated with women. In this regard, capitalism reinforces the oppression of women, by turning something that is already exploited in a non-commercial way – through women doing most domestic labour – into a marketable service. That relatively wealthy, white women are buying the service does not turn the transaction into 'women helping women', although interestingly the surrogates were often encouraged to believe their actions were altruistic: they were 'lifting the curse' of infertility (Deonandan, 2015: 113).

## Conclusion

Liberal feminism seeks to give women the same political and legal rights that men enjoy so that women can be regarded as rational and autonomous individuals. Liberal feminists are accused by their critics of disregarding the negative impact of capitalism on women's lives; of ignoring male oppression in the so-called private sphere; and of embracing an ideology that is abstract and absolutist in tone.

Socialist feminism argues that questions of gender must be considered alongside questions of class. Marxist feminism particularly emphasises the problem posed by capitalism to the interests of women. Liberal critics contend that women can legitimately display their equality through becoming executives in business and argue it is wrong to assume that all women should work outside the home. Other feminists feel that socialists ignore the general problems faced by women in all societies, while postmodernists feel that the socialist 'metanarrative' is as abstract as the liberal one.

Radical feminists pride themselves on concentrating exclusively on women's problems and insist that male oppression manifests itself in interpersonal relations as well as in more conventionally political arenas. They are accused by their critics of an authoritarian disregard for the individual and a prejudice against men. The differences between women, whether racial or class-based, must be taken into account, and it is wrong to assume that a scientific view expresses masculinist values.

Black feminists take the view that ethnic outsiders must be explicitly considered, and generalised views of women are unacceptable. Their critics feel that black feminists focus one-sidedly upon what is one form of oppression among many and that they are guilty of essentialising blackness.

The philosophical feminisms stress either the importance of rigorous scientific methods (the feminist empiricists); the need to understand the distinctive character of a woman's outlook (the standpoint feminists); or the importance of plurality and difference (the postmodern feminists).

Their critics feel that empiricism is vulnerable to the argument that facts themselves imply values, that a woman's standpoint varies dramatically according to circumstance, and that an excessive emphasis upon difference casts doubt upon the whole feminist project.

## References

Aquinas, St T. (1953). *The Political Ideas of St Thomas Aquinas*. Ed. D. Bigongiari. New York: Hafner.

Brody, M. (1992). 'Introduction', in M. Wollstonecraft (ed.), *A Vindication of the Rights of Women*. London: Penguin, 1–73.

Bryson, V. (1992). *Feminist Political Theory*. Basingstoke: Macmillan.

Bryson, V. (1999). *Feminist Debates*. Basingstoke: Macmillan.

Coole, D. (1988). *Women in Political Theory*. Hemel Hempstead: Harvester-Wheatsheaf.

Deonandan, R. (2015). Recent Trends in Reproductive Tourism and International Surrogacy: Ethical Considerations and Challenges for Policy. *Risk Management and Healthcare Policy*, *8*, 111.

Eisenstein, Z. (1981). *The Radical Future of Liberal Feminism*. London: Longman.

Fenton-Glynn, C. (2019). Surrogacy: Why the World Needs Rules for 'selling' Babies. *BBC News*, viewed 3 July 2021, https://www.bbc.co.uk/news/health-47826356

French, M. (1978). *The Women's Room*. New York: Jove.

Friedan, B. (1963). *The Feminine Mystique*. Harmondsworth: Penguin.

Gilligan, C. (1992). *In a Different Voice*. London: Harvard University Press.

Greer, G. (1970). *The Female Eunuch*. London: Paladin.

Greer, G. (1999). *The Whole Woman*. London: Doubleday.

Harrison, L. (2014). "I am the baby's real mother": Reproductive Tourism, Race, and the Transnational Construction of Kinship. *Women's Studies International Forum*, *47*, 145–56.

Hartsock, N. (1983). *Money, Sex and Power*. New York and London: Longman.

Hoffman, J. (2001). *Gender and Sovereignty*. Basingstoke: Palgrave.

Humm, M. (ed.) (1992). *Feminisms*. New York and London: Harvester-Wheatsheaf.

MacKinnon, C. (1989). *Toward a Feminist Theory of the State*. Cambridge, MA: Harvard University Press.

Marx, K. and Engels, F. (1975). *Collected Works*, vol. 3. London: Lawrence and Wishart.

Plato (1955). *The Republic*. Harmondsworth: Penguin.

Rowbotham, S. (1972). *Women, Resistance and Revolution*. London: Allen Lane/Penguin.

Rubin, G. (1970). 'Woman as Nigger', in L. Tanner (ed.), *Voices from Women's Liberation*. New York: Mentor.

Sacks, K. (1974). 'Engels Revisited: Women, the Organization of Production and Private Property', in M. Rosaldo and L. Lamphere (eds), *Women, Culture and Society*. Stanford, CA: Stanford University Press, 207–22.

Shanley, M. and Pateman, C. (1991). 'Introduction', in M. Shanley and C. Pateman (eds), *Feminist Interpretations and Political Theory*. Cambridge: Polity, 1–10.

Whelehan, I. (1995). *Modern Feminist Thought*. Edinburgh: Edinburgh University Press.

Wollstonecraft, M. (1992). *A Vindication of the Rights of Women*. London: Penguin.

## Further reading

Overviews and histories: Lorna Finlayson, *An Introduction to Feminism* (Cambridge University Press, 2016); Margaret Walters, *Feminism: A Very Short Introduction* (Oxford University Press, 2005); Sally Scholz, *Feminism* (OneWorld, 2012); Deborah Cameron, *Feminism: A Brief Introduction to the Ideas, Debates, and Politics of the Movement* (University of Chicago Press, 2019); Lucy Delap, *Feminisms: A Global History* (Pelican, 2020); Rosemarie Tong, *Feminist Thought: A More Comprehensive Introduction* (Routledge, 2017). A good collection: Tasha Oren and Andrea Press (eds.), *The Routledge Handbook of Contemporary Feminism* (Routledge, 2020). On gender: Mary Evans (ed.), *Gender: The Key Concepts* (Routledge, 2012); Raewyn Connell, *Gender: In World Perspective* (Polity, 2020). More focused on philosophy: Alison Stone, *An Introduction to Feminist Philosophy* (Polity 2007); Elinor Mason, *Feminist Philosophy: An Introduction* (Routledge, 2021).

# Chapter 16

# Multiculturalism

## Introduction

Beliefs and values, language and family traditions, dress and diet are central to an individual's sense of identity. Most people would say that these things should be respected, and liberal democracy has developed into an ideology that places great stress on respecting diversity of belief and lifestyle. A fully human existence entails the freedom to live according to your cultural traditions. But what if a particular cultural tradition is hostile to liberalism? What if, for example, it holds that girls should be educated to fulfil a subservient role, limited strictly to the private sphere of the family? What if it advocates discrimination, or even violence, against adherents of other religions, or gay and lesbian people, or different ethnic groups? What if it privileges some ethnic groups over others? These are questions raised by multiculturalism, an ideology that has emerged since the 1960s, but which stands in a complex relationship to older ideologies.

## Key questions

- What is multiculturalism?
- Is multiculturalism a development of liberalism, or a challenge to it?
- Is multiculturalism compatible with feminism?

## Multiculturalism and political theory

If we take the word multiculturalism at face value, it implies a multiplicity of cultures, but that gets us only so far in understanding it. We need to define culture and explain the political significance of the idea of multiplicity – multiplicity relative to what?

The term has gained wide currency in both academic and popular debate, and its employment is not restricted to political theory or political science: there are multicultural perspectives not only in other social sciences, but also in the humanities, and even in the natural sciences. For this reason, it is important to demarcate the debate in political theory. Let us make some distinctions:

a) *Multiculturalism as an attitude* Although it is more usual to describe a person as cosmopolitan than multicultural, the two can be taken as synonyms, indicating either a positive and open

DOI: 10.4324/9780429424106-21

Case study 16.1

# Is multiculturalism bad for women?

**PHOTO 16.1** © Peter Macdiarmid/Getty Images.

Should the following practices be tolerated in Western countries?

- *Polygyny*: the right of a man to have more than one wife.
- *Arranged marriage*, where a degree of family pressure is applied to daughters to marry a certain man.
- *Female circumcision* (also known as genital mutilation; clitoridectomy): this is practised (although not necessarily legally) in around 30 countries and affects 8 million women worldwide. It is illegal in every Western country, but women who send their daughters abroad for such an operation are often not prosecuted: should they be?
- *Religious segregation*: religious groups – including the Christian churches – are exempt from certain kinds of anti-discrimination legislation. This exclusion is often extended to educational establishments, where girls are not educated in the same way as boys.
- *Dress*: should families be permitted to determine how their daughters dress, particularly in respect of wearing the burqa?
- *Marriage law*: should domestic law 'respect' law emanating from specific cultures, which may, for example, not treat men and women equally?
  We will return to these questions at the end of the chapter.

attitude to different cultures or, at least, respect for people, where such respect means recognising their rights to make choices about how they live their lives.

b) ***Multiculturalism as a tool of public policy*** If you do an online search of university library holdings using the word 'multiculturalism', many items will be concerned with education policy, followed by other areas of public policy, such as health and social services. Multicultural education policy is concerned with school organisation and curriculum; health and social policy focuses particularly on social inclusion and identifying the special needs of different cultural groups.

c) ***Multiculturalism as an aspect of institutional design*** Whereas policy questions assume the existence of a particular set of political institutions, the question here is what kind of institutions we should have. Examples of institutional design that make explicit the concern with cultural diversity include the allocation of political representation in national parliaments to identified groups and even control over a specific territory.

d) ***Multiculturalism and moral justification*** Institutions are important, but political theory is not concerned merely with what political institutions should exist, but how they are justified. People might support the same institutional arrangements – for example, special seats in parliament – but for different reasons. We need to understand *why* people support a particular policy.

Much of the discussion in this chapter will focus on (d), but with some attention to (c). But before exploring the various theories of, and justifications for, multiculturalism, we need to define and distinguish culture, race, and religion.

## Culture

Will Kymlicka, in the opening lines of his book *Multicultural Citizenship*, makes the following claim:

> Most countries are culturally diverse. According to recent estimates, the world's 184 independent states contain over 600 living language groups, and 5,000 ethnic groups. In very few countries can the citizens be said to share the same language, or belong to the same ethnonational group.
>
> (Kymlicka, 1995: 1)

In a few short sentences, it is implied culture equates to a language group, an ethnic group, and an ethnonational group. He goes on to define the kind of culture with which he is concerned as an 'intergenerational community, more or less institutionally complete, occupying a given state territory, sharing a distinct language and history' (Kymlicka, 1995: 18) and further suggests a culture provides 'meaningful ways of life across the full range of human activities' (Kymlicka, 1995: 76). The problem is that there is a proliferation of concepts with which culture is equated but this simply pushes the problem of definition onto these other, equally problematic, concepts.

Some help in defining culture might be found in anthropology, where culture is a central concept. Anthropologists attempt to explain why, given a shared biological nature and largely similar physical needs, there is so much cultural diversity. Responses fall into two categories: universalist and relativist. Universalists include Marxists, who argue culture is to be explained by underlying material forces, and most nineteenth century liberals; Mill, for example, argued human beings have innate rational capacities that can only be realised under particular cultural conditions (Mill, 1991: 231). Universalism need not take an evolutionary form: functionalists argue that diverse cultural practices can be explained by underlying, universal needs (Malinowski, 1965: 67–74). Relativists, on the other hand, take culture to be fundamental and not derivative. Ruth Benedict maintained that a culture is an integrated pattern of intelligent, albeit often unconscious, behaviour (Rosenblatt, 2004: 461–2). Pattern theory implies there can be no cultural *diversity* within a society, for culture is integral, and those political theorists, such as James Tully (1995), who draw on work in anthropology, appeal to an alternative and more recent form of cultural relativism advanced by, among others, Clifford Geertz (1993). Culture for Geertz is a complex of signs, whose meaning is dependent upon perspective, not in the sense that an 'outsider' cannot understand the signs, but rather that such understanding – *interpretation* – must refer to the context of the participants (1993: 110).

The difference between Kymlicka on the one side and Tully (and Geertz) on the other is that Kymlicka appears to be asserting cultural diversity as a norm against cultural homogeneity, whereas Tully maintains that culture is by its nature diverse and multiculturalism as a political strategy is not the creation of diversity but its recognition. However, despite the reference to culture in the term multiculturalism, it may be that it is not culture but race or religion that is at its heart.

# Race

Discussion of race in the social sciences focuses on whether it is a biological category (naturalism) or predominantly a social construction (constructivism). There is a tendency for one side in this debate to paint the other in crude terms: constructivists are thought to reject any biological differences, while naturalists treat racial boundaries as impermeable. Neither of these presentations is correct. The starting point for both naturalism and constructivism is the idea that in everyday life we tend to assort people into races, such as black or white or Asian (we can call these 'conventional races'):

> **Constructivism** Conventional races are determined primarily by social (and historical) criteria. Biological correlates – for example, skin colour – may be among the criteria, so constructivists do not reject biological criteria but argue they are endowed with social meaning.
>
> (Hochman, 2013: 334)

> **Naturalism** Our everyday categorisation of races corresponds to biological criteria. Races are sub-species categories. While there are not sharp boundaries between races, if you take a random person from one conventional race and compare her to a random person from another, she will have more in common with a member of her own race than a member of the other race.

One of the standard arguments against naturalism was advanced by biologist Richard Lewontin. In an influential article he poses the question: how much of human genetic diversity between populations is accounted for by conventional racial classifications (Lewontin, 1972: 386)? He maintains that the total diversity of the human species contained within populations is 85.4%. In other words, a member of the same race – for example, a white – is more different to another white than he is to a black. And there is a 30% chance of a person's race being miscategorised. He concludes by saying that:

Human racial classification is of no social value and is positively destructive of social and human relations. Since such racial classification is now seen to be of virtually no genetic or taxonomic significance either, no justification can be offered for its continuance.

(1972: 397)

Lewontin has been criticised for comparing individuals locus-by-locus (that is, looking at a gene at a single locus). If this method is acceptable, then Lewontin is right and subsequent studies have proven this (Hochman, 2013: 337). However, an alternative method is to correlate the differences: a genetic variation in one locus will correlate with a variation at another. If you compare multiple loci, misidentification will drop to almost zero (Edwards, 2003). Using this method, you can achieve very high levels of concordance between a person's self-identified race/ethnicity (SIRE) and his or her genetic profile (Tang et al., 2005: 271).

Most naturalists accept the 'out of Africa' thesis (possibly with some Neanderthal admixture once out of Africa), but argue the human species forms clades or branches. Like a tree, there is a trunk – a common source (Africa) – but the branches become increasingly distant from one another. Biologically informed critics of naturalism counter that there is considerable gene flow between groups, so rather than thinking of the relationship between individuals as having a branch structure it is better understood as a network, with some clustering, but a lot of back and forth between groups.

What is more, while the correlation argument is reasonable, naturalists overestimate the degree of clustering. Wright's Fixation Index is used to compare the amount of genetic variation within a subpopulation (e.g., a conventional race) with that found in all populations combined:

$$F_{ST} = (T - S) / T$$

T is the average difference between genes (alleles) selected randomly from the total population while S is the average difference within a subpopulation. If mating is random, then T and S will have equal value and $F_{ST}$ will be zero. With some non-random mating, it will rise above zero. While the standard number for sub-species division is 0.25 or above, the $F_{ST}$ for humans is between 0.05 and 0.15 (Hochman, 2013: 340).

Both constructivism and naturalism are reasonable positions. But even if the constructivists are correct, then the concept of race still plays a role in politics – as they themselves acknowledge – because so long as people are conventionally placed in racial groups, this will have effects on the distribution of resources and the possibilities for cooperation.

## Religion

Much debate about cultural diversity is about the relationship of religion and politics – that is, of the consequences of the existence of different belief systems, including secular ones, within a political territory. Given that liberalism itself has its roots in the settlement of the Wars of Religion (see pp. 158–9), we have to establish whether multiculturalism is a rearticulation of older debates over religious toleration or if it offers a novel perspective on the relationship between religion and the state.

Religion is a complex phenomenon. Eric Sharpe identifies four 'modes' of religion, that is, ways in which human beings are religious: (a) the *existential* mode, in which the focus is on faith; (b) the *intellectual* mode, which gives priority to beliefs, in the sense of those statements to which a person gives conscious assent; (c) the *institutional* mode, at the centre of which are authoritative organisations that maintain and transmit doctrines; and (d) the *ethical* mode, which stresses the behavioural relationships between members of a religious community, and those outside it

(Sharpe, 1983: 91–107). What differentiates religions and sects is the centrality of one mode relative to another.

In thinking about the relationship of religion and politics, it is important to keep in mind the dominant mode of a religion or sect, as well as the content of its beliefs or practices. For example, there is a popular image of Islam as a radical, proselytising religion, and yet there is a stream of Islam – Sufism – which is inward-looking, mystical, and so relatively unpolitical. Viewing religion in terms of modes allows us to see both divergences *within* a religion as well as commonalities *across* religions. Those commonalities can generate conflict – as when, for example, two opposed proselytising religions face one another – as well as facilitate reconciliation.

We also need to work out whether a conflict that appears to be religious in character is really about something else, such as race or class. Take the concept of radicalisation; that is, the process by which a person comes to adopt increasingly extreme views, to the point where he is prepared to commit terrorist acts. Rather than being triggered by exclusion in the sense of a lack of human resources, such as income, education, or linguistic competence, radicalisation may be tied up with identity. This could be especially the case with second-generation Muslim migrants, who are alienated from their families and the religious practices of their parents, but also do not identify with the majority culture of the land into which their parents immigrated. The parents' version of Islam may appear distant and irrelevant, and the religious leadership at the local mosque is poor, with Imams often unable to speak English. In many ways, radical Islam is Western: it addresses the needs of Muslims who have been socialised in the West, as distinct from immigrants to the West.

## Arguments for and against multiculturalism

In the rest of the chapter, we discuss a range of arguments for and against multiculturalism. Inevitably, justification also entails conceptualisation: not only will theorists disagree about the benefits and costs of multiculturalism but will also in the process disagree about its nature. So definition and justification (or critique) are interrelated.

We present six ways of understanding and justifying (or criticising) multiculturalism. As a way of orientating the reader, we set them out in summary form below. It should be noted that most are arguments for multiculturalism, although often there is a degree of ambivalence. The final one – multiculturalism as intergroup conflict – is almost entirely negative (although with a caveat).

1. Multiculturalism as a struggle for recognition.
2. Multiculturalism as an extension of liberal rights.
3. Multiculturalism as legal pluralism.
4. Multiculturalism as hybridity.
5. Multiculturalism as allocative efficiency.
6. Multiculturalism as intergroup competition.

## Multiculturalism as a struggle for recognition

There is much talk of identity politics. The term tends to be used pejoratively – identity politics is a reversion to tribalism, which is assumed to be a bad thing. This negative idea is explored later, but in this section we look at a philosophical defence of identity, advanced by Canadian political theorist Charles Taylor.

Taylor argues that who we feel we are is constructed in the eyes of others so that to fail to be recognised by others is to be denied the basis of one's identity (Taylor, 1994: 25). The politics of recognition is a modern concept, developing out of the collapse of hierarchies in the eighteenth century. Hierarchies were the basis of honour, and honour was linked to distinction, and hence inequality. In a hierarchy, people 'know their place' and their identity – their psychological sense of who they are – is derived from that hierarchy. Against honour we now have dignity, which Taylor takes to be the basis of a liberal society.

As we shift from honour to dignity, we also experience individualisation: morality is no longer about *mores* – social expectations derived from your place in the hierarchy. Rather, individual conscience – an inner voice – is the basis of morality. But that inner voice is not primarily telling us what to do, but is an end in itself. We must be true to our inner voice if we are to be full human beings. The conjunction of inwardness and authenticity – following that inner voice – creates a danger that we lose sight of the fact that our identity is only possible through other people's recognition of us: we need to reconcile the inwardness of authenticity with the outwardness of recognition. In the days of honour, the two were unproblematic because 'general recognition was built into the socially derived identity by virtue of the very fact that it was based on social categories that everyone took for granted' (Taylor, 1994: 34): the nobility possessed authenticity and lower orders deferred to them. Inwardly derived, as distinct from externally imposed, identity does not enjoy this automatic recognition, but must win it, and that process may fail. Recognition is recognition of *difference*, but this is combined with a traditional liberal emphasis on equality:

> The politics of difference often redefines non-discrimination as requiring that we make these distinctions the basis of differential treatment. So members of aboriginal bands will get certain rights and powers not enjoyed by other Canadians . . . and certain minorities will get the right to exclude others in order to preserve their cultural integrity, and so on.
>
> (Taylor, 1994: 39–40)

Although Taylor's reflections long predate the Black Lives Matter (BLM) movement, we can see the dynamic at work in the conflict between the expressions 'black lives matter' and 'all lives matter'. The latter statement appears to accord with a traditional liberal emphasis on human equality – who would disagree that all lives matter? – but in the struggle for recognition, the statement fails to acknowledge the historical circumstances of black people and is a withholding of recognition.

There are difficulties with Taylor's argument. There is a problem of conflicting identities: you could be a member of a Canadian First Nation, but at the same time a woman, or young, or gay. Authenticity requires integrating multiple perspectives, but these do not map onto physical communities. It is true that a person can belong to multiple communities, such as territorial and virtual (online) ones, but for reasons discussed in Chapter 1, the state is focused on control of territory, and a multicultural state is one in which power is devolved to sub-state cultural groups. What if a group is patriarchal, or hostile to sexual minorities?

An extension of this problem is the existence of deeply conflicting identities sharing a common space. This is illustrated most dramatically in the city of Jerusalem, which is a holy city for both Jews and Muslims, and also contains important Christian sites. Again, we face the problem of how the subjectivity of authenticity corresponds to the objectivity of physical space.

Less dramatic examples would be the everyday displays of flags. The public square is by definition public, and so different identities, as expressed through flags and other symbols, jostle for recognition.

A final problem is that there is a kind of multicultural equivalent of 'my country, right or wrong'. That phrase has an unclear provenance, but is an indictment of blind patriotism. The utterer of the phrase is incapable of critical reflection on his or her country. The danger is that expressions of identity similarly become unreflective, something beyond criticism: 'my identity, right or wrong'. On the other hand, identity could be used to counter the normativity of majorities. For example, the idea that the only valid expression of sexuality is heterosexuality is challenged by the assertion of, and positive evaluation of, gay and lesbian identity.

## Multiculturalism as an extension of liberal rights

In his first book, *Liberalism, Community, and Culture* (1989), Will Kymlicka argued that John Rawls's theory of justice could, with a few revisions, accommodate the value of community (1989: 162). Recall from the discussion of distributive justice (see p. 136) that Rawls argues principles of distribution should be agreed from an imaginary situation (original position) in which we do not know our identities (veil of ignorance). While we are denied knowledge of our identities, we do know we value certain things – primary goods; these include rights, income, and the bases of self-respect. Kymlicka argues that cultural membership should be added to the list, maintaining that culture provides a 'context of choice'.

There is an immediate difficulty with this argument. For Rawls, the primary goods are of instrumental value. You do not know whether you will end up as Amazon boss Jeff Bezos or a Jain mendicant, but you will still seek to maximise your income. But income cannot be treated as valuable in itself. Likewise, if cultural membership is added to the list it is unclear whether this is because there is something about 'culture' in general that is valuable or because specific cultures have value. If the former, then this seems to be covered already in the concept of 'rights', including the rights to associate, practice one's religion, and so on. If, however, it is a specific culture that is valuable, then this is ruled out by the veil of ignorance.

Kymlicka argues that individuals should have rights to cultural membership. A right is an advantage held against another (or others), and he distinguishes three types: self-government rights, polyethnic rights, and special representation rights. Self-government rights usually entail the devolution of power to a political unit 'substantially controlled by the members of an ethnic minority' (Kymlicka, 1995: 30). Examples would be state funding of 'cultural institutions' and exemptions from certain policies, such as those relating to the slaughter of animals (1995: 31). Special representation rights are intended to ensure the fair representation of minority groups (1995: 32). Each of these types of rights, but especially the first two, can take the form of an 'internal restriction' or an 'external protection' (1995: 35–44). He maintains that empirical evidence shows most campaigns for cultural recognition take the form of a demand for external protections from wider society, rather than restricting the freedom of the members of that culture, and so are compatible with liberalism (1995: 38–40). The basic problem is that rights are a specific cultural form, and the effects of rights on a culture depend on how one conceptualises culture. If cultures are integral patterns – as argued by Benedict – then rights may well upset those patterns.

Although Kymlicka makes clear that it is the ends we choose which matter, rather than our capacity to choose, the idea of culture as a context of choice does suggest that oppressive and illiberal cultures are less valuable than those which permit freedom, and so human autonomy – the capacity to choose – must have some intrinsic value (see pp. 99–100). Kymlicka avoids addressing this tension within his theory and instead appeals to empirical examples to show that culture need not be oppressive. He cites Quebec as a culture that has 'liberalised':

> Before the Quiet Revolution [1960–6], the Québécois generally shared a rural, Catholic, conservative, and patriarchal conception of the good. Today, after a period of liberalization, most people have abandoned this traditional way of life, and Québécois society now exhibits all the diversity that any modern society contains . . . to be a Québécois today, therefore, simply means being a participant in the francophone society of Quebec.
>
> (1995: 87)

In the absence of an adequate theorisation of culture, it is not clear whether the example of Quebec can help us to see whether 'cultural membership' enhances or diminishes freedom. After all, the struggle within Quebec is fundamentally over language, and although the freedom of one linguistic community is threatened by the other, the capacity to use language, whether it is French or English, is fundamental to human autonomy. Other dimensions of culture, such as religion, may not contain the same freedom-enhancing potential. Quebec shows that a culture *can* be liberal, but it does not establish that a culture is *necessarily* liberal.

## Multiculturalism as legal pluralism

As we have seen in previous chapters, there is a strong tendency in political theory to conceptualise the state as sovereign. Power may be devolved to individuals or sub-state units, such as provinces, but unless there is a clearly articulated legal right to secede, then power devolved is power retained. The sovereignty argument is expressed in its most trenchant form in the work of Hobbes, for whom the sovereign (Leviathan) is not bound by law.

Although defenders of multiculturalism are not alone in challenging the idea of sovereignty, they offer a distinct perspective, which draws on a specific understanding of culture. James Tully combines Geertz's semiotic theory of culture and Ludwig Wittgenstein's later language theory to develop interculturalism (a label he prefers to multiculturalism). The target of his attack is constitutional uniformity (or modern constitutionalism). Modern constitutionalism stresses sovereignty, regularity, and uniformity, and this contrasts with the implied rejection of sovereignty and with the irregularity and pluralism of 'ancient constitutionalism'. Although there are notable exceptions, Tully maintains that the process of colonisation involved the confrontation of these two forms of constitutionalism, and contemporary cultural conflicts in, for example, the Americas have their roots in the imposition of an alien constitutional form on Native Americans (Tully, 1995: 34). This imperial legacy is still with us, not simply in political practice, but also in political theory. Writers such as Kymlicka, while arguing for cultural diversity, do so in the language of modern constitutionalism (Tully, 1995: 44).

Tully contrasts two models of intercultural communication. The first requires shared terms of reference – so, for example, we might disagree about what rights people have, but we implicitly assume that rights have certain features (1995: 85). The second is based on 'family resemblances' between cultures: we find common ground not through an implicitly agreed, shared language, but by a piecemeal case-by-case agreement, based on affinities between our different cultural traditions (1995: 120). This suggests that constitutional formation cannot be understood from an abstract standpoint, such as utilitarianism or contractarianism (see pp. 164–6). And Europeans have resources within their own culture(s) to engage in such case-by-case communication. English Common Law is an example of an ancient constitution, and Tully considers it significant that there were examples of interaction between Europeans and Native Americans based on recognition of the *affinities* between their legal systems.

There are a number of weaknesses with Tully's argument. First, there is a tension between his espousal of a semiotic theory of culture, which stresses looseness of cultural boundaries, and his talk of 12,000 'diverse cultures, governments, and environmental practices' struggling for recognition (Tully, 1995: 3) (he provides no source for that figure) and '15,000 cultures who demand recognition' (Tully, 1995: 8) (again, no source). To count something you have to identify it, and identification implies 'hard boundaries'. Second, he says very little about how cultural conflicts can be resolved in the contemporary world, despite the aim of his work being to show the relevance of ancient constitutionalism. It is not clear what institutional forms would express cultural diversity, especially for geographically dispersed minorities. Third, and most important, he fails to address the charge that protection of culture can have detrimental consequences for individual freedom. He does maintain that culture is the basis of self-respect, such that to be denied recognition is a serious thing, but he offers only metaphorical observations to support the claim that interculturalism is not a threat to individual freedom (Tully, 1995: 189).

## Multiculturalism as hybridity

Jeremy Waldron takes as his starting point the controversy surrounding Salman Rushdie's novel *The Satanic Verses*. That novel, published in 1988, offended many Muslims and resulted in a *fatwa* being proclaimed the following year against the author by Ayatollah Khomeini. Waldron quotes from an essay in which Rushdie describes *The Satanic Verses* as a 'migrant's-eye view of the world'. It is, Rushdie says, written from the experiences of 'uprooting, disjuncture, and metamorphosis'. He goes on to say that 'the Satanic Verses celebrates hybridity, impurity, intermingling, the transformation that comes of new and unexpected combinations of human beings, cultures, ideas, politics, movies, songs' (Rushdie, cited in Waldron, 1995: 93). Rushdie argues that 'mongrelisation' is the way that 'newness enters the world'.

The concepts of hybridity and cosmopolitanism are at the heart of Waldron's understanding of multiculturalism. Hybridity is a challenge to both liberalism and communitarianism. Against liberalism, it implies a less rigid conception of what it means to live an autonomous life: 'if there is liberal autonomy in Rushdie's vision, it is a choice running rampant, and pluralism internalized from relations *between* individuals to the chaotic coexistence of projects, pursuits, ideas, images, and snatches of culture *within* an individual' (Waldron, 1995: 94).

Communitarians, on the other hand, fail to define community: is it a neighbourhood or the whole world? For the purposes of his argument, Waldron defines community as an ethnic community – 'a particular people sharing a heritage of custom, ritual, and way of life that is in some real or imagined sense immemorial' (Waldron, 1995: 96). Although we may need culture in a wide sense, we do not need to exist in a single culture, such as an ethnic community. Indeed, he goes further and argues that the only authentic response to modernity is the recognition of cultural hybridity: 'from a cosmopolitan point of view, immersion in the tradition of a particular community in the modern world is like living in Disneyland and thinking that one's surroundings epitomize what it is for a culture really to exist' (Waldron, 1995: 101).

Waldron recognises the counter-charge to cosmopolitanism: that living with fragments of culture generates incoherence. As Benedict argued, the meaning of a particular item of culture depends on the whole, for a culture is all of a piece. Waldron argues, however, that real communities are disparate and overlap and are nothing like the aboriginal hunting bands or the 'misty dawn in a Germanic village' (Waldron, 1995: 102). Respecting culture does not entail valuing an entire culture, as if a culture were a self-contained thing, but rather 'meaningful options' come from a variety of cultural sources, and 'cultural erosion' is the key to cultural evaluation: the failure of a culture to survive indicates that one culture – or cultural trait – is better than another. Waldron's argument can be read either as a critique of multiculturalism or as a particular model of multiculturalism. It is a critique, if multiculturalism is meant a deliberate policy of maintaining, through either financial support or the restriction of individual freedom, a particular culture, where culture is understood as an organic whole. It is a theory of multiculturalism insofar as it presents a model of political society in which cultural diversity is valued.

Stanley Fish, in an article which also references the Rushdie affair, distinguishes what he terms boutique multiculturalism from strong multiculturalism. Although he does not discuss Waldron, the former label could be a synonym for hybridity. Boutique multiculturalism is 'the multiculturalism of ethnic restaurants, weekend festivals, and high profile flirtation with the other in the manner satirized by Tom Wolfe under the rubric "radical chic"' (Fish, 1997: 378). The boutique multiculturalist, however, draws the line at ritual sacrifice of animals, or the practice of polygyny, or *fatawa* against novelists. He resists a cultural practice 'at precisely the point it matters most to its strongly committed members' (1997: 379). He cannot take seriously the core values of the culture he superficially values. The real core for boutique multiculturalism is humanity, which it takes to be universal. The strong multiculturalist, on the other hand, acknowledges the importance of a culture's core values to its members, but because she values diversity, she cannot accept the exclusionary claims of a culture – the view held by a cultural group's members that their culture is superior – and so in the end, she too cannot take culture seriously (1997: 384). Fish concludes that there is no such thing as multiculturalism understood as a theory, but rather there is simply the lived experience – or demographic reality – of cultural diversity. Taking a term from Taylor (discussed earlier), Fish talks of 'inspired adhoccery': each conflict situation calls for improvisation and not the application of rules or principles (1997: 386).

## Multiculturalism as allocative efficiency

Human behaviour is affected by legal and non-legal sanctions. For example, gossip can keep people in line by contributing to their reputation, but it has no legal force. Much of our interaction takes place in groups, membership of which is normally voluntary, but which is nonetheless affected by law. The state can draw on the non-legal sanctioning power of groups to achieve good social outcomes, but laws can also undermine those groups, even when that is not the state's intention. Multiculturalism can be understood as the attempt by the state to draw on the bonding and binding power of non-state groups, such as religious communities. As Eric Posner argues, there is a paradox: how can the state use the law to promote cooperation that is spontaneous, not enforced?

Posner is not in fact advancing a theory of multiculturalism, but his argument provides the basis for one. He outlines three concepts: (a) *cohesion* – the ability to cooperate in the absence of law; (b) *group* – a collection of people who choose to cooperate; and (c) *category* – a set of people who share a characteristic. If a group is cohesive and has aims consistent with the state, it is better to transfer resources to the group. If the state tries to improve the position of individuals directly, it may have the perverse effect of reducing welfare. Indeed, even if the state attempts to replicate the work of a group, it may undermine that group and reduce welfare (Posner, 1996: 135–6). Health is an example of group action. Some minorities may be unwilling to seek preventative care or are distrustful of vaccination programmes. The state could try to reach minorities directly through individual contact – a category-based approach – or it could fund group-based activity by, for example, giving religious groups funds to run campaigns to persuade their members to get vaccinated. This may be more effective because community leaders command higher levels of trust.

All groups face a free-rider problem: gaining the benefits from collective action without paying for that benefit. Free-riding can be reduced by, for example, communal living (or at least living within geographically circumscribed areas), encouraging confession, facilitating gossip, and tasking certain group members with detecting free-riders (1996: 140). Reducing contact with other groups – and the possibility of exit – also increases the costs of free-riding. And size matters: the group needs to be large enough to generate goods but not so large that it is difficult to monitor behaviour. What determines group cohesion is the difference between the pay-off for the individual from cooperation and the pay-off from defection. Importantly, a reduction in external hostility – for example, racial hostility – may reduce the effectiveness of the group.

The state can regulate groups through three types of rules. Group-based rules transfer resources to groups, examples being tax breaks and subsidies. Category-based rules transfer resources to categories of people from whom groups draw their members. These might take the former of transfer payments which intentionally or unintentionally have a disparate impact on particular categories; for example, if a particular ethnic group has a relatively high fertility rate, then increasing child support payments will affect its members more than the general population. Dispute resolution rules settle disputes among group members, such as those regulating marriage and child custody. These three kinds of rules will affect group cohesion. Giving groups resources will likely increase cohesion, unless those resources become the focus of conflict among group members. Category-based rules will reduce cohesion if individuals become less dependent on the group. And dispute resolution rules may weaken cohesion, if they reduce the ability of the group to punish free-riders.

While liberalism emphasises the individual and so category-based policies, such policies might undermine groups. And groups may in fact be more effective in achieving socially desirable outcomes, such as crime reduction, health improvements, or educational achievement. The trade-off between category-based state intervention and group-based devolved strategies will depend on the overall level of confidence people have in state institutions, such as the legal system.

Take as an example the importance for business of suppliers and customers honouring their contracts. If legal institutions are perceived as strong and relatively free of corruption, then breaches of contract can be remedied by going to law. But if the institutions are weak and corrupt, then other mechanisms are required, and this is where groups, which often have an ethnic character, are important. Janet Tai Landa has studied the diaspora Chinese communities of Southeast Asia, such as those in Malaysia and the Philippines. In these countries, the Chinese are middleman minorities, meaning that they play a dominant role in facilitating trade, through, for example, offering credit (Landa and Wang, 2001).

Landa focuses specifically on the rubber business in Southeast Asia, which is dominated by the Chinese (2001: 227–31). There are five clans of Hokkien Chinese, originating from the Fukien province of China. Trust in business transactions – for example, by extending credit – is determined by how closely related two individuals are within seven concentric circles: (1) nuclear family; (2) extended family; (3) clansmen (surname); (4) fellow-villagers; (5) Hokkien-Chinese speaking the same dialect; (6) Chinese speaking another dialect; and (7) Non-Chinese.

The sanction for breaching contractual promises is 'expulsion' from the cultural group, which is painful for the person concerned. Clearly, the sanctions get weaker the further you move from inner core, and so the extent of the trust placed in an individual will be calibrated against his or her distance from the core. In effect, trust in ethnic groups is a club good, whereas trust through legal institutions is a public good (see pp. 13–14). The downside is that ethnic exclusivity breeds resentment, and as Amy Chua argues, this can lead to extreme intergroup violence (Chua, 2002).

## Multiculturalism as intergroup competition

This is the most negative of the perspectives, but there are two variants of it. The first comes from traditional liberals who are concerned that the emphasis on cultural diversity is a rejection of individualism – a rejection of Martin Luther King's sentiment that a person should be judged by the content of his character, not the colour of his skin. The second is less prominent in mainstream debate, but comes from white advocates (mostly on the radical right), who argue straightforwardly that multiculturalism is an ideological strategy for dispossessing white people, and is shot through with double-standards, whereby all groups except whites are permitted to organise on the basis of ethnic identity. While they are basically negative about multiculturalism, some on the radical right argue that white people should 'play the game' – they should use the language of identity (identitarianism) to promote white interests.

To illustrate both variants of this critique, consider critical race theory, which first emerged in the early 1990s in university law schools and until a few years ago was a rather obscure movement. According to Delgado and Stefancic (2017: 6–9), its main tenets are as follows:

1. Racism is an ordinary, everyday phenomenon, and not aberrational. It is woven into majority white society, rather than simply being the expression of a few racists.
2. Race is socially constructed.
3. White ascendency serves important purposes, psychic and material.
4. Whiteness is normative – that is, it is taken to be the norm against which other racial identities are judged. There is a process of marginalising and 'othering' non-white people.
5. Being 'colour-blind' does not address whiteness as power. When confronted with this, white people are defensive – they manifest 'white fragility' (DiAngelo, 2011).
6. Minority status brings with it a presumed competence to speak about race and racism.
7. Crucially whiteness is not an ethnicity, but a power structure.

The last of these points is particularly important. Is whiteness an ethnicity or something else? A small illustration of this debate is the decision of the *New York Times* to capitalise Black, but not white (Coleman, 2020). One writer on the *Times* argued:

> "The lowercase B in Black has never made sense to me as a Black woman, and it didn't make sense to me as a Black girl," said Destinée-Charisse Royal, a senior staff editor in the Graphics department and one of the editors consulted on the change. "My thought was that the capital B makes sense as it describes a race, a cultural group, and that is very different from a color in a box of crayons".

The above sentiment is reasonable enough, but the justification for not capitalising white is that it 'doesn't represent a shared culture and history in the way Black does, and also has long been capitalized by hate groups'. Language matters, and the difference between 'Black' and 'white' indicates an ambivalence at the heart of the concept of race. There are three options:

1. Nobody has a race or ethnicity. We are just individuals. This is the liberal position.
2. Everybody has a race or ethnicity. This is the position of white advocates.
3. Some people have a race or ethnicity, but others do not. This – at least implicitly – is what critical race theorists claim.

It might be that 'white' lacks specificity, and as a matter of good grammar English, French, Canadian and so on would be capitalised. But then people are clear these are not racial categories, and indeed to refer to them as such would itself be deemed racist. The strongest argument for resisting whiteness as a racial category is that it is taken to be the norm against which other racial (or racialised) groups are judged, and furthermore, whites do not experience racism, or at least not in the same way and to the same extent that people of colour experience it.

There may be a force in these points, but then we need to conceptualise a society without white racism – without 'structural racism'. There are clearly people who are identified as white – they are, after all, the target of, and presumed audience for, diversity trainer Robin DiAngelo's white fragility theory. Where would they go in a post-racist society? The far right, at its most apocalyptic, argue they would be extinguished. But presumably that is not the aim of critical race theory. The feasible options are either that nobody would be categorised by race – we would all be individuals – or there would be ethnic groups, and individuals would have an ethnic identity, but the structure defined by whiteness (whiteness as power) would disappear. Societies would be majority-minority.

It might have been simpler if critical race theorists had argued whites are an ethnic group, but an oppressive one. The problem with this is that overcoming the power of a group – any group – will be most successful when its members have weak cohesion or a negative identity. Denying the very existence of a group is the most effective way to disable it.

The treatment of whiteness is the most significant problem at the heart of critical race theory, but there are others. It is perverse to argue that a middle-aged, unemployed white man in a deindustrialised town far from the centres of cultural and political power is more privileged than an Ivy League-educated woman of colour working for the government or a major media outlet. It is for this reason that critical racist theorists define the benefits of whiteness as material *and psychic*. However, the more complex you make a theory, the less likely it is to be valid. If every problem a theory encounters – such as explaining away poor whites – requires an additional concept, such as psychic benefit, to patch it up, it looks like the theory is not very good.

There are other methodological problems with critical race theory. There is no testing of the claim of structural racism. Any unequal outcome between groups is taken as evidence of discrimination, and alternative explanations are discounted without consideration. And DiAngelo's white fragility theory is unfalsifiable. If a white employee required to attend a race equality training course reacts negatively to being 'confronted with' white fragility, then that is taken as further evidence of white fragility. To avoid her thesis being pseudoscientific, DiAngelo would have to provide examples of criticism of her theory which were not evidence of fragility.

Ultimately, the focus on whiteness as power – and the associated denial of whiteness as an ethnicity – combined with the widespread dissemination of critical race theory in educational and employment settings may have the unintended effect of raising white consciousness. The more you talk about something – even in highly negative terms – the more people become conscious of it. This is what liberals fear, and white nationalists welcome.

## Women and multiculturalism

Susan Okin argues that multiculturalism is bad for women. The problem is that in liberal societies culture is treated as part of the private sphere. This requires correction, and once corrected, we have to face up to two important connections between gender and culture. First, the sphere of personal, sexual, and reproductive life functions as a central focus of most cultures. Many cultural groups are intensely concerned with family law issues – divorce, child custody, family property, and inheritance. Such a focus has a differential impact on boys/men and girls/women. Second, most cultures have as one of their principal aims the male control of women (patriarchy):

> Consider, for example, the founding myths of Greek and Roman antiquity, and of Judaism, Christianity, and Islam: they are rife with attempts to justify the control and subordination of women. These myths consist of a combination of denials of women's role in reproduction; appropriations by men of the power to reproduce themselves; characterizations of women as overly emotional, untrustworthy, evil, or sexually dangerous; and refusals to acknowledge mothers' rights over the dispositions of their children.
>
> (Okin, 1999: 13)

Okin argues that while discrimination and gender-stereotyping exist in Western liberal democracies, the worst forms of discrimination have been removed – at least at the level of law. Women from minority cultures in Western societies should not be denied the rights enjoyed by the majority culture.

Her critique of multiculturalism generated a significant debate, and responses to her essay are contained in the book *Is Multiculturalism Bad for Women?* (Okin, 1999). Below, we explore the most interesting of the responses to Okin from that book. We are not necessarily endorsing all (or any) of these counter-arguments; rather, our aim is to stimulate debate.

1. **Valid and invalid cultural defences**. If we are studying minority cultural practices, then it is important that we are sensitive to the context. As Katha Pollitt argues, if a man murders his wife because he believes she has been unfaithful, and then appeals to 'his culture' as mitigation, we can reasonably ask the question – is he telling the truth? Are men allowed to do this 'back home' (Pollitt, 1999: 28–9)?

2. **Source material**. Related to the last point, Okin culls her examples from criminal cases in the United States. As Homi Bhabha argues, this distorts the cultural context because 'cultural information' is being used for very specific ends (Bhabha, 1999: 81). Furthermore, the forum is alien to those cultural practices.

3. **Is multiculturalism *especially* bad for women?** You could argue that culture is *especially bad* for women and not just quantitatively but qualitatively – that is, culture is gendered – or you could maintain that culture is bad *for everyone*. To say it is bad for everyone might seem a bizarre defence of multiculturalism, but it could be used in order to move to a more sophisticated idea of the relationship between culture and gender. Take the example of circumcision. Boys are also circumcised: is male circumcision 'genital mutilation'? We need to consider the reasons for male circumcision: medical grounds in specific cases (everywhere), on general medical grounds (particularly in the United Sates), and on ritual/religious grounds. Female circumcision takes three forms (Parekh, 2006: 275–6), of which two are not equivalent to male circumcision. What reasons are given for these practices? Control of sexuality dominates reasoning, but then the great monotheistic religions have all been concerned with controlling sexuality, not just of women, but also of men.

4. **Experience.** Okin makes some rather patronising remarks about older women. She argues – quite rightly – that cultural recognition gives power to certain people, usually older men, and that intercultural communication should involve asking women what they think, but she then says that it should be 'younger women' because 'older women often are co-opted into reinforcing gender inequality' (Okin, 1999: 24). This raises questions about who has the right to speak. Okin seems to be attributing false consciousness to women, but this contradicts one of the major

components of the feminist movement: namely, to ask women what they want. Furthermore, feminists stress that white, Western, middle-class women should not assume that their voice is identical to that of, say, black, working-class, non-Western women (see pp. 271–2).

Despite these criticisms, Okin is right to argue that minority cultures focus their self-defence very strongly on the private, domestic sphere. For example, the cultural defence that Islam prohibits the charging of interest on money is never used when somebody is in court for failure to pay off his credit card. The domestic sphere is conservative in all societies, but what makes minority cultures appear especially conservative is that they are cut off from the wider structure of social institutions.

## Conclusion

Multiculturalism emerged in the 1960s as a distinct area of academic debate. Given the dominance of liberalism as an ideology, much discussion in the field of multiculturalism has revolved around the relationship between liberalism and multiculturalism, with the two standing in a complex relationship to one another. Multiculturalists reaffirm the values of freedom and equality but rearticulate these as equality in difference, and freedom in context. Although there are continuities with earlier debates over religious difference and toleration – debates that dominated political discourse in the seventeenth and eighteenth centuries – multiculturalism cannot be understood as simply a return to these earlier disputes, but rather it is post-liberal, in the sense that it has absorbed the liberal emphasis on human self-expression, but challenges liberals to provide a more adequate understanding of self-expression, one that places greater emphasis on cultural identity. On the radical right multiculturalism is interpreted as a strategy intended to undermine the 'majority' group in society and permit minority groups to maintain their own particularist strategies.

## References

Bhabha, H. (1999). 'Liberalism's Sacred Cow', in S. Okin et al. (eds.), *Is Multiculturalism Bad for Women?* Princeton, NJ: Princeton University Press.

Chua, A. (2002). A World on the Edge. *The Wilson Quarterly* (1976–), *26*(4), 62–77.

Coleman, N (2020). Why We're Capitalizing Black. *New York Times*, viewed 25 July 2021, https://www.nytimes.com/2020/07/05/insider/capitalized-black.html

Delgado, R. and Stefancic, J. (2017). *Critical Race Theory.* New York University Press.

DiAngelo, R. (2011). White Fragility. *International Journal of Critical Pedagogy*, *3*(3), 54–70.

Edwards, A. W. (2003). Human Genetic Diversity: Lewontin's Fallacy. *BioEssays*, *25*(8), 798–801.

Fish, S. (1997). Boutique Multiculturalism, or Why Liberals Are Incapable of Thinking about Hate Speech. *Critical Inquiry*, *23*(2), 378–95.

Geertz, C. (1993). *The Interpretation of Cultures: Selected Essays.* London: Fontana.

Hochman, A. (2013). Against the New Racial Naturalism. *The Journal of Philosophy*, *110*(6), 331–51.

Kymlicka, W. (1989). *Liberalism, Community, and Culture.* Oxford: Clarendon Press.

Kymlicka, W. (1995). *Multicultural Citizenship*. Oxford: Clarendon Press.

Landa, J. T. and Wang, X. T. X. (2001). Bounded Rationality of Economic Man: Decision Making under Ecological, Social, and Institutional Constraints. *Journal of Bioeconomics*, 3(2), 217–35.

Lewontin, R. C. (1972). 'The Apportionment of Human Diversity', in T. Dobzhansky, M. K. Hecht and W. C. Steere (eds), *Evolutionary Biology*. New York: Springer, 381–98.

Malinowski, B. (1965). *A Scientific Theory of Culture, and Other Essays*. Chapel Hill, NC: North Carolina University Press.

Mill, J.S. (1991). *On Liberty and Other Essays*. Ed. J. Gray. Oxford: Oxford University Press.

Okin, S. (1999). *Is Multiculturalism Bad for Women?* Ed. J. Cohen, M. Howard and M. Nussbaum Princeton, NJ: Princeton University Press.

Parekh, B. (2006). *Rethinking Multiculturalism: Cultural Diversity and Political Theory*, 2nd edn. Basingstoke: Palgrave Macmillan.

Pollitt, K. (1999). 'Whose Culture', in S. Okin et al. (eds.), *Is Multiculturalism Bad for Women?* Princeton, NJ: Princeton University Press.

Posner, E. A. (1996). The Regulation of Groups: The Influence of Legal and Nonlegal Sanctions on Collective Action. *The University of Chicago Law Review*, 63(1), 133–97.

Rosenblatt, D. (2004). An Anthropology Made Safe for Culture: Patterns of Practice and the Politics of Difference in Ruth Benedict. *American Anthropologist*, 106(3), 459–72.

Sharpe, E. (1983). *Understanding Religion*. London: Duckworth.

Tang, H. et al. (2005). Genetic Structure, Self-Identified Race/Ethnicity, and Confounding in Case-control Association Studies. *The American Journal of Human Genetics*, 76(2), 268–75.

Taylor, C. (1994). 'The Politics of Recognition', in A. Gutmann (ed.), *Multiculturalism: Examining the Politics of Recognition*. Princeton, NJ: Princeton University Press.

Tully, J. (1995). *Strange Multiplicity: Constitutionalism in an Age of Diversity*. Cambridge: Cambridge University Press.

Waldron, J. (1995). 'Minority Cultures and the Cosmopolitan Alternative', in W. Kymlicka (ed.), *The Rights of Minority Cultures* Oxford: Oxford University Press, 93–119.

## Further reading

Introductions include: Ali Rattansi, *Multiculturalism: A Very Short Introduction* (Oxford University Press, 2011); George Crowder, *Theories of Multiculturalism: An Introduction* (Polity, 2013); Michael Murphy, *Multiculturalism: A Critical Introduction* (Routledge, 2011). A useful collection is Duncan Ivison (ed.), *The Ashgate Research Companion to Multiculturalism* (Routledge, 2017). Other works, focused on various aspects of multiculturalism: Rita Chin, *The Crisis of Multiculturalism in Europe: A History* (Princeton University Press, 2019); Tariq Madood, *Multiculturalism* (Polity, 2013); Anne Phillips, *Multiculturalism without Culture* (Princeton University Press, 2009); Sarah Song, *Justice, Gender, and the Politics of Multiculturalism* (Cambridge University Press, 2007); Göran Adamson, *Masochistic Nationalism: Multicultural Self-Hatred and the Infatuation with the Exotic* (Routledge, 2021). A data-based study of increasing white identity in the United States: Ashley Jardina, *White Identity Politics* (Cambridge University Press, 2018).

# Chapter 17

# Ecologism

## Introduction

Ecologism has only emerged as a fully-fledged ideology since the 1960s. As with all recent ideologies, it has intellectual roots stretching back centuries, but the construction of a relatively autonomous set of ideas and prescriptions for action is a recent occurrence. Ecologism should be distinguished from environmentalism – for environmentalists, the desire to protect the environment is based primarily on concern about the consequences of environmental degradation on human beings, whereas for ecologists, something called 'ecology', or 'nature', is the source of value. It follows from this distinction that whereas environmentalism can be combined with other ideologies, ecologism is distinct. In terms of political practice, politicians from across the political spectrum have embraced the rhetoric and sometimes the policies, of environmentalism, but this does not mean they have endorsed ecologism.

## Key questions

- What is ecologism and is it different to environmentalism?
- Is there an ecological crisis and does that demand new ways of organising political life?
- Is ecologism compatible with the modern world?

## Ecologism or environmentalism?

Giving a name to this chapter is a challenge. At least three possibilities suggest themselves as names – ecologism, environmentalism, or green thought – and these differing possibilities carry distinct ideological implications. In the view of those who call themselves ecologists, environmentalism denotes an attitude compatible with almost all the competing ideologies discussed in this book. Environmentalists attach value to the 'environment' or 'nature' but only in relation to human consciousness and human concerns, and as such, the environment is slotted in as a subordinate component of alternative ideologies, such as liberalism, socialism, or feminism. Environmentalism is anthropocentric – that is, human-centred. Ecologists, on the other hand, assert that nature has intrinsic value, and the task of ecologism is to engage in a critique of the anthropocentric world-view, which in socio-economic terms manifests itself as industrialism. Ecologism is eco-centred. While ecologists embrace values and perspectives derived from other

DOI: 10.4324/9780429424106-21

Case study 17.1

## Is there an argument for nuclear power?

**PHOTO 17.1** © Chris Ratcliffe/Bloomberg via Getty Images.

In the 1980s, plastered on cars and on lapel badges was the German slogan around a smiley 'sun' face: 'Atomkraft? Nein, Danke' ('Nuclear Power? No Thanks'). Central to the German Green movement – and virtually all Green movements – is the rejection of nuclear power as expensive, dangerous, and inextricably linked to the nuclear weapons industry. It therefore came as a shock to many Green activists when one of its leading theorists, James Lovelock – the man who had coined the word 'Gaia' to describe the mutual dependence of all life-forms – came out in favour of nuclear power. Lovelock argued that the threat from global warming is now so great that 'nuclear power is the only green solution' (*Independent*, 24 May 2004). The 'great Earth system' – Gaia – is, he says, 'trapped in a vicious circle of positive feedback': extra heat from any source is amplified, and its effects are more than additive. This means that we have little time left to act. The Kyoto Protocol, which aimed to cut omissions, is simply a cosmetic attempt 'to hide the political embarrassment of global warming'. If we had 50 years to solve the problem, then it might be possible to switch from fossil fuels to 'renewables' such as wind and tide power, but realistically those sources will only make a negligible contribution to the world's energy needs over the next 20 or so years. There is, Lovelock claims, only one immediately available source of energy which does not contribute to global warming and that is nuclear power. Opposition to nuclear power is based on an 'irrational fear fed by Hollywood-style fiction, the Green lobbies and the media'. These fears are, according to Lovelock, unjustified: 'we must stop worrying about minuscule risks from radiation and recognize that a third of us will die from cancer, mainly because we breathe air laden with "that all pervasive carcinogen, oxygen"'. Do you agree with Lovelock?

ideologies those perspectives are assessed from the standpoint of the ecosystem, or earth, as an irreducible and interdependent system. Whereas environmentalists share a post-Enlightenment belief in the uniqueness of the human perspective on the world – they place human beings above, or outside, nature – ecologists challenge that philosophical position, maintaining human life only has value insofar as it is a 'knot' in the 'net' of life, a net which connects together not only non-human animals, but non-sentient entities, such as trees, rivers, and mountains. Indeed, it is the net rather than the knots that is of ultimate value.

Students of politics are most likely to have encountered the political face of the green movement rather than be aware of the underlying philosophical differences within environmentalism (or ecologism), and one of our aims in this chapter will be to connect the philosophical ideas to the political movements. The links are less direct than some writers on environmentalism recognise. To illustrate, consider the idea of an environmental crisis. Many people argue that industrialisation, urbanisation, and population growth have either brought about or threaten to bring about, irreversible changes to the natural environment such that the future of life on earth beyond more than 100 or 200 years is in jeopardy. Some writers maintain the difference between ecologism and environmentalism rests, in part, on attitudes to the seriousness of this crisis, with ecologists being very pessimistic, and environmentalists more optimistic. There is some validity in this characterisation of the differing attitudes, in that ecologists maintain the causes of the crisis are not simply scientific-technical; the roots of the crisis lie in human attitudes to nature – we see nature as a resource to be exploited for our benefit.

However, a human-centred approach to the environment may also explain the crisis. Microbiologist and environmental theorist Garrett Hardin argued that overpopulation will have catastrophic consequences and that food aid to the developing world should be ended so that population levels can be allowed to fall 'naturally' (Hardin, 1974: 564). Hardin is often thought of as an ecologist, and his apparently misanthropic argument is used against ecologism, but, in fact, Hardin reasons from straightforwardly human-centred premises: human beings will suffer from overpopulation.

## Environmental crisis

Most popular discussion of environmentalism – and ecologism – takes place within the context of a discussion of the environmental crisis. The first point to note is the singularity of the phrase: there is *a* crisis. This is controversial, for it may be that there is a series of distinct environmental problems. However, virtually all ecologists, and many environmentalists, argue these problems are interconnected, and a coherent engagement with the environment must recognise this fact. Among the specific environmental problems are the following:

- *Global warming*: This is acknowledged by most, but not all, scientists as the most serious environmental problem facing the planet – the minority who challenge the consensus do not question the evidence of global warming, but its causes, arguing either that warming is not primarily caused by human activity or that its effects are manageable (Lemonick, 2009; Lomborg, 2016). However, most scientists do believe humans are largely responsible for global warming. The earth's temperature is maintained by the greenhouse effect: a layer of gases in the atmosphere traps a small percentage of the sun's radiation, but the burning of fossil fuels increases the greenhouse effect, with the result that sea levels are rising due to the melting of the ice caps, with obvious consequences for low-lying land areas. At a certain point in the process of global warming, many life-forms will be threatened.
- *Resource depletion*: Some resources, such as fish, are, with careful stewardship, naturally replenished; other resources, such as coal and gas, are not. Both types of resources are threatened by excessive demand.
- *Localised pollution*: This may not cause a global crisis, but poor air in places such as Mexico City can have a debilitating effect on inhabitants. Localised pollution is also likely to increase migration.
- *Decline in species*: Although the effects of species loss – or a decline in biodiversity – are unclear, many ecologists argue that the loss of species is bad in itself, regardless of its wider impact. The use of agricultural chemicals and the genetic modification of crops are identified by some environmentalists as the cause of the decline in biodiversity.
- *Nuclear war*: This will not, of course, be a direct environmental problem unless nuclear weapons are used (although nuclear weapons testing has had environmental consequences). In the 1980s, when the consciousness of the threat of nuclear war was much higher than it is today, scientists speculated that the use of intercontinental ballistic missiles could result in a 'nuclear winter': atmospheric pollution caused by dust, soot, smoke, and ash would prevent the sun's rays from penetrating for a period of time long enough to eradicate most plant life and create a new ice age. Since the 1980s, there has been a proliferation of states with nuclear weapons.

Students of political theory cannot be expected to be experts on the scientific causes of environmental problems, and the focus of this chapter is on the philosophical ideas behind, and ethical issues raised by, ecology, many of which can be understood without reference to the environmental crisis. However, the crisis does raise interesting questions about the relationship between science and politics. Ecologists are critical of scientific rationality and yet employ scientific evidence to support their arguments. Furthermore, while there is widespread distrust of scientists employed by multinational companies, and to a lesser extent by government agencies, scientists who speak on behalf of environmental groups enjoy a high level of trust.

## Green politics

Green political parties and movements emerged in the 1970s. In terms of political influence, the most successful Green party is the German Green Party (Die Grünen/Bundnis 90). By 1982, they were represented in the parliaments of six of West Germany's regions (Länder), and they entered the Federal Parliament (Bundestag) in 1983, winning 5.6% of the vote. In the following election, their support rose to 8.3%, and other parties began to adopt environmental policies. However, during the 1980s, it became clear there was a major schism between *Realos* (realists) and *Fundis* (fundamentalists); the former wanted power within the existing political system, while the latter challenged that system. Opposed to German unification in 1990, the Greens fell below the 5% of the vote required for seats in the Bundestag (although their Eastern equivalent – Bundnis 90 – won 6% of the Eastern vote, and thus seats). The internal dispute within the party was won by the Realos and the party – now in alliance with Bundnis 90 – grew in strength through the 1990s. Between 1998 and 2005, the Greens were in coalition with the Social Democrats at the federal – national – level. More recently, they have led the administration in the federal state of Baden-Württemberg, are in coalition in most other federal states, and have consistently outpolled the Social Democrats at the national level in opinion polls.

The German Greens, as with other European Green parties, draw their strength dispropor-tionately from young, public sector middle-class workers. One explanation that is often advanced for the rise of the Green movement is the emergence of 'post-materialist values': quality of life issues is more important than increasing income and enhanced career status (Close and Delwit, 2016: 253–4). Such a view presupposes that a society has achieved a certain level of material comfort, and so the Green phenomenon may rest on a contradiction: the possibility of a Green politics depends on the generation of surplus goods and, therefore, the consumer society of which Greens are so critical.

## Environmentalism and other ideologies

Below are outlined possible links between the ideologies discussed in this book and environmen-talism – what we are identifying are the affinities between environmentalism and the ideology in question. It should be stressed, however, that some of the affinities identified below also hold between *ecologism* and these other ideologies. This does not, however, undermine the claim that ecologism is distinct.

- *Liberalism*: Liberals tend to be universalists. They argue that human beings have rights in-dependently of the culture to which they belong. Just as individuals have rights across space (culture, geography) so they have rights across time: future – that is, not-yet-existing – gen-erations have moral claims. If we leave the world more degraded than we found it, then we are violating their rights.
- *Conservatism*: At a simplistic level, conservatives and environmentalists share a belief in con-servation. Although conservatives focus on the preservation and transmission of cultural tra-ditions, respect for the environment – the maintenance of a sense of place – is also important. At a deeper philosophical level, conservatives share with many ecologists a scepticism towards rationality (see pp. 173).
- *Socialism*: Environmentalists oppose the exploitation – in the pejorative sense of that word – of the natural world. Socialists oppose the exploitation of human beings. There is more than a metaphorical equivalence between socialist and environmentalist opposition to exploitation: the people most likely to suffer the consequences of environmental degradation are the poor, especially the poor in the global south.
- *Anarchism*: Anarchists share with some environmentalists a hostility towards authority, and some anarchists join forces with environmentalists in their opposition to what they see as the authoritarian character of globalisation. Anti-globalisation anarchists tend to stress the im-portance of self-sufficient communities of freely associating individuals, although this brings them closer to ecologism than environmentalism.
- *Nationalism*: Some of the concerns mentioned above – the loss of a sense of place due to globalisation – also inform nationalism and provide a link between nationalism and

environmentalism. More specifically, many nationalists are concerned with the effects on the nation of migration, which itself can be a product of both globalisation and the environmental crisis. Immigration is viewed as a threat to the cultural integrity of the nation-state.

- *Fascism*: Polemical opponents of environmentalism (and ecologism) sometimes talk of 'eco-fascists', and the links between nazism and early twentieth century green movements are highlighted (see pp. 247). The idea of an organic and hierarchical order in nature is, it is claimed, mirrored in a social hierarchy. Sometimes, it is simply the perceived fanaticism of the Green movement, and its utopian desire for a 'clean world' that motivates the charge of fascism. But this is just name-calling, rather than a claim based on serious philosophical reflection.
- *Feminism*: The links between feminism and environmentalism (and ecologism) seem more metaphorical than real. The idea of Mother Earth implies the femininity of nature. Ideas of growth and nurturing also summon up notions of motherhood and of the mother–child relationship. In contrast, the rationalism which some environmentalists, and most ecologists, oppose is masculine. Of course, it is precisely such essentialism that many feminists oppose: the characterisation of women as nurturing and not rationalistic contributes to women's oppression.
- *Multiculturalism*: Multiculturalists value cultural diversity. Environmentalists and ecologists value natural diversity. As a multiculturalist might seek the preservation of a minority language, so an environmentalist seeks to preserve an endangered species.

It is clear there are links and affinities between these various ideologies and both environmentalism and ecologism, but there is a distinctive core to ecologism which can be summed up in the distinction between an anthropocentric ethic and an ecocentric ethic. This is illustrated in the work of two important ecologists: Aldo Leopold and Arne Næss.

## Aldo Leopold and the land ethic

Aldo Leopold (1887–1948) is important as a precursor of ideological ecologism. The essence of his land ethic was that land was an interdependent system and not a commodity; human beings were part of the 'land community' and not masters of it. For human beings to understand themselves, they must grasp the whole of which they are a part. And 'a thing is right when it tends to preserve the integrity, stability, and beauty of the biotic community . . . it is wrong when it tends otherwise' (Leopold, 1987: 150). What Leopold called 'land' later ecologists would call the ecosystem, biosphere, Gaia, Spaceship Earth, and by 'community' Leopold meant an interdependent whole, the members of which were not simply human beings, or even all sentient beings, but all life-forms.

Underlying the land ethic was a controversial philosophical claim: from observation of the empirical world, human beings can derive reasons for action. This violates Hume's naturalistic fallacy argument: claims about how people should behave cannot be generated from observational facts – the moral 'ought' cannot be derived from an observation of what 'is'. This is a recurrent problem with ecologism, and we discuss it in more detail later. Another philosophical, or ethical, claim is that the history of morality is characterised by an expanding circle of concern, whereby we now consider the ownership of other human beings – slavery – wrong, but we have not yet expanded the circle of concern to include the land. The land ethic enlarges the boundaries of the community to include soils, waters, plants, and animals. In fact, Leopold links these two philosophical claims by arguing that morality has undergone an ecological evolution, suggesting the moral ought emerges over time from a growing realisation of what is. Such evolution has its origins in:

. . .the tendency of interdependent individuals or groups to evolve modes of co-operation. The ecologist calls these symbioses. Politics and economics are advanced symbioses in which the original free-for-all competition has been replaced, in part, by co-operative mechanisms with an ethical content.

(Leopold, 1987: 143)

The extension of ethics to land is an 'evolutionary possibility and an ecological necessity'. Certainly, Leopold argues, individual thinkers have condemned the abuse of the land, but society at large has yet to embrace the land ethic. The conservation movement is the embryo of such social affirmation. Leopold's land ethic was shaped by his experiences of the state-led conservation of the 1930s and 1940s in the United States, and this led him to a salutary conclusion: respect for the land cannot be achieved if the state assumes sole moral responsibility for the environment. Rather, *individuals* must change their motivations, and this is a powerful and central claim of the ecological movement. Leopold noted that farmers were prepared to take ecologically friendly measures so long as those measures were consistent with their profit margins. He observes that the existence of obligations is taken for granted when what is at issue are better roads or schools but 'their existence is not taken for granted, nor as yet seriously discussed, in bettering the behaviour of the water that falls on the land, or in the preserving of the beauty or diversity of the farm landscape' (Leopold, 1987: 145).

A difficulty which Leopold observes in moving from dominion over the land, driven by the desire for profit, to stewardship of the land, is that many members of the land community have no economic value: 'of the 22,000 higher plants and animals native to Wisconsin, it is doubtful whether more than 5 per cent can be sold, fed, eaten, or otherwise put to economic use' (Leopold, 1987: 145). But such plants and animals have, Leopold claims, 'biotic rights'. This would seem to entail a rejection of a human-centred attitude to the environment, but it is unclear whether this is really the case, with Leopold suggesting that if a private landowner were ecologically minded, he would be proud to be the custodian of an ecosystem that adds 'diversity and beauty' to his farm and community (Leopold, 1987: 146). Furthermore, the assumed lack of profit in 'waste' areas has proved to be wrong, but only after the destruction of most of it.

To express the interdependence of nature, Leopold uses the image of a pyramid, with a plant layer resting on the soil, an insect layer on the plants, a bird and rodent layer on the insects, and so on up through various animal groups to the apex layer, which consists of the larger carnivores. There exist lines of dependency between these layers, largely determined by the need for food and energy. Industrialisation has changed the pyramid in several ways. First, by reversing evolution: evolutionary change lengthened the food chain through the emergence of more complex life forms; industrialisation shortens the chain by the elimination of both predators and of seemingly useless organisms. Second, by the exploitation, which puts geological, and other formations, to new uses, such as the generation of energy, and removes them from the 'natural chain'. Third, transportation disconnects the chain and introduces forms from one environment to a new, quite different, one, and with sometimes unintended consequences. Leopold summarises the idea of the pyramid as an energy circuit in three basic ideas:

1. Land is not merely soil.
2. Native plants and animals keep the energy circuit open.
3. Man-made changes are of a different order than evolutionary changes and have effects more comprehensive than is intended or foreseen (Leopold, 1987: 148).

Leopold does not assert dogmatically that human-made changes necessarily threaten the continuation of life. He concedes Europe has been transformed over the last two millennia, but that the 'new structure seems to function and to persist'; Europe, he concludes, has a 'resistant biota . . . its inner processes are tough, elastic, resistant to strain' (Leopold, 1987: 148). However, the correct perspective for an ecologist to adopt is global, and the earth is like a diseased body, where some parts seem to function well, but the whole is threatened with death. As with many ecologists, he identified population growth as a major cause of this 'disease':

> The combined evidence of history and ecology seems to support one deduction: the less violent the man-made changes, the greater the probability of successful readjustment in the pyramid. Violence, in turn, varies with human population density; a dense population requires a more violent conversion.
>
> (Leopold, 1987: 149)

Conservationists fall into two groups, labelled by Leopold A and B: group A regards the land as soil and its function as a commodity, whereas group B regards the land as a biota, and its function as 'something broader', but 'how much broader is admittedly in a state of doubt and confusion' (Leopold, 1987: 149). While he may not have been aware of it, this distinction is an early statement of a divide which becomes clear after the 1960s – that between environmentalists and ecologists. Crucial to the coherence of ecologism is an explanation of that 'broader' function or value which troubled Leopold.

## Arne Næss and deep ecology

Arne Næss is credited with coining the contrasting phrases 'deep ecology' (more precisely: 'long-range deep ecology movement') and 'shallow ecology', with the spatial language intended to denote the depth of questioning of human values and reasons for action. Næss presents the idea of depth and comprehensiveness in the form of a table with four levels, with Level 1 being the most comprehensive, or 'deepest':

| Level 4 | Actions | Individual behaviour |
|---|---|---|
| Level 3 | Policies | Particular policies carried out by governmental and non-governmental agencies |
| Level 2 | Platform principles | Packages of policies derived from an ideological standpoint or movement |
| Level 1 | Ultimate values | Grounded in, for example, a comprehensive philosophical or religious position |

Næss argues that we do not have to agree on ultimate values in order to engage in deep ecological action. There is a process of moving up and down the stages, such that action can be guided by a plurality of different sets of ultimate values. The coherence of this idea will be discussed shortly, but the point to make here is that the criticism that deep ecology is intolerant because it fails to respect the pluralism which exists in a modern society is not necessarily valid. Næss's emphasis on the plurality of ultimate values was, in part, born out of his experience in creating cross-cultural peace and ecological activist movements. As Næss argues:

> . . .ecologically responsible policies are concerned only in part with pollution and resource depletion. There are deeper concerns which touch upon principles of diversity, complexity, autonomy, decentralization, symbiosis, egalitarianism, and classlessness.
>
> (Næss, 1973: 95)

What Næss sought to do was develop a set of 'platform principles' (Level 2) – in other words, a manifesto, albeit a non-dogmatic one – around which people with diverse ultimate values can unite. Below are eight principles formulated by Næss and his friend and fellow deep ecologist George Sessions while out on a hiking trip in Death Valley, California:

1. The well-being and flourishing of human and non-human life on Earth have value in themselves (synonyms: intrinsic value, inherent value). These values are independent of the usefulness of the non-human world for human purposes.
2. Richness and diversity of life-forms contribute to the realisation of these values and are also values in themselves.
3. Humans have no right to reduce this richness and diversity except to satisfy vital human needs.
4. The flourishing of human life and cultures is compatible with a substantial decrease of the human population. The flourishing of non-human life requires such a decrease.
5. Present human interference with the non-human world is excessive, and the situation is rapidly worsening.
6. Policies must therefore be changed. These policies affect basic economic, technological, and ideological structures. The resulting state of affairs will be deeply different from the present.
7. The ideological change is mainly that of appreciating life quality (dwelling in situations of inherent value) rather than adhering to an increasingly higher standard of living. There will be a profound awareness of the difference between big and great.
8. Those who subscribe to the foregoing points have an obligation to directly or indirectly try to implement the necessary changes.

(Næss and Sessions cited in Devall and Sessions, 1985: 70)

Unlike Leopold, Næss was a trained philosopher, and so shows a greater awareness of the need for a credible philosophical basis for ecologism. Deep ecology requires an explanation of how particulars, such as individual animals, fit into the whole. He argues that part of the definition of an organism, such as a human being, is that it exists only in relation to something else. He uses the metaphor of the knot – a knot exists only as part of a net, and human beings are knots in the biospherical net (Næss, 1973: 95). Human beings are intrinsically valuable, but any statement of that value must refer to the whole.

Næss accepts that any realistic form of social organisation requires some 'killing, exploitation, and suppression' (1973: 95). However, in principle, we should be biospherical egalitarians, meaning that we ought to have deep respect for all forms of life – to restrict that respect to human beings is to mis-recognise humans, for the value we attach to each other depends on a full understanding of who we are – 'knots in the biospherical net'. Diversity enhances the potential for survival and the chance of new modes of life. Ecological diversity should translate into respect for cultural diversity. However, diversity must be of the right kind – diversity due to class hierarchy is incompatible with the symbiosis inherent in the biospherical net. This is important because it is possible to read into nature hierarchy rather than equality. What Næss must show is that mutual dependence really does imply equality. After all, there is a sense in which a master is dependent on his slave.

Deep ecologists, Næss argues, must fight pollution and resource depletion, and in this struggle, they have found common cause with shallow ecologists, or environmentalists. But such an alliance can be dangerous because it distracts from the comprehensive concerns ecologists should have. For example, if prices or taxes are increased in order to reduce pollution we need to know who will bear the cost – if it is the poor, then the egalitarianism implicit in the biospherical net is not being respected. Deep ecology favours 'soft' scientific research that limits disturbances to the environment, respects traditions, and is aware of our state of ignorance.

Autonomy and decentralisation are central to Næss's understanding of the forms of political organisation appropriate to deep ecology: 'the vulnerability of a form of life is roughly proportional to the weight of influences from afar, from outside the local region in which that form has obtained an ecological equilibrium' (Næss, 1973: 98). A self-sufficient community produces less pollution, and depletes fewer resources, than the existing interdependent world. Such a community is more democratic because the chain of decision-making is much shorter – if decisions are made through a chain of authorities, such as local, national, and supra-national, then the chances of local interests being ignored increase with the addition of every link in the chain.

## Garrett Hardin and the ethics of the lifeboat

Garrett Hardin was a highly influential environmentalist. Although his arguments were neither original, nor profound, there are good reasons for discussing his work. First, he was concerned with a major issue for environmentalists: population growth and control. Second, he is sometimes, and quite erroneously, labelled an ecologist, as distinct from an environmentalist, and his arguments are quoted in political debates against ecologists. Third, he challenged one of the fundamental human rights – the right to procreate – and more generally, his work raises important questions about global justice, questions to which we return in Chapter 19.

Hardin's most famous essay was 'The Tragedy of the Commons', which was based on a presidential address delivered at a meeting of the Pacific Division of the American Association for the Advancement of Science at Utah State University in June 1968. In the following 30 years, it was reprinted in many collections, and Hardin himself revised it several times. The central problem is, by Hardin's own admission, not original; indeed, it is simply a statement of the prisoner's dilemma, which we discussed in Chapter 1, and of the associated problem of common pool (or congestible) goods (see pp. 11–12).

We are to imagine common lands on which herdsmen graze their cattle. So long as the numbers of herdsmen and cattle are low, the commons will recover from the effects of grazing, new grass will grow, the cattle will be fed, and the herdsmen will make a living and not starve. However, if the number of herdsmen and cattle grow – perhaps because population growth is no longer kept in check by war and disease – there will come a point at which the commons will not recover, and indeed deteriorate to the point where even the original low level of grazing would not be supported. As we saw in our analysis of the prisoner's dilemma, even if an individual herdsman recognises the consequences of his actions – that is, can see clearly the 'tragedy' before him – it is in his interests to continue grazing.

Hardin makes a point that appears to echo those of deep ecologists: the harm from an individual action cannot be 'pictured' – the effects may not be discernible for years, and effects are, in any case, cumulative. Such is the case with the tragedy of the commons. Morality must consider the full effects of an action; it must be 'system sensitive' (Hardin, 1974: 562). Without questioning the validity of Hardin's argument, it is important to distinguish his 'system' from that of Leopold or Næss – the long-term effects that concern Hardin are the effects on *humanity*. Hardin's argument, while concerned with environmental degradation, is thoroughly anthropocentric.

Almost all moral and political theorists have accepted that actions have to be assessed against their full consequences, so Hardin's argument is directed much more at popular moral beliefs, rather than at previous thinkers. Hardin argues that a popular morality focused simply on the rights of individuals, without regard to the system will have catastrophic consequences. In particular, he objects to the claim made by the United Nations, as restated in the Declaration on

Social Progress and Development (1969) that 'parents have the exclusive right to determine freely and responsibly the number and spacing of their children' (Article 4):

> If each human family were dependent only on its own resources; if the children of improvident parents starved to death; if, thus, overbreeding brought its own 'punishment' to the germ line – then there would be no public interest in controlling the breeding of families. But our society is deeply committed to the welfare state, and hence is confronted with another aspect of the tragedy of the commons.
>
> (Hardin, 1994: 334–5)

Hardin's comment makes reference to 'our society' – meaning the United States – and its commitment to the welfare state. The tragedy of the commons is, of course, a metaphor for the world's resources, and not every society has a welfare state. However, Hardin's audience is his own people, and the question of population growth is, for Hardin, closely linked to that of immigration. Since population growth is much higher in the developing world than in the developed world, migration from the former to the latter is a consequence of population growth. And Hardin has three fairly straightforward policy proposals: end the despoliation of the 'commons' insofar as this is within the power of the United States and other developed countries to do; stop food aid to the developing world; and severely restrict migration to the developed world.

We will say something about these proposals shortly, but we need to consider Hardin's underlying philosophical position. Hardin is not a philosopher, and so we have to engage in some speculation to capture his basic position, but it seems to amount to this: human beings are naturally selfish, or at least, they are overwhelmingly concerned with their own survival. That some people are lucky to live in relatively wealthy societies and others in poor societies may be cause for a bad conscience, but it does not change the ethical situation. That most Americans are descended from people who 'stole' from Native Americans does not mean that they have an obligation to help the less fortunate:

> We are all the descendants of thieves, and the world's resources are inequitably distributed. But we must begin the journey to tomorrow from the point where we are today. We cannot remake the past. We cannot safely divide the wealth equitably among all peoples so long as people reproduce at different rates. To do so would guarantee that our grandchildren and everyone else's grandchildren, would have only a ruined world to inhabit.
>
> (Hardin, 1974: 567)

Hardin employs the analogy of a lifeboat to illustrate his argument. Two-thirds of the world is desperately poor, while a third is relatively wealthy. Each of those wealthy nations can be likened to a lifeboat. In the ocean outside the lifeboat swim the poor of the world, who would like to clamber on board. If there are 50 people on a boat designed for 60, and a hundred swimming in the water around the boat, what are we – where 'we' means those in the boat – to do? We could respond to the Christian call to be 'our brother's keeper' or the Marxist injunction to give to each 'according to his needs', but since all 100 are our brothers (and sisters) and all are equally in need, we have to choose: we could choose ten, which would leave us with no emergency capacity and would require us to explain why we did not admit the other 90, or we could take all hundred, with the consequence that the boat will sink. Alternatively, each of the 50 could choose to sacrifice their life, but that altruistic act will not solve the global crisis.

The 'harsh ethics' of the lifeboat become harsher when population growth is taken into account. The people in the boat are doubling their numbers every 87 years. Those swimming on the outside are doubling their numbers every 35 years. Hardin argues that it is misleading to talk about satisfying human needs, as if needs were minimal conditions, such as basic food and health care, which once met left a surplus to be distributed. Rather, because the satisfaction of needs has the effect of increasing the population, there is no end to their satisfaction. The only ethical response is to refuse to satisfy the needs by restricting immigration – stopping people getting on the lifeboat – and not giving food aid to those 'outside the boat'. A consequence of this harsh policy would be that countries, once solely responsible for their own well-being, would learn to manage, albeit after a great deal of suffering.

## Joseph Tainter – energy, complexity, and sustainability

Sustainability is a concept much used by ecologists and environmentalists, but what is it? To get a better sense of it, we need to link it to energy and complexity. One way to characterise human history is as the increasing exploitation of energy. All living things require energy. Energy is defined by physicists as 'work': if you pick up a chair the work done on the chair is the force required to lift it. The first law of thermodynamics states that energy is never lost from a closed system (conservation of energy). The second law states that entropy never decreases, meaning, in effect, that in a closed system life will run down. Without food, human beings will die. Energy is locked up in food and released slowly. The production of food itself requires energy. The earth is not, however, a closed system because it gains energy (primarily) from the sun and life-forms survive because they capture energy. However, ecologists argue there are limits to energy. Humans have exploited the energy bound up in dead organisms (fossil fuels). While there are 'renewable' sources of energy, these are often less easily exploited than fossil fuels and they actually require non-renewable sources of energy to produce them: wind turbines must be built and moved into place such that they already embody energy before they start producing it.

Perhaps the most important transition in the use of energy was the agricultural revolution (or Neolithic Revolution) that first began in the Fertile Crescent (modern Syria and Iraq) around 10,000 years ago. That revolution brought in its train greater technological and social complexity. There was a rudimentary division of labour; not everybody had to work on the land. But energy and complexity are not straightforwardly connected. Theorists of complexity used to argue that excess energy – for example, food beyond what is required for basic survival – enabled the development of more complex societies. However, complexity can sometimes drive the search for new sources of energy (Tainter, 2006: 92).

As Tainter argues, increasing complexity can be a way of solving problems, but there are diminishing returns. Both hunter-gatherer and peasant-based societies experience underproduction: the working day is surprisingly short and there is much leisure and rest-time. This is because without complex industrialised agriculture there are diminishing gains from each extra hour of production. Likewise with knowledge: early science was characterised by rather general problems and scientists were not highly specialised. As scientific enquiry advances so do the complexity of the problems and marginal productivity falls (Tainter, 2006: 94–5).

Thomas Malthus (1766–1834) famously argued that population increases geometrically while subsistence (energy) grows only arithmetically. Every advance in productivity is consumed by population growth; per capita income never increases. And indeed without 'checks', the population will outstrip energy resources, such as food. Inevitably, checks do operate. They take the form of 'positive checks', such as famine, disease, and war, and 'preventative checks', such as self-assumed or imposed population controls (Habakkuk, 1959: 100–1).

Many economists argue Malthus was wrong in his predictions; he failed to see how changes in social structures might bring down the birth rate while people can at the same time enjoy the benefits of increased productivity (Trewavas, 2002). Other economists say Malthus was right about some parts of the world, but not others (Weil and Wilde, 2009). But there is another way of interpreting Malthus: he was not predicting what would happen with population growth, but rather posing a challenge: population growth might outstrip energy resources, so how is a society going to respond? It is a problem-solving question.

Tainter argues there are three possible consequences of stretched energy resources: societal collapse; resiliency and recovery through simplification; and sustainable problem-solving based on increasing complexity subsidised by new resources (Tainter, 2006: 98). Drawing on historical examples, he identifies collapse with the Roman Empire, simplification with the early Byzantine recovery of the early fifth century, and complexity with Europe (continuing into the present). The Romans tried to solve their energy challenges by creating ever more complex bureaucratic structures, including punitive forms of taxation. The Byzantines retrenched and simplified, thus cutting their costs. The Europeans from the Renaissance onwards engaged in seemingly costly military competition, but it drove global expansion and the discovery of new sources of energy. In England, forests were cleared to provide energy, but this was a finite resource and so coal was mined. When shallow seams had been exhausted, deep mines were required, but these easily flooded, and so steam power was required to pump the water out. And steam powered the industrial revolution. The potential exhaustion of fossil fuels – combined with war technology – led to the development of nuclear energy.

Some interesting conclusions can be drawn from the ideas of complexity and sustainability (Tainter, 2006: 99):

- Sustainability is about problem-solving, not consuming less.
- Complexity is a primary problem-solving tool.
- There can be diminishing returns to complexity; it can become ineffective.
- Sustainability may require more consumption of resources, rather than less: you have to be able to afford sustainability.

## The argument so far

From our discussion of Leopold and Næss, and drawing on other ecological writings, we can summarise the key components of ecologism as follows:

1. The belief that there is something which can be called 'ecology' or the 'biosphere'; this is an interconnected whole on which all life depends.
2. The natural world, which includes all forms of life, has intrinsic value and should not be used as an instrument to satisfy human wants. There is much debate within the ecological movement about the nature of this value, and we discuss this below. However, there is an intuitive sense that ecologism requires being 'in touch' with nature.
3. The quality of human life will be enhanced once human beings recognise 1 and 2: ecologism is not concerned to devalue human beings, but rather to get us to think about who we really are.
4. The structure of the natural world should be mirrored in the social and political world; the interdependence – but diversity – of the former translates into a commitment to a more equal society, respectful of difference.

5. To achieve ecological and social justice requires not simply a change in the social, economic, and political organisation of society, but a fundamental change in human motivation.
6. Ecologism is a distinct ideology, which sees in both liberalism (capitalism) and socialism a common enemy: industrialism. Industrialism *by definition* cannot be compatible with an ecological consciousness. For ecologists, the earth is a physical object, with natural physical limits; industrialism, which is committed to economic growth, cannot respect the integrity and finitude of the earth.
7. Ecologists seek a sustainable society – that is, one which is in tune with nature. In practical terms, this requires a reduction in consumption.
8. Although there is a division within deep ecology, a strong theme in ecological thought is distrust of technological fixes – that is, a belief that advances in technology will overcome environmental problems. However:
9. Sustainability might require increasing, not decreasing, complexity.

## Critique of ecologism

We have set out the central elements of ecologism. In this final section, we explore some of its ethical and political weaknesses. Our aim is not to provide conclusive objections but to raise problems, with the intention of stimulating debate. We pose a series of questions, which we then discuss.

## Do ecologists have a plausible account of why we should value 'nature'?

The central claim of ecologism is that there is value in the natural world that cannot be explained simply by reference to human wants, needs, or consciousness: nature, or the environment, or the ecosystem has *intrinsic value*. The difficulty with this claim is that to say something has value is to make an evaluation, and such evaluation presupposes a capacity to evaluate, and arguably only humans possess such a capacity; therefore, values are human-centred.

An ecologist might respond by asking us to imagine a beautiful valley that no human being has ever seen – would something be lost if that valley ceased to exist? If we conclude that something would be lost, then does that not show that value is independent of human consciousness? The difficulty is that the question asks us to *imagine* such a valley; while it is possible that a valley exists which no human eyes have ever seen, we nonetheless have the *concept* of a valley and criteria for evaluating its beauty. Perhaps, however, the ecologist is making a different claim: value does indeed depend on the human capacity to evaluate, but it does not follow that values are human-centred.

## Can ecologists respect the created world – that is, culture?

Throughout this chapter, there has been an implied distinction between nature and society (or culture), or the natural world and the human world. This accords with the everyday sense that there is a distinction: imagine looking out of the window at a tree-lined street of apartment blocks. Human beings have constructed the apartments and planted the trees, but because the apartments function according to human design, whereas the trees, despite being planted in neat lines, develop according to processes understood, but not set in motion, by human beings, we reasonably enough say the trees are part of nature, and the apartments are part of the artificial, human world.

That distinction is valid, but difficulties arise for ecologists when they make further claims: (a) that the natural world forms an interconnected whole *set apart from* the human world, and on which the human world is dependent; (b) that the natural world has intrinsic value, whereas the human world does not. The interconnectedness–separateness thesis can be challenged in the following way: there is no part of the globe untouched by human activity, and therefore insofar as there are connections, these are between the two worlds. Of course, the ecological critique rests precisely on accepting as a fact that human beings have transformed the world, and for the worse! Their point is that we depend on the natural world, understood as connected through complex processes, such that the human world is secondary. This claim could be accepted by *environmentalists*: certainly, if we do not allow, say, fish stocks to be replenished because of over-fishing or marine pollution, there will be no fish in the supermarket, and no profits to be made from fish.

An *ecological* argument would require accepting not simply (a), but also (b): the natural world is separate and valuable in a way the human world is not. This is open to challenge. Venice is clearly one of the great human creations – a world heritage site – built on a lagoon and requiring considerable human intervention in the natural environment. That city is under threat of sinking due to the combined effects of subsidence and rising sea levels; in addition, the lagoon is polluted through heavy industrial activity in the region. That there are natural processes at work, which are in part the result of a global environmental crisis, can be accepted by *environmentalists*, but that Venice itself has less value than naturally occurring phenomena is surely open to challenge. That, however, is the conclusion that an ecologist must draw.

The priority given to the natural world by ecologists rests in part on a 'hierarchy of needs', with physical reproductive needs at the base, and other needs, or 'wants', of lesser importance. For example, many ecologists regard food production as more important than tourism, and indeed, many are hostile to tourism. Yet in an advanced capitalist system tourism satisfies the needs of those economically dependent on it.

Ecologists sometimes suggest we can have the benefits of the modern human world even if we remove the material conditions – industrialism – for modernity. Kirkpatrick Sale argues for a self-sufficient community, which does not engage in significant trade with other communities; such a community would ensure 'a wide range of food, some choices in necessities and some sophistication in luxuries, [and] the population to sustain a university and large hospital and a symphony orchestra' (Sale cited in Dobson, 2000: 118). Setting aside economic considerations about whether a low-trade world could sustain a high level of medical care, the social world that gives rise to relatively cosmopolitan institutions such as universities or orchestras has been one in which there is interaction between communities and cultures. Perhaps, the argument is that we should preserve the cultural achievements of a modern industrial society, but without the costs; if that were Sale's point, then it would amount to a much more generous compliment to an industrial society than most ecologists are prepared to pay.

## Are ecologists hostile to human rights?

Ecologists maintain that the language of rights – of individual entitlements held against other people – is part of a false, anthropocentric view of the world. Not only are rights – and especially rights to private property – destructive of nature, but they present a flawed model of human relations. People would be happier in more communal relations. It is interesting that many ecologists are sceptical about animal rights. Certainly among those most hostile to the notion that animals have rights are the anthropocentric theorists of the traditional ideologies, such as socialism or liberalism, but the extension of rights from human beings to non-human animals derives from an individualist world-view: the theory of animal rights does not challenge anthropocentrism. Ecologists, on the other hand, tend to have a robust attitude to animal life, accepting that all animals are locked into a cycle of life and death, and the whole – Gaia – is more important than the parts.

Ecologists must have an account of human motivation, for presumably something must change in terms of the relationship between human beings and nature. There are three possibilities: (a) changes in technology that conserve resources, slow down depletion or allow for economic growth without serious environmental consequences; (b) changes in the way we organise society, providing incentives or sanctions so as to alter behaviour; (c) changes in human motivation, which alter behaviour without requiring external incentives or sanctions. Ecologists are sceptical about (a), and prefer that (b), social and political changes, follow from (c), changes in motivation. It is significant that Hardin rejects (a) and (c) but endorses (b), arguing that only coercive measures will avert a global disaster.

A thread that runs through ecologism is that human behaviour in an industrialised society is bad for the environment, but also bad for human beings. This suggests there is a 'real' human nature, which is fundamentally good, but is distorted by human acquisitiveness, fed by, for example, advertising. Since the achievement of a sustainable society depends on a change in motivation, a great deal depends on the plausibility of this view of human nature. Furthermore, ecologists must show it is impossible to create and maintain a sustainable society without a change in motivation: technology will not fix environmental problems, and coercion is unacceptable and will lead to authoritarian regimes. Ecologists must argue that the real human nature will emerge quickly as we move towards sustainability, perhaps because the benefits of such a society will soon be apparent.

## Are ecologists hostile to reason and rationality?

It was argued that ecologists have to make some concession to human-centredness: for nature to have intrinsic value, there must exist beings capable of evaluation. Yet there is, arguably, a further concession to be made to anthropocentrism: the capacity to evaluate depends upon complex rational machinery that connects different values, experiences, and actions. Rationality requires language and not simply a non-linguistic observation of nature. The idea of interconnectedness, which is a core doctrine of ecologists, is made possible by human reason; arguably, there is no interconnectedness in the world, except what the human mind produces. This is not saying there is no physical world external to the mind, nor that its value depends on the subjective attitudes of individual human beings, but rather the human mind, defined as a set of capacities shared by individual human beings, and made possible through language, is the means through which the world is viewed as interconnected.

More specifically, ecologists have an incoherent attitude to natural science. A major aspect of natural science is the acquisition of knowledge through repeatable experiments – experiments that must take place in a controlled environment. Science necessarily abstracts from the particular and seeks to acquire knowledge by finding something which is not unique to a particular thing – the individual rat in the laboratory is only of scientific interest insofar as its physiological or psychological behaviour is generalisable, meaning that its behaviour must not be peculiar to that particular rat. This observation is not about the ethics of vivisection, but rather about how we acquire knowledge of the world: natural science is advanced through distance from nature, and not by being in touch with it. Yet at the centre of ecologism as a political movement is a continual appeal to the scientific evidence of environmental degradation – evidence acquired through a fundamentally anti-ecological rationality.

In part, the ambivalent attitude to natural science has its roots in the ecologists' conflation of science and technology and, relatedly, of human rationality in general with a particular variant of it: instrumental rationality. Science developed in the early modern period as the result of changes in humans' understanding of their place in the world – only once the material world is seen as lacking in intrinsic spiritual qualities is it possible to treat it in an experimental way (Kuhn, 1962: 111–35). Technology, on the other hand, dates to the earliest human activity – it is simply the marshalling of natural processes to serve human ends. Of course, advances in scientific understanding have aided technological advance, and many ecologists will argue that neither science nor technology are in themselves to be rejected, but rather it is the degree of intervention in, and alteration of, natural processes that is at issue. The danger with ecologism is that it fails to distinguish human enquiry – the drive to understand the world – and human wants, that is, the desire to use the natural world for human ends. Human-centredness is narrowly defined by ecologists as instrumental reason; nature is used as a means, or instrument, for human ends. But you do not need to be an ecologist in order to challenge instrumental reason; you can move completely within a human-centred view of the world and still raise *rational* objections to the idea that because we have the scientific knowledge to do something, such as clone human beings, we should do it.

## Is ecologism compatible with human equality?

As has been argued, ecologists tend not to respect the distinction between facts and values – is and ought. Of course, we should not accept uncritically the claim that the distinction cannot be bridged, but here we are concerned with ecologists' arguments. The approach adopted by many ecologists is to draw *analogies* between the natural world and the social world. Andrew Dobson offers the following (Dobson, 2000: 22):

| Nature | | Society and politics |
|---|---|---|
| Diversity | → | Toleration, stability, and democracy |
| Interdependence | → | Equality |
| Longevity | → | Tradition |
| Nature as 'female' | → | A particular conception of feminism |

In effect, ecologists are asking us to look at nature, consider its intrinsic value, and draw conclusions about how we should behave to it, and to each other. The problem, which Dobson acknowledges, is that people can draw quite different conclusions from nature: interdependence can imply hierarchy rather than equality, and the supposed femininity of nature may imply natural roles that restrict human autonomy. Dobson talks about 'lessons from nature', but it is not simply that we disagree about the social implications of our observation of the natural world, but rather there are no lessons – or, in more philosophical language, reasons for action – to be derived from such observation.

At a more practical level, there are concerns about the impact of Green policies on the poor – that is, the poor in developed countries and the poorest nations. The demand made by the developed world that the Global South severely curb their carbon emissions is regarded by the latter as hypocritical: Western Europe and North America have enjoyed the benefits of pollution as a result of their early industrialisation and are now denying the majority world the possibility of economic growth. Within the industrialised West, the imposition of green taxes impacts disproportionately on the poor, because they must commit a greater proportion of income to paying for energy. These problems are not insuperable, but it is significant that Green parties across all the developed countries draw their support primarily from the better off.

## Is ecologism compatible with value pluralism?

Critics argue that ecologism, unlike environmentalism, is not simply a political programme, but requires individuals to endorse religious or spiritual beliefs they might reasonably reject. Despite Arne Næss's insistence that ecologists can come together from a variety of different religious and philosophical perspectives, the ecological critique of industrialism identifies human motivation as the source of acquisitive attitudes, demands very significant changes in the way society is organised, and holds out the prospect of a reconciliation between human beings and nature that extends beyond political ideas. Most orthodox monotheists – Jews, Christians, Muslims – would interpret ecological ideas as a form of pantheism (earth as God) or panentheism (earth as part of God), standing against the metaphysical separation of God as creator from His creation. Many atheists would treat ecologism with the same suspicion that they treat other religions.

### Nuclear power

Civil nuclear power cannot historically be separated from military nuclear power. For example, the United Kingdom's early civil nuclear programme was largely driven by military requirements, to such an extent that it almost resulted in a catastrophe at Windscale in 1957 (Jones, 2016; Behind Designs, 2020). The fear of another Chernobyl-type accident somewhere in the world cannot be discounted.

Renewables are often the preferred energy option for Greens. But wind and solar power are less easily exploited than nuclear power and actually require non-renewable sources of energy to produce them: wind turbines have to be built and moved into place, such they already embody energy before they begin producing it. In addition, they are less reliable than traditional energy sources and can be detrimental to the environment. To calculate the benefits of an energy source, you have to calculate the Energy Returned on Energy Invested (EROI).

Charles Frank calculated the EROI of different forms of energy (Frank, 2014). Costs include capital (time and cost of building a plant), intermittency (unreliability), and emissions. A cost-benefit analysis shows that in the cases of wind and solar, the costs outweigh the benefits. Hydro is efficient. Nuclear has huge capacity costs – it is expensive to build a nuclear power station – but it yields considerable benefits in terms of avoided emissions. Combined Cycle Gas is also cost-effective.

The resistance among ecologists to nuclear power rests on its connection to nuclear weapons programmes, the very long time-frame for storing radioactive waste, and the risk of another Chernobyl or Fukushima, and perhaps an intuitive feeling that it is the least 'natural' form of energy, in that it has required the greatest human intervention in nature. But the harm resulting from a nuclear catastrophe has to be balanced against its likelihood. And the risks of further global warming if we do not use nuclear power have to be placed on the benefit side of the case for nuclear.

## Conclusion

Ecologism's distinctiveness can be found in its emphasis on the interconnectedness of life on earth and the demand for a fundamental change in the human relationship to nature – where nature, of course, is part of humanity and humanity part of nature. It offers a critique of both liberalism and socialism, and while recognising the important differences between those ideologies, it finds commonalities: a commitment to economic growth that is incompatible with the finite nature of the earth. Humanity's ambitions exceed the resources of its home.

## References

Behind Designs (2020). Windscale Disaster: How the British Chernobyl Was Stopped. Behind Designs YouTube Channel, viewed 3 July 2021, https://www.youtube.com/watch?v=daXkyKUSknE

Close, C. and Delwit, P. (2016). Green Parties and Elections. In *Green Parties in Europe*. Routledge, 255–78.

Declaration on Social Progress and Development (1969), accessed 9 July 2021, Office of the High Commissioner, https://www.ohchr.org/Documents/ProfessionalInterest/progress.pdf

Devall, B. and Sessions, G. (eds) (1985). *Deep Ecology*. Salt Lake City, UT: Gibbs Smith.

Dobson, A. (2000). *Green Political Thought*. London: Routledge.

Frank, C. R. (2014). The Net Benefits of Low and no-Carbon Electricity Technologies. *The Brookings Institution*.

Habakkuk, H. J. (1959). Thomas Robert Malthus, FRS (1766–1834). *Notes and Records of the Royal Society of London, 14*(1), 99–108.

Hardin, G. (1974). Living on a Lifeboat. *Bioscience, 10*(24), 561–8.

Hardin, G. (1994). 'The Tragedy of the Commons', in C. Pierce and D. Ven de Veer (eds.), *People, Penguins and Plastic Trees: Basic Issues in Environmental Ethics*. London: Wadsworth, 330–8.

Kuhn, T. (1962). *The Structure of Scientific Revolutions*. Chicago, IL and London: University of Chicago Press.

Jones, S. (2016). Health Effects of the Windscale Pile Fire. *Journal of Radiological Protection, 36*(4), E23.

Lemonick, M. (2009). Freeman Dyson takes on the Climate Establishment. *YaleEnvironment360*, accessed 9 July 2021, https://e360.yale.edu/features/freeman_dyson_takes_on_the_climate_establishment

Leopold, A. (1987). *A Sand Country Almanac, and Sketches Here and There*. New York and Oxford: Oxford University Press.

Lomborg, B. (2016). Impact of Current Climate Proposals. *Global Policy, 7*(1), 109–18.

Lovelock, J. (2004). Nuclear Power Is the Only Green Solution. *Independent*, 31.

Næss, A. (1973). The Shallow and the Deep, Long Range Ecology Movements. *Inquiry 16*, 95–100.

Tainter, J. A. (2006). Social Complexity and Sustainability. *Ecological Complexity, 3*(2), 91–103.

Trewavas, A. (2002). Malthus Foiled Again and Again. *Nature*, *418*(6898), 668–70.

Weil, D. N. and Wilde, J. (2009). How Relevant Is Malthus for Economic Development Today? *American Economic Review*, *99*(2), 255–60.

## Further reading

Overviews and histories of environmentalism, ecologism, and green political theory: Andrew Dobson, *Green Political Thought*, Third Edition (Routledge, 2012); Steve Vanderheiden, *Environmental Political Theory* (Polity, 2020); David Pepper, *The Roots of Modern Environmentalism* (Routledge, 2019; originally published 1984). Two useful collections of essays: Teena Gabrielson et al. (eds.), *The Oxford Handbook of Environmental Political Theory* (Oxford University Press, 2019); Tom Perreault (ed.), *The Routledge Handbook of Political Ecology* (Routledge, 2019). Other works: Robin Kimmerer, *The Democracy of Species* (Penguin, 2021); Adrian Parr, *Birth of a New Earth: The Radical Politics of Environmentalism* (Columbia University Press, 2017); Keith Woodhouse, *The Ecocentrists: A History of Radical Environmentalists* (Columbia University Press, 2020).

**Part 5**

# Global political theory

# Chapter 18

# Human rights

## Introduction

A human right is an entitlement to treatment that a person enjoys simply by virtue of being a human being. Although the concept can be traced back to the eighteenth century Enlightenment – the 'rights of man' – it is only in the twentieth century that human rights became a major concept in political discourse. The widespread ratification by states of the Universal Declaration of Human Rights (UDHR), which was created in 1948, three years after the end of the Second World War, has changed world politics. Although individuals are frequently denied their human rights, even by states purporting to respect them, the fact of the existence of human rights has shifted international politics from being based simply on states' interest to one based on the recognition that individuals have claims against their own state. But human rights are open to the criticism that they are the product of a particular time and place – post-eighteenth century Europe, or the West – and their 'imposition' is a form of imperialism.

## Key questions

- What is a human right? Is it a moral, legal, or political concept (or all three)?
- Are human rights a Western, liberal imposition?
- Must human rights be absolute? Are there any absolute human rights?

## What are human rights?

Human rights are requirements to be treated in a certain way which derive their legitimacy simply from the fact of humanity. As such they are applicable irrespective of time and place. If we were to say that a person's rights are conditional on her being a citizen of a particular state, or belonging to a particular culture, then the rights would not rest simply on the fact of being a human being, and they would not be universal. This raises a difficulty for human rights discourse. The language of human rights is a modern phenomenon, traceable to the eighteenth century Enlightenment, but only embodied in legal documents in the twentieth century. This suggests that human rights are culturally specific – the product of a particular time (the modern period) and a particular place (Western Europe). For critics of human rights, the problem of cultural relativism is thought to be fatal – the alleged universalism of human rights simply masks a form of cultural imperialism.

DOI: 10.4324/9780429424106-24

Case study 18.1

# Is torture ever right?

**PHOTO 18.1**  Here. A vigil on United Nations (UN) International Day, 2015, London, England. © Peter Marshall / Alamy Stock Photo.

The United Nations Convention against Torture defines torture as:

> . . .any act by which severe pain or suffering, whether physical or mental, is intentionally inflicted on a person for such purposes as obtaining from him, or a third person, information or a confession, punishing him for an act he or a third person has committed or is suspected of having committed, or intimidating or coercing him or a third person, or for any reason based on discrimination of any kind, when such pain or suffering is inflicted by or at the instigation of or with the consent or acquiescence of a public official or other person acting in an official capacity. It does not include pain or suffering arising only from, inherent in, or incidental to, lawful sanctions.

The Convention, which has been signed by 171 countries, requires signatories to take effective measures to prevent torture on their territory. It cannot be qualified or suspended (derogated). Subordinate officials cannot evade legal responsibility for their actions on grounds that they were only following orders. States cannot send people to countries where they would be tortured.

Some human rights, as a matter of legal fact, can be overridden on occasion, or suspended, or limited. In these cases, the right can be derogated. In the case of the Convention, torture is absolutely prohibited.

Question: Should there be an absolute prohibition on torture?

# Human rights after Nuremberg

There is no doubt that while human rights are claimed to be universal, the widespread use of the concept is a relatively recent phenomenon. It is only with the formulation and signing of the Universal Declaration of Human Rights (UDHR) that respect for human rights has become a significant consideration in domestic and international politics. And alongside the philosophical discourse and political rhetoric, there has also developed a body of international human rights law and a set of international legal institutions, such as the International Criminal Court (ICC) in The Hague (Netherlands). So there is a history to human rights.

The UDHR was 'adopted and proclaimed' by the General Assembly of the newly formed United Nations on 10 December 1948. It was developed against the background of the Nuremberg War Crimes Trials, which followed the defeat of Germany and its allies in May 1945. There were two sets of trials: those of the 'major war criminals', before the International Military Tribunal (1945–46), and those of the 'lesser war criminals' before the US Nuremberg Military Tribunals (1946–49). The Nuremberg process was criticised as a series of show trials based on 'victor's justice'. After all, among the indictments were acts that had undoubtedly been carried out by the Allies, such as the British air war against Germany, which deliberately targeted citizens, and the murder of German prisoners of war by the Soviet Union. However, Nuremberg is significant for the study of human rights, in part because of its flaws and, in part, because it introduced novel concepts. The legally significant features of the Nuremberg process were as follows:

- The indictment, or charges made against the defendants, were created *ex-post facto* and were not related to the laws of Germany. The indictment contained four counts (types of charge): (a) conspiracy to wage an aggressive war; (b) planning, preparation, and waging of an aggressive war; (c) war crimes, that included, for example, the mistreatment of prisoners of war; and (d) crimes against humanity.
- The compulsion defence – 'I was only obeying orders' – was removed.
- The *tu quoque* defence was removed – *ad hominem tu quoque* means 'at the person, you too' and effectively amounts to the defendant saying: 'you committed the same crimes, so you have no authority to judge me'.
- The indictment made reference to violations of 'international conventions', but there is no citation of those conventions, with the implication that it was a loose term meaning the 'general standards of criminal law in civilised societies'.

Although the motivation among the leadership of the Allied powers to create the Nuremburg process was largely political, there was a kind of moral consciousness at work, a consciousness that became stronger in later decades. Consequently, Nuremberg posed a problem: on the one hand, there was a sense of what can be termed the 'objective wrongness' of what the German regime had done. On the other hand, the trials seemed to depend on the creation of *post hoc*, or retroactive, laws. Retroactive laws violate the principle that there can be no crime without an antecedent law: if you do something that is legal at the time, you should not be prosecuted. With retroactive laws power is arbitrary. (Other troubling aspects of Nuremberg included the rejection of the *tu quoque* and compulsion defences.) There has been considerable debate among legal and political theorists about the retroactivity. Some theorists argue German law was suspended at some point during the 1930s, and therefore, the laws of Weimar Germany (1918–33) should form part of the basis of the indictment. Other theorists appeal to conventions, such as the prohibition on murder, which all 'right-thinking' human beings, and all properly functioning legal systems recognise as valid.

The point about Nuremberg is that German law of the nazi period could not form the basis of the judgement, and so other laws or conventions, not rooted in a particular legal system, had to be used. And Nuremberg is not simply an interesting historical case. It has relevance for contemporary debates about human rights. If there are human rights as defined at the beginning of this section, then they are universal, and that universality extends across national boundaries and across times. The Nuremberg problem will not disappear when the last alleged nazi war criminal has died, for it is fundamentally a philosophical problem: how can there be human rights if there are no laws embodying those rights? But if human rights only exist where there are laws stating those rights, how can they be universal? The post-Nuremberg codification of human rights in the UDHR and the Genocide Convention (1948) helps to solve a legal problem, but not the political–philosophical one. The UDHR was (eventually) signed by the governments of most states, and through the force of treaty law, human rights have been given legal validity. Had there been such a declaration in the 1920s to which Germany had signed up, and that was not rescinded by the Hitler regime, there would have been a clearer legal basis for Nuremberg (there was a basis for the third count of war crimes: the Geneva Conventions of 1864, 1906, and 1929). However, this does not solve the philosophical problem: if a nation refuses to sign up to any human rights conventions, does that mean it is not obliged to respect human rights?

## Conceptual ambiguities

This last question – and the distinction between legal and philosophical problems – reveals an ambiguity at the heart of human rights discourse. When we use the term human rights are we referring to a set of legal rights, or to moral rights, or perhaps, to some form of political rhetoric that is based neither on legal nor moral grounds? If human rights equate to certain legal rights enjoyed by individuals through international law, then disputes about human rights will take place in a legal framework, by reference to legal documents and judgements. If, however, human rights are moral rights, then disputes are settled by reference to moral concepts and moral arguments. Put simply, as legal rights human rights are individual entitlements backed up by the force of law; as moral rights, they are individual entitlements supported by the force of argument. As tools of international politics, human rights are intended to secure certain outcomes: a state widely recognised as violating human rights may find itself shunned by other states, and consequently, its interests damaged. Many advocates of human rights rely on a mixture of treaty law and 'shame' to advance their cause. However, the political uses of human rights can generate cynicism. One of the justifications given for the bombing of Serbia in 1999 was that it was an 'exceptional measure to prevent an overwhelming humanitarian catastrophe', namely the mass deportation and killing of Kosovars (Greenwood, 2002: 158). Yet the same description could have applied to the situation from 1995 to 2009 in the province of Chechnya, where Russia attempted to suppress – ultimately successfully – a breakaway movement and engaged in a serious violation of human rights. The reasons for action in Kosovo and inaction in Chechnya are, in small part, logistical, but mainly the recognition of realpolitik: Russia has nuclear weapons.

The best approach for further study of the morality, legality, and politics of human rights is a consideration of human rights documents, and in the next section we focus on two: the UDHR and the European Convention on Human Rights (ECHR). However, before discussing these documents, some comments on the pre-twentieth century origins of human rights are in order. Certainly, the idea that humans have rights by virtue of their humanity can be traced back to the eighteenth century 'rights of man' and these rights are grounded in the Enlightenment conception of the human being as a rational agent. However, while many Enlightenment thinkers were reluctant to extend such rights to non-European peoples, and in some cases to women, it could be argued that the logic of rational agency implies that *prima facie* all human beings have rights. But there are attempts to trace the origins of human rights much further back in time and, what is more, demonstrate they have both Western and non-Western sources. Religious documents, such as the Vedas, the Bible (Hebrew and Christian), and the Qur'an, it is argued, either make it explicit or at least imply standards of treatment, and duties and obligations that are universal. These attempts to show human rights have plural sources of justification are really motivated by a contemporary concern to dispel the impression that human rights are a Western, imperialistic imposition on non-Western cultures. Such a discourse may, in fact, serve a useful function in generating respect for human rights, but there is a problem: a proselytising religion, such as Christianity or Islam, is implicitly universal, but it does not follow that the 'rights' it accords are based on 'humanity'. Rather, a person is equal as a Christian or a Muslim, and insofar as Christianity respects non-Christians or Islam non-Muslims that respect is grounded in a view of the 'other' as a potential convert.

## Human rights conventions

Literature on human rights tends to fall into two groups, with limited crossover between them: human rights law and philosophical discussions of human rights. While respecting the difference between these approaches it is useful for students of political theory to establish the connections between them, because legality and morality are both important in debates about the relationship between the state and citizen.

## Universal Declaration of Human Rights (1948)

The UDHR consists of a Preamble and 30 articles (see UDHR). The Preamble asserts that the 'inherent dignity and of the equal and inalienable rights of all members of the human family is the foundation of freedom, justice and peace in the world'. Without specifying the events, it acknowledges the 'barbarous acts which have outraged the conscience of mankind' and asserts that human rights must be protected through law.

The 30 articles are reproduced in summary form below. We have grouped them together for the purpose of discussion; they are not, in fact, grouped in this way in the UDHR.

| Article(s) | |
| --- | --- |
| 1–2 | Human beings should be treated equally, irrespective of personal characteristics or citizenship. |
| 3 | Right to life, liberty, and security of person. |
| 4–5 | Prohibition on slavery and torture. |
| 6–11 | Equality before the law: equal protection by the state; right to an effective remedy for violation of one's rights; prohibition on arbitrary arrest and detention; right to a fair trial; presumption of innocence until guilt is proven; and prohibition on retroactive laws. |
| 12 | Prohibition on arbitrary interference in private life. |
| 13–14 | Freedom of movement, including emigration; right to asylum in another country. |
| 15 | Right to nationality; prohibition on deprivation of nationality. |
| 16 | Right to marry; prohibition on forced marriage. |

| 17 | Right to own property; prohibition on arbitrary seizure of property. |
|----|----|
| 18–20 | Freedom of thought, conscience and religion; freedom of opinion and expression; right to peaceful assembly; and prohibition on compulsion to belong to an association. |
| 21 | Right to political participation; equal access to public service; and 'the will of the people shall be the basis of the authority of the government'. |
| 22–26 | Right to social security; right to work, and the free choice of employment; equal pay for equal work; right to 'just and favourable remuneration'; right to join a trade union; right to rest and leisure; right to an 'adequate' standard of living; 'motherhood and childhood are entitled to special care and assistance'; equal protection of children; right to education; and right of parents to determine the kind of education their children receive. |
| 27 | Right freely to participate in the cultural life of the community. |
| 28 | 'Everyone is entitled to a social and international order in which the rights and freedoms set forth in this Declaration can be fully realized'. |
| 29 | Everyone has duties to his or her community; the exercise of the above rights can only be limited in order to meet the 'just requirements of morality, public order and the general welfare in a democratic society'. |
| 30 | Nothing in the Declaration should imply that any state, group or person can engage in actions destructive of any of the rights and freedoms set out in it. |

Several important points can be drawn from this document:

1. Although reference is made to the importance of legal protection, the document provides for no legal mechanisms, such as courts, to enforce human rights. And the linguistic style of the document lacks the precision a good legal document should possess.
2. Many of the rights themselves can be grouped: (a) rights that essentially amount to being left alone; (b) rights to participate in the political structure of the country, and to enjoy the protection of its laws; (c) rights to associate with people of your own choosing; and (d) social rights, such as employment protection and a minimum level of resources. The first three groups clearly reflect the ethos of a liberal-democratic society, whereas the last was a concession to the realities of power politics in the post-war period, where the Soviet Union was keen to stake out a distinct moral position, one that stressed social goods.
3. The rights are limited by articles 29 and 30, which talk of the duties of individuals – the reference to the 'requirements of morality' leaves open the possibility that the rights could be interpreted in significantly different ways in different cultures.

## European Convention on Human Rights (1950)

The European Convention on Human Rights – officially the Convention for the Protection of Human Rights and Fundamental Freedoms – was adopted in 1950 by the Council of Europe, an international organisation that began with ten member states and now has 47. The Preamble to the ECHR makes explicit its relationship to the UDHR by stating as its aim the 'collective enforcement of certain rights stated in the Universal Declaration' (ECHR: 5). There are, however, several important features that distinguish the ECHR from the UDHR. These differences flow from the fact that the ECHR is intended as a legal document, whereas the UDHR is a general statement of aspiration:

1. Many of the articles of the ECHR are double-headed, meaning that the first part sets out the right, but the second states a limitation on the right. For example, Article 10 is concerned with freedom

of expression, but this is then limited by various considerations, including 'national security', 'public safety', 'protection of health and morals' and the 'protection of reputation' (ECHR: 12).

2.  Section I of the document sets out the rights and freedoms of individuals, but Section II – which is about half the document – is concerned with the powers of the European Court of Human Rights, which was established by the Convention. Part III – 'Miscellaneous Provisions' – deals with various issues relating to the obligations of the contracting states.

3.  The ECHR has been amended – through 'protocols' – many times since its creation; in most cases, this has entailed strengthening, or extending, the rights contained in it. For example, Protocol 6 (1983) restricted the use of the death penalty to times of war or national emergency; Protocol 13 (2002) prohibits the death penalty in all circumstances (not all Council members have ratified Protocols 6 and 13) (ECHR: 40–3; 54–7).

4.  Although there is, unsurprisingly, a strong overlap between the rights contained in both documents, the ECHR omits the 'social rights' (Articles 22–26) of the UDHR. Given that the ten founding members of the Council were all Western European, this is to be expected ('Eastern' states joined only after the collapse of state socialism in 1989 – Russia, for example, joined in 1996).

## The significance of the UDHR and ECHR

The Declaration and the Convention are important in what they reveal about the nature and justification of human rights, and in the rest of this chapter we will pursue these further:

1.  Human rights privilege certain values over others: there can be no doubt that human rights are individualist, in the sense that the integrity of the individual – her body and mind – and the choices she makes are the object of protection. Certainly, Articles 22–26 of the Declaration stress the social conditions for action, but the 'core' human rights are individualist. This raises the question of whether human rights are compatible with cultures that do not place stress on individualism. Would it matter if they were not compatible? We pursue these questions later in this chapter.

2.  The differences between the two documents are interesting and important and raise the issue of what happens to the concept of a human right when we try to apply it in a concrete legal–political situation: must a human right be a legal right? Even if a human right need not be a legal right, might it not be that the only human right worth having is one that can be enforced in law?

3.  Rights will conflict – they can conflict with one another and with certain duties. A system of rights must, therefore, be compossible, meaning mutually possible. Furthermore, rights must be actionable – the fulfilment of the right cannot require impossible actions. The ECHR strives for compossibility and actionability.

## Justifying human rights

## Rights – some conceptual issues

We have approached the concept of human rights by looking at actual documents rather than justifications for human rights. The rest of this chapter will be devoted to the question of justification, but as a preliminary, it is important to make some conceptual distinctions regarding rights – that is, rights in general, rather than specifically human rights. We focus on three aspects of the concept of rights: types of rights; the nature of the right-holder; and conflicts between rights.

- *Types of rights*: A generic definition of a right is an 'entitlement', but legal theorist Wesley Hohfeld argued that there are, in fact, four distinct types of right – claims, privileges (or liberties), powers, and immunities (Hohfeld, 1923: 12). A right is a relationship: correlating to a claim is a duty; a privilege a 'no-claim'; a power a liability; and an immunity a disability. So if you have a claim, someone else (one person or a group) has a duty. Drawing on Hohfeld, we can make two points: (a) rights carry 'costs' for others; (b) what is called a right in the UDHR or ECHR is often a 'bundle' of Hohfeldian rights with an internally complex structure – for example, the 'right to marry' involves exercising *powers* and through those powers generating *claims*, and insofar as the right to marry is constitutionally protected, the state is disabled from interfering, meaning that you have an *immunity* against the state.
- *The nature of the right-holder*: Can very young children – conceptually – have rights? Can non-human animals have rights? Those who reject children's rights or animal rights argue that only a being capable of exercising choice (more technically: exercising a power) can have rights (although in a rudimentary way children and animals do express choices). It does not follow that there are no duties towards children and animals, but simply that those duties do not 'correlate' to rights. Such a theory of rights is called the will theory (it is also known as the choice theory). Theorists who argue that children and animals can – conceptually – have rights argue that to have a right is to be the *beneficiary* of the performance of a duty. A child need not be capable of 'exercising' a right in order to have rights. Benefit theory (or interest theory; recipience theory) takes a much wider view of who can have rights, although at the expense of weakening the distinctiveness of rights. This argument is important not so much in justifying human rights as in explaining what can count as a human right.
- *Conflicts between rights*: We have suggested that a scheme of rights must be compossible and that the ECHR, as a legal document, pays much more attention to this than does the UDHR. It is important to make a distinction between the *violation* of a right and the *overriding* of a right. Violation is simply the arbitrary setting aside of a right. If a right is overridden, then this entails providing reasons for setting that right aside. Such a reason will make appeal to weights between different considerations, such as individual freedom as against collective security. Importantly, human rights need not be absolute: it is a mistake to confuse universality with absoluteness. A human right is a consideration that must always be taken into account irrespective of cultural differences, but it does not follow that a particular human right cannot be overridden. Perhaps some human rights are absolute, but absoluteness is not a necessary feature of a human right.

## Relativism versus universalism

So far we have talked about the concept of a right and discussed the historical origins of human rights documents and mechanisms of enforcement. What we have not discussed is the justification of human rights. The *fact* of law does not necessarily *justify* a law. Once we accept this, we are forced to confront the cultural relativism thesis, which can be stated thus:

Values have to be understood as part of a complex whole; that complex whole is 'culture'. When discussing the universal applicability of 'human rights' we must take into account the impact they have on particular cultures. For some cultures those rights express central values, for others they may, with some revision, be compatible with that culture, but for others they may be wholly inappropriate and damaging.

Cultural relativism does not necessarily entail the rejection of morality: the UDHR may be valid for certain cultures. What cultural relativists challenge is the claim to *universal* application. This raises the question of whether a relativist can endorse some form of human rights. One possibility is to distinguish 'state' and 'culture': the Council of Europe is composed of 47 states, but it could be argued there is a single European culture, which has its roots in Christianity (mediaeval Europe was often referred to as 'Christendom'). Similarly, the Islamic world is composed of many states bound together by Islamic culture (it might also be argued that the Arab world, as part of the wider Islamic world, is a distinct culture). If we endorse the separation of state and culture, then it might be possible to talk of transnational standards of treatment. Those standards would allow a distinction to be made between two ways of rejecting human rights: (a) *violation* of culturally accepted human rights by a particular regime; (b) *legitimate rejection* of human rights on cultural grounds. For example, it could be debated whether Saudi Arabian penal policy, such as public beheadings and the amputation of hands, is grounded in Islamic teaching and Arab custom or it simply serves the interests of the Saudi state to have such draconian forms of punishment.

This argument, while plausible, is difficult for a defender of human rights to embrace. As we suggested in the first section of the chapter, human rights are rights that individuals have by virtue of their humanity. The cultural argument makes rights, or any other standard of treatment, contingent on a person's culture. While there may be a role for culture in the justification, formulation, and implementation of human rights, the radical 'culturalism' that forms the basis of the cultural relativism thesis is incompatible with human rights. We need then to consider arguments against cultural relativism or, put another way, arguments for universalism. We set out five theories.

## Intuition and consensus

Jack Donnelly, in his book *Universal Human Rights in Theory and Practice*, defends what he terms weak cultural relativism, which entails strong universalism. Weak cultural relativism assumes that human rights are universally applicable but allows that 'the relativity of human nature, communities and rules checks potential excesses of universalism'. Strong cultural relativism holds that culture is the principal source of the validity of a right or rule, and 'at its furthest extreme, strong cultural relativism accepts a few basic rights with virtually universal application but allows such a wide range of variation that two entirely justifiable sets of rights might overlap only slightly' (Donnelly, 2003: 90).

The looseness of the language of the UDHR Donnelly regards as a strength. The UDHR is a general statement of orienting value, and it is at this level – and only at this level – that a moral consensus exists. For example, Articles 3–12 'are so clearly connected to basic requirements of human dignity, and are stated in sufficiently general terms, that virtually every morally defensible contemporary form of social organization must recognize them' (2003: 94). Below we discuss the 'rational entailment' argument, of which there are several versions, but the central idea is that certain standards of treatment can be derived from the conditions which humans require for action, and as such a society cannot deny those standards without also denying the preconditions for its own existence. Donnelly's statement has the appearance of such an argument, but in fact he then goes on to appeal to human intuition. By 'intuition' is meant a strong sense of, or belief in, the rightness or wrongness of something, but without the ability to give a complete explanation of that sense or belief. Donnelly identifies the intuition that people should be treated in a certain way irrespective of their culture by means of a question:

In twenty years of working with issues of cultural relativism, I have developed a simple test that I pose to sceptical audiences. What rights in the Universal Declaration, I ask, does your society or culture reject? Rarely has a single full right (other than the right to private property) been rejected.

(2003: 94)

He recalls a visit to Iran in 2001, where he posed the above question to three different audiences. In all three cases, discussion moved quickly on to the issue of freedom of religion, and in particular to atheism, and to apostasy by Muslims, which the UDHR permits, but Iran prohibits. Donnelly observed that the discussion was not about freedom of religion, but rather about Western versus Islamic interpretations of that right.

Particular human rights are like 'essentially contested concepts' in which there are differing interpretations but strong overlap between them. So long as 'outliers' are few, we can talk about a consensus around human rights. Such outliers would be cultures that do not accept a particular human right. The fact that increasing numbers of states are prepared to sign up to the UDHR, and to later, and more specific, United Nations conventions Donnelly takes to be evidence of a dynamic consensus in favour of human rights. He also observes that when Western states criticise non-Western states for apparently barbaric practices that criticism is sometimes accompanied by a lack of self-awareness. In 1994, 18-year-old American Michael Fay was convicted by a Singaporean court of vandalising hundreds of thousands of dollars worth of property. He was sentenced to three months in jail, required to pay a fine and, most controversially, condemned to six strokes of the cane (the cane would leave permanent scars). There was widespread condemnation in the United States. Donnelly tersely observes that President Clinton, while condemning the sentence 'failed to find it even notable that in his own country people are being fried in the electric chair' (2003: 99).

To sum up, Donnelly's observations are interesting, but two points are problematic. First, an intuition in favour of human rights at best indicates that there may be something underlying those rights which is, in some sense, universal. But if this is so, then it should be possible to move beyond intuition and provide reasons for respecting human rights. Second, the fact that *states* have signed up to human rights conventions does not entail *cultural* agreement: human rights must be recognised as valid by large parts of the populations of states and not simply by the leadership. In many states, the governing elites are disconnected from their peoples, and although states may be considered the main actors with regard to human rights, respect for such rights does depend on popular recognition.

## Contractualism

The fact that increasing numbers of states are prepared to sign up to human rights conventions does not in itself amount to an argument for the universality of human rights, but it may provide an element in an argument. In previous chapters, we have discussed the idea of the social contract (see pp. 165–6), which has been a device used by liberal political theorists to justify state power. Our discussion focused on the 'domestic' use of the contract: political theorists such as Hobbes, Locke, Rousseau, and Rawls were concerned with the relationship of the individual to the state. This contrasts with an 'international contract', which is a contract not between individual human beings but between states. We also made a distinction between a quasi-historical contract, whereby we could imagine that people could have agreed to create a state, and the hypothetical contract in which the contractors are 'idealised' and the contract is a thought-experiment rather than a historical event.

Interestingly enough, whereas defenders of the historical contract do not claim there was actually an agreement to enter the state – simply that it was imaginable – international legal institutions can plausibly be described as the product of an agreement between the member states of the international community: agreements to create international institutions. Of course, there is not a single 'moment' of agreement, for the ratification of a convention can take place over decades. Furthermore, there has never been an international agreement to create a single state. Such an agreement would constitute the dissolution of all existing states. The closest the international community has come to the creation of a single, multinational global power has been the formation of the United Nations, with the commitment by member states to provide military personnel to enforce international law.

The problem of enforcement may be thought a serious deficiency of international law, and one that can only be remedied through the creation of a single state. However, there is a considerable body of international law, such as commercial law, which states respect without recourse to a global enforcement agency. As Locke argued, enforcement, while important, is not the main deficiency evident in the state of nature, for a more significant deficiency is the absence of a body capable of interpreting, and indeed determining, the law (see p. 167). Even if all states subscribed to the UDHR, its wording is so general as to require a third-party judgement on its meaning. In practice, the United Nations effectively 'contracts out' the interpretation of human rights to bodies such as the European Court of Human Rights. The general point is that a hypothetical international contract differs from a domestic one in that its object is not the creation of a world state, but is a device for creating a charter of human rights and associated multinational institutions. States will not then be able to violate human rights on grounds of disagreement about their interpretation and will have incentives – such as the desire for reputation – to respect them.

John Rawls offers a philosophical defence of international contractualism in his book *The Law of Peoples* (1999). The underlying aim of that book is to outline the just foreign policy of a liberal society: when is intervention in the affairs of another state justified? And what duties do liberal societies have to non-liberal ones? Although that aim is quite narrow, in the course of the book Rawls presents an argument to show that non-liberal, non-Western societies can respect human rights. He distinguishes four types of society or 'people': (a) *Liberal societies*, which (largely) respect human rights conventions; (b) *Decent non-liberal societies*, of which there can be several variants, but the one type Rawls discusses possesses a 'decent consultation hierarchy' (hereafter referred to as 'decent societies'); (c) *Outlaw states* – states that violate the law of peoples, by, for example, waging aggressive wars or engaging in serious violations of human rights; (d) *Burdened societies*, where poor socio-economic conditions make respect for international law difficult.

Rawls applies the idea of the original position and the veil of ignorance developed in his theory of domestic justice to international law, but there are important differences between how these devices are used in Rawls's theory of (domestic) justice and in his theory of international justice. Liberal societies agree among themselves a 'law of peoples', and then decent societies endorse those same principles (Rawls argues that liberal-democratic societies, by their nature, will tend to respect the human rights of their own peoples and the sovereignty of other peoples). The law of peoples consists of eight principles: mutual recognition of each people's independence; honouring of agreements; legal equality of peoples; duty of non-intervention (except in the case of dealing with outlaw states and grave violations of human rights); right to self-defence; respect for human rights; respect for the rules of war; and, a duty to assist peoples living under conditions that prevent them from becoming just (liberal) or decent societies. The law requires liberal societies that they do not seek to change the fundamental character of a decent society.

To understand how a decent society could endorse the law of peoples, and consequently why a liberal society should tolerate a decent one, we need to know the characteristics of the latter.

Rawls argues that a decent society is peaceful in that it pursues its interests through trade and diplomacy. The domestic laws of such a society are guided by a 'common good conception of justice', meaning that while it may not grant the freedoms to individuals enjoyed in a liberal society, in a fundamental sense all citizens are treated equally. There should exist a 'decent consultation hierarchy', which permits the possibility of dissent (the Arab–Islamic concept of *shura* would be one example of a consultation hierarchy). Importantly, the common good conception of justice entails respect for human rights, including the right to life, liberty (freedom from slavery and forced labour), personal property, and equality before the law. Although a decent society may not permit apostasy and proselytisation, it must accord a degree of religious freedom to minorities, and because that right is limited it must also allow citizens the possibility of emigration. The fundamental philosophical point Rawls makes about human rights is that they should not depend on a particular conception of the human agent as autonomous, but rather 'human rights set a necessary . . . standard for the decency of domestic political and social institutions' (Rawls, 1999: 80).

Human rights fulfil three roles: (a) they are a necessary condition of a regime's legitimacy; (b) they determine the limits of sovereignty – the law of peoples prohibits intervention in the affairs of another state except when that state is violating human rights; (c) they set a limit on the pluralism among peoples. Even if Rawls is correct in arguing that a decent society can respect human rights, are there any grounds for believing that they will do so for reasons other than state interest? Do they respect human rights for the 'right reasons', or because such respect is useful to establishing a reputation in international politics? A similar argument could be applied to the international behaviour of liberal states, but the difference between liberal and non-liberal societies is that human rights are deeply embedded in the culture of the former. Even if the leaders of liberal societies are cynical in their use of human rights rhetoric in international politics – intervening in Kosovo but not Chechnya – they may well (largely) respect human rights in their domestic political systems.

## Rational entailment

The 'rational entailment' argument identifies certain conditions for the existence of social order and from them derives standards of treatment all societies should respect. The argument can take two forms – empirical and logical. The empirical version observes actual societies and claims that the long-term survival of a society depends on the recognition of human rights. This version has only limited plausibility – many societies function without respect for human rights. It is somewhat more plausible to maintain that human rights-respecting societies are more successful than human rights-violating ones, where success is measured by economic growth and political stability.

The logical version does not deny that social life is possible without human rights, but rather that a human rights-violating society cannot justify its own political and legal organisation without falling into contradiction. In Chapter 5, we discussed the citizenship laws of Nazi Germany which effectively stripped Jews of their citizenship (see p. 86). Legal theorist Lon Fuller argued that nazi law could not respect certain principles internal to law, such as the prohibition on non-retroactivity. Fuller is not suggesting that Nazi Germany did not 'function', but rather that it could not justify its laws. Implicit in Fuller's argument is a belief in human rights, to which he is offering a logical entailment defence. Of course, a regime can simply choose not to justify its actions – although that is extremely rare. But refusal to engage in the justification process does not undermine the logical entailment argument.

Jürgen Habermas offers the best contemporary statement of logical entailment. Before we get to his defence of human rights against cultural relativism, it is necessary to set out briefly Habermas's rather complex theory of social change. If we define 'culture' as the 'taken-for-granted horizon of expectations' (what is termed the *lifeworld*), then under conditions of modernity culture is 'threatened' by rationalisation in the form of money (or the market) and bureaucratic power – relations between human beings become instrumental, rather than implicit and 'taken for granted'. There is a diminution of trust. Many theorists, especially in the German philosophical tradition in which Habermas was formed, are pessimistic about the consequences of modernity. However, Habermas argues that the emphasis on instrumentalisation – or what he calls 'systemic rationality' – ignores the positive achievements of modernity, expressed in 'communicative rationality' (Habermas, 1984: 8–22). The growth in consciousness of human rights is one of the achievements of communicative rationality.

What does Habermas mean by 'communicative action'? People engage in speech-acts: person A *promises* to meet person B on Thursday, *requests* B stop smoking, *confesses* to find B's actions distasteful, and *predicts* it will rain. Implicit in each speech-act is an offer or claim. In the first two cases, A is making a claim to normative rightness, in the third a claim to sincerity, and in the final case, a claim to truth. B can contest all three 'validity claims' (Habermas, 1984: 319–28). The success of each speech-act depends upon both parties orienting themselves to principles of reason that are not reducible to individual intentions: in addressing B, person A treats her as an end in herself. The validity claims are implicit in all human action; that is, they are universal. This seems a promising basis for defending universal human rights against the challenge of cultural relativism. However, the validity claims are abstracted from everyday life, and so to redeem them requires an appeal to a stock of culturally specific values. That means the content of human rights is dependent on culture.

One way to address this problem of cultural dependence is to maintain that politics is a dialogue, in which people bring to bear their different cultural perspectives, such that what emerges from the dialogue is something pluralistic yet coherent. For example, Muslims may be criticised by Western feminists for projecting a patriarchal conception of gender relations. By engaging in dialogue, Muslims may reform their view of women's rights, but Westerners might also be obliged to recognise the deficiencies in their own understanding of family relations, by, for example, acknowledging the costs entailed in the commodification of sex in a liberal society.

Habermas argues there is a tradition in Anglophone legal and political theory of conceiving of the state as grounded in the protection of individual 'private' rights – rights derived from the market contract model. Hobbes is the *locus classicus* of this conception of individual–state relations. If we operate with such a theory then it is inevitable that individual rights will be a threat to cultural reproduction. In effect, increasing reliance on rights would be another example of systemic rationality eroding the lifeworld. We are then left with a choice: either we assert the primacy of individual rights at the expense of cultural interaction or maintain the authority of the collective over the individual. Private rights entail the assertion of personal autonomy, but they ignore the other half of the concept of autonomy – public autonomy:

> . . .from a normative point of view, the integrity of the individual legal person cannot be guaranteed without protecting the intersubjectively shared experiences and life contexts in which the person has been socialized and has formed his or her identity. The identity of the individual is interwoven with collective identities and can be stabilized only in a cultural network that cannot be appropriated as private property any more than the mother tongue itself can be.
>
> (Habermas, 1994: 129)

The implication of Habermas's argument is that universal human rights are, contrary to Rawls's theory, grounded in human autonomy, but autonomy itself has a collective dimension which must take into account cultural interpretations of human rights. Legality is central to the realisation of human rights, and Habermas's theory of law bears some resemblance to Fuller's. Law is not reducible to the assertion of will – people are not simply subjects of law – but the formation of law is a discursive process. The legal realisation of human rights will inevitably involve 'local interpretation' – for example, Muslim societies will interpret human rights differently to Western societies – but human beings are bound together through discourse, and discourse presupposes a conception of the human agent as autonomous.

## Natural right and natural rights

We touched on Finnis' work in our discussion of legal moralism in Chapter 6 (see p. 110). Although he devotes only one chapter (of 13) of his book *Natural Law and Natural Rights* explicitly to human rights, he argues that 'right' is central to his entire argument, and it is important to understand the relationship between the singular 'right' and the plural 'rights'. The plural results from 'reporting and asserting the requirements or other implications of a relationship of justice from the point of view of the person(s) who benefit(s) from that relationship' (Finnis, 1980: 205). Surveying the development of the concept of right from its classical antecedent *jus*, Finnis notes that for Thomas Aquinas (1225–74) *jus* meant 'the fair' or 'fairness'. Relationships of justice – who is owed what – are secondary. By 1610, the Spanish Jesuit writer Francisco Suarez (1548–1617) has reversed the priority and defines *jus* in terms of a moral power which each person possesses, and this way of thinking about justice is developed a short time later by Hugo Grotius (1583–1645): *jus* is essentially something a person has – it is a power (1980: 206–7). What we see is the development of rights from right. For Finnis, this takes a damaging turn in the work of Hobbes, who argues that a person has rights in the state of nature – that is, a situation in which there is no state, or political authority: since nobody is compelled to do anything each is free. The state for Hobbes is the rational outcome of the exercise of these 'natural rights'. But since nobody has any duties in the state of nature – for example, nobody is under a duty not to kill you – then we could, Finnis suggests, just as well say that there are no rights outside the state.

While Finnis accepts the post-Thomist pluralisation of rights, he argues that the Hobbesian tradition loses sight of the connection between right and rights. The justification of human rights depends upon understanding that connection. The limitations on the rights contained in the UDHR and the ECHR are significant: they demonstrate that rights derive their validity from an underlying structure of 'right'. Were the only limitation on your rights the rights of others, then Finnis' observation would not be particularly interesting, but others' rights do not constitute the only limits: there is also reference to public morality, public health, and public order. These considerations cannot be reduced to the effects on *identifiable* individuals, but are 'diffuse common benefits in which all participate in indistinguishable and unassignable shares' (1980: 216). A scheme of human rights, such as the UDHR or the ECHR is:

> Simply a way of sketching the *outlines of the common good*, the various aspects of individual well-being in community. What the reference to rights contributes to this sketch is simply a pointed expression of what is implicit in the term '*common* good', namely that *each* and everyone's well-being, in each of its basic aspects, must be considered and favoured at *all* times by those responsible for co-ordinating the common life.
>
> (1980: 214, his emphases)

It may be true that there is a necessary connection between right and rights, and that others' rights are not the only limitation on rights, but we need to establish in what sense rights are *natural*, and thus *universal*. Finnis maintains that there are goods which all cultures value: (a) life (including self-preservation and procreation); (b) knowledge (considered valuable in itself); (c) play (activities enjoyed for their own sake, lacking any point beyond their own performance); (d) aesthetic experience (appreciation of beauty); (e) sociability (including friendship, which is a non-instrumental relationship); (e) practical reasonableness; and (f) religion (even if one rejects religious claims, to ask questions about the origin and purpose of life is essential to a 'full life') (1980: 83–4). Human rights protect these goods.

There are several problems with Finnis' argument. First, even if we can identify cross-cultural activities, such as the pursuit of knowledge or play, it does not follow that what we have characterised as 'common' to different cultures amount to 'goods' which can be pursued. Does the scientific knowledge of Western societies correspond to the voodoo knowledge of some African societies? Does the Netherlands fail to uphold respect for life because – under strict conditions – it permits a doctor to assist a person to die? Second, Finnis – like Habermas – wants to argue that we can derive these goods from reason. But unlike Habermas, he generates a substantive list of goods which we 'ought' to pursue and protect. Furthermore, although Habermas can be criticised, at least his theory derives from formal aspects of communication. Finnis, on the other hand, continually appeals to the intuitions of his reader. He has nothing else in his intellectual armoury. Third, the value of a particular activity is not as straightforward as Finnis suggests. For example, the 'pursuit of knowledge' may be motivated not by a search for truth but a desire for entertainment, and people often have sex for pleasure rather than procreation. Overall, even if Finnis is right to argue that there are goods that transcend 'cultures', his argument lacks the binding quality necessary to generate a set of actionable, universal human rights.

## Cruelty and solidarity

What motivated the UDHR and what moves people most strongly to protest against regimes that violate human rights is revulsion at cruel practices, such as torture. The difficulty with at least three of the other four theories – Donnelly's theory may be the exception – is that they abstract too much. We do not reason our way to human rights from an abstract standpoint of 'duty', but from imaginative identification with the victims of abuse. As Judith Shklar argues, we 'put cruelty first'. That slightly odd formulation – it might imply valuing cruelty – is intended to convey a sceptical, negative basis for human rights and to stress that considerations of cruelty take priority in the articulation of our sense of justice and injustice.

Cruelty Shklar defines as the 'willful inflicting of physical pain on a weaker being in order to cause anguish and fear'. By putting cruelty first, 'with nothing above it, and with nothing to excuse or forgive acts of cruelty' one 'closes off any appeal to any order other than that of actuality' (Shklar, 1984: 8). In understanding human rights as the political expression of our revulsion towards cruelty, we avoid appeal to human essences, or reason, or a positive set of virtues, all of which carry the danger of ethnocentrism. Richard Rorty developed this idea in his book *Contingency, Irony and Solidarity* (Rorty, 1989). By 'contingency', Rorty means opposition to any idea of human essence, or nature, or any other ideas that supposedly provide the 'foundations' for law, morality, and politics. In rejecting philosophical universalism, Rorty recognises the danger that anything will be 'justifiable', or more accurately, since no beliefs or values have a privileged status, there is nothing that can be said against torture or genocide. To address this charge, it is necessary to consider the other two concepts that appear in the title of Rorty's book: irony and solidarity.

Irony is the capacity to recognise that one's own values may not be ultimate – that it is always possible to describe the world in another way. To be ironic is to continue to hold on to one's beliefs and values *and at the same time* acknowledge the force of other 'conversations'. Although we cannot provide any philosophical 'grounding' for respect or tolerance, the ironist will tend to recognise the rights of others. The ironist does not reason from an abstract standpoint but is capable of emotional identification. Such identification might, for example, come through an appreciation of literature. Picking up on Shklar's idea of the 'actual', the ironist will have special sensitivity to cruelty. Recognising the limitations of one's own beliefs and being sensitive to cruelty provides hope for an expanding circle of *solidarity*.

Rorty observes that if you were in Jew in nazi-occupied Europe your chances of avoiding deportation were greater if you lived in Denmark or Italy than if you lived in Belgium (1989: 189). He explains the difference in the following terms:

> Did [Danes and Italians] say, about their Jewish neighbors, that they deserved to be saved because they were fellow human beings? Perhaps sometimes they did, but surely they would usually, if queried, have used more parochial terms to explain why they were taking risks to protect a given Jew – for example, that this particular Jew was a fellow Milanese, or a fellow Jutlander, or a fellow member of the same union or profession, or a fellow bocce player, or a fellow parent of small children. Then consider those Belgians: Surely there were some people whom they *would* have taken risks to protect in similar circumstances, people whom they *did* identify with, under some description or other. But Jews rarely fell under those descriptions.
>
> (1989: 190–1, his emphases)

Rorty's interpretation of the rescuers' motivations has been challenged. Norman Geras argues, first, that there were prosaic reasons why a greater proportion of the Jewish population was deported from some countries than from others – sometimes, it came down to the availability of escape routes, such as from Denmark to Sweden in what has become termed the 'Danish rescue', the availability of pre-war records of religious affiliation, and the actual form of administrative occupation, which varied considerably from one country to another (Geras, 1995: 10–11). Second, and more importantly, Rorty quotes no testimonies of rescuers or their friends and family. After working his way through a large number of such testimonies, Geras found only one case in which a rescuer expressed his reasons for rescuing Jews as that they were fellow citizens (in this case, fellow Dutch). Almost all used the language of 'common humanity' – in other words, the kind of universalism which Rorty rejects (1995: 36).

Geras argues for a universalism based on the recognition of a common human nature, but it is not clear why Rorty rejects the *feeling* for humanity as the basis for human rights. Certainly, Rorty rejects any categorically binding conception of human reason, such as that advanced by Habermas, but it is consistent with Rorty's anti-foundationalism to be moved by another's suffering – to feel revulsion at cruelty towards that person – without any appeal to a shared membership of a parochial group. Perhaps what worries Rorty is that the recognition of humanity will take the form of a 'cold' Kantian duty, which we then *apply* to human beings.

## On torture

Do human rights close off political debate? If we say someone has a human right, then we are obliged to treat him in a certain way and not even discuss whether we should do so. This foreclosing of debate is even stronger if the right is absolute. Not everybody accepts shutting down debate. In the case of torture, some argue there are situations in which torture would be justified, and so there cannot be an absolute prohibition of it (Dershowitz, 2003). There is a famous ticking bomb scenario:

> A device has been planted, which, if it explodes, will kill thousands of people. The interrogators know it will go off within an hour and mass evacuation is impossible. They need to find the bomb and deactivate it. They have in custody a person whom they strongly suspect of planting the bomb. To save thousands of lives they need to do some terrible things to this person.

Critics argue that this is a philosophy classroom example that only has force if it precisely holds: (a) time is limited – no evacuation is possible; (b) the bomb must be ticking but there must be enough time to stop it exploding; (c) *only* the suspect can stop it (either directly or by providing the necessary information); (d) the suspect must therefore know where the bomb is and how to disarm it; (e) the interrogators must know that this person knows where the bomb is and how to disarm it; (f) the interrogators do not know enough to disarm the bomb themselves but they seem to know enough for (e) to hold true; and (f) only torture will elicit the information.

Critics argue this is not only an unrealistic example but also a dangerous one. In using the example in the public arena the unrealistic aspects of the example are suppressed such that people really believe that it is not at all far-fetched. Police in London or New York could be faced with such a situation. Furthermore, the example is presented in isolation – as if nothing but the disarming of the bomb mattered. But you cannot move from this particular case to the institutionalisation of punishment – it is a *non sequitur* to say (a) it would be right to torture in this case; therefore, (b) torture is justified. What defenders of torture want is the *institutionalisation* of torture, but you cannot derive, or justify, an institution on the basis of a very unusual case.

A significant motivation for human rights is to put certain things beyond debate. The ticking bomb example undermines this, by allowing people to consider what human rights advocates argue should be beyond discussion. However, even if we reject the ticking bomb scenario, we cannot avoid discussing the boundaries of torture. What is, and what is not, torture? Indeed, the UN Convention against Torture has a definition, which we cited at the start of the chapter.

Jeremy Waldron argues it is invidious even to attempt a definition. Why would we want a definition? He thinks that what motivates the demand for a definition is that a state official wants to know where he is on a spectrum: '[the official] knows he is on a spectrum and that there is a point at which his conduct might be stigmatized as criminal; and the question is whether he has a legitimate interest in being able to press up as close to that point as possible, in which case he needs to know exactly where it is' (Waldron, 2005: 1701). Some spectra are legitimate: a taxpayer needs to know what things are tax-deductible. But other spectra are not: the husband who enjoys 'pushing his wife around a bit' would like to know how far he can go before what he is doing counts as domestic violence, or the university professor who likes flirting with his students needs to know at what point his behaviour becomes sexual harassment (2005: 1701). Torture, like domestic violence or sexual harassment is, Waldron thinks, a scale on which we simply should not be.

But without a definition we weaken the fight against very extreme forms of torture. In the 1970s, the United Kingdom was taken to the European Court of Human Rights (*Ireland v UK*, 1977). The litigants sought a judgement on interrogation practices used by the United Kingdom in Northern Ireland, specifically five practices: sleep deprivation, hooding, white noise, stress postures, and severe limitations on food and water. One of the judges, Sir Gerald Fitzmaurice, in rejecting the case argued that if these practices were to be defined as torture, then how does one characterise 'having one's finger-nails torn out, being slowly impaled on a stake through the rectum, or roasted over an electric grid?' (Fitzmaurice, cited in Waldron, 2003: 9). In other words, if what the British were doing in Northern Ireland was torture, then what name do we give to these much more extreme practices?

The absolute prohibition on torture raises two important issues. Should some things be beyond political debate – in other words, is it wrong even *to discuss* whether the prohibition on torture should be absolute? Should it also be out of bounds to define torture, even though we need to know what this practice is that is absolutely prohibited?

## Conclusion

The fundamental philosophical debate around human rights is concerned with their alleged 'parochialism': that is, their origins in a particular culture. That something has a history does not, in itself, invalidate its claim to universality, but there is a particular problem about human rights even in those cultures from which they emerged: critics argue that human rights place a great moral weight on individual autonomy to the detriment of other values, such as welfare, community, and democracy. For defenders of human rights, the increasing spread of human rights discourse indicates a welcome development in humanitarian moral consciousness. For opponents, human rights go hand in hand with the growing power of Western liberalism.

## References

Dershowitz, A. M. (2003). The Torture Warrant: A Response to Professor Strauss. *New York Law School Law Review, 48*, 275.

Donnelly, J. (2003). *Universal Human Rights in Theory and Practice*. Ithaca, NY: Cornell University Press.

ECHR. European Convention on Human Rights, Council of Europe, viewed 26 July 2021, https://www.echr.coe.int/documents/convention_eng.pdf

Finnis, J. (1980). *Natural Law and Natural Rights*. Oxford: Clarendon Press

Geras, N. (1995). *Solidarity in the Conversation of Humankind: The Ungroundable Liberalism of Richard Rorty*. London and New York: Verso

Greenwood, C. (2002). Humanitarian Intervention: The Case of Kosovo. *Finnish Yearbook of International Law, 10*, 141–75.

Habermas, J. (1984). *The Theory of Communicative Action*, Vol. 1: *Reason and Rationalization of Society*. London: Heinemann.

Habermas, J. (1994). 'Struggles for Recognition in the Democratic Constitutional State', in A. Gutmann (ed.), *Multiculturalism: Examining the Politics of Recognition*. Princeton, NJ: Princeton University Press.

Hohfeld, W. (1923). *Fundamental Legal Conceptions as Applied in Judicial Reasoning*. New Haven, CT: Yale University Press.

Rawls, J. (1999). *The Law of Peoples*. Cambridge, MA and London: Harvard University Press.

Rorty, R. (1989). *Contingency, Irony, and Solidarity*. Cambridge: Cambridge University Press

Shklar, J. (1984). *Ordinary Vices*. Cambridge MA: Harvard University Press

UDHR (1948). Universal Declaration of Human Rights, United Nations, viewed 26 July 2021, https://www.un.org/en/about-us/universal-declaration-of-human-rights

Waldron, J. (2005). Torture and Positive Law: Jurisprudence for the White House. *Columbia Law Review*, *105*(6), 1681–750

## Further reading

Overviews: Thomas Martens, *A Philosophical Introduction to Human Rights* (Cambridge University Press, 2020); Michael Freeman, *Human Rights*, Third Edition (Polity, 2017); Andrew Clapham, *Human Rights: A Very Short Introduction* (Oxford University Press, 2015); Kerri Woods, *Human Rights* (Palgrave, 2014). Useful collections of essays: Michael Goodhart (ed.), *Human Rights: Politics and Practice* (Oxford University Press, 2016); Costas Douzinas and Conor Gearty (eds.), *The Meanings of Rights: The Philosophy and Social Theory of Human Rights* (Cambridge University Press, 2014); Reidar Maliks and Johan Schaffer (eds.), *Moral and Political Conceptions of Human Rights* (Cambridge University Press, 2018). More focused: Alison Brysk, *The Future of Human Rights* (Polity, 2018); Angelika Nussberger, *The European Court of Human Rights* (Oxford University Press, 2020).

# Chapter 19

# Global justice

## Introduction

The term global justice encompasses debates over human rights, the justification of military intervention, and the international distribution of resources. In this chapter, we focus on the last of these: the just, or fair, allocation of resources between nations, and between individuals across national boundaries. Arguments over global justice emerged from, and took issue with, claims made in debates over domestic justice (discussed in Chapter 8). Three positions on global justice have emerged: *cosmopolitans* maintain that it is incoherent to restrict justice to the sphere of the nation-state. *Particularists* (or partialists) argue it is legitimate to show special concern for one's compatriots and the claims of justice can justifiably be restricted. *Institutionalists* argue for differential treatment of the domestic and global spheres, but they do so by stressing the complexity of morality and the importance of the political.

## Key questions

- What is global justice?
- When there are human catastrophes – such as famines – who should help? Who is responsible for preventing famine?
- Should principles of justice be restricted to fellow compatriots?

## Domestic versus global justice

The debate over global justice[1] within political theory is a relatively recent development. It has been stimulated in large part by arguments over domestic justice, which we outlined in Chapter 8. Although the global justice debate encompasses discussion of human rights and just war, we will be concerned in this chapter with the question of international wealth distribution. We outline three perspectives: cosmopolitanism, particularism, and institutionalism. As a way into the debate, we start with famine.

DOI: 10.4324/9780429424106-25

## Case study 19.1

## Famine

**PHOTO 19.1**  The Red Crescent delivering famine relief. © Colin McPherson/Corbis via Getty Images.

Famine provides the clearest and most compelling illustration of global inequality. That the wealthy enjoy luxury goods while others starve to death is, at least for most people, a demonstration of human immorality. But what responsibilities do the rich nations (or states) bear for famine? Garrett Hardin, in outlining his 'lifeboat ethics' (see pp. 305–7), argued the poor in developing countries bear responsibility for having too many children. Giving aid simply exacerbates the situation. Others argue that famine is the consequence of economic forces set in train by the industrialised, capitalist countries, such that 'we' – the wealthy – have caused famine and so have a responsibility not simply to relieve it when it happens, but to ensure that it never in fact happens.

Understanding the causes of famine is a useful way into exploring issues of global justice, and we discuss those causes – and the rich countries' moral responsibilities – in the first section of this chapter. Before reading that section, consider these questions:

- What is famine?
- What causes famine?
- Who should be responsible for preventing famine?
- Who should be responsible for helping those affected by famine?

## Singer on famine

Peter Singer, in an influential article (Singer, 1972), argues that if you are passing a pond and see a drowning child, then so long as you are not in danger of sacrificing something morally equivalent to that child's life, you have an obligation to wade in and save the child. There may be a cost – perhaps you will ruin your expensive suit – but that has to be weighed against the loss of a life, and in the balance, it is clear what you should do. The failure to make a significant financial contribution to relieve famine on the other side of the world is in all important respects no different to the refusal to jump in and save the drowning child.

Singer's argument is built on two assumptions that any reasonable person would accept: (a) 'suffering and death from lack of food, shelter, and medical care are bad'; (b) 'if it is in our power to prevent something bad from happening, without thereby sacrificing anything of comparable moral importance, we ought, morally, to do it' (Singer, 1972: 231). Proximity to suffering is irrelevant – the child starving 7,000 kilometres away is no less important than the child drowning 50 metres from you. The number of rescuers is of no moral significance – that potentially millions could help the starving child but only you can save the drowning child may alter *how* you assist but not that you *should* assist. Imagine that you are among a group of onlookers seeing the child drowning: that others could help but are not helping in no degree reduces your responsibility to save the child. That there are millions of potential donors capable of relieving a famine does not reduce your obligation to donate to famine relief.

There are, of course, coordination problems in the case of famine that – assuming you are the only potential rescuer – do not exist in the pond example. The cost of saving the drowning child can be calculated as the loss of your $1,000 suit, while the costs of relieving famine are less clear. If we are all willing to give whatever is required to end famine but lack the ability to communicate, we may end up giving too much. However, the existence of a mass media solves this problem. And prisoner's dilemma-type situations do not arise here, because we are assuming that we have a moral obligation to help, such that even if nobody else gave any money, you should still donate. The only sense in which the non-donors are free-riding on your donation is that they are relying on *you* to fulfil *their* obligations to the starving.

## Sen on famine

To explore the problems with Singer's argument, we can contrast it with another discussion of famine, advanced by Amartya Sen. Sen's work is not a response to Singer, and the two explorations of famine are different rather than mutually incompatible. Singer is advancing an argument in moral philosophy about our duties as individuals, whereas Sen is offering an economic and political analysis of the causes of famine. Nonetheless, Sen's emphasis on the 'political' is important in allowing us to see that what may be required of us as *individuals* does not necessarily correspond to what is required of us as *citizens*, such that the cases of the starving child and the drowning child are not analogous. This is not to argue that we should not help people who are starving, but, rather, that a straightforward derivation of politics from morality is simplistic.

Sen distinguishes famines from endemic hunger, defining the former as a 'sudden eruption of severe deprivation for a considerable section of the population' (Sen, 1999: 160). He makes a number of empirical claims, the most striking of which are the following: (a) there is no connection between starvation and lowered food production, and (b) famines do not occur in democratic countries. Even when there is enough food in a country to feed everyone, there can be starvation, because it is the *capacity* to buy food rather than its *availability* that is the key determinant of adequate nutrition. In a competitive democracy, with a free press and media, pressure is placed on the government to put in place measures to deal with the immediate food needs of the population and institute longer-term economic measures to restore the purchasing power of the affected group. Non-democratic regimes lack both the information flows and political incentives to respond properly to food crises (Sen, 1999: 180–1).

Famine cannot be understood, Sen maintains, out of the context of the entire social, economic, and political structure of a country. Food is not distributed through charity or a system of automatic sharing, but rather the ability to acquire food must be earned. What matters is not food production but entitlement, meaning the ownership and command of commodities (Sen, 1999: 162). Entitlement is determined by endowment, production possibilities, and exchange conditions. Most people's endowment is limited to their labour power, meaning that they are dependent on others for employment. Should employment possibilities disappear, then they are vulnerable to a complete loss of entitlement. Those employment possibilities are largely determined by production conditions, such as the development of technology, and exchange rates, meaning the price of goods relative to wages. Exchange rates can change significantly, leading potentially to famine. In the 1943 Bengal famine, in which between 2 and 3 million people died, the exchange rate between food and other types of goods altered radically; for example, as people forwent having haircuts, the rate of exchange between haircutting and staple foods fell in some districts by between 70% and 80% (Sen, 1999: 164).

Crucially, there is not always a direct causal relationship between food availability and famine. The Bangladesh famine of 1974 occurred in a year of higher food production than any other year between 1971 and 1976 (Sen, 1999: 165), and where there is a link between food production and famine, some sections of the population are unaffected, with food moving from poorer to richer areas. A boom in one area can lead to prohibitively high food prices in another. The 1943 Bengal famine was caused, in part, by a war boom in urban Bengal. In summary, famine can only be explained within the context of the total economic structure of a society. The ethical significance of this will be discussed after we have considered the importance of the *political* structure of a society to causing or preventing famine.

Famine prevention is dependent to a significant extent on entitlement protection. After all, in the absence of social security payments, some people in rich, Western nations would starve. The willingness of the wealthy in the West to contribute through redistributive taxation to help their poor compatriots may depend on a mixture of self-interest – fear of social unrest – and genuine compassion, but whatever the motivation there must be a background sense of obligation. The Irish famine of the 1840s provides an illustration of what happens when that sense is absent. For Irish nationalists, the famine became symbolic of British attitudes to Ireland. The fact that food was shipped out of Ireland has led to the accusation that the famine was not only an act of omission – a failure to assist – but tantamount to act of commission: there was a deliberate policy of starvation, which, in effect, was genocide. Sen argues that there is nothing mysterious about food exports during time of famine. Market forces determine that food goes to places where people can afford it. Preventing market interaction is not, Sen suggests, the answer; rather, intervention to enable people to acquire the ability to buy food is the correct response, and here politics and mutual sympathy are important. The British response to the Irish famine – just like their response to the Bengal famine a hundred years later – was not marked by a genocidal mentality, but by an absence of sympathy which, had it existed, would have led to pressure on the

British state to put in place remedial and preventative measures. That British rule in India was not democratic and that Ireland did not enjoy the status of Scotland within the United Kingdom was relevant, but what was significant in the Irish case – especially given that Ireland was not technically a colony – was cultural alienation (Sen, 1999: 173).

## Ethical and political implications

Sen's analysis of the causes of famine may not appear inconsistent with Singer's: Singer would accept that while we have a moral duty to relieve famine how we fulfil that duty is a technical matter. Sen, on the other hand, is concerned with empirical, rather than moral, questions (although implicit in his discussion are moral claims, which he makes explicit in other writings). But there are three important points:

1.  Once we recognise there is a political dimension to famine Singer's simple analogy between the drowning child and the starving child breaks down. The duty to rescue the child is straightforwardly a moral one: we do not wait to find out the child's nationality. There may be a moral duty to help a starving child, but in this case there is also a political dimension that alters the moral duty. While starvation is, almost by definition, suffering caused by the absence of food, and as such analogous to drowning, famine is the absence of the means of acquiring food. This point cannot be dismissed simply as one about means – that is, saving the famished child is just a lot more complex than saving the drowning child – rather, the fact that the world is organised into nation-states means there are other people who have a greater duty to save the famished child. This is a qualitative difference and not just a quantitative one of proximity.
2.  Singer suggests that communication enables us to recognise the needs of starving people; we cannot hide behind a 'lack of knowledge'. The needs of the starving child are just as obvious as those of the drowning child. In Sen's analysis, the causes of famine are complex. Certainly, there are situations in which people are clearly starving and direct food aid is required. The cost of the aid is quantifiable, and the media can report how much has been raised through private donation and state aid. However, preventing famine requires more complicated coordination, which even states and non-governmental organisations may find difficult to achieve. This is not simply a secondary point about how we fulfil our moral duties, but a fundamental one about morality: because complex situations require coordination, we have to hand over responsibility to the state.
3.  Faced with a world of suffering, it is unclear what is required of us. It may be reasonable to ask someone to sacrifice his $1,000 suit in order to save a drowning child, but is it reasonable to hand over all your goods in excess of your basic needs so as to feed the starving of the world? One response is to say that so long as each person – through tax-generated development aid – gives (say) 1% of their income, the duty to help the starving is fulfilled. It would be easy to be cynical: people are just looking for excuses not to give up their luxuries for the sake of the victims of famine. But a moral theory can be too demanding. To say that we ought to do something implies that we are able to do so – 'ought implies can' – and that means not only can we calculate what is required of us, but the demands made on us are not excessive.

There is an important respect in which Sen's analysis does support a moral duty to prevent famine and that is the recognition of the role that economic forces – supply and demand – play in causing famine. If the world is a single interdependent economic system, albeit with some capacity on the part of individual nations to manage their internal socio-economic relations, then we are all responsible for the conditions which lead to famine. As we will see, the interaction argument is an important one in the global justice debate.

In summary, the debate over famine opens up a number of issues: what the relationship between morality and politics should be, and what the demand for global redistribution presupposes about the nature of human agency. The complexity of the causes of, and solutions to, famine may mean that how we behave in our everyday lives does not translate directly or straightforwardly into duties to redistribute goods across national communities. It is these issues that are at the heart of arguments about global justice.

## Cosmopolitanism

Interest among political philosophers in global justice is a relatively recent development and has been strongly influenced by work on domestic justice, inspired above all by Rawls's *A Theory of Justice* (see pp. 135–9). Although there are internal differences, we can identify three distinct positions: cosmopolitanism, particularism, and institutionalism. Defenders of cosmopolitanism have forced the pace in this debate, but the other two positions are not merely reactions to cosmopolitanism, but represent self-subsistent perspectives on global distribution. We start with cosmopolitanism, focusing on the work of Charles Beitz and Thomas Pogge.

Both Beitz and Pogge are strongly influenced by Rawls but criticise his refusal to extend his theory of domestic justice to the international sphere. However, as Beitz acknowledges, Rawls's position on global redistribution has its roots in his assumptions about the circumstances of justice, meaning the circumstances under which it makes sense to talk about justice and injustice. A starting point for Rawls is the idea that justice is about the fair distribution of the benefits and burdens of a *scheme of social cooperation* (Beitz, 1999: 131). This introduces elements of a social ideal into what should be a mere description of a social condition. Slaves in ancient Greece were part of society but neither willingly cooperated nor (arguably) benefited from the polis: 'it would be better to say that the requirements of justice apply to institutions and practices (whether or not they are genuinely cooperative) in which social activity produces relative or absolute benefits or burdens that would not exist if the social activity did not take place' (Beitz, 1999: 131). The international economy is not a cooperative scheme in Rawls's narrow sense but is one in Beitz's wide sense of 'cooperation'. This has radical implications: Rawls's two principles of justice cannot be restricted to the nation-state but must – in some form – be implemented globally.

Although Beitz later weakened the requirement for cooperation from actual cooperation to the capacity for cooperation, he accepts that the absence of cooperation reduces the duty to redistribute wealth between states. In an imaginary world of self-contained – autarkic – states redistribution would be limited to providing states lacking natural resources with the ability to develop just political institutions and satisfy its citizens' basic needs. Where countries are not autarkic and thus potentially cooperative, a stronger principle of distribution is required. Rawls's difference principle – whereby the poorest class must be made as well off as possible – should be extended globally.

Thomas Pogge digs further down into what he sees as the incoherence of Rawls's non-extension of domestic justice to the world. The moral universalism implicit in Rawls's theory should, he argues, commit us to the position that all persons should be subject to the same system of fundamental moral principles and thus to the same assignment of the benefits and burdens arising from the application of those principles. Of course, at a less fundamental level people may be treated differently, but that differential treatment must be justified by reference to the fundamental principles. Equality is the default position. Inequalities that cannot be justified within a particular nation-state should not in principle be justified between nation-states. The task for critics of cosmopolitanism is to find principled reasons for treating the cases differently.

To explore the possibility that such principles might be established, he imagines a country called Sub-subbrazil (Pogge, 2002: 100). As its name suggests, it is modelled on Brazil which, by various measures, such as the Gini Index, is one of the most unequal in the world and thus can be used as a domestic counterpart to the global inequality that exists between the rich West (or North) and the Global South. Subbrazil might not be objectionable if the economic order was accepted by the majority, so we have to imagine that peaceful change from below is not possible, and it is therefore not meaningful to talk of majority support for the existing economic system: Sub-subbrazil is just such a country.

A Rawlsian would regard Sub-subbrazil as unjust, but then they should also regard the world economic system as unjust, because it is, in effect, Sub-subbrazil. So how can Rawls set the minimum criteria for justice in the domestic sphere so much higher than in the global sphere? Put more simply, how can people in the West (North) consider severe poverty in their own country unjust but consider it morally acceptable for such poverty to exist in the Global South? Pogge considers a number of possible responses: (a) we can surrender the discrepancy between domestic and global standards of justice by either weakening the minimum criteria for domestic justice or raising them for international justice; (b) defend the discrepancy; and (c) insist on the discrepancy but reject the universalist demand to justify it (Pogge, 2002: 101). Even if you disagree with Pogge's cosmopolitan position, this is a useful way of setting out the terms of the debate. Advocates of strategies (a) and (b) operate within a universalist moral theory, while defenders of (c) reject universalism.

Pogge is less radical than Beitz in that he argues we have only a negative duty to eradicate world poverty and not a positive one. Were there no global economy there may be a moral duty to assist those in need but it would not be equivalent to the duties owed to those with whom we interact. It is because the rich have contributed to a world economy that has generated not only poverty, but also bad government, that there is a strong duty to redistribute wealth (Pogge, 2002: 197–9). In effect, continuing to cause suffering is a violation of a negative duty owed to one another not to cause suffering.

## Particularism

The two alternatives to cosmopolitanism are particularism (also known as partialism) and institutionalism. Following Pogge's framing of the debate over Sub-subbrazil, both positions insist on, or defend, the discrepancy between domestic and global justice, but they differ in how they go about it. Institutionalism adopts strategy (b) – it accepts the need for a universalist defence of the discrepancy. Particularism maintains the discrepancy but rejects the need for a universalist justification of it.

Alasdair MacIntyre offers a radically particularist defence of patriotism and, by extension, rejects global justice. The defence is 'radical' in that he eschews appeal to universalism with regard to justice in general: universalism is false at the domestic level as well as in the global sphere. Patriotism should not, MacIntyre maintains, be defended by appeal to ideals: American politicians who claim the United States deserve our – or Americans' – allegiance because it champions freedom, are defending the ideal of freedom, and not the United States as a nation (MacIntyre, 1995: 210). MacIntyre undercuts the cosmopolitans' strategy of forcing liberals to face up to the universalism implicit in their claims. Pogge argues that liberals are committed to moral universalism, such that their failure to extend justice globally is a moral blind spot. MacIntyre simply rejects universalism: patriotism is a 'kind of loyalty to a particular nation which only those possessing that particular nationality can exhibit' (MacIntyre, 1995: 210). Two nations may have achieved the same things – for example, economic prosperity – but those achievements are valued not just as achievements, but as the achievements of this particular nation. Patriotism belongs to a class of loyalty-exhibiting virtues, along with marital fidelity, love of one's family, and friendship.

MacIntyre contrasts these virtues with the derivation of value – valuing one's nation, family, friends, and so on – from an impartial, or impersonal, standpoint. The latter would require that partiality towards one's nation, or one's compatriots, be justified universally. This might be done by arguing that patriotism is indeed a virtue but one which commits us to enabling citizens of other nations to value *their* nations. This generates a conflict between partiality and impartiality:

> What your community requires as the material prerequisites for your survival as a distinctive community. . . may be exclusive use of the same or some of the same natural resources as my community requires for its survival and growth into a distinctive nation. When such a conflict arises, the standpoint of impersonal morality requires an allocation of goods such that each individual person counts for one and no more than one, while the patriotic standpoint requires that I strive to further the interests of my community and you strive to further the interests of your community.
>
> (MacIntyre, 1995: 213)

The impersonal standpoint – which translates politically into cosmopolitanism – has, MacIntyre argues, five features: (a) morality is composed of rules to which any rational person would assent; (b) the rules are neutral between rival interests; (c) the rules are neutral between rival beliefs; (d) the basic moral unit is the individual human being and individuals count equally; (e) the standpoint of the moral agent is the same for all and is independent of any social particularity. According to this view *where* and *from whom* you learn the principles of morality are as irrelevant as to where and from whom you learn the principles of mathematics (MacIntyre, 1995: 214–15). For MacIntyre, this is mistaken. Justice is concerned with the distribution of goods but those goods are enjoyed in particular social settings: 'what I enjoy is the good of *this* particular social life inhabited by me and I enjoy *it* as what *it* is' (MacIntyre, 1995: 217, his emphases). That such goods could be enjoyed in other national communities does not diminish the fact that they are enjoyed *here*. It follows – and this is a big claim – that '*I* find *my* justification for allegiance to these rules of morality in *my* particular community; deprived of the life of that community, *I* would have no reason to be moral' (MacIntyre, 1995: 217, his emphases). He makes a further, but actually quite different point, about the relationship between morality and community. Being moral is not easy, for too often our self-interested desires conflict with what we know we ought to do, so 'it is important to morality that *I* can only be a moral agent because *we* are moral agents. . . I need those around me to reinforce my moral strengths and assist in remedying my moral weaknesses' (MacIntyre, 1995: 217, his emphases). MacIntyre summarises his defence of patriotism and thus partiality to compatriots in this way:

> *If*. . . it is the case that I can only apprehend the rules of morality in the version in which they are incarnated in some specific community; and *if*. . . it is the case that the justification of morality must be in terms of particular goods enjoyed within the life of particular communities; and *if*. . . it is the case that I am characteristically brought into being and maintained as a moral agent only through particular kinds of moral sustenance afforded by my community, *then* it is clear that deprived of this community, I am unlikely to flourish as a moral agent.
>
> (MacIntyre, 1995: 218, his emphases)

He goes on to argue that this dependence on community places limits on rational criticism of it (MacIntyre, 1995: 220). MacIntyre's argument is confused. First, he conflates the dependence on a community with dependence on a particular community – the excessive use of italics to emphasise pronouns (I and we) and indexicals (this, it, and here) is really a way of driving a point home in the absence of an argument. Certainly, morality depends on socialisation, but liberals are right to argue that moral consciousness points beyond 'this' community. A person who values her own community will be capable of recognising that others will value their communities. Where MacIntyre is correct is in arguing that such recognition cannot lead to pure impartial treatment: a parent who recognises the rights of other parents cannot commit himself to impartiality between his children and other children without thereby contradicting the universal 'good' of parenthood. Partiality is intrinsic to parenthood. MacIntyre is also right to emphasise the social dimension of 'goods', but his objection to the impersonal treatment of goods is overstated: some goods are tied up with a particular community – it is not easy to export political stability or non-corrupt administration – but others are less marked by particular cultures: material aid being an example of an 'exportable' good.

A less radical, and for that reason, more credible defence of particularism is provided by David Miller. In a manner seemingly similar to MacIntyre, he distinguishes two positions, which he terms ethical universalism and ethical particularism. Universalists can accept agent-relative considerations only so long as they do not conflict with universalism at a basic level. So a universalist would endorse as a basic principle 'relieve the needy', but maintain that this is best achieved if each of us takes care of the needy in our immediate environment (Miller, 1995: 51). The justification of this restriction is that we know better how to address the needs of those close to us, as against those further away. This is not, however, a defence of distance *per se*: for a universalist, distance is a morally arbitrary fact. Another way in which a universalist can generate particularist duties is through contract: each person is assigned rights (more precisely, powers) to enter contracts of various kinds and the exercise of these rights (or powers) generates relationships which are necessarily partial. For a universalist, the existence of a system of rights must itself be justified as valuable for all.

Miller argues that universalism relies upon an implausible picture of moral agency: it draws a sharp line between moral agency and personal identity, and between moral agency and personal motivation (Miller, 1995: 57). Applying these concerns to nationality and global justice, Miller rejects two ways in which partiality might be justified from a universalist standpoint. The first models the nation-state on a club – just like we choose to join and benefit from a tennis club and thus acquire obligations to the club, so we join, or could join, a state. Even if we reject contractualism as implausible, it could still be argued that obligations arise from enjoyment of the benefits of cooperation. The problem is that this might justify an individual's obligation to the state, but it does not justify the world system of states, with its relatively strong obligations to compatriots and weak obligations to foreigners. Furthermore, contractualism does not capture the sense of 'belonging' that characterises national allegiance – we might develop allegiance to the tennis club but it is unlikely to be a major part of our identities because we were not socialised as members of the club.

An alternative argument is from specialisation: although we all have an obligation to save a life (if our own is not threatened), it is better that we leave the saving of life to those best qualified. So at the beach we leave it to the lifeguard to save a drowning person. However, the analogy with partiality towards compatriots does not work: 'why does it make sense to assign responsibility for the rights and welfare of Swedes to other Swedes and the rights and welfare of Somalians to other Somalians, if we are looking at the question from a global perspective? What is the equivalent here to the selection and training of the lifeguard?' (Miller, 1995: 63).

As with the previous argument, this defence of the nation does not account for our emotional attachment to the nation.

Miller argues that differential treatment depends on recognising the importance of particularist claims at a basic level. Of two students asking for academic advice, given restraints on his time, Miller would favour the student from his own (Oxford) college. This seems reasonable, but only because entry to an Oxford college is the result of a contract and because the good which is being distributed – advice – is very closely bound up with the nature of the institution. Miller's extension of the example is less defensible: if two students need to be driven to the hospital for urgent treatment and only one can be taken, Miller would again favour the student from his college. Even in the absence of any other differentiating features between the students, it does not seem a relevant difference that one student belongs to his college and the other does not, and the hospital example is closer to the case of global aid than the academic advice one.

In fact, the hospital example does not serve Miller's case for particularism well. Part of what motivates particularistic attachments is the presence of reciprocity, such that 'outsiders' – members of other colleges, or citizens of other nations – are not isolated individuals, but members of other national communities (Miller, 1995: 73). We do not relate to outsiders simply as human beings, but as citizens of other countries. In the advice example, the distribution of the good – advice – is conditioned by the fact that the student from the other college will be privileged in her dealings with tutors from her college. An analogous situation does not arise with the drive to the hospital: here Miller is faced with a 'human being' rather than a 'college student'.

Unlike MacIntyre, Miller does not claim that moral agency is only possible within the particular community in which you are born. Indeed, living in a community relieves the individual of the pressure of excessive demands for impartiality. He does, however, develop the idea that the goods which are up for distribution have to be conceptualised in context, and furthermore, the criteria for distribution must also be understood contextually. Attitudes to money, work, honours, status, and political power are determined by our culture, and thus, the values we attach to these things are culturally determined. The criteria for a just distribution of the goods also vary: all societies have some notion of merit, but what in fact is meritorious differs between them (Miller, 2000: 169). How we measure deprivation can depend on intersubjective considerations: lacking a television or access to the internet might be a deprivation for children in a society where these things are valued.

Miller acknowledges there are millions of people in the world who are disadvantaged relative to others in an across-the-board sense – they score lower on every measure that corresponds to a significant good: money, housing, education, healthcare, and political rights (Miller, 2000: 173). But given conflicting interpretations of the 'goods' which are to be distributed and of the criteria for distribution, the task of developing a global, transcultural conception of justice would likely result in a minimal set of basic goods and correspondingly a relatively weak principle of global distribution. Miller sums up what he thinks are the demands of global justice: (a) the obligation to respect basic human rights; (b) the obligation to refrain from exploiting vulnerable communities and individuals; and (c) the obligation to provide all political communities with the opportunity to achieve self-determination and social justice (Miller, 2000: 177).

What cosmopolitanism and particularism share is a collapsing of the distinction between the level of individual morality and politics. Although Miller comes closest to recognising that distinction with his emphasis on reciprocity, both positions seek to derive political principles – principles of justice – from claims about the nature of the individual. Of course, they come to different conclusions about the nature of those principles, but nonetheless there is a conceptual similarity between them. Institutionalism, on the other hand, is based on an explicit distinction between justice and other virtues or between justice as applied at the domestic level as against the international level. In the next section, we discuss the work of two institutionalists: John Rawls and Thomas Nagel.

# Institutionalism

Rawls argues that relatively well-ordered societies have a duty to bring burdened societies, along with outlaw societies, into the society of peoples (Rawls, 1999: 106). A well-ordered society is one which is stable and respects both basic human rights and the sovereign status of other nations. Such a society need not be liberal (see pp. 135–9). It does not follow from what Rawls terms the law of peoples that existing well-ordered societies must transfer resources to burdened societies in order to achieve the goal of bringing them into the society of peoples. Part of the reasoning is that transfers are indeterminate – we do not know at what point transfers must cease. This seems an odd point – surely, so long as we know our transfers are having some effect we should make them? A second, and more substantial, argument against transfers is that a society with few resources can be well-ordered if 'its political traditions, law, and property and class structure with their underlying religious and moral beliefs and culture are such as to sustain a liberal or decent society' (Rawls, 1999: 106). Rawls goes on to make a subtly different point: the culture of a society is a very significant determinant of the wealth of that society. These are indeed distinct points. The first establishes the limits of a well-ordered society's duties to a burdened society – transfers are aimed at creating a well-ordered society and not directly at benefiting the individual members of that society. The second is an observation – grounded in Sen's work – on the causes of poverty. Rawls elaborates: a society's population policy is extremely important; failure in food distribution rather than food decline is the cause of most famines; and the unemployed in *prosperous societies* would starve without domestic income transfers (Rawls, 1999: 9, 109–10).

Rawls rejects the extension of the difference principle to international relations, arguing that the target of distribution is the achievement of a society's political autonomy and consequent upon that its joining the society of peoples. This argument fits with his rejection of the extension of domestic liberal justice to the international sphere: peoples are represented in the society of peoples, not individual human beings. A practical result of Rawls's position is that while he has a relatively egalitarian theory of domestic justice, he has a relatively inegalitarian theory of international justice. One might admire Rawls's hard-headedness: it is extremely difficult to motivate citizens in prosperous societies to accept income transfers to poor societies, and that reluctance is not based solely on a lack of confidence in recipient governments to ensure the money benefits the worst-off in those burdened societies. Although Rawls does not make this point, a further argument for an inegalitarian theory of global justice is that in the absence of global economic institutions, it is very difficult to determine when duties correlated to 'socio-economic rights' have been fulfilled. This contrasts with so-called 'negative' human rights, such as the right to practise one's religion or marry a partner of your choice. However, there are more fundamental objections to global egalitarianism at the heart of Rawls's theory of international relations, and to grasp these requires distinguishing three levels of justice: local, domestic, and global.

An illustration of local justice is the distribution of resources within a family; other examples include the rules governing voluntary associations, such as clubs or churches. Domestic justice is concerned with the distribution of resources at the level of the nation-state. This will affect local justice: the state will not tell families how to distribute housework and child-rearing duties, but it must ensure women get fair equality of opportunity. Likewise, domestic justice will *indirectly* affect the third level of justice: the global. For Rawls, the primary ethical relationship holds between the individual and the state. Ethical issues in international relations – military intervention, global distributive justice, human rights – are only of indirect concern for individuals. It is interesting that Rawls's stated reason for writing *The Law of Peoples* was to establish whether or not liberal democracies should tolerate non-liberal societies and, by extension, whether individual citizens of a liberal democracy have an obligation to support military intervention by their state in the affairs of another state.

The assumption that principles of justice are operative in a self-contained, closed society should not be understood as an endorsement of the *nation* as intrinsically valuable. The principles of justice will necessarily be coercively enforced, and that presupposes the existence of a *state*, but the state is a juridical and not a cultural concept. This distinguishes his position from the patriotism of Alasdair MacIntyre and even from the more moderate ethical particularism of David Miller. That 'peoples' rather than individuals are the primary ethical entities in international politics does not contradict Rawls's 'individualism'. Rawls's aim in *The Law of Peoples* is to show that a liberal society can tolerate a non-liberal one:

> To tolerate means not only to refrain from exercising political sanctions – military, economic, or diplomatic – to make a people change its ways. To tolerate also means to recognize these non-liberal societies as equal participating members in good standing of the Society of Peoples, with certain rights and obligations, including the duty of civility requiring that they offer other peoples public reasons appropriate to the Society of Peoples for their actions.
>
> (Rawls, 1999: 59)

Many liberal political theorists – Nagel, whose work we discuss below, is among them – would reject this second idea of toleration. Certainly, the stability of the international order may require refraining from what is commonly referred to as 'regime change', but we have no reason to tolerate non-liberal societies at that deeper level of 'civility'. Since a non-liberal people does not treat their citizens as free and equal, then it cannot *itself* be treated as an equal among the community of peoples.

Rawls is not, however, advocating a MacIntyrian communitarianism. His refusal to extend the individualism of domestic justice to international politics can be explained by his rejection of a teleological view of the world, and of history. The 'society of peoples' does not serve an end, such as the inculcation of liberal values, even though adopting the law of peoples might have that consequence.

Nagel rejects Rawls's toleration of non-liberal peoples but does endorse his institutional conception of (global) justice. Although there may be good, practical reasons for not intervening in the affairs of another sovereign state there are no principled reasons: 'it is more plausible to say that liberal states are not obliged either to tolerate non-liberal states or try to transform them, because the duties of justice are essentially duties to our fellow citizens' (Nagel, 2005: 135).

Nagel argues that sovereignty is the missing link in discussions of global justice. Justice, he suggests, applies only to a form of organisation that claims political legitimacy and the right to impose decisions by force and not to voluntary associations (Nagel, 2005: 140). Both cosmopolitans and particularists fail to recognise this, and Rawls does not make it sufficiently clear. Sovereignty puts the 'political' into justice. As an empirical observation, unjust and illegitimate regimes have for the most part been the necessary precursors of progress towards legitimacy because they created the centralised power that became the object of contestation (Nagel, 2005: 146). In itself, this argument is not persuasive against cosmopolitanism, but if we follow Hobbes and argue that even an unjust state fulfils a coordination role, then we have made the first step towards separating the domestic and global spheres. The state answers the need for a solution to the prisoner's dilemma, such that an extra level of morality – a specifically political morality – is generated.

To illustrate this, we briefly digress from Nagel's discussion to an argument for political obligation advanced by Richard Hare. Hare asks us to imagine that we are part of a 100-strong group that finds itself stranded on a desert island with no prospect of being picked up (Hare, 1989: 11). In short, we are stuck there and must make decisions about how we are to organise ourselves. Hare argues that we have a pre-political duty to wash and delouse ourselves to prevent the spread of typhus. That duty is most effectively exercised by creating hygiene laws which are necessarily coercively enforced, and so requires the creation of a 'state'. If we then survey the reasons why we obey the law they break down, first, into prudential (that is, self-interested) reasons: (a) you do not want to catch typhus, and (b) you do not want to be punished for disobeying the law. Second, there are moral reasons unrelated to the existence of law and the state: (c) you will harm others if you do not delouse, and (d) if you get typhus you will be a burden to others. Third, there are moral reasons that are related to the existence of law and the state: (e) the existence of a law *significantly* increases – relative to (c) – the harm you cause to others by not delousing; (f) you impose costs on the law enforcement agencies by disobeying the law; (g) you will encourage others to break laws; (h) you are taking advantage of those who obey the law (Hare, 1989: 11). Crucially, the third group of reasons depend for their force on the second group – we create law to solve a moral problem and to augment pre-political moral duties.

Hare is concerned with the problem of political obligation rather than global duties, but his argument usefully illustrates how the political duties can be moral and yet distinct from 'general' moral duties. Much of Nagel's work has been concerned with elaborating two standpoints: the partial and the impartial. We discussed these in Chapter 13 (see pp. 231–2). The chief point made there was that the two standpoints are mutually entangled: a parent who cares for his child is committed to the recognition that other parents stand in a special relationship to their children. The weakness of MacIntyre's particularism lay in his failure to recognise that partiality points beyond itself to impartiality, and a fully socialised moral agent recognises this. Of course, it is also the case that the standpoints conflict – recognising the claims of other parents does not resolve the conflict between the distribution of resources between children. The exercise of partiality will benefit some children more than others, and likewise, partiality towards compatriots will disadvantage some individuals relative to others – for example, Swedes in relation to Somalians.

In his book *Equality and Partiality* (Nagel, 1991), Nagel is pessimistic about resolving this problem, but his argument about sovereignty does suggest a way forward. He advocates dualism against monism: in this context, a dualist is someone who argues that morality has more than one level, while the monist maintains there is but one level (Nagel, 1991: 122). Political institutions, Nagel argues, create 'contingent, selective moral relations, but there are also noncontingent, universal relations in which we stand to everyone, and political justice is surrounded by this larger moral context' (Nagel, 1991: 131). Those universal relations are equivalent to the duties owed by parents to all other parents (and their children) and take the form of respect for the 'most basic human rights against violence, enslavement, and coercion, and of the most basic humanitarian duties of rescue from immediate danger' (Nagel, 1991: 131).

Nagel advances an interesting response to the charge that national boundaries are morally arbitrary. Cosmopolitans pick up on a point made by Rawls in *A Theory of Justice* in which he argues that a person's native endowments – intelligence, physical strength, and good character – are from a moral standpoint arbitrary and should not determine the distribution of natural resources. If a person's natural abilities and resources should not affect distribution between citizens of a state, then why should it be thought legitimate for a state to benefit from its natural resources? Indeed, given the role that natural abilities play in a person's sense of their identity, it seems more legitimate for individuals to benefit from the exploitation of those abilities than for nations to be advantaged. Having huge gas reserves may have done wonders for Russian self-confidence but possession of those reserves is not essential to Russian identity. Nagel argues that Rawls's objection to arbitrary inequalities only has force because of the societal context: 'what is objectionable is that we should be fellow participants in a collective enterprise of coercively imposed legal and political institutions that generate such arbitrary inequalities' (Nagel, 1991: 128).

## Conclusion

We have explored three positions on global justice. The first position – cosmopolitanism – argues for an extension of the universalism of domestic justice to the global sphere. The discrepancy between domestic and global justice is, cosmopolitans argue, morally and intellectually unsustainable. The second position – particularism – maintains the discrepancy is justifiable because universalism is, at a basic level, false. The third position – institutionalism – recognises the force of universalist arguments but claims that morality has different levels and the fact that in a nation-state we are subject to coercive authority generates special duties in the domestic sphere that have no global equivalents.

## Note

1   A comment on terminology: some theorists prefer the term 'international justice', as global justice implies there is a global moral standpoint from which we should view the world. In titling the chapter the way we have it should not be assumed we are taking a specific position on this question – our aim is to discuss this and competing positions.

## References

Beitz, C. (1999). *Political Theory and International Relations*. Princeton, NJ: Princeton University Press.

Hare R. (1989). *Essays on Political Morality*. Oxford: Clarendon Press.

MacIntyre, A. (1995). 'Is Patriotism a Virtue?', in R. Beiner (ed.), *Theorizing Citizenship*. Albany: State University of New York Press.

Miller, D. (1995). *On Nationality*. Oxford: Clarendon Press.

Miller, D. (2000). *Citizenship and National Identity*. Cambridge: Polity Press.

Nagel, T. (1991). *Equality and Partiality*. Oxford and New York: Oxford University Press.

Nagel, T. (2005). The Problem of Global Justice. *Philosophy and Public Affairs, 33*(2), 113–47.

Pogge, T. (2002). *World Poverty and Human Rights: Cosmopolitan Responsibilities and Reforms*. Cambridge: Polity Press.

Rawls, J. (1999). *The Law of Peoples*. Cambridge, MA: Harvard University Press.

Sen, A. (1999). *Development as Freedom*. Oxford: Oxford University Press.

Singer, P. (1972). Famine, Affluence, and Morality. *Philosophy and Public Affairs, 1*(3), 229–43.

## Further reading

James Christensen, *Global Justice* (Red Globe Press, 2020); Kok-Chor Tan, *What Is this Thing called Global Justice?* (Routledge, 2017); Jon Mandle, *Global Justice: An Introduction* (Polity, 2006); Gillian Brock, *Global Justice: A Cosmopolitan Account* (Oxford University Press, 2009); Thom Brooks (ed.), *The Oxford Handbook of Global Justice* (Oxford University Press, 2020); Matthias Risse, *On Global Justice* (Princeton University Press, 2012); Uchenna Okeja (ed.), *African Philosophy and Global Justice* (Routledge, 2020); Huw Williams and Carl Death, *Global Justice: The Basics* (Routledge, 2016); Chris Armstrong, *Global Distributive Justice: An Introduction* (Cambridge University Press, 2012).

# Chapter 20

# Migration

## Introduction

Immigration has become a significant issue in political debate across the Western world. It was a signature theme of Donald Trump's candidacy and presidency and explains the rise of populist parties across Europe. Even though immigration is the issue of the day, this chapter is deliberately entitled *migration*, in order to capture the importance of all kinds of movement – away from your state (emigration) and within your state.

Although the debate over migration bears some similarity to the global justice one (Chapter 19), it is possible to be an egalitarian in the justice debate – believing rich countries have obligations to transfer resources to poor ones – and yet 'restrictivist' on immigration. Conversely, you can be anti-egalitarian on global transfers, but an advocate of 'open borders'.

## Key questions

- Why is immigration across international boundaries treated as problematic, but not other kinds of movement, such as migration within a country?
- How do we assess the costs and benefits of migration?
- Should there be 'open borders'?

## Emigration and immigration

Immigration is a significant issue in many Western countries. Surveying European politics from 1980 to 2015, political scientists Christoffer Green-Pedersen and Simon Otjes argue that immigration has risen up the political agenda in many countries, in line with increases in migration levels and alongside the rise of radical right political parties (2019: 432).

There has also been increasing interest among political theorists in a hitherto neglected topic. That neglect was in part the result of a narrow focus on the relationship between the individual and the state, rather than considering the relationship between states or between individuals across state boundaries. For theoretical purposes, individuals were taken to form a self-contained group. Even as late as Rawls's 1971 *A Theory of Justice*, principles of justice were assumed to apply to a closed society, entered at birth and exited at death. Of course, Rawls knew there was

DOI: 10.4324/9780429424106-26

## Case study 20.1

## The EU – an experiment in open borders?

**PHOTO 20.1** The border wall intended to stop irregular migrants entering the port of Calais, France. © PHILIPPE HUGUEN/AFP via Getty Images.

The European Union (EU) is a large-scale experiment in 'open borders'. All 27 countries are required to subscribe to the so-called four freedoms: goods, services, capital, and persons should be free to move without restriction (Europa Briefing, 2017).

It is often asserted that the four freedoms are inseparable, even though classical free trade theory does not assume that labour – or even capital – is mobile. It may be that the insistence on all four freedoms is political, rather than economic: it is an attempt to create a deeper supra-national entity, which can rival the United States and China.

A common criticism of free movement of people is that it leads to the undercutting of wages in higher wage countries. The difference between the richest and poorest country in the EU is significant: the gross monthly wage is €5,179 in Denmark against €690 in Bulgaria (Reinis Fischer, 2020). Of course, one of the aims of the EU is to level the differences between its member states – to bring the poorer countries up to the position of the wealthier ones. And arguably it has had some success, especially with Poland, the Czech Republic, and Estonia.

Could the EU's real-world experiment in free movement provide a model for the rest of the world? What would happen if it were applied globally – that is, all states implemented the four freedoms? A starting point is to look at the wage ratio between the richest and poorest countries. Then think about the cultural barriers – such as language – that might impede movement. You could also look at surveys: a Gallup poll in 2013 found that 630 million people (13% of the world's population) expressed a desire to move, with 138 million wanting to go to the United States and 42 million to the United Kingdom (Economist, 2017). What would be arguments against the global four freedoms?

immigration – and later, he had things to say about it – but it was something that fell outside ideal theory (of which, more later in the chapter).

Despite the neglect of migration among political theorists, some classical thinkers certainly made claims relevant to the debate. Locke's theory of tacit consent (see p. 136) rests on the assertion that by remaining in a territory we are consenting to obey the state, an argument that only makes sense if we can in fact leave. Kant's idea of perpetual peace (see pp. 21–2) emphasises the importance of states protecting merchants as they cross national boundaries in search of trade and markets.

But it is only relatively recently that migration has been discussed directly, rather than as an aspect of other issues. While the focus is on immigration from outside the state's territory, it is important to distinguish all the ways in which people move across physical space:

1. Entering the private property of another person, with or without the consent of that person. This can apply to private individuals, who you invite onto your property, or trespassers, who you do not. It can also apply to state officials, with or without authorisation. The Fourth Amendment of the US Constitution was intended to protect citizens 'against unreasonable searches and seizures'.
2. Using public property, such as roads, to travel within the territory of the state of which you are a citizen.
3. Relocation within your state's territory – for example, moving from California to Texas.
4. Travel across international boundaries, legally or illegally, with the intention of returning to your home state. There can be a range of reasons for such movement, including leisure, study, business, and crime.
5. Travel across international boundaries with the intention of permanent relocation. Again, this may be legal or illegal[1] and motivated by (for example) a desire for economic betterment, or escape from persecution, war, or environmental degradation.

Most discussion focuses on the last of these types of movement, and particularly on immigration rather than emigration. Furthermore, migration within a territory is taken as unproblematic, whereas migration across international boundaries requires justification. These asymmetries – between immigration and emigration, and between internal and external movement – are reflected in Article 13 (Parts 1 and 2) of the Universal Declaration of Human Rights, which asserts free movement and residence within a state, and the right to leave and return to your country (see UDHR). But with the exception of refugees – protected under a later Convention (see Refugee Convention, 2020) – there is no obligation on a state to accept a foreign citizen.

Ilya Somin criticises the emphasis on the nation-state, arguing that freedom of movement should be encouraged at all levels, local, federal, and international (2020: 1–4). If we allow movement within a state's territory, we should, for the same reasons, permit it across international boundaries. We discuss his arguments later, but he makes an important point: the nation (and its territory) cannot be taken as a given – as something that limits movement – but rather, the morality of stopping people crossing borders requires justification.

## Empirical evidence

Political theory is concerned with broad principles, rather than detailed empirical discussion of the effects of migration. Nonetheless, it is inevitable that factual claims will be made. Some argue that immigration reduces wages, others that it generates economic growth. There are debates over the costs and benefits to the welfare state of immigration, and of the negative effects on cultural cohesion or the positive effects for innovation and diversity. There are also projections of how many people would move were countries to 'open' their borders. It is impossible within the scope of this chapter to assess these claims, but we can provide a framework for assessing the evidence:

1. How do we measure the costs and benefits of migration? What is the metric? Is it economic growth, cultural integrity, genetic continuity, or something else? Many arguments assume the only metric is wealth, but this is a very narrow basis on which to assess the effects of migration.
2. What is the time-frame over which we assess the costs and benefits? If, for the sake of argument, we do take wealth as the metric, then should we consider the annual contribution of migrants, or their lifetime contribution? What about their children – do we assess *their* contribution?
3. Do we focus only on the effects on the recipient country, or also consider the impact on the country from which a person migrated? Are there effects on third countries and indeed the globe? For example, does the possibility of migration increase or reduce population pressures?
4. What does history tell us about the effects of migration? That history may be relatively recent – such as the nineteenth century – or it could be a deeper history, revealed by population genetics. Are there historical examples of free movement?

The everyday debate over immigration – on, for example, social media – is not particularly sophisticated. Often the focus is on things unrelated to migration, such as alleged security threats from insecure borders or – on the pro-immigration side – generalisations from food and football. If England had won EUFA EURO 2020 (which took place in 2021), much would have been made of how migration was central to the team's success (Liew, 2021).

Other stratagems employed in the migration debate are appeals to personal experience – 'I wouldn't be here if my parents had not been allowed in' – and claims that we are all mixed, and populations, even in Europe, are the result of 'wave after wave' of migration. The personal biography point may be true, but it will not persuade a person who does not have a migration background to accept migrants. The argument about demographic history needs supporting evidence, which is often not provided, but even if true would not in itself be an argument for opening the borders. Indeed, it could lead to the opposite conclusion. If evidence from population genetics and archaeology – such as burial sites – showed that an in-migrating population violently displaced the existing population, then one would think that the 'lesson from history' would be to resist immigration.[2]

## Theoretical perspectives

Many of the philosophical perspectives familiar from previous chapters – utilitarianism, libertarianism, contractarianism, and so on – can be applied to the immigration debate. However, there will be internal disagreements. A utilitarian (or consequentialist), after defining utility (or good consequences), would have to assess the evidence as to which level of migration (if any) maximises utility (or brings about good consequences), and there will not necessarily be a consensus on this. There are pro-migration and anti-migration libertarians. And some contractarians (contractualists) argue for a global contract leading to a commitment to open borders, while other contractarians argue the contract is a device for generating domestic, not global, principles, and it is legitimate to restrict immigration.

## Global contractarianism

Two claims underlie the global contractarian argument for open borders. First, that immigration controls – stopping somebody crossing a border – is an act of coercion. And, second, those subject to coercion should consent to it. As we have seen, it can be rational to consent to coercion, if by doing so we assure one another of our compliance to law, with all the mutual benefits that come from that (see pp. 11–13). But everyone must be a winner from the contract – in the language of game theory, consenting to coercion must be a positive-sum game. The problem is that migrants from Latin America stopped by ICE (Immigration and Customs Enforcement) from crossing the southern border into the United States gain nothing from ICE's action, so why would they consent? The obvious response is to say that American citizens do not have to get the consent of migrants in order to close the border to them. However, for globalists, this is incompatible with moral equality. As Joseph Carens argues: 'we can take it as a basic presupposition that we should treat all human beings, not just members of our own society, as free and equal moral persons' (1995: 335).

Carens criticises contractarians, such as Rawls, with his ideas of the original position and veil of ignorance (see pp. 136–7), who do not follow the logic of their political theory. They would not allow factors such as race or gender to determine domestic political principles, since a person's race and gender are 'morally arbitrary' characteristics. So why should the contingent fact of being born into a wealthy society rather than a poor one be morally significant? Membership of a particular society is, he argues, morally irrelevant: 'we should take a global, not a national, view of the original position' (1995: 335). Carens advocates a global original position and a global application of (Rawls's) two principles of justice:

> Those in the original position would be prevented by the 'veil of ignorance' from knowing their place of birth or whether they were members of one particular society rather than another. They would presumably choose the same two principles of justice. (I will simply assume that Rawls's argument for the two principles is correct, though the point is disputed). These principles would apply globally, and the next task would be to design institutions to implement these principles – still from the perspective of the original position.
>
> (1995: 335)

Carens grants that there is a 'general case for decentralization of power' which would justify the existence of 'autonomous political communities comparable to modern states' (1995: 335). The question is whether such communities would have the right to limit entry and exit. His answer is that controls on immigration are only justified if they are compatible with the application of a global difference principle. Recall that the difference principle requires the worst-off to be as well off as possible. If immigration controls achieve that, then they may be justified.

The argument is simple and powerful, resting as it does on equality and universalisation. There are, however, difficulties with it. First, moral arbitrariness can mean different things. At its most basic, something is 'arbitrary' if there is no reason underlying it. If an ICE official stopped one person crossing, but not another, without any reason, that would be arbitrary. If he allowed red-headed people to cross, but not brunettes, that would *not* be arbitrary. Yet it would not be a good reason, and this is what Carens means by arbitrariness. The power of Carens' objection rests on analogising something ruled out by Rawls, and other contractualists, as relevant at the domestic level, namely race and gender. But it is not clear that place of birth is analogous to (say) race. Given the entire world is covered by states, then place of birth, and the privileges that flow from that, are dependent on institutions, whereas race is not.

Second, moral equality might require less than open borders. Possibilities include ensuring a baseline level of welfare, or the protection of fundamental human rights, of which the right to immigrate is not one, or insisting that everybody has the right to be the citizen of a country, and thus statelessness is prohibited. Respect for human rights, or a minimal level of resources necessary to function as a human being, or the right to citizenship – of *a* country, not *this* country – could be ensured by something less than open borders.

Third, because there has never been open borders it is difficult to predict with much precision its effects. Proponents tend to think the problems caused by large-scale migration will be modest, short-term, and manageable. But one scenario is intense intergroup conflict, which drives down wages and benefits the super-rich. If the United States shut its borders to people and tried to enact Rawls's difference principle, there would likely be some modest transfer of wealth from Jeff Bezos to the poorest class. Bezos could move his money offshore, and so there are limits to transfers, and overall there need to be incentives to produce, so transfers cannot be too great. If the United States had open borders and there was a global difference principle, then one would think Bezos would pay more because there is now a bigger class at the bottom: it is composed of the world's poor and not just poor Americans. And if there are effective global institutions, then capital flight would be controlled. It is unlikely there will be effective global institutions, but the more interesting question is about incentives. Reconciling equality and efficiency is central to the difference principle, but in a fully globalised world, efficiency might be a race to the bottom, with Bezos much better off than in a closed-borders Rawlsian America.

## Restrictivist contractarianism

As we have seen above – and in the discussion of the previous chapter on global justice (see p. 348) – Rawls's work has been both inspiration for other political theorists and a target for criticism, with commentators arguing that he does not follow the logic of his own argument and ends up with a decidedly inegalitarian theory of international relations. This applies also to his brief comments on immigration. Those comments need to be understood against three aspects of his political theory. First, principles of justice only have a place in the context of a 'scheme of justice' – that is, where people find themselves in a cooperative context – and the world is not a cooperative scheme, so there are no global principles of justice applying directly to individuals. A second point follows: the international law of peoples governs relations between peoples, and not between individuals across international boundaries, although individuals' interests are protected in as far as respect for human rights forms part of that law. Third, large-scale immigration is a problem of non-ideal theory. Ideal theory assumes full compliance with principles of justice (at the domestic level) or the law of peoples (at the international level). In an ideal world, there would be no significant migration.

Rawls argues that 'an important role of government, however arbitrary a society's boundaries may appear from a historical point of view, is to be the effective agent of the people as they take responsibility for their territory and the size of their population, as well as maintaining the land's environmental integrity' (1999: 8). Unless a defined agent is made responsible for maintaining an asset, it will tend to deteriorate, and the asset 'is the people's territory and its potential capacity to support them *in perpetuity*; and the agent is the people itself as politically organized' (1999: 8; his emphasis). The 'in perpetuity' condition is important to the legitimacy of immigration control. The law of peoples precludes dealing with the problem of population growth through conquest in war or 'by migrating into another people's territory without their consent' (1999: 8). Rawls makes clear that people are morally entitled to limit immigration and adds that it can also be limited to protect a people's culture and its constitutional principles (1999: 39n).

Immigration is caused by unjust and unfavourable conditions. The persecution of religious and ethnic minorities understandably causes people to seek sanctuary. Starvation – as in the Irish famine of the 1840s – also triggers the mass movement of people. But following the arguments of Amartya Sen (Sen, 1999: 180–1), Rawls argues that famine is not caused by an absolute shortage of food, but by political failure to provide a safety net when a loss of income results in the inability to buy food (see pp. 340–2). Population pressures often have their roots in gender inequality; as men and women become more equal, the birth rate falls. And Rawls concludes: 'religious freedom and liberty of conscience, political freedom and constitutional liberties, and equal justice for women are fundamental aspects of sound social policy for a realistic utopia. The problem of immigration is not, then, simply left aside, but is eliminated as a serious problem in a realistic utopia' (1999: 9).

## Liberal communitarianism

Liberal communitarianism describes a commitment to moral equality and distributive justice, combined with the importance of national communities. David Miller argues that a justice-compliant immigration policy should take account of the physical location of the migrant – inside the state's territory, outside of it, or at the border – and the nature of the claim to be admitted (Miller, 2015). On the first of these aspects, he argues the state should protect all those resident in its territory. This is because the state asserts its authority over them. A tourist who commits a crime should be provided with all the same legal protections – such as due process – as a citizen. But the state does not (normally) claim authority over non-residents, and so there is no right to cross the border into the territory.

On the second aspect – the nature of the claim to entry – he distinguishes three categories of people who may seek entry: refugees, economic migrants, and those with particularist claims (2015: 394). The claims of the first two groups could be fulfilled by any competent state, whereas the third is a claim against a specific state. Examples of actions triggering a particularist claim might be recompense for the stripping of citizenship from a parent or grandparent, or an entitlement based on military service rendered to the state in question, such as the Gurkhas' service to the United Kingdom (2015: 402).

Refugees may have stronger claims than economic migrants to immigrate, but consideration should still be given to those seeking better economic prospects. In both cases, we start from a global perspective, rather than duties against specific states. We ask: what global actions could satisfy the claims of these two groups? (2015: 395) Miller does not discuss this, but there is a second-order justice issue, and that is fairness to those countries that because of geography disproportionately bear the burden of dealing with refugees and economic migrants. Many relatively poor countries take in a large number of people escaping armed conflict, and in Europe Greece and Italy are the often first port of call for migrants from Africa and the Middle East.

Having narrowed down the obligations of states to accept migrants, there is the question of entry criteria. In the case of those claiming refugee status, this may be relatively straightforward: there is a moral obligation to take them, alongside a legal one, grounded in the ratification of the 1951 Refugee Convention (Refugee Convention, 2020: 2–5). Under the Convention, a refugee is defined as 'someone who is unable or unwilling to return to their country of origin owing to a well-founded fear of being persecuted for reasons of race, religion, nationality, membership of a particular social group, or political opinion' (2020: 14). More challenging are economic migrants. Here, a state has the discretion to judge whether accepting them will be beneficial to the host society.

Would race or religion be acceptable selection criteria? Anti-racism is now a defining norm of Western societies, and those advocating restrictions often go to great lengths to avoid the charge of racism. We discuss ethnonationalist views of immigration later in the chapter, but it is clear Miller is not an ethnonationalist. One argument against race-based selection is the global commitment on the part of states to racial equality, as expressed in the International Convention on the Elimination of all Forms of Racial Discrimination. While the Convention does not provide for the free movement of people, it could be interpreted as prohibiting a race-based immigration policy. And racial discrimination at the border implies that current citizens from that ethnic or racial group have lesser status (Miller, 2015: 399).

## Utilitarianism and consequentialism

All utilitarians are consequentialists, but not all consequentialists are utilitarian. Utilitarians argue that principles, such as an individual's right to immigrate, or a state's right to restrict immigration, should maximise utility. Utilitarians disagree on the definition of utility. Common definitions have been happiness, pleasure, the avoidance of pain, or the satisfaction of preferences (see pp. 164–5). Whereas utilitarianism is necessarily maximising, consequentialism need not be: there could be a plurality of goods, which cannot all be put on one scale or converted into a single metric. For example, in assessing immigration we might consider its effects on security, economic growth, social cohesion, cultural reproduction, and freedom, without trying to put a single value on all these things. In other words, we need to trade off these goods.

Much of the popular debate over immigration is implicitly consequentialist. But it does not follow that this is the correct moral standpoint. Carens' argument is non-consequentialist – it is based on the rights of individuals, rather than the overall costs and benefits of migration. Nonetheless, utilitarianism and consequentialism are moral theories, so what would a utilitarian or a consequentialist say about migration?

Once we have defined utility – or if we are non-maximising consequentialists, what goods should be considered – we then need to consider geographical range and time scales. Utilitarians tend to assess actions on a large geographical scale, so they are globalists. All humans count, and each human counts equally. But what about future (not-yet-existing) people? Actions of contemporaries, including immigration policies, will affect who comes into existence. For rights-based – 'deontological' – theorists (see p. 16), this is a real difficulty: you have duties to people who may not ever exist. Possible people are less of a challenge to utilitarians. Classical utilitarians simply add up instances of utility, which would suggest the more people the better, although more people may mean less utility per capita, if population density makes people less happy. Average utilitarians calculate utility per head, and if density reduces happiness, then this will feed through to a reduction in overall utility much more quickly than is the case with classical utilitarianism. The relevance of this is that migration policies will almost certainly affect how many people exist. If, for example, there was widespread migration from high fertility to low fertility countries that could increase global population levels. Migration would act as a safety valve for the former, while increasing the population of the latter. This was Garrett Hardin's argument (see pp. 305–6).

Intuitively you would think utilitarians would favour open borders, as escaping from poor and unstable countries will significantly increase the utility of migrants. It might also increase the utility of natives of the host countries, through economic productivity gains, but even if their utility was reduced their loss is likely to be less than the migrants' gain. Likewise, even if the global population increased as a result of freer migration, this is unlikely to reduce average utility, since the movers are made happier. However, all these are empirical claims, and we would need to consider the evidence.

We have assumed that only humans generate utility. But non-human animals have experiences (and also perhaps preferences). So they should count. And we need to assess the effects of migration on them. Migration can include not only human migration, but also the invasive effects of non-human species, often as a result of human activity. What is more, if population pressure is a cause of the climate crisis (see pp. 298–9), then it will likely reduce biodiversity, and thus the utility of non-human life-forms. Indeed, while they are not necessarily utilitarians, some ecologists make the case for immigration controls in order to protect the environment and species diversity (Cafaro and O'Sullivan, 2019).

And finally, we need a time-frame. While classical utilitarians define utility in experiential terms – happiness, pleasure, the avoidance of pain – they do not calculate utility based simply on what is immediately experienced. Indeed, if they did, the moment of experience would disappear as quickly as it appears. If someone threatens you with violence you will *now* experience fear, and if they carry out the threatened act, *in the future* you will feel physical pain. Both should be counted into the maximand (that which is being maximised). The only grounds for discounting an experience in the future is uncertainty over whether it will in fact occur. The threat of violence now is real, but it might only be a threat and so you will not experience pain in the future. Because of uncertainty, a utilitarian will apply a discount rate, whereby the further in the future an effect is, the less weight is placed on it (see p. 107). Causal complexity is another reason to discount the future.

We can apply both considerations – uncertainty and causal complexity – to immigration. If we relax border controls, we cannot be sure how many people will migrate, and that uncertainty is greater the further we project into the future. And once migration has taken place, we cannot be sure what effects are due to migration, and what are due to other causal factors. For example, when assessing the effect of migrants do we focus on the immediate impact of their arrival in the host country – say, the first year, or five years – or do we consider their lifetimes (or what is left of them)? What about their children? We inherit genes and cultural traits from our parents, and so second-generation migrants should be included in the utilitarian calculus of the effects of migration. But those children will also be influenced by the wider 'host' society, and so will their behaviour.

## Libertarianism

Libertarians begin from the premise that humans have rights in their bodies, and either through first ownership or through the mutual exercise of rights can acquire rights in external objects. The only grounds for interfering in a person's actions is if she coerces another person. On the face of it, libertarians should favour unrestricted movement, except in cases where such movement is coercive. Indeed, restrictions on movement – stopping someone crossing a border – are coercive and thus a violation of rights (Block, 2008: 168).

Open borders libertarians argue that so long as a migrant is invited by a property-owner, migration is non-coercive (2008: 173). For example, a landowner in the United States invites workers from Mexico to labour on his land. Neither the landowner nor the workers are coercing others. Nobody's rights are violated. But what if there were effects from employing the workers? For example, they might undercut the wages of local workers. Or they might make neighbours feel their culture is under threat. Or the migrant workers may commit crimes, or neighbours fear they will commit crime. The libertarian response to the wages argument is that you have a right to an object – for example, the right to your labour – but not to its value (2008: 177). What you get for your labour is the result of supply and demand, which itself reflects the exercise of individuals' rights – in this case, the rights of the landowner and migrant workers to enter a contract. If crime is committed then compensation is due, but that applies to everyone and not specifically to migrants. And the fear of crime is not coercive, nor is the fear of cultural dislocation.

Another restrictivist argument is that migrants will be attracted by generous welfare spending. But libertarians maintain that the coercive redistribution of resources required to support a welfare state is a violation of property rights. The state should either not exist – the position taken by anarcho-capitalists – or should be reduced to its security functions, which is the stance of minarchists, such as Nozick (see pp. 209–10). The existence of an illegitimate scheme of forced redistribution should not be used as an argument for a further violation of rights, namely, restrictions on free movement (2008: 178–9).

There are, however, libertarian restrictionists, such as Hans-Hermann Hoppe (2002). The starting point is the problem of roads and other infrastructure. If somehow the Mexican workers could be brought onto the private property of the employer without traversing other people's property and without drawing on any other jointly owned facilities, then no rights would be violated. But in practice this is impossible. To develop the restrictivist argument, we need to distinguish between different types of ownership: (a) private (individual), (b) private (joint), (c) state, and (d) unowned. At a stretch, state ownership (category (c)) could be described as joint private ownership, with 'the people' the owners. But their names do not appear on the title deeds, they did not sign a contract, and their consent is not sought for the use of such property, except through the very inadequate mechanism of an election. On category (d), following Locke's argument, libertarians argue that property rights can be established in unowned property if by labouring on it value is added (see pp. 141–3). This is termed 'homesteading' and is an option for migrants.

If we ignore homesteading and assume there is no state ownership, we are left with individual and joint private ownership. Imagine an independent town of 20,000 people. Each street has 200 houses, and those 200 houses jointly own their highway (street). Each of the 200 households has the right to travel along the street and can grant permission to others to do so. Since unanimity is cumbersome, there might be a rule built into the title deeds of the street allowing any townsperson to use any of the streets in the town – indeed, householders would be reluctant to buy a house in a street that did not allow such ease of movement. But what about outsiders (non-townspeople)? This would depend on the nature of the joint title. The title might stipulate that a majority should consent. Or a super-majority. Or there should be unanimity.

It might be objected that the movement of *anything* across the town's borders and along the streets violates another person's rights. For example, the transportation of goods may create pollution. But what is crucial is consent. The townspeople might consent to free trade with other towns, but not the free movement of people, unless temporarily for the purposes of business. A leisure resort might welcome tourists, but not permanent residents. A university town needs students, but would require them on leave on graduation.

Hoppe recognises that in reality the state owns the streets (2002: 81). This he thinks is a usurpation of power, but nonetheless it is a fact which any credible theory of migration must accept. Given this, he argues that only the full consent of the people legitimates allowing migration, and the state violates that right every time it admits migrants.

## Libertarian consequentialism

Most libertarians are deontologists: the exercise of rights, and not the consequences of actions, determines the legitimacy of an outcome. Of course, individuals may seek to bring about good consequences, but they do so by using their rights. For example, free trade has good consequences, but a person cannot be forced to trade. Retail price maintenance, whereby a manufacturer dictates the retail price of a good is bad for consumers but is compatible with the exercise of property rights. Making retail price maintenance illegal is an interference in consensual transactions.

There are, however, libertarian consequentialists: freedom is a good that should be maximised and opening the borders is a way of achieving this. Bryan Caplan argues that open borders would double global GDP and virtually eliminate poverty (2012: 6). This assumes migration does not undermine the trust that makes the legal institutions of Western countries effective. Caplan seems to recognise this and uses the not entirely convincing example of the housing market as an illustration: migration increases property values, which would not happen if neighbourhood trust fell (2012: 12).

Responding to the charge that migrants might import decidedly anti-libertarian preferences, such as the desire for an authoritarian state or big spending programmes, Caplan cites as an example immigrants to the United States from Bismarckian Germany at the turn of the twentieth century. They did not import their values. Migrants tend to favour the status quo – the status quo in their country of origin may be authoritarian, but if the status quo in the country of immigration is liberal, there is no problem. He even makes a virtue of evidence that people in racially and culturally diverse countries are less willing to pay for an extensive welfare state (2012: 15) (because they are reluctant to transfer resources to people who are different from themselves).[3] As an anti-welfare state libertarian, he welcomes this! The implication is that even if migrants want high levels of state expenditure, their presence – the increasing diversity they bring – will reduce it.

And on one issue – immigration itself – migrants are more liberal than the native population, despite the fact that they have the most to lose from further immigration. The problem with this argument is that it assumes the only metric is money. It might well be that further migration reduces recent migrants' wage levels, but they benefit in other ways. Chain migration helps their families, and large co-ethnic communities increase culturally specific goods, such as cuisine. Perhaps, most important of all, ever-increasing racial diversity makes them feel safer. Being one minority among many is preferable to being an exposed minority facing what they perceive to be a hostile 'native' majority. They want to transition from a majority society to a majority–minority one. So the desire for more migrants does not stem from individualist, liberal values.

Somin (2020) argues that freedom would be massively enhanced if people could 'vote with their feet'. In America, competition between states (that is, federal units), benefits individuals, and, of course, American citizens are free to move around the country. He also argues that markets permit foot voting Logically, people should also be free to move across international boundaries. In effect, these forms of movement maximise freedom. It certainly seems plausible that having an exit option from oppressive and dysfunctional regimes would enhance both political and economic freedom.

A problem with this argument is that it precludes the right to exclude and so undermines freedom of association. Associations both facilitate and restrict freedom: insofar as the preferences of members of an association can only be satisfied by excluding non-members, they enhance the members' freedom at a cost to non-members. Restricting foot voting *is* a loss of freedom, but then so is forced association. Restrictive associations are often the only way to realise certain goods. A minority language group may within a defined geographical space restrict house sales to those who speak the language. People within a locality may seek to preserve its rural character by imposing zoning (a greenbelt). A group could try to achieve and maintain herd immunity in the face of a virus by demanding proof of vaccination status. All of these have public good characteristics and are vulnerable to free riders: vendors who want a good price for their property, landowners on the greenbelt who want to sell to housebuilders, and anti-vaxxers who get protection from the vaccinated.

The tragedy of the commons (see pp. 305–6) illustrates the problem of free movement. Somin suggests that private property rights may be a solution to exploitation of the commons, while also acknowledging that this might not always work (2020: 141). In fact, as Elinor Ostrom argued, community governance is often necessary. Such a governance structure – which is distinct from state coercion or a regime of property rights – depends upon a common understanding of how the resource should be used, a low discount rate, trust and reciprocity, and experienced leadership (Ostrom, 2002: 5). Although she does not say it, these things depend upon a stable population and the capacity to exclude those who have not been socialised into these practices.

## Ethnonationalism

We discussed ethnonationalism in a previous chapter (see pp. 233–6). One writer who, from an ethnonationalist perspective, has made a distinctive contribution to the immigration debate is Frank Salter. Recall that he argues that humans have genetic interests – interests in the reproduction of their genes. He prefers the term 'ethny' to 'race', but we can treat these as synonyms. Much of the debate in academic political theory ignores race-based arguments. This may be because race is regarded as beyond the pale of discussion or because 'appeals to blood' are primitive, both in the moral sense of being crude and in the sense that race-based arguments are 'unthinking' – it is assumed that no *reasoned* argument about immigration can appeal to race. Race, it is claimed, is a spurious concept. No boundaries can be established for groups conventionally defined as races. As Richard Lewontin argued, there is more diversity within conventional races than between them. We discussed these arguments in the chapter on multiculturalism (see pp. 282–3).

While Salter is certainly a 'realist' (or naturalist) with regard to race, he claims we do not need to place boundaries around races (or ethnies). We simply take two individuals from within an ethny (a conventional race) and calculate the genetic distance between them, and we do the same for two individuals from different ethnies. The genetic interests of the first pair – the co-ethnics – are determined by the competition they face from members of other ethnies. If there is no competition, then your genetic interests are best served by your immediate reproduction, although there are gains from cooperation with your co-ethnics, such that it might be in the interests of the wealthy to transfer resources to the poor. Funding a decent health system may be adaptive (meaning, the most effective way to reproduce your genes). Also, an ethny must anticipate conflict with other ethnies, and that motivates collective action – action beyond simply promoting the interests of your immediate family.

Where there is intergroup competition, humans can increase their fitness by helping *a lot* of co-ethnics *a little* rather than helping *a few* family members *a lot*. Inclusive fitness is a term from evolutionary biology, meaning the reproduction of copies of your genes. Since you share copies of your genes with co-ethnics, if you help them reproduce, you increase your fitness. Interestingly, as suggested in a previous chapter, given the vagaries of genetic recombination, your fitness may be more effectively increased by aiding co-ethnics rather than your family (see p. 236).

The loss of territorial control is, Salter argues, the most serious threat to a person's genetic interests. Large-scale immigration, combined with higher fertility rates of immigrant groups, will lead to the displacement of the indigenous population. While obviously this argument is influential on the radical right, as it lends support to the 'replacement thesis' (see p. 252), Salter is keen to stress he is a universalist: all humans have genetic interests, and all nations are equal in the sense that they provide the political–institutional conditions for the pursuit of those interests. Salter describes himself as a universal nationalist (Salter, 2007: 185–7).

We highlighted some problems with Salter's argument in our previous discussion: we might not care about our genetic interests, and there is a reliance on the emotional bonding power of the family to persuade us that we ought to care (especially) for our co-ethnics. This second point is brought out dramatically in the following statement:

> [it is] more adaptive for an Englishman to risk life or property resisting the immigration of two Bantu immigrants to England than his taking the same risk to rescue one of his own children from drowning... The same applies in the reverse direction, two Englishmen migrating to Bantu Africa constitute a greater loss of long-term genetic interest than does a random Bantu losing a child.
>
> (Salter, 2002: 124–5)

The difference, for Salter, between the population-level loss of fitness and the loss of your child is that the former is a dispersed loss, while the latter is concentrated. We suggested in our previous discussion that there are emotional aspects to a parent–child relationship – including, importantly, adoptive ones – which make this kind of comparison problematic.

Indeed, even operating within an evolutionary (Darwinian) framework, human psychology may be tuned to distinguish in-groups and out-groups, without necessarily tracking genetic closeness. Groups can form relatively easily, as can intergroup conflicts. If we accept the claims of evolutionary psychology that the mind has been shaped by our long history of living in hunter-gatherer bands, then groupishness has evolutionary roots.[4] But group-formation may 'hitch a ride' on these evolved capacities (or adaptations), such that a group of very genetically diverse individuals can form a cohesive group, and in reverse, genetically close individuals can assort into highly conflictual and competing groups, as is evident in Northern Ireland and in the Balkans.

Even if most people do not care about their genes – or clusters of single nucleotide polymorphisms (SNPs) – it could be argued that those who do should be free to act in ways that promote what they perceive to be shared interests. This argument would no longer make the claim to the objectivity of genetic interests, but rather it would be the case that race is what you make it. If you believe races exist and you seek to promote racial (ethnic, genetic) interests, then you should be free to do so. In effect, this argument is the libertarian restrictivist one discussed earlier. Indeed, Hoppe thinks that, as a matter of fact, people do prefer to be with their co-ethnics (however defined), and given the opportunity will resist the diversity created by immigration (2002: 77).

## The scramble for Europe

At the start of the chapter, we asked whether the EU's experience of free movement should be extended globally. To make this discussion more concrete, let us compare Sub-Saharan Africa and the EU. The current population of Sub-Saharan Africa is about 1.1 billion. It is projected to increase to 2.12 billion in 2050 (Ezeh, Kissling, and Singer, 2020: 1132). The EU's population is around 449 million and will fall slightly to 441 million in 2050 and 416 million in 2100 (Projections, 2020). The two regions have dramatically different age structures. Forty-two per cent of the population of Sub-Saharan Africa is aged 14 years or under, compared to 15% in the EU. The total fertility rate (TFR)[5] for the region is 4.7, while for the EU it is 1.53. The per capita Gross Domestic Product (GDP) of Sub-Saharan Africa is around $1,600, compared to about $34,700 in the EU.

As Stephen Smith argues in his aptly named book *The Scramble for Europe: Young Africa on its Way to the Old Continent* (Smith, 2019), there is likely to be enormous migratory pressure from Africa to Europe over the next 40 or so years. What has been experienced at the Spanish enclave of Ceuta and over the Mediterranean routes to Italy is only a foretaste of what may come. Smith has intimate knowledge of Africa and his book is a down-to-earth assessment of the pros and cons of migration between the two continents, rather than an abstract philosophical discussion. One very important point he makes is that economic development in Sub-Saharan Africa will increase migration, not reduce it. The very poor lack the wherewithal to get to the border. It is those with some resources – but who believe, in a perhaps inchoate way, that they will prosper in Europe – who will make the journey. They will be young, and largely male.

At the end of his book, Smith outlines a number of scenarios for how things might work out over the next several decades:

1. *Eurafrica*: Europe – the old and ageing content – embraces the youth and vitality of Africa and opens its borders. This may be underpinned by a universalism (which we discussed earlier). The problem is that those at the forefront of such pro-migrant activism do not bear the full consequences of their ethical position – they assert what Max Weber terms an 'ethics of conviction' over an 'ethics of responsibility'. Smith argues the European welfare state would not survive open borders, because the 'contract of intergenerational solidarity on which it rests can only apply within a demarcated area' (2019: 168).
2. *Fortress Europe*: This is effectively the current policy – the double, six metre high, barbed wire fence at Ceuta is a visual expression of this policy. Smith thinks this policy is 'not indefensible'. It allows Europe to sustain a credible distinction between refugees and economic migrants, and it fits with an ethics of responsibility: why open the borders, then suddenly shut them in response to popular hostility? Consistency would be a better policy (2019: 170–1).
3. *Mafia drift*: Criminal elements, such as people traffickers, determine policy. If the European underworld finds a 'right-wing political patron', then the politics of migration – the far left versus the far right – will be conducted through competing criminal gangs and networks (2019: 172–3).
4. *Return of the protectorate*: European states will adopt a divide-and-rule strategy, forming pacts with African leaders, whereby they offer no-strings-attached aid, perhaps combined with visas for the children of the African elites. In return, African states prevent their own populations from migrating (2019: 173).

5. **Bric-a-brac politics**: A mix of all of the above. Given competing ideologies and the electoral cycle, there will be mish-mash of stop-go policies, whereby sometimes the borders are opened, and sometimes closed (2019: 174–5).

Smith expresses his views on migration from Africa to Europe:

> The massive migration of Africans to Europe is in the interest of neither Young Africa nor the Old Continent. For Europe, only the very selective entry of a limited number of Africans will provide any benefit because of its highly competitive and vertical job market, which is likely to contract further as automation and especially robotics continue apace: in the end, the decline in its working population will almost certainly be a net gain for Europe, not a loss. Africa, on the other hand, has far more to lose than to win from the large-scale 'exportation' of its youth. They are its hope for a better future and will be the key to its success as soon as conditions on the continent allow them to 'grow up', when there is enough remunerative work for them to become productive and independent.

(2019: 165)

## Conclusion

Multiple perspectives can be brought to bear on the question of migration. Key issues are the extent to which moral obligations extend beyond national boundaries, who benefits from migration and how we measure those benefits. Much of the popular debate – and some of the academic debate – focuses very narrowly on short-term, economic benefits. But part of the discussion must be about what counts as a benefit, how we measure costs and benefits, and over what time-frame. What is clear is that there will be significant migration over the next 50 years, and this issue will increase in importance.

## Notes

1   Actually, the language is politically fraught. The United Nations urges countries to avoid the words 'legal' and 'illegal', instead suggesting 'undocumented' or 'irregular' (UNHCR, 2019).
2   In relation to English history see, for example, Thomas, Stumpf, and Härke (2006), who argue that migrating Anglo-Saxons imposed an 'apartheid' system on the native Britons. Other researchers have challenged this, but that shows the complexity of the evidence.
3   Moving from minimum to maximum racial fragmentation reduces redistribution as a share of GDP by an estimated 7.5% (Caplan, 2012: 15).
4   Evolutionary psychologists argue the mind is modular – there are different modules for dealing with problems our ancestors repeatedly faced, such as working out what food is edible, finding your way when you are lost, getting a sexual mate, detecting whether someone is lying to you, and keeping track of who has treated you well (or not).
5   The TFR is the age-specific fertility rate of women in their 'child-bearing years' (normally set as 15 to 45). It is a statistical construct rather than the actual number of births per year. A key number is the replacement level fertility rate of 2.1 – resulting in a stable population.

# References

Block, W. (2008). A Libertarian Case for Free Immigration. *Labor Economics from a Free Market Perspective: Employing the Unemployable, 13*(2), 175.

Cafaro, P. and O'Sullivan, J. (2019). How Should Ecological Citizens Think about Immigration? *The Ecological Citizen, 3*(1), 85–92.

Caplan, B. (2012). Why Should We Restrict Immigration? *Cato Journal, 32*, 5.

Carens, J., (1995). 'Aliens and Citizens: The Case for Open Borders', in W. Kymlicka (ed.), *The Rights of Minority Cultures.* Oxford: Oxford University Press, 331–49

Economist (2017). A World of Free Movement Would be $78 Trillion Richer. *Economist*, viewed 14 July 2021, https://www.economist.com/the-world-if/2017/07/13/a-world-of-free-movement-would-be-78-trillion-richer

Ezeh, A., Kissling, F., and Singer, P. (2020). Why Sub-Saharan Africa Might Exceed its Projected Population Size by 2100. *The Lancet, 396*(10258), 1131–33.

Europa Briefing (2017). The Four Freedoms in the EU: Are they Inseparable? Jacques Delors Institut, viewed 14 July 2021, https://institutdelors.eu/wp-content/uploads/2018/01/171024jdigrundfreiheitenenwebeinzelseitena4.pdf

Green-Pedersen, C. and Otjes, S. (2019). A Hot Topic? Immigration on the Agenda in Western Europe. *Party Politics, 25*(3), 424–34.

Hoppe, H. H. (2002). Natural Order, the State, and the Immigration Problem. *Journal of Libertarian Studies, 16*(1), 75–97.

Liew, J. (2021). The England Squad Is Built on Immigration – Yet Our Xenophobic Government Dares to Cheer it on. *New Statesman*, viewed 27 July 2021, https://www.newstatesman.com/politics/sport/2021/07/england-squad-built-immigration-yet-our-xenophobic-government-dares-cheer-it

Miller, D. (2015). Justice in Immigration. *European Journal of Political Theory, 14*(4), 391–408.

Ostrom, E. (2002). Reformulating the Commons. *Ambiente & sociedade*, (10), 5–25.

Population Projections (2020). Population Projections in the EU. *Eurostat*, viewed 27 July 2021, https://ec.europa.eu/eurostat/statistics-explained/index.php?title=Population_projections_in_the_EU#Population_projections

Rawls, J. (1999). *The Law of Peoples.* Cambridge, MA: Harvard University Press.

Refugee Convention (2020). *Convention and Protocol Relating to the Status of Refugees*, United Nations High Commissioner for Refugees, viewed 27 July 2021, https://www.unhcr.org/uk/3b66c2aa10

Reinis Fischer (2020). Average Monthly Salary in European Union 2020. *Reinis Fischer*, viewed 14 July 2021, https://www.reinisfischer.com/average-monthly-salary-european-union-2020

Salter, F. (2002). Estimating Ethnic Genetic Interests: Is it Adaptive to Resist Replacement Migration? *Population and Environment, 24*(2), 111–40.

Salter, F. (2007). *On Genetic Interests: Family, Ethnicity, and Humanity in an Age of Mass Migration.* New Brunswick and London: Transaction Publishers.

Sen, A. (1999). *Development as Freedom.* Oxford: Oxford University Press.

Smith, S. (2019). *The Scramble for Europe: Young Africa on its Way to the Old Continent.* Cambridge: Polity.

Somin, I. (2020). *Free to Move: Foot Voting, Migration, and Political Freedom.* New York: Oxford University Press.

Thomas, M. G., Stumpf, M. P., and Härke, H. (2006). Evidence for an Apartheid-like Social Structure in Early Anglo-Saxon England. *Proceedings of the Royal Society B: Biological Sciences, 273*(1601), 2651–7.

UDHR (1948). *Universal Declaration of Human Rights*, United Nations, viewed 26 July 2021, https://www. un.org/en/about-us/universal-declaration-of-human-rights

UNHCR (2019). *Why 'undocumented' or 'irregular'?* United Nations High Commissioner for Refugees, viewed 27 July 2021, https://www.unhcr.org/cy/wp-content/uploads/sites/41/2018/09/Terminology-Leaflet_EN_PICUM.pdf

## Further reading

It is a reflection of how the debate over immigration in political theory has taken off that all these books have appeared relatively recently (most of them since 2019). They tend to argue a line, rather than offer an overview of the debate.

Adam Hosein, *The Ethics of Migration: An Introduction* (Routledge, 2019); Christopher Bertram, *Do States have the Right to Exclude Immigrants?* (Polity, 2018); David Owen, *What do we Owe Refugees?* (Polity, 2020); Sarah Fine and Lea Ypi (eds.), *Migration in Political Theory: The Ethics of Movement and Membership* (Oxford University Press, 2019); Michael Blake, *Justice, Migration, and Mercy* (Oxford University Press, 2020); Gillian Brock, *Migration and Political Theory* (Polity, 2021); Chandran Kukathas, *Immigration and Freedom* (Princeton University Press, 2021); Sarah Strong, *Immigration and Democracy* (Oxford University Press, 2021); David Miller, *Strangers in our Midst: The Political Philosophy of Immigration* (Harvard University Press, 2016).

# Index

Note: *Italic* page numbers refer to figures and page numbers followed by "n" denote endnotes.